WA 1423464 5

KU-052-249

Research Methods and Methodologies in Education

Education at SAGE

SAGE is a leading international publisher of journals, books, and electronic media for academic, educational, and professional markets.

Our education publishing includes:

- accessible and comprehensive texts for aspiring education professionals and practitioners looking to further their careers through continuing professional development

- inspirational advice and guidance for the classroom

- authoritative state of the art reference from the leading authors in the field

Find out more at: **www.sagepub.co.uk/education**

Research Methods and Methodologies in Education

Edited by

**Professor James Arthur, Dr Michael Waring,
Professor Robert Coe and Professor Larry Hedges**

Los Angeles | London | New Delhi
Singapore | Washington DC

© Editorial material James Arthur, Michael Waring, Robert J. Coe and Larry V. Hedges 2012

Chapter 1 © James Arthur 2012
Chapter 2 ©Robert J. Coe 2012
Chapter 3 © Michael Waring 2012
Chapter 4 © Larry V. Hedges 2012
Chapter 5 © Laura Day Ashley 2012
Chapter 6 © Robert J. Coe 2012
Chapter 7 © Marilyn Leask 2012
Chapter 8 © Carol Munn-Giddings 2012
Chapter 9 © Rob Walker 2012
Chapter 10 © Ghazala Bhatti 2012
Chapter 11 © Robert Thornberg 2012
Chapter 12 © Jenni Karlsson 2012
Chapter 13 © Laura Day Ashley 2012
Chapter 14 © Ian Davies and Andrew Peterson 2012
Chapter 15 © Anne Vignoles 2012
Chapter 16 © Stephen Gorard 2012
Chapter 17 © Emma Smith 2012
Chapter 18 © Steve Higgins 2012
Chapter 19 © Peter Tymms 2012
Chapter 20 © Mark Newman and Kelly Dickson 2012
Chapter 21 © Gert Biesta 2012
Chapter 22 © Richard Pring 2012
Chapter 23 © Michael V. Angrosino 2012

Chapter 24 © Carolyn L. Mears 2012
Chapter 25 © Rosalind Hurtworth 2012
Chapter 26 © Anita Gibbs 2012
Chapter 27 © Rhona Sharpe and Greg Benfield 2012
Chapter 28 © Axel Bruns and Jean Burgess 2012
Chapter 29 © Gary McCulloch 2012
Chapter 30 © Carole Torgerson, Jill Hall and Kate Light 2012
Chapter 31 © Peter Tymms 2012
Chapter 32 © Ron K. Hambleton 2012
Chapter 33 © Graham R. Gibbs 2012
Chapter 34 © Paul Connolly 2012
Chapter 35 © Elaine Vaughan 2012
Chapter 36 © Michael Atkinson 2012
Chapter 37 © Claudia Mitchell 2012
Chapter 38 © Michael Waring 2012
Chapter 39 © Judith L. Green, Audra Skukauskaite and W. Douglas Baker 2012
Chapter 40 © MIchael Tedder 2012
Chapter 41 © Michael Borenstein 2012
Chapter 42 © Harvey J. Keselman and Lisa Lix 2012
Chapter 43 © Stephen Gorard 2012
Chapter 44 © Michael Seltzer and Jordan Rickles 2012
Chapter 45 © Robert J. Coe
Chapter 46 © Larry V. Hedges

First published 2012

Apart from any fair dealing for the purposes of research or private study, or criticism or review, as permitted under the Copyright, Designs and Patents Act, 1988, this publication may be reproduced, stored or transmitted in any form, or by any means, only with the prior permission in writing of the publishers, or in the case of reprographic reproduction, in accordance with the terms of licences issued by the Copyright Licensing Agency. Enquiries concerning reproduction outside those terms should be sent to the publishers.

All material on the accompanying website can be printed off and photocopied by the purchaser/user of the book. The web material itself may not be reproduced in its entirety for use by others without prior written permissoin from SAGE. The web material may not be distributed or sold separately from the book without the prior written permission of SAGE. Should anyone wish to use the materials from the website for conference purposes, they would require separate permission from us. All material is © James Arthur, Michael Waring, Robert J. Coe and Larry V. Hedges, 2012.

Los Angeles | London | New Delhi
Singapore | Washington DC

SAGE Publications Ltd
1 Oliver's Yard
55 City Road
London EC1Y 1SP

SAGE Publications Inc.
2455 Teller Road
Thousand Oaks, California 91320

SAGE Publications India Pvt Ltd
B 1/I 1 Mohan Cooperative Industrial Area
Mathura Road
New Delhi 110 044

SAGE Publications Asia-Pacific Pte Ltd
3 Church Street
#10-04 Samsung Hub
Singapore 049483

Library of Congress Control Number: 2011927306

British Library Cataloguing in Publication data
A catalogue record for this book is available from the British Library

ISBN 978-0-85702-038-3
ISBN 978-0-85702-039-0 (pbk)

Typeset by Kestrel Data, Exeter, Devon
Printed in Great Britain by
CPI Group (UK) Ltd, Croydon, CR0 4YY
Printed on paper from sustainable resources

Contents

PART III: KEY METHODS

DIMENSION 1: RESEARCH DESIGNS

DIMENSION 2: DATA COLLECTION TOOLS

DIMENSION 3: ANALYSIS METHODS

Acknowledgements

The editors would like to thank all of the contributors for the work they have done in writing and creating the chapters which make up this text. The editors appreciate the time and dedication that has been put into each chapter, and thank contributors for the understanding and diligence shown in responding to feedback during the writing process.

The editors would like to thank Sage for publishing this project. In particular, they would like to show their appreciation to Marianne Lagrange and her assistants who have worked on this project, Monira Begum and Kathryn Bromwich.

Finally, the editors would like to thank Aidan Thompson who, in his role as administrator for the project, has performed a truly excellent job in bringing this text together.

List of figures and tables

Figures

Tables

List of abbreviations

AIDS	acquired immune deficiency syndrome
ANCOVA	analysis of covariance
ANOVA	analysis of variance
APA	American Psychological Association
AR	action research
ASC	Annual Schools Census
BECTA	British Educational Communications and Technology Agency
BERA	British Educational Research Association
CA	conversation analysis
CAQDAS	Computer-Assisted/Aided Qualitative Data Analysis
CHASS	Council for Humanities, Arts and Social Sciences (Australia)
CMC	computer-mediated communication
CONSORT	Consolidated Standards of Reporting Trials
CoPE	Certificate of Personal Effectiveness
CPD	continuing professional development
CSDP	Comer's School Development Program
DCSF	Department for Children, Schools and Families
ECLS	Early Childhood Longitudinal Study
Edna	Education Network Australia
ELESIG	Evaluation of Learners' Experiences of e-learning Special Interest Group
EPPI Centre	Evidence for Policy and Practice Information and Co-ordinating Centre
ERA	Excellence in Research for Australia
ERIC	Education Resources Information Center
ESDS	Economic and Social Data Service
ESL	English as a Second Language
ESRC	Economic and Social Research Council
FSM	free school meals
GNVQ	General National Vocational Qualification

GPA	grade point average
GPS	global positioning system
GT	grounded theory
GTCE	General Teaching Council for England
GTM	grounded theory method
HE	higher education
HEFCE	Higher Education Funding Council for England
HIV	human immunodeficiency virus
HSB	High School and Beyond
ICC	intra-class correlation
IDeA	Improvement and Development Agency
IEA	International Association for the Evaluation of Educational Achievement
IPRN	ITT Professional Resource Networks
IRF	Initiation, Response, Feedback/Follow-up
ITT	initial teacher training
IWB	interactive whiteboard
LTE	language teacher education
NFER	National Foundation for Educational Research
NHST	null hypothesis significance testing
OECD	Organisation for Economic Cooperation and Development
ONS	Office for National Statistics
PAR	participatory action research
PICOS	participants, interventions, outcomes, study designs
PISA	Programme for International Student Assessment
PRISMA	Preferred Reporting Items for Systematic Reviews and Meta-Analyses Statement
QCA	Qualifications and Curriculum Authority
QCDA	Qualifications and Curriculum Development Agency
QUOROM	Quality of Reporting of Meta-analyses
RAE	Research Assessment Framework
RCT	randomised controlled trial
RDI	Researcher Development Initiative
RSA	Royal Society of Arts
SDM	standard mean deviation
SDQ	Strengths and Difficulties Questionnaire
SES	socio-economic status
SETT	Self-Evaluation of Teacher Talk
SIVS	strategically important and vulnerable subject
STEM	science, technology, engineering and mathematics
TDA	Training and Development Agency for Schools
TESL	Teaching English as a Second Language
TM	Transition Mathematics
UCAS	Universities Central Admissions Service
VLE	virtual learning environment
VSFG	very small focus group

About the editors

Professor James Arthur, Head of School of Education, University of Birmingham. He has written widely on the relationship between theory and practice in education, particularly the links between communitarianism, social virtues, citizenship, religion and education. He is director of citizED, sits on the executive of the *Society for Educational Studies* and is editor of the *British Journal of Educational Studies*.

Professor Robert J. Coe, Durham University, Professor of Education and Director of the Centre for Evaluation and Monitoring. His research interests include evaluation methodology, evidence-based education and the involvement of practitioners in research, school effectiveness and improvement including the methodology of school effectiveness research, the use and effects of feedback especially in performance monitoring information systems, and the statistical comparability of examinations in different subjects and over time.

Professor Larry V. Hedges, Northwestern University, Professor of Statistics and Social Policy. A national leader in the fields of educational statistics and evaluation, his research is in the fields of sociology, psychology and educational policy. He is best known for his work to develop statistical methods for meta-analysis in the social, medical and biological sciences.

Dr Michael Waring, Loughborough University, Senior Lecturer. He is on the editorial board of the *British Journal of Educational Studies*. His research interests focus on teaching and learning, the critique and development of grounded theory methodology, and the level and determinants of young people's involvement in physical activity.

Notes on the contributors

Dr Michael V. Angrosino, University of South Florida, Professor Emeritus. He teaches on cultural anthropology, qualitative methods and rethinking anthropology modules and his research interests are in organised religion in secular society, symbolic interactionism, psychological anthropology and ethnography.

Dr Michael Atkinson, University of Toronto, Associate Professor. He is associate editor of *Deviant Behavior* and assistant editor of *International Journal of Qualitative Methods.* His research interests include physical activity, health, bioethics and social policy, violence, crime and exploitation in sport, and poststructuralism, existentialism and physical cultural studies.

Dr W. Douglas Baker, Eastern Michigan University, Associate Professor. He is an associate professor in the department for English Language and Literature. He teaches courses that focus in some way on writing and instructional methods for secondary school teachers and students. He coordinates accreditation demands of the National Council for Accreditation of Teacher Education (NCATE), co-directs the Eastern Michigan Writing Project (EMWP) and co-edits *Language Arts Journal of Michigan.*

Dr Greg Benfield, Oxford Brookes University, Educational Development Consultant. His work focuses on supporting e-learning and he is a tutor on the Postgraduate Certificate of Teaching in Higher Education. He is a Fellow of the Assessment Standards Knowledge exchange (ASKe). His research interests include learner experiences of e-learning, computer-aided assessment and computer-mediated communication.

Dr Ghazala Bhatti, University of Southampton, Deputy Director of Postgraduate Research Degrees. She is a founding member of the Network for Social Justice and Intercultural Education of the European Conference on Educational Research. Her research interests include social justice, ethnographic research, bilingualism in schools, comparative education research and the educational achievements of children from minority ethnic backgrounds.

Professor Gert Biesta, University of Stirling, Professor of Education and Director of Research. He is the editor of Studies in Philosophy and Education. He conducts theoretical and empirical research on a range of topics but is particularly interested in the relationships between education, democracy and citizenship. He is also interested in the educational potential of complexity theory.

Michael Borenstein, BioStat, Expert. He is an expert in meta-analysis working for BioStat, a programme funded by the National Institutes of Health in the United States for the purpose of developing computer programs for statistical power analysis and for meta-analysis.

Dr Axel Bruns, University of Queensland, Associate Professor. He is associate professor in the Creative Industries Faculty at Queensland University of Technology in Brisbane. He is a chief investigator in the ARC Centre of Excellence for Creative Industries and Innovation (CCi). He is a co-founder of the premier online academic publisher M/C – Media and Culture. His research interests are in produsage (or collaborative user-led content development), social media, blogging, social network mapping, citizen journalism, online communities, creative industries and popular music studies.

Dr Jean Burgess, Creative Industries Faculty, Queensland University of Technology, Deputy Director, CCI, and Senior Research Fellow. Her research includes communication and media studies, cultural studies, film, television and digital media. She obtained her PhD from Queensland University of Technology and is a member of the ARC Cultural Research Network and Association of Internet Researchers.

Professor Paul Connolly, Queen's University Belfast, Professor of Education. He is director of the Centre for Effective Education as well as Improving Children's Lives: An Inter-Disciplinary Research Initiative at Queen's University Belfast, and is editor of the *Effective Education* journal. His research interests include diversity and social inclusion in early childhood and quantitative methods and statistics in educational research.

Professor Ian Davies, University of York, Professor of Education. He is the editor of the citizED and CiCea journal *Citizenship Teaching and Learning.* Publications include the *Sage Handbook of Education for Democracy and Citizenship.* His research interests include citizenship education, history of education and social studies education.

Dr Laura Day Ashley, University of Birmingham, Research Fellow. She has a background in social anthropology and a particular interest in anthropological, sociological and historical approaches to the study of education. She leads the Masters module Practitioner Inquiry in Education and the undergraduate module Schooling: A Social and Cultural History. Her research interests include education for marginalised groups, education in India and private/non-state sector education.

Kelly Dickson, Institute of Education, University of London, Research Officer. Her background is in applied psychology and sociology and social research methods. She teaches the Institute of Education MA module in Systematic Research Synthesis and her current work includes leading systematic reviews in education and social care and working with review groups to undertake systematic reviews.

Dr Anita Gibbs, University of Otago, Associate Professor. She supervises postgraduate research related to adult criminal justice and probation, social work research methods, inter-agency collaboration and family practice areas. Her research interests are in mainstream, alternative and indigenous social work theories and methodologies, probation and criminal justice, especially alternatives to custody, and home detention and electronic monitoring.

Mr Graham R. Gibbs, University of Huddersfield, Reader in Research Methods. He is course co-ordinator for MSc Social Research and Evaluation. His research interests include computer-assisted learning and the use of computers in the social sciences. He has published on the sociology of the state and computer-assisted learning and been involved in a number of local environmental projects.

Professor Stephen Gorard, University of Birmingham, Professor of Education Research. He has conducted studies of primary education, early childhood, secondary education, FE, HE, adult and continuing education, and informal learning in the home. His research approach is multi-method, combining large-scale surveys, focus group work, complex statistical modelling and historical archive analysis, among others. He is the associate editor of *Evaluation and Research in Education*, editor of Continuum Publishers' *Empirical Studies in Education*, and *Trials in Public Policy*.

Professor Judith L. Green, University of California, Santa Barbara, Professor of Education. She is Director of Center for Literacy & Inquiry in Networking Communities, Gevirtz Graduate School of Education. Her research interests include learning within and across disciplines, literacy across disciplines, research methods – qualitative and ethnographic, cross case research, action research and early childhood education.

Ms Jill Hall, University of York, Research Fellow. She works as a Research Fellow in Health Sciences, and has written and co-written numerous publications around her research interests in complex wounds, patient involvement in patient safety, clinical trials in fracture prevention and podiatry, and systematic reviews of the effectiveness of interventions.

Professor Ronald K. Hambleton, University of Massachusetts Amherst, Distinguished University Professor. He is also Co-Chairperson of the Research and Evaluation Methods Program, and Executive Director of the Center for Educational Assessment. He teaches graduate-level courses in educational and psychological testing and educational research methods including survey research. He has served as editor or co-editor of many special issues of journals including the *European Journal of Psychological Assessment*, *Applied Psychological Measurement* and *Language Testing*.

Professor Steve Higgins, Durham University, Professor of Education. His research interests include the areas of effective use of information and communications technology (ICT) and digital technologies in schools, understanding how children's thinking and reasoning develops, and how teachers can be supported in developing the quality of teaching and learning in their classrooms. He was previously the founding Director of the Research Centre for Learning and Teaching at Newcastle University.

Dr Rosalind Hurworth, University of Melbourne, Associate Professor. She is Director at the Centre for Program Evaluation and Cluster Leader in the Graduate School of Education. She teaches on postgraduate courses including a a module in Research Methods in Education: Qualitative Methods. She has led, taken responsibility for, or made a major contribution to over one hundred local, state and national projects.

Dr Jenni Karlsson, University of KwaZulu-Natal, Deputy Head: School of Education and Development. Her research interests span education policy, school space and visual methods. She is a member of an international team researching how the global mandates about gender equality and poverty reduction are treated in policy and practice within the education systems of Kenya and South Africa. She also teaches Education and Policy modules at postgraduate level.

Professor Harvey J. Keselman, University of Manitoba, Professor of Psychology. He is Head of the Department of Psychology at the University of Manitoba. His current research program involves developing statistical tests that will be insensitive (robust) to non-normality and variance heterogeneity in independent and correlated groups designs. He would like to initiate in the future testing of social scientists' use of statistical tests to assess whether or not the effect of an experimental manipulation is significant.

Professor Marilyn Leask, University of Bedfordshire, Dean. She is well known for her work on knowledge management in education and in building the evidence and knowledge base for teacher education and classroom practice. Her current work includes developing national and international models for scaling up promising small-scale research. She is co-editor of the Learning to Teach in the Secondary School series of text books which are widely used for teacher training and which cover all subjects.

Ms Kate Light, University of York, Information Specialist. She is an information specialist at the Centre for Reviews and Dissemination (CRD), University of York. She is responsible for contributing to systematic reviews, mainly through the design and running of complex search strategies. She also contributes to the production of CRD's DARE and HTA databases and teaches on systematic review training courses run by CRD.

Dr Lisa Lix, University of Saskatchewan, Associate Professor. She is also Centennial Chair at the School of Public Health, Site Director at the Western Regional Training Centre for Health Services Research and Adjunct Scientist, Health Quality Council, Saskatoon. Her research interests include analysis of longitudinal/ repeated measures data and multivariate analyses of quality of life and behavioural health outcomes.

Professor Gary McCulloch, Institute of Education, University of London, Brian Simon Professor of History of Education. He teaches History of Education and Understanding Education Research. He is a member of advisory boards of *History of Education*, *History of Education Review*, *History of Education Quarterly*, *Journal of Educational Administration and History*. His research interests are in the history of education, including curriculum history, the history of secondary education and documentary research methods.

Dr Carolyn L. Mears, University of Denver, Affiliated Faculty and Guest Lecturer. Carolyn L. Mears holds a research appointment and is dissertation advisor and adjunct faculty at the University of Denver. She serves on the Expert Council of Firestorm Solutions, an organisation dedicated to risk mitigation and crisis recovery. Her research interests include qualitative research, school violence and its prevention, social research methods and methodologies and trauma. Her recent publication, *Interviewing for Education and Social Science Research: The Gateway Approach*, was selected by AERA as a finalist for the Outstanding Qualitative Book of the Year Award 2010.

Professor Claudia Mitchell, McGill University, Professor of Education. She is a professor in the McGill University Department of Integrated Studies in Education. Her research interests include youth, gender and AIDS, visual and arts-based research methodologies, girls' education in development studies and teacher identity.

Professor Carol Munn-Giddings, Anglia Ruskin University, Professor in the Department of Social Work and Social Policy. She was previously Head of the Research Section at Essex Social Services and has worked as a researcher in various health and social care settings. Her research interests are in self-help/ mutual aid groups, user-run organisations (self-help organisations) and practitioner, user and carer involvement in research and action research.

Dr Mark Newman, Institute of Education, University of London, Reader in Evidence-informed Policy and Practice in Education and Social Policy. He teaches on several postgraduate modules. His background includes health, social sciences and education. His academic interests include developing methods and processes for policy and practice decision-making across different areas of social policy and methods for the design and evaluation of effective learning environments in professional and clinical education.

Dr Andrew Peterson, Senior Lecturer in Education, Canterbury Christ Church University. He works in the field of the education of citizenship teachers and has published in the field of civic and moral education. He sits on the executive of the Society for Educational Studies and on the editorial board of the *British Journal of Educational Studies*.

Professor Richard Pring, University of Oxford, Senior Research Fellow. Formerly Director of the Department of Educational Studies, a position that he held for 14 years. He was Lead Director of the Nuffield Review of 14–19 Education and Training, a £1 million six-year project, funded by the Nuffield Foundation. His research interests include philosophy of education,

education and training of 14–19 year olds and studies of faith-based schools.

Jordan Rickles, UCLA, Fellow, Department of Education. His research interests include quasi-experimental design and causal inference. Jordan is developing a study to identify the factors associated with enrolment in 8th grade algebra and estimating the effects of 8th grade algebra on high-school performance in the US. He previously spent three years as a research analyst within the Los Angeles Unified School District.

Professor Michael Seltzer, University of California, Los Angeles, Professor of Education. He has published widely in the areas of growth modelling, hierarchal models and sensitivity analysis. His research interests include hierarchical models, methods for Bayesian analysis, methodology for multi-site evaluations and longitudinal analysis.

Dr Rhona Sharpe, Oxford Brookes University, Educational Development Consultant. She is a staff and educational consultant with particular responsibility for promoting the effective use of technologies within teaching, learning and assessing in order to meet the university's strategic aims. She is a tutor on the Postgraduate Certificate in Teaching in HE. Her current research interests are in online professional development and the implementation and evaluation of learning technologies. She is currently associate editor of the *International Journal for Academic Development* and holds a SEDA Fellowship.

Dr Audra Skukauskaite, University of Texas at Brownsville, Associate Professor. She is an associate professor of research, with emphasis on qualitative and interpretive research methodology. She teaches research on the doctoral programme and works with the faculty on their research at the UTB Department of Curriculum and Instruction. Her research involves examining access to education afforded diverse students and the impact of reforms on teachers, as well as discourse and video analyses of interviews, documents and classroom data.

Professor Emma Smith, University of Birmingham, School of Education. Her research interests are in equity issues in the field of education and in the role that educational policy can play in reducing inequalities and closing achievement gaps. She is Head of Department for the Department of Education and Social Justice. She also teaches on a range of undergraduate and postgraduate courses. She is on the editorial board of the *British Educational Research Journal* and is executive editor of *Educational Review*.

Dr Michael Tedder, University of Exeter, Research Fellow. He has taught Liberal Studies and been responsible for teacher education for many years. His research interests include life history and biographical research, adult and community learning, the experiences of young people on vocational courses in FE, and notions of professionalism in post-compulsory education.

Dr Robert Thornberg, Linköping University, Associate Professor of Education. His main focuses are on bullying and peer harassment among children in school settings, school rules, moral practices, student participation and social interactions in everyday school life, and student perspectives on bullying as well as on school rules and teachers' discipline practices. He is also co-ordinator for Empirical Research on Value Issues in Education.

Professor Carole Torgerson, University of Birmingham, Professor of Medical Education. Previously, she held a Readership in Evidence-based Education at the University of York. Her main methodological research interests are in experimental methods (randomised controlled trials and quasi-experiments) and research synthesis. She is particularly interested in applying methodological work in experimental research previously undertaken in the field of health care to the field of education.

Professor Peter Tymms, Durham University, Professor of Education. He is Head of Department and Chair of the Board of Studies in the School of

Education. He is on the Expert Board of the European Science Foundation and is an adviser to the German NEPS project. His main research interests include monitoring, assessment, performance indicators, ADHD, reading and research methodology.

Dr Elaine Vaughan, Mary Immaculate College, Teaching and Learning Advocate. She works in the Centre for Teaching and Learning at Mary Immaculate College. Her research interests include institutional and professional discourse, humour in discourse, the profession of English language teaching both inside and outside the classroom, and spoken language and corpus analysis.

Professor Anna Vignoles, Institute of Education, University of London, Professor of Economics of Education and Deputy Director of the Centre for the Economics of Education. She has written widely on the subject of the quantitative evaluation of education policy, the economic value of education and skills and the use of longitudinal data in education research.

Professor Rob Walker, University of East Anglia, Professor of Education. He teaches and researches in the area of 'higher education practice', dealing both with the practicalities of day-to-day teaching in lecture theatres, seminars and on websites, and acknowledging the growing debates about research, teaching and curriculum. He works in the Centre for Applied Research in Education (CARE) and is a member of the Learning Technology Group.

PART I

INTRODUCTION TO RESEARCH METHODS AND METHODOLOGIES IN EDUCATION

1

Introduction
How this book can help you

James Arthur

Using a variety of methodological approaches and research techniques in education, this book sets out to provide students with the theoretical understandings, practical knowledge and skills which they need to carry out independent research.

The editors bring together an array of international contributors, all of whom identify key research methodologies, data collection tools and analysis methods, and focus on the direct comparisons between them.

The editors have ensured that each chapter is written in an accessible and informative way, with each chapter setting out the strengths and weaknesses of key research methods by:

- identifying specific research designs;
- presenting a series of relevant data collection tools;
- highlighting the various analytical methods which can be used.

The chapters cover the full range of methodologies and methods, including Internet research, mixed methods research and the various modes of ethnographic research. All chapters provide the reader with an introduction describing the method, technique or approach (and identifying associated methodology);

detailed guidance on the method or approach; examples of the application in process; summaries regarding ethics, data collection, sampling and reliability, as well as the advantages and disadvantages of different techniques; and good practice in presenting findings.

The chapters in Part III of the book all provide readers with annotated further reading and questions for further investigation, aimed to stimulate ideas and discussion.

This book is an essential text for M-level students and other postgraduates involved in Education and Educational Research Methods programmes.

Chapters and layout

There are three parts to this text:

I   Introduction to research methods and methodologies in education
II Basic principles and practice in conducting research
III Key methods
    Research designs
    Data collection tools
    Analysis methods.

Part I contextualises educational research, high-lighting the various forms, purposes and demands that it faces today. It provides the reader with an overview of associated notions of criticality, truth and information, and Rob Coe's chapter on 'The Nature of Educational Research' explores the different understandings of educational research, clearly and logically presenting different ways in which the researcher might see the world.

Part II identifies the relationship between the four key building blocks of research (ontology, epistemology, methodology and methods). It begins with Larry V. Hedges' chapter on the 'Design of Empirical Research'. This section links a student's or researcher's perceived nature or assumptions around educational research with the practicalities of designing a research project, planning your research (Day Ashley) and conducting the research (Coe). Having linked the first three building blocks of research, the relationship with the final block is made and the process of selecting and using appropriate techniques to collect data are explored. As this section of the text leads the reader through the design of a research project, the planning, inferences and interpretations involved in conducting research in the field, it progresses to look at the necessary dissemination and impact of the research findings, once the research is complete (Leask).

The text moves on to highlight the use of key research methods. It does this by drawing on a range of international researchers who have been involved in an array of recent and current research projects and who have implemented different methods to obtain their research data. These chapters, which form Part III, Dimension 1 of the book, provide a unique and unmatched showcase of different methods of research by providing an insight into current educational research projects. These 'mini-chapters' offer showcases of recent research, as well as philosophical insights into different aspects of educational research. These chapters form a fascinating prelude

to Dimensions 2 and 3 of the text, which provide a range of contributions detailing introductions on both the tools required for data collection and relevant methods for analysing data obtained. These chapters form the main body of the book and have been written by leading academics, experts in each of the various methods of data collection and data analysis.

Those data collection tools identified range from those which are well established in many aspects of educational research such as observations in classrooms and other educational settings, in-depth interviews and focus groups, to newer techniques involving online and Internet-based approaches. Within these chapters the reader is given precise information regarding the potential advantages and disadvantages of employing each of the data collection tools, as well as being provided with selections of suggested further reading from the author, who also sets a number of challenging questions for further investigation should the reader wish to follow up their interest in a particular area of research.

The methods of analysis discussed in Part III, Dimension 3 acknowledge the importance and value of both qualitative and quantitative methods of analysis. It also highlights the tremendous value of using these methods of analysis in conjunction with each other within a research project.

This text provides a wealth of material which is accessible to all levels of student and educational researchers who are seeking to conduct almost any type of educational research. The text provides a fresh and current view of the educational research landscape, ensuring that the theoretical aspects are fully supported by numerous and 'real' practical examples, as well as the precise unassuming guidance from world-leading academics. Those examples of research design 'showcased' really do allow the reader to appreciate the outcomes of a well considered and designed research project.

The nature of educational research

Robert J. Coe

Introduction

Many books on research methods start with a section that describes a range of different views about what research is. For some, understanding these different views is a prerequisite to thinking about doing any kind of research: you cannot do or understand research unless you are clear about fundamental philosophical issues of ontology, epistemology and axiology. Moreover, these issues really are fundamental in the sense that the philosophical position you adopt determines the kinds of research that is worth doing, the kinds of questions you can ask and the methods you will use. The different positions are often presented as a package, with a collection of apparently coherent views about different aspects of research combining to form a 'paradigm' – a world-view or perspective – being shared by groups of researchers who adopt the whole paradigm as the one true way and defend it in opposition to any other set of views.

Our approach here is pragmatic and eclectic. Whether or not the philosophical positions determine the research approach, it is important for researchers to understand their own and others' views about the nature of reality (ontology), how we can know about it (epistemology) and the different values (axiology) that may underpin enquiry, along with a number of other differences. It probably is true that certain

views tend to go together and will influence choices about what kinds of questions a researcher believes to be interesting and important, as well as the methods they adopt to answer them. It may be important for researchers to understand how alternative positions have arisen as a reaction to what was seen as the constraining dominance of a particular view. It is true that researchers are influenced by each other and tend to gravitate to common understandings across a range of issues. However, it is also true that in practice many researchers are often not as consistent as the philosophers might exhort them to be; although allegiance to a particular 'paradigm' may be a fundamental commitment for some, others can see the merits of both sides of an argument about opposing views, and may be willing to move between positions and back again.

In the next section we present an outline of some of the different positions researchers may take along a number of dimensions. Next we discuss different views about how, if at all, these positions can be reconciled. A third section discusses different aims for educational research. The last two sections of this chapter present, respectively, an attempt to define what distinguishes research from other forms of enquiry and what distinguishes good research from bad.

Dimensions of difference: paradigms?

In Table 2.1 below each row represents a dimension or aspect of difference in views about the nature of research. The two columns present the extreme or opposing views on this dimension. A simplistic interpretation would be to identify the positions outlined in the left-hand column with 'positivism' and quantitative research, while those on the right present the 'constructivist', qualitative paradigm. However, as we discuss below, the whole notion of a 'paradigm' is problematic and should probably be treated somewhat more critically than it often is.

What is a paradigm?

The use of the word paradigm to describe a particular way of seeing the world derives from the work of the philosopher of science, Thomas Kuhn. Kuhn (1970) explained the development of new ideas in science in terms of shared understandings or 'paradigms' within the social community of scientists. At any time there are known inconsistencies, but these are generally treated as 'puzzles' to be worked on within the rules of 'normal science'. Periodically, they become 'anomalies' that are so troublesome they trigger a 'scientific revolution' in which the dominant paradigm is replaced by a new one, generally as an older generation of scientists is replaced by a new generation rather than a result of individuals being persuaded. The old and new paradigms are 'incommensurable' in the sense that they offer wholly different ways of understanding the world and there is no higher set of values or logic by which their relative merits can be easily or objectively compared.

Although it had not always been the case, by the time Kuhn was putting forward these ideas in the 1960s and 1970s the dominant view of educational research in countries like the UK and US was essentially a scientific perspective, with most research adopting statistical, experimental and hypothesis-testing approaches (Nisbet, 2005). Kuhn's work was seen as supporting a challenge to this hegemony, a challenge which also drew on established qualitative traditions in anthropology and sociology, and new (or newly applied) ideas from other disciplines, such as phenomenology, poststructuralism, postmodernism and critical theory. These new approaches were (and still are) often presented as new paradigms, though the use of this word is not really consistent with Kuhn's original use (Hammersley, 2007). Moreover, Kuhn argued that his account of scientific revolution did not apply to the social sciences which are characterised by a lack of consensus on the appropriateness of different procedures, theories and metaphysical assumptions, and hence may more appropriately be seen as an immature science in a 'pre-paradigm' period (Bird, 2009).

Despite this distortion of Kuhn's use of the word, it is still common to see particular collections of philosophical and methodological preferences for educational research described as paradigms. Hammersley (2007) describes a number of different ways of classifying educational research, including a standard two-paradigm typology (quantitative/positivist vs. qualitative/interpretive/constructivist), a three-paradigm typology (the previous two, with the addition of a critical/emancipatory paradigm) and various typologies that subdivide further into multiple paradigms (including participatory research, mixed-methods, human ecology, ecological psychology, holistic ethnography, (cognitive) anthropology, ethnography of communication, symbolic interactionism, sociolinguistics, ethnomethodology, qualitative evaluation, neo-marxist ethnography and feminist research – see Tashakkori and Teddlie, 2003; Jacob 1987; Atkinson et al., 1988; Hammersley, 2007).

Reconciling the different views

There are a number of different possible ways of dealing with the existence of different paradigms.

Incommensurability

The first is to accept the fundamental nature of these paradigms along with the need for consistency within each, and to see them as basically incommensurable. Under this view it is not possible to pick and mix from the available options; a philosophical commitment to a particular way of seeing the world necessarily implies the adoption of certain approaches and the rejection of others. If you believe, for example, that

Table 2.1   Differences in views about the nature of research

The world and phenomena are real and exist independently of perception.	Social phenomena are always perceived in a particular way; they have no 'reality' independent of perception.
There is truth and objective knowledge about the world.	All knowledge is subjective and socially constructed.
It is possible to find universal laws and knowledge that are generalisable.	Individual social contexts are unique; generalisation is neither desirable nor possible.
Research should aim to discover general (generalisable) explanations for phenomena and to make generalisable predictions.	Research should aim to understand individual cases and situations and to focus on the meaning that different actors bring to them.
The kinds of objective knowledge and facts discovered by research are not dependent on the values and beliefs of particular researchers.	Understanding the values and beliefs of researchers is crucial to understanding their claims.
Power relationships are not relevant to the truth.	Power, and particularly imbalances of power, are central to understanding social phenomena. A key purpose of research is to emancipate and transform.
Research aims to develop and test hypotheses. Hypotheses must be clearly stated before a study can be designed to test them.	Research is inductive, following an unending dialectical cycle of thesis, antithesis, synthesis. Hypotheses and theory emerge in the course of researching; they are critically tested and refined against data and theory. Researchers aim to avoid making assumptions before collecting data.
The world is fundamentally mechanistic and deterministic, in which human behaviour is governed by general laws and is capable of manipulation.	Human beings are active participants in the researched world, interacting with rather than reacting to their environment, constructing situations by bringing their own meanings and acting freely.
Phenomena can be understood by analysis of their component parts (reductionist).	Social phenomena are more than the sum of their parts and can be understood only holistically.
Causal laws exist, determine behaviour and can be discovered by the methods of science (e.g. experiments).	The complexity, level of interactivity, situational specificity and contextual dependence of social phenomena prevent the traditional concept of causation from being useful or appropriate.
Constructs must be operationalised to be used in research. Many constructs can be quantified and treated as having measurement properties. Characteristics such as validity and reliability are crucial.	Many constructs cannot usefully be quantified; only rich qualitative description can capture their essence. Representations of phenomena must be authentic, based on studying things in their natural settings.
Generalisation from observed samples to wider populations is justified in terms of statistical representativeness and probability sampling.	Observed cases can be a basis for generalisable theory and understandings, even where the number of cases is small (perhaps even one) and they are selected for some particular characteristics.
Quantitative.	Qualitative.
Positivist, neo-positivist, post-positivist	Anti-positivist, constructivist (constructionist) , interpretivist (interprevist).

our knowledge of social phenomena is inevitably subjective and socially constructed then it makes no sense to seek general laws to describe the world. Nor is it possible to compromise between these discrete defensible positions. Either you believe the world exists independently of our knowledge of it, or you don't; there is no middle way.

One consequence of the belief that different paradigms are incommensurable is that there is no way to compare or evaluate the relative merits of the approaches and results of research conducted under different paradigms. The choice to adopt, or believe the findings from, one particular paradigm over another cannot in principle be justified logically, since by definition such a logical argument can only be made within a particular paradigm (Pring, 2000).

Compatibility

A second approach allows that researchers must take a philosophical stance on fundamental issues such as the nature of reality and knowledge and on core values, but that these do not necessarily constrain other choices about the kinds of questions and methods they adopt. In this view, the differences are real and important but, in the words of Gage (1989), 'Paradigm differences do not require paradigm conflict.' For example, one may believe in a realist ontology but still emphasise an interpretive approach, focusing on the meanings that participants bring to a situation and using naturalistic observation with qualitative data to study them. Or a feminist/emancipatory researcher may adopt the use of randomised controlled trials (e.g. Oakley, 2006; Mertens, 2005).

There is arguably some asymmetry in this perspective, however, since it may be harder to imagine a researcher who believes all knowledge is subjective and personal wanting to conduct large-scale surveys involving statistical analysis of quantitative data. For this reason, this perspective might be seen as a kind of positivism, albeit softened by the adoption of qualitative methods and the inevitable acceptance of subjectivity they imply, but in which those qualitative methods are essentially subservient to the quantitative. Certainly, an acceptance of compatibility is likely to depend on an environment in which researchers with different perspectives are able to respect the differences of others and feel confident enough of the security of their own position to be tolerant of others.

Pragmatism

A third perspective adopts the philosophical stance of pragmatism, rejecting the traditional philosophical dichotomies of realist vs. idealist ontology and subjective vs. objective epistemology. Some have linked pragmatism with an explicitly mixed-methods approach and even argued that the use of mixed-methods is a paradigm in its own right (e.g. Johnson and Onwuegbuzie, 2004). However, another reading of the pragmatic approach is to see the whole notion of paradigms as problematic and unhelpful. In this sense, pragmatism is not just another philosophy, but is itself an anti-philosophy – not another paradigm, but a challenge to the whole notion of paradigms. According to this view, research may be conducted for particular reasons, for example to find answers to certain questions or to redress key inequities or injustices. The choice of those reasons is likely to be influenced by the values and beliefs of the researchers (including their, perhaps implicit, metaphysical beliefs); the particular questions or aims they select will also influence the research methods they use.

There are therefore practical and logical reasons why philosophy and methodology are not independent. However, it is an oversimplification, and unnecessary constraint, to see all research as having the characteristics of one of a small number of paradigms.

Different aims for educational research

Alongside the different paradigms and different approaches to reconciling them, it is important to recognise that research is conducted for a range of very different reasons. As mentioned above, in some presentations of the different paradigms these reasons or research aims are combined with the philosophical and methodological differences outlined above to form further paradigms, such as the emancipatory paradigm or feminist research. Identifying a particular research aim with its own paradigm may be a way of emphasising the importance of that aim, since for those who adopt it, it fundamentally transforms everything they do. However, it is also clear that a single piece of research often has a mixture of aims of different kinds, and that different research studies with very different approaches may nevertheless overlap in their aims. For this reason we see the aims of a piece of research as a separate dimension from its values, assumptions and methodology, and present the following typology of different aims for educational research.

Scientific

The first set of aims for research may be described as scientific, in the broadest sense. This kind of research sets out to understand the world, to build, test and support theory, to discover or create knowledge. 'Scientific' here is not meant to imply a preference for a particular approach, such as quantification, or even a preference for empirical enquiry, but simply a search for knowledge. It is probably unusual for any educational research not to include some scientific aims.

Political

A second category of research aims is essentially political, in the sense that the research aims to change the world. If we hope our research may be used to help improve education in some way then it has at least partially political aims. Although research may not have explicitly political aims, it is perhaps unusual for these not to be at least implied; research funders increasingly call for research to have 'impact'.

Therapeutic

A third class of aims covers research that sets out to help individuals. The distinction between this and the previous category is that the individuals are in some sense participants in the research. This would be the case, for example, in action research, in which a practitioner-researcher works in a particular context alongside other actors to help address particular problems in that context.

Aesthetic

A final category of research aims may be described as aesthetic. Research with this kind of aim attempts to express, affirm or represent human experience, to 'engage, surprise, attract, shock, delight, connect the unconnected, stir the memory and fertilise the unconscious', or to 'communicate something ultimately unsayable' (Saunders, 2003). The research may have a poetic or literary quality, setting out to tell a story, perhaps using arts-based forms to present its messages, and aiming to connect with readers on an emotional or spiritual level (Barone and Eisner, 2006).

Other ways of classifying different types of educational research

There are a number of other distinctions that can be made and it may be helpful to understand these differences.

Applied vs. basic

This distinction is made by many writers. Applied educational research is focused on questions of practice or policy, with the intention of informing or improving some aspect of them and often containing explicit recommendations for action. Reports are likely to be publicly available and may be written for a lay audience. Applied research is sometimes commissioned by a particular agency with a specific agenda and is governed by an explicit contract with the researchers.

Basic research, by contrast, is conducted for the advancement of knowledge, with no concern about whether the research is directly or immediately useful in any way. This kind of research is typically conducted within an academic community, often within a particular disciplinary structure; reports of the work are written primarily for other scholars and there is less direct accountability for the delivery of any specific, pre-determined outcomes.

Empirical vs. theoretical

Empirical educational research is grounded in observation. It takes phenomena (things that exist or happen), or at least our perceptions of phenomena, as its starting point, and attempts to represent them as data which can then be analysed. In this way, empirical research aims to represent, describe and understand particular views of the educational world.

Theoretical research focuses on ideas rather than phenomena, though of course both kinds of research require both. Theoretical educational research may present, for example, a philosophical argument, a critique or a methodological advance.

Nomothetic vs. idiographic

Nomothetic educational research seeks understanding of the general case (*nomos*, 'the law' in Greek). It aims to discover general (and explicitly generalisable) explanations for phenomena and to make generalisable predictions to further cases. Theory consists of sets of such rules, together with the conditions under which they apply. Idiographic research, on the other hand, focuses on the individual case (*idios*, 'belonging to an individual' in Greek). It aims to describe and understand what is unique and distinctive about a particular context, case or individual.

Intervention vs. descriptive

A final distinction is less commonly made but is perhaps at least as important as any of the others listed here. Intervention research actively sets out to introduce some change into the educational world, then studies the reaction. It includes types of research that may traditionally not usually have been put together, such as action research (which often has a critical, emancipatory emphasis – see Carr and Kemmis, 1986) and randomised controlled trials (generally advocated from a scientific, positivist perspective). Nevertheless, these approaches share a belief in the importance of change and the view that we can really only fully understand the world if we understand how to change it.

Descriptive research simply describes what is, without directly attempting to change it. Again, diverse approaches may be grouped together here, from ethnography (with a focus on natural settings and rich description) to large-scale surveys (characterised by generalisable, quantified measures). Of course, much apparently descriptive educational research actually has an (explicit or implicit) intention to provoke or support changes in the educational world. The point of making the distinction between intervention and descriptive research is to emphasise that we should not underestimate the difficulties of inferring implications for making changes from research that has not itself involved changing anything.

Characteristics of research

Given the variety of different kinds of educational research, the different reasons for doing it, beliefs underpinning it and methods employed to conduct it, we may question whether there are any common elements that distinguish research from other kinds of activity. We would argue that research generally has the following characteristics, though we acknowledge that not all educational research will necessarily exhibit all these qualities (for other attempts to define or discuss the characteristics of research, see, for example, Kerlinger, 1970; Bridges, 2006).

Critical

Educational research is critical in the sense that it actively seeks to question its own claims, assumptions and methods, and those of others. Where explanations are offered, the research process seeks to verify them, generating and testing alternatives. Obvious and popular perceptions or explanations are treated with caution and subjected to scrutiny. Attempts are made to identify and remove extraneous influences and confounded explanations.

Systematic

Educational research is a deliberate, planned, intentional activity. It takes a specific question or questions which provide its focus and direction. Questions may be pre-determined or emergent. Research sets out to exhaust those questions, providing answers that are as full as possible. Research aims to consider all the evidence that may be relevant to its questions, not just what is easy to access or supports a particular view.

Transparent

Educational research is transparent in the sense that its aims, methods, assumptions, arguments, data and claims are stated explicitly and clearly. Results, and their supporting justifications, are disclosed fully, taking care to minimise the danger of misinterpretation, and made widely available. Prior beliefs, conflicts of interest and biographies of researchers are disclosed, where appropriate. Sufficient information is given that the work could be replicated or checked by another researcher.

Evidential

Educational research appeals to evidence, not opinion, authority or common sense, as the basis of its justification. Empirical research is grounded in phenomena and their authentic representation as data. Clear, logical arguments link those phenomena, or other premises, to their interpretations and the claims made.

Theoretical

Educational research is guided by theory, but also seeks to build and test theory. Theory attempts to help make sense of phenomena, to allow predictions to be made, to clarify thinking, to provide conceptual tools and to enable subsequent research to build cumulatively on what has been done before.

Original

Educational research aims to add to existing knowledge in some way, either through new discovery, confirmation of previous findings, new theory or enhanced understandings. Research does more than simply re-present existing ideas, even if communicated in new or more effective ways.

How is educational research different from other kinds of research?

Defining what makes educational research different from any other research is not straightforward. Indeed, the most defensible answer may be that it is not different in any fundamental way. The notion of an academic discipline – a community of scholars who share common methods of investigation of particular types of questions, with agreed rules and criteria for judging the strength and quality of their claims – may be employed to try to define the discipline of education. Yet, as has been discussed above, such agreement about methods, questions, rules and criteria may be hard to find among those who would describe themselves as educational researchers.

We might try to avoid these differences by identifying as 'educational' any research that seeks to understand, inform or improve the practice of education. But education itself is hard to define in a way that is broad enough to include all the different kinds of activity that might come under this heading, while still retaining some common set of distinguishing characteristics.

Ball and Forzani define education as 'the deliberate activity of helping learners to develop understanding and skills' (Ball and Forzani, 2007: 530). Where this occurs in schools or similar institutions they say it is characterised by interactions among four elements: teachers, students, content and environments. These multiple interactions ('active processes of interpretation') constitute the 'instructional dynamic', which is the defining feature of education.

One problem in defining educational research is that research questions that relate to education can be found in many other, generally longer established, disciplines. For example, significant parts of psychology are concerned with learning and much psychological research addresses questions on this issue. Claiming this research as educational might be seen as an unnecessary and unwelcome attempt to appropriate something that already had a perfectly good disciplinary home. Similar arguments could be made about the existence of educational research questions in older disciplines such as sociology, philosophy, history, economics, anthropology, geography, linguistics, political science, business and health sciences. Ball and Forzani (2007) make a distinction between 'research related to education' that adopts a perspective from another discipline and 'research in education' that focuses on the 'instructional dynamic' of education by considering the multiple interactions among all four elements. Even if this definition is useful, however, it seems likely that it might include quite a small proportion of the research that is conducted by people who would describe themselves as educational researchers or that is published in educational research journals.

When education began to stake its claim to be seen as a discipline in its own right in the 1960s it became common to present it as built on the four 'foundation disciplines' of philosophy, history, psychology and sociology. The development of education as a university subject was, in the UK at least (according to Simon, 1983), a response to a political drive to establish teaching as a graduate profession, and hence to locate the professional training of teachers in universities. In a search for academic respectability beyond what R. S. Peters (cited in Bridges, 2004) had described as the 'undifferentiated mush' of existing teacher education, education studies drew on these more established disciplines. In the 1970s, a focus on the curriculum as an object of study, the rise of classroom action research and the flourishing of new research methodologies (Bridges, 2004) contributed to a weakening of the foundation disciplines. Later developments, such as the increasing demands of research funders (including governments) for educational research to have direct applications in policy or practice, the increasingly instrumental focus of teacher training and the influence of a much wider repertoire of methodologies and theories on educational research have further displaced the original four disciplines. Today, whether education is itself a discipline and, if so, what differentiates it from other disciplines is very much open to debate.

Research quality

Perhaps even harder than defining educational research is defining good research. Given the breadth of approaches to doing educational research, it seems unlikely that there will be any universal set of quality criteria. We present here a list of questions that it may be appropriate to ask in evaluating the quality of a piece of research.

- What are the research questions/aims?
- Are they clearly stated?
- Are they relevant/important?
- Does the research actually address them?
- Is the methodology appropriate to them?
- Could the research add to existing knowledge?
- Does the research build systematically on what is already known?
- Are any assumptions or beliefs of the researcher(s) made clear?
- Is it clear who funded or supported the research and whether there are any potential conflicts of interest?
- Are any definitions of terms or constructs clear?
- Are these definitions appropriate (not too broad/ narrow)?
- Is it clear how phenomena have been represented?
- Are any constructs operationalised appropriately?
- Is any interpretation of constructs (e.g. measures, scores, variables) supported by a convincing validity argument?
- How realistic or representative are the contexts in which the research was done? Are they described adequately?
- Are any samples adequate? In what sense are they representative?
- Is there enough information about the participants? Who were they? Are we told what the study meant to them?
- How were participants chosen? Who is included/ excluded? Is any non-response disclosed?
- Are the claims clear and explicit?
- Are there implicit causal claims?
- Does the evidence support the claims?
- How far are the claims generalised? Is any generalisation justified?
- Are alternative explanations offered/challenged?
- What is arbitrary? How might things have been done otherwise? Are the choices made by the researchers transparent?
- Has there been any selection in what is reported?
- If the data might have been interpreted or analysed differently, could this have led to different conclusions?

Questions for further investigation

1. In each row of Table 2.1 we have presented two opposing views. Is it helpful to see these as simplistic, caricatured extremes rather than strongly defensible alternative positions? Is it possible to agree with both positions in a row, or are they mutually contradictory?
2. To what extent should researchers be consistent in their adoption of the views presented in either column of Table 2.1? Is it possible to mix elements from the right- and left-hand columns and still be philosophically coherent?
3. Is it possible to define research in a way that distinguishes it from other forms of enquiry or writing? What distinguishes educational research from other research?
4. Of the questions listed under 'research quality', which are the most important?

Suggested further reading

Gendron, S. (2001) 'Transformative alliance between qualitative and quantitative approaches in health promotion research', in Rootman, I. et al. (eds) *Evaluation in Health Promotion: Principles and Perspectives*. World Health Organization Regional Publications, European Series, 92.

Guba, E. G. (ed.) (1990) *The Paradigm Dialogue*. Thousand Oaks, CA: Sage.

Hammersley, M. (1992) 'The paradigm wars: reports from the front', *British Journal of Sociology of Education*, 13(1): 131–43.

Lincoln, N. K. and Guba, E.G. (2000) 'Paradigmatic controversies, contradictions, and emerging confluences', in Denzin, N. K. and Lincoln, Y. S. (eds) *Handbook of Qualitative Research* (2nd edn). Thousand Oaks, CA: Sage, pp. 163–88.

Ragin, C. C. (2003) 'Making comparative analysis count'. Available at: http://www.compasss.org/RaginDayOne.PDF (accessed 4 March 2011).

Schwandt, T. A. (2000) 'Three epistemological stances for qualitative inquiry', in Denzin, N. K. and Lincoln, Y. S. (eds) *Handbook of Qualitative Research* (2nd edn). Thousand Oaks, CA: Sage, pp. 189–213.

References

Atkinson, P., Delamont, S. and Hammersley, M. (1988) 'Qualitative research traditions: a British response', *Educational Researcher*, 58(2): 231–50.

Ball, D. L. and Forzani, F. M. (2007) 'What makes education research "educational"?', *Educational Researcher*, 36(9): 529–40.

Barone, T. and Eisner, E. (2006) 'Arts-based educational research', in Green, J., Camilli, G. and Elmore, P. (eds) *Complementary Methods in Research in Education*. Mahwah, NJ: Lawrence Erlbaum Associates.

Bird, A. (2009) 'Thomas Kuhn', in *The Stanford Encyclopedia of Philosophy*, Zalta, E. N. (ed.). Available at: http://plato.stanford.edu/archives/fall2009/entries/thomas-kuhn (accessed 12 March 2011).

Bridges, D. (2004) *The disciplines and discipline of educational research*. Paper presented at the Annual Conference of the British Educational Research Association, Manchester Metropolitan University, September 2004.

Bridges, D. (2006) 'The disciplines and discipline of educational research', *Journal of Philosophy of Education*, 40(2): 259–72.

Carr, W. and Kemmis, S. (1986) *Becoming Critical: Education, Knowledge and Action Research*. Lewes: Falmer.

Gage, N. L. (1989) 'The paradigm wars and their aftermath', *Educational Researcher*, 18(7): 4–10.

Guba, E. G. (2005) 'Paradigmatic controversies, contradictions, and emerging confluences', in Denzin, N. K. and Lincoln, Y. S. (eds) *Handbook of Qualitative Research* (3rd edn). Thousand Oaks, CA: Sage.

Hammersley, M. (2007) *Methodological Paradigms in Educational Research*. London: TLRP. Available at: http://www.tlrp.org/capacity/rm/wt/hammersley (accessed 12 March 2011).

Jacob, E. (1987) 'Qualitative research traditions: a review', *Review of Educational Research*, 57(1): 1–50.

Johnson, R. B. and Onwuegbuzie, A. J. (2004) 'Mixed methods research: a research paradigm whose time has come', *Educational Research*, 33(7): 14–26.

Kerlinger, F. N. (1970) *Foundations of Behavioral Research*. New York: Holt, Rinehart & Winston.

Kuhn, T. S. (1970) *The Structure of Scientific Revolutions* (2nd edn). Chicago: University of Chicago Press.

Kuhn, T. S. (1991) 'The natural and the human sciences', in Hiley, D., Bohman, J. and Shusterman, R. (eds) *The Interpretative Turn: Philosophy, Science, Culture*. Ithaca, NY: Cornell University Press, pp. 17–24.

Mertens, D. M. (2005) *Research Methods in Education and Psychology: Integrating Diversity with Quantitative and Qualitative Approaches* (2nd edn). Thousand Oaks, CA: Sage.

Nisbet, J. (2005) 'What is educational research? Changing perspectives through the 20th century', *Research Papers in Education*, 20(1): 25–44.

Oakley, A. (2006) 'Resistances to "new" technologies of evaluation: education research in the UK as a case study', *Evidence and Policy*, 2(1): 63–87.

Pring, R. (2000) 'The "false dualism" of educational research', *Journal of Philosophy of Education*, 34(2): 247–60.

Saunders, L. (2003) 'On flying, writing poetry and doing educational research', *British Educational Research Journal*, 29(2): 175–87.

Simon, B. (1983) 'The study of education as a university subject in Britain', *Studies in Higher Education*, 8(1): 1–13.

Tashakkori, A. and Teddlie, C. (eds) (2003) *Handbook of Mixed Methods in Social and Behavioral Research*. Thousand Oaks, CA: Sage.

Finding your theoretical position

Michael Waring

Introduction

This chapter highlights the relationship between the four 'building blocks' of research (ontology, epistemology, methodology and methods) (Grix, 2002). It begins with an exploration of the nature of educational research, presenting different ways in which the researcher might see the world. It then links those assumptions with how the researcher sees what is possible with knowledge of that world. The text will then explore how this relates to certain procedures or logic to be followed in association with their views of the world and notions of knowledge within it. Having linked the first three building blocks of research, the relationship with the final block is made: the process of selecting and using appropriate techniques to collect data are explored.

Fundamentally, research is about disciplined, balanced enquiry, conducted in a critical spirit (Thomas, 2009). However, the nature of educational enquiry and subsequently those attempts to define educational research have been and continue to be problematic (see Phillips, 2005, 2006). The debate revolves around a number of issues but mainly relates to the complexity of the educational context, conceptual confusion, inappropriate adoption of positivistic interpretations of 'scientific' method and notions of rigour, as well as the dichotomy between practice and theory. Cohen et al.'s (2011: 1) definition of educational research is an acceptable one in that it acknowledges and accommodates many of the contentious issues: 'The systematic and scholarly application of the principles of a science of behaviour to the problems of teaching and learning within education and the clarification of issues having a direct and indirect bearing on those concepts.' Importantly, the use of the term science here is taken to imply both normative and interpretive perspectives.

Over recent decades there has been, and continues to be, a debate and competition over the foremost set of beliefs which will inform and guide enquiry over and above all others (Entman, 1993; Denzin and Lincoln, 2002). The debate will not be continued or reiterated to any great extent here – others offer a more comprehensive account of this (McNamara, 1979; Bradley and Sutton, 1993). The purpose here is to identify the fundamental set of assumptions that underpin all research and to make clear their interrelationship and implications.

Ontology, epistemology, methodology and methods

All researchers need to understand that their research is framed by a series of related assumptions. These assumptions can be framed around four key questions, as identified in a simplistic fashion in Figure 3.1. These questions have an order.

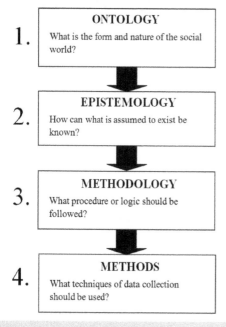

1.

ONTOLOGY
What is the form and nature of the social world?

2.

EPISTEMOLOGY
How can what is assumed to exist be known?

3.

METHODOLOGY
What procedure or logic should be followed?

4.

METHODS
What techniques of data collection should be used?

Figure 3.1   The relationship between ontology, epistemology, methodology and methods

Question 1

The first question that a researcher needs to ask relates to 'ontology'. That is: what is the nature or form of the social world? These assumptions will form the starting point for all research. Ontological positions can be seen to exist in a simplistic fashion along a continuum from left to right from realism to constructivism. In realism there is a singular objective reality that exists independently of individuals' perceptions of it. At the other end of the continuum, under constructivism reality is neither objective nor singular, but multiple realities are constructed by individuals. It is on the

basis of the answers to the ontological question that the epistemological question can be asked and assumptions are made.

Question 2

Epistemology relates to knowledge and the researcher should ask the question: how can what is assumed to exist be known? Taking the same continuum and extreme positions as identified above, the corresponding epistemological positions to realism and constructivism would be positivism and interpretivism respectively. Existing within a realist ontology, positivism sees it as possible to achieve direct knowledge of the world through direct observation or measurement of the phenomena being investigated. At the other end of the continuum, existing under a constructivist ontology, interpretivism does not see direct knowledge as possible; it is the accounts and observations of the world that provide indirect indications of phenomena, and thus knowledge is developed through a process of interpretation.

Question 3

Methodological assumptions are a reflection of the ontological and epistemological assumptions. Methodology asks what procedures or logic should be followed? Developing the notion of the continuum, to the left (under realist ontology/positivist epistemology) is nomothetic and experimental in nature. To the right (under constructivist ontology/interpretivist epistemology) is ideographic, dialectical and hermeneutical in nature.

Question 4

Often confused with methodology is the final question associated with method. This asks what techniques of data collection should be used? These will be the techniques or procedures used to gather the data. They will take various forms from questionnaires, interviews, observations, video and still images, etc. As part of Grix's (2002: 179) illustration of the interrelationship between the building blocks of research, he identifies that the method(s) are closely linked with the research questions posed and to the sources of data collected.

He also considers that methods are free of ontological and epistemological assumptions, which relate to the researcher. The immediate relationship determining the methods to be used should be (but is not always) with the research question. However, Sparkes (1992), acknowledging the confusion over terminology and the way in which it exacerbates a fundamental misunderstanding with regard to epistemological assumptions underpinning the researcher and the research, considers the researcher's ontological and epistemological assumptions to influence all aspects of research. Consequently, to say that the nature of the problem of the research will determine the overall approach and the methods of investigation, he would consider misguided.

Any researcher should fully appreciate the research process and so should be able to understand and acknowledge the fundamental relationship between the ontological, epistemological and methodological assumptions that underpin their research and inform their choice of methods. Grix (2002: 176), in his paper about the need for clarity in the use of generic research terminology, reinforces this when he says that

> . . . a clear and transparent knowledge of the ontological and epistemological assumptions that underpin research is necessary in order:
> (1) to understand the interrelationship of the key components of research (including methodology and methods);
> (2) to avoid confusion when discussing theoretical debates and approaches to social phenomena; and
> (3) to be able to recognise others', and defend our own, positions.

The nature of paradigms – making sense of reality

Kuhn (1962) is commonly associated with the notion of the paradigm and believed it to be a set of interrelated assumptions about the social world which provides a philosophical and conceptual framework for the organised study of that world. Over time numerous authors have similarly defined it as a set of 'belief systems' (Guba and Lincoln, 1989), a 'world view' (Patton, 1978; Guba and Lincoln, 1994) and a particular 'lens for seeing and making sense of the world' (Sparkes, 1992), all of which emphasise the many definitions that mark out a paradigm.

A paradigm represents a person's conception of the world, its nature and their position in it, as well as a multitude of potential relationships with that world and its constituent parts. Therefore, as the person brings along with them the 'baggage' of their previous life experiences and knowledge base to any research context, it is this very amalgamation which constructs their competence and credibility as a member of any given research community, as well as their answers to certain fundamental questions which will determine such acceptance in and of that community. Proponents of any given paradigm can summarise their beliefs relative to their responses to those ontological, epistemological, methodological and methods questions identified.

Table 3.1 outlines those basic responses which proponents located at either end of a continuum of paradigms (from positivist to interpretivist) would make in reaction to those fundamental questions. This table is intended to be a basic framework/continuum which offers extreme positions (responses) to assist the reader in their discussion to locate themselves.

It is discerning while at the same time encouraging to know that many researchers experience and acknowledge confusion over the terminology employed in this whole paradigmatical debate (Cohen et al., 2011). A host of authors (Tesch, 1990; Blaikie, 1993; Grix 2002; Weed, 2009) have identified a multiplicity of labels which have been attached to research resulting in a confusion over the meaning and conceptual level of such terminology. 'Sometimes it is difficult to distinguish clearly labels that denote an epistemological stance and those that refer to method' (Tesch, 1990: 58). One final point on terminology relates to the use of the terms qualitative and quantitative research. These do not actually exist. Qualitative and quantitative refer to data which can be gathered and used in combination or singularly in any form of research.

Table 3.1 Basic assumptions fundamental to the positivist and interpretive paradigms

Assumptions	Positivism[1]		Interpretivism[2]	
Ontology	External realist	Basic posture is reductionist and deterministic. Knowledge of 'the way things are' is conventionally summarised in the form of time- and context-free generalisations, some of which take the form of cause-and-effect laws.	Internal-idealist, relativist (local and specific constructed realities, holistic and dynamic)	Realities are apprehendable and mind-dependant.[3] There are multiple realities with the mind playing a central role by determining categories and shaping or constructing realities. We cannot see the world outside of our place in it. There is no separation of mind and objective since the two are inextricably linked together – the knower and the process of knowing cannot be separated from what is known and the facts cannot be separated from values.
Epistemology	Dualist objectivist	The investigator and investigated 'object' assumed to be independent entities; enquiry takes place as if in a one-way mirror. Investigator does not influence or is influenced by the object. Replicable findings are 'true'.	Subjectivist, transactional, interactive	The investigator and the object of the investigation are assumed to be interactively linked so that the 'findings' are literally created as the investigation proceeds. Therefore, conventional distinction between ontology and epistemology dissolves.[4]
Methodology	Nomothetic, experimental, manipulative: verification of hypotheses	Questions and/or hypotheses are stated in proportional form and subjected to empirical test to verify them; possible confounding conditions carefully controlled (manipulated) to prevent outcome from being improperly influenced.	Ideographic, dialectical, hermeneutical	The variable and personal nature of social constructions suggests that individual constructions can be elicited and refined only through interaction between and among investigator(s) and respondent(s). Conventional hermeneutical techniques are used in interpretations and compared and contrasted through a dialectical interchange. It is not a matter of eliminating conflicting or previous interpretations, but to distil a more sophisticated and informed consensus construction.
Inquiry aim	Explanation, prediction and control	Over time attempt to increasingly explain so that ultimately one can predict phenomena be they human or physical.	Understanding, interpretation and reconstruction	Over time, everyone formulates more informed and sophisticated constructions and becomes more aware of the content and meaning of competing constructions.

1. Elsewhere (Denzin and Lincoln, 1994) a post-positivist paradigm has been added to break the paradigms down further.
2. The term 'interpretivism' has been chosen because, as Sparkes (1992) has identified, it refers to a whole family of approaches which are in direct contrast to a positivist sense of social reality.
3. Mind-dependence here does not mean that the mind 'creates' what people say and do, but rather how we interpret their movements and utterances; the meaning we assign to the intentions, motivations and so on of ourselves and others becomes social reality as it is for us. In other words social reality is the interpretation (Smith, 1989, in Sparkes, 1992: 27).
4. The dashed line represents the challenge which such a posture represents between ontology and epistemology; what can be known is inextricably linked with the interaction between a particular investigator and a particular object or group.

Based upon Guba and Lincoln (1994) and Sparkes (1987, 1992).

Conclusion

Educational research is complex and there continue to be a host of debates about the nature of the educational enquiry and associated terminology. However, regardless of the definition of educational enquiry adopted, all researchers should appreciate how the research process and their research is framed by a series of fundamental questions associated with ontology, epistemology, methodology and methods. Having ownership of the process of generating assumptions allows the researcher to be informed about the interrelationship between the key components of research, to minimise confusion and to enhance their ability to critique their own research position and that of others.

Questions for Further Investigation

1. Where do you stand as an educational researcher between the different paradigms? What philosophical standpoints inform your position?
2. Why are research paradigms relevant in thinking about research processes and methods in education?
3. With regard to epistemological and ontological assumptions, what differences and commonalities underpin various research paradigms?

Suggested further reading

Conrad, C. F. and Serlin, R. C. (eds) (2006) *The Sage Handbook for Research in Education: Engaging Ideas and Enriching Inquiry*. Thousand Oaks, CA: Sage. This is a comprehensive text which identifies different issues the educational researcher faces in their research endeavours. It explores the multiple purposes and challenges of enquiry by offering many examples of how researchers have addressed the key questions in their research.

Denzin, N. K. and Lincoln, Y. (eds) (2005) *The Sage Handbook of Qualitative Research*. Thousand Oaks, CA: Sage. This book rehearses at length the paradigm debate, offering the reader an illustration of critical issues associated with a host of differing research perspectives.

Thomas, G. (2009) *How to Do Your Research Project*. London:

Sage. This is an accessible text which addresses many of the fundamental questions and issues facing the researcher conducting a research project. It provides an engaging and practical source of information for any researcher.

References

Blaikie, N. (1993) *Approaches to Social Enquiry*. Cambridge: Polity.

Bradley, J. and Sutton, B. (1993) 'Reframing the paradigm debate', *Library Quarterly*, 63(4): 405–10.

Cohen, L., Manion, L. and Morrison, K. (2011) *Research Methods in Education*. London: Routledge.

Denzin, N. K. and Lincoln, Y. (eds) (2002) *The Sage Handbook of Qualitative Research*. London and Thousand Oaks, CA: Sage.

Entman, R. M. (1993) 'Framing: toward clarification of a fractured paradigm', *Journal of Communication*, 43(4): 51–8.

Grix, J. (2002) 'Introducing students to the generic terminology of social research', *Politics*, 22(3): 175–86.

Guba, E. and Lincoln, Y. (1989) *Fourth Generation Evaluation*. Beverly Hills, CA: Sage.

Guba, E. G. and Lincoln, Y. S. (1994) 'Competing paradigms in qualitative research', in Denzin, N. K. and Lincoln, Y. S. (eds) *Handbook of Qualitative Research*. Thousand Oaks, CA: Sage, pp. 105–17.

Khun, T. (1962) *The Structure of Scientific Revolutions*. Chicago: University of Chicago Press.

McNamara, D. R. (1979) 'Paradigm lost: Thomas Khun and educational research', *British Educational Research Journal*, 5(20): 167–73.

Patton, M. (1978) *Qualitative Evaluation Methods*. Beverly Hills, CA: Sage.

Phillips, D. C. (2005) 'The contested nature of empirical educational research (and why philosophy of education offers little help)', *Journal of Philosophy of Education*, 39(4): 577–97.

Phillips, D. C. (2006) 'Exploring the multiple purposes of inquiry and key stake holders: introductory essay', in Conrad, C. F. and Serlin, R. C. (eds) *The Sage Handbook for Research in Education: Engaging Ideas and Enriching Inquiry*. Thousand Oaks, CA: Sage, pp. 3–5.

Sparkes, A. C. (1987) *The Genesis of an Innovation: A Case of Emergent Concerns and Micropolitical Solutions*. PhD, Loughborough University.

Sparkes, A. C. (ed.) (1992) *Research in Physical Education and Sport – Exploring Alternative Visions.* London: Falmer Press.

Tesch, R. (1990) *Qualitative Research: Analysis Types and Software Tools.* London: Falmer Press.

Thomas, G. (2009) *How to Do Your Research Project: A Guide for Students in Education and Applied Social Sciences.* London: Sage.

Weed, M. (2009) 'Research quality considerations for grounded theory research in sport and exercise psychology', *Psychology of Sport and Exercise*, 10: 509–10.

PART II

BASIC PRINCIPLES AND PRACTICE IN CONDUCTING RESEARCH

4

Design of empirical research

Larry V. Hedges

Introduction

Research design is the organisation of data collection so that the data collected will support unambiguous conclusions about the problem being studied. This definition focuses on empirical studies. There are other forms of research that do not centrally involve empirical evidence, such as deductive mathematical or statistical research or philosophical research, but this chapter does not speak to the issues of that research. The perspective of this chapter is that empirical research studies are designed to support arguments. The data collected is linked to the conclusions by a warrant that gives a logic explaining why the empirical evidence collected supports the validity of those conclusions.

A crucial objective of empirical research designs is to ensure transparency of the research process. That is, research designs help make explicit what research data is considered relevant, the process by which that evidence is collected, and the relation between that evidence and how it is organised in the analysis to support research conclusions. Transparency helps other scholars understand one another's work, enables it to be subjected to public scrutiny, and enables future research to build on that work.

Many different research designs are used in various traditions of educational research, so many that it would be difficult to adequately characterise them. Instead, we will focus on general principles that may be relevant to research designs that arise in many research traditions.

Problem formulation

Research design cannot be conceived in isolation from the problem the research is intended to investigate. Sound research design proceeds from an understanding of the question, problem or issue that the study addresses. Such an understanding of the problem situates the problem in a relevant context and relevant intellectual traditions. Such situation of the problem suggests what kinds of empirical evidence might be relevant, and what kinds of logics of enquiry might be employed.

Some research traditions require rather extensive specification of problems in terms of contexts, relevant empirical evidence and logics of enquiry. Other traditions frame problems in a broader context and relevant empirical evidence. For example experimental traditions often specify rather detailed specification of how the data collection will be organised, what will be measured and how the data that is collected will be analysed. On the other hand, ethnographic traditions offer much more flexibility in how the data collection is organised, what evidence may be relevant and how it will be organised in analysis.

Different problems require different research designs. The problem of understanding the normal developmental of certain intellectual skills (e.g. language development in pre-school children) may suggest research designs that passively observe development over time. The problem of determining if a particular intervention has a causal effect might suggest quite different research designs such as an experiment. Much of wise research strategy involves matching the research design to the question or research problem.

Logic of enquiry

While it is essential that research designs be well suited to the research problem, they must also be well suited to the way in which the empirical evidence will be used to draw conclusions – to the logic of enquiry used in the research. The logic of enquiry for a particular problem will be shaped by the intellectual traditions in which the researchers are working and by how they conceive the particular problem being studied. This will determine what kinds of evidence might be relevant in supporting the conclusions of the research, as well as how they might be organised in analysis.

Many logics of enquiry involve implicit or explicit comparisons of units being studied (which may be individuals or collectives such as classrooms, schools or even countries). Some logics of enquiry involve comparisons of a unit or units with external standards, conventions or ways of understanding. This is most obvious in studies like experiments or quasi-experiments that compare one group of individuals with another as an essential feature of their logic of enquiry. Such studies compare groups that are intended to be the same in every important respect except the intervention or treatment they are evaluating, arguing that any difference observed must be caused by the treatment or intervention.

A similar logic of enquiry involving comparisons motivates some kinds of research that do not manipulate or intend to draw causal conclusions. For example, survey research that attempts to describe populations often involves comparisons of one part of the population to another to give meaning to both or to define new comparative concepts, like gaps between societal groups in academic achievement. Another kind of comparison that gives meaning in logic of research arises in studies of a single unit, where the comparison is with the unit itself at a different point in time, for example a single subject time series that traces behaviour over time using comparison of the unit with itself over time to gauge progress or decline in desired behaviour. The same logic applies to time series representing the performance of aggregate units like schools over time.

Even studies that investigate a single unit (whether individual or aggregate) like intensive case studies use comparisons to give meaning to the evidence about that unit. Such studies often use internal comparisons as part of their logic of enquiry. They may also use comparisons to external standards or broader experience to give meaning to the evidence even if it is never explicitly compared to another unit. Such use of comparisons with external standards is also part of the logic of other research designs, such as surveys (e.g. assessments) that include measures with externally referenced performance standards.

In many quantitative research traditions, the logic of enquiry involves highly specific logics involving statistical methods for data analysis and hypothesis testing. For studies in these traditions, important considerations in research design involve ensuring that the data collected will support the validity of inferences drawn using the statistical analyses, for example statistical power analysis to ensure that the sample size is adequate for the hypothesis tests to have a high likelihood of detecting effects if they are present. In survey research methods for drawing probability samples are highly specified to ensure that findings will be generalisable to the appropriate population.

In many qualitative research traditions, the logics of enquiry are less specifically technical but are none the less highly evolved. For example, some logics of enquiry used in ethnography involve the idea that the process of developing descriptions, claims and interpretations must be based on evidence, subject to searches for alternative interpretations and attempts at disconfirmation.

Table 4.1 A typology of types of research design and some prominent examples of each type

	Focus of study			
	Single unit		Multiple units	
	Type of design	**Objective**	**Type of design**	**Objective**
Passive observation	Case study	Describe	Survey	Describe
	Time series	Describe	Cross sectional comparative	Describe
			Longitudinal/panel study	Describe
			Natural experiments	Infer causal effect
Manipulated treatment	$(AB)^k$ designs	Infer causal effect	Randomised experiments	Infer causal effect
	Interrupted time series	Infer causal effect	Assignment by covariate (RDD)	Infer causal effect
			Quasi-experiments	Infer causal effect

Varieties of research designs

There are many kinds of research designs, but they differ on at least two dimensions. One dimension is whether the research design involves manipulation of putative independent variables or passive observation. The other dimension is whether the research design involves a single unit (which may be a person or an aggregate unit such as a classroom or school) or multiple units. While there are sometimes ambiguities (such as designs that involve multiple intensive case studies), these dimensions are useful as principles to subdivide research designs for the purposes of discussion. This classification of research designs is summarised in Table 4.1.

Single units no manipulation

Some research designs are organised to study single units. Sometimes the purpose of the study is simply to describe the unit at one point in time. More often, designs study single units over time. For example, passive developmental studies might study the behaviour of a single individual over time, observing language or other behaviour over time in order to understand the development of cognitive skill or other concepts thought to generate behaviour. No intervention or manipulation (other than the observation) might be used nor would it be appropriate if the purpose of the study was to understand how 'normal' development unfolded. Similarly, some studies focus on an aggregate unit such as a school as it changes over time.

Intensive case studies, both contemporaneous and retrospective, fall into this category of designs. Quantitative studies such as time series designs that observe one or more variables over time for a single unit also fall into this category.

Single units with manipulation

Some research designs focus on a single unit but involve an attempt to determine if manipulating one (or more) putative independent variables will have a causal effect on another variable. For example, classic studies of single subject behaviour (often grounded in behavioural psychology) observe the behaviour of a single individual over time, but do so as different interventions are applied to try to influence that behaviour. The timing of the application of different interventions may be arbitrary or it may be highly formalised, even determined under a random allocation scheme.

Interrupted time series where outcome variables are measured over time both before and after an intervention is introduced fall into this category. The simplest of these interrupted time series designs is when there is only one observation before and one observation after the intervention is introduced (this is often called the pre-test/post-test design). In behavioural psychology, interventions are typically different reinforcement conditions. A common single subject design emphasises the differential response of outcomes to treatments, tracking the outcome under one reinforcement condition, then introducing an intervention, then removing the intervention and returning to the original reinforcement condition, then returning to the intervention. This is called the $(AB)^2$ design, mnemonic for the idea that condition A is followed by condition B and that this sequence is repeated twice. If this sequence is repeated k times, it is called an $(AB)^k$ design.

Multiple units no manipulation

Several research designs focus on *multiple* units but involve no attempt to determine if manipulating one (or more) putative independent variables will have a causal effect on another variable. These designs can be described as using passive observation, although the data collection itself may involve questionnaires, interviews, the collection of administrative or even biologic data (such as blood or saliva samples). However, the more intrusive the measurement process, the more likely it is to have effects of its own and the notion that these designs do not involve manipulation becomes more questionable.

Cross sectional surveys focus on the measurement of a collection of units at one point in time, supporting logics of enquiry that focus on comparisons between individuals at one point in time. Longitudinal surveys (also known as panel studies) collect data on the same units at several points in time to allow comparisons not only between different units at one point in time, but also the same units across time.

While surveys are among the most common research designs in this category, there are other important designs. Natural experiments are one of the most important. A natural experiment arises when existing differences in policies or practices create a situation in which naturally occurring groups that are quite similar on many variables except a key policy or practice (herein labelled the 'treatment') that is the focus of the research problem. Such natural experiments often occur when similar administrative entities adopt different policies or practices, such as when adjacent schools or school districts that are similar in other ways adopt different curricula or programmes. Natural experiments are so named because they resemble artificial experiments that (randomly) assign units to different interventions, policies or practices.

Natural experiments are difficult to distinguish from quasi-experiments using a comparison group that did not arise from manipulation by the researcher (sometimes called the non-equivalent control group design or an observational study). In both designs, the logic of enquiry is to try to deduce whether the causal effect of an intervention differs from that of another (the comparison condition) by comparing the groups on one or more outcome variables. The fundamental validity problem is to ensure that the groups being compared are alike in every way that might cause differences in outcome other than the intervention itself.

Validity claims require that extensive information be collected on the individuals in both the treated group and the comparison group on variables that could not be affected by the treatment. Variables that could not have been affected by the treatment are called *covariates*. Covariates are typically variables that have been measured before the treatment group receives the treatment (such as pre-tests), but can also be measured after the treatment has begun if they are unlikely to change (such as gender or social class). Naturally occurring comparison groups (even in natural experiments) rarely are sufficiently similar enough to the treated groups to support treatment effects without further refinement of the project's design.

The most important refinement in design is to use covariates to evaluate the equivalence of the treated and comparisons groups and to use measured values of the covariates to improve the matching of the groups. One strategy for improving the matching of groups is to construct a more closely matched comparison group by explicitly matching (on covariate values) units in the comparison group with units in the treated group. Such matching can substantially improve the pre-treatment equivalence of the comparison group to the treated group and consequently strengthen validity claims. Explicit matching works best if the distribution of covariate values in the treated and comparison groups overlap considerably and if there are considerably more potential comparison units than treated units. Even then, technical tools to facilitate multivariate matching (such as propensity scores) are often needed because units are being matched on not one but several covariates at the same time. Another strategy to improve matching of groups, which is often used in conjunction with explicit matching, is the use of statistical adjustment using the covariate values. While statistical adjustment is technically straightforward, it is viewed by many statisticians as inferior to explicit matching because it relies strongly on modelling assumptions that are often difficult to empirically falsify.

Multiple units with manipulation

Research designs in which the researcher manipulates the value of an independent variable so that different units have different values of that independent variable can provide strong evidence about the causal effects of independent variables on outcomes. There are principally two kinds of designs that rely on manipulation of independent variables by the researcher. The most prominent designs are experiments with random assignment. A lesser known alternative is the class of designs in which treatment assignment is based strictly on the value of a covariate, but where there is no random assignment.

Randomised experiments have a distinctive role in scientific enquiry because, in principle, they can provide valid inferences about the causal effect of treatments without requiring any statistical modelling assumptions. Natural experiments and other study designs that involve matching provide valid causal inferences only if all of the covariates that affect outcome have been measured and properly matched between the treatment and comparisons groups. Randomisation achieves (on average) matching on all

the covariates that a researcher may have imagined, and all the covariates the researcher *has not* imagined as well. Consequently, randomisation is a powerful tool for assuring the validity of causal inferences.

There are many varieties of experimental designs involving random assignment of units to different treatments. Individual persons can be randomly assigned to treatments, but so can aggregate units such as classrooms or schools. Random assignment of groups such as classrooms or schools to treatment often has advantages in educational studies. For example, it may be practically difficult to assign different treatments to individual students in the same classroom. It may be politically difficult to assign different treatments to different individuals or classrooms within the same school, particularly if one of the treatments seems more desirable (regardless of whether there is any actual evidence that it is superior). In some cases the theory of the treatment is that it functions through the entire unit (e.g. whole-school reforms such as school-wide positive behaviour support programmes). In such cases, assignment of treatments to aggregate units such as classrooms or schools may be desirable or even essential.

Designs that assign treatment strictly on the basis of a covariate are an alternative to randomised experiments that can also provide very strong evidence about causal effects. The most prominent of such designs in education and the social sciences is the regression discontinuity design. The regression discontinuity design with two treatments involves assignment to one treatment of individuals with a covariate score less than a certain cutpoint and assignment to the other treatment of those whose scores exceed the cutpoint. This design was first used to evaluate the effects of fellowships and prizes (which were assigned according to a score used for selection). However, this design is well suited to other situations in which allocation decisions are made via a formula involving an explicit score (such as sorting into curricula or programmes).

Validity considerations

The principle function of research design is to support validity claims about the findings of research studies. The dominant perspective on validity of research designs in quantitative social science grew out of an important paper (later published as a small book) by Campbell and Stanley (1963) that has been elaborated since then (see Shadish et al., 2002). The key to this framework is the idea that conclusions reached from research design are subject to potential threats to their validity. If we think of the research process as developing an argument supporting conclusions, these threats to validity are like counter-arguments. While their framework was developed in the quantitative domain, the general thrust of their analysis is quite general.

In the Campbell-Stanley-Cook-Shadish framework, there are four classes of threats to the validity of research designs, which we have generalised slightly below to stress their general applicability.

Data analysis validity

Cook and Campbell (1978) originally called this class of threats to validity 'statistical conclusion validity', but the idea is clearly more general. All empirical research designs involve the collection of empirical materials which are organised by the analysis in order to draw conclusions. If the design does not assure that the empirical materials used in the analysis are adequate to draw conclusions or if the analysis is not organised to permit drawing valid conclusions even if the materials collected are sufficient to do so, then the conclusions drawn from the research design will be invalid.

The specific threats to data analysis validity include:

- unreliable data elements (which might include measurements, notations of occurrences from field notes, incorrect observations of participants). Often this will occur due to too few observations, too little time spent observing or poor choices of what to observe (e.g. intrinsically variable as opposed to more stable characteristics);
- incorrect analysis, meaning an invalid summary of data elements (which could include the use of improper statistical methods, relying on impressions on memory when more verifiable means are available, such as counting instances in field notes);
- incorrect data elements (including using invalid measurements, focusing data collection on the

wrong participants or being deceived by informants).

Internal validity

This was one of the two original classes of threats to validity mentioned by Campbell and Stanley (1963). It refers to the issue of whether the relation observed between putative independent and dependent variables is a causal relation as opposed to just an association that is not causal. Obviously this class of threat applies only to research designs that are seeking to identify causal relations. Research designs or research traditions that seek just to identify associations are not subject to threats to internal validity. For research traditions that do make claims about cause and effect, achieving internal validity is a fundamental (and often daunting) validity challenge.

There is a long list of threats to internal validity in quantitative studies. Some of these threats apply only to specific types of designs, others apply more generally. For example, consider the threat of maturation given below. The threat is that individuals may have changed as part of a natural process over the period of the study and this might undermine the validity of causal claims made based on the design. Clearly this threat is more serious in a design such as the pre-test/post-test design (where it is completely indistinguishable from a change caused by the treatment) than in a design with a comparison group (where the comparison groups would also be subject to maturation and so could provide an indication of any maturation effects). Moreover, these threats are more important when a design is used to study some types of problem than when it is used to study others. For example, consider the threat of maturation again. Clearly this threat is more serious over a year-long study than a two-week study and more serious when the outcome being measured is one that is changing rapidly in the natural development of individuals like those in the study.

Important threats to internal validity include the following:

- *Ambiguous temporal precedence.* Because causes must precede their effects, any claims of causality in which the putative cause does not unambiguously precede the putative effect is suspect.

- *Observation effects.* The act of observing (or measuring or interviewing) changes the phenomenon being observed in substantial ways. This presents a threat to internal validity when observation effects might be confused with relations between putative independent and dependent variables.
- *Maturation.* Individuals grow older, wiser and more experienced over time for reasons that have nothing to do with interventions. This presents a threat to internal validity when maturation effects might be confused with relations between putative independent and dependent variables.
- *Selection.* When groups are being compared that are not randomly assigned it is possible that the groups differ in ways other than the putative independent variable which is the presumed cause of group differences in outcomes. This presents a threat to internal validity when the pre-existing differences between groups induced by selection could cause one of the groups to have higher outcome scores irrespective of the treatment.
- *Mortality.* Often, not every unit (e.g. person, classroom, or school) that begins the study persists throughout the study. This presents a threat to the internal validity of the study if the units that drop out do so in ways that are related to the putative independent variable. For example, in studies comparing two groups receiving different treatments, if the more able individuals tend to drop out of one group more frequently, and those who drop out differ from those who persist, this is a threat to the internal validity.

Generalisability

This was one of the two original classes of threats to validity mentioned by Campbell and Stanley (1963), where it was described as external validity. It refers to the issue of whether the relation observed between independent and dependent variables can be generalised from the settings, persons and contexts studied to those that are part of the scope of application intended by the researcher. Representative (that is probability or random) sampling can ensure external validity, but this is seldom a viable option outside survey research. Probability sampling requires the precise specification of the sampling frame that is the intended scope of generalisation. While external validity is often discussed in rather vague terms, the concept can be sharpened by specific explication of the intended scope of applicability of the study results.

In the absence of probability sampling, one line of argument supporting external validity is based on the similarity of the study sample to the intended scope of application. Within this scope of application, it is helpful if the research design can provide information about whether there are variations in findings across subgroups (that is interactions). Another line of argument supporting generalisability is based on the mechanism by which the independent variable has an effect on the dependent variable. To the extent that a research design can provide any information to support the mechanism, it may also support the generalisability of the findings.

Construct validity of explanation

Cook and Campbell (1978) called this threat to validity 'construct validity of cause and effect' because they focused on empirical studies of causal effects, but the idea is clearly more general. This validity threat concerns whether the explanation of the study has correctly identified the constructs in the interpretation. This concept of validity draws its inspiration from the measurement concept of construct validity and in some it ways resembles the measurement concept of consequential validity (whether the interpretations of a measurement 'as used' are correct). For example, a research design might identify a generalisable causal relation between an intervention and an outcome, but misinterpret the construct causing the effect. Hawthorne effects or novelty effects where the actual cause of the effects is attention or a change in routine rather than the attributed type of attention or the particular attributed change in routine are examples of how explanations can lack construct validity. Construct validity of explanation is not a property of designs, but of interpretation of evidence from designs, which inevitably involve the theoretical framework in which the research is embedded. However, certain design features can support the construct validity of explanations. For example, having several variations of the treatment in the design can make it possible to determine whether the effects of particular variations of the treatment are consistent with an explanation in terms of treatment constructs.

Suggested further reading

Kirk, R. E. (1995) *Experimental Design* (3rd edn). Belmont, CA: Brooks-Cole.

Kratochwill, T. (ed.) (1978) *Single Subject Research*. New York: Academic Press.

Rosenbaum, P. R. (2002) *Observational studies* (2nd edn). New York: Springer-Verlag.

Rubin, D. B. (2006) *Matched Sampling for Causal Effects*. Cambridge: Cambridge University Press.

Shadish, W. R., Cook, T. D. and Campbell, D. T. (2002) *Experimental and Quasi-Experimental Designs for Generalized Causal Inference*. New York: Houghton Mifflin.

References

Campbell, D. T. and Stanley, J. (1963) *Experimental and Quasi-experimental Designs for Research*. Chicago: Rand McNally.

Cook, T. D. and Campbell, D. T. (1978) *Quasi-experimentation*. New York: Houghton Mifflin.

Rubin, D. B. (1977) 'Assignment to treatment on the basis of a covariate', *Journal of Educational Statistics*, 2: 2–16.

Shadish, W. R., Cook, T. D. and Campbell, D. T. (2002) *Experimental and Quasi-experimental Designs for Generalized Causal Inference*. New York: Houghton Mifflin.

Thistlewaite, D. L. and Campbell, D. T. (1960) 'Regression-discontinuity analysis: an alternative to the ex post facto experiment', *Journal of Educational Psychology*, 51: 309–17.

Planning your research

Laura Day Ashley

Why is planning important?

Embarking on a research project can be overwhelming; particularly if it is the first time you have ever done such a thing. Planning is an important skill which can help you progress your research from the initial inception of an idea through to the collection and analysis of data and writing up your project. Rather than simply approaching the project in a linear fashion undertaking one task at a time in sequence, planning can encourage you to think ahead to future stages of your research and conceptualise your project as a whole. It can also enable you to anticipate potential problems you may face during the research process and consider potential resolutions to these problems in advance; as the old saying claims: 'forewarned is forearmed'. Through the process of planning you can start to take ownership of your research and realise that effectively *you* are the 'manager' of your project. As Jennifer Mason has argued, research demands 'a highly active engagement from its practitioners' (Mason, 2002: 4) as opposed to a 'passive following of methodology recipes' (ibid.) and '[i]t is vital . . . that researchers are fully conscious of the decisions they are making, and that these are informed and strategic rather than *ad hoc* or straightforwardly reactive' (ibid.: 5). By planning you can start to prepare and equip yourself for the difficult decisions you may have to make along your research journey.

Starting to plan early on

Planning is especially relevant in the early stages to help you think about the range of tasks you will need to complete before you actually start collecting your data. This section details a number of 'prestudy tasks' (Glesne, 2006) that you may need to consider, and suggests some strategies and techniques to aid your planning activities. There is some logic to the sequence in which these tasks are presented; however, they may not be carried out in this precise order. As each element of research connects with the next, you may find that you need to consider tasks further down the list before you can adequately plan for earlier ones.

Being strategic about choosing your topic

Since you will be spending a considerable amount of time investigating your research topic it helps enormously if you choose a topic that interests and motivates you. You might additionally consider how it relates to your previous experiences or future plans, perhaps in terms of your career development. It is also important that your topic does not only interest *you* but is of interest, relevance and significance in wider terms.

To help you decide on your research topic you may consider discussing your ideas and plans with various people, such as colleagues in your institution or fellow

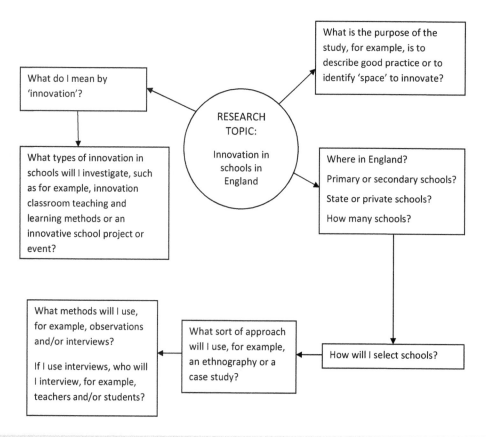

Figure 5.1   Example of a brainstorm of a research topic

students on your course, your tutor or supervisor, or practitioners and specialists in your potential field of study. Listening to their comments and questions and responding to them can be useful to help you clarify what you are planning to research and why.

Mapping out your research: research design and research questions

While it may be relatively easy to decide on a broad topic to research, it is a far more difficult task to develop focused research questions relating to your topic and design a research project that can address and answer them (Mason, 2002). Clearly defining specific research questions is an important part of planning; this set of research questions will express what you are researching and how, and will serve as an important

guide for your research project. Once you have a clear idea about the type of research questions you will be asking, you will then be able to think about the type of research design that is most suited to answer them (e.g. action research, ethnography, case study, historical research, survey, evaluation etc.). Conversely, it is possible that you already had a type of research design in mind when you decided on your topic – in this case your research questions will need to be consistent with that type of design.

Brainstorming using mind maps and spider diagrams (see Figure 5.1) is a useful technique for moving from your broad topic to starting to think about designing your research project. This can allow you to interrogate your topic from different angles, consider various possible routes, and also decide which paths you definitely do not want to pursue. It can help

Activity for drafting research questions

1. Write a long list of questions that you would like to ask about your research project – don't limit the list at this stage.

2. Go through the list and underline the questions you think are the most important.

3. Use the following checklist – based on Keith Punch's criteria for good research questions (2005: 46) – to consider whether your questions are:

- 'Clear'?
- 'Specific'?
- 'Answerable'?
- 'Interconnected'?
- 'Interesting and worthwhile' researching?

4. Adapt, refine and eliminate questions accordingly until you have a set of approximately two to five research questions (depending on the size of the project).

Figure 5.2   Drafting research questions

you to refine your focus and lead you to starting to think about the different elements of your research design, for example, its purpose, selection and sampling strategies, and methods of data collection and analysis. You could do this brainstorming on your own or, perhaps, with a peer who can bring a different perspective to your research plans by asking questions and making suggestions that you may not have considered (Blaxter et al., 2006).

This brainstorming exercise can also provide a launch pad from which to start formulating relevant research questions. One approach to getting started with drafting research questions is detailed in Figure 5.2. This exercise may help you to generate an initial set of research questions; however, it is important to recognize that arriving at a set of research questions that can effectively articulate and guide your research may take time, and it is likely that you will continue to refine your research questions as you plan your research and read around your topic. You should also attempt to compose a single overarching research question which encompasses your set of research questions and encapsulates your research project; this

research question might become the basis of the title for your dissertation, thesis or research report.

Planning your literature review

It is likely that you will have already read about your topic before you sit down to plan your literature review. For example, you may have originally become aware of, or interested in, your topic through reading; and it is likely that reading helped you develop your research questions. When conducting a literature review you are concerned with two key questions:

(i) What is already known about my topic (i.e. what has already been researched)?
(ii) How will my research project contribute to existing knowledge?

Planning your literature review can help you to identify fields of research that relate to your topic; it can also enable you to see how these fields and sub-fields interrelate. Again, visual displays such as mind maps can help you to start to plan your literature review. Figure 5.3 illustrates how a research project might draw on broader fields of research to inform the specific topic and how the topic relates to sub-fields. It also shows that it might be useful to look at research literature surrounding similar topics which, although not directly related to your topic, might be of interest to compare with your own. You may additionally consider the role that theory will play in your research and the theoretical literature you could draw on. In this way you will be able to build up a picture of the existing body of knowledge in relation to your topic and identify gaps. In the early stages of research, carrying out such an activity might lead you to revisit your original research ideas and refine your research focus; it may also help you to justify your research rationale, for example, that your research project will fill a gap in the existing literature, or build on what is known from previous studies.

Planning the literature review also helps you to consider the sources available to you; typically these include books, chapters in edited books, journal articles, and unpublished theses and dissertations. You may also decide to look at other media in which research is disseminated e.g. newspaper articles, radio programmes and websites. Searching for research literature today invariably involves using online resources, such as online library catalogues or electronic databases, to search for relevant books and journal articles or theses and dissertations. Key to the

success of this process of searching is the identification of appropriate search terms related to your topic that enable you to access the relevant materials.

You might plan your literature search by first listing the key terms related to your research – these may be terms you are using to articulate your research questions and plans. When listing these terms you should consider the following: *Are they widely used by the public / research community? Are there alternative terms that you could use?* Searching is a process of trial and error – you may try a key word or combination of key words that yield very few titles or even none; alternatively, your initial search might result in far too many titles to browse through. In such cases you would need to adapt and refine the key words you are using in your searches accordingly.

When you do have a reasonable selection of titles relating to the various aspects of your research, you should then read through their abstracts to judge whether or not they are relevant to read in full. As part of your planning process you might consider printing the abstracts you have selected and cutting and pasting them onto a larger version of your mind map of your literature review. This will help you to see the existing research related to your topic at a glance. It will also enable you to see in more detail the interrelationships between existing research fields and identify where your research project fits into this picture.

This process of planning your literature review

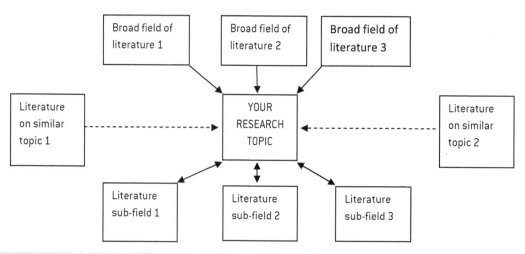

Figure 5.3   A mind-map of a literature review

will help you considerably when you come to write it up in your dissertation, thesis or research report. As Gary Thomas (2009) stresses, a good literature review should not just be a summary of the existing literature but also an analysis (i.e. indicating how the parts relate to one another) and a synthesis (i.e. bringing the parts together to create something new). The mind mapping processes described in this section should help you in this endeavour.

Anticipating ethical issues

As part of your planning tasks it is important to give thorough forethought to the ethical issues you may face at different stages in the research process. When designing your research and framing your research questions, you may ask yourself: *What is the purpose of my research in ethical terms? What are the implications of my research – is it likely to benefit to a particular group of people or wider society?* Ethical considerations are particularly important if your research involves people. You will need to gain the *voluntary informed consent* of all participants in your research. This involves ensuring that you provide them with adequate information about the nature of your research, how it will be used and reported, its benefits, as well as any potential harm that could arise from it, to enable them to decide whether or not to agree to take part. It also involves specifying what participating in the research means (for example, being interviewed or observed and whether or not this will involve audio or video recording) why it is important, and clarifying that participants have the right to withdraw themselves (or data relating to them) from the study at any time.

During the process of data collection you will need to continue to engage with the ethics of what you are doing; for example, you might find yourself considering:

- How can I observe this classroom with minimal disruption to the lesson?
- How can I ask questions about a potentially sensitive topic without causing distress and anxiety to interviewees?
- If I introduce this educational intervention to one group of students, should I ensure that the control group also benefit from the intervention after I have collected my data?

Finally, you should continue your ethical thinking and practice through to the appropriate handling and storage of data and its analysis, and during the writing and dissemination of your research. An ethical matter particularly relevant to these research processes is respect for the privacy of your research participants, paying special attention to issues of confidentiality and anonymity.

Thinking ahead about the potential ethical issues that may arise in your research project can help you to address them appropriately. It is also crucial to build ethical considerations into the early planning stages of your research as it is likely that you will be required by your institution and/or funding body to complete a formal ethical review process before commencing your research. As part of your early planning tasks you will need to find out what the process requires you to do, and the timescales you will need to meet. You may well need to go through the ethical review process before you make contact with your research site(s) and/or participant(s). You should also familiarise yourself with the ethical guidelines of your institution as well as those of the professional organisations in your subject area, such as the British Educational Research Association's *Revised ethical guidelines for educational research* (2004).

Giving forethought to access considerations

It is likely that you will have already considered some of the issues around access when you decided on your research topic. However, it is important to give this more thought at the planning stage, not least because your project may well depend on your gaining access to appropriate research sites, participants, documents etc.

The first task is to identify the key individuals (often referred to in research methods literature as 'gatekeepers') who are in the position to give you the access that you need for your research. It is beneficial if you have some prior knowledge of these individuals; for example, you may have been put in contact by a colleague, a friend or your supervisor. If this is the case, you could ask them what they think might be an appropriate way to make initial contact with the individual – for example, by letter, telephone or email – and whether you could use their name in your first communication to indicate your existing connection.

The purpose of the initial contact with the gatekeeper(s) should be ideally to arrange a face-to-face meeting (Walford, 2001). Such a meeting can be important in building trust as it enables the gatekeeper to find out who you are and ask questions about your research and the access you require. It can also prove beneficial for you to learn more about the site, participants and/or documents you are seeking to access which may help to inform your selection and sampling decisions. This meeting, and indeed the initial contact, should be carefully planned. Such investment of time and effort in planning is likely to pay off by increasing your chances of securing access. Figure 5.4 lists some points worth considering when planning your first contact or meeting with gatekeepers.

Preparing for data collection and analysis

Jennifer Mason draws our attention to an important, but sometimes neglected, point in planning research – that early decisions about research design and methods involve, to a degree, 'anticipating the process of data analysis' (2002: 37). Data analysis, then, should not be a process that is only thought about and carried out after data collection has occurred. Instead, the analysis of data is central to the research process with a main focus being: *How to collect data that can be meaningfully analysed to build descriptions and explanations that answer the research questions?*

An important point to make here is that planning should involve checking the internal consistency of your proposed research project so that the mode of data analysis that you intend to use is coherent with your methods of data collection which, in turn, are appropriate given your research design and research questions. Jennifer Mason (*ibid.*: 30) suggests an activity to help with this which involves drawing up a grid in which you list your research questions and then match each of these research questions to the data sources and methods you intend to use, and justify why these methods and sources will help you to answer the research questions.

- Have a clear idea of how you are going to introduce yourself and your research project succinctly; if necessary, write notes that you can look over beforehand.

- Plan to listen to gatekeepers; anticipate concerns and questions that they may have and consider how these might be addressed. You might also ask what aspects of your topic interest them or would be useful from their perspective to find out more about (Blaxter et al., 2006) and then consider incorporating this into your research plans.

- Consider how you can 'sell' your research project (Walford, 2001); for example, you might already have good reason to believe that your topic is something your gatekeeper is interested in – if so, share your interest and talk about the research purpose and possible outcomes. You can also offer to share research products, such as copies of research reports and publications, or you may be able to offer to provide a workshop (Blaxter et al., 2006). However, you should be realistic and not offer anything you will not be able to deliver. You should also be mindful of ethics: attempting to gain access should not involve either coercion or concealing aspects of your research.

- Find out in advance what you can about the site, documents, etc. you are seeking to access. This can help you to ask informed questions and gauge what sort of access would be reasonable to request.

- Be prepared to negotiate the access you need. You might be granted partial access and you will need to decide whether or not this would be sufficient – and what you plan to do if it is not, e.g. identify other research sites, participants and gatekeepers to approach, or adapt the focus of your study (Glesne, 2006).

- Finally, be aware at this early stage that access is an ongoing process (Blaxter et al., 2006). Even if you have been granted initial access, it is likely you will need to maintain and renegotiate it throughout the process of research.

Figure 5.4 Planning your communication with gatekeepers

Once you are happy with your selection of methods of data collection and analysis, a *pilot study* can help you to refine the techniques and tools you plan to use. You should plan to conduct the pilot study in a situation as close as possible to that of the actual research (Glesne, 2006), and preferably where participants are willing to play an active role in suggesting improvements to research instruments. This process will take you away from the 'drawing board' and bring you closer to the research context, enabling you to fine tune your research plans to the realities of the research situation. You may also decide to pilot your intended data analysis methods by conducting analysis on a section of the data collected during the pilot study.

Carefully planning your data collection and analysis can prevent you making a common research error – collecting more data than you will have time to analyse. Planning can help you remain focused on collecting data that directly addresses your research questions and helps you keep in mind what you will be doing with this data in terms of analysis.

Planning your writing

During the research process it can be easy to lose sight of the fact that the research project in which you are absorbed will actually need to be written up. How you will present your research project and findings in your research report, dissertation or thesis (as well as journal articles, book chapters and conference papers) is of paramount importance. Therefore, it is good practice to engage with the idea of writing at the planning stage. This will enable you to consider how you will translate your project into words on a page, and to whom you will be communicating your research, e.g. your dissertation examiners, commissioners of the research project, practitioners, policy makers and/or the wider research community.

Starting to write about your project at an early stage will help you to articulate and develop your ideas. It will also enable you to consider when the most productive time for you to write is. This might depend on whether you feel you have more energy in the morning or later on in the day, or it might be a case of finding time in the day or week when you can write undisturbed, perhaps in the evening or at the weekend. Whichever you decide upon will depend on your particular circumstances and preferences. By engaging with writing early on, you will also gain an indication of the time you will require for writing; do remember to factor in the time it takes to draft, redraft, proofread, edit, provide a list of references and arrange for printing/binding processes – all of which can take longer than anticipated.

A number of research methodology books demonstrate how a dissertation might be structured in terms of the content to include and the percentage of the finished written product to allocate to each section (see for example, Blaxter, et al., 2006: 236 (citing Barnes); Edwards and Talbot, 1999: 17; and Thomas, 2009: 24). Although they differ slightly in terms of the content and written percentages, they are really variations on a theme. However, all stress that their suggestion is a basic guide only and should not be rigidly adhered to. The final structure is likely to be modified in accordance with (a) the nature of your research project and (b) regulations or guidelines provided by your institution.

Managing your time and resources

The time and resources available to you will shape both the scale of your study and your research design. You will need to give consideration to both at the very beginning of your research. Resources include books and journals; equipment such as computers, digital voice recorders and cameras; consumables such as office supplies, postage, photocopying; services such as transcription or administrative assistance; travel expenses etc. Your first job is to find out what is available for your use in your institution (Bryman, 2008) – both those resources that are freely available (perhaps as a loan service) and those which require additional payment. Then you need to identify the gaps: consider the costs of the resources you require and the funds available to you – perhaps funds that you have secured from a funding body; you may even consider identifying funding bodies to whom you could apply. However, if there is a gap between the resources you need and those which you have and you cannot be certain to secure the funding required to cover their costs, you should be prepared to adapt your research design so that it depends on fewer resources.

The time you will have for your research project will be constrained by its submission date as well as the other demands on your time. When conducting educational research you should also be aware of the time constraints of your research participants, such as teachers and students whose activities and availability are shaped by school timetables. When you are planning the timescale for your research project – and particularly the data collection phase – you will need to accommodate these time limitations into your schedule.

It cannot be emphasised enough how important it is to draw up a timetable for your research – this is a useful tool that you can use and modify throughout your project to help you keep on track and meet your deadline. A useful place to start is with your submission date, then work backwards plotting the big tasks you will need to achieve perhaps on a month-by-month basis. There are many ways of doing this; my preferred approach is simply to draw up a table that lists the months of the year in the first column with the tasks I plan to carry out in the second column. I prefer to organise my table in this way on the basis that the months will not change but the activities might; for example, as the project becomes more focused and defined over time, the order of tasks may change, new tasks may be added and others discarded, some may take longer than anticipated and others surprisingly less time. This timetable should be regarded as a working tool that is regularly revised and updated.

It is important to note that while these practical issues require careful consideration, your project should not be led by them. Research decisions should be made first on sound academic grounds, but you may need to make realistic compromises in the face of obstacles. You should therefore ensure that you are able to justify why your research design was the best available option given the practical circumstances.

The research proposal or plan

The culmination of your planning processes in the early stages of research should be to write a research proposal or plan that sets out what your research is about and how you intend to carry it out. The research proposal is a very good preparation for research: it can

help you to identify weaker areas to work on, check the internal consistency of the design, justify your research decisions and start to take ownership of the project. It will also get you writing and you might even use relevant sections of your proposal as starting points for chapters of your dissertation, thesis or research report.

If writing a research proposal is a requirement of your course, or if you are writing a research proposal for a prospective funder, you will probably be required to follow guidelines provided by your institution or funding body about the structure and content of the proposal. These may cover similar points to those set

- Your research topic and your rationale for choosing this topic.

- The purpose of your research.

- The research questions you are seeking to answer (or research problem you are aiming to solve).

- The literature that already exists on your research topic and/or fields of research related to your topic and how your research project will contribute to this existing body of knowledge.

- The research design you will use to address your research questions and why this is the most appropriate design for your project.

- Your methods of data collection and analysis and rationale for your selection.

- The practical (e.g. access) or ethical issues you might face in your research and the measures you intend to put in place to address them.

- The resources your research project will need and how you will fund them.

- The outputs you plan to generate from your research in terms of publications or other forms of dissemination.

- The timescale for completing the different phases of your research project.

Figure 5.5   Points to consider in a research proposal or plan

out in Figure 5.5; you may also notice that these points broadly relate to issues and tasks we have discussed so far in the chapter.

While the proposal serves as an excellent basis for your research project, you should not feel overly constrained by it – it should incorporate some flexibility to enable appropriate tailoring to the research context as necessary. However, it is important to warn against making too many changes after you have written your proposal as this will entail the loss of precious time for carrying out your research (Bryman, 2008) and you should check if you need to gain approval from your course tutor or supervisor and/or funding body to do so. An important message is this: the more you have done in terms of planning tasks *before* you write your proposal, the closer your proposal will be to what you will actually end up doing.

Planning as an ongoing activity

Planning is not something that you do once before you actually start your research and never again. You will need to draw on this important skill throughout the research process and it will come in particularly handy when you arrive at junctures in your research where you face new dilemmas and need to make new decisions. You can draw on and adapt some of the strategies and techniques suggested in this chapter to help you with this process. Figure 5.6 sets out three suggestions for planning strategies you might consider using as you conduct your research.

For first time researchers in particular, the perceived enormity of the task of conducting a research project can feel overwhelming and anxiety provoking; often there are several different elements of the project to keep an eye on and different tasks to juggle at the same time – many of which you may not feel in complete control of. During my doctoral research I learnt to live with this feeling and began to welcome it as I saw it as being alert to the possibility of things not always going exactly to plan! This chapter has highlighted the importance of careful planning for research. However, it is also important to be aware that even with the best laid plans you may not always be able to anticipate every problem that may arise. Being aware of this may

help you to be ready to respond and draw on your planning skills to decide on an appropriate resolution should an unexpected problem occur, as Blaxter et al. (2006: 150) remark: 'Research is really about getting misdirected, recognizing this as such, understanding why it happened, then revising our strategy and moving on'.

1. Pose yourself 'difficult questions' (Mason, 2002) about your research as you carry it out. Such questions should be probing and critical to encourage you to think about the very things that you might prefer to brush under the carpet! This will help you to anticipate potential problems or inconsistencies in your research and address them sooner rather than later. You may also consider meeting with peers on a regular basis to discuss each other's research.

2. Keep a research diary in which you can note down these difficult questions along with other reflections on your research progress, including new ideas or doubts you are having about the direction of your research or a particular research tool. You might use the diary to start to form arguments in relation to a key issue or even make some tentative interpretations about what appears to be going on in your research.

3. Each month revisit your timetable and the tasks you have set yourself. How long is each of these likely to take? How many days do you have available this month? Plot your tasks in a diary, setting yourself targets and mini-deadlines for that month.

Figure 5.6   Suggestions for ongoing planning activities

Suggested further reading

British Educational Research Association (2004) *Revised Ethical Guidelines for Educational Research*. Available at: http://www.bera.ac.uk/files/guidelines/ethica1.pdf. Clear ethical guidelines for educational research as set out by BERA. Recognises diversity of members' research and the ethical concerns shared about the relationship between the work, those who have participated in it and those who will use it.

Thomas, G. (2009) *How to Do Your Research Project: A Guide for Students in Education and Applied Social Sciences*. London: Sage. Important, accessible and clear text on beginning a research project. Well structured and insightful.

Walford, G. (2001) *Doing Qualitative Educational Research: A Personal Guide to the Research Process*. London: Continuum. A reflection on the trials and tribulations and the problems and promises of conducting research – and also on the links between the idiosyncrasies and circumstances of researchers and what is possible in research from a respected scholar.

References

British Educational Research Association (2004) *Revised Ethical Guidelines for Educational Research*. Available at: http://www.bera.ac.uk/files/guidelines/ethical.pdf (accessed 27 January 2011).

Blaxter, L., Hughes, C. and Tight, M. (2006) *How to Research* (3rd edn). Maidenhead: Open University Press.

Bryman, A. (2008) *Social Research Methods*. (3rd edn) Oxford: Oxford University Press.

Edwards, A. and Talbot, R. (1999) *The Hard-pressed Researcher* (2nd edn). Harlow: Pearson Education.

Glesne, C. (2006) *Becoming Qualitative Researchers: An Introduction* (3rd edn). Boston, MA: Pearson Education.

Mason, J. (2002) *Qualitative Researching* (2nd edn). London: Sage Publications.

Punch, K.F. (2005) *Introduction to Social Research: Quantitative and Qualitative Approaches* (2nd edn). London: Sage Publications.

Thomas, G. (2009) *How to Do Your Research Project: A Guide for Students in Education and Applied Social Sciences*. London: Sage Publications.

Walford, G. (2001) *Doing Qualitative Educational Research: A Personal Guide to the Research Process*. London: Continuum.

6

Conducting your research

Robert J. Coe

The importance of inference and interpretation

This chapter addresses an important issue in the conduct of research: *How can we establish the strength and applicability of claims about interpretations and inferences?* The somewhat cumbersome wording of this question to include these four elements (strength, applicability, interpretations and inferences) allows it to encompass a wide range of issues, including those often considered under headings such as validity, reliability, generalisability (in the quantitative tradition), credibility, authenticity, trustworthiness, transferability (in the qualitative tradition), sampling and representativeness (in both traditions). This attempt at unification is deliberate: although the words used in different traditions may be different, we believe the fundamental issues broadly overlap. Of course, the kinds of claims made, justifications given, importance attributed to different qualities, types of threats, etc., will vary greatly in the different traditions. But research of all types involves making interpretations and inferences whose validity (or credibility) must be established, along with some justification for the nature and extent of the domains to which those interpretations and inferences are, and are not, applicable.

Confusion over 'validity'

Validity is one of the fundamental concepts in research, yet also one of the most often confused. Within the quantitative tradition, some writers list a number of different types of validity, such as 'internal validity', 'statistical conclusion validity', 'face validity', 'criterion-related validity', 'construct validity' and many others. Textbooks and courses on quantitative research often present definitions and discussion of validity alongside reliability, sometimes presenting reliability as an aspect of validity, sometimes as a necessary but not sufficient condition for validity, sometimes arguing that they operate in tension: that more of one is achieved at the expense of the other. The widely quoted common-sense definition of validity as telling us 'whether an instrument measures what it is intended to measure' fails to capture a crucial aspect of validity: that it applies not to tests, assessments, questionnaires or other data collection instruments, but to particular interpretations or uses of them. Furthermore, measures of internal consistency such as Cronbach's alpha, which are the most commonly used indicators of reliability used in quantitative research, are widely interpreted as indicating the extent to which items in a test measure a common, unidimensional construct; this is properly an aspect of validity, not reliability. The novice researcher can be forgiven for being somewhat confused about exactly what 'validity' means and how it relates to other aspects of quality.

In the qualitative tradition, many writers (e.g. Lincoln and Guba, 1985) have eschewed the word validity altogether as tainted with a legacy of positivistic thinking, and put forward alternatives that better capture the equivalent idea for qualitative data and an interpretative or naturalistic view, such as credibility, transferability or authenticity. Some have presented these alternatives as direct translations of each concept from the quantitative paradigm into the qualitative. Others have added to this list of alternatives to quantitative validity additional concepts (e.g. catalytic validity or paralogical validity) that do not have equivalents in the quantitative tradition but capture important quality concerns in at least some parts of the qualitative tradition.

Nevertheless, there is a core idea, that interpreting data in particular ways should be explicitly justified, which is essentially common to both traditions and a requirement for any good research, whatever its paradigmatic stance. Whether more is gained in emphasising the different traditions than is lost in the confusion engendered by using different words for broadly the same thing may be open to argument.

Teddlie and Tashakkori (2003) observe that, 'With so many types of validity, the term has lost meaning ... validity has become a catch-all term that is increasingly losing its ability to connote anything. When a term is used with other words to connote so many meanings, it essentially has none' (2003: 12, 36). To illustrate this they (2003: 13) provide a list of different types of validity in both qualitative and quantitative traditions, which is reproduced here in Table 6.1. As an alternative to the word validity, they suggest the use of the general term 'inference quality' as a way of emphasising the fact that all the different types of validity relate to different aspects of the quality of inferences that can be made from a collection of data.

In the following sections we draw on this attempt to unify the language of 'QUAL' and 'QUAN' in the context of mixed-methods research. We focus on particular types of claims that researchers make and the threats or challenges that may undermine those

Table 6.1   Types of validity

Quantitative	Qualitative
Internal validity (causal, relationship definitions)	Catalytic validity
Statistical conclusion validity	Crystalline validity
External validity 　　Population 　　Ecological	Descriptive validity
	Evaluative validity
Construct validity (causal)	Generalisability validity
Consequential validity	Interpretative validity
Validity (measurement) 　　Face 　　Content 　　Criterion related 　　Predictive 　　Concurrent 　　Jury 　　Systemic	Ironic validity
	Neopragmatic validity
	Rhizomic validity
	Simultaneous validity
	Situated validity
	Theoretical validity
	Voluptuous validity
Construct validity (measurement) 　　Convergent 　　Divergent 　　Factorial	Plus terms associated with authenticity: Educative 　　Ontological 　　Catalytic 　　Tactical

Source: Teddlie and Tashakkori (2003: 13).

claims as a way of structuring an analysis of the different kinds of inferences and interpretations that can be made and the arguments that can be used to support them. Focusing on claims, and on the justifications that must be given to support them, we identify two general types of claims:

- *Interpretation claims.* These include simple descriptive claims, but also the issue of 'interpretive validity' (ensuring that interpretations are consistent with the understandings of research participants). Interpretation claims also incorporate the idea of 'construct validity' in quantitative research, which addresses the kinds of arguments that are required to justify interpreting quantified measures (such as test scores, grades, ratings or scales) in particular ways.
- *Transfer claims.* These include any claims that a particular result, interpretation or inference is applicable to a setting other than the one in which it has been directly evidenced. Arguments about the representativeness of samples (generalisation), the theoretical applicability of particular explanations or understandings (transferability) and the extent to which findings may be sensitive to particular arbitrary or contingent features of the research (which includes the concept of reliability in quantitative research) are relevant here.

Interpretation claims

All empirical research involves the interpretation of data and a good deal of reporting of research can be classified as making interpretation claims. These may be simple descriptive claims, such as a verbatim transcript of words spoken or the presentation of a written answer given in response to a test question. The claim here is 'this is what happened' and the kinds of warrant or justification for the claim are generally fairly straightforward. Slightly more problematic would be interpretation claims that depend on an analysis, reduction or interpretation of the original data. For example, if part of a transcript is claimed as an example of a person expressing a particular view, or if answers are coded as right or wrong, the process of analysis must be understood before the reader can accept this interpretation as legitimate. At this point all data are essentially qualitative, even if subsequent analysis may involve quantification.

As the analysis becomes more complex, so too does the argument required to justify its interpretation. To continue our first example, if an analysis of a series of interviews is claimed to show that a person's strength of feeling about an issue is related to their past experience, we would need to follow a complex argument which would include more extensive data (such as multiple excerpts of text), details of methodology (how the text was coded), context (where and when the research was conducted), and no doubt many other things, in order to be convinced of such a claim. In the second example, right/wrong codings of a series of questions might be combined to assign an overall score to a person and this score might then be interpreted as a measure of their 'intelligence'. Before accepting this interpretation as valid, we would need to consider a range of supporting evidence, including procedural details about the kinds of questions asked, the context in which they were asked, and how they were coded and combined. Evidence about the defensibility of interpreting responses to the different questions in the test as indicating a single trait would be needed. Evidence that the trait, or more appropriately the claimed interpretation of that trait, is fully represented by the set of questions asked and that the score being interpreted as a measure of that trait is not affected by other spurious factors, biases or confounds would also be required. Finally, in judging the appropriateness (validity) of the claim that a score represents a person's 'intelligence', we might want to examine the intended and unintended consequences of this interpretation and the ways it may be used. If we judge that its use brings worthwhile benefits without significant harm, then the validity will be endorsed; if the risk of harm is judged to be a concern, the validity of this interpretation is more problematic.

Establishing these kinds of interpretation claims may be seen as a process of answering a number of questions, each of which raises a particular concern about the interpretation. Examples are considered in the further detail in the sections which follow.

Is the interpretation plausible?

This question is a major focus for justifying interpretation claims in the qualitative tradition. For example, Guba and Lincoln define 'credibility' as the match between an evaluator's representation and the 'constructed realities' of respondents or stakeholders (1989: 237). They offer a range of techniques the evaluator can use to verify this, including *prolonged engagement* ('substantial involvement at the site of enquiry'), *persistent observation* ('to add depth to the scope which prolonged engagement affords'), *peer debriefing* (discussing the work with another disinterested researcher), *negative case analysis* (revising hypotheses to account for all known cases), *progressive subjectivity* (checking developing ideas against what was believed at the outset to demonstrate responsiveness to the data) and *member checks* ('testing hypotheses, data, preliminary categories, and interpretations with members of the stakeholding groups from whom the original constructions were collected', 1989: 238). Other methods of verifying the plausibility of interpretations include providing full and explicit *audit trails* of the processes of data collection, analysis and interpretation.

In the quantitative tradition, the plausibility of interpretations of scores and scale measures comes under the heading of *face validity*. At its simplest this means looking at a test or instrument and making a judgement about how appropriate it would be to interpret responses to it as a measure of the intended construct. Related to face validity is *content validity* – indeed sometimes these terms are used interchangeably. A tighter definition of content validity restricts it to situations where the judgements are made by 'subject-matter experts' and/or when systematic procedures are used to examine individual questions or test items for suitability and relevance to the intended construct. Subject-matter experts may be asked to rate each item for its alignment with the construct and its suitability for inclusion in the measure. This practice may include examining the process by which responses are coded and the codes combined to form an overall score (the mark scheme). Another aspect of content validity relates to whether the whole of the target domain is covered by the assessment process. If some parts of the intended construct are not assessed, that interpretation cannot be said to have content validity (see discussion of construct under-representation, below).

Is the interpretation corroborated by other evidence?

A second question looks for convergence with other evidence. The word *triangulation* is widely used here, borrowing a metaphor from the world of surveying in which the precise location of a geographical feature such as a mountain can be found by observing it from two distinct fixed points. In a research context these two views may come from different methodologies, sources of data, methods of analysis, theoretical perspectives or observers, among other differences (Denzin, 1978). For example, in a study of bullying we might observe children in a playground and interpret one individual's behaviour as an instance of bullying, but then triangulate by asking the children for their interpretations, or getting another observer to give an interpretation. Or we might use member checks, sharing the transcripts or analyses of interviews with the participants to verify that researchers' interpretations are appropriate.

The method of *constant comparison* may also be seen as an example of this kind of corroboration of interpretations. In this process, newly collected data are constantly compared with existing data and theory. In this way theory is built on data, and both theory and interpretations of data (codings) are revised to ensure overall consistency.

In the quantitative tradition, the extent to which a measure corresponds with other things that we would expect it to correspond with is known as *convergent validity*. The process of *construct validation* (leading to evidence of *construct validity*) consists of making predictions, ideally based on explicit and defensible theory, about other measures with which we would expect the new measure to correspond, and estimating the strength of the expected correlation. These predictions are then tested empirically. If the measure behaves as we expected a measure of the intended construct should, then we can say it has construct validity. In the full construct validation process we would look for evidence not only of convergent validity, but also of *discriminant validity* – the extent to which the measure is distinct from (i.e. not correlated with) other measures that might be expected to be confused or confounded with it, but which logically and theoretically should not be (Campbell and Fiske, 1959). This aspect of the process is described in more detail below.

A specific form of the quantitative corroboration of the agreement between a new measure and its intended interpretation is known as *criterion-related validity*. If we want to be able to interpret scores from some instrument (such as a test or questionnaire) in a particular way and already have an existing validated measure of the target construct (the criterion measure) then the correlation between the putative measure and the criterion measure is an estimate of the criterion-related validity of the former. In this case it is common to express the strength of validity as a number: a validity coefficient, which is the correlation coefficient between the measure and the criterion. There are a number of different kinds of criterion-related validity, including *concurrent validity* (where the putative measure and the criterion are measured at the same time) and *predictive validity* (where the new measure is used to predict a criterion that is measured later). An example would be a selection examination that is used by universities to decide which applicants should be offered a place. If the selection examination is found to correlate well with later performance at university then it may be judged to have good predictive validity: it helps to predict who will do well and hence to decide who should be offered a place.

Of course the whole idea of criterion-related validity begs the question of how we know the criterion measure is valid. If claims about the interpretation of one measure can only be supported by presupposing the validity of another we are left with a chain of claims that are dependent on each other and hence at best conditionally valid, but for which full validation could only be achieved by drawing on some additional source of support. Furthermore, in many cases there is no suitable criterion measure.

Is the interpretation based on an adequate range of supporting data, methods and contexts?

This question is often a high priority in the qualitative tradition, with its focus on naturalistic settings, 'thick description' and rich data. Qualitative researchers often adopt strategies such as prolonged engagement and persistent observation (see above) and approaches to data collection that are detailed, intensive and set out to be exhaustively comprehensive within a particular setting or group, rather than to sample a wider range of settings but treat them more superficially. The limits of applicability of interpretations are determined by theoretical sampling strategies that actively seek potential counter-examples or negative cases, and regard the continuing generation of significant new categories, themes or theoretical explanations as an indication that the breadth of the evidence-base still needs to be extended (*saturation sampling*).

In the quantitative tradition this question addresses the issue of *construct under-representation*. For example, if a mathematics test contains only questions involving numerical calculations it might be appropriate to interpret the score as a measure of arithmetic, but not as a measure of general mathematical understanding, since most interpretations of mathematics would include aspects other than just arithmetic (for example, algebra, geometry, statistics, modelling, etc.). Similarly, if the test contained only short-answer questions we might argue that it failed to reflect a candidate's ability to solve more extended problems, which could be seen as a vital element of mathematics. If we judged that the test questions could be answered by a candidate who had simply memorised a set of procedures, we might challenge the interpretation of test performance as an indication of 'understanding'. Further, we might object if the test used only written questions and answers and we took the view that mathematical understanding should encompass the ability to speak about mathematical ideas or solve problems in your head without writing anything down. We might also argue that the context of a school mathematics classroom imposes constraints on the ways children think about problems (for example, seeking simplistic right/wrong answers and drawing on a range of unstated conventional assumptions) which we might want to transcend in making claims about a person's 'mathematical understanding' that we hope would be applicable to a wider range of contexts. In all these cases the full construct is under-represented in what is measured and interpreting these test scores as an indicator of 'mathematical understanding' would not be appropriate.

It is also clear that in all these cases there is a considerable role for judgement, creativity and critical thinking in the validation process. Validating the interpretation of a measure requires us to start by thinking hard about what that interpretation should mean. We then need to think creatively and critically about possible ways in which we might have failed to capture some aspect of the intended interpretation in the process we have actually followed. We may, for example, have inadvertently narrowed the range of knowledge, skills, attitudes or behaviours from what was intended to what has actually been assessed. Often this will have been for compelling pragmatic reasons: some aspects may be much easier to assess than others.

We will also have used particular methods to capture the intended knowledge, skills, attitudes or behaviours, the results from which would not generalise to, or correspond with, the results we would have achieved by other methods. For example, if we have used multiple-choice tests, self-completion questionnaires or responses to simulated situations, we might find that had we used open-response questions, peer-ratings or naturalistic observation, our results might have been quite different. If we want to be able to interpret a measure as indicating 'knowledge' without having to qualify it as 'knowledge (as demonstrated in a multiple-choice test)' we must either ensure that the measure incorporates a broad range of methods or show that the different methods agree well enough to be interchangeable.

This importance of demonstrating that quantitative measures represent some quality that transcends a particular method of collecting them is often overlooked in the validation process. The analysis of a range of different measures shows, rather disturbingly, that the correlations between measures of completely unrelated traits that have been collected using the same method are often about as high as the correlations between the same trait measured using different methods (Cote and Buckley, 1987). In other words, *method variance* (the spurious correspondence between measures of unrelated constructs that are assessed using the same method) is often at least as large as *trait variance* (the extent to which the measure is actually determined by the trait it is intended to measure).

For example, suppose we want to measure two traits of children in schools that we believe should not be strongly related: their learning motivation and social connectedness. We might decide to use two methods to capture each: a self-report questionnaire and teacher ratings based on observation. What we would hope to find is that the two measures (self-report and teacher ratings) of the same trait would correspond well, while measures of the two traits (learning motivation and social connectedness) should correlate weakly, if at all. In practice what we often find is rather different: that measures of what is supposed to be the same trait captured using different methods correlate only moderately well, while theoretically unrelated traits, when measured using the same method, are found to be correlated. For example, the average cross-method, same-trait correlation found by Cote and Buckley (1987) in educational studies was only 0.35, hardly bigger than the average (0.31) for same-method, cross-trait correlations.

Could the interpretation have been influenced by other spurious or inappropriate features of the research process?

Again, this question is relevant in both qualitative and quantitative traditions, though the approach will differ.

In qualitative research the focus is often on the processes by which an interpretation has been made and on the researcher's awareness of the features that may influence that interpretation. The words 'spurious' or 'inappropriate' may not really apply here, since it is recognised that there is not necessarily any 'correct' (or incorrect) interpretation. Different perspectives or beliefs may lead to different interpretations; in order to make sense of a particular interpretation we may need to understand the perspectives and beliefs that led to it and how they might have been influential. One of the approaches used to do this is *bracketing*. Here the researcher attempts to identify, state, suspend or dissociate from the research process aspects such as their own ontological and epistemological positions and theoretical frameworks, suppositions based on the researcher's personal knowledge, history, supposition culture, assumptions, beliefs, experiences, values and viewpoints, suppositions based on the their academic and scientific theoretical orientations and theories, and pre-existing assumptions about the phenomenon being investigated. Approaches to bracketing may differ in the extent to which it is aimed to remove these aspects, which aspects are chosen, how permeable the brackets are around them and when in the research process bracketing is applied (Gearing, 2004).

Other methods used in qualitative research to identify or eliminate unwanted influences on interpretation have already been mentioned above. These include peer debriefing and progressive subjectivity. Audit trails also focus on the data collection and interpretation processes and may identify such influences.

In the quantitative tradition the influence of these spurious or inappropriate features is characterised as *construct-irrelevant variance*. If values of a score or measure are influenced by something other than the intended construct then we might say that the measure is biased or contaminated by another construct. For example, if we want to interpret scores on a written mathematics test as measuring mathematical ability, it might be a problem if we found that performance on the test was determined partly by a candidate's reading ability. This kind of problem would be harder to detect if we believed, as seems likely, that in general even a true measure of mathematical ability would be correlated with reading: people who are good at maths are often good readers too.

Test bias would be diagnosed if people who should have the same measure on the intended construct (i.e. whose underlying mathematical ability is the same), but who differ on the contaminating construct (one is a good reader, the other less good) were found to have different scores on the test. This means that bias can only ever be identified relative to something else: a criterion measure. Unless we already have a pure, unbiased measure of mathematical ability against which to compare a new instrument, we cannot say whether two people whose test scores differ should really have the same measure on the construct.

In practice, we can estimate the relative biases of different items in a test, or the relative biases of different tests for different groups. There might also be cases where the equality of measures across groups was part of the definition of the construct. For example, empirically we might find that some items in

a mathematics test are easier for females while others are easier for males. If we were developing a new test we might find it easier to generate the latter kind of items, so a lazy test developer might conclude that males were better at maths than females. On the other hand, we might incorporate in the definition of the construct of 'mathematical ability' the principle that on average the two groups should perform equally. Such a definition would allow us to identify test bias without requiring an additional 'unbiased' criterion measure.

Establishing that a measure is independent of things that it should not be related to provides evidence of its *discriminant validity*. To investigate this, we need to have a clear and detailed theory that allows us to predict how we would expect the construct that we are hoping to measure to be related to other things. Testing these predictions is the process of construct validation that establishes, if the predictions are confirmed, the *construct validity* of the interpretation.

Does the interpretation, or its likely uses, lead to any desirable or undesirable consequences?

This question relates to the issue of *authenticity* in the qualitative tradition. As well as responding to traditionally quantitative concerns of reliability and validity by developing equivalent notions more applicable to their aims, qualitative researchers have initiated a further list of quality criteria 'which spring directly from constructivism's own basic assumptions' (Guba and Lincoln, 1989).

Guba and Lincoln (1989) list five quality criteria under the heading of authenticity. The first is *fairness*, which concerns whether the research represents and honours the beliefs, values and understandings of all participants appropriately. To do this it must actively seek the constructions of all potential stakeholders and conduct open, balanced negotiation of the whole evaluation process. The second is *ontological authenticity*. This is the extent to which involvement in the research enhances the way participants experience the world, by enabling them to better assess and situate their own experiences and awareness. *Educative authenticity*, the third criterion, is the extent to which participants are helped by the research to understand and appreciate how others see the world. The fourth criterion, *catalytic authenticity*, concerns whether the research stimulates action or decision-making by participants. Finally, *tactical authenticity* relates to 'the degree to which stakeholders and participants are empowered to act' (Guba and Lincoln, 1989: 250).

In the quantitative tradition, the equivalent notion is captured by the idea of *consequential validity*. Championed by Messick (1989), this idea is still controversial, with some quantitative researchers arguing that it is not properly an aspect of validity. Messick – and others since – argued that if validity relates to a particular interpretation or use of a score rather than to the instrument itself, then a judgement about the appropriateness of that interpretation or use must include consideration of its consequences. If we want to use test scores in particular ways then we must provide evidence of the relevance and utility of the scores for those purposes. But interpretations themselves have consequences: different ways of interpreting the same test score may rest on different values and have different implications. For example, if we produce an intelligence test which is biased against candidates from a particular ethnic, racial or cultural minority, to describe this as a test of 'intelligence' would involve making the implicit assumption that the kinds of intelligence (and methods of assessing it) valued by the majority are more important than those that might be more appropriate for that minority. To interpret performance in that test as a measure of 'intelligence (as valued by the majority)' would be more honest – hence more valid – and makes its value-dependence clearer. Whether or not we think it would be appropriate to use that test score to make selection decisions among applicants from both majority and minority groups for employment or higher education opportunities depends crucially on how we interpret the meaning of the score.

Transfer claims

If a particular researcher conducts a study with a particular group of participants in a particular context on a particular occasion, then the claims that can be made about the interpretation of what was observed must be validated according to the processes described above. However, if we claim that a phenomenon, interpretation or inference has applicability or meaning beyond the particular occasion, context or persons that have been directly studied then we make a transfer claim. Some of the key points of disagreement between researchers in the qualitative and quantitative traditions concern the extent to which such transfer claims are appropriate and desirable (or even possible) and, if they are, how they may be justified.

If we want to make these kinds of transfer claims, there are broadly two kinds of errors we could make. On the one hand, if we underestimate the importance of the differences that distinguish contexts and the individual human beings that conduct and participate in research, we may make sweeping over-generalisations, stretching too far beyond what our evidence can safely support. On the other hand, if we overstress these differences, we will be limited to reporting what a specific researcher subjectively perceived to have happened on a unique occasion in a particular context with a precise set of individuals, with no basis on which to claim that this reflects any more than the idiosyncrasies of an individual researcher or that it has any relevance to any other situation.

Rejecting generalisation

Within the qualitative tradition some have argued that it is not appropriate for researchers to make generalised claims about the applicability of their work to other contexts. For example, Lincoln and Guba (1985) state that 'the only generalisation is: there is no generalisation', since the classical concept of generalisability depends on unwarranted assumptions of determinism and reductionist and inductive logic, and because of the impossibility of time- and context-free understandings and the difficulties of applying probabilistic generalisations to specific cases.

According to Lincoln and Guba (1985) it may be possible for research conducted in one context to be applicable to another, but at best this can be in the form of a 'working hypothesis', not a generalised claim. Moreover, the work of applying a working hypothesis from one context to another must often be done by the reader, not the original researcher. The latter can only provide sufficient 'thick description' to enable the former to judge whether the two contexts are sufficiently congruent. Only a person who has detailed knowledge of a particular context can make a judgement about whether what has been studied in another context has any relevance to it. Hence, in reporting the research that was conducted in one context, the researcher must resist the temptation to make any kind of general claims about its relevance or applicability, and must limit any specific claims of transferability to contexts that have been described in similar levels of detail to the originally studied context.

Naturalistic generalisation, which develops within a person as a product of experience, is a process of assimilating new experiences and knowledge with existing ones, expanding and accommodating existing constructions and understandings to incorporate the new. This kind of 'generalisation' is conducted by the reader of research and their reading can be seen as a form of learning. Research connects with the reader to provoke new insights, understandings, connections and explanations, which the reader may apply to their past experiences, their constructions of reality and their explanations of phenomena.

It follows that the selection of cases and contexts for study in qualitative research is guided not by their representativeness of some wider group, but for their potential to contribute information in their own right: their ability to provoke new insights, understandings, connections and explanations. Purposive sampling strategies, such as *intensity sampling* (choosing the most information-rich cases), *maximum variation sampling* (choosing cases to illustrate a wide range of the dimensions of interest), *critical case sampling* (choosing cases that deliberately test the theory), *extreme or deviant case sampling* (choosing unusual, extreme or exotic cases) or *typical case sampling* (choosing cases to illustrate what is normal) are likely to be the methods of choice (Patton, 1990). The sample may also be selected *contingently*, with each new case chosen in the light of what has been gained from existing cases. Although many authors suggest otherwise, strategies such as *snowball sampling* (identifying new cases from recommendations of those already chosen) or *convenience sampling* (using cases that are easy to identify, access or co-opt) are not really purposive in the same sense; they are simply pragmatic ways of achieving a sample.

Types of transfer claims

For the kinds of research that do set out to claim that interpretations and inferences from a particular context can be transferred to a range of other contexts, it is important to identify quality criteria for judging these claims. For transfer claims in general the question we need to address is: *Is the claim dependent on particular choices of appropriate, but arbitrary or contingent, features of the research?* If the interpretations and inferences that have been made in relation to the particular context studied are appropriate, we still need to know whether they would be equally appropriate in other contexts. The research we carried out took place on particular occasions, made use of particular data collection methods and observers, and was conducted with particular participants in particular contexts. There may be no reason to challenge the use of these particular features, but if we want to be able to claim generalisability or transfer to what might be expected to happen on other occasions, using different methods or data collection instruments, observed by different researchers, carried out with different groups of participants or in different contexts, we must provide evidence that our interpretations and inferences are not sensitive to these particular choices. These five elements of arbitrariness in the research enable us to differentiate five different kinds of transfer claims relating to the transfer across occasions, instruments, observers, participants and contexts.

In the quantitative tradition, the first three of these forms of generalisability (transfer across occasions, instruments and observers) are conventionally listed under the heading of *reliability*, while the last two (transfer across contexts and participants) relate to the issue of sample *representativeness*, sometimes referred to as *external validity* or just *generalisability*.

Transfer across occasions

Evidence that some observed phenomenon, such as a performance or score on some test or assessment, is not just a 'one-off' but would be expected to be replicated on future occasions is an important part of justifying interpreting it as a characteristic of the person who took the test. If we want to be able to claim that what has been measured is a stable trait, rather than just a temporary state, we must provide evidence of its stability and consistency over time.

The stability over occasions of a measure is referred to as its *test-retest reliability*. It is generally estimated as the correlation between the same candidate's scores on a test or measure on successive occasions. The shorter the time interval between testing occasions, the higher the correlation is likely to be, since there is less time for the trait to genuinely change. On the other hand, the correlation may be spuriously affected by the candidate's memory of having taken the same test a short time ago. One way round this is to use two versions of the test instead of repeating the identical test. The correlation between scores on these similar versions is known as *parallel-forms (or equivalent-forms) reliability*.

Transfer across instruments

If two parallel forms of the same test are given in quick succession then we are no longer assessing stability over time but are effectively estimating the equivalence, or interchangeability, of two different versions of the same instrument. Hence *parallel-forms reliability*, if taken on the same occasion, provides evidence of the consistency of scores across different versions of the instrument. More generally, we might want to be able to claim that a candidate's score on a test was not just a reflection of the particular questions asked, but could be interpreted as indicative of their likely performance on similar tests containing different questions. If the two parallel forms of the test are constructed by creating a larger item-bank of questions and then randomly allocating items to one or other version, we may interpret the correlation between their scores as an indicator of the robustness of the measure to arbitrary choices of particular items, taken from a universe of all the possible questions we could have asked on the same topics.

A clever way to estimate this without having to go to the trouble of creating two parallel forms of the test would be to treat the two halves of the test as if they were two parallel forms of a shorter test, administered in quick succession. Because shorter tests are less reliable than longer, we must apply a correction (the Spearman-Brown formula) to the correlation between

the two halves if we want an estimate of what the correlation would be between two tests of twice the length. This would be the *split-half reliability*.

We might realise that there are many other ways we could split the test into two halves, for example counting all the odd-numbered items as one half and the even-numbered the other. If we were to calculate the average of all the possible split-half correlations we would have arrived at perhaps the most commonly cited estimate of reliability, *Cronbach's alpha* (in practice there is a much simpler formula to calculate it). Cronbach's alpha can therefore be interpreted as an indicator of how sensitive the overall test score is to the particular choice of items in the test. High values of alpha (close to 1) indicate that replacing the actual test items with equivalent items (e.g. items from a bank from which the actual items were a random sample) would not make much difference to the overall scores: the particular items are highly interchangeable.

If the test construction process had consisted of listing all the possible questions that could be used to assess the intended construct and then putting a random sample of them into the actual test, Cronbach's alpha could be interpreted as an indicator of the adequacy of that sample to be used as an estimate of what a candidate's score would have been across all the questions. In particular, if we use Cronbach's alpha to calculate the standard error of measurement of the test score, we can interpret this as an indication of the precision implied in using the observed test score as an estimate of the score that would have been achieved if the candidate had been able to answer all the possible questions.

Another way to interpret Cronbach's alpha is as an indicator of how well correlated all the test items are with each other. For this reason, it is often referred to as a measure of *internal consistency*. High values of alpha (close to 1) indicate that the items are highly inter-correlated, hence they are all measuring the same thing. This is sometimes taken as evidence that the construct being measured is unidimensional, though this is far from a guarantee: it is possible to get very high values of alpha in a test in which the main construct is confounded with one or more other constructs.

Transfer across observers

The third aspect of reliability relates to measures that depend on the judgement of an observer or rater. Some tests, such as an objectively marked multiple-choice test, may require no judgement at all. Others, such as a closed-answer mathematics test, may require minimal judgement. Still others, such as a test containing short-answer factual questions, may require some judgement. And some, such as essay questions, may require considerable judgement to mark. Other measures, such as ratings of behaviour by observers, may also depend on judgement.

If we want to be able to claim that a score based on such a judgement is not just a feature of the subjective perceptions or idiosyncratic marking of that particular rater then we need to provide evidence that scores are consistent across observers. Getting two raters to rate the same behaviour or performance independently would allow us to demonstrate this consistency. The correlation between scores derived from different raters is known as *inter-rater reliability*, and this provides evidence of the transferability of the interpretation of those scores across observers.

Transfer across participants

The fourth kind of claim that we can transfer interpretations from what was specifically studied to some wider set of cases or situations relates to research participants, and takes us out of what is traditionally labelled as reliability into *generalisability* and sampling. How do we know that what we found with a particular sample of respondents or research participants can be applied to a wider group that we have not directly studied?

Most textbook discussions of sampling make a distinction between *probability sampling* and *non-probability sampling*, with the latter including purposive and pragmatic approaches, as discussed above. What is not always clear is that the approach to sampling we choose should depend on the aims for our research and the kinds of claims we want to be able to make. If our aim is to describe a particular context in rich detail, to make sense of the interpretations and constructions that people in that context make and to analyse them in ways that promote insightful and deep

understanding, then a purposive sample is likely to be best. On the other hand, if our aim is to use the sample that we can access for study to make claims about a wider group that is of interest to us, then it is vital that the sample is representative of that wider group.

The starting point for thinking about sampling in the latter case is defining that wider group or *population* about which we want to find out. Unless we know who we want to be able to make claims about, we cannot choose a sample that is representative of them. Once that population is defined, we can then list its members: the *sampling frame*. A statistically representative sample is achieved by using some kind of random sampling, such as *simple random sampling* (each member of the population has an equal chance of being selected), *stratified random sampling* (the population is first subdivided to ensure that all important subgroups are captured adequately) or *cluster sampling* (sampling first clusters, such as schools, and then sampling individual students from each).

If we achieve a random sample, then we can use the information we collect from that sample to estimate the equivalent parameters for the whole population and apply some standard statistical analyses to indicate the precision of those estimates. Hence we can make precise claims about the population in which we were interested, with known levels of confidence. In practice, quantitative researchers often apply those analyses without worrying too much about the fact that they did not actually achieve a random sample. Even if a full sampling frame, which listed every unit in the population, was available (and it often isn't), as soon as a single person declines or fails to take part in the research we can no longer claim to have a random sample. Response rates to invitations to take part in educational research are often disappointingly low – or not even reported – which makes any kind of inference about the population quite problematic.

Transfer across contexts

The final type of transfer claim relates to the context in which the research was done and the contexts to which we want to claim its applicability. In educational research the issue of contexts is often subsumed under the issue of sampling participants, on the assumption that if we get an adequate, representative range of participants, the contexts from which they come will also have been sampled adequately. Sometimes a cluster or *multi-stage sample* will be used to sample context units (such as schools or neighbourhoods), then participants (e.g. students, teachers, families) are selected from them. Provided the analysis respects the multilevel structure of the data and the sample size is adequate for both contexts and participants, this kind of approach is appropriate.

Suggested further reading

Kemper, E. A., Stringfield, S. and Teddlie, C. (2003) 'Mixed methods sampling strategies in social science research', in Tashakkori, A. and Teddlie, C. (eds) *Handbook of Mixed Methods in Social and Behavioral Research*. Thousand Oaks, CA: Sage. Provides an accessible overview of sampling strategies in both quantitative and qualitative traditions, together with arguments for their combination in mixed-methods approaches and illustrative examples.

Kane, M. T. (2006) 'Validation', in Brennan, R. L. (ed.) *Educational Measurement* (4th edn). Westport, CT: American Council on Education and Praeger. Traces the history of the development of thinking about validity from a quantitative perspective and gives a clear account of modern ideas within this tradition. In particular, he stresses the process of validation and the kinds of arguments and evidence that are likely to be required. This is a long chapter and hard going in parts, but a key reference.

References

Campbell, D. T. and Fiske D. W. (1959) 'Convergent and discriminant validation by the multitrait-multimethod matrix', *Psychological Bulletin*, 56(2): 81–105.

Cote, J. A. and Buckley, R. (1987) 'Estimating trait, method, and error variance: generalizing across 70 construct validation studies', *Journal of Marketing Research*, 24(3): 315–18.

Denzin, N. K. (1978) *The Research Act: A Theoretical Introduction to Sociological Methods*. New York: McGraw-Hill.

Gearing, R. E. (2004) 'Bracketing in Research: A Typology', *Qualitative Health Research*, 14(10): 1429–52.

Guba, E. G. and Lincoln, Y. S. (1989) *Fourth Generation Evaluation*. Newbury Park, CA: Sage.

Kane M. T. (2006) 'Validation', in Brennan, R. L. (ed.) *Educational Measurement* (4th edn). Westport, CT: American Council on Education and Praeger.

Kemper, E. A., Stringfield, S. and Teddlie, C. (2003) 'Mixed methods sampling strategies in social science research', in Tashakkori, A. and Teddlie, C. (eds) *Handbook of Mixed Methods in Social and Behavioral Research*. Thousand Oaks, CA: Sage.

Lincoln, Y. S. and Guba, E. G. (1985) *Naturalistic Enquiry*. Newbury Park, CA: Sage.

Messick, S. (1989) 'Validity', in Linn, R. L. (ed.) *Educational Measurement* (3rd edn). Washington, DC: American Council on Education/Macmillan.

Patton, M. Q. (1990) *Qualitative Evaluation and Research Methods* (2nd edn). Newbury Park, CA: Sage.

Teddlie, C. and Tashakkori, A. (2003) 'Major issues and controversies in the use of mixed methods in the social and behavioral sciences', in Tashakkori, A. and Teddlie, C. (eds) *Handbook of Mixed Methods in Social & Behavioral Research*. Thousand Oaks, CA: Sage, pp. 3–50.

7

Research impact and dissemination

Marilyn Leask

Introduction

This chapter explores current controversies and emerging practices which affect the impact and dissemination of social science research findings.

The chapter challenges the reader to consider their views about the purpose of research, the contractual and moral obligations of academic researchers and the potential for impact if research commissioning practices operated by charities, government and private organisations are reformed to take account of e-research tools.

Across the world, the autonomy of universities and academics is being challenged by governments wanting to keep pace with changes in societies brought by globalisation and e-communications. In increasing numbers of countries, academic researchers are expected to provide evidence of the impact of their work for national research assessment exercises which rate the research of universities and individual staff.

The argument is made in this chapter that modern technologies pose such serious challenges to traditional academic research communities and their practices that academic research practice must evolve to produce significant, impactful research – or be seen to be irrelevant. Increasingly sophisticated electronic search tools and systematic review methods (EPPI-Centre;[1] Campbell Collaboration;[2] Cochrane Collaboration;[3] Davies et al., 2000; GTCE, 2006; TDA, 2004a, 2004b) used by policy-makers in the UK in searching for evidence to underpin policy-making and practice (Hu et al., 2000) revealed that academic practice was leading to the production of a plethora of small-scale social science research. At the same time, an expectation that universities must engage in knowledge transfer and ensure research has impact has emerged (Australian Government, 2005; Howard Partners, 2005; Leask, 2010a; OECD, 2007a, 2007b) which was of minimal significance beyond the immediate context. In the UK, guidelines to improve the potential impact of research were produced as a result and discussed with academic journal editors (Newman et al., 2004; Newman and Elbourne, 2005).

A second argument is made that those commissioning research such as government agencies, charities and private organisations also need to reform their commissioning practices to avoid funding research using methods that are out of date and unnecessarily expensive. Much government commissioned research could be undertaken by academic and practitioner research networks of the sort described by Hopkins (1989: 90–2) and McLaughlin et al. (2006) which nowadays can be supported by e-tools such as those described later in this chapter. Knowledge management has emerged as a discipline across the public and private sectors

(Collinson and Parcell, 2006; Davenport and Prusak, 1998; IDeA, 2006, 2008; Henley, 2008; OECD, 2003; Oakley, 2003; Newman and Holzman, 1997).

To maintain any respect and indeed funding for their work, it is argued that academic researchers must adapt to new forms of online collaboration, engaging practitioners and policy-makers who support dissemination and impact and must adopt research approaches which yield results which can be considered significant nationally and internationally (see also Lucas, 2007).

Forms of publication too are changing and require academics to change existing practice. New open-access online journals challenge traditional models of publishing and peer review as do new models of research such as 'translational research' which have grown from earlier attempts to ensure research findings are accessible by practitioners and which require a researcher to take responsibility for ensuring publication and dissemination of results in ways which impact on practice (Wellcome Trust, 2011; Stanford Center for Clinical and Translational Education and Research, 2011; BERA, 2000; Leask and White, 2004; Leask and Jumani, 2011).

The following sections in the chapter explore these issues in more depth:

- judging the impact of research;
- autonomy versus accountability – changing roles for universities and academics;
- e-research tools;
- practitioner access to research and practitioner researcher approaches;
- commissioning research to underpin policy and practice.

The chapter concludes with an invitation to the reader to reflect on their views on the autonomy or accountability of researchers.

Definitions

Demands for research to have an impact are currently directed by governments at the work of *academic researchers*. Governments are holding university staff to account for the volume, impact and quality of their published outputs – funding and status follow such assessments. That this accountability is not extended to *contract researchers* even where they operate in a competitive environment with academic researchers is an anomaly in terms of value for public money gained by those commissioning research for the public good. It appears to mean that where public funds are invested in research, lower expectations are placed on contract researchers than on academic researchers who have an extra level of accountability and work to do beyond the research contract.

For the purposes of this chapter, three categories of researcher are defined as follows:

- **Academic researchers**, i.e. university staff required to add to the body of knowledge in their field through research and publications. Such researchers are required, as part of their academic role to demonstrate deep expertise and knowledge in particular fields.
- **Contract researchers**, i.e. researchers commissioned by an external body to undertake research. Researchers in this category have no contractual commitment to building the body of knowledge in the area they are researching. They are typically commissioned to undertake time-limited research in an area in which they may or may not have specific expertise. They may work as consultants or in research institutes independent of universities. At the end of a research project they move on to another contract which may or may not be related.
- **Practitioner researchers**, i.e. non-university staff who are engaged in research in the field in which they practice. They may be in a network of researchers which includes academic staff and may include policy-makers or may be undertaking research for their organisation or as part of higher study.

The argument is made in this chapter that e-tools can support different ways of undertaking research which supplant older, slower, more costly methods which have in the past had limited impact and yielded little of significance at the national and international and level. Cost-effective collaborations between policy-makers, practitioner researchers and academic researchers can be particularly supported through the use of a range of e-tools which can lead to rapid and timely impact on practice through e-data collection, analysis and dissemination techniques.

Judging the impact of research

Any beginning researcher would be wise to examine how the different ontological and epistemological stances which they might adopt are likely to help or hinder them in this high-stakes accountability environment. Decisions made early on in a research career about specialisms, methodologies and forms of publication all affect the impact of a researcher's work, the researcher's reputation and the likelihood of the researcher gaining funding to undertake research, i.e. career advancement. But the criteria for evaluating an academic's research are not stable.

Criteria for judging high-quality research are becoming increasingly more sophisticated as governments from countries across the globe as far apart as the UK, Finland, Netherlands, Germany, Romania, Thailand, Australia and New Zealand develop measures to judge the quality of academic research (HEFCE, 2006, 2008; Aalto University, 2009; Australian Research Council, 2009; Hutchson, 2009, Sheehan et al., 2008). Such scrutiny is high-stakes resulting in increased status and in some countries the allocation of significant amounts of funding for organisations and individuals. In the 1980s in the UK, university research assessment exercises were initially carried out by academic researchers, i.e. peer review was used. By the 2008 exercise, user reviewers were included on the panel and by the 2013 exercise, explicit review of impact was to be included. (Bernard (2000) and Chatterji and Seaman (2007) provide an overview over 30 years of the UK research assessment exercises.) By contrast, the model used for the Australian ERA exercise in 2011 abandoned attempts by an earlier Australian administration to assess impact (Allen Consulting Group, 2005; CHASS, 2005) and appeared to focus judgements on volume, excluding assessments of impact as did the NZ exercise (Willis, 2009). For the 2011 exercise in Australia a league table of journals and conferences was compiled which was intended to provide a coherent way of judging the

significance of research but which does not appear to recognise the complexity of knowledge across disciplines nor the sub-communities of researchers which exist (Australian Government, 2011). In the UK in 2008, the Research Assessment Exercise, which judged the standard of research publications in social work, sport and related studies and education decided to place no significance on the place of publication, preferring to focus on the international relevance and quality of research (Bernard, 2000; Blyth et al., 2010). It was recognised that some research might best be reported to a small group of specialists through their professional journal rather than in a journal with a more general audience.

In the UK, the Australian work on impact was noted in reports emanating from government-funded ESRC workshops held in 2005 and 2007 on the measurement of impact (ESRC, 2005, 2011). Many forms of impact were discussed – academic, non-academic, societal, economic and so on. The ESRC workshops focused on economic impact measurement, although significant problems arose – easy, cost-efficient, reliable measures could not be identified. The workshops:

> . . . identified two main kinds of problems besetting attempts at economic impact measurement. The *first* problem relates to the setting up of reliable indicators of relevant output and outcome variables . . . there is no obvious solution to the identification of indicators related to more intangible social benefits . . . for many of the eventual welfare benefits (e.g. improved quality of life, better environment), it is often impossible to quantify the effects. Thus, there are no perfect measures of the impacts from research . . . only a number of imperfect or partial indicators (e.g. scientific publications, citations, patents, licensing revenue, spin-off companies) . . . The *second* type of problem is derived from the complexity of any quantitative model that can capture research inputs and reliably relate them to relevant outcome indicators . . . (Molas-Gallart and Tang 2007: ii)

The Australian impact work is explicitly referenced in the UK reports:

A large study, *Measuring the Impact of Publicly Funded Research*, was undertaken in 2005 for the Australian Department of Education, Science and Training to develop a new approach to measure the impact of publicly funded research (Allen Consulting Group, 2005). It identified four key challenges to its development. First, the limited availability of research output data that can be measured. Second, the time lags involved before any impact can be identified. Third, the continuing difficulty in dealing with the issue of attribution. Fourth, the importance of the contextual environment under which the research was undertaken: 'identical sets of indicators are not applicable for different research groups if they are doing research for different purposes' (Allen Consulting 2005: viii) . . . The Australian Department of Education, Science and Training also commissioned another large study, *Measures of Quality and Impact of Publicly Funded Research in the Humanities, Arts and Social Sciences* (CHASS, 2005). This study stated, like the Allen Consulting report, that assessing impact of academic research must extend beyond the 'pure economic' to include societal benefits, and recommended that appropriate measures be developed on a discipline-by-discipline basis – 'no set of metrics can be common to all disciplines or research units' (CHASS, 2005: 40–1). The study suggested that assessment should be conducted under an 'audit' model, in which academic institutions can compile evidence-based cases demonstrating the impact of their research. (Molas-Gallart and Tang, 2007: 2)

The recommendations from the Australian reports for impact case studies to be developed were taken forward into a UK pilot impact study. Oancea (2010) summarises the findings from the UK pilot as follows:

- identification of impact is difficult;
- issues about selection of cases and construction of stories [are still to be resolved];
- validation/evidence of impact where possible is needed;
- case studies need to be written in similar format;
- a mechanism to collect data relating to impact is needed;

- entire process needs to be guided and time managed carefully. (Oancea, 2010)

The fine detail of the criteria used in the 2013 research impact assessment in the UK is likely to be determined in the end through moderation exercises between the peers and users on the research assessment panels after submissions have been made. This is the opposite of best practice in assessment which is to make the criteria for assessment clear to those being assessed before they are assessed.

Many proxy measures for impact could be used and researchers would be wise to gather these for their own research. Examples include: web statistics (for article downloads); citations, e.g. in systematic reviews used for policy formation (citations in other journals are not considered a reliable indicator – for example, the citation might be because the research is not acceptable); book sales, invitations to join national committees related to an academic's research. There is some cross-over with indicators of esteem.

Autonomy versus accountability – changes in the role of the university and the academic

That academics should be able to demonstrate that their research has impact is controversial because there is a long European tradition of university autonomy. This autonomy is being challenged as governments striving to maintain international standing and economic strength place demands on universities to demonstrate economic impact from the investment of public funds. A 2011 Europe-wide study into university autonomy (Jongsma, 2009) builds on concerns expressed over decades.

For example, Australian academics Anderson and Johnson's (1998) review of university autonomy in 20 countries outlines the tensions between academics in western countries who are the inheritors of a tradition of freedom and independence of thought and action and the needs of governments which fund higher education to have a higher education system which supports national objectives.

That this is an international issue is illustrated in a

speech given by the vice chancellor of the Canadian Simon Fraser University in 2004 to a university audience in Indonesia:

> . . . in all universities around the world we are all dealing with very important issues of how to strike the proper balance between universities and governments, how to strike the proper balance between the autonomy of universities and the reasonable accountability of universities for the public funds that sustain much of their activity. (Stevenson, 2004: 1)

Stevenson reminded his audience that university autonomy:

> . . . is grounded in the history of the classical western university as adapted through three very distinct periods . . . the classical model . . . thirteenth century . . . until the nineteenth century. It was grounded on a very restrictive model of learning both with respect to curricula in theology, philosophy and other 'classic' subjects, and in terms of accessibility to a very small and elite proportion of the population . . . The original universities were founded on a principle of collegial self-governance, a very incipiently democratic system of control by tenured scholars . . . This model began to change only in the nineteenth century with the origin of the research university . . . relate[d] first of all to the scientific and industrial revolution, to the growth of the national warfare state, and to the recognition that the state increasingly requires investment in certain kinds of practical knowledge and higher learning, that only the universities can produce . . . the mass university evolved in the aftermath of the Second World War, funded by formidable public investments oriented towards broader access and enrolment. (Stevenson, 2004: 1)

By 2011 in England, the government agency responsible for universities (HEFCE, 2011) identified five core strategic aims for its work with universities: improving the quality of teaching, widening participation, employer engagement and knowledge transfer, research and contribution to the economy.

By 2011 in Australia, universities were required to sign three-year 'mission-based' compacts with the government with goals not dissimilar to those identified in England by the HEFCE above:

> Each compact will contain a mission statement that will show how the institution plans to align its aspirations and major priorities with the Commonwealth's goals for higher education, research, research training and innovation. The compacts will include specific sections on teaching and learning, research, research training and innovation, and information on funding provided by the Commonwealth [Government] to each of the universities. (Australian Government, 2011b: 2)

In the US, the picture appears to be different with university engagement in national agendas around the knowledge economy appearing to be voluntary, presumably because of the independence of the university sector from federal government control (US Government, 2010).

These demands for increased accountability of universities and academics are occurring at a time when new communications technologies mean that the outputs of academics' work can be easily and cheaply found and assessed by practitioners and policymakers, by potential users and funders. Questions are raised about practitioners' access to research, the small-scale nature of much social science research undertaken by academics and forms of publication which mean research cannot easily be built on (BERA, 2000; TDA, 2004a, 2004b).

New expectations and ways of working are emerging around knowledge management and knowledge mobilisation (University of Toronto, 2011; Oakley, 2003; MacGregor et al., 2006). These include expectations that policy and practice should be research and evidence based (OECD, 2003, 2007a, 2007b), that systematic review systems should be developed to enable access to existing knowledge (EPPI-Centre;[4] Campbell Collaboration;[5] Cochrane Collaboration;[6] Davies et al., 2000; GTCE, 2006; TDA, 2004a, 2004b; Leask and White, 2004) and that user engagement at all stages of research is possible in ways heretofore not possible.

E-tools supporting research impact and dissemination

In England in 2004 prior to the government making a multi-million pound investment to improve the quality of teacher training via professional knowledge networks (ITT Professional Resource Networks), an analysis was undertaken of practitioners' access to research by the government agency responsible. This report (Leask and White, 2004) described the traditional research process as limited in impact on practice (Figure 7.1) and what now might be described as a translational research approach (Figure 7.2) as a way of embedding research findings in practice, i.e. ensuring the dissemination and adoption of best practices emerging from research.

The traditional research process forms only part of the cycle necessary to support embedding new practices suggested by research evidence.

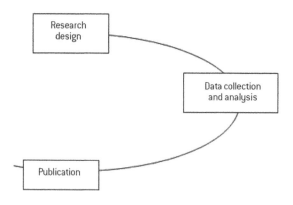

Source: TDA (2004b).

Figure 7.1 The traditional research process

The purpose of the TDA IPRN (ITT Professional Resource Networks) process was to complete the cycle from review of the evidence base and identification of gaps in knowledge and commissioning of research to embedding new knowledge in practice and reviewing the evidence for the knowledge base regularly (Leask and White, 2004: 3). Figure 7.2 provides an illustration of the process.

This process operated in England for six years be-fore being cut by the incoming administration in 2010. The commissioning of the Teacher Training Resource Bank and associated specialist networks (http://www.ttrb.ac.uk) was based on this analysis.

The 'translational research' approach now adopted by some medical researchers takes research 'from the bench to the bedside'. It has similarities with the process outlined in Figure 7.2 and now can be facilitated by software provided by online communities which allows cost-effective ways of engaging researchers and practitioners in co-researching and in dissemination and impact.

E-tools now allow academic researchers to do more with less resource. Table 7.1 provides examples of e-tools and new ways of working facilitated by such tools together with comments about the implications for research approaches for the use of these e-research tools.

Online networking to support professional communities of practice as mentioned in Table 7.1 is bringing about significant changes in the ways researchers work and engage with practitioners, with many governments supporting this way of working. At the time of writing, calls by major funders for submissions for networking projects were found in the UK, Australia and across the EU. Table 7.2 outlines a proposal put to the UK Universities Council for the Education and Training of Teachers in 2010 requesting the organisation to support professional networking as a way of scaling up small-scale educational research and providing a new way of working for educational researchers so that their research can be based on significant sample sizes, i.e. be significant enough to influence practice nationally and internationally.

Practitioners' access to research and engagement of practitioners in research

In many areas of knowledge there is a large body of practitioners on whose practice research might potentially impact – health, policing, the hundreds of functions of local government, including social work and education. In the UK alone, there are over two million practitioners in local government and education.

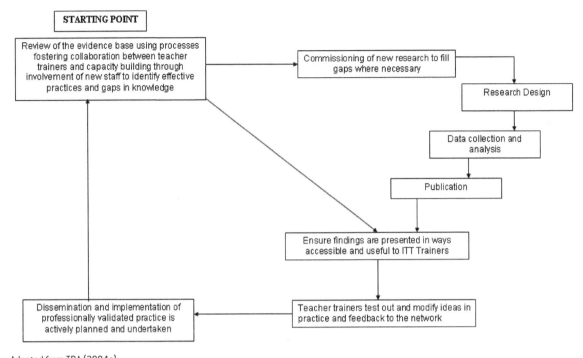

Adapted from TDA (2004c)

Figure 7.2   A translational research approach for initial teacher training

Until access to the Internet became widespread (around the year 2000), access by such practitioners to research was very restricted. Within a decade, initial training and continuing professional development was transformed with online training, online access to knowledge bases and the possibility of taking part in professional forums and sharing knowledge between experienced and inexperienced practitioners. Building knowledge through professional 'communities of practice' had been recognised before the Internet as a key method of developing professional practice (Schön, 1987; Wenger et al., 2002; Wenger, 1998; Lave and Wenger, 1991).

Two major challenges yet to be resolved which affect the impact and dissemination of research and the adoption of new ways of working are as follows:

- The attitudes and understanding of policy-makers, politicians and academic researchers, particularly senior members of these professional communities themselves who were trained and studied in the pre-Internet age.

- The lack of a coherent e-infrastructure available to support new ways of working. In some professions, e.g. accountancy and law, the private provision of knowledge repositories and organisational subscription models works well – organisations and individuals subscribe to the services. In education, current models of the privatisation of knowledge excludes those on whom the knowledge is likely to have most impact, e.g. practitioners and policy-makers responsible for sector improvement. In the education sector perhaps more than any other many benefit by educational knowledge being widely available – to teachers, teacher trainers, parents, students, providers of CPD.

In some countries, for example the USA and Australia, a sustained commitment by government to the

Table 7.1 E-research tools and implications for researchers and commissioners of research

E-tools and new ways of working facilitated by technology	Notes and details of application Implications for policy and practice
E-surveys, e.g. Bristol Online surveys (http://www.survey.bris.ac.uk/), Survey Monkey (http://www.surveymonkey.com)	E-questionnaires linked automatically with databases and e-communications tools such as professional association or school email lists allow collection of data from significant sample sizes (1,000 plus) within 24 hours and dissemination of findings within 48 hours. Low-cost longitudinal studies can be undertaken and annual repeat surveys on individual topics would be similarly cost-effective.
Mind-mapping software as a research tool for use with focus groups	The use of this software provides for a new intensive approach to the running of focus groups. See the PIMS approach (Leask and Preston, in preparation).
E-access to research databases and efficient search mechanisms	Research databases can now be linked and be cross-searchable (such as the Education Evidence Portal in the UK (http://www.eep.ac.uk)). Literature searches and the gathering of copies of articles for literature reviews, which once would have taken researchers weeks if not months, now take minutes. E-collections of articles can also be archived for others to build on.
E-infrastructure exists which supports researcher networking,e.g. online communities of practice linking practitioners, policy-makers and researchers to share and build knowledge and to undertake research collaboratively	Provides cost-effective methods for: – collective knowledge building; – scaling up small-scale research; – e-dissemination; – users to contribute to decisions on topics; – users to be co-researchers. For example, http://www.educationcommunities.org – networking researchers to do research leading to efficiencies, distributed knowledge, collective knowledge building (see Figure 7.2.).
Rapid publication through new forms of publishing	Publication in forms easily usable by a range of users can be cost-effectively provided. New forms of publication through open-access websites such as the Durham University e-journal (http://www.oerj.org).
Systematic reviews to build knowledge	Systematic review approaches are now influencing expectations of how literature reviews might be constructed and reported so that they can be shared and built on. Guidelines for the writing of articles so that they can be included in systematic reviews can be found in the REPOSE guidelines: http://eppi.ioe.ac.uk/cms/Default.aspx?tabid=759.
Translational research practice – obliges translational researchers to commit to ensuring their research can be accessed by users	BERA guidelines written in 2000 presage this 'benchtop to bedside' approach (http://www.bera.ac.uk/publications/guidelines/) which is gaining ground in medicine. The Map of Medicine approach provides an example of how research-based knowledge can be made easily accessible to practitioners and other researchers (http://www.mapofmedicine.com/).

Table 7.2   A model for scaling up small-scale educational research via collaborative research networks

---

Why create interlinked national and international collaborative research networks?
The goal of such networks is to improve the quality of the evidence base underpinning educational practice in schools and in teacher education in order to strengthen the claim of the sector to be professional so that the sector is less vulnerable to the 'eureka' moments of policy-makers.

The context in which educational research is conducted and funded means that:
A major source of funding for educational research is academic staff time. Combining some of this resource through collaborative projects to scale up promising small-scale research could create a powerful research tool producing findings of national and international significance, the outcome of such collaboration being greater than that which each partner could produce individually.

Would the network favour one method of research over another?
The network would recognise that teaching is both an art and a science and that the evidence base for professional practice includes case studies and conceptual papers as well as large-scale studies including randomised controlled trials where appropriate.

The research methods used would be down to the network working on the topic. The research could be around attitudes or structures for example. A small-scale study might find that underachieving boys find factors such as x, y and z about school organisation really prevent them learning. A finding of this scale among 100 boys in one school is interesting. If, say, something like 80 per cent of boys from a structured sample of 4,000 across a structured sample of schools across the country or across a number of countries agreed, then there might be a case for national pilots, changing practice in school structures in a sample of schools and testing out if this was more conducive to them. The form of test would be down to the research group and what they think will lend weight to their results. The figures here are just matters of professional judgement of course.

Adapted from from Leask (2010b)

provision of online access to knowledge in education since the mid-1990s has meant that knowledge repositories such as Edna[7] in Australia and the What Works Clearing House[8] and ERIC[9] in the USA have survived changes in administration and have continued to build resources over time which are freely available to all with, it could be expected, consequent impact on practice.

Changes of government in Sweden in 2006 and the UK in 2010 saw the closing of online knowledge repositories supported by education ministries. These were the first changes of government since the Internet became widely available. In Sweden government-supported educational websites disappeared overnight. In England, the first steps of the education ministry were to cut the resources supporting dissemination of research to education practitioners such as Teachers TV, the Qualifications and Curriculum Agency,

BECTA, the education communications technology agency, and the Teacher Training Resource Bank and accompanying subject-specific resource networks. Major web-based resources in other public sectors such as social work and in health are also at risk. Experiences from these countries point to the need for any national e-infrastructure, whether this is for research repositories or online communities, to be established on a basis capable of surviving changes in administration. It can be argued that providing access to knowledge via appropriate e-infrastructure is a responsibility of national government in much the same way that in the past governments have provided national infrastructures to support national postal and telephone services and road networks.

Commissioning research to underpin policy and practice

Policy-makers, i.e. politicians and their civil servants, could have considerable influence on improving research impact and dissemination through their decisions about:

- the provision of a national e-infrastructure for the dissemination of research and for collaborations between practitioners and researchers;
- the criteria for accountability for academic researchers;
- the guidelines set for government bodies dispensing research funds;
- the requirements for research tenders;
- accountability for practitioners to demonstrate research- and evidence-informed practice.

The first three points are addressed elsewhere in this chapter.

When commissioning research, tenders can be written to include requirements which ensure impact and dissemination of the outcomes. An example of a missed opportunity in this regard in England was a reportedly one million pound contract awarded some years ago to a consultancy firm to find out what makes for effective teachers. The research was duly carried out and reported to government. This provides an example of the minimal impact of research of the type Leask and White (2004) refer to in Figure 7.1 above. Those undertaking the research had no engagement with the education sector so did not use the avenues for impact and dissemination expected of academic researchers, e.g. engagement with users, conference presentations, article and book publications.

Today, similar work could be undertaken using online communities and various e-tools at a fraction of the cost and yielding impact across the sector. A network of practitioner researchers from a stratified sample of, say, 10% of the 150 local authorities could be granted short secondments to gather data in their local area through observations and focus groups. A centrally coordinated e-survey could feed back the findings to every school and teacher training institution in the country via email. Requirements to report findings via professional networks could

be included and cost little. If a translational research approach was used web publications, perhaps linked with videos demonstrating particularly effective approaches, would provide an effective training resource for new teachers.

Your stance on impact and dissemination?

In the different sections of this chapter the roles of universities and academic researchers and the behaviours of those commissioning research, particularly policy-makers, are explored along with the potential for twenty-first-century technologies to revolutionise approaches to research, research costs and impact through rapid widespread dissemination of research which has engaged practitioners from the start.

What is certain about the expectations of researchers is that change in the ways professionals access, present, publish, share and build knowledge is happening now. What is less certain is which governments, organisations and professional associations will adapt to new methods for commissioning, undertaking and publishing research and which will continue with practices which ossified perhaps some time in the early twentieth century. Decisions taken by individual researchers to move their practice into the twenty-first century or stay in the twentieth century will have a cumulative effect on how their professional group is viewed by users of their research – government and practitioners.

However, the major opportunities identified in this chapter depend on the existence of an e-infrastructure to support rapid publication and collaborations between policy-makers, practitioners and researchers in online communities of practice which allow members to be part of multiple communities and to play different roles in each community. The need for the creation of such an e-infrastructure is akin to the needs for connectivity which led to the creation of the national telephone, road and rail networks. Publicly visible examples of interconnected professional networks open to professionals are provided by http://www.educationcommunities.org for educators and http://www.communities.idea.gov.uk for local government in the UK. Glow in Scotland and Ultranet in Victoria,

Australia are private communities funded for the education sector by government which potentially provide this service to their closed communities. Individual subject-based communities abound but interconnectedness allowing users to be engaged in a variety of communities and to find others with similar interests from around the world is a major value of the online connected professional community approach. Practitioners, policy-makers and researchers are rarely interested in just one aspect of professional knowledge.

Countries able to implement such an e-infrastructure can expect to see significant changes in the speed and extent of dissemination of research and its consequent impact. However, researchers have to produce research which is significant enough to be worth disseminating and worth practitioners and policy-makers considering acting upon.

The attitudes and expectations of those commissioning research and those setting the criteria for assessing research quality will have a major effect on how quickly practice in terms of research methods, types of publication and the engagement of users change in a country. A note of caution is needed for national research assessment exercises as these can promote ways of undertaking research which in fact work against impact, e.g. if volume of publications is the main criterion, then researchers would be sensible to leave impact to someone else and focus on the production of articles.

Conclusion

If you are a researcher, you have a very personal professional decision to make: what kind of a research profession do you want to belong to – one that adapts to change and plays a full role in providing the research and evidence base for policy and practice, or one which stays with the outmoded models of practice of yesteryear? Your actions, or lack of actions, will influence the outcome for your country. Considering to whom you feel accountable – contractually, professionally and morally – may help you decide where you stand on the issues outlined in this chapter about academic autonomy or accountability. Researchers who do not recognise the new world order are likely

to find their work and ideas sidelined or buried in outmoded processes not fit for the information age.

Notes

1. http://eppi.ioe.ac.uk
2. http://www.campbellcollaboration.org/
3. http://www.cochrane.org/
4. http://eppi.ioe.ac.uk
5. http://www.campbellcollaboration.org/
6. http://www.cochrane.org/
7. http://www.edna.edu.au
8. http://ies.ed.gov/ncee/wwc/
9. http://www.eric.ed.gov/

Suggested further reading

Training and Development Agency for Schools (TDA) (2004) *Initial Teacher Training (ITT) Professional Resource Networks (IPRNs) – Rationale and Development*. Paper presented at the British Educational Research Association Annual Conference, University of Manchester, UK, 16–18 September 2004. Available at: http://www.leeds.ac.uk/educol/documents/00003667.htm (accessed 14 February 2011). Paper addressing one of the major challenges to those wishing to improve the quality of education: the embedding in educational practices of new professional knowledge validated through research and evidence.

EPPI Centre (2009) *EPPI-Centre* [online]. Available at: http://eppi.ioe.ac.uk. The EPPI Centre at the Institute of Education, University of London has been at the forefront of carrying out systematic reviews for nearly 20 years. The website provides access to reliable research findings and resources and offers support and expertise to those undertaking systematic reviews.

Blyth, E., Shardlow, S. M., Masson, H., Lyons, K., Shaw, I. and White, S. (2010) 'Measuring the quality of peer-reviewed publications in social work: impact factors – liberation or liability?', *Social Work Education*, 29(2): 120–36. Interesting recent article on the measurement of peer-reviewed articles in social work.

References

Aalto University Research Assessment Exercise (2009) *Finland: Rector Matti Pursula's (TKK) Presentation for Assessment Panels 8th June 2009*. Available at: http://www.aaltoyliopisto.info/en/view/innovaatioyliopisto-info/research-evaluation (accessed 15 February 2011).

Allen Consulting Group (2005) *Measuring the Impact of Publicly Funded Research*. Report prepared for the Australian Government Department of Education, Science and Training.

Anderson, D. and Johnson, R. (1998) *University Autonomy in Twenty Countries*. Centre for Continuing Education, Australian National University. Available at: http://www.magna-charta.org/pdf/University_autonomy_in_20_countries.pdf (accessed 15 February 2011).

Australian Government (2005) *The Emerging Business of Knowledge Transfer: Creating Value from Intellectual Products and Services*. Canberra: Department of Education, Science and Training.

Australian Government (2011) *Mission Based Compacts with Universities*. Available at: http://www.innovation.gov.au/RESEARCH/MISSIONBASEDCOMPACTS/Pages/default.aspx (accessed 15 February 2011).

Australian Research Council (2009) *The Excellence in Research for Australia (ERA) Initiative ERA Indicator Descriptors*. Available at: http://content.cqu.edu.au/FCWViewer/view.do?page=10856 (accessed 15 February 2011).

Bernard, G. W. (2000) 'History and research assessment exercises', *Oxford Review of Education*, 26(1): 95–106.

Blyth, E., Shardlow, S. M., Masson, H., Lyons, K., Shaw, I. and White, S. (2010) 'Measuring the quality of peer-reviewed publications in social work: impact factors – liberation or liability?', *Social Work Education*, 29(2): 120–36.

British Educational Research Association (BERA) (2000) *Guidelines for Good Practice in Educational Research*. Available at: http://www.bera.ac.uk/files/guidelines/goodpr1.pdf (accessed 15 February 2011).

Chatterji, M. and Seaman, P. (2007) 'Research assessment exercise results and research funding in the United Kingdom: a regional–territorial analysis', *Education Economics*, 15(1): 15–30.

Collison, C. and Parcell, G. (2006) *Learning to Fly*. London: Wiley.

Council for Humanities, Arts and Social Sciences (CHASS) (2005) *Measures of Quality and Impact of Publicly Funded Research in the Humanities, Arts and Social Sciences*. Australian Department of Education, Science and Training.

Davenport, T. and Prusak, L. (1998) *Working Knowledge*. Boston: Harvard Business School Press.

Davies, H., Nutley, S. and Smith, P. (eds) (2000) *What Works? Evidence-Based Policy and Practice in Public Services*. Bristol: Policy Press.

ESRC (2005) Approaches to Assessing the Non-academic Impact of Social Science Research. Available at: http://www.esrc.ac.uk/_images/non-academic_impact_symposium_report_tcm8-3813.pdf (accessed 15 February 2011).

ESRC (2011) *Impact Toolkit*. Available at: http://www.esrc.ac.uk/funding-and-guidance/tools-and-resources/impact-toolkit/index.aspx (accessed 14 February 2011).

General Teaching Council for England (GTCE) (2006) Synthesis of Research and Evaluation Projects Concerned with Capacity-building Through Teachers' Professional Development: Full Research Report. Available at: http://www.gtce.org.uk/research/commissioned_research/cpd/synthesis_cpd_projects/ (accessed 15 February 2011).

HEFCE (2006) '*2008 RAE Panel Criteria and Working Methods Panel K*. Available at: http://www.rae.ac.uk/pubs/2006/01/byuoa.asp?u=k (accessed 14 February 2011).

HEFCE (2008) *RAE 2008*. Available at: http://www.rae.ac.uk/ (accessed 14 February 2011).

HEFCE (2011) *Higher Education Funding Council for England Mission Statement*. Available at: http://www.hefce.ac.uk/aboutus/mission.htm (accessed 14 February 2011).

Henley Knowledge Management Forum (2008) *Sharing Knowledge with Other Organizations*. Henley: Henley Management College.

Hopkins, D. (1989) *Evaluation for School Development*. Milton Keynes: Open University Press.

Howard Partners (2005) *The Emerging Business of Knowledge Transfer: Creating Value from Intellectual Produces and Services*. Canberra: Department of Education, Science and Training.

Hu, T. O., Davies, S. M. and Smith, P. C. (2000) *What Works? Evidence-Based Policy and Practice in Public Services*. Bristol: Policy Press.

Hutchison, H. (2009) *Humanities and Creative Arts: Recognising Esteem Factors and Non-Traditional Publication in Excellence in Research for Australia (ERA) Initiative*. Advocacy paper. Available at: http://www.chass.org.au/papers/PAP20090820HH.php (accessed 14 February 2011).

Improvement and Development Agency [for local government] (IDeA) (2006) 'Knowledge Management Strategy: Board Paper'. IDeA internal document. London: IDeA.

Improvement and Development Agency [for local

government] (IDeA) (2008) *Knowledge Management Tools and Techniques: Helping You Find the Right Knowledge at the Right Time*. London: IDeA.

Jongsma, A. (2009) 'Europe: scoring university autonomy', *University World News*, 100. Available at: http://www.universityworldnews.com/article.php?story=20091106120156959 (accessed 14 February 2011).

Lave, J. and Wenger, E. (1991) *Situated Learning: Legitimate Peripheral Participation*. Cambridge: Cambridge University Press.

Leask, M. (2010a) *Higher Education in a World Changed Utterly: Doing More with Less*. Paris: OECD/IMHE, 13–15 September 2010.

Leask, M. (2010b) *A Model for Scaling Up Small-Scale Research Through Collaborative Research Networks*. Paper presented to UCET Research Sub-Committee, London.

Leask, M. and Jumani, N. B. (2011) *Translational Research and Online Learning Communities: Moving the Dominant Paradigm for Teacher Education Research from the 19th to the 21st Century*. Paper presented at the Computer Assisted Learning Conference, Manchester, April 2011.

Leask, M. and Preston, C. (2011) 'Being Observed or Being Involved: PIMS – An Innovative and Timely Research Method Linking Policy Makers, Practitioners and Pupils as Co-researchers'. Unpublished paper.

Leask, M. and White, C. (2004) Initial *Teacher Training (ITT) Professional Resource Networks (IPRNS) – Rationale and Development: Using Research and Evidence to Improve Teaching and Learning*. London: Teacher Training Agency Paper presented at the British Educational Research Association Annual Conference, University of Manchester, 16-18 September 2004. Available at: http://www.leeds.ac.uk/educol/documents/00003667.htm (accessed 5 November 2011).

Lucas, L. (2007) 'Research and teaching work within university education departments: fragmentation or integration?', *Journal of Further and Higher Education*, 31(1): 17–29.

MacGregor, R., Rix, M., Aylward, D. and Glynn, J. (2006) 'Factors associated with research management in Australian commerce and business faculties', *Journal of Higher Education Policy and Management*, 28(1): 59–70.

McLaughlin, C., Black Hawkins, K., Brindley, S., McIntyre, D. and Taber, K. (2006) *Researching Schools: Stories from a Schools – University Partnership for Educational Research*. London: Routledge.

Molas-Gallart, J. and Tang, P. (2007) *Report of the ESRC Impact Evaluation Methods Workshop 20th March 2007*. Available at: http://www.esrc.ac.uk/_images/ESRC_Impact_

Evaluation_Methods_Workshop_tcm8-3814.pdf (accessed 15 February 2011).

Newman, F. and Holzman, L. (1997) *The End of Knowing*. London: Routledge.

Newman, M. and Elbourne, D. (2005) 'Improving the Usability of Educational research: Guidelines for the Reporting of Primary Empirical Research Studies in Education (The REPOSE Guidelines). Available at: http://eppi.ioe.ac.uk/cms/Default.aspx?tabid=759 (accessed 14 February 2011).

Newman, M., Elbourne, D. and Leask, M. (2004) *Improving the Usability of Educational Research: Guidelines for the Reporting of Empirical Primary Research Studies in Education*. Roundtable discussion paper presented at the 5th Annual Conference of the Teaching and Learning Research Programme, Cardiff, 22–24 November 2004.

Oakley, A. (2003) 'Research evidence, knowledge management and educational practice: early lessons from a systematic approach', *London Review of Education*, 1(1): 21–34.

Oancea, A. (2010) Beyond Impact: Connecting Research to Policy and Practice? Presentation at the Society for Education Studies Annual Seminar, London, 4 November 2010.

OECD (2003) *Knowledge Management: New Challenges for Educational Research*. Paris: OECD Publishing.

OECD (2007a) *Evidence in Education: Linking Research and Policy*. Available at: http://www.oecd.org/document/56/0,3343,en_2649_35845581_38796344_1_1_1,00.html (accessed 14 February 2011).

OECD (2007b) *Taking Stock of Educational R&D: Joint OECD-CORECHED International Expert Meeting*. Available at: http://www.oecd.org/document/36/0,3343,en_2649_35845581_39379876_1_1_1_1,00.html (accessed 14 February 2011).

Schön, D. (1987) *How Professionals Think in Action*. New York: Basic Books.

Sheehan, J. et al. (2008) *Practices and Perspectives of Research Evaluation*. Amsterdam: IOS Press.

Stanford Center for Clinical and Translational Education and Research (2011) *Mission Statement*. Available at: http://scter.stanford.edu/about/ (accessed 14 February 2011).

Stevenson, M. (2004) *University Governance and Autonomy: Problems in Managing Access, Quality and Accountability*. Keynote address to ADB Conference on University Governance, Denpasar, Indonesia. Simon Fraser University. Available at: http://www.sfu.ca/pres/president/speeches/20045.html (accessed 14 February 2011).

Training and Development Agency for Schools (TDA) (2004a) *Using Research and Evidence to Improve Teaching and Learning in the Training of Professionals – An Example from Teacher Training in England*. Paper presented at the British Educational Research Association Annual Conference, University of Manchester, UK, 16–18 September 2004. Available at: http://www.leeds.ac.uk/educol/documents/00003666.htm (accessed 14 February 2011).

Training and Development Agency for Schools (TDA) (2004b) *Accumulating the Evidence Base for Educational Practice: Our Respective Responsibilities*. Paper presented at the British Educational Research Association Annual Conference, University of Manchester, UK, 16–18 September 2004. Available at: http://www.leeds.ac.uk/educol/documents/00003665.htm (accessed 14 February 2011).

University of Toronto (2011) *Annotated Bibliography – Knowledge Mobilization*. Available at: http://www.oise.utoronto.ca/rspe/Free_KM_Resources.html (accessed 14 February 2011).

US Government Department of Education (2010) *The Role and Responsibilities of States in Increasing Access, Quality, and Completion: Under Secretary Martha J. Kanter's Remarks at the SHEEO Higher Education Policy Conference*. Available at: http://www.ed.gov/news/speeches/role-and-responsibilities-states-increasing-access-quality-and-completion-under-secret (accessed 14 February 2011).

Wellcome Trust (2011) *What Is Translational Research?* Available at: http://www.wellcome.ac.uk/Funding/Technology-transfer/WTD027704.htm (accessed 14 February 2011).

Wenger, E. (1998) *Communities of Practice: Learning, Meaning, and Identity*. Cambridge, MA: Cambridge University Press.

Wenger, E., McDermott, R. and Snyder, W. (2002) *Cultivating Communities of Practice: A Guide to Managing Knowledge*. Cambridge, MA: Harvard Business School Press.

Willis, D. (2009) 'Disciplines, institutions and the performance-based research fund: the scholarship of teaching and learning from a New Zealand perspective', *International Journal for the Scholarship of Teaching and Learning*, 3(2): 1–6.

PART III

KEY METHODS

Dimension 1

Research designs

Action research

Carol Munn-Giddings

What is action research?

Action research (AR) has a long history in education and community development and is becoming increasingly popular in a range of other disciplines including health, social care and business studies. Trying to get an agreed definition can be very frustrating for students as there are many, in large part due to the number of disciplines involved. However, if we look a little more closely at a number of abridged definitions we can see some common themes that help us both discern its core characteristics and distinction in relation to other research approaches.

For example, Kurt Lewin (a psychologist) first described it as a way of generating knowledge about a social system while, at the same time, attempting to change it (Lewin, 1946). John Elliott (an educationalist) described it as 'the study of a social situation with a view to improving the quality of action within it . . . providing the necessary link between self evaluation and professional development' (1991: 69) while Ernest T. Stringer (in relation to community action research) defined it as 'an approach to research that potentially has both practical and theoretical outcomes . . . in ways that provide conditions for continuing action – the formation of a sense of community. It is . . . rigorously empirical and reflective and engages people who have traditionally been called "subjects" as active participants in the process . . .' (1996: xvi).

We can see from these definitions that action research is considered to be based in practice or a community and not separate from it – it is the antithesis of 'ivory tower' research. Rather than a 'technical' activity that is carried out by 'expert researchers' it is a form of research that can be undertaken by practitioners such as teachers, social workers, community development workers as well as students and service users.

In contrast to most other forms of research, action research is often led by 'insiders', defined as those facing the situation or trying to develop their practice, as opposed to an external 'outside' research expert who does research 'on' other people's problems or practices. However, in many contexts (e.g. health, social care and community development) a model exists whereby social researchers act as 'facilitators' in the action research process, bringing a knowledge of research methods to the enquiry process but working alongside people who have lived experience of the situation being enquired into. In this latter mode the role of the researcher is more like a catalyst and co-ordinator of projects (Winter and Munn-Giddings, 2001).

Another key feature of the above definitions, as the term suggests, is that the research is action not description orientated. This distinguishes AR from purely quantitative and qualitative approaches since the purpose of AR is to work towards practice change during the research process, not merely to explore and describe a situation 'as it is', for example involving teachers and students or mental health service users in a process of change to their practice or community. This is why AR is claimed to bridge the theory–practice gap as there is technically no problem in having to implement findings as the process is educative for all involved and learning and change occurs within the AR process.

Although AR studies can be carried out by a single teacher or community worker the research process generally aims to be collaborative. Sometimes the term 'co-researcher' is used to describe collaborators on the project. Some writers make a distinction between 'action research' and 'participatory action research' (PAR), where the former is primarily seen as being about practice change and not necessarily involving participants throughout the research process, whereas PAR aims towards broader social or systemic change and more consciously involves participants in each stage of the research process. Other authors, however, use these terms interchangeably and Hart and Bond have set out a useful typology of types of AR in their 1995 text.

AR does not fit neatly into academic debates about 'paradigms'. It shares some features with the interpretivist paradigm in that the value base of AR would always have a commitment to understanding the meanings that participants and groups in the research attach to events and situations, that is the way in which individuals and groups construct their world. Some might locate AR in what Ernest (1994) defines as the 'critical theoretic paradigm' which goes beyond finding out and understanding but is also concerned with the search for improvement of aspects of social life or social institutions. Heron and Reason (1997) suggest that all forms of participatory research (including AR) can be seen as fitting into a 'participatory paradigm' that is always concerned with a 'participative reality' co-created with others, such as knowing in conceptual terms that something is the case (propositional knowing) and the knowledge creation that comes with actually doing what you propose (practical knowing).

The above discussion suggests that AR is a developmental process and research questions in AR reflect this, for example:

- How can I improve the way I work with large groups of students?
- How do we create a culturally sensitive online forum?
- In what ways do postgraduate students become each other's critical friends and how can this process be developed?

Research design

Typically the AR process is one that continually alternates between enquiry and action. This is often conceived of and illustrated as a series of stages, spirals or cycles. For example, Zuber-Skerritt (1992) outlines four stages in an AR cycle: planning, acting, observing and reflecting. There may be many cycles in any one project. Unlike most other forms of research data collected in one stage/cycle informs the development of the next stage of the project (as illustrated in the example below).

Action researchers use any methods that are relevant to their research question. It is very common therefore to use a mixed-method approach combining both quantitative and qualitative data. Because AR is based in or close to practice, often the existing practice materials/resources are incorporated into the research design as 'data', for example minutes from meetings. A number of researchers use methods from the creative arts as part of their studies to collect data, for example dance, collage work and poetry.

When we are 'analysing' data within an AR project we are concerned with learning and implementing change, rather than (as in most other forms of social research) on description or constructing an interpretation. So we need to think about the data in terms of new possibilities for action. In terms of design, the cyclical nature of AR requires analysis and reflections on data collected at each stage of the project to be used to inform the next stage and practical step in the research process.

It can be easier to understand these characteristics through a concrete example, so the following sections provide a synopsis of a cross-disciplinary project that involved academics, practitioners and managers in a workplace setting; the principles would readily translate into an education setting.

Example: stress in the workplace

In the project a team from Anglia Ruskin University worked with two large-scale organisations that had shown an interest in attempting to address the negative consequences of stress in their workplace. The organisations were a healthcare trust and a social services organisation in the United Kingdom (England). Workplace stress and burn-out are recognised phenomena which impact negatively on the delivery of care by health and social work organisations. In 2007/8 it was estimated that workplace stress, depression or anxiety in the UK resulted in a loss of 13.5 million working days (Health and Safety Executive, 2009). The aim of the project was to develop a bespoke mental well-being strategy in each of these workplaces based on the concerns and ideas of the organisations' employees and senior managers. The research question was typically developmental in nature and for both organisations was: 'How do we best address staff stress in our organisation?'

The methodological approach

The project was based on a participatory action research (PAR) approach since it involved a change or development during the research process and actively engaged stakeholders in the development of the project and in generating shared solutions to shared problems. The collaboration was twofold within the project. The university project team (10) was multidisciplinary and included staff from various backgrounds such as social work, mental health, health psychology, social policy and business, and ranged from senior lecturers to professors. As a team we worked as facilitators with frontline practitioners, middle and senior managers in the two organisations both of which were undergoing structural change (see Ramon and Hart, 2003).

Because of the hierarchal nature of the organisations the lead researcher had to first negotiate access to staff members as well as agreeing on the overall purpose and format of the research. Ethics approval was gained via the university approval process. Once this stage was complete, in both organisations we recruited staff who showed an interest in the project and who would be prepared to actively contribute to five participatory workshops at fortnightly intervals, each lasting two

and a half hours. These workshops were structured around some key exercises covering different aspects of stress; the methods included the use of small-group exercises and discussions related to presentations (by the university team plus invited speakers), vignettes and role-play. The 'data' were the issues and discussion points that derived from these methods. At each workshop notes and flipcharts of the core issues were recorded and the contents were written up as 'themes' and disseminated to group members before the next meeting. The subsequent workshop would begin with participants' observations or queries arising from the last session. On occasion participants were sometimes requested to do some work between sessions related to the issues being raised, for example writing examples from their work which highlighted relevant issues and strategies. Although each session had a pre-defined format and content the university team responded to issues raised by participants during the workshop sessions and adjusted future sessions accordingly.

Alongside these workshops which yielded qualitative data we undertook in both organisations an anonymous quantitative survey of all staff based on the Maslach Burnout Inventory (Maslach and Jackson, 1986) to ascertain the wider staff groups' views on stress at work.

As we saw earlier it is the sequence of several phases of critical reflection within an AR project that carries forward its development (Winter and Munn-Giddings, 2001: 235). That is, each stage of data analysis helps in the next practical step of the project. The data analysis techniques were similar to those used in some other types of projects. The qualitative data were analysed thematically (Aronson and Calsmith, 1990) to draw out the key issues. However, in contrast to some other methodologies in this project, the six workshops were used as building blocks and the analysis that was done after each workshop informed the debate in the subsequent workshop. Thus each session built towards finalising the data and suggestions that formed the final strategy document presented to senior managers. The results of the survey were analysed in the statistical package SPSS, Inc., an IBM Company,[1] for both descriptive and inferential statistics and these data were also included in the final well-being strategy document.

In AR, data analysis is a collaborative process of

negotiation. In this example study, participants were agreeing the core themes on flipcharts at the end of each session. One of the university team took these interpretations, revisited the data collected in each session and wrote these up for all involved. As above these were revisited at the start of each session. At the end of the project the university team were involved in looking across the data from all six workshops and giving their overall interpretations as well as making suggestions about the practical implications from the data. These were then taken back to be firmed up with the participants. In some action research studies participants in the situation are much more actively involved in that process. Ours was a pragmatic solution to working with organisations where staff time was limited.

The primary outcome of the study was an organisationally bespoke strategy document which contained staff perspectives on the core issues causing or aggravating mental distress at work and suggestions for short/medium and long-term actions to be carried out. These action areas also identified a process by which issues could be resolved and by whom. A secondary and unanticipated outcome emerged from the process which was to use the data to inform a returning-to-work support group together with a self-management pack primarily informed by the data collated during the project (see Backwith and Munn-Giddings, 2003).

For a reflective and more detailed account of the content, process and outcomes see Munn-Giddings et al. (2005).

Note

1. SPSS was acquired by IBM in October 2009.

Suggested further reading

The project description I have provided above is illustrative of some key features of the action research approach. However, to get a feel for the range of approaches it is important to look at different examples of AR projects and design. A good starting point would be the specialist journals in the area such as *Educational Action Research, Action Research and Systemic Practice* and *Action Research*. It is worth getting a feel of projects that involve singular or small groups of practitioners examining their practice (see, for example, Bana, 2010) and comparing this with projects that involve collaborations between different groups (see Bland and Atweh's 2007 account of students, teachers and university researchers working together). It is also useful to look at articles where collaborators work in different organisational settings – a particularly interesting and innovative example of a project sustained over many years that began as an educational curriculum project and developed into an action-based group in a hospital can be found in Jayne Crow et al's account (2005, 2009). How to engage people in AR projects is an ongoing issue. Cotterell (2008) provides an interesting account of involving people with life limiting conditions as co-researchers throughout the research process focusing on the data analysis stage of the project. As mentioned earlier some writers use the creative arts as part of their methodology; for students interested in this area see for examples Burchell (2010) who uses poetic expression and form as part of her methodology. Finally, many of the AR textbooks provide very useful 'how to' guides for those new to AR (as well as reminders for more experienced researchers!) – see Winter and Munn-Giddings (2001) and Stringer (1996) and the recent McNiff (2010).

References

Aranson, E. and Calsmith, J. (1990) *Methods of Research in Social Psychology*. New York: McGraw-Hill Education.

Backwith, D. and Munn-Giddings, C. (2003) 'Self-help/mutual aid in promoting mental health at work', *Journal of Mental Health Promotion*, 2(4): 14–25.

Bana, Z. (2010) '"Great Conversation" for school improvement in disadvantageous rural contexts: a participatory case study', *Educational Action Research*, 18(2): 213–17.

Bland, D. and Atweh, B. (2007) 'Students as researchers: engaging student voices in PAR', *Educational Action Research*, 15(3): 337–49.

Burchell, H. (2010) 'Poetic expression and poetic form in practitioner research', *Educational Action Research*, 18(3): 389–400.

Cotterell, P. (2008) 'Exploring the value of service user involvement in data analysis', *Educational Action Research*, 16(1): 5–17.

Crow, J., Smith, L. and Keenan, I. (2005) 'Journeying between the Education and Hospital Zones in a collaborative action research project', *Educational Action Research*, 14(2): 287–306.

Crow, J., Smith, L. and Keenan, I. (2009) 'Sustainability in an action research project: 5 years of a Dignity and Respect action group in a hospital setting', *Educational Action Research*, 15(1): 55–68.

Elliott, J. (1991) *Action Research for Educational Change.* Buckingham: Open University Press.

Ernest, P. (1994) *An Introduction to Research Methodology and Paradigms*, Educational Research Monograph Series. Exeter: University of Exeter.

Hart, E. and Bond, M. (1995) *Action Research for Health and Social Care.* Milton Keynes: Open University.

Health and Safety Executive (2009) *Health and Safety Statistics 2007/8 Labour Force Survey* [online]. Available at: http://www.hse.gov.uk/statistics/overall/hssh0708.pdf (accessed 12 December 2010).

Heron, J. and Reason, P. (1997) 'A participative inquiry paradigm', *Qualitative Inquiry*, 3(3): 274–94.

Lewin, K. (1946) 'Action research and minority problems', *Journal of Social Issues*, 2(4): 34–46.

McNiff, J. (2010) *Action Research for Professional Development.* Dorset: September Books.

Maslach, C. and Jackson, S. (1986) *The Maslach Burnout Inventory.* Palo Alto, CA: Consulting Psychologists Press.

Munn-Giddings, C., Hart, C. and Ramon, S. (2005) 'A participatory approach to the promotion of wellbeing in the workplace: lessons from an empirical research', *International Review of Psychiatry*, 17(5): 409–17.

Ramon, S. and Hart, C. (2003) 'Promoting mental wellbeing in the workplace: a British case study', *International Journal of Mental Health Promotion*, 5: 37–44.

Stringer, E. T. (1996) *Action Research: A Handbook for Practitioners.* London: Sage.

Winter, R. and Munn-Giddings, C. (2001) *A Handbook for Action Research in Health and Social Care.* London: Routledge.

Zuber-Skerritt, O. (1992) *Action Research in Higher Education: Examples and Reflections.* London: Kogan Page.

9

Naturalistic research

Rob Walker

Naturalistic enquiry

The immediate appeal of naturalistic methods is that they are readily accessible and available without special equipment or facilities. Primarily based on participant observation and informal interviewing, they extend practices that are a normal part of social life. They appear to require little training and no specialised resources. The forms of writing and analysis used (descriptive, narrative, interpretive) are familiar and much like those we encounter day-to-day in other aspects of our lives. Naturalistic methods appear based on common sense and report their explorations of the social world in forms that avoid esoteric concepts, speaking directly to those Jean Lave, with an ironic sideways glance at conventional social science, calls jpfs ('just plain folks') (Lave, 1988).

But all is not what it seems. Observation of social settings turns out to be a conceptually complex process; interviewing is not quite the same as conversation (and conversation itself is more problematic and less transparent than we might think). And description too is more problematic than first impressions might suggest. What we take to be 'natural' when we start out quickly trips us up once we begin using its methods for research. Small wonder that a disproportionate amount of the research literature is devoted to problematic issues of methodology and ethics.

A brief history

Naturalistic methods derive primarily from the work of the Chicago School (Adelman, 2010; Norris and Walker, 2005). The Chicago School was a collection of social scientists, including criminologists, geographers, city planners and journalists, who combined to study the city from the 1920s up to the present. They sought to understand the dramatic social changes they saw in the urban environment and introduced to social science ideas from ecology. In particular they adapted the idea of 'succession' to changes in land use and occupation – an idea that is current today as patterns of urban land use continue to change. The Chicago sociologists also focused on studying occupations and careers, both formal and informal, and were drawn to the methods of journalism and documentary reporting.

In education, key works of the School include an evocative study of public school teaching (Waller, 1932), which remains a classic in the field of teaching. In the 1950s, Howard Becker introduced the idea of 'horizontal mobility' (Becker, 1952), identifying the ways in which teachers would move 'sideways' in the career structure to take jobs in better schools. He also studied the occupations and 'careers' of university students, particularly medical students (Becker et al., 1961) and of jazz musicians (Becker and Faulkner, 2009). In the 1960s Philip Jackson, a Chicago psychologist, made an influential 'naturalistic' study of school classrooms (Jackson, 1968) based on long periods of observation in elementary school classrooms to study of the occupations of both teachers and students.

Aside from their detailed attention to the observation of behaviour in a particular social environment, a key aspect of the methods used in these studies is that the personal experiences and life stories of the researcher are incorporated into the studies. The researcher does not stand apart from data collection but is intimately involved in it and in many cases the questions they choose to pursue derive from personal experience. Willard Waller drew heavily on his family experiences (his father was a teacher and school superintendent), Howard Becker's studies of jazz musicians are strongly connected to his own practice as a musician and Philip Jackson later became Director of the University of Chicago Laboratory School, founded by John Dewey.

The work of the Chicago School inspired a move among educational researchers to extend the use of qualitative methods in educational research. From the 1960s researchers became seriously interested in the long-term participant observation of schools, classrooms and other educational settings. In the UK, the pioneering studies of Lacey (1970) and Hargreaves (1967) were followed by a succession of PhD studies (notably Stephen Ball at Sussex, David Hamilton, Sara Delamont and Michael Stubbs at Edinburgh and Martyn Hammersley at Leeds). From a starting point in sociology and using methods partially derived from ethnography, influences from elsewhere were adapted – from sociolinguistics, from ethnomethodology and from history. In turn this was succeeded by more strongly critical influences from participatory action research (Carr and Kemmis, 1986) and from feminist theory (Kenway and Bullen, 2001; Davies, 1993).

The consequence of these developments for naturalistic enquiry is that it can no longer be reduced to a simple collection of readily available methods, but needs to engage with social theory; otherwise it becomes vulnerable to the critique of empiricism, the very point from which it first developed.

Methods of naturalistic enquiry

In terms of methods, naturalistic enquiry can be seen as a subset of qualitative research. It differs from other qualitative methods in that it relies more heavily on the social and interpretive skills of the human observer and on the vernacular methods of enquiry. These include the analysis of found documents, reported conversations, descriptions of events, locations and the actions of individuals, all often linked by narrative. In this it is less empiricist than some other qualitative methods (for example, the use of Computer-Assisted Qualitative Data Analysis (CAQDAS) in analysing transcripts), more reliant on the interpretive work of the researcher and, at least at first sight, less driven by theory.

An example: the David Medd study

This was an interdisciplinary study, funded by the Faculty of Education, University of Cambridge, and carried out in 2009–10 by a team led by Catherine Burke, a historian. There were five other members of the team, Peter Cunningham, also an educational historian from Cambridge; Alison Clark, a psychologist from the Children's Research Centre at the Open University; Rachel Sayers, an architect from the practice Fielden, Clegg & Bradley; Dominic Cullinan, a partner in an architecture practice (SCABAL); and Rob Walker, an educational sociologist from the University of East Anglia. They were supported by two video-makers, Audrey Destandau and Jun Keung Cheung.

The context of the study was a strong policy interest in rebuilding and renovating the stock of primary school buildings in England, partly because the buildings themselves were moving beyond their planned life but also because building standards and materials had advanced (heating, lighting, insulation) and needed modernising. Linked to this effort was a perceived need to incorporate new media technologies – mobile and ubiquitous computing, display technologies, digital resources and communications, all of which were believed to be leading changes in educational practice.

David Medd (and his wife Mary Medd, née Crowley) were significant figures, for they had been at the forefront of educational architecture in the post-war period, when many existing schools, now due for renewal, were first built. They had been particularly active in Hertfordshire, in Oxfordshire and at the Architect and Buildings Branch of the Ministry of Education, where David had drafted the chapter on school building design for the Plowden Report in the 1960s (Plowden, 1967).

Recovering the work of the Medds (and other influential educators of the time) was a continuing project for Catherine Burke, part of which was this project, in which she invited members of the team to accompany David Medd (then in his nineties) to visit some of his most important schools and to see how they were being used currently. In each visit the researchers were accompanied by one of the video-makers.

The study lent itself to naturalistic enquiry. The methods available – observing the schools at work, talking to teachers and others, taking notes and photos and using video to capture David Medd's impressions – are all 'natural methods' in the sense that they do not require research training.

Since the aim of the study was to encourage discussion among the professions and the public, including planners, education managers, teachers, parents, architects and researchers, it was important that the language of the study was not seen as too esoteric or its concerns too distant from those with everyday involvement in the schools. While each member of the team came to the study with theoretical preoccupations and concerns, in communicating with others, these needed to be treated as background rather than foreground.

We also needed to be able to talk to each other. In practice this took some time. We were each doing this in time we set aside from our own work and it was through a series of relatively informal meetings that we evolved ways of working that related in different but complementary ways to one another. It was only when we did public presentations, one at a half-day conference in Cambridge, one to architects in London, that we realised, on reflection, how far we had developed a shared set of values and complementary practices.

Finding appropriate ways to report this study presented a challenge that was resolved by a decision that each of us should make a short film using the video we had collected during the school visits. These short films were packaged with a booklet that described the project and added further information on particular themes. This form of publication in itself reflected a feature of naturalistic enquiry, which is that it is adapted to the needs of potential audiences. For the architects, the booklet with its CD was a form that could be given to potential clients to demonstrate involvement in research and a serious interest in educational issues. For the academics, the CD was a resource that could be used in lectures and conference presentations, or given to students to view in their own time.

Issues in naturalistic enquiry

Participatory research

Naturalistic enquiry is often the design of choice for those working in participatory projects. Because the methods are immediately available this means that 'plain folks' can quickly engage with research – collecting data, analysing it and incorporating it into their projects. They can also bring to bear specialised skills and knowledge that may be beyond the researcher. There are though some dangers in this, since commitments and bias are never far from the stage. Using naturalistic methods requires constant attention to self-reflection, self-critique and concurrent active reading to keep the study intellectually mobile and sharp.

Training

Getting started with naturalistic enquiry requires no specialised training, but doing it well requires a level of awareness, a capacity for self-reflection, a range of experience and a facility with the written word. Frequent problems involve issues of fieldwork ethics, conducting effective interviews, accumulating excessive data and rushing to closure. The problems are less technical than ethical and interpretive, and require critical reflection on experience rather than skill training.

Design

Naturalistic methods do not fit well with rational design. Critical variables are discovered rather than preordinately determined. Interpretation is emergent rather than driven by extant substantive theory. What they do well is identify unforeseen outcomes in specified contexts and uncover hidden influences in particular settings. They resist generalisation and reduction to simple causes and effects. Somewhat perversely in the eyes of some, their value is that they tend to make interpretation more complicated and decision-making more difficult.

Suggested further reading

Greene, J. C. (2004) 'Memories of a novice, learning from a master', *American Journal of Evaluation*, 29: 322. The online version of this article can be found at: http://aje. sagepub.com/content/29/3/322.citation. By way of an obituary for Egon Guba, one of the leading advocates of naturalistic enquiry in evaluation, this short personal account describes the development of qualitative methods in educational evaluation in the US.

Stake, R. *University of Illinois, Course EDPSY 490E Case Study Methods*. Available at http://www.ed.uiuc.edu/circe/EDPSY490E/Index.html. Robert Stake is perhaps the single most significant figure in naturalistic methods in educational research, especially in his advocacy of 'case study'. His book, *The Art of Case Study* (Sage, 1995) is a key text. This outline of his course (which he has taught for many years at the University of Illinois) reveals something of his intellectual style – concise, principled, yet (somewhat paradoxically) terse to the point of enigmatic. There is a useful reading list, a description of the tasks set for students and an insistence on studying the particular and individual case rather than attempting to generalise from observations.

Cambridge Evaluation Conferences. Available at: http://groups.tlrp.org/access/content/group/e0462675-d837-46dd-00b5-403deb2957b7/EdEval_2.0/edeval_2.0.html. This series of conferences brought together educational researchers, evaluators and policy people from the US and UK over a thirty-year period from the early 1970s. Robert Stake, mentioned above was a key contributor. As part of an ESRC TEL Project, this recently developed online resource has archived some of the key naturalistic case studies associated with the conference group, many of which are unpublished or difficult to obtain through libraries.

References

Adelman, C. (2010) 'The Chicago School', in Mills, A. J. et al. (eds) *Encyclopedia of Case Study*, Vol. I. Thousand Oaks, CA: Sage, pp. 140–4.

Becker, H. S. (1952) 'The career of the Chicago public school-teacher', *American Journal of Sociology*, 57(5): 470–7.

Becker, H. S. and Faulkner, R. R. (2009) *Do you know . . .? The Jazz Repertoire in Action*. Chicago: University of Chicago Press.

Becker, H. S., with Geer, B., Hughes, E. C. and Strauss, A. (1961) *Boys in White: Student Culture in Medical School*. Chicago: University of Chicago Press.

Burke, C. et al. (2010) *Principles of Primary School Design*. Cambridge: ACE Foundation.

Carr, W. and Kemmis, S. (1986) *Becoming Critical: Education, Knowledge and Action Research*. Geelong: Deakin University Press.

Davies, B. (1993) *Shards of Glass*. New York: Hampton Press.

Hargreaves, D. (1967) *Social Relations in a Secondary School*. London: Routledge & Kegan Paul.

Jackson, P. W. (1968) *Life in Classrooms*. New York: Holt, Rinehart & Winston.

Kenway, J. and Bullen, E. (2001) *Consuming Children: Entertainment, Advertising and Education*. Milton Keynes: Open University Press.

Lacey, C. (1970) *Hightown Grammar*. Manchester: Manchester University Press.

Lave, J. (1988) *Cognition in Practice*. Cambridge: Cambridge University Press.

Norris, N. and Walker, R. (2005) 'Naturalistic enquiry', in Somekh, B. and Lewin, C. (eds) *Research Methods in the Social Sciences*. London: Sage, pp. 131–7.

Plowden, B. (1967) *Children and their Primary Schools* (The Plowden Report). London: HMSO.

Waller, W. (1932) *Sociology of Teaching*. New York: John Wiley.

Ethnographic and representational styles

Ghazala Bhatti

Definition and brief history

Ethnography has a long history which can be traced back to the late nineteenth and early twentieth century and has its roots in anthropology, which involved travelling to distant places to collect insiders' accounts of what were then colonial outposts (Gobo, 2011). From 1930s onwards sociologists at the University of Chicago employed methodologies which were exploratory both conceptually and empirically, leading to innovative ways of representing the realities of local communities. The work of the Chicago School encapsulates research about aspects of society which were both familiar and taken for granted and yet unfamiliar to the society where they were embedded. The exploration of the diffuse and difficult to pin down realities were presented from the point of view of the people under scrutiny. These studies held up a mirror to society. This chapter will look at ethnography as a tool and as a methodology and a way of researching everyday reality.

Ethnography has made a significant contribution to our understanding of participants' worlds through offering new insights and providing in-depth insider accounts. It has gained in popularity among researchers who wish to conduct qualitative studies of

naturally occurring phenomena in everyday settings. Ethnography cannot happen in an artificial and contrived environment, nor as an experiment specially set up to investigate a situation. The very process of an ethnographic enquiry would soon uncover the artifice and name it for what it is, through describing what the 'norm' is in a given setting. This is because ethnographic research emerges from the researcher's sustained interest and engagement with the field. The ethnographic gaze captures the reality as experienced by the participants and recorded by the researcher at a particular historical moment.

Ethnographic research has enriched our understanding of how individuals and groups behave in various communities and organisations; how they make sense of their everyday lived realities, what choices they make and how they present themselves. An ethnographer is an observer of people and events as they unfold. Ethnographic research has been located in a variety of settings such as schools, hospitals, jazz clubs and street corners. Ethnography relies heavily on the researcher's interaction with and commitment to the field of enquiry, so that the researchers become, as far as possible, a part of the world they are trying to study. Ethnography seeks to represent the realities of participants in a way that the participants would recognise to be true. However, the final analysis which the ethnographer presents may not echo the subjective realities of each individual participant. It is more likely to be a combination of many perspectives. Ethnographic research is built on a systematic enquiry which seeks to incorporate different views and perceptions, and describes the messy nature of everyday life. It captures high and low moments, the harmony as well as the discord and contradictions revealed in the tales from the field (Van Maanen, 1988). A criticism that has been levelled against ethnography is that of researcher bias (Hammersley, 1992). Ethnographers address this by describing in detail how the data was collected and analysed and what role they adopted in the field. This is in turn connected to the power they may or may not have, the quality of their interactions with those in different hierarchical positions and a combination of the researchers' personal attributes and overall reach and capacity for data capture. It is impossible to predict in advance exactly what the ethnographer will discover.

Methodologically, ethnographic research can take different turns. It does not have a fixed and inflexible parameter. Those new to ethnography might like to consider some basic questions such as:

1. *Is the ethnography meant to be an exploration?* For example, what is it like to be 10 years old and in care? What do children feel? What do their carers think? What do social services personnel who organise placements think about this and what do they do when things go wrong?
2. *Is it a piece of research about a situation/phenomenon?* For example, how does an organisation deal with making senior staff redundant? How do people positioned at different levels react? Is the union effective in overturning decisions and negotiations? Does it matter if this happens in a car factory, hospital or a bank?
3. *Is the ethnography about investigating the impact of policy on practice?* For example, will more young people from poor backgrounds in England apply to study in a particular university if the fees are trebled in 2013? How do young people feel/act? What do their parents think? Does it really matter if higher education is 'rationed' – to borrow a term from Gillborn and Youdell (2000).

The research design adopted in any of the above cases would be directly connected to the research focus, as well as the time available for research. If the same ethnographer were to conduct all of the above studies one after another – for they cannot all be conducted simultaneously – he or she is bound to write different kinds of ethnographies about each, depending on what actually happens in the field. As explained above, the outcome of ethnographic research is not predictable as it is a combination of what is discovered and how the researcher is perceived. Ethnography must be composed of 'thick descriptions' (Geertz, 1973) contextualising both behaviour and the values implicit in the behaviour. The values a researcher brings to the field influence the final text and how it is documented. Sometimes these are implicit in the text and at others researchers openly declare their standpoint.

Research question and paradigmatic location

Ethnographers usually begin with an open-ended question and try to explore what is happening in the field. It is not uncommon for researchers to start with one set of questions but then end up describing a different set of findings which have a tenuous connection with the researcher's original starting point. Ethnography is unpredictable. A good example is the story Burgess (1987) tells of a casual meeting with a headmaster which led to 15 years of productive research. What actually happens in the field defines the final focus of the research and the way in which it is written up and presented.

For researchers who are considering ethnography some of the questions worth considering might be:

1. What am I going to study in general terms?
2. How strongly should I define a clear focus right from the outset?
3. How am I going to choose a place to site my study?
4. Who will help me gain access to the site?
5. Why this site and not another site?
6. Why am I studying these people/places/phenomena at this moment?
7. Will I be able to choose a sample or will the sample choose me?

At the outset the researcher may not be in a position of control and must be prepared to work with whatever is open to negotiation. What a new researcher or their more experienced supervisor/tutor may encounter might be qualitatively different, though equally valid, provided due care is taken in ethical and methodological terms. Access is the key to good ethnography. And yet access can be very problematic. For example, access may be gained to a particular institution but not to everyone within that institution.

Most importantly, the main tool or instrument of data collection is the researcher's own self (Eisner, 1991). A successful ethnographer is one who is self-aware and reflexive, someone who has the capacity for both empathy and distance. The need to nurture these simultaneously brings its own set of contradictions and conflicts which may be written up in field notes, but which the ethnographer is not always able to share with the researched at the time. Many ethnographers have felt the tension which is inevitable when they have to be insiders and outsiders simultaneously (Hammersley and Atkinson, 1983). Ethnographers need to cultivate the ability to live with uncertainty and self-doubt, as well as the ability to collect evidence which can convince their readers, who never having stepped into the field with the ethnographer, should nevertheless get a feel of the place, events and people. An ethnographer can only be effective if he or she can communicate the findings accurately and with a sense of conviction.

Methods, data collection and analysis

The research question which is under consideration will define exactly how a researcher may go about collecting the data. For example, if a piece of research is about how English is taught in a secondary school over a year, it would be important for the researcher to be familiar with the demands on teachers at different stages and ages – from the beginning of the year to the end. The researcher will need to know about any changes in the laws governing the acquisition of English, both on a national and on a local school level. Syllabi, curriculum content, the choice of books and other materials, the school budget in general and with reference to English in particular, the relative

experiences of different teachers – all these factors will define what the researcher must rehearse before entering the field. What kinds of questions must be asked at what frequency and of whom during the field work must be considered carefully. Are some children struggling with basic literacy when their peers are fluent readers? What sort of help is available or affordable? Who decides which student deserves a certain number of hours of individual teaching? The researcher would need to find out about teacher autonomy. Where do they site control of the subject (English) – within the school, the classroom or in government departments? This would also depend on the 'status' of the subject in the school in relation to other subjects. Are these questions relevant for all classes in the school? So even before drawing up a list of teachers to approach and students to observe, there is a lot of groundwork which needs to be covered. Data can be collected through participant and non-participant observation, interviews and documentary analysis. Grounded theory is quite useful for ethnography where the theory emerges from the data and is not imposed on the data from the outset (Glaser and Strauss, 1967; Charmaz, 2006).

An example: an ethnographic journey

My ethnographic research was based in a secondary school. Initially I wanted to capture the lived experiences of white, African Caribbean and South Asian young people at the time of transition during their first year at a mixed secondary school. However, as the study developed and access was gained to totally unexplored areas, I found myself increasingly torn between where I wanted to go and, instead, where the data was really leading me. Despite the cross-cultural data I originally gathered for many months, the final focus rested on the experiences of 50 South Asian young people, their teachers and parents. I had to consider the world I was facing rather than the world I had hoped to encounter. The research design had to be adaptable to take account of what I found during my fieldwork. I spent several months in a secondary school before being invited home by the teenagers where I was able to gather data from their parents. Instead of being an ethnography about transition it became an ethnography about the experiences of young people at home and at school (Bhatti, 1999). In another study about literacy and dyslexia conducted over a shorter period of time I could not gain direct access to the research community – illiterate prisoners who are dyslexic (Bhatti, 2010). However, the experiences of the teachers who choose to work with this community were fascinating. These teachers are marginalised by 'other' types of teachers precisely because they work with prisoners. This was an unexpected finding. I expected imposition of discipline and control in this particular setting, but not prejudice against the teachers. Ethnographic research can be full of surprises.

Other resources

There are many ethnographies of educational institutions such as schools. However, each might deal with a totally different aspect. From Colin Lacey, David Hargreaves and Stephen Ball who studied how schools affect the kinds of experiences children have to more recent studies, it is possible to see the wide range of possibilities. Ethnographic research can be about labelling and bullying, racism, gender, sexuality, religious education, special education and other areas. For example, Benjamin (2002) looked at the experiences of young women who struggle at school because of their learning difficulties. Race has been studied by researchers such as Wright (1992) and Gillborn (1990). Skelton (2001) looked at the schooling of boys. If we extend the meaning of education to include out-of-school activities then there are many studies on a variety of people such as dancers (Delamont, 2006), musicians (Buscatto, 2007) and others.

Ethnographies are informative, meaningful and interesting to read. The close engagement and immersion in the field and the immediacy of the world they describe is what draws researchers to the field of enquiry. According to Walford (2002)

> doing ethnographic fieldwork, analysing the data and writing the full account [require] personal commitment of a very high order and a vast amount of sheer hard work.

It may be very hard work but it takes the ethnographer on an unforgettable, transformative journey!

Suggested further reading

McCall, M. (2000) 'Performance Ethnography', in Denzin, N. and Lincoln, Y. (eds) *Handbook of Qualitative Research*, (2nd edn). London: Sage. This is an interesting and unusual article which looks at ethnography's connection with performance and the theatre. Bertolt Brecht's epic theatre was meant to shake the audience out of their complacency by taking them out of their comfort zone. McCall's contribution is an invitation to look at the dramatic manifestation of ethnography and the different ways of sharing ideas with the community from which the data emerged.

Silverman, D. (2007) 'Instances or sequences?', in *A Very Short, Fairly Interesting and Reasonably Cheap Book about Qualitative Research*. London: Sage, pp. 61–84. This is an accessible chapter on data analysis written in a fluid and user-friendly style covering complex ideas which need to be taken into account when analysing data. There is a necessity to think carefully about the 'whats' and 'hows' in qualitative research rather than just focusing on the 'whys'. Silverman explains what he means by 'sequential organisation' by drawing attention to and building on the work of Sacks and Sassure.

Whyte, W. F. (1984) 'Planning the project and entering the field', in *Learning from the Field: A Guide from Experience*. Beverly Hills, CA: Sage, pp. 35–63. Accessing an unknown territory for research is always a challenge, no matter how experienced a researcher might be. This book, Whyte tells the reader, is 'not a text book'. It is based on Whyte's experience spanning over half a century in different settings. This chapter uses an autobiographical style to demystify research by explaining what happened to Whyte during his own research. He also makes references to other researchers who conducted original work in community settings.

References

Benjamin, S. (2002) *The Micropolitics of Inclusive Education*. Buckingham: Open University Press.

Bhatti, G. (1999) *Asian Children at Home and at School*. London: Routledge.

Bhatti, G. (2010) 'Learning behind bars', *Teaching and Teacher Education*, 26(1): 31–6.

Burgess, R. G. (1987) 'Studying and Restudying Bishop McGregor School', in Walford, G. (ed.) *Doing Sociology of Education*. London: Falmer Press.

Buscatto, M. (2007) 'Contributions of ethnography to gendered sociology: the French jazz world', *Qualitative Sociology Review*, 3(3): 46–58.

Charmaz, K. (2006) *Constructing Grounded Theory: A Practical Guide Through Qualitative Analysis*. London: Sage.

Delamont, S. (2006) 'The smell of sweat and rum: teacher authority in *capoeira* classes', *Ethnography and Education*, 1(3): 161–75.

Eisner (1991) *The Enlightened Eye: Qualitative Inquiry and the Enhancement of Educational Practice*. New York: Macmillan.

Geertz, C. (1973) 'Thick description: towards an interpretive theory of cultures', in Geertz, C. (ed.) *The Interpretation of Cultures*. New York: Basic Books.

Gillborn, D. (1990) *'Race', Ethnicity and Education*. London: Unwin Hyman.

Gillborn, D. and Youdell, B. (2000) *Rationing Education*. Buckingham: Open University Press.

Glaser, B. G. and Strauss, A. (1967) *The Discovery of Grounded Theory: Strategies for Qualitative Research*. Piscataway, NJ: Aldine Transaction.

Gobo, G. (2011) 'Ethnography', in Silverman, D. (ed.) *Qualitative Research*. London: Sage.

Hammersley, M. (1992) *What's Wrong with Ethnography?* London: Routledge.

Hammersley, M. and Atkinson, P. (1983) *Ethnography: Principles in Practice*. London: Tavistock.

Skelton, C. (2001) *Schooling the Boys*. Buckingham: Open University Press.

Van Maanen, J. (1988) *Tales of the Field: On Writing Ethnography*. Chicago: University of Chicago Press.

Walford, G. (2002) 'Introduction', in *Doing a Doctorate in Educational Ethnography*. Oxford: Elsevier.

Wright, C. (1992) 'Early education: multiracial primary school classrooms', in Dawn, G., Mayor, B. and Blair, M. (eds) *Racism and Education*. London: Sage and Open University Press.

Grounded theory

Robert Thornberg

Introduction

Everyday life at school consists of a lot of individual and collective actions as well as social processes. Grounded theory (GT) is a qualitative and inductive research approach which is designed to explore, analyse and generate concepts about individual and collective actions and social processes. As a research approach, GT offers systematic and at the same time flexible guidelines for collecting and analysing data to construct middle-range theories which consist of 'abstract conceptualizations of substantive problems that people experience, rather than explaining the structure of an entire society' (Thornberg and Charmaz, 2011). Examples of educational research questions in which a GT approach might be useful are:

- What happens in everyday classroom life?
- How do interactions take place between students in the schoolyard?
- What goes on while students are doing group work?
- How can the teaching, classroom management, or educational assessment taking place in the classroom be understood and explained?
- What hinders learning in classrooms?
- What happens in conflicts between students or between students and teachers?

- What kinds of norms and values are displayed and mediated in the everyday life of school, and how and why does this take place?
- How can school bullying be understood and explained as a social process?
- What happens when students display disruptive behaviour in the classroom?

GT was originally developed by the sociologists Glaser and Strauss (1967) as a new research approach defined as 'the discovery of theory from data' (Glaser and Strauss, 1967: 1) and was at the same time a reaction to the dominant hypothetico-deductive use of 'grand theories' in the social research of the 1960s. In contrast to only verifying theories by quantitative methods, they offered a set of qualitative methods for generating inductive theories from data. Since 1967, GT has been further developed in different versions, such as the classic or Glaserian GT (e.g. Glaser, 1978, 1998, 2005), Straussian GT (Corbin and Strauss, 2008; Strauss and Corbin, 1990, 1998), constructivist GT (Bryant, 2002; Charmaz, 2000, 2003, 2006, 2008), multi-GT (Goldkuhl and Cronholm, 2010; Lind and Goldkuhl, 2006), Dey's (1999) version with an elaborated view on categorisation, process, causality and structure/agency in GT, and Clarke's (2003, 2005) postmodern version called situational analysis.

Data collection and theoretical sampling

In contrast to many other research traditions, in which one first collects data and then does the analysing, when doing a GT study, data collection and analysis go hand in hand throughout the whole research project (Charmaz, 2000, 2006; Glaser, 1979, 1998; Glaser and Strauss, 1967; Strauss and Corbin, 1990, 1998). Grounded theorists use data collection methods that best suit the research problem and the ongoing analysis of the data. This approach is therefore open to many methods of data collection (frequently used methods in GT studies are field observations, interviews and different forms of written reports from participants; for collections of GT research examples see Glaser and Holton, 2007; Strauss and Corbin, 1997). At the outset, the research problem may point to one method or a combination of methods for data collection. During the research process, the analysis of data evokes insights, hunches, 'Aha!' experiences or questions, which might lead the researcher to change or add a new data collection method. This interplay between data collection and analysis is essential in GT and is called *theoretical sampling* (see Figure 11.1).

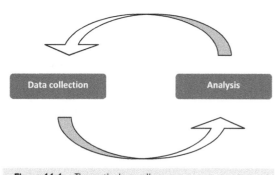

Figure 11.1   Theoretical sampling

Glaser and Strauss define theoretical sampling as 'the process of data collection for generating theory whereby the analyst jointly collects, codes, and analyzes his data and decides what data to collect next and where to find them' (Glaser and Strauss, 1967: 45). Theoretical sampling prevents researchers from becoming unfocused and overwhelmed in the practice of data collection and analysis. Note that theoretical sampling is not a type of initial sampling. Whereas initial sampling, such as convenience sampling, is used to begin collecting the very first data in a study (e.g. choosing a particular school, classroom, activity or group of students), theoretical sampling directs the researcher with regard to where to go, where to gather data next. In a research project aiming to explore values and norms in everyday school life (e.g. Thornberg, 2007, 2008, 2009, 2010a), I began gathering data by doing field observations in classrooms and schoolyards in two Swedish elementary schools. I took field notes and conducted audio recordings. I also began coding and analysing my field notes and I transcribed audio recordings directly as the first data started to emerge in the study. After a while, the ongoing analysis of the data generated a set of codes and questions which led me to start interviewing students and teachers about certain topics.

Coding

Coding begins immediately as the first data is gathered in a GT study. By coding, which is about creating codes and categories grounded in the data, the researchers scrutinise and interact with the data and ask analytical questions. As Charmaz puts it, 'unlike quantitative data, in which *preconceived* categories or codes are applied to the data, grounded theorists *create* their codes by defining what they see in the data' (Charmaz, 2003: 93). Coding in GT consists of three phases: initial coding, focused coding and theoretical coding (there is, however, a variation of coding phases among the different versions of GT). Coding is not a linear process. The researchers move flexibly back and forth between the different phases of coding, although they do more initial coding at the beginning and more theoretical coding at the end of the study.

Initial coding

The first phase in GT coding procedure is termed *open coding* (Glaser, 1978; Strauss and Corbin, 1990) or *initial coding* (Charmaz, 2000, 2003, 2006). In this phase the researchers stay close to the data and remain open to exploring what they define is going on in these data. The researchers ask a set of questions of the data: 'What is this data a study of?' 'What category does this incident indicate?' 'What is actually happening in the data?' (Glaser, 1978: 57); 'What is the participant's main concern?' (Glaser, 1998: 140); 'What do the actions and statements in the data take for granted?' 'What process(es) is at issue here? How can I define it?' 'How does this process develop?' 'How does the research participant(s) act while involved in this process?' 'What does the research participant(s) profess to think and feel while involved in this process? What might his or her observed behavior indicate?' 'When, why, and how does the process change?' 'What are the consequences of the process?' (Charmaz, 2006: 51). These analytical questions are used as flexible ways of seeing – not as forcing applications – and

help the researchers to search for and identify what is happening in the data and to look at the data critically and analytically.

The grounded theorists conduct initial coding by reading and analysing the data word by word and line by line. This approach forces the researchers to verify and saturate their 'emerged' codes and minimises missing important codes or significant details in the data (Glaser, 1978). The example in Table 11.1 illustrates my line-by-line coding of a piece of an early transcription of my audio recordings from a classroom conversation about fear.

The grounded theorists constantly treat their constructed codes as provisional and open for modification and refinement in order to improve their fit with the data. By using the *constant comparative method* (Glaser and Strauss, 1967), the grounded theorists compare data with data, data with code, and code with code, to find similarities and differences. Such comparisons in turn lead to the sorting and clustering of initial codes into new, more elaborated codes. The data collection and coding become more focused and selective through careful word-by-word, line-by-line and incident-by-incident coding, in which the constant comparative method is used. When the researchers have identified and developed a core category or a set of focused codes (see below), they can then enter the next phase of coding.

Table 11.1   Initial coding

Initial coding	Classroom observation data	
Attention-getting in the class	Teacher:	Now listen to me. As homework you get this –
Interrupting teacher, Speaking-out-loud	Daniel:	I know! I want –
Correcting by hushing, Continuing despite teacher correcting,	Teacher:	Shhh!
Sticking to the subject	Daniel:	I would like to say something! I'm scared when someone is dying.
Teacher acknowledgement, Talk-inviting	Teacher:	You are scared when someone is dying?
Interrupting teacher–student dialogue,	Thomas:	Me too!
Speaking-out-loud	Yasin:	Me too!
	Babak:	Yeah, it's no fun.
Correcting by hushing, Teacher Redirecting the talking turn back to the student	Teacher:	Shhh! Daniel, have you felt anytime that someone you knew has died and you became scared?

Focused coding

The next phase of coding is, according to Glaser (1978, 1998), *selective coding*, in which the core category (i.e. the most significant or frequent code that is also related to as many other codes as possible and more than other candidates for the core category) becomes a guide to further data gathering and coding. Instead of one core category and selective coding, Charmaz (2000, 2003, 2006) talks about *focused coding* as a second phase and as a result of identifying the most significant or frequent initial codes, which become treated as focused codes in the study. In focused coding, the researcher uses these codes to sift through large amounts of data. Charmaz' position could be considered more flexible by being open for more than one significant or frequent code in order to conduct this work. This openness also means that the researcher continues to determine the adequacy of those codes throughout the focused coding phase. In my research project on values and norms in everyday school life, data collection and coding were guided by, and more or less limited to, a set of focused codes – codes that had previously been constructed by carefully comparing and clustering a lot of initial codes. Focused codes are more directed, selective, and conceptual than initial codes. The example in Table 11.2 illustrates my focused coding of a piece of a transcription from a group interview with some of the students.

As you can see in Table 11.2, the focused codes capture and synthesise the main themes in the students' statements. During focused coding, the researchers explore and decide which codes best capture what they see happening in the data, and raise these codes up to tentative conceptual *categories*, which means that they give them conceptual definitions and begin to assess the relationships between them (Charmaz, 2003, 2006). For example, the focused code 'not knowing if rule is in force' in Table 11.2 was later conceptualised as the category 'rule diffusion', which refers to students' uncertainty and interpretation difficulties regarding which rules are in force and how they should be applied (Thornberg, 2007). In order to generate and refine categories, researchers have to make a lot of constant comparisons:

- comparing and grouping codes and comparing codes with emerging categories;
- comparing different incidents (e.g. social situations, actions, social processes or interaction patterns);
- comparing data from the same or similar phenomenon, action or process in different situations and contexts (Thornberg and Charmaz, 2011);
- comparing different people (their beliefs, situations, actions, accounts or experiences);
- comparing data from the same individuals at different points in time;
- comparing specific data with the criteria for the category;
- comparing categories in the analysis with other categories (Charmaz, 2003: 101).

Table 11.2 Focused coding

Focused coding	Group interview data	
Inconsistencies in teacher's rule-making	John:	It's strange! Sometimes she [the teacher] gets angry and yelling at a student if he starts to talk without raising his hand, but sometimes she will not react like that. She just, 'Oh, that's right!'
	Interviewer:	Why is that strange?
	John:	Well, but then you don't know what to do.
Not knowing if rule is in force	Robin:	No, if you don't need to put your hand up or if you have to put your hand up.
Difficulties in predicting teacher reactions	Daniel:	Yeah, you don't know if she will get mad or not, how she will react.
	Robin:	Or if she likes that you answered her question.
	Interviewer:	So you don't know how she will react?
	Robin:	No.
Teacher's rule-articulating	John:	She tells us that we have to put up our hands if we want to say something –
	Daniel:	Yeah, she does.
Not knowing if rule is in force	John:	– but you still don't know if you really have to take that rule seriously or not.

Theoretical coding

The third phase of coding is *theoretical coding*. Now the researchers analyse how categories and codes generated from data might relate to each other as hypotheses to be integrated into a theory (Glaser, 1978). In order to do that, the researchers use *theoretical codes*, which refer to underlying logics that could be found in pre-existing theories, as analytical tools to organise their codes and categories with each other or with the core category (see Glaser, 1978, 1998, 2005). Theoretical codes 'give integrative scope, broad pictures and a new perspective' (Glaser, 1978: 72), and 'specify possible relationships between categories you have developed in your focused coding . . . [and] may help you tell an analytic story that has coherence' (Charmaz, 2006: 63). Glaser argues that by studying many theories across different disciplines, the researchers may identify numerous theoretical codes embedded in these theories and thus develop and enhance their own knowledge base of theoretical codes (Glaser, 1998, 2005). 'One reads theories in any field and tries to figure out the theoretical models being used . . . It makes the researcher sensitive to many codes and how they are used' (Glaser, 1998: 164).

To make it a bit easier for grounded theorists to do theoretical coding, Glaser has elaborated a list of theoretical codes organised in a typology of *coding families* (Glaser, 1978: 72–82; Glaser, 1998: 170–5; 2005: 21–30). Examples of coding families presented by Glaser are:

- the *'six C's'* (causes, contexts, contingencies, consequences, co-variances and conditions);
- *process family* (e.g. phases, stages, progressions, passages, transitions, careers, trajectories, sequencings, cycling);
- *degree family* (e.g. limit, range, grades, continuum, level);
- *type family* (e.g. type, styles, classes, genre);
- *identity-self family* (e.g. self-image, self-concept, self-evaluation, identity, transformations of self);
- *cutting point family* (e.g. boundary, cutting point, turning point, breaking points, point of no return);
- *cultural family* (e.g. social norms, social values, social beliefs);

- the *consensus family* (e.g. agreements, contracts, definitions of situation, conformity, non-conformity, homogeneity, heterogeneity, conflict): and;
- *paired opposite family* (e.g. ingroup–outgroup, in–out, manifest–latent, explicit–implicit, overt–covert, informal–formal).

According to Glaser (1978), theoretical codes must not be forced into the analysis but have to earn their way in by constant and careful comparisons between theoretical codes, data, empirically generated codes and categories, and memos (see below). Theoretical codes must work, have relevance and fit with data, focused codes and categories. One must not become blinded by one theoretical code. A combination of many theoretical codes most often captures the relationships between categories and is therefore typically used when relating and organising categories and integrating them into a grounded theory. In my study of values and norms in everyday school life, I took advantage of a lot of theoretical codes to further develop my categories and investigate their relations to each other in order to generate a grounded theory of inconsistent rule-making in school. Examples of theoretical codes that I used during theoretical coding that preceded the findings in Thornberg (2007) were basic social process, explicit–implicit, latent pattern, social norms, causes–consequences, social interaction, negotiation, and perception (see also the memo excerpt and my discussion below).

Memos

During data gathering, coding or analysing, the researchers will likely come up with ideas and thoughts about their codes and relationships between codes, as well as questions they want to get answers to in their further investigation. In order to remember these thoughts and questions, researchers write these down as *memos* (i.e. analytic, conceptual or theoretical notes). According to Glaser, memos are 'the theorizing write-up of ideas about codes and their relationships as they strike the analyst while coding' (Glaser, 1978: 83). By *memo-writing*, grounded theorists step back and ask, 'What is going on here?' and 'How can I make sense of this?' (Thornberg and Charmaz, 2011). Memo-writing drives the researchers to investigate their codes and categories as well as the possible relationships between them, to gain an analytical distance to data and generated codes, and to build up and maintain 'a storehouse of analytical ideas that can be sorted, ordered and reordered' (Strauss and Corbin, 1998: 220). At the outset of a GT study, researchers' memos are usually shorter, less conceptualised and filled with analytical questions and hunches. In my study of norms and values in everyday school life (e.g. Thornberg, 2007), in one of my early memos, I reported that I had observed how teachers often applied rules inconsistently and listed the following analytical questions:

- How are these rule inconsistencies constructed in everyday interactions?
- Why do these rule inconsistencies occur?
- How do teachers make meaning of these rule inconsistencies?
- How do students make meaning of these rule inconsistencies?
- What are the consequences?
- Are there any hidden assumptions and/or latent patterns here?

All the questions in the memo above were expressions of the basic question in initial coding, 'What is happening or actually going on here?' By asking these questions, I formulated hunches and strategies for further data collection and coding. I began to observe and make field notes prompted by these questions and I also began to interview students and teachers afterwards whom I observed participating in such events about their experiences, concerns and meaning-makings of the incident. Later on, when grounded theorists conduct focused and theoretical coding, their memos become longer, more conceptualised and more and more like written findings. The excerpt below is a memo that I wrote towards the end of the study (the excerpt is translated from Swedish and was first cited in Thornberg and Charmaz, 2011).

Applying implicit rules

A deeper analysis of rule inconsistencies indicates a latent pattern or a social process that I would call 'applying implicit rules'. In everyday school life, teachers and students interact as if there were a set of unarticulated supplements or exceptions to the explicit rules. This unspoken set of rules appears to be unnoticed background features of everyday life. These implicit rules form patterned regularities of social interactions in the classroom or other school contexts, produced by teachers' responses to students' behaviour in the everyday stream of activities.

Creating confusion and criticism among students

Informal conversations and focus group interviews with students indicate that many students appear to be unaware of these implicit rules and to perceive the teachers' behaviour as inconsistent and confusing. John in grade 5 tells me, for example, 'Well, but then you don't know what to do,' and his classmate Robin said, 'No, if you don't need to put your hand up or if you do have to put your hand up.' Furthermore, several students claim that some rule inconsistencies result in unfairness.

Alice: It's unfair when she [the teacher] gives them the question, although they haven't put their hands up.
Robert: What do you mean? Why is it unfair?
Alice: That they still get the question. And those kids who have put their hands up, don't get it, although we have this rule.

(From a group interview with Alice and Johanna, fifth grade)

Children's difficulties in making sense of the inconsistencies can, at least in part, be explained by the latent pattern of implicit rules, which remain unarticulated in everyday teacher–student interactions.

*Creating rule diffusion, prediction loss, and
negotiation loss*

Rule inconsistencies and unarticulated implicit rules
create rule diffusion for students (i.e. uncertainty
and interpretation difficulties regarding which rules
are in force and how they should be enforced). This
rule diffusion in turn leads students to a prediction
loss (i.e. they cannot always predict what would
be appropriate behaviour in particular situations,
and how teachers would react to their behaviour
or fellow students' behaviour). By remaining
unarticulated and invisible for the students, the
implicit rules also result in a negotiation loss for
them (i.e. they are not given any opportunity to join
teachers in an open discussion and decision-making
processes for developing and revising these rules).
They cannot have any say in and openly negotiate
rules of which they are unaware.

I had identified a basic social process – applying
implicit rules – as well as its consequences and relations
to other significant categories. The memo begins
with a title, which is the tentative name of the main
category in the memo, and then provides a definition
of this category. This category is also related to other
categories and thus conceptualises in the memo how
this basic social process appears to affect students'
perceptions and the chance of having a say about
these rules. During theoretical coding, the researchers
compare, sort and integrate their memos. Such memo
sorting is the key to constructing a theory and writing
drafts of papers.

Interplay between induction and abduction

GT is usually described as an inductive method in
which a theory is constructed from data. According
to classic GT, the researchers have to be unbiased
and *tabula rasa*, and therefore must delay the literature
review in the substantive area of the actual GT study
until the analysis is nearly complete. The main reasons
behind this strategy are to keep the researchers as
free and open as possible to discovery, and to avoid
contamination, in other words to avoid forcing data
into pre-existing concepts that might distort or do not
fit with data (Glaser, 1978, 1998). However, the very
idea of a researcher who collects and analyses theory-
free data without any prior theoretical knowledge and
preconceptions has been strongly challenged (e.g.
Chalmers, 1999; Kelle, 1995). Moreover, ignoring
established theories and research findings in the
substantive area implies a loss of knowledge. Instead
of running the risk of reinventing the wheel, missing
well-known aspects and coming up with trivial
products or repeating others' mistakes, the researchers
should take advantage of the pre-existing body of
related literature to see further (Thornberg, 2012),
like 'a dwarf standing on the shoulders of a giant may
see further than the giant himself' (Burton, 2007: 27;
for a further discussion of how the classic dictum of
delaying the literature review can be problematised,
see Dunne, 2011; Thornberg, 2012).

In contrast to classic GT, constructivist GT
assumes that neither data nor theories are discovered
but are constructed by the researchers as a result of
their interactions with the field and its participants,
and coloured by the researchers' perspectives,
values, privileges, positions, academic training and
socio-cultural context in which they are embedded
(e.g. Charmaz, 2006, 2008). In accordance with
constructivist GT, researchers should not dismiss the
literature or apply it mechanically to data, but use it as a
possible source of inspiration, ideas, 'Aha!' experiences,
creative associations, critical reflections and multiple
lenses. Abduction is a selective and creative process
in which the researchers carefully investigate which
hypothesis explains a particular segment or set of data
better than any other candidate hypotheses for further
investigation (Douven, 2011; Pierce, 1958).

Different from the situation of induction, in
abduction problems we are confronted with
thousands of possible explanatory conjectures (or
conclusions) – everyone in the village might be
the murderer. The essential function of abduction
is their role as *search* strategies which tell us which
explanatory conjecture we would set out *first* to
further inquiry . . . through the explosive *search
space* of possible explanatory reasons. (Schurz,
2008: 203–4)

Theoretical codes as well as pre-existing theoretical perspectives and concepts and research findings from the substantive area are significant tools in doing abduction in GT. Therefore researchers who conduct a GT study should recognise the analytical power of the constant interplay between induction, in which they are never *tabula rasa*, and abduction, in which pre-existing theories and concepts are treated as provisional, disputable and modifiable conceptual proposals or hypotheses (Thornberg, in press). The ability to draw good abductive inferences is dependent on the researchers' previous knowledge, rejection of dogmatic beliefs and development of open-mindedness (Kelle, 1995).

Conclusion

Because the research aim is to construct theory from data, GT is a particularly useful research approach when we want to investigate a substantive area that is relatively unexplored, whether there are gaps, ambiguities or contradictions in pre-existing theories, whether new data or research findings conflict with pre-existing theories, or if we want to investigate social psychological or social processes without being limited to a certain pre-existing theory. In the context of educational research, this research approach, which is conducted in close conjunction with people and practice, helps us to develop middle-range theories that have great potential to succeed in explaining relevant behaviour in the educational setting, fitting with the educational setting and having relevance to the people (e.g. teachers, students or non-teaching school professionals) in the educational setting (cf. Glaser, 1998).

Suggested further reading

Charmaz, K. (2006) *Constructing Grounded Theory*. London: Sage. This book offers an excellent and practical introduction to constructivist GT.

Corbin, J. and Strauss, A. (2008) *Basics of Qualitative Research: Techniques and Procedures for Developing Grounded Theory* (3rd edn). Los Angeles: Sage. This book

provides an informative and clear description of Strauss and Corbin's version of GT.

Glaser, B. G. (1978) *Theoretical Sensitivity*. Mill Valley, CA: Sociology Press. This book offers the basic statement of Glaser's logic of grounded theory and clear prescriptions of how to do GT according to classic GT.

Glaser, B. G. and Strauss, A. (1967) *The Discovery of Grounded Theory*. New York: Aldine. This book is the original statement of GT.

Thornberg, R. (2012) 'Informed grounded theory', *Scandinavian Journal of Educational Research*. (In press). This article offers arguments concerning data-sensitising principles in using literature in GT.

References

Bryant, A. (2002) 'Re-grounding grounded theory', *Journal of Information Technology Theory and Application*, 4: 25–42.

Bryant, A. and Charmaz, K. (2007) 'Grounded theory in historical perspective: an epistemological account', in Bryant, A. and Charmaz, K. (eds) *The Sage Handbook of Grounded Theory*. Los Angeles: Sage, pp. 31–57.

Burton, R. (2007) *The Anatomy of Melancholy: Vol. 1*. Teddington: Echo Library (original edition 1638).

Chalmers, A. F. (1999) *What Is This Thing Called Science?* (3rd edn). New York: Open University Press.

Charmaz, K. (2000) 'Grounded theory: objectivist and constructivist methods', in Denzin, N. K. and Lincoln, Y. S. (eds) *Handbook of Qualitative Research* (2nd edn). Thousand Oaks, CA: Sage, pp. 509–35.

Charmaz, K. (2003) 'Grounded theory', in Smith, J. A. (ed.) *Qualitative Psychology: A Practical Guide to Research Methods*. London: Sage, pp. 81–110.

Charmaz, K. (2006) *Constructing Grounded Theory*. London: Sage.

Charmaz, K. (2008) 'Constructionism and the grounded theory method', in Holstein, J. A. and Gubrium, J. F. (eds) *Handbook of Constructionist Research*. New York: The Guilford Press., pp. 397–412.

Clarke, A. E. (2003) 'Situational analyses: grounded theory mapping after the postmodern turn', *Symbolic Interaction*, 26: 553–76.

Clarke, A. E. (2005) *Situational Analysis: Grounded Theory After the Postmodern Turn*. Thousand Oaks, CA: Sage.

Corbin, J. and Strauss, A. (2008) *Basics of Qualitative Research: Techniques and Procedures for Developing Grounded Theory* (3rd edn). Los Angeles: Sage.

Dey, I. (1999) *Grounding Grounded Theory*. San Diego, CA: Academic Press.

Douven, I. (2011) 'Pierce on abduction', in Zalta, E. N. (ed.) *Stanford Encyclopedia of Philosophy*. Available at: http://plato.stanford.edu/entries/abduction/ (accessed 1 June 2011).

Dunne, C. (2011) 'The place of literature review in grounded theory research', *International Journal of Social Research Methodology*, 14: 111–24.

Glaser, B. G. (1978) *Theoretical Sensitivity*. Mill Valley, CA: Sociology Press.

Glaser, B. G. (1998) *Doing Grounded Theory: Issues and Discussions*. Mill Valley, CA: Sociology Press.

Glaser, B. G. (2005) *The Grounded Theory Perspective III: Theoretical Coding*. Mill Valley, CA: Sociology Press.

Glaser, B. G. and Holton, J. A. (eds) (2007) *The Grounded Theory Seminar Reader*. Mill Valley, CA: Sociology Press.

Glaser, B. G. and Strauss, A. L. (1967) *The Discovery of Grounded Theory*. New York: Aldine.

Goldkuhl, G. and Cronholm, S. (2010) 'Adding theoretical grounding to grounded theory: toward multi-grounded theory', *International Journal of Qualitative Methods*, 9: 187–205.

Kelle, U. (1995) 'Theories as heuristic tools in qualitative research', in Maso, I., Atkinson, P. A., Delamont, S. and Verhoeven, J. C. (eds) *Openness in Research: The Tension Between Self and Other*. Assen: van Gorcum, pp. 33–50.

Lind, M. and Goldkuhl, G. (2006) 'How to develop a multi-grounded theory: the evolution of a business process theory', *Australasian Journal of Information Systems*, 13: 69–85.

Pierce, C. S. (1958) *Collected papers of Charles Sanders Pierce. Vol. VII: Science and Philosophy* (Burks, A. W. ed.). Cambridge: Harvard University Press.

Schurz, G. (2008) 'Patterns of abduction', *Synthese*, 164: 201–34.

Strauss, A. and Corbin, J. (1990) *Basics of Qualitative Research*. Newbury Park: Sage.

Strauss, A. and Corbin, J. (eds) (1997) *Grounded Theory in Practice*. Thousand Oaks, CA: Sage.

Strauss, A. and Corbin, J. (1998) *Basics of Qualitative Research* (2nd edn). Thousand Oaks, CA: Sage.

Thornberg, R. (2007) 'Inconsistencies in everyday patterns of school rules', *Ethnography and Education*, 2,: 401–16.

Thornberg, R. (2008) 'School children's reasoning about school rules', *Research Papers in Education*, 23: 37–52.

Thornberg, R. (2009) 'The moral construction of the good pupil embedded in school rules', *Education, Citizenship and Social Justice*, 4: 245–61.

Thornberg, R. (2010a) 'A student in distress: moral frames and bystander behaviour in school', *Elementary School Journal*, 110: 585–608.

Thornberg, R. (2010b) 'Schoolchildren's social representations on bullying causes', *Psychology in the Schools*, 47: 311–27.

Thornberg, R. (2012) 'Informed grounded theory', *Scandinavian Journal of Educational Research* (in press).

Thornberg, R. and Charmaz, K. (2011) 'Grounded theory', in Lapan, S. D., Quartaroli M. T. and Reimer F. J. (eds) *Qualitative Research: An Introduction to Methods and Designs*. San Francisco: John Wiley/Jossey-Bass.

Visual methodologies

Jenni Karlsson

The visual turn

Cameras for still and moving film in the nineteenth century, the breakthrough to colour photography and the production of affordable easy-to-operate cameras in the twentieth century paved the way for popular participation in amateur photography (for more about this, see Emmison and Smith, 2000; Kress and van Leeuwen, 1996; Prosser, 1998). The subsequent inventions of television and digital technologies enabled the rapid broadcast, production and exchange of images globally. Thus over two centuries society has increasingly become attuned to communicating and ways of knowing via images rather than through words and preferring an image-based format over written text (Hall, 1997; Kress and van Leeuwen, 1996). As technologies have become available, innovative social scientists have utilised them in their research methods, most notably anthropologists who photographed their study communities extensively (see Banks, 1998; Collier Jr, 1967; Edwards, 2001, 1994; Harper, 1998). Such influences reached even to South Africa: E. G. Malherbe, the South African educationist who completed his graduate studies in New York, compiled a significant collection of field photographs in the early 1930s for the Carnegie Enquiry into the Poor Whites in South Africa (Malherbe, 1932, 1981).[1] However, Malherbe's photographs are mostly illustrative material annexed to his report, and the images themselves are not analysed. Having participants generate their own photographs as part of research projects and social interventions is now common – even in Africa (for example, see de Waal, 2010; Larkin et al., 2007; McLea, 2010; Olivier et al., 2009; Taylor et al., 2007). The reason for this trend lies beyond mere technological access; it is due to researchers seeking to illuminate social life from the standpoint of the insider and increase participants' roles in the research, even when they are children (Fiedler and Posch, 2009).

It is only in the last twenty years that education researchers have taken visual methodologies more seriously, the first significant body of published work being the volume edited by Jon Prosser (1998). In making these comments I distinguish between a supplementary illustrative use of images in research and the conscious, deliberate generation and analysis of data that is in the form of an image – the latter being a key feature in visual methodologies.

I have found that visual methods enable me to explore educational settings, policies and phenomena in ways that extend the reach of interviews, questionnaires, document analysis and narratives. For example, while most critiques of race-based education in South Africa (1948–1990) relied on comparative statistics, documentary and interview data (see Kallaway, 1984; Kallaway et al., 1997; Unterhalter et al., 1991), through a visual methodology I found evidence that during the apartheid era school children learned about South Africa's racialised hierarchy in places beyond their classrooms, and in the post-apartheid era apartheid discourse was residual more in the non-pedagogic spaces of schools than in classrooms. Having outlined the emergence of visual methodologies and pointed to some visual researchers in education, let us consider what defines visual methodologies and how some visual methods are implemented.

Defining visual methodologies

A distinguishing feature of visual methodologies is the foregrounding of methods that involve the study and use of images about social life, based on the assumption that 'images encode data about values, norms and practices that are often inaccessible to other forms of collecting and reporting information' (Grady, 2001: 4). Michael Emmison and Philip Smith (2000) include objects (material culture) and observing place and use of space as a type of visual research. They do not distinguish sharply between the visual and the spatial. Arts-based methodologies have also emerged in recent years (see Finley, 2008) and some visual researchers make little distinction as they move seamlessly between images as data and participants' performance as data (for example, see Mitchell et al., 2006). Douglas Harper (2008) usefully separates visual studies of social life (such as in education and which usually, but not always, entail generating images) from cultural studies that are about the meaning of visual culture. For education researchers the study focus is on social life pertaining to education. It is not easy, nor necessarily desirable, to fence off visual, spatial and arts-based methodologies; indeed, their overlapping and integrated aspects point to the creativity of education researchers and their effort to understand complex educational issues.

Visual researchers use data that are pre-existing images or they generate images or both. Images may take the form of original or published drawings, diagrams, maps, paintings, advertisements and publications, as well as still photographs and movies in film, video and digital formats, or originate as interactive web-based broadcasts. But a methodology is not defined by its predominant type of data; rather, visual methodology concerns the visual researcher's position on knowing through images (epistemology) and how images represent reality (ontology). Thus Gillian Rose (2001) emphasises the researcher's stance, especially in relation to interpreting images. She asserts that the visual researcher 'takes images seriously', 'thinks about the social conditions and effects of visual objects' and 'considers [their] own way of looking at images' (Rose, 2001: 15–16). This focus on the researcher's standpoint and on understanding images as constructed representations of society and social relations pushes visual methodology into the critical paradigm, whereas unreflexive decodings and analysis of image content and descriptions of composition sit more easily in the interpretive paradigm.

Methods of data collection and analysis

Many techniques or methods used by visual researchers are not entirely unique to visual methodology, though they may be adapted to employ new technologies. For example, Jon Prosser (2000) writes about using the observation method to record school life with a camera. In so doing he raises the importance of an ethical practice in generating visual images. Other technologies, such as GPS devices, are being adapted for types of observation such as tracing movement patterns. More recently the SenseCam (Microsoft, 2007), hung around a participant's neck, takes photos at set intervals to passively create a visual log of the participant's context and encounters. As new technologies are employed in research they raise fresh questions about surveillance and consent. Those working with existing images in photo albums, textbooks and art collections share concerns with historians about authorship, authenticity and representivity in selection methods, although their analytical approaches differ vastly. Emmison and Smith (2000) explain how images can be used in the interview method. Rose (2001) and van Leeuwen and Jewitt (2001) provide extensive discussions of different approaches to analysing images. From the array of methods available in visual methodologies, my focus in this chapter is on two generative methods that employ still photographs.

Implementing two approaches to generating visual data

Depending on the nature of the study, images may already exist or are produced by the researcher and/or participants. My interest in visual methodologies began in about 1996 while assisting a visiting scholar from the United Kingdom gather photographs of black South African teachers and learners in classrooms for her photo-elicitation interview instrument. Shortly after that, I was reflecting on post-apartheid legislation about the funding and governance arrangements of schools and how it would slowly smudge the harsh spatial and material inequalities of apartheid-era school types. The idea of harnessing photography for researching inequality in the South African school environment seemed a possibility. My interest piqued when I stumbled across Rieger's (1996) work on photographing social change and I embarked on a visual study of the residual apartheid discourse and emerging post-apartheid discourse in school space, based on a study of six government schools in the city of Durban, South Africa (see Karlsson, 2003). As a South African researcher, I was isolated from the community of visual researchers in the United Kingdom and North America. Thus I devised two complementary instruments using photo-observation and photovoice methods, based on my reading of two articles (Combs and Ziller, 1977; Rieger, 1996) sourced over the Internet. I did not use those method names at the time and it was much later that I became aware of Wang and Burris's (1994) writing about photovoice. My photo-observation and photovoice instruments were designed to generate data deductively and inductively that I could use to compare the spaces of six schools and explore the political discourses in the schools' spatial practices. I found that visual data is a good fit for a spatial study even though such data is insufficient for answering questions about intent. Photographs are also suitable when working with particular categories of participants. For example, when I have worked with young children who are shy and reluctant to express themselves to an unfamiliar adult outsider-researcher, especially when there are racial, linguistic and cultural differences between the children and me, the photographs taken by the learners have given me a window onto their world of experiences that I

Table 12.1 Sample of a photo-observation instrument used for viewing inequality in South African school space

Category	Sub-category views
Resource utility views	Energy-based object
	Water supply
	Toilets
	Telephone
	Library
	Laboratory/specialised room
	Sports fields and playground
Boundary views	School entrance as seen from road
	Road as seen from main entry point of school building
	Main door to school
	Door to principal's office
	Door to classroom
	School as a whole
Views of rituals and routines	Control over movement/routines in the corridor
	Staffroom
	Assembly
	Public representational images
Views of school bureaucracy	Administrative office furniture
	Administrative equipment
	Staffroom noticeboard
Classroom views	First-phase classroom
	Second-phase classroom
Informal social space	Car park
	Tuck shop

would not have had via a conventional interview. Photovoice is also a suitable method when the research concerns an emotionally charged or sensitive topic that participants may struggle to speak about, such as

Table 12.2   Extract from a comparative table of observed forms of energy-based technologies available in six schools in South Africa

	School 1	School 2	School 3	School 4	School 5	School 6
Total forms of technologies	24	32	9	10	9	(9)
Urn	x	x		x	x	x
Microwave	x	x		x		
Washing machine	x					
Hot water pipes/geyser	x	x				
Fridge	x	x				
TV aerial (implies TV and VCR)		x	x			

HIV and AIDS (for example, see Larkin et al., 2007; Mitchell et al., 2007; Olivier et al., 2007; Taylor et al., 2007). Visual methods such as photovoice are also suitable when the researcher wants to narrow her/his power differential with participants and when there is a need to work collaboratively with participants.

I will now explain my approach to the photo-observation and photovoice methods.

Photo-observation method

In this method the researcher generates photographs of what is observed. Still cameras 'fix' what is observed so that the image can be analysed later at length and digital cameras make the storage of images and printing relatively easy. My approach to photo-observation starts with a priori categories gleaned from my problem statement and reading of relevant literature. Using the categories I systematically plan standardised observations of particular places or things rather than haphazardly snapping anything seen during a school visit.[2] Apart from providing dependability, being systematic is vital for comparing schools, as was my task in studying the spatialised discourse of race-based schooling at six schools. Thus I devised a structured instrument of standardised views for each a priori category (see Table 12.1).

I usually take several photographs (long shots and close-ups) for a full observation of one view. For example, using an instrument with six categories and 24 sub-category views, I generated a data-set

of about 500 images for my comparative analysis of political discourses in the spaces of six schools. Depending on the research question, I have used various analytical methods for making meaning of the photo-observations. For example, to understand the spatiality of a race-based funding differential to schools in the apartheid era I used content analysis to compile inventories and counts of energy-consumptive technologies in each school (see Table 12.2). These lists reveal the apartheid discourse of racial hierarchy in privileged schools, previously for white middle-class learners, compared to township schools that served learners from African working-class families.

The drawback of photo-observation is when the researcher is an outsider to a school and does not know the place well. To offset this limitation it is worthwhile collaborating with participants through drawing tasks or photovoice. I have employed both participatory methods successfully with young learners even in contexts fraught by linguistic and other social barriers.

Photovoice method

In this method participants collaborate with the researcher by generating photographs and accompanying text. The value of this is that participants are insiders to the site or phenomenon under investigation. For example, for my study of school space I thought it worthwhile to ask school learners to photograph their schools because they knew their schools intimately and by spending more time at school than my occasional visits, their photographs would cover a greater range of spatial practices as well as places that I would not know about. In this way I generated a data-set of about 500 images from 24 learners' photovoice accounts. Their insider photos revealed things such as school food gardens and misdemeanours and incidents that they regarded as important yet which I had not seen via my outsider photo-observations.

I follow a seven-step process to generate school learners' photovoice accounts.

1. I prepare myself by purchasing disposable cameras and developing a pamphlet which introduces me and explains how to use the camera. The pamphlet also includes a paragraph in which I tell the learners in their own language what I want them to do with the camera. The task instruction is purposively vague so that it is not leading and avoids prompting or restricting the learner-photographer to take particular shots. I also prepare letters to parents and to learners, in which I explain the study and address ethical issues and request participation. The letters include informed consent reply forms and envelopes for return to me.

2. I engage in preparations with the class teacher. Using the class register I sample the requisite number of boys and girls and seek the teacher's confirmation that my sampled names suit the purpose of my study. Once the names are finalised, my letters are distributed to the selected learners and their parents. The returned letters are checked for consent.

3. I convene a briefing meeting with the selected learners. Each learner is presented with a disposable camera and pamphlet, and I go through the pamphlet, checking that they know how to use the camera and understand their task. I also assure them about my ethical responsibility in writing about them and their photographs. The meeting ends with the learner-photographers posing and taking one practice shot with each other's cameras. This ensures that later I have a first frame that identifies the learner-photographer's set of photographs.

4. The learner-photographers spend about a week using their cameras.

5. Then I collect the cameras to develop, digitise and print two sets of the photographs (one set being a memento for the learner). At this stage I label and file the negatives and digital copies, and label my set of the photograph prints, giving each a unique code to identify information such as school, learner-photographer and sequence in the set.

6. I meet with each learner-photographer to give them their set of prints and to talk about the photographs, which I lay out sequentially on a table. The learner-photographer talks about each photo, explaining what is represented and responding to my questions, when necessary with an interpreter on hand. This 'talk' is recorded.

7. The recordings are transcribed and, where necessary, translated. The digitised photos are then embedded at the appropriate point of the transcript file to accompany the learner-photographer's account (see Figure 12.1). With this stage the process to generate photovoice accounts is complete and analysis can begin.

The analytical phase involves a relatively intuitive interpretive process that is a confluence of prior knowledge, theoretical understanding, content analysis and reflection. First, there is an inter-textual reading of the photovoice account that flags recurring elements. In the second stage the identified elements are reduced to themes. The third stage involves a deeper thematic reading of the photovoice accounts to add texture, depth and coherence to the thematic finding. Finally, meaning is attributed to the finding in relation to the theoretical framework.

Lastly, there are thorny ethical issues when using photovoice, which have led me to caution novice researchers about this method (Karlsson, 2007). These issues are heightened when participants are vulnerable and who may perceive that they cannot contest the researcher's request, such as children, the poor, under-educated people, and so on. In such cases, have participants fully understood how researchers use photovoice accounts and disseminate findings? How are other members of the community giving their consent and being protected from harm when they appear in participants' photos? How is anonymity

CL1m:23

'I've formed friendships [on the bus]. Some of them we do spend time with them here at school. Yeah, some of them are in the same class. We take the same bus, same class . . . I'm always talking and interacting.'

Figure 12.3   Extract from a learner's photovoice account of his trip to and from school

possible when a place is recognisable? The question of ownership of photographs and recognition of participants is also vexed (for further discussion see Banks, 2001; Pink, 2001). As the researcher who originates and designs the photovoice task, I assert intellectual property rights over the data; nevertheless I acknowledge the learner-photographers by providing them with a set of prints and I indicate their photographic 'authorship' in the encoded labelling assigned to each image (see Figure 12.1).

Conclusion

Visual methodologies appeal to critical education researchers because they offer a means to enter into dialogue with participants in ways that privilege those participants' experiences and understandings, the insiders with knowledgeable insight and expertise, and they provide avenues to research spatiality and delve into issues often left unspoken. Such approaches chime with the intent of critical education researchers who seek a rigorous research practice as well as research that advances social justice.

Notes

1. E. G. Malherbe's two photo albums from the Poor White study are housed in the Campbell Collections of the University of KwaZulu-Natal in Durban, South Africa.
2. Although my generative technique is structured, this does not imply that I am not spontaneous if I see something in the field that I think may be significant.

Suggested further reading

Those who are interested in broadening their understanding of visual research should turn to *Visual Studies*, a journal that is entirely dedicated to things visual within social science research. Douglas Harper is a leading sociologist who uses and writes about visual research. He has a worthwhile chapter entitled 'What's new visually' in Sage's third edition of *Collecting and Interpreting Qualitative Materials* edited by Norman Denzin and Yvonna Lincoln (2008).

One can also learn a lot of lessons from reading about how other people have applied photovoice in different contexts and for different purposes. One book that includes several chapters by authors who have employed this method is *Putting People in the Picture: Visual Methodologies for Social Change* edited by Naydene de Lange, Claudia Mitchell and Jean Stuart (Sense Publishers, 2007).

References

Banks, M. (1998) 'Visual anthropology: image, object and interpretation', in Prosser, J. (ed.) *Image-Based Research: A Sourcebook For Qualitative Researchers*. London: Falmer Press, pp. 9–23.

Banks, M. (2001) *Visual Methods in Social Research*. London: Sage.

Collier Jr, J. (1967) *Visual Anthropology: Photography as a Research Method*. New York: Holt, Rinehart & Winston.

Combs, J. and Ziller, R. (1977) 'Photographic self-concept of counselees', *Journal of Counseling Psychology*, 24(5): 452–5.

de Waal, S. (2010) 'Shot on the spot', *Mail & Guardian Friday*, pp. 10–11.

Edwards, E. (ed.) (1994) *Anthropology and Photography 1860–1920*. New Haven, CT: Yale University Press.

Edwards, E. (2001) *Raw Histories: Photographs, Anthropology and Museums*. Oxford: Berg.

Emmison, M. and Smith, P. (2000) *Researching the Visual: Images, Objects, Contexts and Interactions in Social and Cultural Inquiry*. London: Sage.

Fiedler, J. and Posch, C. (eds) (2009) *Yes, They Can! Children Researching Their Lives: A Selection Of Articles based on the 2nd International Conference on Research with and by Children, 10–12 December 2007 [at the] SOS Children's Villages, Hermann Gmeiner Academy, Innsbruck*. Baltmannsweiler: Schneider Verlag Hohengehren.

Finley, S. (2008) 'Arts-based inquiry: performing revolutionary pedagogy', in Denzin, N. and Lincoln, Y. (eds) *Collecting and Interpreting Qualitative Materials* (3rd edn). Los Angeles: Sage, pp. 95–113.

Grady, J. (2001) 'Sociology's new workshop: the visual challenge to sociology', *Sociological Imagination*, 38(1/2): 4–6.

Hall, S. (ed.) (1997) *Representation: Cultural Representations and Signifying Practices*. London: Sage/Open University.

Harper, D. (1998) 'An argument for visual sociology', in Prosser, J. (ed.) *Image-Based Research: A Sourcebook for Qualitative Researchers*. London: Falmer Press, pp. 24–41.

Harper, D. (2008) 'What's new visually?', in Denzin, N. and Lincoln, Y. (eds) *Collecting and Interpreting Qualitative Materials* (3rd edn). Los Angeles: Sage, pp. 185-204.

Kallaway, P. (ed.) (1984) *Apartheid and Education: The Education of Black South Africans*. Johannesburg: Ravan.

Kallaway, P., Kruss, G., Donn, G. and Fataar, A. (eds) (1997) *Education After Apartheid: South African Education in Transition*. Cape Town: University of Cape Town Press.

Karlsson, J. (2003) *Apartheid and Post-Apartheid Discourses in School Space: A Study of Durban, A Thesis Submitted for the Degree of Doctor of Philosophy*. London: University of London.

Karlsson, J. (2007) 'The novice visual researcher', in de Lange, N., Mitchell, C. and Stuart, J. (eds) *Putting People in the Picture: Visual Methodologies for Social Change*. Rotterdam: Sense Publishers.

Kress, G. and van Leeuwen, T. (eds) (1996) *Reading Images: The Grammar of Visual Design*. London: Routledge.

Larkin, J., Lombardo, C., Walker, L., Bahreini, R., Tharao, W., Mitchell, C. et al. (2007) 'Taking it global xpress: youth, photovoice and HIV & AIDS', in de Lange, N., Mitchell, C. and Stuart, J. (eds) *Putting people in the Picture: Visual Methodologies for Social Change*. Rotterdam: Sense Publishers, pp. 31–43.

McLea, H. (2010) 'Diepsloot kids say it in pictures', *The Times*, 18 October, p. 8.

Malherbe, E. G. (1932) *Education and the Poor White: Report of the Carnegie Commission* (Vol. 3). Stellenbosch: Carnegie Commission.

Malherbe, E. G. (1981) *Never a Dull Moment*. Lansdowne: Howard Timmins Publishers.

Microsoft (2007) *Introduction to SenseCam* [online]. Available at: http://research.microsoft.com/en-us/um/cambridge/.../sensecam (accessed 1 November 2010).

Mitchell, C., Walsh, S. and Moletsane, R. (2006) '"Speaking for ourselves": visual arts-based and participatory methodologies for working with young people', in Leach, F. and Mitchell, C. (eds) *Combating Gender Violence in and around Schools*. Stoke-on-Trent: Trentham Books, pp. 103–111.

Mitchell, C., de Lange, N., Stuart, J., Moletsane, R. and Buthelezi, T. (2007) 'Children's provocative images of stigma, vulnerability and violence in the age of AIDS: Re-visualisations of childhood', in de Lange, N., Mitchell, C. and Stuart, J. (eds) *Putting People in the Picture: Visual Methodologies for Social Change*. Rotterdam: Sense Publishers, pp. 59–71.

Olivier, T., Wood, L. and de Lange, N. (2007) '"Changing our eyes": seeing hope', in de Lange, N., Mitchell, C. and Stuart, J. (eds) *Putting People in the Picture: Visual Methodologies for Social Change*. Rotterdam: Sense Publishers, pp. 11–29.

Olivier, T., Wood, L. and de Lange, N. (2009) *Picturing Hope in the Face of Poverty, as Seen Through the Eyes of Teachers: Photo Voice – A Research Methodology*. Cape Town: Juta.

Pink, S. (2001) *Doing Visual Ethnography: Images, Media and Representation in Research*. London: Sage

Prosser, J. (ed.) (1998) *Image-Based Research: A Sourcebook for Qualitative Researchers*. London: Falmer Press.

Prosser, J. (2000) 'The moral maze of image ethics', in Simons, H. and Usher, R. (eds) *Situated Ethics in Educational Research*. London: Routledge, pp. 116–32.

Rieger, J. (1996) 'Photographing social change', *Visual Sociology*, 11(1): 5–49.

Rose, G. (2001) *Visual Methodologies: An Introduction to Interpreting Visual Objects*. London: Sage.

Taylor, M., de Lange, N., Dlamini, S., Nyawo, N. and Sathiparsad, R. (2007) 'Using photovoice to study the challenges facing women teachers in rural KwaZulu-Natal', in de Lange, N., Mitchell, C. and Stuart, J. (eds) *Putting People in the Picture: Visual Methodologies for Social Change*. Rotterdam: Sense Publishers, pp. 45–58.

Unterhalter, E., Wolpe, H., Botha, T., Badat, S., Dlamini, T. and Khotseng, B. (eds) (1991) *Apartheid Education and Popular Struggles*. Johannesburg: Ravan Press.

van Leeuwen, T. and Jewitt, C. (eds) (2001) *Handbook of Visual Analysis*. London: Sage.

Wang, C. and Burris, M. (1994) 'Empowerment through photovoice: portraits of participation', *Health Education Quarterly*, 21(2): 171–86.

Case study research

Laura Day Ashley

Case study research: an outline

The case study is a popular research design in the social sciences and has been defined by Robson as:

> . . . a strategy for doing research which involves an empirical investigation of a particular contemporary phenomenon within its real life context using multiple sources of evidence. (Robson, 2002: 178)

What may constitute a 'case' for empirical research is wide ranging: it may be an individual, such as a teacher or student; an institution, such as a school; an event, project or programme within an institution; it may be a policy, or other types of system. A case may be described as 'a bounded system' (Smith, cited in Stake, 1995: 2) whereby its 'parameters of particularity are set by spatial, temporal, personal, organizational or other factors' (Thomas, 2012: 5); and it is studied with reference to the specific context in which it is situated.

The purpose of case study research might be to *explore* a phenomenon about which not much is known, or to *describe* something in detail. Yin (2009) suggests that case studies have a particular ability to answer *why* and *how* research questions rather than simply *what* and, therefore, they have the potential to *evaluate* or *explain*, for example, why a particular programme did

or did not work. The strength of case study research lies in its ability to enable the researcher to intensively investigate the case in-depth, to probe, drill down and get at its complexity, often through long term immersion in, or repeated visits to/encounters with the case.

Case study research includes single case studies, and multiple case studies involving a small number of cases that are often related in some way. The case study might be differentiated from '"variable-led" research' (Thomas, 2012: 4, citing Ragin) since it places a focus on 'the complex interaction of many factors in few cases' rather than on 'few variables in a large number of cases' (Thomas, 2012: 4). For both types of case study a key design issue involves the selection of the case(s). Yin (2009: 47-9; 52) sets out five key rationales for selecting a single case:

1. the 'critical' case that seeks to test theory;
2. the 'extreme', 'unique' or 'rare' case;
3. the 'representative' or 'typical' case;
4. the 'revelatory' case that is important because it may not have been previously investigated;
5. the 'longitudinal' case which is studied at different moments in time with a focus on change.

That a case might be 'representative' or 'typical' is questioned by Thomas (2011: 31) who emphasises that the case study is limited to 'a particular representation given in context and understood in that context'. Related to this, is the limited potential of case studies in terms of generalisation, particularly to larger populations. For example, Yin (2009: 54) asserts that a 'sampling logic' is irrelevant to case selection in a multiple case study and instead suggests that multiple cases should be selected because either they are expected to lead to similar findings, or because they are expected to lead to different findings for particular reasons.

Case study research allows for a certain degree of methodological eclecticism which typically includes asking people questions, observing what happens and analysing documents (Bassey, 1999). Multiple methods and sources are often made use of to achieve in-depth understanding of cases through the triangulation of methods and sources to confirm emerging findings and to point to contradictions and tensions – an 'awareness of anomaly' (Kuhn, cited in Thomas, 2010: 580) that may highlight areas for analysis and help draw insights and interpretations. A particular data collection and analysis concern for multiple case studies is: How to preserve in-depth understandings of the uniqueness of individual cases – their 'meaning in context' (Mishler, 1979, cited in Noblitt and Hare, 1988: 17) – and at the same time ensure a consistency of approach across the cases to enable cross-case comparison? In the following section I will discuss how I addressed this and other design issues mentioned above in a multiple case study research project of my own.

A multiple case study of private school outreach in India

This doctoral research (conducted in 2000-2003) focused on a phenomenon in the Indian context that I have termed 'private school outreach' (Day Ashley, 2005; 2006; 2010) and defined as follows:

Private schools that extend their activities beyond the usual remit of providing middle-class children with fee-charging education and additionally provide education free of charge (or for a nominal fee) to socio-economically disadvantaged children who would otherwise be out of school.

Despite its apparent increasing incidence, the phenomenon of private school outreach had barely been researched at the time – only a couple of short descriptions about this type of activity existed within other works (Jessop, 1998; Tooley, 2001). Therefore, I decided upon a case study strategy to explore this phenomenon and gain an in-depth understanding of its complexities and, in particular, the dynamics of the attempt to educate children from very different socio-economic backgrounds by the *same institution*. In this respect, private school outreach presented an unusual case in the Indian context, where the education system has been described as the grouping of children into 'different types of institutions according to their socio-economic background' (Kumar, 1987: 38), a situation that was exacerbated with the mushrooming of low-fee private schools (De, et al., 2000) at the time of research adding another layer of institution catering for a specific socio-economic group. However, in private school outreach, although educated by the same institution, private school students and out-of-school children were not usually educated together in the *same classrooms* but separately with the former receiving a formal English-medium private education and the latter being given a non-formal education in their local languages in what I refer to as 'outreach programmes'. This anomaly of the same institution educating diverse children - but separately - led to the development of the overarching research question:

Does private school outreach in the Indian context contribute to bridging educational and social divides, or does it serve to maintain and reinforce them?

I decided to carry out a multiple case study rather than a single case study because I was interested to make some broad comment about what characterises private school outreach; in a single case study it would be difficult to separate private school outreach as a phenomenon from what was idiosyncratic about that particular case. A multiple case study then would transcend 'the radical particularlism' (Firestone and Herriott, 1983) of the single case and ask the question:

OVERARCHING RESEARCH QUESTION: ASKED OF ENTIRE STUDY	
Does private school outreach contribute to bridging educational and social divides in the Indian context, or does it serve to maintain and reinforce them?	
INSTRUMENTAL QUESTIONS POSED TO EACH CASE	**MAIN METHODS OF DATA GENERATION**
Q1. What factors have shaped the origin and development of private school outreach?	• Documents • Semi-structured interviews (*staff*) • Ethnographic methods
Q2. How does private school outreach operate, particularly in terms of the interface between the private school and outreach programme?	• Ethnographic methods • Semi-structured interviews (*staff*) • Documents
Q3. What are the forms and meanings of interactions between students of the private school and outreach programme?	• Focused observations (*interactions*) • Focus group discussions (*students*) • Semi-structured interviews (*staff*)
QUESTIONS ASKED OF FINDINGS ACROSS MULTIPLE CASES	
Q4. How can variation between the three cases be best explained? Q5. What do the findings suggest about the distinctive role of private school outreach?	

Figure 13.1 Set of research questions

'Do these findings make sense beyond a specific case?' (Miles and Huberman, 1994: 173).

Since private school outreach was relatively new research terrain, the strategy of 'maximum variation' (Patton, 1990) was adopted for case selection. This allowed for common patterns across the diverse cases to be traced, leading to the identification of key characteristics of private school outreach. It also enabled an exploration of variation – to investigate the different conditions in which variation between cases occurred (Becker, 1990), as well as its meaning and effects. Of the ten examples of private school outreach identified during a pre-study visit, three of these were selected for the multiple case studies. This was considered a sensible number of cases given the size of the project and time available to balance an in-depth understanding of each case with the breadth of understanding gained by investigating multiple cases (Schofield, 1990). The first criterion was that the three cases were not directly influencing each other and so cases were selected that were not part of the same network. Other criteria included: variation in the philosophical foundations of the schools; variation in the length of time since the schools had been founded; variation in the physical set up of the outreach programmes in relation to the private schools; variation in the student clientele of both private school and outreach programme; and variation in their geographical location, i.e. to include both urban and rural cases.

EXPLORATORY PHASE		
Documentary analysis	Ethnographic methods	'Outwards mapping'

SECOND SEMI-STRUCTURED PHASE		
Semi-structured interviews	Focus group discussions	Focused observations

Figure 13.2   Progressive structuring of the research process

A set of research questions served as a guiding framework for the data collection and analysis (see Figure 13.1). In order to answer the overarching research question, instrumental research questions were used to guide the empirical data collection in each case. The types of methods of data collection used to address each instrumental research question are indicated in the right hand column, with data sources in brackets. This data was drawn on to answer the research question asked of findings across the multiple cases which in turn served as a vehicle for answering the overarching question asked of the entire study.

A data collection procedure based loosely on Yin's concept of 'case study protocol' (2009) was devised which served as a practical guide to the collection of data in all three cases and was piloted and subsequently refined during a visit to the field in a private school outreach setting separate from the three actual cases for the study. This procedure (see Figure 13.2) involved progressive structuring of the research process, inspired by Firestone and Herriott's (1983) formalization of qualitative research processes. In each case it comprised two phases of research over a six-week to two-month period: an exploratory phase, followed by (and overlapping with) a semi-structured phase, with each phase lasting approximately 3-4 weeks. The exploratory phase involved a period of looser, more unstructured methods of data collection which included sourcing, reading and analysing

documents relating to the schools and their outreach work, and ethnographic methods. The process, which I describe as 'outwards mapping' (inspired by the 'backward mapping' used by Dyer (2000, citing Elmore, 1980) to research policy by starting at the grassroots level) was used as a technique to explore the possible vantage points from which the researcher could be positioned during the semi-structured phase. Taking the outreach programme in each case as a starting point and working outwards it involved the strategic identification of people, places and practices associated with it.

As well as being a source of richly contextual data about each case, in many ways the exploratory phase provided the groundwork for the semi-structured phase, in terms of establishing rapport with key informants, identifying participants and settings for selection, and generally understanding how the cases worked. This informed the questions posed during the semi-structured interviews, focus group discussions and focused observations of interactions, which could be more deeply probing and strategic in their nature. Understandings derived from the exploratory phase also informed how the data collection methods in the semi-structured phase might be tailored in ways that were more suited and sensitive to specific cases. Equally, this data collection procedure ensured that during the semi-structured phase the same types of questions were asked of all three cases in broadly similar ways and provided a 'coherent system … for collecting information from a range of informants, across a potential range of sites, in a roughly comparable format' (Huberman and Miles, 1994: 430).

Initial data analysis of individual cases began in the field; this enabled me to return to each case to check emerging findings and to explore issues that had been drawn to my attention in one case but not in the other two. This strengthened the more intense within- and cross-case analysis that followed on return from the field. At this stage the data had been organised into various forms: individual case study reports, the semi-structured data (both that acquired through semi-structured research methods and the transformed unstructured data) and the original unstructured data. Initially, a rereading of the entire data set was conducted to bring the researcher close to the data to discover areas which may not have been dominant in the emerging analyses whilst in the field. During this rereading a 'cross-sectional indexing system' (Mason, 2002) was developed which was applicable to the whole data set. Thus, the data set was reduced to a system of categories which revealed broad conceptual patterns across the three cases as well as areas of variation. This was followed by in-depth within-case analyses to view the categories in the context of the complexities and dynamics pertaining to each case and relate them back to original field notes, interview transcriptions and documentary sources (Coffey and Atkinson, 1996). Connections between the categories were investigated and during this process displays were used in order to see more clearly the associations and configurations (Miles and Huberman, 1994). Finally, the displayed data from each of the cases was compared. This phase involved the researcher in the process of interpretation: 'drawing meaning from the displayed data' (Huberman and Miles, 1994: 429). In this way an explanatory picture for the variation between the three cases was built and findings which emerged were verified through processes of triangulation.

This description of my own case study research is intended to provide the reader with an example of how a multiple case study might be done; however, it is important to note that this is just one specific case study design tailored to a particular research focus and there are many other types of design possibilities. Recent examples of multiple case studies include research by Coronel et al. (2010) on the leadership roles of eight female school principals in Spain, and Meirink et al.'s (2010) study of five teacher learning and collaboration teams in Dutch secondary schools; the latter study involved a combination of qualitative and quantitative methods. In terms of single case studies, some recent examples include ethnographic case studies such as that by Theodorou and Nind (2010) of a young child with autism in England, and by McKinney (2010) of a desegregated girls' school in South Africa. The last example given is Nilholm and Alm's (2010) case study of an inclusive classroom in Sweden which explicitly attempts to develop a methodology to study inclusiveness transparently to include pupil experience, and creatively makes use of a range of data collection methods including sociograms and children's poetry. As a final note, I would suggest (following Mason, 2002) that this type of creative thinking, as well as strategic thinking, is key to research design (not only case study research) since it can help the researcher formulate the best available research design for the specific research project.

Suggested further reading

Day Ashley, L. (2005) 'From margins to mainstream: Private school outreach inclusion processes for out-of-school children in India', *International Journal of Educational Development*, 25(2): 133–44.

Day Ashley, L. (2010) 'The use of structuration theory to conceptualize alternative practice in education: the case of private school outreach in India', *British Journal of Sociology of Education*, 31(3): 337–51. Two articles based on the research case study presented in this chapter, for further information and expansion.

Stake, R. (1995) *The Art of Case Study Research.* Thousand Oaks, CA: Sage. This book presents a disciplined, qualitative exploration of case study methods by drawing from naturalistic, holistic, ethnographic, phenomenological and biographic research methods.

References

Bassey, M. (1999) *Case Study Research in Educational Settings*. Buckingham: Open University Press.

Becker, H.S. (1990) 'Generalizing from Case Studies', in Eisner, E.W. and Peshkin, A. (Eds.) *Qualitative Inquiry in Education: The Continuing Debate*. New York, N.Y: Teachers College Press.

Coffey, A. and Atkinson, P. (1996) *Making Sense of Qualitative Data: Complementary Research Strategies*. Thousand Oaks, CA: Sage.

Coronel, J.M., Moreno, E. and Carrasco, M.J.(2010) 'Beyond obstacles and problems: women principals in Spain leading change in their schools', *International Journal of Leadership in Education*, 13(2): 141–62.

Day Ashley, L. (2005) 'From margins to mainstream: Private school outreach inclusion processes for out-of-school children in India', *International Journal of Educational Development*, 25(2): 133–44.

Day Ashley, L. (2006) 'Inter-school working involving private school outreach initiatives and government schools in India', *Compare*, 36(4): 481–96.

Day Ashley, L. (2010) 'The use of structuration theory to conceptualize alternative practice in education: the case of private school outreach in India', *British Journal of Sociology of Education,* 31(3): 337–51.

De, A., Majumdar, M., Samson, M. and Noronha, C. (2000) *Role of Private Schools in Basic Education*. New Delhi: NIEPA (National Institute for Educational Planning and Administration) and Indian National Commission for Cooperation with UNESCO, Ministry of Human Resource Development, Government of India.

Dyer, C. (2000) *Operation Blackboard: Policy Implementation in Indian Elementary Education*. Oxford: Symposium Books.

Firestone, W.A, and Herriott, R.E. (1983) 'The formalization of qualitative research: an adaptation of "soft" science to the policy world', *Evaluation Review*, 7(4): 437–66.

Huberman, A.M. and Miles, M.B. (1994) 'Data management and analysis methods', in Denzin, N.K. and Lincoln, Y.S. (Eds.) *Handbook of Qualitative Research*. Thousand Oaks, CA: Sage Publications.

Jessop, T. (1998) *A Model of Best Practice at Loreto Day School, Sealdah, Calcutta*. Occasional Paper No.1, Education Sector Group, Department for International Development, India.

Kumar, K. (1987) 'Reproduction or change? Education and elites in India', in Ghosh, R. and Zachariah, M. (Eds.) *Education and the Process of Change*. New Delhi: Sage Publications.

Mason, J. (2002) *Qualitative Researching* (2nd edn). London: Sage Publications.

McKinney, C. (2010) 'Schooling in black and white: assimilationist discourses and subversive identity performances in a desegregated South African girls' school', *Race Ethnicity and Education*, 13(2): 191–207.

Meirink, J.A., Imants, J., Meijer, P.C. and Verloop, N. (2010) 'Teacher learning and collaboration in innovative teams', *Cambridge Journal of Education*, 40(2): 161–81.

Miles, M.B. and Huberman, A.M. (1994) *Qualitative Data Analysis: An Expanded Sourcebook*. London: Sage Publications.

Nilholm, C. and Alm, B. (2010) 'An inclusive classroom? A case study of inclusiveness, teacher strategies, and children's experiences', *European Journal of Special Needs Education*, 25(3): 239–52.

Noblitt, G.W. and Hare, R.D. (1988) *Meta-Ethnography: Synthesising Qualitative Studies*. Newbury Park, CA: Sage Publications.

Patton, M.Q. (1990) *Qualitative Evaluation and Research Methods* (2nd edn). Newbury Park, CA: Sage Publications.

Robson, C. (2002) *Real World Research: A Resource for Social Scientists and Practitioner-Researchers* (2nd edn). Oxford: Blackwell.

Schofield, J.W. (1990) 'Increasing the generalizability of qualitative research', in Eisner, E.W. and Peshkin, A. (Eds.) *Qualitative Inquiry in Education: The Continuing Debate*. New York, N.Y: Teachers College Press.

Stake, R. (1995) *The Art of Case Study Research*. Thousand Oaks, CA: Sage.

Theodorou, F. and Nind, M. (2010) 'Inclusion in play: a case study of a child with autism in an inclusive nursery', *Journal of Research in Special Educational Needs*, 10(2): 99–106.

Thomas, G. (2010) 'Doing case study: abduction not induction, phronesis not theory', *Qualitative Inquiry*, 16(7): 575–82.

Thomas, G. (2011) 'The case: generalisation, theory and phronesis in case study', *Oxford Review of Education,* 37(1): 21–35.

Thomas, G. (2012) 'A typology for the case study in social science following a review of definition, discourse and structure'. *Qualitative Inquiry*, 15(5): in press.

Tooley, J. (2001) *The Global Education Industry: Lessons from Private Education in Developing Countries*. London: The Institute of Economic Affairs.

Yin, R.K. (2009) *Case Study Research: Design and Methods* (4th edn). Thousand Oaks, CA: Sage Publications.

14

Issues of truth and justice

Ian Davies and Andrew Peterson

Citizenship education, and research upon it, is fundamentally and obviously concerned with social justice; it is also concerned with discovering, discussing and enacting truth. As such the issues – or, as some would have it, the tensions – regarding truth and justice can be illustrated and illuminated through a consideration of researching citizenship education. There has been a great deal of interest in research in the field of citizenship education over the last three decades. This has included international comparative work (principally, the International Association for the Evaluation of Educational Achievement (IEA) civic education study and the IEA international civic and citizenship education study, a large-scale longitudinal study in England (conducted by the National Foundation for Educational Research (NFER)), formal systematic reviews (for example, as part of the EPPI initiative), as well as a large amount of individual theoretical/conceptual work and small-scale empirical research and development projects.

In this chapter we refer to a style of collaborative research and development (illustrated through one case study), and use this in order to reflect on issues of truth and justice. The projects in which we have been involved were designed to achieve impact in the form of quality education programmes and were constructed in three interacting and overlapping stages: collegial professional investigations into what

teachers and students want to achieve; the formulation of resources and strategies to help achieve those ends; and evaluations resulting in refinements to project resources, guidelines for professionals and academic discussions to provide indications of where further research and development are needed. As such, we see research as being concerned with helping to clarify our understanding of specific concepts and practices with particular purposes in mind.

Truth and justice in educational research: fundamental considerations and practical influences

Citizenship education is necessarily entangled with real-world events and, therefore, there is a need to accept the connection between academic knowledge and social purpose – in other words, to relate truth to justice. Some (for example, see Weis and Fine, 2004) accept this position. Mirza argues that:

> Research by its very nature is political and it is about the nature of power as well as the access to power. (1995: 165)

Others disagree. Gorard (2000), for example, by referring to the work of Griffiths (1998), opposes approaches which he sees as being principally committed to a particular view of society:

> . . . their justified concerns for justice may lead [researchers] to take sides *before* collecting the necessary empirical evidence, as actually advocated by some 'researchers' (e.g. Griffiths 1998).
>
> I reject absolutely Griffiths's principles for researching social justice in education. The researcher cannot afford to take sides with anything but the truth. (Gorard, 2000).

This is a hugely complex matter. Insights into citizenship education are not always achieved through the application of what all would see as being true, nor necessarily aligned with ideas of justice in contemporary liberal democracies. Some researchers in the field, such as those influenced by neo-Marxism or postmodernism, may be seen crudely as being deterministically committed to particular positions on the nature and possibility of truth and objectivity. While the influence of these standpoints is waning (or has already waned), the force of their positions still seems to provide a background to current debates. Fundamental and wide-ranging controversies across the social sciences and humanities concerning, for example, the truth of history (Jenkins, 1991, 1995; Appleby et al., 1994; Evans, 2002) certainly relate directly to these discussions. More precise details about research procedures for gathering and analysing data show different approaches which nevertheless relate to the search for 'truth'. (For example, Walkerdine's recent work on researching affect and affective communication (http://www.ncrm.ac.uk/research/other/NMI/2009/) is clearly not conducted in the same way as other types of work on social justice such as Gorard et al. (2009) or Gillborn's (2008) work on racism.) There exists, then, fundamental philosophical disagreement about what researchers can and should do in regard to truth, and at times these differences lead to a great deal of contestation between researchers as to what constitutes 'legitimate' research in education (see Barnhouse Walters et al. (2009) for a discussion of these in the context of the US).

Similar issues arise in connection with debates over justice and, as with truth, researchers concerned with social justice have to be aware of important philosophical positions. Simply stated, justice can be expressed as a commitment to fairness. The aim for many researchers is to ensure that the voice of all groups in society is represented fairly and with equity in the research process, and in a way which involves a commitment to certain substantive ideas and beliefs which relate to ideas of a good society. There is a need for reflection, however, on the extent to which conceptions of a good society are mutually exclusive. This matter hinges, in relation to citizenship education, essentially around two axes: notions of liberalism and civic republicanism (where the former emphasises the value of the rights of individuals in private contexts and the latter stresses the need for a sense of collective identity and action in public contexts and, at least to some proponents, to a unified conception of a good society). There is also a need to reflect on whether education, and research on it, should aim at personal growth, intellectual rigour and/or societal benefit (or indeed at a combination of these).

These fundamental, essentially philosophical, positions concerning truth and justice cannot be fully discussed here; to do so would require consideration of these concepts within the context of a range of different approaches to epistemology, political philosophy and public philosophy. It would also be necessary to explore sociological matters through reflections on contextualised theorising on feminism, 'race' and postcolonialism. Instead, given the confines of this chapter, we do wish to make some comment about four related practical matters that apply to research in citizenship education.

Firstly, that the relationship between research, policy and practice is complex. Increasingly, education research in the UK and elsewhere has been subject to debates about scientific rigour (and here the links to truth and social justice are clear) and about the impact of research on policy and practice. The ESRC's Evaluation Strategy and overviews of research impact in the UK are relevant here (http://www.york.ac.uk/iee/research/o_policysurvey.htm) as are the debates about the need to emphasise quality as well as (or, instead of) impact (Gorard, 2008). If impact is important then we must be required to consider the criteria that are used to develop judgements and the extent to which these link to ideas of truth and/or justice.

Secondly, there are difficult issues about who is, and should be, seen as researchers and what sort of relationships they should seek to achieve with those from whom data is gathered. If justice is important it is necessary to ask what sort of characterisation of it is being developed through the process of recognising and educating researchers. Generally, there may be a decreasing adherence to the notion of expert and subject in a move to be – or at least to appear to be – non-hierarchical (although some of the jargon associated with research suggests otherwise). There is, simultaneously, an increased emphasis on the need for specialised research training which suggests a professionalisation of research which is not necessarily inclusive. Further there are deeper (and not always positive) issues to do with the nature of expertise and how we all (researchers and the researched) may be seen as experts (Rose, 1999). In research on citizenship education, this has involved understanding 'young people as actively constructing meaning' (Hahn and Alviar-Martin, 2008: 81), which itself raises questions pertinent to conceptions of the truth as an objective (rather than socially constructed) entity.

Thirdly, it is important to reflect on the nature of education as an academic and professional field of enquiry. If we are concerned with truth and justice then we need to ask about the extent to which inter-disciplinarity (or borrowing) can take place. Work that has taken place in relation to systematic reviewing is relevant here (Andrews, 2005; Hammersley, 2001; MacLure, 2005), as is the increased importance placed on randomised controlled trials (Tymms et al., 2008). These moves, and the scientific methods which they claim to uphold, have been claimed positively by some (e.g. Torgerson et al., 2005), as a useful connection between health and education research, but are seen rather negatively by others (see Barnhouse Walters et al., 2009).

Finally, the structures in which research on citizenship education takes place are very important. Developments in technology make publication easier and so there is now available a large amount of material rather than a few select accounts. Neither the 'truth' nor justice is not to be found in a limited number of sources. Further, pressures on researchers associated with such initiatives as the Research Assessment Exercise (RAE) (and the forthcoming Research Excellence Framework) and the scope of research funding will also affect what is researched and by whom, and there is perhaps a need to generate revisions of currently accepted positions about where and why researchers undertake their work (see Lucas, 2006; Carnell, 2008).

An example of a recent research and development project

We have been involved in a variety of projects which have been developed in an attempt to develop good practically useful and thoughtfully considered work with teachers and learners concerning the concept of 'active citizenship'. This has involved working closely with a team of curriculum or other developers to explore and contribute to what they think and what they do and to look for questions and issues that require further investigation and promotion.

One such project (see Davies et al., 2009) began from the idea that the subtitle of the Crick Report ('The Teaching of Democracy') would need to be monitored and developed as well as the (possibly) more limited aim to develop lessons about citizenship that would enable National Curriculum targets to be met. The project developed a working definition for 'Active Citizenship' and focused on the need to achieve democracy through citizenship. The leaders of the project asserted that this meant 'young people, working within the context of – and hoping to learn about, and develop further – a pluralistic democracy': this seems a very clear commitment to justice. As such they outlined the following aspirations for young people taking part in project activities:

- having their say;
- being involved in their community;
- making things happen;
- making decisions about their community be that their class, school, neighbourhood, city or country;
- becoming involved in the political process.

Several mini projects were developed around themes including individual and group advocacy in social and political contexts within, and for, the community. For each mini project that took place within the whole initiative, students were perceived to need: a broad knowledge and understanding of the issues relevant to the notion of active citizenship; the skills to research further into the topic; and a method by which students can influence and take responsible action. The project team developed resources and events involving young people from a wide range of local and other communities.

The thinking about the evaluation of the project was influenced by the tradition of condensed fieldwork (SAFARI, 1974) and illuminative evaluation (Parlett and Hamilton, 1976: 89). It is strongly related to other research in which collaboration between researchers and practitioners is deemed necessary and valuable (Harland and Kinder, 1989) and was mindful of the need to avoid an overly individualist approach to research methods (see Biesta and Lawy, 2006). Prior to the beginning of the three-year project a feasibility study took place to investigate what was currently happening for citizenship education, what plans had already been made for the future and what (if anything) would be preferred if a project were to be established to promote democratic thinking and participation. The findings and recommendations emerging from this feasibility study were later published (Davies and Evans, 2002). In the main, project data were collected from six schools, including one special school, a college of further and higher education, ten community organisations; the project advisory group, representatives of the funding body and managing institution, and project staff.

The practical work undertaken in the form of projects supplied the key point of interest for the evaluation team. Samples of young people (reflecting, broadly, the range of age and gender of those involved) and other key personnel within the initiative (e.g. a coordinating teacher) were the principal sources of data. Interview data from young people were normally achieved through focus groups. Observations of at least four mini-project events took place each year. The evaluation team took into account other evidence such as the amount and nature of media coverage.

It is important to clarify the style of evaluation. First, we aimed to establish a collaborative approach between the project team and evaluation team. Second the feedback given by the evaluators occurred throughout the project as attempts were made to avoid simple summative statements. Third, although we include references to the numbers of people involved to give a sense of the scale of the project, we were keen to avoid placing too great an emphasis on potentially misleading quantitative data. We wanted to develop a sense of the context that was significant for the work of the project while devoting particular attention to the meaning of precise initiatives. As such we were prepared to see a project that had broad goals with a gradually developing sense of its characterisation of citizenship; we respected the project team's advice about what would be analysed in depth; and we did not attempt to undertake potentially misleading activities in which, for example, we would evaluate impact merely by noting the numbers of people that had been affected, perhaps superficially, by the project. This approach allowed us to see what project staff could do and to help them reflect on what that work meant and how it could be further developed.

There were two main aspects to the process of data gathering. First, discussions between the project team and evaluators led to sampling of activities with data from the lead adult, representative young people, written material (hard copy or electronically based) and observations of key events. We wanted to look at activities that were current, were contributing over time to different aspects of citizenship, and in which the project team were attempting a variety of strategies to promote engagement. Second, at the end of each academic year, all citizenship coordinators in the schools in the local area were surveyed (including the target six schools as well as others which had fewer formal expectations in relation to project aims). Interviews were conducted with people who had continuous involvement with the overall project (i.e. one formal interview with one member of the project team, members of the advisory group and funder). The questionnaire and interview schedules focused on the perceptions of project aims, the involvement (extent and type) of young people and adults, organisational matters including the development and use of resources, and the challenges. All interviews and questionnaires explicitly included the encouragement of open-ended responses.

The process of data analysis involved four stages: the generation of categories and initial interim reports produced by one member of the evaluation team; a second person reviewed all the data and then met with the author of the draft paper to suggest revisions; that revised paper was then discussed with the project team and without further modification presented to the steering group for discussion (involving the project team). The interim reports were written with a developing sense of what was being achieved by the project team and the final report was again drawn up by one person, checked by a second member of the evaluation team and presented as a final report. In particular the argument and the representative nature of the selected quotations were regarded as key features for discussion as drafts were modified.

The above does not indicate work that cannot be challenged. It is not purely objective or to everyone's taste in terms of its educational goals. It is, though, an honest attempt to help develop educational practice that is deliberately designed to achieve specific identifiable goals and to reflect on the extent those goals were achieved. It is not narrowly asserting that some form of pure truth or particular notion of justice has been targeted, but rather that the research had both these objectives in mind in an implicit sense. This was messier, more practical but, hopefully, helped in the development of fair and useful processes and outcomes which have been accurately reported and discussed.

Conclusion

All (or almost all) university-based education researchers (and many others) are committed to truth and justice. Within a democratic society there are in reality few who wish to ignore either or both. Truth and justice are not incompatible. Instead heated debates develop among researchers principally by reference to and because of rather practical matters as discussed above. When those arguments occur researchers cast their position in relation to truth and justice (and are right to do so in the sense that these things are what really matters). They are not, however, convincing when they argue that other researchers are fundamentally opposed to what they are doing. Thrupp (2006) has raised issues about the nature of social justice research in which there may be a complex

picture involving interplay between utopians who emphasise justice and rationalists who emphasise the quality of research. In practice these positions are not as exclusive as is sometimes suggested. It is necessary to identify common ground between education researchers, and take issue with the extent to which the dichotomy between truth and social justice may serve to detract from, or complicate, other concerns which are highly significant in the day-to-day experience of professional researchers. One way to appease these contentions is to make clear the boundaries between, and the relationship between, broad commitments to truth and justice and more day-to-day issues which impact on education research. Through disentangling such issues, and seeking to understand the multifarious and complex connections, educational researchers will be better placed to conceptualise the field and to identify and employ appropriate methodologies.

Suggested further reading

Evans, R. (2002) *Telling Lies About Hitler: History, the Holocaust and the David Irving Trial*. London: Verso. This book tells the fascinating story of David Irving's libel suit against historian Deborah Lipstadt. Evans explores the issues that led to Irving losing the case and as such losing anything of a reputation that he had left as a historian. The very challenging issues raised at the trial related to the need for historians to tell the truth about the past. This seemingly obvious point raises by implication (at the very least) issues about what is regarded as truth and the extent to which deeply held values may be asserted.

Harvard University's 'Justice' with Michael Sandel: http://www.justiceharvard.org/. Michael Sandel's course on justice at Harvard University is internationally renowned. He deals with the big questions of justice, equality, democracy and morality. Sandel is an excellent communicator and this very lively website is full of engaging resources dealing with controversial challenges. Stimulating video material provides insights into key issues to do with truth and justice and how they may be debated and resolved.

Weis, L. and Fine, M. (eds) (2004) *Working Method: Research and Social Justice*. London, Routledge. In the introduction to this book the editors explain that they offer 'a theory of method for conducting critical theoretical and analytic work on social (in)justice . . . we have tried to write with communities under siege and to document the costs of oppression and the strengths of endurance that circulate among poor and working-class youth and young adults in America'. This is a good example of a book that explicitly attempts to do the sort of research that matters to the authors and to do it in ways that reflects their conception of social justice.

References

Andrews, R. (2005) 'The place of systematic reviews in education research', *British Journal of Educational Studies*, 53(4): 399–416.

Appleby, J., Hunt, L. and Jacobs, M. (1994) *Telling the Truth about History*. London: Norton.

Barnhouse Walters, P., Lareau, A. and Ranis, S. H. (eds) (2009) *Education Research on Trial: Policy Reform and the Call for Scientific Rigor*. New York: Routledge.

Biesta, G. and Lawy, R. (2006) 'From teaching citizenship to learning democracy: overcoming individualism in research, policy and practice', *Cambridge Journal of Education*, 36(1): 63–79.

Canandine, D. (1987) 'British history: past, present and future', *Past and Present*, 116: 169–91.

Carnell, E., MacDonald, J., McCallum, B. and Scott, M. (2008) *Passion and Politics: Academics Reflect on Writing for Publication*. London: Institute of Education.

Davies, I. and Evans, M. (2002) 'Encouraging active citizenship', *Educational Review*, 54(1): 69–78.

Davies, I., Flanagan, B., Hogarth, S., Mountford, P. and Philpott, J. (2009) 'Asking questions about participation', *Education, Citizenship and Social Justice*, 4(1): 25–40.

Evans, R. (2002) *Telling Lies About Hitler: History, the Holocaust and the David Irving Trial*. London: Verso.

Gillborn, D. (2008) *Racism and Education: Coincidence or Conspiracy?* London: Routledge.

Gorard, S. (2000) *Education and Social Justice: The Changing Composition of Schools and Its Implications*. Cardiff: University of Wales Press.

Gorard, S. (2008) 'Research impact is not always a good thing: a re-consideration of rates of "social mobility" in Britain', *British Journal of Sociology of Education*, 29(3): 317–24.

Gorard, S., See, B. H. and Shaheen, R. (2009) 'Educating for citizenship: some lessons from England 2008', *Citizenship Teaching and Learning*, 5(1): 35–45.

Griffiths, M. (1998) *Educational Research and Social Justice: Getting Off the Fence*. Buckingham: Open University Press.

Hahn, C. and Alviar-Martin, T. (2008) 'International political socialization research', in Levstik, L. S. and Tyson, C. A. (eds) *Handbook of Research in Social Studies Education*. New York: Routledge, pp. 81–108.

Hammersley, M. (2001) 'On "systematic" reviews of research literatures: a "narrative" response to Evans & Benefield', *British Educational Research Journal*, 27: 543–54.

Harland, J. and Kinder, K. (1989) 'Can Evaluation Contribute to an Improvement in Practice?' Unpublished paper presented to the Education Research Group, University of York, 5 November.

Jenkins, K. (1991) *Re-Thinking History*. London: Routledge.

Jenkins, K. (1995) *On 'What is History?'* London: Routledge.

Lucas, L. (2006) *The Research Game in Academic Life*. Maidenhead: Society for Research in Higher Education/ Open University.

MacLure M. (2005) '"Clarity bordering on stupidity": where's the quality in systematic review?', *Journal of Education Policy*, 20: 393–416.

Mirza, M. (1995) 'Some ethical dilemmas in fieldwork: feminist and antiracist methodologies', in Griffiths, M. and Troyna, B. (eds) *Antiracism, Culture And Social Justice in Education*. Stoke-on-Trent: Trentham Books.

Parlett, M. and Hamilton, D. (1976) 'Evaluation as illumination', in Towney, D. (ed.) *Curriculum Evaluation Today: Trends and Implications*. London: Macmillan Education.

Rose, N. (1999) *Powers of Freedom*. Cambridge: Cambridge University Press.

SAFARI (1974) *Innovation, Evaluation, Research and the Problem of Control: Some Interim Papers*. Norwich: Safari Project Centre of Applied Research in Education, University of East Anglia.

Thrupp, M. (2006) 'Editorial', *British Journal of Educational Studies*, 54(3) 269–71.

Torgerson, C. J., Torgerson, D. J., Birks, Y. F. and Porthouse, J. (2005) 'A comparison of randomized controlled trials in health and education', *British Educational Research Journal*, 31(6): 767–91.

Tymms, P. B., Merrell, C. and Coe, R. J. (2008) 'Educational policies and randomized controlled trials', *Psychology of Education Review*, 32(2): 3–7 and 26–9.

Weis, L. and Fine, M. (eds) (2004) *Working Method: Research and Social Justice*. Abingdon: Routledge.

15

Surveys and longitudinal research

Anna Vignoles

Longitudinal data and research designs

There are various different types of data that a researcher can use. Cross-section data are the most common type, which are data collected at one point in time. Examples of cross-section data include the Labour Force Survey,[1] which tells you about people currently in the UK labour market, or opinion polls, which tell you about people's opinions at a given point in time. Another type of data that is collected over several points in time, such as throughout a person's life, is called longitudinal data. Longitudinal data are extremely useful for research purposes because they help researchers to better address issues of causality.

To take a specific example, imagine you want to determine whether unemployment causes poor health. If you use cross-section data, you will be able to determine whether people who are currently unemployed also have poor health. You will not, however, be able to tell whether unemployment actually leads to poor health. Longitudinal data by contrast can tell you whether the health problem occurred before the period of unemployment rather than the other way around. Of course cross-section surveys can always ask respondents about the past. In this example, one could ask the respondent whether the spell of unemployment came about after the health problem started. However, retrospectively asking

people about things that happened a long time ago is often unreliable.

Longitudinal data can enable the researcher to model the impact of an event at one point in time on outcomes that happen later in an attempt to determine cause and effect. A longitudinal research design can be used with either qualitative or quantitative survey data and a discussion of both types of data can be found in Creswell (2003). With quantitative data, there are numerous complex statistical and econometric models that can be used to improve the researcher's ability to establish causality using longitudinal data (see, for example, Baltagi, 2001, or for an easier introduction to some basic longitudinal models see Gujarati, 2003).

Applications of longitudinal research designs

Longitudinal research designs are often used in policy research, i.e. when the government has introduced a particular policy and wants to determine whether it has had a positive effect. If one simply uses cross-section data to undertake policy evaluation it is often not clear whether the policy is actually causing a positive effect as both the implementation of the policy and the outcome are observed simultaneously. Ideally one might use an experiment to measure the impact of a particular policy. So if, for instance, the government wants to introduce a parenting support programme, one might randomly allocate mothers to the programme or to a control group (a group that does not get the programme). One could then compare the outcomes of children whose mothers went through the programme with the outcomes of children whose mothers did not. Since the mothers are allocated randomly to the programme one can say with some certainty that if their children do better than those whose mothers did not go through the programme, the policy is having a positive impact. If mothers were not allocated randomly to the programme but rather *chose* to participate, there would be concern that better mothers are more likely to choose to take the programme and hence their children will do better not due to the programme but rather because their mothers are inherently better at parenting.

However, a purely experimental approach is often not feasible in real-world policy-making. For instance, in our example it would not necessarily be seen as fair to randomly allocate some mums to receive help while others lose out. If an experiment is not possible, one might instead adopt a longitudinal research design. In this instance one would survey the mothers and their children prior to the programme and then see if the children of mothers who took the programme *make more progress* than children of mothers who did not. Even if the behaviour of children whose mothers participated in the programme is better to start with, the longitudinal approach will take this into account by measuring differences in the progress made by children in the programme and those who did not participate (this modelling approach is called difference in difference).

This is just one example of an application of longitudinal research design, and some further practical illustrations are given below after discussion of data issues.

Data

There are different types of longitudinal data and the terminology can be confusing. One important type of longitudinal data is cohort data, which are data collected over time about a group of individuals of the same age. These data are powerful when analysing factors that impact over the life course (e.g. the impact of education on later earnings). Cohort data only provide information on one cohort, however, and cannot be used to study events that may affect different cohorts differently (e.g. economic recessions). Panel data are collected over time about a group of individuals of mixed ages and enable us to determine both time and cohort effects, such as the impact of a recession on different age groups. Both types of data are generally collected using survey methods.

Longitudinal data does suffer from some difficulties. When surveying individuals throughout their lives with long gaps between surveys, longitudinal surveys require individuals to remember events that happened in the past. This is problematic as there may be recall bias, i.e. when individuals do not recall an event a long time in the past accurately. Cross-section data always suffers from this potential problem. Longitudinal data is also extremely costly to collect as one has to follow the same individuals or families or schools over a long period of time. Remaining in touch with these subjects over time is problematic. Furthermore, some people will drop out of the study, leading longitudinal studies to suffer from what is known as attrition (see Olsen, 2005, for a full discussion).

Despite these limitations, longitudinal survey data remain a powerful tool for research, as illustrated by the applications discussed in the next section.

Applications of longitudinal research

One practical application of a longitudinal research design is some recent work undertaken by Chowdry et al. (2010) to identify the determinants of higher education (HE) participation. The research was asking: why are poorer children less likely to enroll in HE? This work made use of a series of linked English administrative data sets to construct a longitudinal record of each individual pupil's schooling. The study used longitudinal data on two cohorts of students (each cohort had around half a million pupils each), with information on their schooling dating back to primary school. A longitudinal research design was crucial since there is clear evidence from other studies that socio-economic gaps in education achievement emerge early in children's lives (Cunha and Heckman, 2007). Hence it was essential that the research made use of data on children's early childhood achievement in order to understand why they did not go to university.

The research followed two cohorts of students in England – those who took GCSEs in 2001–2 and 2002–3 – from age 11 to age 20. The findings from this research indicated that there are extremely large differences in the likelihood of going to university for students with different socio-economic backgrounds. As illustrated in Figure 15.1, the likelihood of a young person going to university is considerably higher if they come from a less deprived family background.

However, the research also indicated that the large gaps in HE participation between rich and poor students substantially reduced once allowance was made (in a longitudinal model) for pupils' prior attainment in both primary and secondary school. Figure 15.2 on p. 117 shows that the likelihood of going to university for poor and rich students is quite similar

for a given A level point score. Hence if a poor student achieves well in primary and secondary school, ending up with a good set of A levels, they have a similar chance of going to university as compared to a richer student. This suggests that poor attainment in primary and secondary schools is more important in explaining lower HE participation rates among students from disadvantaged backgrounds than barriers arising at the point of entry into HE. These findings highlight the need for earlier policy intervention to raise HE participation rates among disadvantaged youth.

The above example is one of many studies that have made use of longitudinal research designs in the field of education. Another example is work investigating the impact of education on individuals' earnings. This work aims to measure the genuinely causal impact of education on earnings. This is difficult to do as individuals who are socially advantaged and more able also tend to get more education. Such advantaged people would earn more in the labour market with or without this education and hence getting at the causal impact of education on earnings is problematic. One

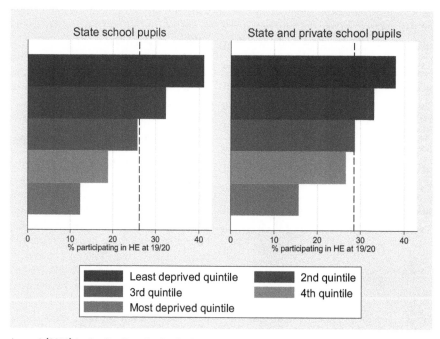

Source: See Chowdry et al. (2010) for details of how deprivation is measured in this study.

Figure 15.1 The likelihood of enrolling in HE by socio-economic background

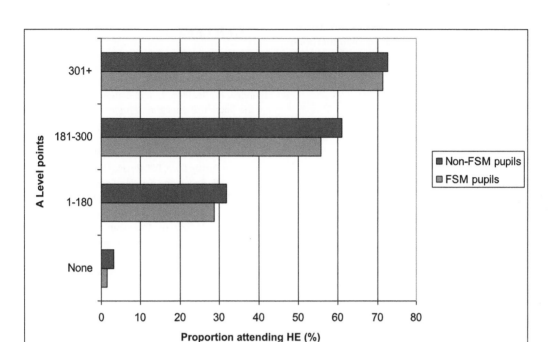

Figure 15.2   The likelihood of going to university for FSM and non-FSM pupils

approach to overcome this methodological challenge is to have longitudinal data on individuals' family background and early IQ/ability and use this to identify the additional impact of education on earnings. A key study that used this approach with British cohort data (the 1958 National Child Development Study) is Blundell et al. (2005). They showed that education has a genuinely causal impact on individuals' wages, over and above any impact from ability and family background.

Longitudinal research designs have also been used in child development research. A number of studies have examined the impact of different childcare settings on children's cognitive and non-cognitive achievement. In the US, Currie and Thomas (1995) looked at the impact of a parenting programme called HeadStart on children's cognitive achievement. Sylva et al. (2004) did the same for the UK's SureStart programme. Both these studies required information not just on the child's involvement in the programme but also details of their family background and early

ability, to allow for other differences between children that might explain differences in outcomes. Both studies found positive effects from these programmes.

Longitudinal research designs have been used in school effectiveness research. The difficulty of establishing the impact of schools on pupil performance using a cross section has long been recognised. In a cross section, the researcher simply observes that some schools have high performing pupils and others low performing pupils. One needs longitudinal data to measure the progress made by pupils in different schools before one can deduce that some schools are more effective than others (Goldstein and Blatchford, 1998).

Conclusion

The examples discussed above illustrate the powerful way in which a longitudinal research design, along with quantitative or qualitative longitudinal data, can help researchers identify the causal impact of government policy. While longitudinal data has its own methodological challenges such as attrition, there is no doubt that rich longitudinal data and longitudinal methods of analysis often enable researchers to get much closer to establishing causal relationships.

Note

1. Although this survey also has a longitudinal element over five quarters.

Suggested further reading

Dale, A. and Davies, R. B. (1994) *Analyzing Social and Political Change*. Online at: http://srmo.sagepub.com/view/analyzing-social-and-political-change/n2.xml?rskey=kWinQS. This book includes a number of excellent chapters which provide empirical applications of longitudinal research methods and tell the reader how one goes about analysing socio-economic and political change.

Kalaian, S. A. and Kasim, R. M. (2008) 'Longitudinal studies', in Lavrakas, P. (ed.) *Encyclopedia of Survey Research Methods*. Online at: http://srmo.sagepub.com/view/encyclopedia-of-survey-research-methods/n280.xml?rskey=UYmFQo. This online encyclopaedia provides a number of concise entries on the major research methods. Of particular relevance is this entry on longitudinal studies by Kalaian and Kasim.

Ployhart, R. and Vandenberg, R. J. (2010) 'Longitudinal research: the theory, design, and analysis of change', *Journal of Management*, 36(1): 94–120. An article covering not just a description of how one might use longitudinal data in research but, more specifically, effective longitudinal research design.

Ruspini, E. (2003) 'Longitudinal research', in Miller, R. L. and Brewer, J. D. (eds) *The A–Z of Social Research*. Online at: http://srmo.sagepub.com/view/the-a-z-of-social-research/n1.xml?rskey=uuzhGh. This dictionary provides an accessible introduction to longitudinal research and is used widely in undergraduate and postgraduate teaching of research methods.

References

Baltagi, B. (2001) *Econometric Analysis of Panel Data*. Chichester: John Wiley & Sons.

Blundell, R., Dearden, L. and Sianesi, B. (2005) 'Evaluating the impact of education on earnings in the UK: models, methods and results', *Journal of the Royal Statistical Society, Series A*, 168(3): 473–512.

Bound, J., Brown, C. and Mathiowetz, N. (2001) *Measurement Error in Survey Data*, PSC Research Report No. 00-450. Ann Arbor, MI: Population Studies Center at the Institute for Social Research, University of Michigan.

Chowdry, C., Crawford, C., Dearden, L., Goodman, A. and Vignoles, A. (2010) *Widening Participation in Higher Education: Analysis Using Linked Administrative Data*, Department of Quantitative Social Science Working Paper No. 8. Institute of Education. Available at: http://repec.ioe.ac.uk/REPEc/pdf/qsswp1008.pdf (accessed 7 November 2011).

Creswell, J. W. (2003) *Research Design: Qualitative, Quantitative, and Mixed Methods Approaches*. Thousand Oaks, CA and London: Sage.

Cunha, F. and Heckman, J. (2007) 'The technology of skill formation', *American Economic Review*, 92: 31–47.

Currie, J. and Thomas, D. (1995) 'Does Head Start make a difference?', *American Economic Review*, 85(3): 341–64.

Goldstein, H. and Blatchford, P. (1998) 'Class size and educational achievement: a review of methodology with particular reference to study design', *British Educational Research Journal*, 24(3): 255–67.

Gujarati, D. N. (2003) *Basic Econometrics*. New York: McGraw-Hill.

Olsen, R. J. (2005) 'The problem of respondent attrition: survey methodology is key', *Monthly Labor Review*, February.

Ruspini, E. (2002) *Introduction to Longitudinal Research*. London: Routledge.

Sylva, K., Melhuish, E., Sammons, P., Siraj-Blatchford, I. and Taggart, B. (2004) *The Effective Provision of Pre-School Education (EPPE) Project: Final Report. A Longitudinal Study Funded by the DfES 1997–2004*. London: Department for Education and Skills.

Statistical and correlational techniques

Stephen Gorard

Introduction

This chapter presents a simple introduction to using numbers in education research, illustrating a few of the many and varied research questions that can be addressed with numeric evidence. The chapter clarifies that using numbers involves no kind of paradigmatic or epistemological assumptions – these are just red herrings. Some common sources of data and methods of analysis are outlined, before a simple example is presented from my own work. The bulk of the analysis was completed under my supervision by a Masters student in less than two months and has already led to several articles in high-prestige journals. Shorn of the schismic and other barriers that some commentators write about apparently instead of doing research itself, doing research is really rather easy. And this is true even of work involving large-scale numeric datasets. The chapter ends by suggesting a few further applications of similar simple techniques.

Statistical and correlational research

It is not possible to do justice to all of the approaches that might come under the heading of statistical and correlational research in a chapter of this brevity. There *is* a sub-set of statistical work that is based on random sampling theory and that is intended to help analysts estimate whether a result they have for a random sample is also true for the population from which that sample was drawn. I do not intend to cover this kind of work here for a number of reasons. The whole approach is often unrealistic since true random samples are so rare and because it relies on a number of prior assumptions about measurement accuracy and a complete response rate that are even rarer in practice. I also believe the approach to be based on a fundamental error of confusing the probability of the data observed given a pre-specified hypothesis with the probability of that hypothesis being true given the data observed. The two values are very different, and one cannot be converted into the others without a third and unknown value (Gorard, 2010a). Finally, the approach is very limited in only being concerned with generalisability to a population. It does not help analysts decide the really important point, which is whether the result is substantively important (and this is what they have to do subsequently, whether they want to generalise that conclusion or not).

So, in this chapter I focus on the latter issue which is common to, and faced by, all analysts at some stage. And when I say all analysts, I do mean all. The same kind of judgement about the importance and robustness of a numeric result is made when considering a non-numeric result (Gorard, 2010b). This logic of analysis is universal, and there are no paradigmatic differences in education research, any more than there are in real life. Take something everyday like the use-by date on food products in the UK. This is numeric information that requires no epistemological commitment or paradigmatic beliefs. Stores can use it to ensure produce is fresh and customers can use it to help decide whether to buy the product. All will realise, if they think about it, that the date could be in error (mislabelled in printing for example), that nothing dramatic happens on that date (it is a limit stamped onto a continuous process of food becoming less fresh over time), that due to circumstances (like poor storage) the food may be beyond use before that date, and otherwise that much foodstuff is still safely edible the day after the use-by date. A customer using the date information to decide whether to buy or eat the product makes a subjective judgement. This, in summary, is what numeric analysis in social science also involves, and very similar steps can be used to describe textual and all other analyses. For example, a textual analyst knows that what they read could be a misprint, it could represent exactly what the writer intended to convey or it could be an attempt to mislead. In coding, they must make a subjective judgement about what the text portrays and hope that this does not mislead their own readers, and so on.

However, some different techniques of analysis *are* differentially suitable for certain kinds of research questions. Correlational research, for example, addresses questions about the relationship between two or more variables, and the extent to which they co-vary. The most commonly used technique for correlation/regression is based on the Pearson's R correlation coefficient. An R score of 1 means perfect correlation or even identity, an R of −1 means perfect inverse, and an R of 0 means no correlation at all between the two variables. Usually you will uncover R values between these extremes. (See my Chapter 43 on 'Multiple Linear Regression' in this volume or Gorard (2001) for further explanation of correlation coefficients and examples of using Pearson's R.)

Correlation is the basis of many more advanced techniques for analysis, such as factor analysis, regression and structural equation modelling. Here it is used to help see the possible common patterns in 12 trends over time.

An example: correlational research

Previous international work has shown that clustering pupils with similar characteristics in particular schools yields no clear academic benefit and can be disadvantageous to pupils both socially and personally (Gorard and Smith, 2010). Understanding how and why this clustering happens, and how it may be reduced, is therefore important for policy. Yet previous work has tended to focus on only one kind of clustering at a time. In the USA, for example, black–white segregation of pupils has been the key issue. In the UK, and across Europe, the focus has been on social background, especially on the clustering or segregation in specific schools of pupils living in poverty. In the UK, segregation by poverty has been considered an outcome of the regional stratification of economic activity, housing prices and social housing policies, increased diversity of schools and the process of school place allocation (Gorard et al., 2003). There is also evidence that changes in the overall number of schools, and changes in the prevalence of poverty, are related to the precise level of local segregation. In the limited sense that segregation other than by poverty (such as by ethnicity) has been considered in the UK, it has been assumed that the same kinds of reasons apply. So the assumption has been that segregation by ethnicity and by poverty have the same determinants. But is this true? Is there one process, perhaps involving a number of indicators of disadvantage, that clusters similar pupils together in schools however their similarity is measured? Or do these factors operate differently, or perhaps not operate at all, in separate processes of segregation depending on which pupil characteristics are considered?

The new analysis presented here is based on figures from the Annual Schools Census (ASC) for all state-funded secondary schools in England. It used official school-level figures for the number of full-time equivalent pupils on roll in each school for January

Table 16.1   Segregation 1996–2009, all indicators, secondary schools in England

	1996	1997	1998	1999	2000	2001	2002	2003	2004	2005	2006	2007	2008	2009
FSM takeup D	0.35	0.34	0.35	0.36	0.37	0.37	0.39	0.38	0.38	0.38	0.39	0.39	0.38	0.38
FSM takeup GS	0.30	0.30	0.31	0.32	0.33	0.33	0.34	0.34	0.34	0.34	0.35	0.35	0.35	0.34
FSM eligible D	0.38	0.38	0.38	0.39	0.39	0.39	0.39	0.39	0.39	0.40	0.39	0.39	0.39	0.39
FSM eligible GS	0.31	0.31	0.32	0.32	0.33	0.33	0.33	0.34	0.34	0.34	0.34	0.34	0.34	0.33
SEN statement D	0.30	–	0.28	0.28	0.27	0.27	0.27	0.26	0.25	0.25	0.24	0.24	0.25	0.25
SEN statement GS	0.29	–	0.28	0.27	0.27	0.26	0.26	0.25	0.25	0.24	0.24	0.24	0.24	0.24
SEN no statement D	0.32	–	0.28	0.26	0.25	0.25	0.27	0.28	0.27	0.26	0.26	0.26	0.26	0.26
SEN no statement GS	0.27	–	0.24	0.22	0.21	0.21	0.22	0.24	0.24	0.23	0.22	0.22	0.22	0.21
Non-white D	–	0.68	0.67	0.65	0.65	0.64	0.65	0.59	0.57	0.55	0.54	0.54	0.54	0.55
Non-white GS	–	0.60	0.60	0.56	0.56	0.55	0.54	0.48	0.46	0.45	0.44	0.43	0.43	0.43
ESL D	–	–	–	–	0.70	0.70	–	0.66	0.66	0.66	0.64	0.63	0.63	0.63
ESL GS	–	–	–	–	0.65	0.64	–	0.61	0.60	0.60	0.59	0.56	0.56	0.55

Notes:

Figures are presented to only two decimal places for ease of reading.

The DfE figures for SEN in 1997 are only half those of 1996 and 1998, yielding much higher levels of segregation. They cannot be correct, and so we exclude them from our analysis.

DfE can provide no figures for first language in 2002. Ethnicity was collected from 1997 onwards, and language from 2000 onwards.

of each year, the number eligible for and taking free school meals (FSM) which is a measure of family poverty, and those with a declared additional or special educational need with or without a statement (SEN), in each minority ethnic group, and those speaking a first language other than English. These are all indicators of possible educational disadvantage. For each indicator, there are two estimates of how clustered each pupil characteristic is. These estimates are the Gorard segregation index (GS) and the dissimilarity index (D). The two indices are very similar, with a higher value (nearer one) representing a very segregated system, while both would be zero if all schools have their proportionate share of potentially disadvantaged pupils. There is no space here to explain

the calculation of these indices in more detail (but see Gorard et al., 2003; or Cheng and Gorard, 2010). The six indicators of disadvantage each summarised in two indices yield 12 measures of pupil segregation between schools which have been tracked for 14 years from 1996 to 2009.

The trends in between-school segregation, in terms of pupil backgrounds from 1996 to 2009, show several different characteristics (Table 16.1). Both indices (GS and D) tend to give very similar results for each indicator. However, the levels of clustering between schools in terms of different indicators are very different. Segregation by poverty is about 0.3, meaning that around a third of pupils with free school meals would have to exchange schools for poverty to be distributed between schools in proportion to their size. Segregation by pupil special need is a little less than this but is of the same order of magnitude (around 0.28). Segregation by minority ethnic group and for those not speaking English as a first language is around twice these values, however (0.6 or more). Another difference is that segregation by FSM increased from 1996 to 2005/6 and subsequently dropped a little. All other indicators, on the other hand, have shown an annual decline in segregation.

So, perhaps there are three kinds of segregation going on here. The first is for FSM which shows a different level to ethnicity and language and a different trajectory of change over time to SEN. The second is SEN which shows a very different level of segregation to the third group of ethnicity and language but a similar trajectory over time. Why has segregation by poverty risen while segregation by ethnicity and language has fallen? Many of the kinds of factors that might affect segregation by poverty, including increased diversity in types of school or school closures, would surely also influence segregation in terms of other pupil characteristics. So are there genuinely different patterns of clustering in schools depending upon the kinds of pupil background measures used, with different determinants? One way of investigating this further is to calculate the *correlation* between the changes over time in each measure.

Table 16.2 shows the correlation coefficients for all 12 national measures of segregation over time (as in Table 16.1). A correlation of 1 means that the two variables are, in effect, measuring the same thing (like Centigrade and Fahrenheit for temperature). Of course, each variable has a correlation of 1 with itself (the shaded diagonal). We also learn from Table 16.2 that, for most practical purposes, the two indices of D and GS serve the same purpose. Whatever their theoretical differences, their values for each of the six indicators correlate very highly. Indeed, the correlation between D for segregation by free school meal take-up and GS for the same indicator is 1 (top left of table). The correlation between D for segregation by English as a second language and GS for the same indicator is +0.99 (bottom right of table).

Table 16.2 Correlations between trends in all 12 measures of segregation, secondary schools in England

	FSM takeup D	FSM takeup GS	FSM eligible D	FSM eligible GS	SEN statement D	SEN statement GS	SEN no statement D	SEN no statement GS	Non-white D	Non-white GS	ESL D	ESL GS
FSM takeup D	1	1	0.79	0.96	−0.93	−0.93	−0.54	−0.47	−0.82	−0.87	−0.83	−0.79
FSM takeup GS	1	1	0.79	0.97	−0.95	−0.95	−0.58	−0.51	−0.86	−0.89	−0.86	−0.82
FSM eligible D	0.79	0.79	1	0.89	−0.7	−0.72	−0.62	−0.47	−0.54	−0.54	0.29	0.36
FSM eligible GS	0.96	0.97	0.89	1	−0.96	−0.97	−0.65	−0.55	−0.87	−0.89	−0.66	−0.61
SEN statement D	−0.93	−0.95	−0.7	−0.96	1	1	0.59	0.53	0.97	0.98	0.88	0.84
SEN statement GS	−0.93	−0.95	−0.72	−0.97	1	1	0.6	0.54	0.96	0.97	0.86	0.82
SEN no statement D	−0.54	−0.58	−0.62	−0.65	0.59	0.6	1	0.98	0.07	0.05	−0.2	−0.16
SEN no statement GS	−0.47	−0.51	−0.47	−0.55	0.53	0.54	0.98	1	0.03	0.01	−0.02	0.03
Non-white D	−0.82	−0.86	−0.54	−0.87	0.97	0.96	0.07	0.03	1	0.99	0.92	0.89
Non-white GS	−0.87	−0.89	−0.54	−0.89	0.98	0.97	0.05	0.01	0.99	1	0.94	0.92
ESL D	−0.83	−0.86	0.29	−0.66	0.88	0.86	−0.2	−0.02	0.92	0.94	1	0.99
ESL GS	−0.79	−0.82	0.36	−0.61	0.84	0.82	−0.16	0.03	0.89	0.92	0.99	1

Table 16.3   Correlations between trends in all six indicators, using GS index of segregation, secondary schools in England

	FSM takeup	FSM eligible	SEN statement	SEN no statement	Non-white	ESL
FSM takeup	1	0.97	−0.95	−0.51	−0.89	−0.82
FSM eligible	0.97	1	−0.97	−0.55	−0.89	−0.61
SEN statement	−0.95	−0.97	1	0.54	0.97	0.82
SEN no statement	−0.51	−0.55	0.54	1	0.01	0.03
Non-white	−0.89	−0.89	0.97	0.01	1	0.92
ESL	−0.82	−0.61	0.82	0.03	0.92	1

For ease of analysis, therefore, Table 16.3 shows the same values as 16.2 but with the duplication of indices eliminated (only GS is retained). For a fuller analysis, see Gorard and Cheng (2011). What becomes clearer in this simplified table is that the values of GS for free school meal take-up and for eligibility are very strongly related (top left of table). Whichever way we measure free school meals, the results and their correlations with the other four indicators are similar. So using correlation, making some justifiable assumptions about correlations near 1 and ignoring FSM eligibility, we have 'reduced' 12 measures to five only. This kind of data reduction can make seeing the patterns in the data much easier.

A fairer estimate of the strength of the relationship between any two variables is the effect size found by squaring the R correlation coefficient. R-squared shows how much of the variance in one variable is common to the other. Table 16.4 shows the R-squared

values from Table 16.3, but ignoring the second measure of free school meals. Many of these values are very small. For example, the R-squared between special needs with no statement and non-white ethnic origin is 0.0001. All such values less than 0.5 have been ignored for ease of analysis. What Table 16.4 now makes clear is that measures of segregation by special needs with no statement are unrelated to any other measure used here. This is a somewhat different and more sophisticated analytical conclusion than that suggested by Table 16.1 which initially led to both indicators of SEN being treated together (see above). This finding could be important, because it suggests that whatever causes changes in segregation by SEN without statements is not the same thing that causes segregation by poverty, language and ethnicity.

The other four indicators have substantial variance in common over time, and so it may be that whatever causes change in these values has some similarity for

Table 16.4   R-squared between trends in five indicators, using GS index of segregation, secondary schools in England

	FSM takeup	SEN statement	SEN no statement	Non-white	ESL
FSM takeup	1	0.90	–	0.79	0.67
SEN statement	0.90	1	–	0.94	0.67
SEN no statement	–	–	1	–	–
Non-white	0.79	0.94	–	1	0.84
ESL	0.67	0.67	–	0.84	1

Note: Values less than 0.5 have been suppressed.

all of them. The values for free school meal segregation and the other three measures are negatively related (see Table 16.3), which means that whatever drives changes does so in opposite directions for these two groups of indicators. It is reasonable to assume, for simplicity at present, that whatever causes segregation by ethnic origin is also related to what causes segregation by language in England. Segregation of pupils from families living in poverty (FSM) is to some extent a separate process from segregation by language/ethnicity, having a very different scale and a near opposite trend over time, and to some extent it is an inverse. So, their determinants might be related but in an opposite direction, although this seems an unlikely situation. For example, if selection by aptitude is a process likely to segregate pupils by poverty, it seems unlikely that it would also *desegregate* them by language/ethnicity (since origin and socio-economic status (SES) are often strongly related).

Although simple, this is a valuable analysis which will assist in the search for the causes of, and so the solutions to, segregation by disadvantage in schools because it shows that the clustering of pupils with similar characteristics in schools is not just one process, but at least two. It is important because segregation is important, and because understanding how it occurs is a key part of overcoming its dangers. What these processes are and how they differ cannot be estimated using these same data, so as usual numeric analysis is not the end of an investigation but merely the start of a more detailed study.

Suggested further reading

Department for Education, England, School Performance Tables – online at: http://www.education.gov.uk/performancetables/. This fantastic UK website provides data relevant to the performance of every school and college in England for as many years as these are available. Try some of the ideas in this chapter, by correlating scores for schools over time, for progress from one formal assessment to another, or examine the results in terms of other useful data provided, such as the level of student absence. Many other countries will have their own versions of this dataset.

Gigerenzer, G. (2002) *Reckoning with Risk*. London: Penguin. This is a brilliant book for anyone who wants to think more clearly about numbers and the use of numeric evidence in social science. It shows how experts and advisers frequently present real evidence in ways that are deeply misleading. And it does so in a way that is easy for any reader. Primary school arithmetic only required.

Gorard, S. (2001) *Quantitative Methods in Educational Research: The Role of Numbers Made Easy*, London: Continuum. This is a popular introduction to reasoning with statistics, including how to calculate and use correlations. The book has become a standard for many courses because it presents everything from the outset so simply and without the clutter of technical language.

References

Cheng, S. C. and Gorard, S. (2010) 'Segregation by poverty in secondary schools in England 2006–2009: a research note', *Journal of Education Policy*, 25(3): 415–18.

Gorard, S. (2001) *Quantitative Methods in Educational Research: The Role of Numbers Made Easy*. London: Continuum.

Gorard, S. (2010a) 'All evidence is equal: the flaw in statistical reasoning', *Oxford Review of Education*, 36(1): 63–77.

Gorard, S. (2010b) 'Research design, as independent of methods', in Teddlie, C. and Tashakkori, A. (eds) *Handbook of Mixed Methods*. Los Angeles: Sage.

Gorard, S. and Cheng, S. C. (2011) 'Pupil clustering in English secondary schools: one pattern or several?', *International Journal of Research and Method in Education* (in press).

Gorard, S. and Smith, E. (2010) *Equity in Education: An International Comparison of Pupil Perspectives*. London: Palgrave.

Gorard, S., Taylor, C. and Fitz, J. (2003) *Schools, Markets and Choice Policies*. London: RoutledgeFalmer.

Secondary data

Emma Smith

Introduction

This chapter provides a brief introduction to using secondary data in educational research. Secondary data analysis is a relatively under-used research technique in the field of education yet the potential for its use, among novice researchers in particular, is huge. From a nation's population census to public opinion polls about the outcome of TV talent show competitions, there are not many aspects of the social world that have not been covered by some type of survey or opinion poll. Indeed, it is very likely that whatever your research topic, the answers to at least some of your research questions can be found by analysing secondary data.

What is secondary data analysis?

Secondary data analysis is 'an empirical exercise carried out on data that has already been gathered or compiled in some way' (Dale et al., 1988: 3). In other words, it is an approach where the researcher analyses data which has already been collected, usually by someone else. The analysis may involve using the original, or novel, research questions, statistical approaches and theoretical frameworks. Secondary data comes in many forms. It can include the data generated from systematic reviews, through documentary analysis as well as the results from large-scale surveys such as the National Census or the Programme for International Student Assessment (PISA). Secondary data can be numeric or non-numeric. Non-numeric, or qualitative secondary data, can include data retrieved second-hand from interviews, ethnographic accounts, documents, photographs or conversations. In the UK, an excellent source of archived qualitative data is provided by the Economic and Social Data Service (ESDS) *Qualidata* facility. Data available through *Qualidata* includes in-depth interviews, field notes and observations, as well as personal documents. The service provides support and training, as well as access to classic postwar studies of British society including the research papers and data for Dennis Marsden and Brian Jackson's classic 1962 study, *Education and the Working Class*.

However, our interest in this chapter is with numeric secondary data, examples of which might include the following:

- census data such as the decennial National Population Census or annual school censuses;
- government surveys such as the Labour Force Survey or the ONS Opinions Survey;
- other regular or continuous surveys, such as the World Values Survey;
- cohort and other longitudinal studies, such as the Millennium Cohort Study;

- administrative data such as those collected on applications to UK higher education courses or by government organisations such as the Department for Education.

This focus on numeric secondary data is important. According to the Economic and Social Research Council (a key funder of training and research in the economic and social sciences in the UK) 'the lack of quantitative skills is endemic in many areas of Social Science' (ESRC, 2006: 12). Indeed quantitative social science in higher education is one of four strategically important and vulnerable subjects (SIVS) targeted by the government for additional support and training. However, as we shall show in this chapter, one of the key attractions of secondary data analysis is that you do not have to be a statistician to access and engage with this type of data. Some of the most powerful and useful analyses can be done by using relatively straightforward arithmetic techniques which are well within the capabilities of even the most stats-phobic educational researcher. In the next section we will briefly consider some of the advantages of the technique before providing some illustrations of how secondary data might be used in research.

The promises of secondary data analysis

The promises of secondary data analysis are many. It can allow researchers to access data on a scale that they could not hope to replicate first hand; and the technical expertise involved in developing good surveys and good datasets can lead to data that is of the highest quality. Secondary data can be analysed from different empirical or theoretical perspectives and in this way provides opportunities for the discovery of relationships not considered in the primary research. In addition secondary analysis is also a very democratic research method. The availability of low-cost, high-quality datasets means that secondary analysis can ensure that 'all researchers have the opportunity for empirical research that has tended to be the privilege of the few' (Hakim, 1982: 4). As 'it is the costs of data collection that are beyond the scope of the independent researcher, not the costs of data analysis' (Glaser, 1963: 12), the very accessibility of the data enables novice and other researchers to retain and develop a degree of independence. Often when researchers are employed on busy projects (or undertaking Masters or doctoral level study) there is limited time and resources to apply for grants or other funding and, if successful, there are likely to be difficulties in securing opportunities for fieldwork. By circumventing the data collection process, secondary analysis can enable novice researchers, including students, to gain valuable experience in undertaking independent research in an area of their own interest, as well as presenting opportunities to publish and present their findings as independent researchers. In this sense secondary data analysis has a valuable role in the capacity building of research skills as well as in developing an early career researcher's theoretical and substantive interests (for example, Smith, 2005, 2008). In the following section I will provide two examples of how secondary data might be used in educational research.

Using secondary data in mixed methods research

One excellent application of secondary data analysis is its use in mixed methods research. An example of this might be to use data from the UK National Census to characterise the population of the area in which a small-scale piece of work will take place; another might be to use secondary data to draw a sample from a larger population for more in-depth research.

The following illustrates the use of Census data to characterise the local population of an area which is the focus of a small-scale case study. This study is concerned with examining the interactions between users and providers who are involved in one Sure Start children's centre in one English city. Sure Start is an intervention aimed at providing integrated support for families by bringing together local childcare, early education, health and family services. Its range of programmes is primarily targeted at families living in disadvantaged areas in England. The study that is being introduced here involved a longitudinal examination of the experiences of the practitioners and users at the children's centre. In order to situate the study in the wider context of who might access the service in terms of their social and economic characteristics, a useful place to start is with the UK National Census data. Using a tool called CASWEB it is possible to access aggregate data from the 2001 Census (the most recent at the time of writing). Although a large range of data are available through CASWEB, in this example we only consider the ethnic composition of the area in which the Sure Start Centre is located. CASWEB is relatively straightforward to use and step-by-step instructions are provided to lead you through each stage in retrieving your data. The CASWEB homepage can be accessed from http://casweb.mimas.ac.uk/.

Table 17.1 Ethnic group composition of Sure Start location and city

	Sure Start location (%)	City (%)
White British	25	60
White Irish	0.6	1
White Other	0.8	2
White and Black Caribbean	0.9	1
White and Black African	0.1	0.2
White and Asian	1	0.7
White and Other	0.5	0.4
Indian	63	26
Pakistani	1	1
Bangladeshi	0.6	0.7
Asian Other	40	2
Caribbean	1	2
African	0.5	1
Black Other	0.2	0.2
Chinese	0.2	0.5
Other ethnic group	0.2	0.3
Total (N)	10,297	27,9921

Source: Census 2001.

The data presented in Table 17.1 were retrieved from CASWEB and can provide us with some basic contextual information about the local area that is covered by the Sure Start children's centre. The table shows us that the majority ethnic group in the Sure Start location is Indian (63%), compared with a white British majority in the city as a whole (60%). Only around a quarter of residents in the Sure Start area are of White British origin. The ethnic profile of the other residents of the Sure Start area suggests a predominately Asian population.

In addition to demographic data, CASWEB will also provide data on the health, housing and occupational characteristics of a local population. So, for example, it is possible to examine the composition of households in the Sure Start location in terms of how many children are present and the employment status of all adults. Thus this brief analysis will enable the researcher to provide an indication of the types of family that might be using the Sure Start centre and the extent to which they are representative of the wider city.

Data of this type could be very useful for providing a context to the more in-depth data that would be derived from more detailed accounts of life at the Sure Start centre. This sort of secondary data is also useful for providing a framework for drawing the sample for a study. For example, in the scenario just examined, if researchers wished to interview a sample of users or potential users of the children's centres, they might wish to ensure that their sample is representative of the local population. One way of doing this would be to ensure that a representative proportion of people of Indian origin were identified for inclusion in the study.

Using secondary data to monitor trends over time

The second example comes from my own recent research into participation in science subjects in higher education (Smith, 2010, 2011). Over the past few decades, there have been numerous initiatives to increase recruitment into the sciences (DCSF, 2006) particularly among groups, such as women and non-traditional age students, who have tended to be under-represented in many science subject areas. Using data on applications and acceptances to university it is possible to examine trends in the proportions of candidates who choose to study science and science-related degree programmes and consider the impact that such initiatives may have had on recruitment at the aggregate level. The data needed to undertake this analysis was accessed at no cost from the Universities Central Admissions Service (UCAS: the main body for administering recruitment to undergraduate higher education courses in the UK). While a considerable amount of work was required to enter and prepare this data, the analysis was relatively straightforward and required only a fairly rudimentary knowledge of the SPSS computer package.

The results in Figure 17.1 show that gender stereotyped patterns of participation still persist in subjects such as physics and engineering. They also show a remarkable stability in the numbers of women who study these subjects at undergraduate level, despite a large increase in the overall proportion of women at university over the last twenty or so years. So, for example, in 1986, 423 women were accepted to study an undergraduate degree in physics, in 2009, despite a fivefold increase in the total number of female students, the number studying physics was only 620.

UCAS also provides data on the age of applicants and this enables us to examine the extent to which the agenda to widen access to university for non-traditional aged students has been successful in recruiting to the pure sciences. As Figure 17.2 shows, the proportions of non-traditional aged students entering key science subjects have hardly changed over the past two decades. In chemistry, physics and mathematics, for example, the figures have varied by only a few percentage points in almost 25 years and remain consistently low at around 6% of the cohort. Mechanical engineering has fared better than these other three subjects but levels of non-traditional aged participation have not followed a consistent pattern, with levels in 2009 comparable to those in 1986.

This relatively straightforward secondary analysis of participation rates in higher education has suggested that policies aimed at increasing or widening participation in science in UK higher education appear to have had limited impact on the social composition of the full-time undergraduate science population in terms of their age and sex. From a relatively simple dataset and straightforward analysis it is possible to build a powerful picture of how participation has varied over a 25-year period.

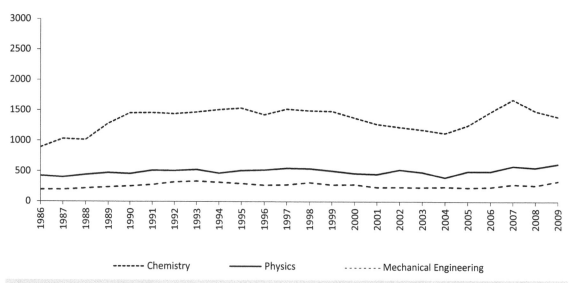

Figure 17.1   Variation in the number of female candidates accepted to study selected STEM subjects 1986–2009

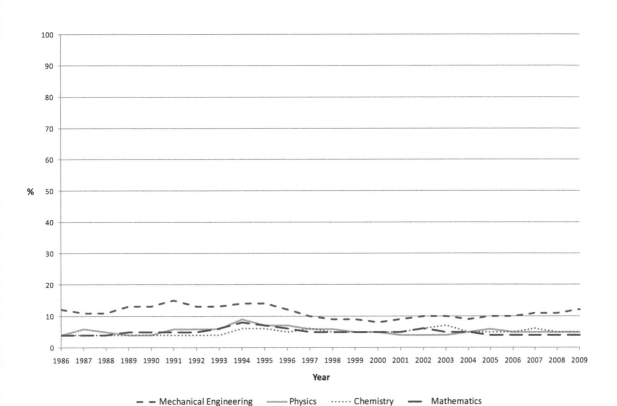

Figure 17.2   Non-traditional aged acceptances as a proportion of all acceptances, selected STEM subjects 1986–2009

Conclusion

This chapter has attempted to introduce the reader to some of the key advantages of undertaking secondary data analysis in educational research. Of course there are many more complex applications of the technique, but the aim here has been to demonstrate the potential of secondary data analysis in mixed-method research and also as a primary method in its own right.

Suggested further reading

Economic and Social Data Service. The ESDS provides an access and support gateway to a wide range of economic and social data. It also links to the UK Data Archive. Access to the ESDS datasets requires registration but is free to academic users. The Nesstar analysis tool is also worth looking at – this enables researchers to analyse data without needing to download whole datasets. Data accessible through the ESDS and the UK Data Archive include:

- British Social Attitudes Survey;
- Labour Force Survey;
- ONS Opinions Survey;
- Millennium Cohort Study;
- Youth Cohort Study;
- Longitudinal Study of Young People in England.

UK Data Archive. The UK Data Archive curates the largest collection of digital data in the social sciences in the UK. It is part-funded by the ESRC and is a lead partner of the Economic and Social Data Service (ESDS). Its data catalogue provides access to over 5000 datasets for research and teaching purposes across a range of disciplines. It is well worth accessing the UK Data Archive and browsing through its list of datasets, just to appreciate the variety and range of resources that are available. The homepage for the Data Archive is at http://www.data-archive.ac.uk/.

Organisation for Economic Cooperation and Development. The Organisation for Economic Cooperation and Development (OECD) is well known for its publications and statistics covering economic and social issues including trade, health and education. There is a huge amount of data available through the OECD website (http://www.oecd.org) including e-books, annual compendia of data, aggregate. Selected original datasets can also be downloaded, including those linked to the Programme for International Student Assessment (PISA). A good place to start is with the Education at a Glance publication which is a useful comparative resource on areas such as financial and human investment in education, access to education, learning conditions and educational outcomes.

Smith E. (2008). Using Secondary Data in Educational and Social Research. This book provides an introduction to using secondary data in social and educational research. It assumes no prior mathematical expertise and is intended as a practical resource for researchers who are new to the field of secondary data analysis. It provides an overview of the field, lists resources and provides step-by-step instruction on accessing and preparing secondary datasets for analysis.

http://www.secondarydataanalysis.com. This website provides links to a large range of national and international sources of secondary data in the field of education.

References

Dale, A., Arber, S. and Procter, M. (1988) *Doing Secondary Analysis*. London: Unwin Hyman.

DCSF (2006) *The Science, Technology, Engineering, and Mathematics Programme Report*. Available at: http://www.nationalstemcentre.org.uk/res/documents/page/050110114146stem_programme_report_2006.pdf (accessed 8 November 2011).

ESRC (2006) *Economic and Social Research Council Delivery Plan 2006*. Available at: http://www.esrc.ac.uk/_images/ESRC_Delivery_Plan06_tcm813460.pdf (accessed 8 November 2011).

Glaser, B. G. (1963) 'Retreading research materials: the use of secondary analysis by the independent researcher', *American Behavioral Scientist*, 6(10): 11–14.

Hakim, C. (1982) *Secondary Analysis in Social Research: A Guide to Data Sources and Methods with Examples*. London: Allen & Unwin.

Smith, E. (2005) *Analysing Underachievement in Schools*. London: Continuum.

Smith, E. (2008) *Using Secondary Data in Educational and Social Research*. Buckingham: Open University Press.

Smith, E. (2010) 'Do we need more scientists? A long-term view of patterns of participation in UK undergraduate science programmes', *Cambridge Journal of Education*, 40(3): 281–98.

Smith, E. (2011) 'Women into science and engineering? Gendered patterns of participation in UK STEM subjects', *British Educational Research Journal*, http://www.tandfonline.com/doi/pdf/10.1080/01411926.2010.515019 (accessed 20 September 2011).

18

Impact evaluation

Steve Higgins

Impact evaluation: a case study of the introduction of interactive whiteboards in schools in the UK

The aim of this case study is to present the evaluation, design rationale and overview of outcomes from a large-scale project in the UK where interactive whiteboards (IWB) were introduced into about 250 classrooms of the teachers of 9–11 year olds in England (Higgins et al., 2005). The initiative was designated as a national pilot project with the key goal of raising levels of attainment in literacy and mathematics, which were at the heart of the UK government's Primary National Strategy. The tensions inherent in evaluating a high-stakes, government-funded pilot project with the provision of rigorous and informative research data as well as the practicalities of evaluation in schools will be explored through the analysis and reflection presented below.

Evaluation rationale and aims

The evaluation had an implicit rationalist paradigm (Young, 1999), but was influenced by post-positivist approaches such as scientific realism (Pawson and Tilley, 1997) and responsive evaluation (Stake, 2004). The key objectives were to identify any effect from

the use of IWBs on literacy and mathematics teaching and learning. The model of impact involved checking implementation fidelity (teachers' weekly logs of IWB use) and identifying short-term indicators focusing on teaching and learning processes (participants' perceptions and observed changes in patterns of classroom interaction) and then educational outcomes (students' attainment in literacy and mathematics). The evaluation is therefore similar to other policy-driven evaluations (such as Every Child Counts in the UK: Torgerson et al., 2011) or technology implementation evaluations (such as integrated learning systems (Underwood et al., 1996) or laptop provision (Silvernail and Gritter, 2007)) which adopt multi-method approaches, but with a comparative and quantitative focus.

A review of the available evidence about interactive whiteboards indicated that perceptions were generally very positive, but that data about the impact on classroom interaction or measures of attainment were scarce and inconclusive (Smith et al. 2005). The research design was influenced by this evidence, particularly in terms of the balance of evidence types (Blatchford, 2005) but also included awareness of the importance of teachers' and students' perceptions (van den Berg and Ros, 1999). Other evaluative approaches were discussed with the sponsor (such as cluster randomised trials and regression discontinuity design options).

However, none of these options were acceptable for a range of reasons to do with the selection of schools and a perceived need for all of the project schools to adopt nationally approved approaches to teaching in literacy and mathematics. A further challenge was imposed in terms of timescales in that the evaluation evidence was needed to inform policy decisions about wider roll-out of the technology across England, ideally within 18–24 months of commissioning. Working with schools also had a number of constraints relating to the timing of data collection and permissions for video and audio recording.

Evaluation aims and methods

The initial literature scoping (Smith et al., 2005) was used to identify focal issues at implementation stage, as well as themes to pursue in the structured classroom observations and interview schedules. Three main strands of data were identified as central to the evaluation (see Table 18.1 below). These were, first, tracking use of the technology, as previous studies of teacher use of technology for instruction suggested that this may be relatively low (e.g. Russell et al., 2003). Second, aspects of the process of using

Table 18.1 Evaluation overview

Evaluation approach	Timing/frequency/sample	Evaluation focus
Weekly record of daily IWB use	2 × 6 weeks blocks 12 months apart	Implementation fidelity Changes in patterns of use after 1 year
Structured classroom observation data	*Year 1:* 30 randomly selected teachers observed four times (with and without IWB for both literacy and mathematics)	Impact on classroom interaction IWB/no IWB comparison Literacy/mathematics differences Gender differences
	Year 2: Same 30 teachers observed with IWB for literacy and mathematics	Changes after 1 year – embedding effect Literacy/mathematics differences Gender differences
Lesson videos	15 volunteer teachers videoed twice in second year of the evaluation	Wider aspects of classroom interaction Teacher use of IWB for presentation
Teacher interviews	68 teachers randomly selected, semi-structured telephone interview	Teacher perceptions of IWB impact on classroom interaction, attainment, gender
Pupil interviews	12 focus groups of 6 pupils; schools randomly selected, but pupils selected by schools	Pupils' perceptions of IWB impact on classroom interaction, attainment, gender
	80 pupils completed mediated interviews using pupil views templates (opportunity sample collected by researchers visiting project schools)	Pupils' reflections on impact of IWB on their learning (meta-cognition)
Pupil attitude data	Quantitative attitudinal data collected from 3,042 pupils in Year 1 and Year 2 of the project (12 months apart)	Impact on pupil attitudes to learning
Attainment data	67 project schools matched with a comparison group using national test data from previous year's data (n = 2,900)	Initial impact on pupils' test performance in literacy, mathematics and science (after 6 months' use of IWBs)
	Similar analysis one year later (n = 2,800)	Impact on pupils' test performance in literacy, mathematics and science (after 18 months' use)

the technology in classrooms were studied using structured observations (see Smith et al., 2006; Smith et al., 2007 for full details). The sample size had sufficient power to compare literacy and numeracy lessons and to examine any interaction effect between the technology (lessons with/without an IWB) and subject area (literacy/mathematics) using ANOVA and independent t-tests. Additionally, 15 teachers volunteered to be videoed to ensure other aspects of classroom interaction were not missed (see Smith and Higgins, 2007). Interviews were conducted with teachers, pupils and those responsible for the project at local authority level (Wall et al., 2005; Hall and Higgins, 2005). Finally outcome data on pupils' attitudes and attainment were collected to identify any quantitative impact of the technology on their learning.

There are limitations in this evaluation design in terms of the inferences which can be drawn from the findings. The lack of control over allocation of the technology and absence of randomisation were of particular concern in an evaluation which sought to inform a national expansion of the initiative. We were confident that we would identify any differences at the process or classroom level (i.e. those based on within-sample comparisons) and that the random sampling of project teachers for observation and interview would capture a reasonable snapshot of use and perceptions across the project. However, we were concerned that the attainment data analysis would not provide confidence in any causal link between IWB use and attainment which could be generalised, though if there were differences associated with IWB adoption the sample size and use of a matched comparator sample would be likely to identify the extent of these.

Results of the evaluation

The teachers reported using IWBs initially in about two-thirds of lessons, then nearly three-quarters of lessons one year later. Reported software use indicated they were developing or adapting resources more in the second year, suggesting increased confidence in using the technology. The pilot project was therefore successful in embedding use of the technology in the majority of lessons in project schools.

The use of IWBs also seemed to make a difference to aspects of classroom interaction. There were fewer pauses in IWB lessons and by the second year of the project there were more open questions, repeat questions, probes, longer answers from students and more general talk. There was a faster pace in the IWB lessons with almost twice the amount of evaluative responses from teachers and longer answers from students.

Interpreting these observational findings is challenging. There were clear differences associated with the technology and some of these changes were consistent with more effective teaching (e.g. Nystrand and Gamoran, 1991; Muijs and Reynolds, 2001). In particular the increase in open questions, length of answers and use of 'probes' or follow-up questions indicated a more interactive style of classroom discourse (Galton et al., 1999). Others may or may not be beneficial. Pace of lessons is an example of this (Muijs and Reynolds, 2001: 9). Inspection reports in the UK often comment favourably that one of the benefits of information and communications technology is enabling a faster pace of lessons and it is certainly the case that IWB lessons had a faster pace (at least as measured by the number of interactions).

Overall, the teachers interviewed were extremely positive about the impact of IWBs on their teaching. The students were also very positive about the use of IWBs, and particularly enjoyed the multimedia potential of the technology, believing that they learned better when an IWB was used in the classroom and suggesting the technology helped them to pay better attention.

Data at individual student level from the national tests in English, mathematics and science for 11 year olds were obtained from the UK's Department for Education and Skills (DfES) for the year before the project (for identification of a matched comparison group) and for two subsequent years. These data were then analysed (comparing means, using t-tests and calculating effect sizes) to identify any impact of the use of IWBs in the project schools and to see if there was any difference in impact according to gender or for high- or low-attaining students. The first tests were after about six months of use of IWBs in the project schools. This is a relatively short time for any effect to become apparent, but as shown in Table 18.2,

Table 18.2 Comparison of student attainment data in the first year of the project

Subject	Group	n students	Mean test score	s.d.	t	p	Effect size
English	IWB	2,879	58.69	16.39	1.28	n.s.	0.04
	Controls	2,085	58.09	16.32			
Maths	IWB	2,892	63.93	21.00	3.62	<0.001	0.10
	Controls	2,094	61.75	21.06			
Science	IWB	2,921	59.42	11.94	3.79	<0.001	0.11
	Controls	2,108	58.10	12.30			

(National test scores: IWB and controls – student level)

the mean test scores in the IWB schools are slightly higher than in the control schools, with statistically significant margins for mathematics and science. The effect sizes (the extent of the differences) in all cases are very small, however.

A year later a similar comparison was made after 18 months of technology use (Table 18.3). There were no significant differences between the two groups and the effect sizes are negligible. The small benefit for the IWB schools seen in mathematics and science test results in the first year was not sustained.

The early improvement seen after the first few months may have been a 'halo' or novelty effect of some kind. It did not lead to further improvement in the following year, which might have been expected on the inference from the observations that classes were taught more actively with an IWB.

Challenges for interpretation and evaluation design

One obvious question raised by the evaluation is whether the project was successful. There was evidence that the technology was effectively embedded in teachers' practice and that there were some changes in the patterns of interaction which might be associated with more effective teaching. Participants, both teachers and students, were confident that IWBs improved teaching and learning in their classrooms. However the quantitative attainment data did not show any sustained significant improvement associated with the technology. It may be that the evaluation design was not robust enough to identify differences in test scores as the allocation and matching processes were not ideal. It may also be that the teachers and pupils were mistaken in their belief that learning improved, or that aspects of learning were improved, but not

Table 18.3 Comparison of student attainment data after 18 months

Subject	Group	n students	Mean test score	s.d.	t	p	Effect size
English	IWB	2,763	55.36	15.08	0.63	n.s.	0.02
	Controls	1,965	55.08	14.89			
Maths	IWB	2,824	66.53	21.41	0.09	n.s.	0.00
	Controls	1,980	66.47	21.20			
Science	IWB	2,850	57.29	12.45	1.16	n.s.	−0.03
	Controls	1,944	57.71	11.99			

(National test scores: IWB and controls–students level)

those captured by test scores. We believe that the design was sufficient to identify any quantitative changes associated with the introduction of interactive whiteboards in terms of the project aims, although if a substantial difference had been found, we would have had reservations about any strong causal claims. In terms of the politics of the evaluation, the analysis of the final results came after the decision had been made to expand the pilot, which was based on (or bolstered by) the interaction and perception data available earlier in the evaluation. Of course many of these issues are well known – there are numerous examples of the evaluation of technology use in education (see Weston (2004) for example) and ways to overcome the challenge of 'shoestring' evaluation have been proposed (Bamberger et al., 2004). Good evaluation design therefore attempts to mitigate these challenges to provide as robust an answer to the evaluation research questions as the constraints allow.

socialresearchmethods.net/kb/evaluation.php . It sets out the characteristics which distinguish evaluation research from other kinds of educational research, as well as containing detailed information about other aspects of research design and analysis in social research methods.

van den Berg, R. and Ros, A. (1999) 'The permanent importance of the subjective reality of teachers during educational innovation: a concerns-based approach', *American Educational Research Journal* 36(4): 879–906. Available at: http://www.jstor.org/stable/1163523. This article reviews research conducted over several years to illustrate how teachers express different types of concerns at different stages of the educational innovation process. This indicates the importance of matching or 'attuning' innovation policy and implementation to factors influencing the innovation process with teachers' concerns about the adoption of new practices, as well as highlighting the importance of understanding changes in patterns of teachers' concerns at different stages of implementation, innovation, evaluation and design.

Suggested further reading

Bamberger, M., Rugh, J., Church, M. and Fort, L. (2004) 'Shoestring evaluation: designing impact evaluations under budget, time and data constraints', *American Journal of Evaluation*, 25(1): 5–37. Available at: http://citeseerx.ist.psu.edu/viewdoc/download?doi=10.1.1.115.9518&rep=rep1&type=pdf. This paper outlines the shoestring evaluation approach, developed to assist evaluators conduct evaluations that are as methodologically sound as possible but within budget and time constraints and with limitations in terms of the types of data which are accessible. It also sets out a six-step approach to ensure the most robust evaluation within these different constraints:

1. Planning and scoping the evaluation
2. Addressing time constraints
3. Addressing data constraints
4. Addressing budget constraints
5. Assessing the strengths and weaknesses of the evaluation design
6. Addressing the identified weaknesses and strengthening the evaluation design.

Bill Trochim's research methods website has a useful section of evaluation research methods: http://www.

References

Bamberger, M., Rugh, J., Church, M. and Fort, L. (2004) 'Shoestring evaluation: designing impact evaluations under budget, time and data constraints', *American Journal of Evaluation*, 25(1): 5–37.

Blatchford, P. (2005) 'A multi-method approach to the study of school class size differences', *International Journal of Social Research Methodology*, 8(3): 195–205.

Galton, M., Hargreaves, L., Comber, C., Wall, D. and Pell, A. (1999) *Inside the Primary Classroom: 20 Years On.* London: Routledge.

Hall, I. and Higgins, S. (2005) 'Primary school students' perceptions of IWBs', *Journal of Computer Assisted Learning*, 21: 102–17.

Higgins, S. (2010) 'The impact of IWBs on classroom interaction and learning in primary schools in the UK', in Thomas, M. and Cutrim-Schmid, E. (eds) *Interactive Whiteboards for Education: Theory, Research and Practice.* Hershey, PA: IGI Global, pp. 86–101.

Higgins, S., Falzon, C., Hall, I., Moseley, D., Smith, F., Smith, H. and Wall, K. (2005) *Embedding ICT in the Literacy and Numeracy Strategies: Final Report.* Newcastle-upon-Tyne: Newcastle University. Available at: http://partners.becta.org.uk/page_documents/research/univ_newcastle_evaluation_whiteboards.pdf (accessed 4 January 2011).

Mroz, M. A., Smith, F. and Hardman, F. (2000) 'The discourse of the literacy hour', *Cambridge Journal of Education*, 30(3): 379–90.

Muijs, D. and Reynolds, D. (2001) *Effective Teaching: Evidence and Practice*. London: Paul Chapman.

Nystrand, M. and Gamoran, A. (1991) 'Student engagement: when recitation becomes conversation', in Waxman, H. C. and Walberg, H. J. (eds) *Effective Teaching: Current Research*. Berkley, CA: McCutchan.

Pawson, R. and Tilley, N. (1997) *Realistic Evaluation*. Thousand Oaks, CA: Sage.

Reynolds, D. and Muijs, D. (1999) 'The effective teaching of mathematics: a review of research', *School Leadership and Management*, 19(3): 273–88.

Russell, M., Bebell, D., O'Dwyer, L. and O'Connor, K. (2003) 'Examining teacher technology use: implications for preservice and inservice teacher preparation', *Journal of Teacher Education*, 54: 297–310.

Silvernail, D. L. and Gritter, A. K. (2007) *Maine's Middle School Laptop Program: Creating Better Writers*. Gorham, ME: Maine Education Policy Research Institute, University of Southern Maine.

Smith, H. and Higgins, S. (2007) 'Opening classroom interaction: the importance of feedback', *Cambridge Journal of Education*, 36(4): 485–502.

Smith, F., Hardman, F. and Higgins, S. (2006) 'The impact of IWBs on teacher–pupil interaction in the national literacy and numeracy strategies', *British Educational Research Journal*, 32(3): 443–57.

Smith, F., Higgins, S. and Hardman, F. (2007) 'Gender inequality in the primary classroom: will IWBs help?', *Gender and Education*, 19(4): 455–69.

Smith, F., Hardman, F., Mroz, M. and Wall, K. (2004) 'Interactive whole-class teaching in the national literacy and numeracy strategies', *British Educational Research Journal*, 30(3): 395–411.

Smith, H. J., Higgins, S., Wall, K. and Miller, J. (2005) 'Interactive whiteboards: boon or bandwagon? A critical review of the literature', *Journal of Computer Assisted Learning*, 21: 91–101.

Stake, R. (2004) *Standards-based and Responsive Evaluation*. Thousand Oaks, CA: Sage.

Torgerson, C. J., Wiggins, A., Torgerson, D. J., Ainsworth, H., Barmby, P., Hewitt, C., Askew, M., Bland, M., Coe, R., Hendry, V., Higgins, S., Hodgen, J., Hulme, C., Jones, K. and Tymms, P. (2011) *Every Child Counts: The Independent Evaluation*. York: Institute for Effective Education, University of York.

Underwood, J., Cavendish, S., Dowling, S., Fogelman, K. and Lawson, T. (1996) 'Are integrated learning systems effective learning support tools?', *Computers and Education*, 26(1–3): 33–40.

van den Berg, R. and Ros, A. (1999) 'The permanent importance of the subjective reality of teachers during educational innovation: a concerns-based approach', *American Educational Research Journal*, 36(4): 879–906.

Wall, K., Higgins, S. and Smith, H. (2005) '"The visual helps me understand the complicated things": pupil views of teaching and learning with IWBs', *British Journal of Educational Technology*, 36(5): 851–67.

Weston, T. (2004) 'Formative evaluation for implementation: evaluating educational technology applications and lessons', *American Journal of Evaluation*, 25(1): 51–64.

Young, M. D. (1999) 'Multifocal educational policy research: towards a method for enhancing traditional educational policy studies', *American Educational Research Journal*, 36(4): 677–714.

19

Interventions: experiments

Peter Tymms

Definition and outline of the key research design

An intervention is a deliberate attempt to change the world in some way with a view to assessing the impact of that intervention. The intervention is arranged (designed) so that the researcher can ascribe cause to the results of the intervention. At its simplest this can be done by creating two equal groups by randomly assigning membership of the groups (see, for example, Campbell and Stanley, 1966; Boruch, 1997). There are many variations on this theme but from an educational perspective there are two broad levels: one involves individuals and the other involves groups. The assignment of individuals to different treatments has the longest history. One of the first investigations which could be called a clinical trial was carried out by James Lind. He showed that the eating of oranges and lemons was a clear winner in comparison with alternative suggestions when it came to treating scurvy onboard ships in the eighteenth century (Lind Alliance, 2010). The random assignment of treatments to individuals is very common in, for example, psychological research (see, for example, Abelson and Frey et al., 2004). The second approach involves units made up of individuals such as schools or classrooms. This is known as a clustered randomised control trial and is well suited to assessing the impact for potential policy initiatives.

The kind of associated research questions

The kinds of research questions which might be tackled using the two types of intervention are many and varied. They include:

Individual random assignment:

'What is the impact on pupils' understanding of mathematics when they themselves teach other pupils compared with being taught by teachers?'

'How much difference does giving homework once a week for six weeks in mathematics make to the knowledge of 11 year olds compared to giving no homework at all?'

'What is the impact of arresting someone who has been reported for beating their partner as opposed to simply being warned or cautioned by the police?'

Clusters randomly assigned:

'Does tough inspection improve the examination results of schools?'

'Does the introduction of performance related pay for teachers improve the motivation of teachers generally?'

Paradigmatic location

Intervention research presumes that the world can, at least partially, be understood in terms of cause and effect relationships. It tries to find causal relationships and in doing so it can test hypotheses, help to refine theories and help to evaluate potential policy changes. This is not to suggest that the world is not extremely complex. Indeed in a complex hard-to-predict world there is a great need for research using interventions even when findings may not be applicable across cultures and time. It is worth noting the differing perspectives both for individual trials and clustered trials (see also Tymms et al., 2008 and discussion in the same volume).

Individual random assignment

As noted above, this has a long history in social science and medical research. It seeks either to establish basic psychological, medical or social relationships or to act as a preliminary investigation designed to be followed by larger-scale work. Within the medical world the dominant paradigm is that the fundamental features of the human body hold true for people across the world and across time. It is acknowledged that different people may respond differently to differing treatments but it is still thought that this is predictable. Indeed, there is talk of using individual genomes to target treatment. Within psychological studies a similar view is taken but there is a greater acceptance that contact and culture is important although the ideas are disputed (see, for example, Grigorenko, 2009).

There are some who would argue that it is impossible or foolish to try to find generalisations when researching human interactions. Indeed the famous twentieth-century experimental psychologist from the United States, Lee J. Cronbach, changed his optimistic early view:

> . . . he came to realize that in social, behavioral, and educational research, the standard errors were enormous, contextual factors led to complex interactions between people and their environments that were hard to generalize, and 'facts decay with a short half-life as society changes. (Shavelson, 2009)

Clusters randomly assigned

Clustered trials are designed to investigate the working of systems rather than the individuals within them. Here the artificial world created by humans is being studied (Simon, 1969). There is less expectation that eternal truths will be found and it is acknowledged that it is more likely that solutions to temporal problems will be discovered. But this does not diminish their importance: policy-makers need to know what has been shown to be effective while not assuming that what worked in the past will definitely work in the future.

Methods of data collection and analysis that are typically used for this design

In this kind of design the focus is typically on an outcome which needs to be measured. This might be one or more of a great many constructs such as knowledge or understanding or motivation or anxiety or behaviour. The collection of data might involve questionnaires or tests or observations. These will quantify the outcome that we are interested in and there may also be an initial assessment, a baseline. Such a baseline can enhance the power of the statistical tests of the impact of the intervention when they are used as controls. Additional data on the background of the participants (such as sex, age, social class and ethnicity) are routinely collected and, for groups, measures of the groups are also common (such as size of group, percentage of free school meal entitlement and other aggregate scores of individuals).

One wants to know very clearly what has happened during the intervention. In a short and straightforward intervention with a small number of individual cases a special data collection exercise may not be needed but in a more complex design over a longer period across many sites then it would be vital to assess the extent to which the intervention has actually happened – fidelity to treatment. In order to assess this, there have to be ways to collect that data and typically that would be by observation. The amount of data that is collected would be an important consideration for those designing the experiment because observers can be expensive. Questionnaires to participants can also be used but it is important to doubt their veracity in this situation.

Analysis of the data is typically much simpler than the kinds of modelling that one can expect without intervention. For interventions with individuals a t-test, or possibly a non-parametric alternative, can be used to establish statistical significance and the effect size should also be calculated (see, for example, Fitz-Gibbon and Morris, 1990).

For clustered trials multilevel models (see, for example, Snijders and Bosker, 1999) are appropriate with dummies used to identify the interventions. Effect sizes should also be calculated (Tymms, 2004).

An example of a clustered randomised control trial

One recent example of a clustered randomised control trial involved peer learning within the Fife authority in Scotland. It was decided that there was enough individual experimental evidence to show that peer tutoring had an impact (see, for example, Cohen et al.,1982). What we were concerned to do was to show how this work could be extrapolated into many schools on an authority-wide basis. To find out what worked best in such an approach we were not sure if cross-age tutoring, which is difficult to organise but often produces better effects, would work more sustainably than same-age tutoring which is relatively easy for a teacher to organise in his/her class but isn't as effective. We also were not sure if running peer tutoring in Maths or in Reading would be most effective, or if indeed the two together would work better, or how often it should be done – lightly (once a week) or intensively three times a week.

We invited the heads of all 145 Fife schools to join the project on the understanding that they would be randomly assigned to various modes of intervention. We planned to randomly assign schools either to cross-age or same-age, to Maths or Reading or Maths and Reading, and to light or intensive. One hundred and twenty schools agreed to join the project and on that basis we set up the interventions which were run over two years. The schools were assisted by researchers in preparing material and preparing the tutors. They also carried out observations going into the classrooms and collecting questionnaire data on how the project was working. The outcome measures were collected and analysed separately. The analyses involved multilevel models with pupils nested within schools controlling with dummies for the interventions.

The results indicated what really worked was cross-age peer tutoring with an effect size of 0.2. It was better than same-age peer tutoring and it mostly did not matter if the topic were Reading or Maths or if the approach was intensive or light (Tymms et al., 2011).

Suggested further reading

There is a burgeoning literature on interventions in the social sciences and many different units have been set up to bring these together and to synthesise the results. These include:

- the What Works Clearing House (http://ies.ed.gov/ncee/wwc/);
- the Campbell Collaboration (http://www.campbellcollaboration.org/);
- the Best Evidence Encyclopedia (http://www.bestevidence.org/).

All of these units start by finding high-quality research, commonly well-designed intervention studies and then synthesising the results. As part of the systematic reviews meta-analysis is often used to bring together and understand the results as a whole, each of which, alone, might not tell a stable story (see, for example, Hedges and Olkin, 1985).

References

Abelson, R. P., Frey, K. P. et al. (2004) *Experiments With People: Revelations from Social Psychology*. Mahwah, NJ: Lawrence Erlbaum Associates.

Boruch, R. (1997) *Randomised Experimentation for Planning and Evaluation: A Practical Guide*. London: Sage.

Campbell, D. T. and Stanley, J. C. (1966) *Experimental and Quasi-Experimental Designs for Research*. Chicago: Rand McNally.

Cohen, P. A., Kulik, J. A. and Kulik, C. C. (1982) 'Educational outcomes of tutoring: a meta-analysis of findings', *American Educational Research Journal*, 19: 237–48.

Fitz-Gibbon, C. T. and Morris, L. L. (1990) *Program Evaluation Kit: How to Analyze Data*. Newbury Park, CA: Sage.

Grigorenko, E. L. (ed.) (2009) *Multicultural Psychoeducational Assessment*. New York: Springer.

Hedges, L. V. and Olkin, I. (1985) *Statistical Methods for Meta-Analysis*. New York/Orlando, FL: FLA/Academic Press.

Lind Alliance. Available at: http://www.lindalliance.org/ (accessed 22 December 2010).

Shavelson, R. (2009) *Lee J. Cronbach 1916–2001 A Biographical Memoir*. Washington, DC: National Academy of Sciences.

Simon, H. A. (1969) *The Sciences of the Artificial*. Cambridge, MA: MIT Press.

Snijders, T. and Bosker, R. (1999) *Multilevel Analysis: An Introduction to Basic and Advanced Multilevel Modeling*. London/Thousand Oaks/New Delhi: Sage.

Tymms, P. (2004) 'Effect sizes in multilevel models', in Schagen, I. and Elliot, K. (eds) *But What Does It Mean?* Slough: National Foundation for Educational Research, pp. 55–66.

Tymms, P., Merrell, C. and Coe, R. (2008) 'Open dialogue: educational policies and randomized controlled trials', *Psychology of Education Review*, 32(2): 3–7.

Tymms, P., Merrell, C., Thurston, A., Andor, J., Topping, K. and Miler, D. (2011) 'Improving attainment across a whole district: school reform through peer tutoring in a randomized controlled trial', *School Effectiveness and School Improvement*, 22(3): 265–89.

A systematic review

Mark Newman and Kelly Dickson

Definition and outline of the key research design

Systematic reviews are a family of research technologies that can be used for the task of reviewing the answer provided by existing research to a specific question. The key features of a systematic review are that it:

- brings together and 'pools' the findings of primary research;
- is a piece of research, following standard methods and stages;
- takes steps to reduce/make transparent hidden bias and 'error';
- is accountable, replicable, updatable and sustainable.

Traditionally systematic review technology has been closely associated with answering questions about the effectiveness of interventions (so called 'what works') questions using a specific statistical synthesis technique called meta-analysis. However, the key features shown above could be applied to a greater or lesser degree to the process of reviewing research to all types of research question and even to the synthesis of non-empirical data.

The basic stages of the systematic review process are:

- formulating a review question;
- searching and selecting studies;
- coding to describe studies;
- assessing study quality and relevance;
- synthesising results;
- deriving conclusions and implications.

The details of the methods used in each of these stages are discussed in Chapter 30 by Torgerson et al. in this volume. The remainder of this chapter provides an illustration of the methods used at each of these stages using as an exemplar a systematic review of the evidence about the impact of 'Block Scheduling' on academic attainment that we carried out for the UK government Department for Education and Science (DfES) (Dickson et al., 2010).

Formulating the review question

The organisation of school and how time should be spent during the school day has been under discussion since the education system came into existence. Questions about the optimal length of the school year or school day and how much time is afforded to which subjects continue to be asked by educational policy-makers and educational professionals. Individual schools, in England and Wales, have responsibility for designing, organising and timetabling the curriculum and have a choice about which year pupils take their National Curriculum end of Key Stage tests. Schools can make decisions regarding which subjects they prioritise, the time allocated to each subject and the number of lessons in the school day. Internationally, the traditional school day includes six to eight periods/classes, each lasting for approximately 50 minutes (Scroggins and Karr-Kidwell, 1995). Block scheduling is an alternative to this traditional structure whereby subjects are studied in 'blocks' of time (Trenta and Newman, 2001). One of the cited aims of block scheduling is to allow greater time for student-oriented activities in order to promote in-depth discussion and increased interaction. In line with this, teachers are expected to use a variety of teaching strategies and engage in learning-oriented activities. Through a process of discussion and consultation with the DfES the review team formulated the following systematic review question

Does block scheduling result in higher levels of student attainment than traditional scheduling?

Searching and selecting studies

The processes of searching and selection are clearly linked. The selection criteria determine what you search for and how the search is conducted. The selection criteria to exclude studies are shown in Table 20.1. The criteria used were constructed in order to identify not only the relevant studies but also to identify those which were of a better quality for answering the specific review question.

We searched for studies in the main educational and social science databases, including ASSIA, Australian Education Index, British Education Index, EPPI-Centre database of education research, ERIC, International Bibliography of the Social Sciences, PsycINFO, Social Policy and Practice, Social Science Citation Index and Sociological Abstracts. We also searched on Google Scholar and a number of key websites, and contacted experts in the field.

Table 20.1   Review exclusion criteria

- Not an evaluation of the effect of block scheduling
- Not reporting academic achievement using standardised test(s)
- Not pupils with a mean age between 11 and 16
- No control group in the report
- Not a mainstream, maintained and independent school
- Were of the following study type:
  – descriptive
  – methodology
  – editorial, commentary, book review
  – policy document
  – resource, textbook
  – bibliography
  – theoretical paper
  – position paper
  – reviews (systematic and non-systematic)
- Not reporting data on pupils or the school
- Not published or reported in English
- Not published or reported between 1988 and the present

Coding to describe studies

All of the included studies were coded using a standard coding tool for educational studies developed by the EPPI-Centre[1], supplemented by some subject-specific keywords. This information is used to provide descriptive information about the studies in the study report, to facilitate synthesis and to make judgements about study quality. The broad categories of coding used were:

- Study aims and rationale
- Study policy/practice focus
- Sample descriptions
- Description of programme/ Intervention
- Results

- Study methods
  - groups
  - sampling
  - recruitments and consent
  - data collection
  - data analysis
- Study quality

Assessing study quality

The quality of the included studies was assessed and weighted on three dimensions. The quality of the study execution, i.e. its internal methodological coherence, was assessed using a quality assessment tool that assessed the methodological quality of each study in four key areas: sample selection, bias, data collection and data analysis. A scoring system was used to measure the overall quality, with possible scores ranging from 4 to 20. Studies with the lowest scores are considered to be the most methodologically robust.

The appropriateness of the research design and analysis used for answering the review was assessed according to the methods used for selecting the sample and how studies controlled for baseline differences between the control and intervention groups. Studies which used random allocation were considered to be the most appropriate method for answering the review question and were given a high rating. Studies that used a matched sample design or statistically controlled for differences in the analysis were given a medium rating. Studies that did not control for any baseline differences between the control and intervention were given a low rating.

Synthesis of evidence in the in-depth review

Each included study compared the effect of block scheduling against a control group of students who had undergone a traditional schedule. Studies measured 'academic achievement' in a range of academic subjects (e.g. Mathematics, English, Science) and in some cases across subjects as a grade point average (GPA). We identified from the individual studies all of the outcomes which attempted to measure some form of academic achievement. The necessary data was supplied for only 12 of the 14 studies and thus the synthesis was based only on these 12 studies. The results of these studies were converted into the effect size standard mean deviations (SMD) using Hedges (Hedges, 1981) and then grouped according to type of block scheduling and by subject. The findings were synthesised using the statistical procedure meta-analysis. The meta-analysis was conducted using both fixed and random effect models and tests for heterogeneity undertaken.

Deriving conclusions and implications

An interpretation framework was developed based on the Maryland Scientific Methods Scale (Farrington et al., 2002) in order to help summarize and interpret the strength and outcomes of the evidence provided. The framework was based on the number and quality of the studies that evaluated any particular type of block scheduling and/or type of outcome and the weighted average effect size and/or directions of effect in each individual study.

What did the review find?

There is not space to detail the findings of the review here and interested readers are directed to the full review report (Dickson et al., 2010). The intention here is rather to illustrate what the results of a systematic review of the type presented here might look like. The initial electronic searching identified 8,054 citations, which were screened for potential relevance on the basis of title and abstract. Fourteen studies met the inclusion criteria for answering the review question as given above. All of the studies were published between 1995 and 2004 and evaluated different types of block schedules. All of the studies were conducted in North America (USA n = 13; Canada, n = 1) and investigated the UK equivalent of secondary school pupils aged 11–16. Pupil-level data was collected and examined to evaluate the effectiveness of block scheduling. Most studies evaluated either the 4×4 block schedule (n = 8) or the A/B block schedule (n = 5). Some studies also examined hybrid schedules (n = 3) and the impact of extending a single lesson (n = 2). Of the 14 evaluations included in the in-depth review, only one used a quasi-randomised design. The remaining 13 studies used a retrospective study design whereby the outcomes of students who were already enrolled in schools delivering block scheduling (the intervention group) were compared to the outcomes of students already enrolled in school using a traditional schedule (the control group). In some cases this would be the same school at two different points in time, i.e. comparing the outcomes of a cohort of students before block scheduling had been implemented with a later cohort of students who followed the block schedule.

Overall the individual studies were too dissimilar to combine and thus no 'overall effect' of block scheduling could be computed. Sub-group analyses were carried for different kinds of block scheduling and different kinds of outcome (cross-subject grade averages or single-subject grade averages). By way of illustration eight studies investigated the effect of block scheduling on Science. Five studies investigated the effect of block scheduling on student attainment (test scores)

in science. Of those five, three evaluated the effect of 4×4 block scheduling (Lewis et al., 2005; Marchette, 2003; Zhang, 2001) and four evaluated the effect of A/B block scheduling (DiRocco, 1997; Lewis et al., 2005; Marchette, 2003; McCreary and Hausman, 2001).

Only the studies on the A/B block schedule were sufficiently similar to combine and the forest plot of the results from these individual studies is shown in Figure 20.1. The forest plot shows that in each of the individual studies the students in the block scheduled science classes achieved on average a higher attainment score. The pooled estimate of effect (the black diamond in the forest plot) was positive and the 95% confidence intervals exclude 'no effect'.

Based on these findings our interpretation of the results for the effect of A/B block scheduling on science attainment was that the evidence suggested that, when compared with traditional schedules, block scheduling could improve academic performance in science subjects. But given the low quality rating given to four studies we felt that the evidence was not strong

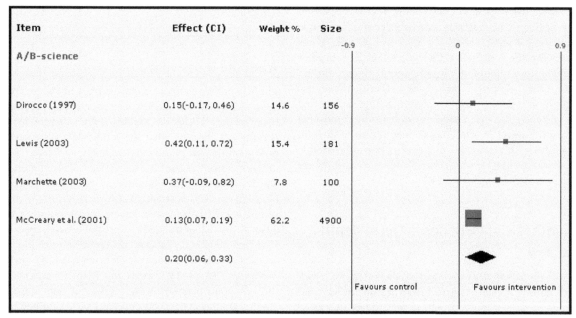

Item	Effect (CI)	Weight %	Size
A/B-science			
Dirocco (1997)	0.15(-0.17, 0.46)	14.6	156
Lewis (2003)	0.42(0.11, 0.72)	15.4	181
Marchette (2003)	0.37(-0.09, 0.82)	7.8	100
McCreary et al. (2001)	0.13(0.07, 0.19)	62.2	4900
	0.20(0.06, 0.33)		

Favours control   Favours intervention

Heterogeneity statistic Q = 4.28 df = 3 p = 0.232 I2 = 30%
Test statistic (combined effect) z = 2.84 p = 0.00456

Figure 20.1 Effect sizes (Hedges' g) of A/B block scheduling on science achievement

enough to support the introduction of policy guidance on the use of block scheduling for science lessons in secondary schools.

Different applications of systematic review methods

In this chapter we have illustrated the application of systematic review technology to one particular kind of research question and effectiveness or what

Table 20.2 Different approaches and questons using systemic review technology

- Narrative numerical synthesis of quantitative studies using non-experimental designs, e.g. What is the relationship between secondary school size and student outcomes? (Newman et al., 2006)

- Systematic narrative synthesis of studies using a mixture of methods, e.g. Can PDP improve student learning? (Gough et al., 2003)

- Meta-ethnography of studies using 'qualitative methods', e.g. What meaning do people with chronic healthcare conditions attach to their medication? (Britten et al., 2002)

- Critical interpretivist synthesis of studies using a mixture of methods, e.g. How can 'access' to healthcare be conceptualized? (Dixon-Woods et al., 2006)

- Thematic synthesis of studies using qualitative methods to understand people's perceptions, e.g. What are young people's views about food and eating? (Thomas et al., 2003)

- Realist synthesis of studies investigating the impact of policy initiatives, e.g. How does public disclosure work to change performance/behaviour? (Pawson, 2002)

- Meta narrative review of mixed literature to identify the narrative of a concept, e.g. What are the storylines in the field of diffusion of innovations? (Greenhalgh et al., 2005)

works question and one particular kind of review and synthesis process, meta-analysis. Systematic review technology is not limited to this type of question or approach; rather it is a family of similar approaches that vary somewhat in their approaches to the different stages of the review process. Examples of different kinds of review question and approaches to synthesis are shown in Table 20.2. It is worth noting firstly that many of these approaches are 'new' or emerging, secondly that very few have been used in what might be regarded as education research and thirdly that the 'distinctiveness' of these approaches is often claimed by the author.

In conclusion we have demonstrated in this chapter that systematic review technology can usefully be applied to education research questions. The application of systematic review processes to 'What works?' type of questions is well established if not 'uncontroversial'. The application of variants of systematic review approaches to other types of educational research question using different methods of synthesis is still in its infancy and much needs to be done to explore, develop and test the validity and utility of these new approaches.

Note

1. EPPI-Centre Data Extraction and Coding Tool for Education Studies V2.0 – contact the authors for further details.

Suggested further reading

Morgen Alwell and Brian Cobb (2009) 'Functional life skills curricular interventions for youth with disabilities: a systematic review', *Career Development for Exceptional Individuals*, 32(2): 82–93. Online at: http://cde.sagepub. com/content/32/2/82.full.pdf+html. This article illustrates the application of systematic review and meta-analysis techniques to a particular sub-field of education where the research question had been addressed using a number of different types of quantitative primary research.

D. Gough, S. Oliver and J. Thomas (eds) (2012) *An Introduction to Systematic Reviews*. London: Sage (forthcoming). Online at: http://www.uk.sagepub.com/books/Book234152. This textbook provides an introductory comprehensive and in-depth guide to the process and methods of systematic review. Written by experts at the UK EPPI-Centre at the University of London who specialise in developing systematic review methods for a range of different research questions and research types, this text provides an accessible overview of the variations in systematic review approaches.

Helen Penn and Eva Lloyd (2006) 'Using systematic reviews to investigate research in early childhood', *Journal of Early Childhood Research*, 4(3): 311–30. Online at: http://ecr.sagepub.com/content/4/3/311.full.pdf+html. This article illustrates how a group of educational researchers with an interest in early childhood used systematic review methods to investigate a number of research questions in their field.

References

Britten, N., Campbell, R., Pope, C., Donovan, J., Morgan, M. and Pill, R. (2002) 'Using meta ethnography to synthesise qualitative research: a worked example', *J. Health Serv. Res. Policy*, 7(4): 209–15.

Dickson, K., Bird, K., Newman, M. and Kalra, N. (2010) 'What is the effect of block scheduling on academic achievement? A systematic review. Technical report', in *Research Evidence in Education Library*. London: EPPI-Centre, Social Science Research Unit, Institute of Education, University of London.

DiRocco, M. D. (1997) *Effects of Alternating Day Block Scheduling on Student Academic Performance, Attendance and Discipline (Alternative Day Scheduling, Intensive Scheduling)*. Pennsylvania State University Dissertation Thesis.

Dixon-Woods, M., Cavers, D., Agarwal, S., Annandale, E. et al. (2006) 'Conducting a critical interpretive synthesis of the literature on access to healthcare by vulnerable groups', *BMC Medical Research Methodology*, 6: 35.

Farrington, D., Gottfredson, D., Sherman, L. and Welsh, B. (2002) 'The Maryland Scientific Methods Scale', in Farrington, D., MacKenzie, D., Sherman, L. and Welsh, L. (eds) *Evidence Based Crime Prevention*. London. Routledge, pp. 13–21.

Gough, D. A., Kiwan, D., Sutcliffe, K., Simpson, D. and Houghton, N. (2003) 'A systematic map and synthesis review of the effectiveness of personal development planning for

improving student learning', in *Research Evidence in Education Library*. London: EPPI-Centre, Social Science Research Unit, Institute of Education, University of London.

Greenhalgh, T., Robert, G., Macfarlane, F., Bate, P. et al. (2005) 'Storylines of research in diffusion of innovation: a meta-narrative approach to systematic review', *Social Science and Medicine*, 61(2): 417–30.

Hedges, L. (1981) 'Distribution theory for Glass's estimator of effect size and related estimators', *Journal of Educational Statistics*, 6(2): 107–28.

Lewis, C. W., Dugan, J. J., Winokur, M. A., Cobb, B. R. (2005) 'The effects of block scheduling on high school academic achievement', *NASSP Bulletin*, 89(645): 72–87.

McCreary, J. and Hausman, C. (2001) *Differences in Student Outcomes Between Block, Semester, and Trimester Schedules*. Salt Lake City, UT: University of Utah.

Marchette, F. (2003) *Impacts of Scheduling Configurations on Mississippi Biology Subject Area Testing*. Paper presented at the Annual Meeting of the Mid-South Educational Research Association Biloxi, MS.

Newman, M., Garrett, Z., Elbourne, D., Bradley, S. et al. (2006) 'Does secondary school size make a difference? A systematic review', *Educational Research Review*, 1(1): 41–61.

Pawson, R. (2002) 'Evidence and policy and naming and shaming', *Policy Studies*, 23(3–4): 211–30.

Scroggins, G. V. and Karr-Kidwell, P. J. (1995) *Implementation of Block Scheduling in a Four-Year High School: A Literary Review and a Handbook for Administrators, Teachers and Parents*. Available at: http://eric.ed.gov/ERICDocs/data/ericdocs2sql/content_storage_01/0000019b/80/14/34/22.pdf (accessed 25 January 2010).

Thomas, J., Sutcliffe, K., Harden, A., Oakley, A. et al. (2003) *Children and Healthy Eating: A Systematic Review of Barriers and Facilitators*. London: EPPI-Centre, Social Science Research Unit, Institute of Education, University of London.

Trenta, L. and Newman, I. (2001) *Evaluation of an On-going Block Scheduling Program*. Paper presented at: the Annual Meeting of the Mid-Western Educational Research Association, Chicago, 24–27 October.

Zhang, G. (2001) *Academic Performance Differences Between Students in Block and Traditionally Scheduled High Schools 1993–2000*. Paper presented at: the Annual Meeting of the American Educational Research Association, Seattle, 10–14 April.

21

Mixed methods

Gert Biesta

Introducing mixed methods research

Since the 1990s mixed methods research has become a popular and increasingly influential way to understand and conduct research in the social sciences, including in the field of education (for the latter see, for example, Gorard, 2004). In its most basic form mixed methods research entails a combination of 'qualitative' and 'quantitative' approaches with the ambition to generate a more accurate and adequate understanding of social phenomena than would be possible by using only one of these approaches. During the second half of the twentieth century the discussion about social research was characterised by strongly opposing views about what counts as good and worthwhile research – a discussion often referred to as the 'paradigm wars'. The advance of mixed methods research has brought about a degree of pacification (see Denzin, 2008), acknowledging that 'qualitative' and 'quantitative' approaches both have their strengths and weaknesses, so that a combination of the two might be a more fruitful option. Proponents of a mixed methods approach thus advocate a *pragmatic* rather than a *principled* approach, arguing that decisions about design and methods should be driven by the aims, objectives and research questions. Johnson and Onwuegbuzie (2004: 17) formulate this as the idea that one should 'choose the combination or mixture of methods and procedures that works best for answering your research questions', while Tashakkori and Teddlie (1998: 20) call it the 'dictatorship of the research question'.

The idea of mixed methods research can be said to have developed from the notion of 'triangulation', which expresses the belief that the convergence of evidence stemming from two or more methods can enhance the strength and validity of research findings. *Triangulation* – seeking convergence and corroboration of results from different methods and designs studying the same phenomenon – is indeed one of the five major purposes or rationales for mixed methods approach as indicated by Greene et al. (1989). The others are *complementarity* (seeking elaboration, enhancement, illustration and clarification of the results from one method with results from the other method); *initiation* (discovering potential paradoxes and contradictions that lead to a re-framing of the research question; *development* (using the findings from one method to help inform the other method; and *expansion* (seeking to expand the breadth and range of research by using different methods for different enquiry components) (see also Johnson and Onwuegbuzie, 2004: 21–2).

There are ongoing discussions about the precise definition of mixed methods research (for the most comprehensive overview of the field see Tashakkori and Teddlie, 2010; for a detailed discussion of different mixed designs see Creswell and Plano Clark, 2007).

Johnson et al., (2007: 123) have suggested to define mixed methods *research* as 'the type of research in which a researcher or team of researchers combines elements of qualitative and quantitative research approaches (e.g. use of qualitative and quantitative viewpoints, data collection, analysis, inference techniques) for the broad purposes of breadth and depth of understanding and corroboration'. They distinguish this from a mixed method *study* which involves 'mixing within a single study' and from a mixed method *programme* which involves 'mixing within a program of research [where] the mixing might occur across a closely related set of studies' (ibid.).

The nature of mixed methods research

While it is relatively easy to say that mixed methods research is about the combination of qualitative and quantitative approaches, it is more difficult to articulate what this exactly means and entails. This has to do with the fact that under the labels 'qualitative' and 'quantitative' a wide range of differing concepts, ideas, values and opinions is clustered together (which is one reason why, in the English-speaking world, authors often speak about two different paradigms of research rather than two different approaches).[1] This not only means that when one claims to be combining 'qualitative' and 'quantitative' approaches it is not immediately and automatically clear what one is actually trying to mix or combine. More importantly, whereas the combination of some aspects of these two approaches is relatively unproblematic, there are also aspects where mixing is far more complicated and perhaps even impossible. Researchers wanting to use a mixed approach therefore at least need to be aware of the different 'levels' at which one might aim to mix or combine. Elsewhere (Biesta, 2010) I have therefore suggested that we should distinguish between seven levels or dimensions at which mixing might take place. At each level one can ask questions about the possibility of mixing. These comprise:

1. *Data* – is it possible to combine text and numbers?
2. *Methods* – is it possible to combine different methods of data collection and/or data analysis?
3. *Designs* – is it possible to combine experimental/ interventionist and naturalist/non-interventionist designs?
4. *Epistemologies* – is it possible to combine different views about knowledge?
5. *Ontologies* – is it possible to combine different views about reality?
6. *Research purposes* – is it possible to combine the intention to generate causal explanation with the intention to generate interpretative understanding?
7. *Practical orientations* – can research be orientated both towards the production of solutions, techniques and technologies and towards the development of critical understanding and analysis?

While it is relatively uncontroversial to combine different data and different data-collection and data-analysis strategies within the same study (levels 1 and 2), and while it is also relatively uncontroversial to combine different designs within the same programme (level 3), things become more complicated when one reaches questions about what knowledge 'is' and what kind of knowledge research is able to generate, or how we should understand the reality that is the object of our investigation (levels 4 and 5). This, in turn, may have an impact on the extent to which different purposes of research can be combined (level 6) – something which is more feasible within a programme than within a study – not in the least because one's answer to the question whether it is possible to provide causal explanations of social phenomena (level 6) strongly depends on one's views about social reality (level 5). All this is, finally, also connected with the way in which one articulates the practical orientations of one's research, that is what one hopes the research will achieve and contribute to fields of practice (level 7) – which is, of course, a crucial concern in the domain of education.

Different mixed designs

Given the foregoing observations, it will not come as a surprise that there are many ways in which one can combine different elements within a mixed research study or research programme. As a result, authors within the field of mixed methods have developed a range of different typologies in order to characterise different mixed approaches (see particularly the contributions by Tashakkori and Teddlie, 1998, 2003; Greene et al., 1989; and Creswell et al., 2003). One important distinction is that between *concurrent* and *sequential* designs. In concurrent designs qualitative and quantitative elements occur within the same study. For example, in a case study of a school, quantitative data may be collected about student performance and interviews conducted with teachers and students, both sources of information being used to build up the case study. Triangulation, where separate studies of the same phenomenon are conducted and the findings of the two studies are brought together after they have been concluded, is an another example of concurrent design. In sequential designs qualitative and quantitative elements alternate. For example, statistical information about the relationship between student characteristics and educational achievement may be collected and analysed first and then, once certain patterns have been identified, these are followed up with in-depth interviews in order to gain a deeper understanding of why these patterns might occur. Alternatively, life-history interviews may be conducted with teachers in order to explore their career development and motivation and then a statistical analysis of population data about teachers' careers could be undertaken in order to expand the insights acquired through the interviews.

In the literature concurrent and sequential approaches are often depicted as 'QUAL + QUAN' and 'QUAL $\rightarrow$ QUAN' or 'QUAN $\rightarrow$ QUAL' respectively. When 'QUAL' and 'QUAN' are both written in capitals it is to indicate that equal status is given to both approaches. If, on the other hand, one of the approaches is given a dominant status, only this approach is written in capitals. In that case there are two potential concurrent combinations – QUAL + quan and QUAN + qual – and four potential sequential combinations – QUAL $\rightarrow$ quan; qual $\rightarrow$ QUAN; QUAN $\rightarrow$ qual; quan $\rightarrow$ QUAL. The issue of dominance might best be understood in relation to dimension 6 discussed above, that is the aspect of the purposes of research. Here one could imagine that a QUAN approach is one that aims to generate causal explanations of social phenomena. If, within such an orientation, qualitative data and analysis are used, it is done to strengthen the explanatory power of the research – and in precisely this regard this approach is different from triangulation. If, for example, one aims to provide an explanation of the factors that cause the underachievement of boys in secondary education one might, to deepen understanding of the causal patterns, conduct interviews with students in order to add qualitative understanding of one's explanations. In that case the design could be depicted as 'QUAN $\rightarrow$ qual'. Creswell and Plano Clark (2007) refer to such a design as *explanatory*. A 'QUAL $\rightarrow$ quan' design, on the other hand, would be one where the overriding aim is to generate interpretative understanding, that is giving an account of why people act as they act, where quantitative information can be added to deepen the interpretation and provide a more robust confirmation of the understandings acquired through the collection of qualitative data. The example mentioned above of a life-history project with additional quantitative information could be constructed in this way. Creswell and Plano Clark (2007) refer to such a design as *exploratory*.

What follows from this is that there are no typical methods for data collection in mixed research. Depending on what one aims to achieve, any method can, in principle, be included. In a sense there are also no typical methods for data analysis, other than that it is of crucial importance that the analysis of the data is congruent with the design of the research and, most importantly, with the overall purpose of the research. This shows that the conduct of mixed methods research depends first of all on one's research purpose and, once this has been clarified, on the particular design that best meets this purpose. This also means, however, that unlike what many authors who write about mixed research maintain, it is not the research question that is the very first step in a mixed process but rather the research purpose – something which can only be stated if one has a good grasp of the problems one wishes to address through research. One could say, therefore, that for mixed research – as for all good research – one should start with identifying a problem. One should then identify to what extent research might make a contribution to addressing the problem – some problems, after all, do not need research to be addressed – after which one can begin to state the overall research purpose and more specific aims and objectives. It is only after this has been done that it becomes possible to formulate research questions, construct a design and decide about methods for data collection and data analysis.

An example: the Learning Lives project

While the inclusion of qualitative and quantitative data in a small-scale research study can in itself already be an example of a mixed approach, my own experience with mixed methods research has been in large-scale educational research projects, one on learning cultures in further education (James and Biesta, 2007) and one on the role of learning in the life course: the Learning Lives project (Biesta et al., 2011). The latter project is interesting from a design point of view as it actually combined *three* different approaches: interpretative life-history research and two forms of life-course research, longitudinal interpretative life-course research and longitudinal quantitative survey research. The life-history research sought, through extensive individual interviews, to understand the role of learning in the lives of the participants up till now, whereas the longitudinal interpretative life-course research aimed to track the role of learning in the lives of the participants during the three years the project lasted. The overall aim of the project was to deepen understanding of the complexities of learning in the life course while identifying, implementing and evaluating strategies for sustained positive impact upon learning opportunities, dispositions and practices, and upon the empowerment of adults. For this we were particularly interested in the interrelationships between learning, identity and agency in the life course.

The project was initially set up as a sequential mixed design where the findings from the two QUAL parts of the project (interpretative life-history research and longitudinal interpretative life-course research) would feed into the construction of a survey, the findings of which would feed back into the next cycle of interpretative research and so on – thus following an extended sequential pattern of QUAL → QUAN → QUAL → QUAN and so on. This, however, turned out to be too complicated, partly because the data collection and analysis of the QUAL phase would take so much time that there would be insufficient time left for survey construction, and partly because

within the resources available for the project it would be too difficult to generate high-quality longitudinal survey data. Instead, therefore, the QUAN part of the project became based on secondary analysis of data from the British Household Panel Survey, thus turning the project from a sequential into a concurrent mixed design.

Although to a certain extent the QUAL and the QUAN parts of the project operated on equal terms, one could argue that the QUAL part was slightly more dominant in that the overall aim of the project was to deepen understanding of the complexity of learning in the life course – a research aim that focuses on understanding rather than causal explanation – albeit that within this wider aim, the project had a clear interest in relationships between learning, identity and agency and in factors that might contribute to the improvement of learning through the life course – which thus added questions about relationships and interactions that moved the overall aims of the project into the direction of explanation. Nonetheless, the main approach for identifying such connections was through interpretative modes of research with additional insights from the survey part of the project. It appears, therefore, that the Learning Lives project was more of a QUAL + quan design than a fully blown QUAL + QUAN, at least, that is, if we focus on the overall aims and purposes of the research.

While informed by the same set of questions, concepts and theories, the QUAL and the QUAN part of the project operated relatively independently with regard to data collection and data analysis. It was only once the analysis within the separate strands had been conducted that insights were brought together – and even then at a relatively high level of abstraction. One could therefore argue that the mixing that took place within the Learning Lives project was a form of triangulation, albeit not in the narrow sense of two approaches investigating the same phenomenon, but in the broader sense of different approaches trying to generate answers to the same set of research questions.

The Learning Lives project is therefore of interest, partly because it provides an example of a more complicated mixed design than most of the literature on mixed methods research assumes, and partly because it reveals that, while in theory mixed designs may be very attractive, in practice they can become quite complicated, particularly if either time or financial resources are limited or if the project is large in scale. This should function as a warning that mixed methods research poses a number of additional challenges to researchers so that it is even more important to think carefully through the design of one's research if one wishes to make use of the unique opportunities of mixed approaches.

Note

1. It is important to be aware of the fact that the idea of 'research paradigms' is a typical Anglo-American way to engage with questions concerning the methods and methodologies of research. In Continental traditions there is a much stronger emphasis on explanation and understanding as two distinctively different orientations in social and behavioural research – a discussion at least going back to the late 1950s (see Frisby, 1972). In this tradition one would often argue that, in addition to an approach focused on explanation and one focused on understanding, there is a third approach focused on emancipation or, in the words of Carr and Kemmis (1986), on 'becoming critical'.

Suggested further reading

The idea of mixed methods is becoming increasingly popular in many areas of social research, including the field of education. But whereas more and more researchers are beginning to characterise their work in terms of mixed methods, the wide variety of approaches that can go under this general label implies that in some cases this means hardly more than that different data are used. Only in a very limited number of cases will researchers be using the full potential a mixed approach can offer. This is why it is important – both for those who read research and those who design and conduct research – not to assume that all research that uses the label is of similar design and, more importantly, of similar quality. For those who wish to read more about mixed methods research, its range of designs and its strengths and weaknesses Plano Clark and Creswell's *Mixed Methods Reader* (2008) provides a good starting point, while much more detailed discussions about the many varieties of mixed methods research can be found in the second edition of Tashakkori and Teddlie's *Handbook*

of Mixed Methods in Social and Behavioral Research (2010). The *Journal of Mixed Methods Research* provides many up-to-date examples of mixed methods approaches from across the social and behavioural sciences. In addition many journals in the field of educational research are increasingly publishing work that uses some form of mixed methods design.

References

Biesta, G. J. J. (2010) 'Pragmatism and the philosophical foundations of mixed methods research', in Tashakkori, A. and Teddlie, C. (eds) *Sage Handbook of Mixed Methods in Social and Behavioral Research.* (2nd edn). Thousand Oaks, CA: Sage, pp. 95–118.

Biesta, G. J. J., Field, J., Hodkinson, P., Macleod, F. J. and Goodson, I. F. (2011) *Improving Learning Through the Lifecourse: Learning Lives.* London and New York: Routledge.

Carr, W. and Kemmis, S. (1986) *Becoming Critical.* London: Falmer Press.

Creswell, J. W. and Plano Clark, V. L. (2007) *Designing and Conducting Mixed Methods Research.* Thousand Oaks, CA: Sage.

Creswell, J. W., Plano Clark, V. L., Gutmann, M. L. and Hanson, W. E. (2003) 'Advanced mixed method research designs', in Tashakkori, A. and Teddlie, C. (eds) *Sage Handbook of Mixed Methods in Social and Behavioral Research.* (2nd edn). Thousand Oaks, CA: Sage.

Denzin, N. K. (2008) 'The new paradigm dialogs and qualitative inquiry', *International Journal of Qualitative Studies in Education*, 21(4): 315–25.

Frisby, D. (1972) 'The Popper-Adorno controversy: the methodological dispute in German sociology', *Philosophy of the Social Sciences*, 2: 105–19.

Gorard, S. with Taylor, C. (2004) *Combining Methods in Educational and Social Research.* Maidenhead: Open University Press.

Greene, G. C., Caracelli, V. J. and Graham, W. F. (1989) 'Toward a conceptual framework for mixed-method evaluation design', *Educational evaluation and policy analysis*, 11(3): 255–74.

James, D. and Biesta, G. J. J. (2007) *Improving Learning Cultures in Further Education.* London: Routledge.

Johnson, R. B. and Onwuegbuzie, A. J. (2004) 'Mixed methods research: a research paradigm whose time has come', *Educational Research*, 33(7): 14–26.

Johnson, R. B., Onwuegbuzie, A. J. and Turner, L. A. (2007) 'Toward a definition of mixed methods research', *Journal of Mixed Methods Research*, 1(2): 112–33.

Plano Clark, V. L. and Creswell, J. W. (2008) *The Mixed Methods Reader*. Thousand Oaks, CA: Sage.

Tashakkori, A. and Teddlie, C. (1998) *Mixed Methodology: Combining Qualitative and Quantitative Approaches*. London: Sage.

Tashakkori, A. and Teddlie, C. (2003) 'The past and future of mixed methods research: from data triangulation to mixed model design', in Tashakkori, A. and Teddlie, C. (eds) *Sage Handbook of Mixed Methods in Social and Behavioral Research*. (2nd edn). Thousand Oaks, CA: Sage, pp. 671–701.

Tashakkori, A. and Teddlie, C. (eds) (2010) *Sage Handbook of Mixed Methods in Social and Behavioral Research* (2nd edn). Thousand Oaks, CA: Sage.

Philosophical research[1]

Richard Pring

Issues which traditionally have concerned philosophers permeate every aspect of educational thinking. This, however, is not generally recognised, as is reflected in the initial and continuing education of teachers, in the development and implementation of policy and in the conduct of educational research. The result is misbegotten certainty where doubt would be appropriate, apparent clarity where there is confusion, conclusions from evidence where evidence does not support the conclusions. This paper seeks to illustrate this from the conduct of the Nuffield Review of 14–19 Education and Training.

Introduction

Philosophy of education needs to be reclaimed for educational research. Increasingly it is seen to be of little relevance – as is reflected in lack of appointments to university departments of education, in submissions to the Research Assessment Exercise and in courses in educational research methodology. Indeed, educational controversies are seen to be resolvable simply by effective and thorough empirical investigation.

Yet, as Alasdaire MacIntyre recently reminds us:

The warring partisans on the great issues that engage our culture and politics presuppose, even when they do not recognise it, the truth of some philosophical theses and the falsity of others. (2010)

Philosophical questions (for example, in ethics, epistemology, philosophy of mind and political philosophy) permeate almost every aspect of educational research, policy-making, educational practice and deliberation. The lack of philosophical thinking is apparent in the government's policy statements, in the many educational White Papers and consultation documents, and in the research which addresses the educational problems.

The significance of this is explored through a reflection upon the work undertaken for the Nuffield Review of Education and Training of 14–19 Year Olds in England and Wales. This £1 million review was the largest in the secondary phase of education and training since the Crowther Report fifty years ago. Such a Review had to be comprehensive, thus embracing (1) the vision of learning which permeates the system, (2) its translation into curriculum, (3) its assessment for both better learning and accountability, and (4) reflection of that assessment in an ever more complex and centrally directed system of qualifications.

This paper focuses in particular upon:

- the overall educational aims which, too often, remain implicit, which are reflected in a language that 'bewitches the intelligence' and which need constantly to be addressed systematically;
- the notion of 'standards' which, though logically related to aims, are treated as objective, clear and disconnected from any deliberation about educational aims and values;
- the different kinds of 'learning', the neglect of whose analysis has resulted, first, in the false dualisms between 'academic' and 'vocational' and between the theoretical and the practical; second, in the neglect of experiential learning; third, in the narrow understanding of assessment which too often impoverishes the quality of learning.

What the Review endeavoured to do, in its comprehensive account of 14–19 education and training, was to show, first, that these key concepts (aims, standards, learning) provide a logical framework through which educational policy and practice are described, evaluated and promoted, and, second, that so much actual descriptions and evaluations are distorted through the failure to look critically at the unexamined and implicit ways in which these words are put to use. Therefore both a critique of the educational system and the recommendations for future improvement require a careful examination of those concepts and the logical interconnections between them.

In many respects there is little new in such an undertaking. Such analysis has been the very stuff of the philosophy of education. But rarely has it been conducted through the context of a detailed account of the system both as it is and as it is planned by policymakers. In some respects, the philosophical critiques of the Plowden Report in the late 1960s engaged in a similar philosophical exercise and demonstrated the valuable contribution of philosophical thinking to unravelling the conceptual complexities which underpin policy and shape practice in primary education. But it was conducted within the examination of a particular text rather than a detailed account of the system as a whole and against an examination of the empirical evidence.

Doing philosophy

First, it is necessary to indicate what I mean by 'doing philosophy', without in any way implying that this is the only way. There is a tradition which focuses on the meaning of the language we use and shows how, unless one is careful, the grammar of that language can belie the more complex usages. In this respect, 'philosophy is a battle against the bewitchment of our intelligence by means of language' (Wittgenstein, 1947).

A highly relevant example is the use of the word 'skill' or the 'skilled person'. 'Skill' is what a good footballer has, but also now the empathic person, the clever thinker, the astute crossword performer, the ballet star. Clearly there are overlapping meanings; the word is not used equivocally. But assimilating these uses from different contexts leads to the wrong belief that there is more in common than there really is.

For example, assumptions are made about 'transfer of learning' or about 'generic powers of the mind' which permeate different kinds of thinking (as in the teaching of 'thinking skills') or about the emphasis upon skills training. Policies are promoted, following the Leitch Report (2006), for the development of skills *as such*, since there will be, so it is declared, only 600,000 jobs in 2020 which require no skills, as opposed to the seven million today. Other research contradicts this; there will remain the seven million jobs requiring workers without skills. Is Leitch right or wrong? The question is posed as though it is an empirical one. But it is in part, if not mainly, a conceptual issue. What is a skill? And, given there are many different kinds and complexities of skill, how can they be added up to get the number 600,000? Is 'street cleaning a skill' (some streets are cleaned more effectively than others). If so, is it one or several skills, and how quickly can each of those component skills be learnt? Are street cleaners included in the overall number of skilled jobs to be trained for? As Wittgenstein asserted:

Assimilating the descriptions of the uses of words in this way cannot make the uses themselves any more like one another. For, as we see, they are absolutely unlike. (Leitch, 2006)

One important function of philosophy therefore is to expose the false implications drawn from the failure to see differences of meaning in the usages of words, such as 'skill', 'education', 'practical capability', 'vocational', 'academic', 'experience', 'personalised learning'. Often (as in the case of the academic/ vocational distinction which pervades policy documents and thereby shapes the curriculum, and the status given to different timetabled activities) that analysis will trace the different usages, locating them in different and wider traditions of human activity. In so doing, it might be critical of those traditions. Perhaps they have been blind to particular values or make wrong assumptions about the kind of knowledge embedded within them.

This chapter pursues this philosophical approach through reflection upon the conduct of the Nuffield Review. In particular, it examines the too often unexamined 'educational aims and values' which are embodied in policy and practice. Second, in the light of that, it focuses on 'standards' which dominate educational discourse and which are logically related to educational aims, although that logical connection is rarely if ever acknowledged. Thirdly, it examines briefly what can be meant by the 'quality of learning' which is supposed to improve through concentration upon 'raising standards', but which, upon examination, seems, in policy and recommended practice, to arise from a narrow understanding of quality. In particular, it argues for a wider understanding of quality of learning – one which meets a more comprehensive view of standards arising from the analysis of educational aims and values.

The aims of education

To review all that is happening within a particular phase of education and training requires some organising principle – some standpoint from which one might see and evaluate the different elements. Such a standpoint, too, shapes how different aspects (standards, quality of learning, assessment, teaching) are logically related to each other. Different aims and values redefine their significance and their interrelationship. What purpose, then, is the system intended to serve? What are the aims and values

which, even not explicit, underpin the educational system in its different aspects?

The Review encapsulated this standpoint by framing the question: *What counts as an educated 19 year old in this day and age?*

There are many answers to this kind of question for the simple reason that 'educated' implies the acquisition of qualities, understandings and aspirations which are judged to be of value and worth pursuing. They are tied to what one sees, implicitly or explicitly, to be the sort of person and the sort of society which, through learning, one would wish to see developed. But there does not appear to be broad consensus on the aims and values which should direct educational choices.

However, despite this lack of consensus, recent government papers pay little attention to the aims of education, and thus to the values which should shape the standards to be achieved, the knowledge to be transmitted and the virtues to be nourished. Of course, there are gestures in this direction. The 14–19 Education and Skills White Paper (DCSF, 2004) insists that we should seek to realise the potential of all young people. But such aspirations hardly do the job. Any newspaper reveals that there is as much potential for evil as there is for good. The problem with such clichés is that they dodge the ethical issues implicit in talking about educating young people.

And yet values are embodied in all that we do in seeking to educate. One can see how implicit and unexamined values shape the educational programme of young people from 14 to 19. For example, the division between the more prestigious academic pathways for some and the vocational studies for the others, the dismissal of the arts and humanities from the core curriculum at 14, the focus on economically relevant skills and on the qualities of entrepreneurship and enterprise, the concentration upon examination grades, the absence of practical and experiential engagement, the proposed designation of maths and science as 'hard subjects' for purposes of league tables (and the arts and drama as 'soft'), the mode through which merit is recognised in formal assessments – all these reflect dominant values and thereby the prevailing aims of education. Practices and policies, too often unquestioned, become problematic against a deeper ethical critique.

The Review, therefore, had to argue for its

understanding of what it means to be a person and to be one more fully, knowing that any such argument would be controversial. Society's disagreement about standards, learning, assessment or role of the teacher stem as much from different ethical views on what it means to be a person as they do from empirical evidence – a point rarely acknowledged.

Hence, the review argued that four aspects distinguish what it means to be a person – and thereby what is required to *develop* as a person:

- The *ability to make sense of the physical, social, economic and moral worlds we inhabit*. That 'making sense' draws upon the concepts, modes of enquiry, explanations which we have inherited through the different traditions and disciplines of thinking. Inevitably, different young people acquire such modes of thinking at different levels of sophistication. But no one should be excluded from entry into these different modes of experiencing and understanding the world in which they live or from the capacity to exercise control over their lives and to be liberated from others' control over their minds.
- The *practical capabilities* that enable one to act in the world – we are 'doers' and creators as well as thinkers. The Review drew upon the traditions of the Royal Society of Arts which for 250 years has emphasised the importance for human achievement and flourishing of the unity of thinking and doing, of imagination and creating, of 'thinking with the hands'. Its 1988 manifesto *Education for Capability* stated:

  > There exists in its own right a culture which is concerned with doing and making and organising and the creative arts. This culture emphasises the day-to-day management of affairs, the formulation and solution of problems, and the design, manufacture and marketing of goods and services. (RSA, 1988)

  And yet, in thinking about the 'educated 19 year old', that 'intelligent doer' is too often neglected – unrecognised in the 'standards' by which learner and school or college are judged.

- The *capacity to take responsibility* for the direction of one's life, for the relationships entered into and for the contribution to the wider community – what the Review referred to as *moral seriousness*. It is not hard to imagine the academically successful being bereft of desirable human sensibility or appropriate dispositions or virtues, and thereby being that much 'less of a person'. And such sensibilities can be learnt through an educational process and ethos which helps shape the personality and goals thought worth pursuing.
- *Community orientation* – that is, the recognition that these young persons' very identity is tied up with being a member of wider communities upon which they are essentially dependent (the language inherited, the traditions into which they are born, the range of human labour sustaining them, the laws providing protection) and to which they can, if so enabled through learning, help shape. Presumably this is what essentially 'citizenship' is about.

All the above need to be learnt through the initiation into the different forms of knowledge and understanding, into moral traditions which can so easily come to be neglected, into practices of doing and making, and into civic and public traditions of service.

It may well be the case that such analysis, general though it is, will have its critics, and such criticism will be reflected in what are accepted as 'educated persons'. There is not, nor will there ever be, unanimity over the aims of education. William Morris (the car maker) was excluded from the local golf club because he was in trade – hardly an educated person. But this brilliant 'doer and maker' demonstrated his practical capability by purchasing the golf club. Was he not really an educated person, despite his lack of formal education beyond the age of 14? ('Certainly not', acclaimed one student of Christ Church, who had known him personally, when I posed this question at an Oxford seminar.)

Moreover, within each of these four aspects there will be disagreement. What are the different disciplines of knowledge and is there agreement about the key ideas and modes of enquiry which they embody? Are there key practical capabilities which all young people should acquire if they are to be called educated (cooking, the use of internet and communication technology, public speaking)?

The key point is that where one stands on these essentially ethical issues affects profoundly what the shape and provision of 14–19 education should be. And this is generally unacknowledged. Initiative and reforms proceed as though the whole matter is ethically neutral.

Standards of performance

The significance of these points arises particularly in the attempt to make sense of the 'standards agenda'. It is a constant theme of educational 'reform' that standards are too low and compare badly with countries elsewhere. It is argued that standards need to be raised. To this end standards have been made much more explicit, set out in 'specifications' for GCE A level grades, for skill performances at Levels 1, 2 and 3 NVQs and for teacher qualifications. (Professor Ted Wragg once counted 181 standards which primary trained teachers had to meet.) Furthermore, as the government tries to tidy up the range of qualifications available, so its agency the QCA (then the QCDA) defined equivalences between standards in quite different activities. For example, standards of ASDAN's Certificate of Personal Effectiveness (CoPE) at Level 2 are declared to be 'equivalent to' a GCSE graded A–C; Diploma Levels 2 and 3 are 'equivalent' in standard across the different lines of Diploma – for example, in hairdressing and in engineering; a Level 3 Diploma is equivalent to three A levels.

However, harking back to the above section entitled, 'Doing philosophy', one might ask in a puzzled sort of way, 'What does this mean?' 'Standards' are the benchmark by which an activity is judged good or bad, fit or not fit for purpose, appropriate or not appropriate. One talks of someone's performance coming up to standard.

Several observations are necessary here as we try to unravel the meaning of 'standard'.

First, it is not clear what could be meant by standards going up or down rather than performance in relation to specific standards. Thus, if a standard has gone down then that must be by virtue of some other standard by which 'up' and 'down' are defined. During the brief life of the Assessment Performance Unit, established to 'monitor standards over time', difficulties were encountered in providing a longitudinal measure of performance in relation to agreed standards because these standards do themselves change in tune with new knowledge, different aims and reformed evaluations of what is worth learning.

Second, therefore, standards must relate to the nature of the activity which is seen to be educationally worth pursuing. What is its purpose? Educational standards relate logically to the aims of education. If those aims are broadened to embrace the sort of qualities referred to above, then the standards do themselves change. It would be wrong, if the pursuit of practical capability or the development of 'moral seriousness' were seen to be a worthwhile educational aim, to ignore such achievements in the assessment of a student's or a school's performance.

Third, it does make sense to say a performance does not come up to standard where the standard is not made (and cannot be made) explicit. Think of an essay judged to be elegantly written, or an argument seen to be incisive, or a painting appreciated as exceptionally beautiful. In pursuit of 'higher standards' there has been an attempt to accept as standards only those aspects of an activity which can be made explicit, easily measured and then 'standardised', dismissing the place of 'judgement'. This in turn makes it possible to 'teach to the standards' in the sense of training to conform behaviour to what has been explicitly laid down as the standardised measure. But part of what it means to learn is to come to see, often through struggling with the criticism of those more expert, what those standards are – as in the writing of history essays or in the appreciation of poetry.

Fourth, the notion of equivalence seems unintelligible. How can there be 'equivalence' between standards of performance in very different activities (in hairdressing and construction, for example – in cutting hair and cementing bricks)? Perhaps meaning could be attached to such 'equivalence' in terms of the amount of difficulty which each respectively demands. But different people in fact find difficulty in different ways and different activities.

Hence, standards are intrinsic to the activity – part of the definition, as it were. The standards in bricklaying relate both to the purpose of the activity and to the endurance and appearance of the product. It requires the expert eye of the bricklayer to assess the level of competence, the insight of the mathematician to assess the quality of the mathematical thinking. In both cases, it is more than a lot of 'can dos' on standardised tests. Historians will themselves disagree on what count as standards in that there are philosophical differences about the nature of historical enquiry.

Who, then, should decide what, in different activities taught in school and college, are 'the standards'? Who are the experts? In one way they must be those who are recognised by their professional and craft peers as the experts and who have demonstrated their expertise through their participation in the relevant discipline or craft, bearing in mind that the prevailing acceptance of standards is always provisional and developing through the arrival of new techniques, new knowledge and new circumstances in the world in which the different activities are engaged.

The Review, therefore, cast doubt on the 'standardisation of standards', on attempts to bring all awards neatly into a 'framework of qualifications', on the exercise of rendering different activities equivalent, on the legacy of maintaining equivalence between the old O level and GCSE grade C, and on the distorting effects of league tables constructed on this misuse of language. There is a disconnection of 'standards' from the different forms of life to which they are logically related, and thus, as a result of this 'bewitchment by the use of the language' of performance management, those activities become impoverished in relation to the very standards by which they should be judged.

Learning

Central to education (in the descriptive sense) is of course the promotion or nurturing of learning. What kind of learning that should be depends on the underlying view of what is worthwhile to learn (education in its evaluative sense) – that is, on the aims of education whether explicit or, as is usual, implicit and unexamined. Presently the responsibility for post-16 learning is in the hands of the Learning and Skills Council which determines what learning activities are worth funding. The Act which, at the time of

writing, was going through Parliament, namely the Apprenticeships, Skills, Children and Learning Act, would transfer the responsibility for this funding to the new Young People's Learning Agency. Here, as in the names of the two departments of state responsible for schools, colleges and universities, the word education was conspicuous by its absence. Learning is the generic term that escapes the ethical difficulties embraced by *educational* assessment.

However, in the absence of any attention to what it means to learn, many different kinds of learning are lumped together despite essential differences characterised, first, by the different forms of life in which that learning occurs, and, second, by the formal properties of that which is to be learnt. Learning history is a different sort of learning from learning mathematics. Learning how to build walls is different from learning how to drive a car. Each incorporates different standards. Each poses different problems to be overcome. General theories of learning or its assessment are misplaced, as indeed are such policy clichés as 'learning how to learn'.

Furthermore, such learning, despite the logical differences between how different kinds of learning might be properly described, is impoverished further by the Orwellian language of 'performance management' through which 'learning' is organised and controlled – that of *inputs* to learning related to *outputs*, learning reduced to *performances* in order to reach pre-specified *targets* or *outputs*, *audits* of those targets or *performance indicators*, teachers as *deliverers* of a curriculum developed elsewhere, learners as *customers*. Such focus on measurable productivity and on the instrumental value of learning has little room for that *struggle to understand*, that *exploration of ideas*, that *trial and error* in experiment, that *engagement* and *intrinsic interest* in a learning activity, or that *search for meaning* in life's experiences. Surely, if anywhere, 'learning policy' (as governed by such bodies as the 'Learning and Skills Council') is a prime example of 'when language is like an engine idling, not when it is doing its work' (Wittgenstein, 1947).

There are two areas in 14–19 provision where this failure to reflect upon important distinctions distorts and impoverishes the aims of education and thereby the standards by which young people's achievements might be recognised.

Academic and vocational

The false distinction is made, in document after document, between academic and vocational attainment and qualifications, the latter being somehow inferior to the former – what you do if you are not capable of academic studies. Yet the distinction, on closer examination, cannot be defended. Is the pursuit of art or drama academic or vocational? Well, the study of the history of art would seem to be in the academic category, but what about *doing* art? What about dramatic performance? What about the writing of poetry, rather than writing critiques of others' poems? What about the thoughtful, tentative creation of an artefact in woodwork? The word 'academic' is used in these contexts as though its meaning is clear, but in fact it would seem to be defined ostensively, that is by pointing to certain subjects which have been traditionally part of the grammar school curriculum. As in the case of 'skill', it lumps together a range of different kinds of knowledge and enquiry as though they had common features – another case of 'assimilating the descriptions of the uses of words' when 'they are absolutely unlike'.

Michael Oakeshott, referred to education as an *initiation into the world of ideas*, a world of ideas which had arisen from *the conversation between the generations of mankind*, in which the young person is *introduced to the different voices in that conversation* – the voices of poetry, of science, of history, of philosophy. The so-called 'academic learning' is *at its best* an introduction to that conversation – an acquisition of those concepts, ideas and modes of enquiry through which we have come to make sense of the world and which are captured in the respective subjects. And these key concepts and ideas can be put across to any child at any age at some level of understanding. The curriculum, according to Jerome Bruner, is ideally spiral in that it constantly revisits the key ideas (Bruner, 1960).

A current example of this would be that of Applied Science (see Nuffield Review, 2007). This involves understanding scientific knowledge and methods of scientific enquiry embodied in techniques used by scientists. These techniques cross areas of application (e.g. in the use of microscopes by public analysts and microbiologists). It develops this understanding through authentic work-related contexts (e.g. a doctor or nurse dealing with cystic fibrosis). It focuses on people who apply scientific techniques and knowledge, looking into the thought processes and skills involved (e.g. questioning the theoretical and practical limitations of a given technique). It provides opportunity for practical problem-solving, emphasising ability to use techniques, skills and knowledge for tackling science-related problems (e.g. in the analysis of blood samples in the diagnosis of an illness). It engages with contemporary scientific issues, especially the relation between science, technology and society. And it requires high-level numeracy because of the centrality of 'quantity' and statistics in the work-related science; accurate measurement is crucial. Applied Science, in emphasising practical and experiential learning, overcomes the false dualism between 'academic' and 'vocational' and has led to an impressively large increase in the number of young people wanting to continue post-16 with the study of science.

The false dualism between the academic and vocational has had four pernicious consequences:

- It has treated as similar, for teaching and assessment purpose, learning activities which are quite dissimilar (for example, the use of multi-choice questions to assess learning both in science and in the humanities).
- It has demoted the arts and the humanities in the education of young people from 14 to 18, who are able to opt out where they choose to pursue so-called vocational options.
- It has helped maintain the tripartite division, explicitly promulgated in the Norwood Report of 1943, between different types of young people: those capable of 'academic success', those good at practising, and the rest.
- It has confused 'vocational' with 'practical' thereby failing to perceive the relevance of the practical activity as a way into theoretical understanding.

Practical learning

The Nuffield Review started with a re-examination of the aims of education and concluded from such considerations that there was a need for a wider vision of learning. Oakeshott's metaphor of the 'conversation between the generations of mankind' could be extended to the traditions of 'practical capability' which can so easily die through neglect – or be identified with the vocational skills associated with the less able. And indeed that is what is happening. There is the gradual demise of practical subjects in secondary schools – no longer the woodwork and metalwork, the technical drawing where hands and brain struggled creatively to make an object and to meet demanding standards. Cookery became domestic science. The General National Vocational Qualification, now given way to the new Diplomas, failed because, although aiming to build on the more occupation-related and practical interests of young people otherwise disengaged from the more 'academic curriculum', it was then assessed through written assignments. Successful 'doing' was supposed to be reflected in successful 'writing about doing'.

Practical knowledge (knowing how) cannot be captured in propositional knowledge (knowing that). That no doubt is why it suffers in a high-stakes assessment system which requires successful learning to be adequately reflected in the written word – essays and multi-choice questions. But the successful carpenter or plumber, the successful engineer or architect, is demonstrating an understanding which cannot logically be reduced to propositional knowledge.

Richard Sennett, in his recent book *Craftsmen* (Sennett, 2008), criticises the dualism between mind and body which, philosophically, we have inherited from Descartes, and which permeates the dualism between theorising (what goes on in the mind) and 'practising' (what goes on in the body) and which creates a hierarchy, within education, between the more prestigious 'academic studies' and the less prestigious 'vocational'. Writing explicitly from within the philosophical tradition of 'pragmatism' (and thereby associating himself closely with John Dewey) he argues for the 'intimate connexion between hand and head' (Sennett, 2008: 9) – the dialogue which all good craftsmen conduct 'between concrete practices and thinking'. The skills of the craftsman begin as a bodily practice, those practices emerging into habits, those habits constantly adapted as new problems are confronted and solutions imagined. He speaks of

knowledge being 'in the hand' through 'touch and movement' – that 'knowing how' embodying ways of seeing the world (concepts, causal connections, imagined ways forward, priorities) which are not necessarily explicit, but which could be so upon reflection or when that practical 'know how' falters.

However, Sennett goes further and argues that this is characteristic not simply of 'knowing how' rather than 'knowing that' – practical knowledge rather than academic knowledge. The latter is grounded in the former. Religious practices precede theology which is an attempt to make sense of them. Practical problem-solving gives rise to theoretical science. And it is important that such theory does not take flight from the material, experienced and practical world to which it logically relates. Here we see the basis of the flight from the so-called academic curriculum from which so many young people come to be disengaged.

In so arguing, he criticises the dualism between theory and practice which 'demeans' practical activity 'divorced from supposedly higher pursuits' – and certainly permeating the curriculum of our secondary schools (though that particular point is not made by Sennett).

Furthermore, this practical and experiential knowledge, developed through different craft traditions, should not be seen simply as a means to an end – the value of which lying in its effectiveness. Within a craft tradition (carpentry, pottery, welding, bricklaying) the worker is dedicated to good work for its own sake. There are standards not only of good workmanship but also of a moral kind (patience, perseverance, honesty, cooperation, aspiration to quality, pride in one's work), reflected, in medieval times, in the creation of guilds. Such practical engagement has its distinctive standards of appropriate behaviour as well as its implicit knowledge through which a more theoretical understanding is made possible.

This embodies, too, a very different understanding of experience from that which is presupposed by those who pay little attention to the importance of experience in formal education, ignoring the experiences which young people bring to school from their homes and communities, not seeing the provision for experiential learning to be important. For Dewey:

An ounce of experience is better than a ton of theory because it is only in experience that any theory has vital and verifiable significance. (Dewey, 1936: 51)

But, in so arguing, Dewey, from within this pragmatist tradition, dismisses that dualism of mind and body within which traditional empiricism has interpreted experience as that which 'happens to one' – an imprint on the mind (on the 'tabula rasa'), upon which the mind (the thinking bit) begins to operate.

Rather is experience already imbued with a way of seeing the world. New experience is filtered through the understandings left by previous experiences and, at the same time, adapts the framework of understanding through which new experiences are made possible. Dewey's pragmatism made experience central to education, not peripheral. Persons are constantly adapting to new situations in the light of previous experiences. Of course, particular bits and pieces of knowledge can be 'stuck on', as it were (as if by chewing gum or sellotape), for the sake of examinations. But, without being linked to deeper understandings, it will remain inert. This was the basis of Dewey's critique of 'traditional education' and so-called teaching.

Such practical and experiential learning might be characterised as learning through doing and experience, being shown rather than being told, deliberating over what is possible and what is desirable to create, involving such virtues as patience, pride in the quality of what has been created, respect for others through the engagement in a common activity. Standards of success are intrinsic to the activity. Motivation lies in successful creation rather than as a means to some further end such as a qualification. There is the growth of theoretical understanding – you can't get far in growing your own vegetables without a basic understanding of different kinds of soil or of the right conditions for the germination of seeds. But this growing understanding is learnt within a context, the experience of which gives the more theoretical concepts meaning.

Sadly, practical learning is seen in the main to be appropriate for those who have failed academically. And yet it is a mode of learning that opens up a way of knowing and understanding ('capabilities' to use the words of the RSA Manifesto), as well as giving entry to more theoretical understanding. But its attainment is to be shown in what is done, not in the writing about what is done. The apprentice had to demonstrate his learning, not through writing an essay about what he had learnt, but by his final *chef d'œuvre*; he became a master craftsman after a long period as a journeyman by presenting his *chef d'œuvre élevé*.

Conclusion

In pursuing the aim of *education for all*, as that is proclaimed or implicit in so many publications and legislations over the last 60 years, we have not escaped from a conception of learning which guarantees that only a relatively small number will and indeed can succeed – namely, those who perform well in a rather narrow understanding of academic studies.

However, reflection on the broader aims of education and the consequent standards and wider vision of the learning which enables us to live fully human lives shows how inadequate that is, not only in the education for all, but also in the education for those few who are deemed to succeed. Such learning must embrace:

- the development of understanding for the intelligent management of life – that initiation into the world of ideas, which enable us to make sense of the social, physical and economic worlds which we inhabit;
- the practical capabilities through which we come to understand the world in a different way and act creatively within it;
- the understanding of what it means to be human and to live a distinctively human form of life;
- a sense of community within which one might flourish and which one is empowered to enrich.

This requires a transformation of our educational ideals and a refusal to have them betrayed by the impoverished language and practices of performance management.

Note

1. This chapter is slightly modified from the paper given to the Annual Conference of the Philosophy of Education Society of GB, March 2010.

Suggested further reading

Pring, R., Hayward, G., Hodgson, A., Johnson, J., Keep, E., Oancea, A., Rees, G., Spours, K. and Wilde, S. (2009) *Education for All: The future of education and training for 14-19 year olds*. London: Routledge.

Shawver, L. (2000) *An Introduction to Reading Ludwig Wittgenstein's Philosophical Investigations*. Available at: http://users.rcn.com/rathbone/lwtocc.htm. A website offering an introduction to Wittgenstein's key text.

Wittgenstein, L. (1947) *Philosophical Investigations*. Harlow: Prentice Hall. Hugely important and influential text.

References

Bruner, J. (1960) *The Process of Education*. Cambridge, MA: Harvard University Press.

DCSF (2004) *14–19: Education and Skills*. London: DCSF.

Dewey, J. (1936) *Experience and Education*. London: Simon & Schuster.

Leitch, S. (2006) *Prosperity for All in the Global Economy – World Class Skills*. London: Home Office.

MacIntyre, A. (2010) *God, Philosophy, Universities*. Lanham, MD: Rowman & Littlefield.

Nuffield Review (2007) Issue Paper, *Applied Science*.

RSA (1988) *Education for Capability*. London: RSA.

Sennett, R. (2008) *The Craftsmen*. London: Allen Lane.

Wittgenstein, L. (1947) *Philosophical Investigations*. Harlow: Prentice Hall.

Dimension 2

Data collection tools

Observation-based research

Michael V. Angrosino

Observation as a technique for data collection in social research: a brief introduction

Researchers who want to learn about the many different kinds of groups that make up human society necessarily use some of the ordinary activities that are naturally part of group behaviour. For example, when we are part of a group, we engage in conversation, which gives us information and also helps us develop the social bonds that hold the group together. In the research context, ordinary conversation is transformed into the asking of structured questions, conducting interviews, and administering surveys. These techniques can all be thought of as formalised, organised ways of having informational and network-building conversations. Perhaps even more basic is observation: the use of our five senses to orient us to the social environment. This chapter deals with the use of observation in social research. It will demonstrate the ways in which this most fundamental of human social activities is transformed into a systematic technique for collecting and analysing information about how people behave.

There are two main approaches to research involving social groups. *Quantitative* research is based on the collection of numerical data (i.e. information about things that can be counted and/or measured) and on the statistical analysis of those data. It is often presented in the form of tables, graphs and charts. *Qualitative* research, by contrast, is based on the collection of verbal data (i.e. information about things that can be described in words); it is often presented in the form of narrative accounts of what people say and/or do. Both forms of research use observation; that is, both quantitative and qualitative researchers collect information through their five senses, although most research seems to emphasise things that can be seen and heard. Observation is rarely a stand-alone technique; it usually constitutes the first phase of a research project, and other data-collection techniques are dependent on the basic information provided by initial observations.

Types of observation-based research

One kind of observation-based research is conducted in *clinical* or *laboratory* settings, which means that researchers set up situations in which they can control what goes on and they bring carefully selected (i.e. randomised and representative) participants into that setting. Their observations will typically be structured so as to fit into predetermined categories that can be coded to facilitate statistical analysis. They strive to end up with measurable, countable data in a way that is as objective as possible. That is, the observations themselves and the recording of the resulting data are designed so that any researcher trained in the method can replicate the conditions of the experiment and generate the same results. The observations must, in other words, be *reliable* in statistical terms. This type of research is known as *experimental observation*. Experimental observational research is almost always quantitative in orientation.

In this chapter, however, we will concentrate on observational research conducted in the settings in which people are found of their own accord. In other words, researchers go to the places where people work, play, worship or conduct the myriad other tasks of daily life. The researchers do not seek to control what goes on at the research site, and so their main task is to observe what happens 'naturally'. This type of research is known as *naturalistic* observation, and it has been used by both quantitative and qualitative researchers. It may seem that naturalistic observation is easier to do than the more controlled, experimental form. But in some ways, qualitative researchers must be even more rigorous than their quantitative colleagues in formalising their data collection and thus approximating the reliability achieved by quantitative researchers. To do otherwise might suggest that they have slipped into biased, unsubstantiated opinion, which would not be useful for scientific purposes.

Naturalistic observations may be grouped into three categories, the first of which is *unobtrusive* or *non-reactive observation*. Researchers in this mode avoid intervening in the action they are observing. When their research uses observations undertaken in some sort of public space, they may not even identify themselves at all.

The second category of naturalistic observation is *reactive observation*, which means that researchers do identify themselves and explain their intentions to those they wish to observe; they may also intervene in the action, although they try to do so in their role as social scientists.

The third category of naturalistic observation is *participant observation*, which means that researchers strive to be active members of the group they are observing. The trick in this case is to become enough of a member to gain an insider's perspective on what is going on, without losing the credibility of the objective scientist. They must, in other words, avoid

'going native', to use an old-fashioned term, although they readily acknowledge that they are interested in getting a subjective, insider's view of the activity being observed; this subjective perspective ideally complements, rather than replaces, the outsider's overview.

Observational research in educational settings

Observation-based research is a well-established technique in educational research; the most frequent site for such research is the classroom. It would be unthinkable for an unidentified researcher to slip unobtrusively into a school, and it would be awkward for teachers or students to conduct research on themselves. For those reasons, most research based on classroom observation takes the form of reactive observation. Several topics have been of particular interest to educational researchers doing classroom observations. The first has been the *description of instructional processes*, often with an eye toward identifying problems. Observations have also been used to *investigate the extent to which technology is used in the classroom*. Based on the assumption that self-reports from administrators and teachers (and even, in some cases, students) are biased and self-serving, researchers prefer to rely on their own, presumably unbiased observations. Observational studies have also been used to *monitor the effectiveness of schools*. The study of *instructional inequities* has also lent itself to classroom observational research. Observation-based educational research has tended to be 'reactive' in nature; its findings were often used to provide feedback to teachers and administrators with the goal of improving teaching.

A checklist for doing observational research

- Decide on a theme or topic for the project and select a site that is accessible and that actually illustrates the issue you are interested in studying.
- Be mindful of *gatekeepers*. Some potential sites

are open to the public and researchers require no special permission to be there. Access to some sites, however, is strictly controlled – classrooms and playgrounds are clear examples. Those who control access to such sites are its *gatekeepers*. Sometimes they occupy a formal role (e.g. the school principal or superintendent) and must be approached through clearly defined 'channels'. In many other cases, however, there are informal gatekeepers – people who are the opinion leaders in a particular community even without holding any official position. You may need to do some prior research in order to identify these informal gatekeepers, perhaps by seeking out someone you know to be a member of the group you want to study and asking him or her for advice about how best to gain entry into the community.

- Decide on a research orientation. Your research topic and the site you have selected will direct your decision about the most appropriate research orientation. You need to ask whether the topic you have chosen lends itself more readily to numerical or to narrative data.

- Carry out your observations, which develop through several phases. The initial phase, *descriptive observation*, is intended to give a broad overview of the physical and social characteristics of the site. The observations next proceed through a *focusing phase* when you begin to recognise patterns in the behaviour you are observing. You are moving from the phase of very general questions ('What is going on here?' 'Who are these people?) to one of ever more pointed enquiry ('Why does the nurse stand there?' 'Whose responsibility is it to notify relatives of the victim?'). Next, your observations enter a *selective phase* because pointed questions can only be addressed with selected observations which allow you to establish and clarify the relationships among elements in the site. Finally, your observations reach a *saturation* point, which occurs when new findings consistently replicate material that has already been discovered and accounted for. It may be appropriate to suspend data collection when saturation is achieved and commence the process of analysing the data.

- The essence of *data analysis* is the highlighting and clarifying of the patterns you have begun to observe. *Pattern-finding* may be done 'manually' (i.e. by reading your notes over and over), although nowadays it is almost always aided by some sort of computerised database management program. Regardless of how you choose to identify patterns, you must carefully distinguish 'real' (what people are observed to do) from 'ideal' behaviour (what they tell you in subsequent interviews they are supposed to do) in those patterns. You might also want to pay attention to patterns that are recognised by the people themselves as distinct from those that might only be noted by the researcher, who has access to comparative data from other studies.

- Your findings are now ready for *representation*. How will you make your material known to your designated audience? The default answer is perhaps the traditional *scientific report* (an article, book or paper read at a professional conference), although there is increasing interest in alternative forms of representation, such as narratives that make use of a personal perspective and those that use the forms of literary fiction, poetry or drama. (Choosing 'fiction' does *not* mean that you are making up your data – only that you are using the stylistic devices characteristic of fiction to present your information.) Beyond the written word, one should consider a film (documentary or 'fictional' in nature), a website or an exhibit/visual display.

The ethics of observation-based research

Because observation-based researchers are dealing with real people who have legal rights and to whom we owe some form of moral obligation, they must pay particular attention to the ethical aspects of their projects. Truly unobtrusive researchers may not need to be concerned with their responsibilities to the people they study, especially since their findings are likely to be reported in the aggregate and cannot be used to identify anyone in particular. The other forms of observation, however, do require some basic precautions. The most fundamental principles of ethical research are *informed consent* and the *protection of confidentiality*. That is, people being studied must be made aware that research is taking place and that it has certain definable processes and expected outcomes. They must be assured that their anonymity will be protected (unless they give expressed permission to the contrary) and that all notes and other materials associated with the project will be kept strictly private.[1] Based on this information, potential participants must be allowed to opt out of the research. Informed consent agreements are usually written (in plain English rather than 'legalese') and signed by all parties. Arrangements should be made for translation into another language whenever necessary. People who are illiterate in any language should be given the option of having the agreement read to them by someone they trust. Special care must be taken when observing groups designated as 'vulnerable' under federal guidelines (e.g. children, people with mental disabilities, people in prison). Every university (or other research institution) that receives federal funding in the United States must have an Institutional Review Board that monitors all research proposals for compliance with these basic ethical principles. The professional associations of most of the social science disciplines have published codes of ethics that spell out these principles in terms specific to the conduct of their own preferred styles of research.

Some points for further consideration

In addition to reliability, discussed above, social scientists must also be concerned with the *validity* of their data, which means that an observation actually demonstrates what it is purported to demonstrate. A quantitative researcher might argue, for example, that student test scores are valid measures when assessing the effectiveness of certain teaching techniques. In the absence of such measurable variables, however, observational researchers may validate their procedures by: (a) working with multiple observers who can cross-check team-mates' data, and thus identify (and, perhaps, rectify) inconsistencies; (b) searching for negative cases whenever an emerging pattern is discerned in the data; (c) representing findings in such a way that they 'ring true' with the audience (admittedly a highly subjective criterion).

The potential for 'observer bias' has always been recognised by researchers, since the method almost always involves some sort of subjectivity. Some sorts of bias, such as rushing to ethnocentric judgements (i.e. assuming that something is 'wrong' because the people being observed do things differently from what the researcher is used to), can be overcome with relative ease once they are recognised. More intractable are the problems associated with the built-in biases that flow from the researcher's gender, race/ethnicity, or social class. In these cases, even if the researcher is aware of such factors, there is little or nothing to be done about them. A white researcher observing a black community will certainly recognise the suspicions arising from such a project, but he or she can hardly change the way his or her race is perceived. While it might be possible to overcome these built-in biases, the very act of discussing them and reaching a mutually satisfying accommodation may well lead to changing the way the 'natural' community that was the subject of the research in the first place actually functions. Restricting observational research to those researchers who share the characteristics of the study community ('insider research') might be one solution, but it is hardly a fully satisfactory one, as insiders bring many biases of their own to the project (e.g. taking too many things for granted; being expected to act and think in a certain way by the members of the community). In any case, limiting research to insiders seems to be a very serious violation of the value of comparativeness that has historically been so important in social research.

Another set of issues has recently come to the fore. It has become more common to conduct research online in 'virtual' rather than 'natural' communities. Even if one is willing to grant virtual communities the same social and cultural status as natural ones, it is clear that the meaning of 'observation' is vastly different when one is by definition unseen. The basic ethical principles of informed consent and confidentiality should remain in effect (although the potential certainly exists for those norms being defied more easily than would be the case in face-to-face encounters). Moreover, the essential principles of conducting observational research, recording notes, finding patterns in the data and representing data remain the same. And yet people in general – and social researchers in particular – have the uneasy feeling that they are nonetheless different in ways we have only begun to realise.

Conclusion

The bottom line: as long as we humans use our powers of observation to orient ourselves to our everyday surroundings, social scientists will continue to find ways to integrate refined, rigorously organised observations into their study of group dynamics.

Questions for further investigation

1. Think about a social issue that you would like to explore. What sort of setting would be an appropriate one in which to conduct naturalistic research? Explain why. What, if anything, do you think you would need to do in order to gain access to that setting?
2. Would the research problem you have identified above be better answered by quantitative or qualitative research? Explain why.
3. Would the research problem you have identified above be best answered by unobtrusive, reactive or participant observation research? Explain why.
4. With regard to the research problem you have identified above, discuss potential areas of ethical concern that you would need to address in carrying out your research.

Note

1. There have been a number of cases in which researchers conducting observations of behaviour that can be construed as criminal or otherwise subject to legal constraint have had their notes subpoenaed by law enforcement agencies. In most cases, researchers do not enjoy the privilege of protecting their sources (as might be the case with attorneys, doctors or clergy) in such circumstances. Disclosing this fact ought to be part of the informed consent agreement if there is even a slight chance of potential participants being up to something they do not want the authorities to know about.

Suggested further reading

Angrosino, M. V. (2007) *Naturalistic Observation*. Walnut Creek, CA: LeftCoast Press.

Angrosino, M. V. (2010) *How Do They Know That? The Process of Social Research*. Long Grove, IL: Waveland Press. These two selections are book-length treatments of the issues dealt with in this chapter; they include more extensive examples, discussion questions, suggestions for student research and extended reading lists.

Buchanan, E. A. (ed.) (2004) *Readings in Virtual Research Ethics: Issues and Controversies*. Hershey, PA: Information Sciences Publishing. This anthology covers the main emergent concerns of doing social research on and about the Internet.

Elliott, D. and Stern, J. E. (eds) (1997) *Research Ethics: A Reader*. Hanover, NJ: University Press of New England. This anthology is a comprehensive guide to the ethical conduct of social research.

Schensul, S. L., Schensul, J. J. and LeCompte, M. (1999) *Essential Ethnographic Methods: Observations, Interviews, and Questionnaires* (Vol. II of J. J. Schensul, S. L. Schensul and M. LeCompte (eds) *Ethnographer's Toolkit*). Walnut Creek, CA: AltaMira Press. This work is the standard professional text for qualitative social research.

Waxman, H. C., Tharp, R. G. and Hilberg, R. S. (eds) (2004) *Observational Research in U.S. Classrooms: New Approaches for Understanding Cultural and Linguistic Diversity*. New York: Cambridge University Press. For those interested in the applications of observation-based research in educational settings, this anthology is an excellent guide to research methods and policy issues.

In-depth interviews

Carolyn L. Mears

Introduction

Educational researchers study the world of teaching and learning in order to understand, inform and improve practice. They often attempt to explain a phenomenon, describe a culture, disclose life experience, predict outcomes or assess variables and impacts. Researchers determine the method for their study by clarifying the questions they want answered and their purpose for asking. Some researchers conduct quantitative studies to reveal broad patterns or trends across populations. Others prefer qualitative study of individuals or small groups to produce a deeper understanding and appreciation for circumstances of people's lives.

If you are entering into the world of educational research, one of your first steps will be to consider what you want to learn from your investigation. Are you looking for broad trends or deep insights, cause and effect or interpretations of meaning, variables or personal stories, or perhaps some combination of pursuits? If you want to learn from the qualities of experience and the significance of events or situations, your methodology will probably involve interviewing. While serving as a primary tool for data collection, in-depth interviewing can also function to clarify or triangulate data obtained through other means.

This chapter introduces you to the practice of interviewing for research, with particular attention to semi-structured, in-depth interviews that are intended to go beyond what can be learned through focus groups or tightly scripted protocols. It provides an overview of a process for using open-ended questions to explore participants' experiences and understandings, and it considers challenges to be faced and standards to be met.

Interviewing: It's more than questions and answers

In-depth interviews are purposeful interactions in which an investigator attempts to learn what another person knows about a topic, to discover and record what that person has experienced, what he or she thinks and feels about it, and what significance or meaning it might have. This process appears to be innately simple and intuitive. After all, we are accustomed to having routine conversations in which information is easily exchanged. Someone asks a question; someone responds; experiences, opinions and perceptions are shared. Graduate students I've worked with often consider an interview-based approach for their research under the mistaken assumption that interviewing is 'easy'. But don't be fooled! Interviewing for research is quite different from common conversation and requires a well-envisioned design, a great deal of preparation, purposeful conduct and attentive listening. You are not just passing the afternoon. You are collecting data that can allow insightful analysis and produce defensible findings.

Several years ago when I studied the aftermath of the Columbine shootings, I discovered a term that has shaped my understanding of research. In preparing for the work, I spent considerable time learning about the impact of trauma. In the process, I found that individuals who survive a traumatic event commonly feel distanced from others because of their own life experience. As a result, victims commonly withdraw behind what psychologists call a *trauma membrane* to avoid further victimisation or misunderstanding (Lindy et al., 1981).

I find this concept of separation serves as a powerful metaphor to describe the challenge of researching *any* lived experience, whether traumatic or mundane. Each of us has a unique awareness and response to life events. What we do, see, think, believe and hope for is distinctive to us, and until we share that perspective with others it remains within our own personal membrane of knowing. An in-depth interview provides a way for a researcher to cross this boundary, to journey into another's perspective about a circumstance or event, so meaning can be learned and significance shared. In this way, in-depth interviews offer a path to discovery and greater understanding.

Before considering the mechanics of interviewing, it is important to address its use in research. If you're about to begin a thesis or dissertation, your first job is not to identify a method but to clarify the question you want your research to answer and the purpose you want it to serve. When you know what you want to learn and why, you can determine your method.

'At the root of in-depth interviewing is an interest in understanding the experience of other people and the meaning they make of that experience' (Seidman, 2006: 9). Research questions that can be answered through interviewing commonly address matters of *what* or *how* related to lived experience, for example:

- *What are the long-term consequences of . . . ?*
- *What is the experience of . . . ?*
- *What characteristics emerge when . . . ?*
- *How does participation in . . . ?*
- *How do changes influence . . . ?*
- *How do students perceive . . . ?*

In the pursuit of a depth of understanding that cannot be accessed through brief interaction, questions like these would require you to decide who holds the needed information, what to ask, how many interviews will be optimal, and how to manage and analyse the data. Your research question guides your design.

For example, if you want to understand situations influencing teacher retention, you would, of course, want to interview teachers, but which ones? Because the goal is depth not breadth, you will spend considerable time with a small number of participants. As a result, you should select 'information-rich cases . . . those from which one can learn a great deal about issues of central importance to the purpose of the research' (Patton, 2002: 230). While not seeking randomness, you need to be intentional in making your selection and that requires preparation. Your research purpose and awareness of context drive your strategies for sampling; for example, you might want to study extreme cases at the far ranges of experience, or a convenience sample of those easily accessed, or a snowball sample in which participants lead you to other informants (see Patton, 2002).

Determining the number of participants for your study is a little trickier, since there is no universal standard for this but is instead relative to the data you collect. Essentially, you are required to collect sufficient data to represent the experience you are investigating and you may stop when you reach saturation (i.e. no longer hear anything new). The proposed number to interview is often expressed as a range (e.g. 6–8 participants). You will negotiate this matter with your research advisor and learn by doing.

Achieving a level of in-depth reflection usually requires multiple interviews with each participant. The first responses you hear undoubtedly will be the oft-told tale, the frequently shared story of events or happenings without much depth, detail or reflection. You want to get beyond these simple facts, which provide context but are unlikely to bring you to enriched understanding or fresh insight. A series of two or three, 90-minute interviews spaced about a week or two apart, for example, will provide greater opportunity to build rapport and achieve deeper reflection. Also, when you ask participants a question, related information may rise in their memory later, and multiple sessions give you the chance to access this.

Conducting the interview

Effective interviewing depends on a well-planned interview guide to ensure that you cover the topics you want your participants to address. For standardised or focused interviews, a structured guide specifies each question to be asked so the exact wording can be used with each participant. Each question is read, the respondent's answer recorded, then the next question is read, and so on.

For in-depth interviews, however, a more open format is employed. Instead of scripted questions, your guide will list primary areas of exploration for each session. You let your study participants know what interests you and invite them to tell you more. For example, to study effects of participation in an adult literacy programme, you might begin with the following plan:

First session: Ask about experiences while in the programme; motivation to enrol; effects; challenges; relationships; employment.

Second session: Clarify points from Session One. Ask about perspective after graduation; overall feelings about how programme affected life, satisfaction, identity; how he/she would describe it to someone considering enrollment.

These general focal points will help you generate the questions to begin your interview, but remember that your research questions are not your interview questions. While you want to answer an overarching research question, it is not your participant's job to answer it for you! You ask participants about related matters and to tell their experiences, share their feelings or thoughts, and reflect on decisions and events. From their narratives, you will be able to analyse the information and answer your research question. For example, if your research question is: 'What is the effect of completion of an adult literacy programme on life satisfaction?' you can't really

expect someone in your study to know the answer to this. However, graduates of such a programme can tell about *their* experience and that will help *you* find the answer. By compiling and analysing stories of all your participants, you will see patterns or themes related to their overall life experience, satisfaction, attitudes, challenges and suchlike.

At the first session, you start by introducing your study: explain its intent, risks, potential benefits; answer any questions the participant has; and ask the participant to sign an *informed consent* to be in the study. Your candour, interest and respect throughout the process help establish the trust and rapport that can create an environment for sharing. If your study includes participants from marginalised or underrepresented groups, pay particular attention to perceived differences in status, power or background. Although you cannot make differences disappear, you can consider how participants might respond to you and attend to perceptions that might negatively affect your research.

In the interview, your job is to invite participants to tell you about matters that interest you and to listen carefully to their response. Your interview guide frames the area to be investigated, but with open-ended or semi-structured questions you can't be certain exactly where the answer will lead. The first response you hear may be a general description, but buried in the response, you find the markers that point to other areas to explore. Noticing these signs requires that you stay aware and that you confirm you understand what you think you are hearing. If something seems contradictory or unclear, express your confusion, or rephrase the question and ask again. Monitor your assumptions and don't take for granted that you understand everything you hear. Words have different meanings in different contexts, so take time to build comprehension. Listen for expressions that challenge what you were thinking, then explore a little further.

To get the most from interviews, it helps to ask questions in a way that first sets a context and then opens avenues for a response (Morrissey, 1987). A closed or tightly scripted question such as 'How long did it take you to complete the literacy programme?' doesn't leave much room for exploration. However, you could learn much more if you phrase your question as 'I am interested in learning about adult literacy programmes. Please tell me about your experience in such a programme.' This defines the area of interest, and instead of limiting the response lets the participant decide what seems most important and worthy of sharing. From this discussion, you will have many paths to pursue.

Be sure to transcribe each interview before conducting the next one. Review your notes and the transcript carefully in preparation for the next interview. Highlight areas of discussion that may have been approached but left incomplete; note topics yet to be covered; identify salient lines of investigation to pursue. Be sure to ask your participant to help you know what you may have overlooked, what questions they expected you to ask, and what seems most important to be included in your report.

In some cases, you may need to conduct your interviews over the telephone. The considerations that apply to face-to-face interviewing also apply to telephone interviews: the need for rapport, careful preparation, purposeful questioning, attentive listening, perceptive follow-up and appreciation for the participant's contribution to your study. The primary difference is that telephones don't provide visual cues of body language or facial expression. This means that you must attend to the voice even more carefully, noting pauses, emphasis, silences and sighs. Emerging technologies such as Skype offer promise in allowing the use of computers to provide video as well as audio connection. However, for some, the technology may be distracting, and you want the attention to be on the dialogue, not on the uniqueness of the experience.

Conducting interviews is merely one phase of interview-based research. Before you can begin the analysis phase, you need to ensure that your data are correct. To do this, you can conduct a member check to confirm accuracy and completeness of the transcripts (Lincoln and Guba, 1985) or perhaps a narrator check in which you meet with each participant for another interview to review and reflect on your interpretation of their meaning (Mears, 2009).

There are many models for data analysis. Some researchers employ qualitative software while some prefer a more hands-on approach for coding and theme-finding. Rather than guiding you through a variety of approaches here, I suggest that you check the resources included in the Suggested Further Reading section at the end of this chapter.

Challenges and dispositions

No discussion of in-depth interviewing would be complete without acknowledging the challenges it poses, namely that it requires patience, demands considerable time and energy, and involves coordinating your schedule with the busy calendars of others. In addition, the 'lack of rules, vast amounts of data to process, the tasks of writing are baffling to some' (Lichtman, 2006: 19). Instead of a simple set of clearly defined steps, interview research is characterised by an emerging design, with data collection blurring into data analysis, countless hours devoted to transcription and no iron-clad rules of what constitutes sufficient data.

In interview research, you cross borders of experience in order to learn from others, and since interviews are interactions with people, there's always an element of unpredictability. 'Research – like life – is a contradictory, messy affair' (Plummer, 2005: 357), yet in this messiness lies the opportunity for discovery and enriched understanding. Interviews may not go as planned; a participant may not have the desired information; someone may cancel or drop out altogether. However, your dedication to learning from others will help you to collect data that inform your topic, to analyse that data to discover meaning and to share that meaning with others.

Before proceeding, it might be wise for you to take a moment to self-reflect and consider your readiness for this type of research. Do you ask the kind of questions that can only be answered by learning from another's perspective? Do you enjoy interacting with people, take a certain pleasure in exploring the unique ways people experience their world, feel comfortable finding your own path on a complex, unmarked journey? In short, do you think you could complete a study that requires you to:

- enter into the complexity of people's lives?
- establish rapport that encourages communication?

- ask challenging questions and pose meaningful follow-up?
- attend to nuances of expression, silences and non-verbal cues?
- hear meaning from another's perspective?
- refrain from judgement and argument?
- organise, manage and analyse an abundance of verbal data?
- synthesise information from a variety of sources?
- accurately report what others express?
- maintain healthy boundaries?
- engage in self-reflection?
- write and communicate effectively?

Certain skills and dispositions can help you meet the challenges. Some of these traits you may already have. Others require practice. I just think it's important that you appreciate what is involved before you begin.

Standards

When you set out to learn from others, it is important to consider how your work will affect them. The imperative of *first, do no harm* should drive every action and decision. Respecting participants in your study, ensuring genuine informed consent, maximising benefits, minimising risks and assuring fairness and equity in selecting participants are mandates of human-subjects review boards governing research. However, an ethics of accuracy and principled conduct is also required. As a visitor in your study participants' world, you are responsible for communicating honestly, treating them fairly, accurately representing their meaning and using their interviews only as promised.

Beyond the issues of ethics, you also need to achieve research standards for quality. Standards traditionally applied to quantitative research, however, mean something different to qualitative researchers.

The validity of interview research is related to its appropriateness for studying what it claims to inform and its veracity in reporting. However much we are committed to achieving this standard, an assessment of qualitative research in terms of validity 'does not lead to a dichotomous outcome (i.e. valid vs. invalid), but represents an issue of level or degree'

(Onwuegbuzie and Leech, 2007: 239). Lummis (2006) observes that 'the validation of oral evidence can be divided into two main areas: the degree to which any individual interview yields reliable information on the experience, and the degree to which that individual experience is typical of its time and place' (2006: 273). These are matters for you to consider as you design your study and select your participants.

Reliability, which 'refers to the trustworthiness of observations or data' (Stiles, 1993: 601), can be measured by how accurately the study reflects the participants' meaning and their authority to comment on matters being studied. Member check and/or narrator check are essential for establishing reliability.

Achieving replicability does not mean that a qualitative study can be exactly duplicated in another setting; instead, it relates to the transparency of the work. By providing a thorough account of your procedures (e.g. participant selection, interviewing, data confirmation, analysis) along with a clear rationale for your decisions at each step of the way, you can provide an audit trail for others to follow and continue or extend your study, a mark of replicability.

For interview-based investigations, rather than questing for objectivity, it is more productive to evaluate the extent to which any preformed opinions may have tarnished the legitimacy of the research. While neutrality may seem a desired stance, subjectivity has its virtues (Peshkin, 1988), and skilled investigators use their prior knowledge and experience to good advantage. Thus 'the real aim [for a researcher] . . . should be to reveal sources of bias, rather than to pretend they can be nullified . . . by a distanced researcher without feelings' (Thompson, 2000: 137). In writing up your research, disclose anything that might have subjectively affected your work and explain what you did to limit its negative impacts.

While interview studies do not aspire to generalisability, their findings can have implications for other settings. Semi-structured or open-ended interviews invite participants to share their experience and understanding, thereby revealing the 'possibilities and limits of what people may do in similar circumstances, even when we cannot predict what they will do. By indicating what might happen, stories enable us to prepare for a range of eventualities' (Stiles, 1993: 601). As you generate your findings, you point out potential significance for other settings and situations.

Conclusion

In-depth interviewing can help us learn about the world in terms of human experience. Skilled and insightful interviews have contributed to discoveries of how we think and what we believe. For example, the ground-breaking work on attitudes about end-of-life experience, *On Death and Dying* (1969) was the product of Elisabeth Kubler-Ross's extensive interviews of terminally ill patients. *Women's Ways of Knowing* by Mary Belenky and colleagues (1997) is another masterful example of the power of interviews, in this case deepening understanding of how women experience and express knowledge. The product of interview research, clearly, is not limited to scholarly tomes lining library shelves but may be easily shaped for a wide audience. By collecting stories, analysing their contents, finding patterns and sharing what is learned, researchers can help us better understand our world and what it means to be human.

I encourage you to consider an interviewer's path in pursuit of learning from the experiences of others. Ask the questions that interest you, and share the answers you hear in ways that illuminate and deepen our understanding.

Questions for further investigation

1. Develop ten research questions that could be answered through in-depth interviewing. List appropriate types of interviewees for each.
2. Write five interview questions to use in researching one of the research questions from 1 above. Meet with another student and take turns interviewing each other for 15 minutes each, taking notes on responses. After completing both interviews, share what you heard each other say. Discuss the process. How did your questions shape the response? What do you feel went well? What changes would you make?
3. With your class, discuss ethical considerations that would require you to terminate an interview.

Suggested further reading

Glesne, C. (2005) *Becoming Qualitative Researchers: An Introduction* (3rd edn). Boston: Allyn & Bacon. An informative introduction to qualitative research practices.

Mears, C. L. (2009) *Interviewing for Education and Social Science Research: The Gateway Approach.* New York: Palgrave Macmillan. A handy guide to in-depth interviewing to create a gateway to deeper understanding.

Miles, M. B. and Huberman, A. M. (1994) *Qualitative Data Analysis: An Expanded Sourcebook* (2nd edn). Thousand Oaks, CA: Sage. A manual on a variety of strategies for organising and processing qualitative data.

Mishler, E. G. (1991) *Research Interviewing: Context and Narrative.* Boston. MA: Harvard University Press. Examination of the process of interviewing for narrative research.

Patton, M. Q. (2002) *Qualitative Research and Evaluation Methods* (3rd edn). Thousand Oaks, CA: Sage. A comprehensive guide to qualitative practice, with sound advice on interview research.

Rubin, H. and Rubin, I. (2004) *Qualitative Interviewing: The Art of Hearing Data* (2nd edn). Thousand Oaks, CA: Sage. A practical resource on interview research.

Saldaña, J. (2009) *The Coding Manual for Qualitative Researchers.* Thousand Oaks, CA: Sage. A helpful guide to multiple strategies for coding qualitative data.

Seidman, I. (2006) *Interviewing as Qualitative Research: A Guide for Researchers in Education and the Social Sciences* (3rd edn). New York: Teachers College Press. Classic resource on interviewing for phenomenology and other applications.

Weiss, R. (1994) *Learning From Strangers: The Art and Method of Qualitative Interview Studies.* New York: Free Press. Handbook offering insights into effective interviewing, its risks and opportunities.

References

Belenky, M., Clinchy, B., Goldberger, N. and Tarule, J. (1997) *Women's Ways of Knowing.* New York: Basic Books.

Kubler-Ross, E. (1969) *On Death and Dying.* New York: Scribner.

Lichtman, M. (2006) *Qualitative Research in Education: A User's Guide.* Thousand Oaks, CA: Sage.

Lincoln, Y. S. and Guba, E. G. (1985) *Narrative Inquiry.* Newbury Park, CA: Sage.

Lindy, J. D., Grace, M. and Green, B. (1981) 'Survivors: outreach to a reluctant population', *American Journal of Orthopsychiatry*, 51: 468–78.

Lummis, T. (2006) 'Structure and validity in oral evidence', in Perks, R. and Thomson, A. (eds) *The Oral History Reader* (2nd edn). London: Routledge, pp. 255–60.

Mears, C. L. (2009) *Interviewing for Education and Social Science Research: The Gateway Approach.* New York: Palgrave Macmillan.

Morrissey, C. (1987) 'The two-sentence format as an interviewing technique in oral history fieldwork', *Oral History Review*, 15: 43–53.

Onwuegbuzie, A. J. and Leech, N. L. (2007) 'Validity and qualitative research: an oxymoron?', *Quality & Quantity*, 41: 233–49.

Patton, M. Q. (2002) *Qualitative Research and Evaluation Methods* (3rd edn). Thousand Oaks, CA: Sage.

Peshkin, A. (1988) 'Virtuous subjectivity: In the participant-observer's I's', in Berg, D. N. and Smith, K. K. (eds) *The Self in Social Inquiry: Researching Methods.* Newbury Park, CA: Sage, pp. 267–81.

Plummer, K. (2005) 'Critical humanism and queer theory: living with tensions', in Denzin, N. K. and Lincoln Y. S. (eds) *Sage Handbook for Qualitative Research* (3rd edn). Thousand Oaks, CA: Sage, pp. 357–73.

Seidman, I. (2006) *Interviewing as Qualitative Research: A Guide for Researchers in Education and the Social Sciences* (3rd edn). New York: Teachers College Press.

Stiles, W. B. (1993) 'Quality control in qualitative research', *Clinical Psychology Review*, 13(3): 593–618.

Thompson, P. (2000) *The Voice of the Past: Oral History.* Oxford: Oxford University Press.

Techniques to assist with interviewing

Rosalind Hurworth

Introduction

Interviewing has always been a core method within qualitative research but there has often been a feeling expressed from some quarters that 'any old fool can go out and ask a few questions'. However, this is a fallacy and many books have been written to demonstrate that interviewing can be full of pitfalls and must be undertaken rigorously if quality material is to be collected and findings accepted. Therefore the process can be trickier than first imagined, especially when attempting to encourage interviewees to talk freely. For instance, difficulties may arise when:

- the subject matter is sensitive;
- dealing with differing attitudes and cultural beliefs;
- events pertinent to the study took place some time ago, so that people find them hard to recall;
- those being studied (including children) are not used to talking to strangers.

So, how can you: help a teacher to think about teaching thirty years ago? encourage small children to reveal their innermost thoughts? make talking about difficult topics easier? or approach abstract concepts in a more concrete way? The answer can be through the use of various stimuli, as these can assist in obtaining rich data as well as making a potentially forbidding process more palatable for participants. This chapter therefore examines the use of:

- the visual, during which the interviewee makes sense of the world through looking at photographs;
- vignettes (short stories) which can be commented upon by individuals or groups; and
- props such as puppets, dolls and drawings in order to talk (particularly) to children.

The use of still photographs and other images as stimuli

Photo interviewing/photo elicitation

Photo-interviewing has been used to encourage talk ever since early anthropologists showed photographs to key informants in order to find out about non-Western cultures and rituals (Chiozzi, 1989). This introduction of photographs into the interviewing process became known as photo-elicitation (Harper,

1984) and has been used for a variety of purposes such as to understand behaviours (Entin, 1979), assist small children to recall events (Ascherman et al., 1998) and to evaluate programmes (Stokrocki, 1984).

Collier found photo-interviewing to be extremely valuable because:

. . . they were flooded with encyclopaedic information whereas in the exclusively verbal interviews, communication difficulties and memory blocks inhibited the flow of information. (Collier, 1979: 281)

Furthermore, interviewees shown pictures often respond to the visual image 'without hesitation. By providing informants with a task such as viewing an album, the strangeness of the interview situation is averted' (Schwartz, 1989: 151–2).

Images can also assist in facilitating rapport, helping those involved to focus and adding meaning that may be lost if researchers simply interview participants in the traditional way.

Use of the visual has also been found to be particularly helpful when working with children/ young people. For example, Diamond (1996) used photos to reveal pre-school children's perceptions of disability, Weiniger (1998) introduced photo-prompts as a way to seek children's beliefs about potential careers and Foster et al. (1999) explored the development of primary children's historical thinking. More recently, Thomsen used selected magazine images to prompt teenager discussion on body image (Hurworth et al., 2005).

Photo-elicitation has also been employed within higher education projects. For instance, Killion (2001) used photographs with nursing students to examine cultural aspects of health, Smith and Woodward (1999) carried out research with media students, Loeffler (2004) undertook a study to understand a college outdoor education programme and Martin described how she used several photographs to determine factors underpinning why some surgeons volunteer to be surgeon trainers (Hurworth et al., 2005).

Photo-elicitation has also been used as a tool for evaluation. For example, Tucker and Dempsey (1991) applied photo-interviewing to evaluate a computer training workshop. They concluded that:

Photo interviewing provided an expedient means of getting inside the program . . . and its consequences, in terms of participants' realities and meaning systems that oral interviewing did not permit. (Tucker and Dempsey, 1991: 652)

Autodriving and reflexive photography

Researchers then began to realise that for certain types of research, better information may be acquired when interviewees take the photos themselves (Heisley and Levy, 1991). This method was first called 'autodriving' as interviews were 'driven by the informants who are seeing their own behaviour' (Heisley and Levy, 1991: 261). First used to study eating at home, autodriving resulted in more complex conversations about family dynamics, meal-time behaviour and beliefs about diet. Most importantly though, it allowed a:

. . . negotiated interpretation of events . . . which gives the informant increased voice and authority while providing a perspective that makes personal systems meaningful to an outsider. It also manufactures distance for the informant so that they see familiar situations in unfamiliar ways (Heisley and Levy, 1991: 257).

The approach then became known as 'reflexive' photography'. For instance, Ziller (1990) requested students from four overseas countries to take pictures about what the USA meant to them and then to explain their choice of images. Later, Douglas (1998) asked African American students to photograph their impressions of a predominantly white university while Berman et al. (2001) sought images reflecting the lives of recently arrived Bosnian refugee children in Canada. The meanings of these photographs were then explored during interviews later.[1]

Reflexive photography has become especially popular for school-based research (especially with the arrival of disposable cameras and cameras in mobile phones). For example, Agbenya (2008) suggests that photographs provide a good tool for understanding the influence of school on a student's identity and learning while Allen (2009) used the approach to study the sexual culture of a school from the students' perspective. Schratz and Löffler-Anzböck (2004) also point out that related discussion can portray the 'micro system' of a school and this can be indicative of the 'macro' (wider) school system.

Photo novella/photovoice

Another form of photo stimulus was termed 'photo novella' (picture stories) by Wang and Burris (1994). While participants were still asked to take photos to portray their lives, the use of image-based talk proved empowering. It enabled those with little money or power to communicate where change should occur. Since then, the term 'photovoice' has now replaced photo novella (Wang and Burris, 1997) and has become a technique embedded within participatory action research (Young and Barrett, 2001) or needs assessments. In this way, the 'photographers' can contribute to policy change or programme improvements. For example, hearing students' 'photo-voices' can lead to more effective school management to meet students' needs (Busher, 2009; Raggl and Schratz, 2004).

Many feel that the use of photovoice contributes to increased literacy skills. Consequently, some studies have required students to mount story boards (Pink, 2009) or keep photo journals which are then discussed at a subsequent interview. Busher (2009) refers to such activity as 'scrapbooking' where pupils label their selected photographs in order to help explain them later.

Photolanguage

Another form of visual stimulus is photolanguage. Originally developed in France, the technique was used with small groups of teenagers who had trouble talking about personal experiences. The facilitators asked questions and then in order to help them answer, the youngsters selected one or two images from a set of 60 black and white photographs of uniform size. It was found that shots depicting people, landscapes and events were able to evoke current or past experience from the subconscious, so that the young people could convey innermost thoughts to the rest of the group (Burton and Cooney, 1986).

Photolanguage can also be a tool for use in evaluation. It can help determine programme outcomes and impacts as well as to ascertain elements of the programme experience. For instance, at the end of a course, students could be asked to select one photo that reflects how they felt before it started and then to choose another to indicate how they feel at its conclusion.

The photolanguage process is designed for use with small groups of 6–15 people. In preparation, the facilitator needs to develop the research question(s), consider participants' ages, abilities and privacy issues, select the photos and determine how to facilitate the sharing of information. Photos need to be laid out on tables surrounded by plenty of space so that participants can walk around easily to see every image before making a selection. While respondents are asked to explain their choices the commentary is taped for later analysis.

Vignettes

Another way to provoke discussion is through the use of vignettes. The latter are short stories or scenes about individuals or situations that can be presented in written, spoken, pictorial or video/film clip format.

Uses of vignettes

Vignettes are useful for revealing participants' perceptions, beliefs and attitudes (Hughes, 1998: 381) and for providing concrete examples about which participants can offer comment or opinion (Hazel, 1995: 2). Also, by selecting particular groups to interview, the researcher can carry out comparisons between various socio-economic, cultural or age groups.

Vignettes have become an especially popular technique when researching difficult/sensitive topics such as bullying, abuse and mental health issues as well as for dealing with ethical or moral dilemmas (Kugelman, 1992) because participants can give accounts of practice and positions taken. So the technique has the capacity to 'get under the skin' of complex 'undiscussables' through prompts such as: how would you react to this situation? what would you do next? or what do you think others would do?

Posing questions in the third person (as in the last question above) can 'desensitise' issues for participants and allow them to answer freely (Hughes and Huby, 2002: 384) because it avoids being personal and so is less threatening.

Advice on creating vignettes

While appearing simple, there is an art to creating a useful vignette. According to Barter and Renold (1999) the story, cartoon, etc. must:

- be credible and based on real-life situations if possible;
- reflect mundane occurrences, otherwise people cannot relate to the scenario;
- have enough detail to be interesting but not be so complex that it is impossible to understand;
- be open enough for people to expand on what is presented;
- be in an appropriate format (e.g. for children, different age groups or non-english speaking groups).

Props and prompts when talking (especially) to children

Brooker (2001: 166) reports that the younger the interviewee, the greater the need for preparation. Consequently, a number of strategies have been used to make the interview process more 'child-friendly'. These include reliance on props and stimuli such as puppets, persona dolls and drawings in order to engage children's attention and interest, enhance reflection and avoid adult dominance.

Puppets

Since a younger child possesses a short attention span and less developed language skills than older interviewees, eliciting reliable information can be challenging (Ablow et al., 1999; Epstein et al., 2006). They also find it difficult to remember things easily (Aldridge, 1998). However, with the aid of puppets, researchers have been able to discover children's knowledge about illnesses, as well as attitudes about school and home (Siegal, 1988; Loveland et al., 1990). Furthermore, the use of puppets can help children to identify, clarify and verbalise feelings and also assist in reducing fears and anxieties about being interviewed (Green, 1975; Hawkins, 1991; Schulz et al., 1981).

The puppet-based research cited above was carried out with children aged 5–9. However, Darmawan et al. (1991) suggests that using a puppet as a way to elicit conversation need not be limited to younger children. For example, older students (11–14 years old) who were illiterate and from low socio-economic status (SES) families provided useful data after they had watched a whole puppet play (Coplin and Hardcastle, 1985).

Another advantage of using puppets is that they can be employed in a variety of research designs and in a variety of ways. For instance, Krott and Nicoladis (2005) introduced a puppet which did not understand some English words. Young children were then asked to explain these and so they 'taught' the puppet. Responses were taped, transcribed and analysed.

Meanwhile Verschueren et al. (2001) provided a crocodile puppet to be manipulated by the children themselves. Through the puppet, children responded to simple interview questions about scholastic competence, social acceptance, athletic competence, physical appearance and conduct. Children's responses were videotaped transcribed and coded before a quantitative analysis was undertaken using the material that had been articulated qualitatively.

(Persona) dolls

Allowing children to play and talk through dolls is another way to elicit information. Recognising this, a Californian kindergarten teacher developed the concept of 'persona dolls' in the 1950s, in order to research and confront prejudice and discrimination. She was prompted to create such dolls because there were few resources that reflected the lives of children from American minority ethnic groups. Therefore she and her colleagues made dolls resembling various features of the children in their care and began using them for research and teaching.

Interestingly, Aldridge (1998) reviewed the literature about using dolls during interviews with sexually abused children and found that children's responses were more accurate when the doll's characteristics closely matched those of the child's in terms of gender, race and physical appearance.

Now commercially produced dolls have become useful for dealing with difficult issues such as disability, sexism, special needs, immigration, class, ageism and being a refugee. For example, Brown described how:

> I've used them to find out about racism because this is what people still find hard to talk about – and also homophobia because this is a research area that has been difficult to confront in the past. Somehow it's easier through a third party such as a doll. (Brown, 2008)

Ebrahim and Frances also used persona dolls to research ideas about race and gender, held by 2–4-year-old South African children. Through the medium of dolls, the children were interviewed about their interpretation of difference.

A teacher-trainer perceived persona dolls to be useful for investigating curriculum development in regard to issues such as bullying, name-calling and being excluded from play – as well as for planning to teach about tolerance of others who appear or behave differently. As she explained:

> When looking at curriculum issues, the dolls are used to address all areas of difference – we then have a platform to investigate how we can apply anti-discriminatory practice in the classroom. For example, I use a doll wearing the Islamic burqua as a way into topical debate on equality. Similarly we can also research issues around children's perception of disability by having a doll who uses a wheelchair and talking about it. (Brown, 2008)

Drawing and other arts-based stimuli

As the saying goes, 'a picture's worth a thousand words' and therefore, drawing can be another way to find out how people make sense of the world (Herth, 1998). So, through the medium of art, in conjunction with interviews, particular research questions can be answered (Williams et al., 1989). This approach also has the advantage of increasing interviewee participation (Kwiatkowska, 1978) and of making abstract concepts more concrete (Sroufe, 1997).

Thus, the researcher can ask interviewees to draw their perceptions, feelings or representations of a situation instead of relying solely on verbal description. For example, a group of health education students were asked to draw a reflection of their work with HIV/AIDS prevention programmes. One woman drew a bridge explaining later that it symbolised the path from 'uninformed' to 'safe and educated'.

Certainly, research findings extracted from drawings can be powerful. For example, it assisted Williams et al. (1989) to study the health beliefs of primary school children. In another Australian study, drawing was used to determine the drug education needs of primary school children. Prior to interview, groups of 9-year-old children, were asked to draw and talk about anything they knew about drugs. Drawings ranged from those of a child who had never heard the word and so drew 'jugs' to one boy who filled a page with drug paraphernalia (such as syringes, packets, phials and a drug holster) while explaining it all to an interviewer. This proved to researchers that introducing drug education at secondary level was far too late!

Drawings have also been used successfully in evaluative exercises. For instance, an evaluator carried out a needs assessment during which children were asked to draw how they feel about going to church in comparison with what it should be like. By analysing the 'gap' (via interviews about the 'before and after' drawings) the evaluator was able to suggest church-going practices which would be more appealing to young people.

In quite a different evaluation, drawings helped to determine the impact of an environmental education programme. Before the programme commenced, the children in a primary school class were asked to draw and talk about 'My local stream'. On paper rolled out on the floor they drew a stylised water course with houses on the bank, children playing, a flower and one fish in the water. During the ensuing weeks the class undertook a programme which involved examining the stream intensively. The children went ponding, caught tadpoles, looked down microscopes, carried out tests on water samples and examined local plants and animals. A few weeks later they repeated the drawing-interview exercise. The change was dramatic. This time rather than drawing an imaginary bank they drew detailed depictions of what they had seen and studied. Also when interviewed, recall was strong and discussion about the drawing animated. The programme was therefore deemed a success.

Issues concerning the use of stimuli

Within this chapter I have indicated various possibilities for enhancing the task of research interviewing by using various stimuli. However, each researcher must assess whether such techniques are useful to them or not. This would depend on the issue and population being studied. For example, with certain participants, such methods might make the interview seem less monotonous, more interesting and more 'doable'. However, with those who are already quite articulate or who feel they are less artistic, the suggested techniques may not be so appealing.

In addition, while these approaches may seem straightforward, they are still subject to the same considerations as other types of research. So, the researcher needs to think about:

- how the method relates to the overall research question(s) and design;
- what resources are needed (e.g. budget, staff available and time);
- what sampling approach is to be used (e.g. how many photos should be taken? who is to take the photos? where should the research take place? what sort of children should be involved in a persona doll study? etc.);
- how analysis should be undertaken and the results interpreted. This will depend on the overarching methodology used as well as the research question.

Analysis and reporting

In many cases, data that is produced using stimuli can be analysed and interpreted in similar ways to other qualitative approaches (see Miles and Huberman, 1994). Most commonly, the researcher would analyse transcripts to discover themes and categories before writing that are supported by evidence (interview quotes, drawings). During this process, the researcher needs to declare and clarify his/her own interpretations of the products (photographs, drawings, etc.) as opposed to those created by the participants. This is especially necessary in collaborative/participatory/empowerment research and evaluation since the researcher and participants often engage in analysis together and so co-create the results. With permission from participants, researchers can then present these 'tangible findings' in reports, theses or presentations.

Ethics

Perhaps the biggest issue likely to arise relates to ethics. During most of what has been described, the interviewer usually holds the power, especially when children and young people are involved. Thus, as Christensen and Prout point out, there is a danger that the powerful can exploit the powerless during an interview. In relation to children, it is emphasised that

> . . . children's vulnerability and relative lack of power therefore present the researcher with challenges as well as responsibilities to protect children's rights within the research process. (Christensen and Prout, 2002)

However, introducing a photograph, doll or puppet or asking for a drawing provides an intermediary agent which can help neutralise the power relationship between the researcher and interviewee (Nunkoosing, 2005).

Conclusion

We have seen that using stimuli to enhance interviews can be particularly powerful for the educational researcher. They can increase the ease of response, challenge participants, provide nuances, trigger memories (Lyle, 2003), lead to new perspectives/explanations and help to avoid researcher misinterpretations. In addition, stimuli provide advantages because they can:

- be used at any stage of research;
- be a component of multi-methods triangulation to improve research rigour;
- assist with building trust and rapport;
- enhance collaborative and participatory research;

- be preferable to conventional interviews for many participants;
- provide a means of 'getting inside' a context;
- bridge psychological and physical realities;
- produce unpredictable information;
- promote longer, more detailed interviews in comparison with traditional interview formats.

Most importantly, though, stimuli offer choices about how to communicate, as well as facilitating a more comfortable atmosphere for discussion.

Questions for further investigation

1. How could any of the suggested stimuli be applied to your own research topic?
2. With this piece of research in mind, what would be some of the advantages of using stimuli for interviewing?
3. What might be some of the issues that you may face?

Note

1. Similar projects are under way in Melbourne Australia. One involves recently arrived Afghani students and another has asked overweight youngsters to portray 'the obese world'.

Suggested further reading

Aldridge, N. (1998) 'Strengths and limitations of forensic child sexual abuse interview with anatomical dolls: an empirical review', *Journal of Psychopathology and Behavioural Assessment*, 20: 1–41. Key article on 'persona dolls'.

Bessell, A. G., Deese, B. and Medina A. L. (2007) 'Photolanguage: how a picture can inspire a thousand words', *American Journal of Evaluation*, 28(4): 558–69. Important article on the use of 'photolanguage'.

Guillemin, M. (2004) 'Understanding illness: using drawings as a research method', *Qualitative Health Research*, 14(2): 272–89. Important article from the *Qualitative Health Research* journal on using drawings as a method of conducting research.

Schulze, S. (2007) 'The usefulness of reflective photography for qualitative research: a case study in higher education', *South African Journal of Higher Education*, 21(5): 536–53. Article detailing the use of reflective photography in educational, qualitative research.

Wang, C. and Burris, M. B. (1997) 'Photovoice: Concept, methodology and use for participatory needs assessment', *Health Education and Behaviour*, 21(2): 369–87. Article regarding the importance and use of 'Photovoice' as a research method.

References

Ablow, J. C., Measelle, J. R., Kraemer, H. C. et al. (1999) 'The MacArthur three-city outcome study: evaluating multi-informant measures of young children's symptomatology', *Journal of the American Academy of Child and Adolescent Psychiatry*, 38: 1580–90.

Agbenya, J. S. (2008) 'Developing the understanding of school place on students' identity, pedagogy and learning, visually', *International Journal of Whole Schooling*, 4(2): 52–66.

Aldridge, N. (1998) 'Strengths and limitations of forensic child sexual abuse interview with anatomical dolls: an empirical review', *Journal of Psychopathology and Behavioural Assessment*, 20: 1–41.

Allen, L. (2009) '"Snapped". Researching the sexual cultures of schools using visual methods', *International Journal of Qualitative Studies in Education*, 22(5): 549–54.

Ascherman, E., Dannenburg, U. and Schultz, A. P. (1998) 'Photographs as retrieval cues for children', *Applied Cognitive Psychology*, 12(1): 55–66.

Barter, C. and Renold, E. (1999) *The Use of Vignettes in Qualitative Research*, Social Research Update 25. University of Surrey.

Berman, H. et al. (2001) 'Portraits of pain and promise: a photographic study of Bosnian youth', *Canadian Journal of Nursing Research*, 32(4): 21–41.

Brooker, L. (2001) 'Interviewing children', in MacNaughton G., Rolfe, S. and Siraj-Blatchford, I. (eds) *Doing Early Childhood Research*. Buckingham: Open University Press.

Burton, K. and Cooney, J. (1986) *Photolanguage Australia*. Sydney: Australia.

Busher, H. (2009) *Using Participants' Photo-Narratives to Elicit Their Perspectives on Social Interactions in Schools*. Paper presented at the 1st International Visual Methods Conference UK, Leeds.

Chiozzi, P. (1989) 'Photography and anthropological research: three case studies', in Boonzajer, F. (ed.) *Eyes Across the Water*. Amsterdam: Het Spinhuis, pp. 43–50.

Christensen, P. and Prout, A. (2002) 'Working with ethical symmetry in social research with children', *Childhood*, 9(4): 477–97.

Clark, C. (1999) 'The auto-driven interview: a photographer's viewfinder into children's experience', *Visual Sociology*, 14: 39–50.

Collier, J. (1979) 'Visual anthropology', in Wagner, J. (ed.) *Images of Information*. Beverly Hills, CA: Sage.

Coplin, R. and Hardcastle, C. A. (1985) 'Communicating through puppets', *Journal of the Medical Association of Georgia*, 74: 228–31.

Darmawan, J. et al. (1991) 'Arthritis community education by leather puppet shadow play in rural Indonesia', *Rheumatology International*, 12: 97–101.

Diamond, K. E. (1996) 'Preschool children's conceptions of disabilities: the salience of disability in children's ideas about others', *Topics in Early Childhood Special Education* (TECSE), 16(4): 458–75.

Douglas, K. B. (1998) 'Impressions: African American first-year students' perceptions of a predominantly white university', *Journal of Negro Education*, 67(4): 416–31.

Emmison, M. and Smith, P. (2001) *Researching the Visual: Images, Objects, Contexts and Interactions in Social and Cultural Inquiry* (Introducing Qualitative Methods series). London: Sage.

Entin, A. D. (1979) 'Reflection on families', *Photo Therapy Quarterly*, 2(2): 19–21.

Epstein, I. et al. (2006) 'Photo elicitation interview (PEI): using photos to elicit children's perspectives', *International Journal of Qualitative Methods*, 5(3): 1–9.

Epstein, I., Stevens, B., McKeever, P., Baruchel, S. and Jones, H. (2008) 'Using puppetry to elicit children's talk for research', *Nursing Inquiry*, 15(1): 49–56.

Foster, S., Hoge, J. D. and Rosch, R. H. (1999) 'Thinking aloud about history: children's and adolescents' responses to historical photographs', *Theory and Research in Social Education*, 27(2): 179–214.

Gauntlett, D. (2009) *Creative and Reflective Production Activities as a Tool for Social Research*. Presentation at the Introduction to Visual Methods Workshop (ESRC Research Development Initiative), University of Leicester.

Green, C. S. (1975) 'Larry thought puppet-play "childish": but it helped him face his fears', *Nursing*, 5: 30–3.

Hammond, J. D. (2004) 'Photography and ambivalence', *Visual Studies*, 19: 135–44.

Harper, D. (1984) 'Meaning and work: a study in photo elicitation', *International Journal of Visual Sociology*, 2(1): 20–43.

Hawkins, N. E. (1991) 'Bravery training: an approach to desensitising young children to fears encountered in a hospital setting', *Archives of Physical Medicine and Rehabilitation*, 17: 10–17.

Hazel, N. (1995) *Elicitation Techniques with Young People*, Social Research Update 12. University of Surrey.

Heisley D. D. and Levy, S. J. (1991) 'Autodriving: a photo-elicitation technique', *Journal of Consumer Research*, 18: 257–72.

Herth, K. (1998) 'Hope as seen through the eyes of homeless children', *Journal of Advanced Nursing*, 285: 1053–62.

Hughes, R. (1998) 'Considering the vignette and its application to a study of drug injecting and HIV risk and safer behaviour', *Sociology of Health and Illness*, 20(3): 381–400.

Hughes, R. and Huby, M. (2002) 'The application of vignettes in social and nursing research', *Journal of Advanced Nursing*, 37(4): 382–6.

Hurworth, R. (2004) Photo Interviewing, Social Research Update 40. University of Surrey.

Hurworth, R., Clark, E., Martin, J. and Thomsen, S. (2005) 'The use of photo interviewing: three examples from evaluation and research', *Evaluation Journal of Australasia*, 1(2): 52–62.

Jenkins, N. et al. (2010) 'Putting it in context: the use of vignettes in qualitative interviewing', *Qualitative Research*, 10: 175–97.

Killion, C. M. (2001) 'Understanding cultural aspects of health through photography', *Nursing Outlook*, 49(1): 50–4.

Krott, A. and Nicoladis, E. (2005) 'Large constituent families help children parse compounds', *Journal of Child Language*, 32: 139–58.

Kugelman, W. (1992) 'Social work ethics in the practice arena: a qualitative study', *Social Work and Health Care*, 17(4): 59–80.

Kwiatkowska, H. Y. (1978) *Family Therapy and Evaluation Through Art*. Springfield, IL: Charles Thomas.

Land, S. M. et al. (2009) 'Supporting school-home connections through photo journaling: capturing everyday experiences and nutrition concepts', *Techtrends* 53(6): 61–5.

Linn, S., Beardslee, W. and Patenaude, A. (1986) 'Puppet therapy with pediatric bone marrow transplant patients', *Journal of Pediatric Psychology*, 11: 37–46.

Loeffler, T. A. (2004) 'Meaning of participating in a college-based outdoor education program: a photo elicitation study of the meaning of the outdoor adventure experience', *Journal of Leisure Research*, 36(4): 536–56.

Loveland, K. A., Fletcher, J. M. and Bailey, V. (1990) 'Verbal and nonverbal communication of events in learning-disability subtypes', *Journal of Clinical and Experimental Neuropsychology*, 12: 433–47.

Lyle, J. (2003) 'Stimulated recall: a report on its use in naturalistic research', *British Educational Research Journal*, 29(6): 861–78.

Measelle, J. et al. (2005) 'Can children provide coherent, stable and valid self-reports on the big five dimensions? A longitudinal study from ages 5-7', *Journal of Personality and Social Psychology*, 89: 90–106.

Miles, M. and Huberman, A. (1994) *Qualitative Data Analysis* (2nd edn). Thousand Oaks, CA: Sage.

Nelson, E. and Christensen, K. (2009) 'Photovoice in the middle: how our students experience learning at school and beyond', *New Zealand Journal of Teachers' Work*, 6(1): 35–46.

Nunkoosing, K. (2005) 'The problems with interviews', *Qualitative Health Research*, 15(5): 698–706.

Pink, S. (2009) *Applied and Participatory Methods in Visual Ethnography*. Presentation at the Introduction to Visual Methods Workshop (ESRC Research Development Initiative), University of Leicester.

Raggl, A. and Schratz, M. (2004) 'Using visuals to release pupils' voices', Pole, C. (ed.) *Seeing is Believing?* New York: Elsevier, pp. 147–62.

Rose, G. (2001) *Visual Methodologies: An Introduction to the Interpretation of Visual Materials*. London: Sage.

Salmon, K. (2001) 'Remembering and reporting by children: the influence of cues and props', *Clinical Psychology Review*, 21(2): 267–300.

Schratz , M. and Löeffler-Anzböck, U. (2004), cited in Raggl, A. and Schratz, M., 'Using visuals to release pupils' voices', in Pole, C. (ed.) *Seeing is Believing?* New York: Elsevier, pp. 147–62.

Schulz, J. B. et al. (1981) 'The effects of a preoperational puppet show on anxiety levels of hospitalized children', *Children's Heath Care*, 9: 118–21.

Schwartz, D. (1989) 'Visual ethnography: using photography in qualitative research', *Qualitative Sociology*, 12(2): 119–54.

Siegal, M. (1988) 'Children's knowledge of contagion and contamination as causes of illnesss', *Child Development*, 50: 1353–9.

Smith, C. Z and Woodward, A. M. (1999) 'A Photo-elicitation method gives voice and reactions of subjects', *Journalism and Mass Communication Educator*, 53(4): 31–41.

Sroufe, A. (1997) 'Children's Representations of attachment relationships in family drawings', *Child Development*, 68(6): 1154–64.

Stokrocki, M. (1984) 'The significance of touching in an art awareness experience: a photographic analysis, elicitation and interpretation', *International Journal of Visual Sociology*, 2: 44–58.

Tucker, S. A. and Dempsey, J. V. (1991) 'Photo-interviewing: a tool for evaluating technological innovations', *Evaluation Review*, 15(5): 639–54.

Verschueren, K. et al. (2001) 'Self-representations and socioemotional competence in young children: a 3-year longitudinal study', *Developmental Psychology*, 37: 126–34.

Wang. C. and Burris, M. B. (1994) 'Empowerment through photo novella: portraits of participation', *Health Education and Behaviour*, 21(2): 171–86.

Weiniger, S. (1998) 'Children living in poverty: their perception of career opportunities', *Families in Society: The Journal of Contemporary Human Services*, May–June, pp. 320–30.

Wilks, T. (2004) 'The use of vignettes in qualitative research into social work values', *Qualitative Social Work*, 3: 78–87.

Williams, D., Wetton, N. and Moon, A. (1989) *A Picture of Health: What Do You Do That Makes You Healthy and Keeps You Healthy?* London: London Health Education Authority.

Young, L. and Barrett, H. (2001) 'Adapting visual methods: action research with Kampala street children', *Area*, 33(2): 141–52.

Zenkov, K. and Harman, J. (2009) 'Picture a writing process: photovoice and teaching writing to urban youth', *Journal of Adolescent and Adult Literacy*, 52(7): 575–84.

Ziller, R. C. (1990) *Photographing the Self: Methods for Observing Personal Orientation*. Newbury Park, CA: Sage.

Focus groups and group interviews

Anita Gibbs

Introduction

Focus groups and group interviews are methods often used synonymously to mean an organised discussion with a selected group of individuals to gain collective views about a research topic. Group interviews are a way to gather many opinions from individuals within a group setting but are largely didactic between interviewer and each individual in the group. The distinguisher of focus groups is that they are *interactive*, the group opinion is at least as important as the individual opinion, and the group itself may take on a life of its own not anticipated or initiated by the researcher. In this chapter I will be primarily referring to focus groups as the more widely used technique in educational-based research and because this term has come to be accepted as the term for research utilising a group method. In educational research focus groups can be used for a multitude of purposes, for example co-constructing new knowledge, gauging opinion, evaluating services, generating theory, learning from experiences, understanding the everyday use of language, interpreting cultures, reshaping people's views, political action and empowerment of marginalised groups (Cousin, 2009; Halcomb et al., 2007; Hopkins, 2007). Perhaps less suitable for focus group study would be: confirmation or disconfirmation of hypotheses, pre- and post- group assessment of interventions, any study where generalisations to whole populations might be required, or studies that are predictive in nature (Vaughn et al., 1996).

Focus groups can be used as a method in their own right but are often used to complement other methods, for example to develop or refine survey questions. Reasons to choose focus groups over other methods might include the need to gather reasonable numbers of people together for a group view on a topic, the need to gauge multiple perspectives about a topic in the emotive and interactive way that only a focus group can achieve, and as a cheaper or speedier way of doing interviews where easily accessible groups of participants can be readily assembled instead of interviewing many individuals.

The rest of this chapter considers the strengths and weaknesses of focus groups, how to set-up and run focus groups, the ethical dilemmas and cultural challenges to consider when undertaking focus group studies, and the use of 'online' focus groups. The chapter also provides two exemplars of educational-based research focus groups and advice on further reading as well as some questions for discussion.

Strengths and weaknesses of focus groups

Halcomb et al. (2007: 1008) discuss the strengths and weaknesses of focus groups. These include the benefits of discovering the collective perspective, the 'synthesis and validation of ideas and concepts', the involvement of diverse groups of people and access to potentially a large number of participants. On the downside, Halcomb et al. (2007: 1008) consider that focus groups have potential for problems with confidentiality (see the section on ethics later), can produce conflicts resulting in problems in managing group interaction, can be poorly run if moderators are not highly skilled, and can sometimes produce complex verbal and non-verbal responses from participants making analysis and interpretation a challenging task. Others have argued that focus groups can also produce shallow or poor quality data thus reducing the quality of insight overall (Hopkins, 2007).

Yet, the benefits to focus group participants themselves should not be underestimated. People may feel strongly about a topic and may enjoy discussing it with others who share some of their concerns; they may also enjoy group debate on a topic in such a way that they feel empowered by the group dynamic. Participants in focus groups may feel able to talk about sensitive topics in a way in which they would not do in an individual interview, and they may gain strength from the energy of a group setting. Of course, the researcher may not be able to predict or control whether focus group participants do have such experiences, and ultimately has to decide if their research questions are best answered by this method. For researchers, a clear strength of focus groups is that they allow information to be collected on *why* an issue is salient, as well *how* it may be salient or in *what* ways it may be salient – all at the same time. Hence the gap between what people say and what they do can be better understood.

Another advantage of focus groups is their potential for change, whether during a group session or post sessions. This could of course be perceived as a disadvantage if change occurs in the negative. Potentially though, changes in education to policy, practice or theory may occur through focus group research because new ideas have emerged during the dialogues between participants who may themselves be capable of initiating change. Researchers also can initiate change in the way they choose to present the analysis from focus group studies.

The context in which a focus group occurs and its influence is particularly pertinent to consider, as potentially the contributions made by participants will be swayed by such factors as location, culture, age and gender balance, status, capabilities, physical abilities and so on. Each focus group meeting needs to be understood in its contextual setting in an entirely different way to that of an individual interview. The timing of a group is also an important contextual consideration: trying to get parents of school-aged children to focus groups during school holidays is a non-starter for example.

On a practical note, focus groups can be difficult to assemble (see next section). It may not be easy to get the sample that is able to answer your research questions, and focus groups may discourage certain people from participating, for example those who are not very articulate or confident, and those who have communication challenges or special needs. People more likely to participate in group-based research will be confident and articulate, although it may be possible to gain more vulnerable or marginalised perspectives if participants are part of a pre-existing group. If the researcher is also part of the marginalised group, perhaps as a service user or as an invited guest, then again it may be possible to obtain the perspectives of less confident participants.

How to set up and run a focus group

Focus groups are particularly suited to qualitative research but that does not mean they cannot complement a quantitative and positivist-oriented study, i.e. survey plus group interviews. Mixed methods are fine but also a stand-alone focus group study can be undertaken. Once a decision has been made that focus groups might best answer a particular research objective or question then initial planning can begin. Selecting the groups of participants is a crucial stage. A focus group researcher will need to decide how many groups, of what size, of what composition and so on. Most texts advise groups composed of between 4 and

12 people but there have been studies outside of these guidelines (Cousin, 2009; Hopkins, 2007; Vaughn et al.,1996). Toner (2009), for example, who used as few as two participants for focus groups studies about women who had abused illegal substances, argues that small groups still follow typical group development and can be analysed in the same way as larger focus groups. Toner (2009) believes that feminist research principles of collaboration and emancipation enable an acceptance of the validity of very small focus groups (VSFGs as they are known), especially with hard to reach groups. As to how many groups, again that depends somewhat on the research questions but from a grounded theory perspective 'how many?' may need to be decided after data collection has begun. Often people conduct one-off groups with three or more different focus groups, but also many meetings of the same group of participants can be undertaken. The researcher will need to decide when they have gathered enough data to achieve their research goals and when they have analysed enough groups to reach saturation and meaning, and are able to justify clear themes and add new concepts.

In order to undertake a focus group study in education the researcher will probably have completed an ethics application and approval process and will have prepared information sheets, consent forms, and letters of invitation. Accessing participants may require the use of key informants or go-betweens who can contact likely participants and recruit them. These recruiters can play a pivotal role and will need to be acknowledged and thanked, perhaps through a gift or financial payment. The participants themselves may need to be offered a small incentive for taking part, or offered food or refreshments during attendance at focus group meetings. The researcher will need to determine the time, place and format of meetings. The selection of participants will need to reflect whether the research question can best be answered with diversity of groups or homogeneity. In the past, focus group researchers were advised to make up the groups with similar kinds of people, e.g. single-sex, same ages, same ethnicities, but nowadays focus groups are full of a greater range of mixed characteristics. Diversity is welcomed but the researcher must always be mindful of the impact of status and power on group dynamics and getting it wrong can result in poor quality interaction

and data. Too many power differentials can mean some people will not speak and may even be upset by comments from powerful others. Can the group mix best answer your research questions and will the focus group experience be safe for participants? These two questions should guide selection. It is always best to over-recruit by as much as 30%, as not everyone will make it. It is quite common to do additional individual interviews with people who agreed to participate in the study but then failed to turn up to the actual group meeting.

The moderator, researcher or group facilitator plays a critical role in determining the outcomes and experiences of the focus group. Nearly every text suggests that they need to be knowledgeable of group processes and skilled in group facilitation (Halcomb et al., 2007; Toner, 2009). Key characteristics of moderators are good interpersonal skills and the ability to handle conflict as well as to nurture contributions, thus enabling interaction between participants while being reflective and non-judgemental. Ultimately, the quality of data produced is dependent on the ability of the moderator to get people talking to each other, in-depth, about the topic in hand. When running the actual focus group the moderator will undertake introductions, setting of groundrules and facilitation of discussion. In some cases he/she will assisted by an observer who might take notes, help with other recording equipment or ask the occasional question of the group. An observer can be very helpful after a group has finished in discussing key themes arising from group interaction. The moderator is likely to have prepared an interview guide but must be fully prepared not to have all their questions covered, so the fewer the questions the better. Focus groups are likely to cover areas of discussion not anticipated by the researcher but a skilled moderator can make the most of these 'new' areas as well as bring the discussion back to the main points. At the end of a group which usually lasts between 45 minutes and two hours (although there have been examples of less than 30 minutes for children, and four hours for Maori – see the Suggested Further Reading section at the end of the chapter), the moderator will thank participants and sum up. It is likely that transcripts of sessions will be prepared and sent to participants for checking and/ or further comment.

For analysis (see the articles by Wilkinson in the Suggested Further Reading) the focus group researcher needs to bear in mind that the unit of analysis is the collective perspective. Too often in the reporting of focus groups the analysis is presented as if there had been only a conversation between the researcher and each individual participant whereas there has mostly been group dialogue. The reporting of findings needs to show the interaction between and influence of participants upon each other to fully represent what has occurred in the focus group. The analysis of focus group data will include deductive reasoning from the original research questions and inductive reasoning to allow new concepts, themes and ideas to emerge. Consensus of views as well as divergence of opinion will all be captured and reported upon in final reports. The validity and reliability of focus group data can include triangulation, audit trails, and respondent and inter-rater checking (Toner, 2009).

Ethical dilemmas

Tolich (2009) and Halcomb et al. (2007) identify many ethical dilemmas peculiar to focus groups. These include issues to do with confidentiality and fully informed consent, arguing that focus groups present extra dilemmas and risks because of their group nature. They argue that it is not possible to ensure confidentiality because all participants hear the discussion in a group even if they do not share it beyond the group. Likewise, the nature of the research questions and actual discussion taking place in a focus group may differ somewhat from the schedule suggested in the information sheets. This is because in a group the interaction levels can change the flow of the topic and the researcher inevitably has less control even if they are highly skilled in group research. Tolich (2009) argues that some of the ethical issues can be overcome by more detailed information sheets which clearly lay out the risks of participation, as well as researchers reiterating at the start of focus group meetings that people should be wary of sharing too much personal information and that the researcher may be limited in their abilities to minimise harm. Tolich also wisely reminds us that viewing focus groups as a kind of *public meeting* rather than a private

meeting is more helpful to participants in enabling them to decide what to say. In any good ethical research participants should be offered the chance to debrief, and/or, contact the researcher to follow-up concerns. In very sensitive research additional services should be offered, for example a counsellor or other professional service for participants who feel they have experienced distress from participating in a focus group. In VSFGs extreme care should be taken to protect the identity of participants through limited reporting of participants' characteristics.

Cultural challenges

Much has been written about the need to ensure the appropriate mix of focus group participants in a way in which is not discriminatory or offensive to different cultural groups, and which also takes account of different cultural practices (Halcomb et al., 2007). Issues of sample size, status, gender, age, location, recruitment and question procedures all need to be reflected upon in culturally appropriate terms. Sometimes, even when appropriate cultural protocols have been followed and participants have felt comfortable to participate in a focus group, unintended consequences will occur. Pere and Barnes (2009) provide an example of a focus group study with Maori where one focus group proceeded well and another one resulted in causing offence to some people, even though the same culturally sensitive practices had been in place prior to the group meeting. Pere and Barnes (2009) conducted a study to ascertain the views of mental health service users on the concept of self-stigma. Pere was Maori and Barnes non-Maori but could speak Maori. The researchers consulted appropriately with, and enlisted the help of, respected Maori leaders to run the focus groups. In one of the focus groups the Maori leader was critical of research procedures which failed to understand the complexities of Kaupapa Maori, that is Maori ways of doing and self-determination. The focus group facilitated by this Maori leader was conducted very differently from other groups but in a way in which participants felt that Maori protocol had been adhered to and useful data was still collected. Pere and Barnes concluded that it is vital to allow Maori to define their own ways of doing research even if it contrasts with the assumed 'normal' western ways of doing it. Other cultures may favour alternative ways of conducting focus group research and it is therefore important for people planning focus group studies to allow extra time for working in culturally appropriate ways.

Online focus groups

While this chapter concentrates on 'traditional' face-to-face group interviewing, future focus group research will increasingly be done on-line, via email, or the Internet, or by using remote audio and video technology. Online focus group research therefore needs to be considered as a potential option. The issues to consider when using distance methods for focus groups will be similar to those when undertaking traditional focus groups but will also involve new challenges for researchers in recruitment, getting people together at exactly the same time or at different times but in different locations, working the equipment and dealing with technology hiccups, and in the recording and management of data. Online focus groups have the potential of convenience for participants and researchers, reduced costs, ongoing dialogue, inclusiveness and greater anonymity. An excellent example of an online discussion board style focus group is provided by Yick et al. (2005) who organised an asynchronous focus group for 28 academics to explore their experiences of distance education and online teaching. The online discussion board ran for three weeks and three researchers posted new discussion questions each week. All the participants were encouraged to respond and also to engage in dialogue with each other (*interaction* in other words). The researchers moderated the discussions and participants were encouraged to revisit any previous discussions and continue current conversations. All discussion postings were downloaded (the data) and analysed using a content analysis to develop key themes. The article by Yick et al. was, not surprisingly, published in an online journal (see References below).

Exemplars

Jinnah-Ghelani and Stoneman (2009) undertook a focus-group study to discover the critical elements of successful inclusion of school-age children with disabilities into childcare settings. This exploratory study involved five focus groups and eight telephone interviews with 37 parents of school-age children with disabilities. The study sought the views of parents on what was needed to ensure their children were included in childcare settings in an appropriate way that enhanced well-being. Jinnah-Ghelani and Stoneman detail how participants were recruited and interviewed, and the article is a good example of reported findings. The focus groups were transcribed and analysed using a grounded theory approach with QSR 6, a non-statistical software package for qualitative data. The findings were reported thematically and detailed quotes from participants were included to illustrate the main themes. The authors were able to conclude from this carefully carried out study that parents of children with disabilities struggle to find appropriate after-school care for their children and that much more needs to be done by childcare centres to improve the services they offer such children.

In a different focus-group study considering discourses and explanations Tett and Riddell (2009) sought educators' views of gender issues in the teaching profession. Tett and Riddell conducted six focus groups with primary and secondary school teachers (n = 38) and 16 individual interviews with key informants involved in education. They gathered data on educators' opinions about the gender balance in teaching, and their views about why men choose teaching and how more men can be encouraged into teaching. Each focus group lasted about 45 minutes and was transcribed and analysed thematically. The main strength of this paper is that it shows how focus groups alongside individual interviews can assist in the furthering of theoretical ideas about a topic. The findings themselves were presented to answer 'why' rather than 'what' questions and this piece adds nicely to what we know about gender imbalances in the teaching profession.

Conclusion

Focus groups are highly suited to many kinds of educational research. When undertaken well they can be rewarding for participants, present exciting challenges for researchers, and produce quality in-depth interactional data of a kind not possible through other methods.

Questions for further investigation

1. What kinds of educational research might be suited to focus-group research?
2. What are the main ethical issues a novice researcher might face when undertaking an education-based focus-group study?
3. How would you prepare and plan for an email, Internet-based or online group-based research meeting?
4. What cultural assumptions do you bring as a researcher to group-interviewing research?

Suggested further reading

Bagnoli, A. and Clark, A. (2009) 'Focus groups with young people: a participatory approach to research planning', *Journal of Youth Studies*, 13(1): 101–19. An excellent report on research undertaken with 12 and 13 year olds demonstrating the empowering and participatory nature of focus groups as well as the *basics* of using focus groups for recruitment and research with young people. Bagnoli and Clark used video excerpts as part of their research and gauged feedback on the usefulness of this as well as young people's views of being involved in focus groups as research participants.

Krueger, R. and Casey, M. (2009) *Focus Groups: A Practical Guide for Applied Research* (4th edn). Thousand Oaks, CA: Sage. The 'nuts and bolts' guide to organising focus groups, with detailed advice on how to think about and run focus groups. The book also contains material on styles of focus groups, cross-cultural focus-group research and telephone and Internet focus groups.

Vaughn, S., Schumm, J. and Sinagub, J. (1996) *Focus Group Interviews in Education and Psychology*. London: Sage. While dated this is a great introductory guide for education

and psychology students. The book covers definitions, rationales for using focus groups, applications, how to prepare for groups, selection of participants, the role of moderator and data analysis. It also explores the use of focus groups with children and young people and potential abuses of focus groups. It is written in an accessible style with thought-provoking activities at the end of each chapter.

Wilkinson, S. (1998) 'Focus groups in health research', *Journal of Health Psychology*, 3(3): 329–48.

Wilkinson, S. (1999) 'Focus groups: a feminist method', *Psychology of Women Quarterly*, 23(2): 221–44.

Wilkinson, S. (2004) 'Focus group research', in Silverman, D. (ed.) *Qualitative Research* (2nd edn). London: Sage. In these readings Wilkinson covers the groundwork of the pros and cons of focus groups. She provides excellent examples from health and social sciences, and gives detailed reported findings from her own studies as well as details on the analysis of focus group data. She also explores focus groups as a feminist method and discusses the power issues involved. She is one of the few authors who also details the interactive nature of focus groups and demonstrates this through evidence and quotes from her own research.

References

Cousin, G. (2009) *Researching Learning in Higher Education*. London: Routledge.

Halcomb, E., Gholizadeh, L., DiGiacomo, M., Phillips, J. and Davidson, P. (2007) 'Literature review: considerations in undertaking focus group research with culturally and linguistically diverse groups', *Journal of Clinical Nursing*, 16(6): 1000–11.

Hopkins, P. (2007) 'Thinking critically and creatively about focus groups', *Area*, 39(4): 528–35.

Jinnah-Ghelani, H. and Stoneman, Z. (2009) 'Elements of successful inclusion for school-age children with disabilities in childcare settings', *Child Care in Practice*, 15(3): 175–91.

Pere, L. and Barnes, A. (2009) 'New learnings from old understandings: conducting qualitative research with Maori', *Qualitative Social Work*, 8(4): 449–67.

Tett, L. and Riddell, S. (2009) 'Educators' responses to policy concerns about the gender balance of the teaching profession in Scotland', *Journal of Education Policy*, 24(4): 477–93.

Tolich, M. (2009) 'The principle of caveat emptor: confidentiality and informed consent as endemic ethical dilemmas in focus groups research', *Journal of Bioethical Inquiry*, 6(1): 99–108.

Toner, J. (2009) 'Small is not too small: reflections concerning the validity of very small focus groups (VSFGs)', *Qualitative Social Work*, 8(2): 179–92.

Vaughn, S., Schumm, J. and Sinagub, J. (1996) *Focus Group Interviews in Education and Psychology*. London: Sage.

Yick, A., Patrick, P. and Costin, A. (2005) 'Navigating distance and traditional higher education: online faculty experiences', *International Review of Research in Open and Distance Learning*, 6: 2.4. Available at: http://www.irrodl. org/index.php/irrodl/article/view/235/320 (accessed April 2010).

Internet-based methods

Rhona Sharpe and Greg Benfield

Introduction

A single chapter cannot hope to encompass the breadth, depth or complexity of 'Internet research methods' and the research design, data-gathering and ethics issues related to them. This chapter examines one aspect of Internet research in education using the example of a national UK project to explore students' experiences of technology-mediated learning. It examines methods from investigations of learners' experiences of e-learning, and the role that the Internet and other digital technology have played in the development of this field. Much of our perspective comes from our role in the JISC Learner Experiences of E-learning programme,[1] working alongside nine research projects over four years as they collected their data and analysed their findings. We also draw on our leadership of ELESIG[2] – a special interest group of learner experience researchers and practitioners.

In this chapter, we show that the Internet has precipitated a change in both research questions and data collection methods. We argue that the pervasive, integrative use of social and personal technology by learners means that the study of educational uses of technology needs to be seen within a wider, holistic context. This chapter explains how such research is being conducted and provides examples of some of the research methods.

The chapter title, 'Internet-based methods', harbours a duality that is central to our discussion: the Internet is both a repository of research tools and an object of research in its own right. Our examples of research methods for investigating learner experiences encompass both aspects of this duality. Thus we explore some of the online tools and techniques that are being used for gathering data and the methodological issues around their use. We also outline the significance and role of digital technologies in the experiences of today's learners and explore how researchers can take account of this.

We use the example of learner experience research to illustrate how Internet technologies may be used to support three key methodological aims in naturalistic research. The first aim is gaining *sustained engagement* (Lincoln and Guba, 1985) with research participants. We show how online methods can facilitate multiple engagements with participants over extended time periods, allowing the researcher to obtain a more complex picture of dynamic behaviours, perceptions and beliefs than is possible with a single interview or questionnaire. Second, we explore how online methods may be used to improve research validity or *trustworthiness*. This includes the notion of triangulation, that is using a variety of different data types and sources and comparing them for consistency, confirming and crosschecking accounts and observations. This is a cornerstone of naturalistic research and an important way of increasing the trustworthiness of interview data (Cohen et al., 2000; Robson, 2002). Finally, we put forward a position of *participatory*, inclusive evaluation and research as the appropriate standpoint for conducting human research in a digital age.

The impact of the Internet on social science research

It is almost trivial to observe that the Internet is having a major impact on social science research. There are several dimensions to this impact. New topics for investigation continually emerge. For example, the meaning of 'learning' in virtual worlds like Second Life (Savin-Baden, 2008), or the effectiveness for learning of gaming and immersive simulations (de Freitas and Oliver, 2006) are current topics that were unheard of ten years ago. Also, the rapid pace of technological innovation spawns new tools and environments for gathering research data. Even five years ago gathering data from social networking sites was unknown to educational researchers.

The other important impact of the Internet on educational research is its pervasiveness in our lives. To take an example: survey data collection has long been an important social science research method. Just ten years ago, online survey administration was available but not common, in good part because the sampling population then was small. Now, 73% of UK homes have Internet access (Office for National Statistics, 2010), online survey research accounts for more than 20% of global data collection expenditure (Vehovar and Manfreda, 2008) and online survey administration tools are readily available to all educational researchers.

For social science researchers, Mann and Stewart's (2000) early methodological work on computer-mediated communication (CMC) as a research tool has stood the test of time, maintaining its relevance as a manual for researchers on using CMC for interviewing, participant observation, collecting documents and linguistic analysis. However, the commonplace Internet communication tools in the world Mann and Stewart wrote about at that time were email, asynchronous text-based conferencing like the

discussion boards found in modern university virtual learning environments (VLEs), and synchronous text-based chat. Ubiquitous social networking, image, video and application sharing, and web-enabled mobile devices were not in existence at that time. As a result, new research tools such as video interviewing and video diaries both remove some of the problems of text-based environments, like establishing participant identity in focus groups, and introduce new issues, such as interpreting data involving significant levels of performance.

The impact of the Internet on researching learners' experiences of e-learning

Learner experience research has prompted a reconsideration of the place and role of technology in students' lives. Previous e-learning research was primarily evaluative, asking questions about the impact of tutor behaviour, e.g. e-moderating (Salmon, 2004) or presence (Garrison et al., 2001; Garrison, 2003); pedagogy, e.g. constructivist (Hughes and Daykin, 2002; Allen, 2005; Gulati, 2008) or collaborative (Hiltz et al., 2000; McConnell, 2000; Macdonald, 2003; Schweizer et al., 2003; Goodyear and Zenios, 2007); and environment, i.e. technology (Freeman, 1998; Lockyer et al., 2001; Crook, 2002; Ellis and Calvo, 2004; Kear, 2004) on student learning and satisfaction within a specific educational context. As we noted at the time:

> There is in general a dearth of studies of the learner experience. In particular there is a scarcity of studies that can be characterised as expressing a 'learner voice', i.e. in which the learners' own expressions of their experiences are central to the study. (Sharpe et al., 2005: 3)

Learner experience research takes a different view, encouraging us to view the experience of being a student from the learner's perspective. Using technology that learners are already familiar with to elicit and record their experiences (such as email, SMS texting and mp3 players), we are prompted to see the role of technology more holistically. We find that learners use technology primarily not to 'learn' but as a source of information and to engage with their social networks (Salaway et al., 2007). We find that technology takes on different roles for various groups of students – having particular significance for disabled and international learners where they have a real need for it (Sharpe et al., 2009). We find also a vast range of individual differences in how learners use technology, from no use at all to extensive, individual choice in creatively appropriating a range of technologies for learning.

This change in the way evaluations of e-learning are conducted is impacting on their research aims and questions. We note a shift from a concern with the actions of course designers and tutors to a focus on the ways in which learners manage their engagement with digital technology (e.g. Davies et al., 2008) and ultimately the study of the development of digitally literate learners (Lankshear and Knobel, 2006; Beetham et al., 2009). Eliciting learners' experiences is helping us to understand how learners develop skills, practices and make choices, and then to design environments and provide tutoring in ways that will support them at critical moments.

Using online research methods to investigate learners' experiences

For these reasons learner experience research is avowedly naturalistic in approach. It should, in so far as is possible, occur in a natural setting and use methods such as 'interviews, observations, document analysis, unobtrusive clues, and the like' (Lincoln and Guba, 1985: 187). In the JISC Learner Experiences of E-learning programme, this approach was a consequence of both the research questions and our understanding of the role technology plays in the life of the modern student. Our aim was to privilege learners' voices and consider their technology use holistically. This section uses examples from the learner experience field to illustrate the use of naturalistic methods to develop an understanding of the learner in context.

Sustained engagement

Technology has been used in imaginative ways to engage learners in data-gathering over a sustained period of time. Dujardin (2009) in her 'conversations with an e-learner' describes a series of interviews conducted via instant messaging over a five-month period. Masterman (2010a) conducted a careful review of the literature on email interviewing in other fields such as health (e.g. Hunt and McHale, 2007) and adapted this for their own project, engaging 23 students in three 'rounds' of questioning over a period of 8–9 months in what they termed the 'pen-pal' method.

> 'Pen-pal' was the name given to the method we devised to meet the challenge of eliciting data from busy students over an extended period with minimal intrusion, and using a simple and robust technology (i.e. email). Each researcher established individual relationships with 6–10 students and conducted an extended email correspondence culminating, as pen-pal relationships can do, in a face-to-face encounter (a semi-structured interview). (Masterman, 2010a: 29)

Here questions were derived from the research questions of the study, knowledge of the students' course context and their previous data responses, e.g. 'I note from your survey response that . . .'. The email correspondence aimed to provide background information to personalise the subsequent interviews and record experiences that might not be remembered in interview.

Sustained engagement has also been achieved through the keeping of diaries or logs. Variants include audio logs (Conole et al., 2007) where students phoned a voicemail service to leave a log entry, and projects where students were given the choice of recording diary entries on a camcorder, webcam or digital voice recorder (Hardy et al., 2008; Jefferies and Hyde, 2009). In the STROLL project at the University of Hertfordshire, students provided diary entries every day for a week, during four weeks spread over 18 months (Jefferies and Hyde, 2009). The videos provide a vivid insight into the worlds, and study bedrooms, of the learners (see Figure 27.1).

Figure 27.1 Screenshot from STROLL video diaries

Trustworthiness

Internet research presents a range of issues around validity or, in naturalistic terminology, the *trustworthiness* of our interpretations of qualitative data. There are different ways of achieving this, which include member checks, debriefings by peers, triangulation, prolonged engagement and persistent observation, the use of reflexive journals and independent audit.

A fundamental principle of learner experience research is that it is holistic. In order to understand how learners experience learning in our technology-rich age, we must ask the participants themselves to define what is talked about. We must go in without preconceptions and ask about all aspects of life. Creanor and her colleagues in one of the first learner experience studies, interviewed learners using an open set of

questions, and improved trustworthiness by engaging three researchers to analyse the resulting transcripts using Interpretive Phenomenological Analysis (see Mayes, 2006; Smith et al., 2009).

Traditionally, validity is improved through the use of mixed methods designs. In learner experience research, this approach is exemplified by the Thema project at Oxford University, through their mix of survey and email interviewing as shown in Table 27.1. The 'pen-pal' correspondence culminated in a face-to-face interview, further improving the trustworthiness of the data.

One of the methods in a mixed-method design is often an interview. In conducting interviews – whether online or face to face – the researcher faces the problems of eliciting complete and accurate information where the artificiality of the interview situation may conspire against these aims. Eliciting tacit understandings is notoriously problematic for researchers and in learner experience research we have found that learners may not associate certain activities or technologies with 'learning'.

To help address these problems, the learner experiences of e-learning programme adopted an approach called *interview plus* (Sharpe et al., 2005; Creanor et al., 2006; Mayes, 2006). The idea is similar to the 'think aloud' observation technique that is used in cognitive psychology (Ericsson and Simon, 1993), where the 'plus' represents some artefact that is chosen to guide recall during the interview. This might be a website, blog, wiki, social networking environment, diary, learner progress files or student work. The

Table 27.1 Example of mixed-methods strategy (adapted from Masterman, 2010a)

Study	Technique	Students involved
Preliminary	Online survey	Undergraduate, taught Master's and graduate research students
Main	Online survey	Case-study contributors plus other students from the courses involved in the main study
	Email 'pen-pal' correspondence	Case study contributors only
	Online survey	Case-study contributors plus other students from the courses involved in the main study
	Face-to-face interview	Case study contributors only

researcher is taken on a 'guided tour' of the artefact by its creator. In doing so, they hear the participant's explanations while simultaneously comparing these accounts with their behaviours at the computer and on-screen evidence. Interview plus is an important tool in revealing hidden practices and a variant is being used in a large study of academic literacy where multiple data is being collected during interviews including documents, screen dumps, photos and students' own work as well as interview transcripts (Lea and Jones, 2011).

As part of mixed-method designs, some studies are adding contemporaneous experience probes to interviews and diaries. This is made easier by the ubiquity of mobile phones. For example, in a study of the Net Generation student's use of technology, Jones and Healing (2010) adapted Riddle and Arnold's (2007) day experience method, sending students text messages throughout the day asking them to respond to prompts such as 'What time is it?', 'What are you doing?', 'Where are you?', 'Who are you with?' and 'Are you using any technology and, if so, what is it?'

Participatory approaches

The final methodological aim of naturalistic research into learners' experiences is a participatory approach where learners are involved at all stages of the research. Seale and colleagues, in a two-year study of disabled learners in higher education, describe such an approach as

> involving disabled learners as consultants and partners not just as research subjects. Where disabled learners help to identify and (re)frame the research questions, work with the researchers to achieve a collective analysis of the research issues and bring the results to the attention of each of the constituencies that they represent. (Seale et al., 2008a: 11)

The challenge for trustworthiness is to not over-interpret the learner's voice, while balancing that with answering the research questions we have in mind. Participatory approaches allow us to check back with the research participants that the data collected is accurate and that we have consent to use it, and also to check our understanding and interpretation of the data. The researcher's personalised requests for information, conversational style and prompt replies are important in eliciting the data needed and improving validity. Some are extending this approach to using students as researchers (e.g. Ainley, 2009).

There are examples of where holistic, participatory methodologies which have engaged learners over extended periods of time have produced unexpected results. The Thema project planned to investigate the use of technology by Masters students; however, their final report also tackles issues like adapting to autonomous learning and joining a research community (Masterman, 2010b). Other projects have benefited from having a contextualised understanding of use of technology within the wider choices learners make, such as the notion of the 'digital agility' demonstrated by learners with disabilities (Seale et al., 2010). Despite their benefits, these methodologies are not without their challenges.

Challenges in learner experience research

One of the challenges of the research approaches described in this chapter is that participants who are articulate, reflective and often skilled learners produce the most detailed and useful data. Dujardin (2009), for example, recognises this and talks about the need to have a 'key informant' willing to engage in reflective conversations with tutors. Other studies purposively sampled learners who were acknowledged as being effective in technology-based learning (e.g. Creanor et al., 2006). Internet-based research methods need to be clear about the extent to which their results can be representative. Those who have used email interviewing, for example, have noted their success in eliciting data from IT literate individuals who have a preference for the written word (Hunt and McHale, 2007).

We have also found that captured learners' voices – whether text, audio or video – can represent their perspectives in powerful and emotive ways. The challenge for researchers is to avoid the temptation to over-emphasise selected verbatim quotes at the expense of the analysis and synthesis of the data.

Table 27.2 Summary of methods used in learner experience research

Method	Description	Strengths	Weaknesses
'Pen-pal' variant of email interviewing (Masterman, 2010b)	Researchers enter into a personal dialogue with learners by email. Collects reflective, written contributions over a period of time.	• Can record experiences that learners might subsequently forget. • Can build up a picture of the process of studying as it happens. • Allows researcher to personalise questions. • Minimal intrusion into learners' time. • Maximises sustained participation through establishing a personal dialogue between researcher and learner.	• Time-intensive for researcher to craft individual questions and follow up responses. • Inconsistency in timing and content of questions across students and courses. • Researchers and learner both subjectively involved in interpretation. Requires careful checking for validity against other sources of data (triangulation).
Audio logs (Conole et al., 2007)	Providing facilities for learners to audio record their daily experiences, e.g. a phone-in voicemail number.	• Can provide rich data about day-to-day events. • Less time intensive for learner than keeping written logs. • Captured voices give insight into the emotion of the experience. • Can provide artefacts for later interviews. • Audio clips can be used in dissemination.	• Instructions need to be clear as researcher is not present to explain. • Participants need to be motivated to stay involved without contact with researcher. • Equipment needs to be easy to use. • Learners need to give informed consent for all possible uses of their voices. • Time-consuming to code data. • Poor recording practice can result in data loss.
Interview 'plus', variant of semi-structured interview (Seale et al., 2008b)	Interview which uses an artefact, selected by the participant, to support guided recall, e.g. a blog, email or laptop.	• Prompts discussion of actual learner behaviours, feelings and beliefs. • Allows learners to set the agenda. • Supports recall of actual incidents. • Less time-consuming for researchers than observation • Allows learner opportunities for reflection.	• Requires skilled interviewer to tease out beliefs, practices and feelings. • Can take more time than other interview techniques. • Some artefacts may be products of group work or held in group spaces, which present ethical difficulties for use as data.
Video diaries (Jefferies and Hyde, 2009; Hardy et al., 2008)	Participants provided with a set of questions and key dates and record diary entries with a webcam, either at their own location or in the study's 'diary room'.	• Recordings can be made at time and place of students choosing. • Elicits detailed information and captures thoughts, feelings and opinions at the time. • Prompts can be given for entries around trigger points and significant events. • Resulting videos are compelling viewing. • Videos can be analysed directly without needing to be transcribed.	• Resulting data files may be too large to upload. • Learners need to give informed consent for all possible uses of their images and understand that they cannot be anonymised. This may involve going back to learners at the end of the study to reconfirm permission to use selected clips.
Synchronous online interviewing (Dujardin, 2009)	One-to-one interviewing using text-based instant messaging software.	• Almost real-time interactions allow for some of the immediacy of face-to-face interactions. • Typing delay gives few seconds for reflection before answering. • Transcript created in real time and can be returned to during the interview.	• Participant may manage their presentation of self in the explicit record.
SMS Prompts (Jones and Healing, 2010)	Participants sent prompts via text message to their mobile phones. Responses to the prompts can be recorded in a voice recorder, video camera or notebook.	• Multiple prompts can be used to capture a day's experience.	• Cost of voice recorders or video cameras in large cohorts. • Produces large volumes of data.

Adapted from the 'Recipe Cards' produced for the JISC Learner Experiences of E-Learning programme at http://wiki.brookes.ac.uk/display/JISCLE2.

Video extracts need to illustrate a story which has been derived from an established methodology. Extracts can, however, produce easily digestible and readable findings from large amounts of data, e.g. such as personalised, vivid case studies of individual learners (see, for example, those produced by the PB-LXP project – see Thorpe, 2009).

Finally, there are clearly ethical issues in obtaining informed consent for video diary extracts which might be disseminated widely. We also found that holistic, participatory methods encourage participants to reveal information which the researcher then has to decide whether it is important to pass on, such as students revealing difficulties with their course and in need of support. We recognise the need to develop better guidelines for the ethical use of the digital data provided by research participants.

Conclusion

We hope that this chapter has demonstrated the benefits of adopting a naturalistic stance in Internet-based research and that readers can see parallels between how such approaches have influenced studies of learner experiences of e-learning and their own areas of interest. As these approaches evolve, we are aware of the need to develop methods which draw together data from multiple qualitative projects, perhaps such as meta-ethnography (Lam et al., 2008). What is needed is a synthesis and conceptualisation of findings that will take us beyond the stories of individual learners to recommendations which can transform learners' experiences in the future. See Table 27.2 for a summary of the methods used in learner experience research.

Questions for further investigation

1. How effectively are e-learning tools used on your course? How suitable are they for your area of research interest(s)?
2. List and discuss the many potential pitfalls that surround Internet-based research.

Notes

1. JISC Learner Experience programme at https://wiki.brookes.ac.uk/display/JISCLE2.
2. ELESIG is an international special interest group for those conducting investigations of learners' experiences of e-learning. See http://www.elesig.ning.com.

Suggested further reading

There are some good books and online resources that the Internet researcher can consult. We recommend in particular:

Mann and Stewart's early work on computer-mediated communication (CMC) as a research tool, in Mann, C. and Stewart, F. (2000) *Internet Communication and Qualitative Research: A Handbook for Researching.* London: Sage.

Fielding, N., Lee, R. M. and Blank, G. (eds) (2008) *The Sage Handbook of Online Research Methods.* London: Sage.

The UK Economic & Social Research Council (ESRC)-funded Research Methods Programme (running from 2002–2007, see http://www.ccsr.ac.uk/methods/), especially the web-sites *Exploring Online Research Methods* at http://www.geog.le.ac.uk/ORM/site/home.htm and *Ethnography for the Digital Age* at http://www.cf.ac.uk/socsi/hyper/p02/index.html.

References

Ainley, P. (2009) 'The varieties of student experience – an open research question and some ways to answer it', *Studies in Higher Education,* 33(5): 615–24.

Allen, K. (2005) 'Online learning: constructivism and conversation as an approach to learning', *Innovations in Education and Teaching International,* 42(3): 247–56.

Beetham, H., McGill, L. and Littlejohn, A. (2009) *Thriving in the 21st century: Learning Literacies for the Digital Age.* Available at: http://www.jisc.ac.uk/publications/reports/2009/elearningllidareport.aspx (accessed 12 October 2009).

Cohen, L., Manion, L. and Morrison, K. (2000) *Research Methods in Education.* London: RoutledgeFalmer.

Conole, G., de Laat, M., Dillon, T. and Darby, J. (2007) '"Disruptive technologies", "pedagogical innovation": what's new?

Findings from an in-depth study of students' use and perception of technology', *Computers and Education*, 50(2): 511–24.

Creanor, L., Trinder, K., Gowan, D. and Howells C. (2006) *LEX: The Learner Experience of e-learning. Final report*. Glasgow Caledonian University.

Crook, C. (2002) 'The campus experience of networked learning', in Steeples, C. and Jones, C. (eds) *Networked Learning: Perspectives and Issues*. London: Springer-Verlag, pp. 293–308.

Davies, C., Carter, A., Cranmer, S., Eynon, R. et al. (2008) *The Learner and Their Context – Interim Report: Benefits of ICT Use Outside Formal Education*. Interim report for Becta-funded project 'The Learner and Their Context'.

de Freitas, S. and Oliver, M. (2006) 'How can exploratory learning with games and simulations within the curriculum be most effectively evaluated?', *Computers and Education*, 46(3): 249–64.

Dujardin, A.-F. (2009) 'Conversations with an e-learner', *Brookes eJournal of Learning and Teaching*, 2(4). Available at: http://bejlt.brookes.ac.uk/article/conversations_with_an_e_learner/ (accessed 31 March 2011).

Ellis, R. A. and Calvo, R. A. (2004) 'Learning through discussions in blended environments', *Educational Media International*, 41(3): 263–74.

Ericsson, K. A. and Simon, H. A. (1993) *Protocol Analysis: Verbal Reports as Data*. Cambridge, MA: MIT Press.

Freeman, M. (1998) 'Video conferencing: a solution to the multi-campus large classes problem?', *British Journal of Educational Technology*, 29(3): 197–210.

Garrison, D. R. (2003) 'Cognitive presence for effective asynchronous online learning: the role of reflective inquiry, self-direction and metacognition', in Bourne, J. and Moore, J. C. (eds) *Elements of Quality Online Education: Practice and Direction*. Newburyport: Sloan-C, Olin College, pp. 47–58.

Garrison, D. R., Anderson, T. and Archer, W. (2001) 'Critical thinking, cognitive presence, and computer conferencing in distance education', *American Journal of Distance Education*, 15(1): 7–23.

Goodyear, P. and Zenios, M. (2007) 'Discussion, collaborative knowledge work and epistemic fluency', *British Journal of Educational Studies*, 55(4): 351–68.

Gulati, S. (2008) 'Compulsory participation in online discussions: is this constructivism or normalisation of learning?', *Innovations in Education and Teaching International*, 45(2): 183–92.

Hardy, J., Haywood, D., Haywood, J., Bates, S. et al. (2008) *Techniques for Gathering Student Views of their Experiences at University*. Edinburgh: University of Edinburgh. Available at: http://www.jisc.ac.uk/media/documents/programmes/elearningpedagogy/leadtechniquesreport.pdf (accessed 31 March 2011).

Hiltz, S. R., Coppola, N., Rotter, N. and Turoff, M. (2000) 'Measuring the importance of collaborative learning for the effectiveness of ALN: a multi-measure, multi-method approach', *Journal of Asynchronous Learning Networks*, 4(2): 103–25.

Hughes, M. and Daykin, N. (2002) 'Towards constructivism: Investigating students' perceptions and learning as a result of using an online environment', *Innovations in Education and Teaching International*, 39(3): 217–24.

Hunt, N. and McHale, S. (2007) 'A practical guide to the email interview', *Qualitative Health Research*, 17(10): 1415–21.

Jefferies, A. and Hyde, R. (2009) 'Listening to the learners' voices in HE: how do students reflect on their use of technology for learning?', *Electronic Journal of e-Learning*, 7(2): 119–26.

Jones, C. and Healing, G. (2010) 'Learning nests and local habitations: locations for networked learning', in Dirckinck-Holmfeld et al. (eds). *Proceedings of the 7th International Conference on Networked Learning 2010*, pp. 635–42.

Kear, K. (2004) 'Peer learning using asynchronous discussion systems in distance education', *Open Learning*, 19(2): 151–64.

Lam, P., McNaught C. and Cheng, K. (2008) 'Pragmatic meta-analytical studies: learning the lessons from naturalistic evaluations of multiple cases', *ALT-J*, 16(2): 61–80.

Lankshear, C. and Knobel, M. (2006) 'Digital literacies: policy, pedagogy and research considerations for education', *Nordic Journal of Digital Literacy*, 1(1): 226.

Lea, M. R. and Jones, S. (2011) 'Digital literacies in higher education. Exploring textual and technological practice', *Studies in Higher Education*, 36(4): 377–93.

Lincoln, Y. S. and Guba, E. G. (1985) *Naturalistic Inquiry*. Newbury Park, CA: Sage.

Lockyer, L., Patterson, J. and Harper, B. (2001) 'ICT in higher education: evaluating outcomes for health education', *Journal of Computer Assisted Learning*, 17(3): 275–83.

McConnell, D. (2000) *Implementing Computer Supported Cooperative Learning*. London: Kogan Page.

Macdonald, J. (2003) 'Assessing online collaborative learning: process and product', *Computers and Education*, 40(4): 377–91.

Mann, C. and Stewart, F. (2000) *Internet Communication and Qualitative Research: A Handbook for Researching*. London: Sage.

Masterman, L. (2010a) *Thema: Exploring the Experiences of*

Master's Students in a Digital Age: Methodology Report. JISC Learner Experiences of E-learning programme, University of Oxford. Available at: https://mw.brookes.ac.uk/download/attachments/918039/Thema+Methodology+Report.pdf?version=1 (accessed 31 March 2011).

Masterman, L. (2010b) *Thema project: Report on Students' Use of Digital Technologies*. JISC Learner Experiences of E-learning programme, University of Oxford. Available at: https://weblearn.ox.ac.uk/access/content/user/5739/Thema%20Project%20Outputs/Thema%20Technology%20Report.pdf (accessed 31 March 2011).

Mayes, T. (2006) *LEX – Methodology Report September 2006*. Available at: http://www.jisc.ac.uk/media/documents/programmes/elearningpedagogy/lex_method_final.pdf (accessed 31 March 2011).

Office for National Statistics (2010) *Internet Access 2010*. Available at: http://www.statistics.gov.uk/pdfdir/iahi0810.pdf (accessed 31 March 2011).

Riddle, M. D. and Arnold, M. V. (2007) *The Day Experience Method: A Resource Kit*. Available at: http://dtl.unimelb.edu.au/dtl_publish/12/67585.html (accessed 31 March 2011).

Robson, C. (2002) *Real World Research* (2nd edn). Oxford: Blackwell.

Salaway, G., Caruso, J. B. and Nelson, M. R. (2007) *The ECAR Study of Undergraduate Students and Information Technology, 2007*. Available at: http://www.educause.edu/ir/library/pdf/ers0706/rs/ERS0706w.pdf (accessed 9 October 2007).

Salmon, G. (2004) *E-moderating: The Key to Teaching and Learning Online* (2nd edn). London: RoutledgeFalmer.

Savin-Baden, M. (2008) 'From cognitive capability to social reform? Shifting perceptions of learning in immersive virtual worlds', *ALT-J: Research in Learning Technology*, 16(3): 151–61.

Schweizer, K., Paechter, M. and Weidenmann, B. (2003) 'Blended learning as a strategy to improve collaborative task performance', *Journal of Educational Media*, 28(2–3).

Seale, J., Draffan, E. A. and Wald, M. (2008a) 'Exploring disabled learners' experiences of e-learning', *LexDis Project Report*. Southampton: LexDis.

Seale, J., Draffan, E. A. and Wald, M. (2008b) 'An evaluation of the use of participatory methods in exploring disabled learners' experiences of e-learning', *LexDis Project Report*. Southampton: LexDis.

Seale, J., Draffan, E. A. and Wald, M. (2010) 'Digital agility and digital decision-making: conceptualising digital inclusion in the context of disabled learners in higher education', *Studies in Higher Education*, 35(4): 445–61.

Sharpe, R., Benfield, G., Lessner, E. and DeCicco, E. (2005) *Final Report: Scoping Study for the Pedagogy Strand of the JISC E-learning Programme*. Oxford: Oxford Brookes University. Available at: http://www.jisc.org.uk/uploaded_documents/scoping%20study%20final%20report%20v4.1.doc (accessed 31 March 2011).

Sharpe, R., Beetham, H., Benfield, G., DeCicco, E. and Lessner, E. (2009) *Learners Experiences of E-learning Synthesis Report: Explaining Learner Differences*. Available at: https://mw.brookes.ac.uk/display/JISCle2f/Findings (accessed 10 June 2009).

Smith, J. A., Flowers, P. and Larkin, M. (2009) *Interpretative Phenomenological Analysis: Theory, Method and Research*. London: Sage.

Thorpe, M. (2009) *JISC learner experience phase 2: PB_LXP: Learners' experience of elearning in practice courses: student case studies*. OU Knowledge Network. Available at: http://kn.open.ac.uk/public/document.cfm?docid=12130 (accessed 31 March 2011).

Vehovar, V. and Manfreda, K. L. (2008) 'Overview: online surveys', in Fielding, N., Lee, R. M. and Blank, G. (eds) *The Sage Handbook of Online Research Methods*. London: Sage, pp. 177–94.

28

Doing blog research

Axel Bruns and Jean Burgess

Introduction

Blogs and other online platforms for personal writing such as LiveJournal have been of interest to researchers across the social sciences and humanities for a decade now. Although growth in the uptake of blogging has stalled somewhat since the heyday of blogs in the early 2000s, blogging continues to be a major genre of Internet-based communication. Indeed, at the same time that mass participation has moved on to Facebook, Twitter and other more recent communication phenomena, what has been left behind by the wave of mass adoption is a slightly smaller but all the more solidly established blogosphere of engaged and committed participants. Blogs are now an accepted part of institutional, group and personal communications strategies (Bruns and Jacobs, 2006); in style and substance, they are situated between the more static information provided by conventional websites and web pages and the continuous newsfeeds provided through Facebook and Twitter updates. Blogs provide a vehicle for authors (and their commenters) to think through given topics in the space of a few hundred to a few thousand words – expanding, perhaps, on shorter tweets, and possibly leading to the publication of more fully formed texts elsewhere. Additionally, they are also a very flexible medium: they readily provide the functionality to include images,

audio, video and other additional materials – as well as the fundamental tool of blogging, the hyperlink itself.

Indeed, the role of the link in blogs and blog posts should not be underestimated. Whatever the genre and topic that individual bloggers engage in, for the most part blogging is used to provide timely updates and commentary – and it is typical for such material to link both to relevant posts made by other bloggers and to previous posts by the present author, both to background material which provides readers with further information about the blogger's current topic and to news stories and articles which the blogger found interesting or worthy of critique. Especially where bloggers are part of a larger community of authors sharing similar interests or views (and such communities are often indicated by the presence of yet another type of link – in blogrolls, often in a sidebar on the blog site, which list the blogger's friends or favourites), then, the reciprocal writing and linking of posts often constitutes an asynchronous, distributed conversation that unfolds over the course of days, weeks and months.

Research into blogs is interesting for a variety of reasons, therefore. For one, a qualitative analysis of one or several blogs can reveal the cognitive and communicative processes through which individual bloggers define their online identity, position themselves in relation to fellow bloggers, frame particular themes, topics and stories, and engage with one another's points of view. It may also shed light on how such processes may differ across different communities of interest, perhaps in correlation with the different societal framing and valorisation of specific areas of interest, with the socio-economic backgrounds of individual bloggers, or with other external or internal factors. Such qualitative research now looks back on a decade-long history (for key collections, see Gurak et al., 2004; Bruns and Jacobs, 2006; also see Walker Rettberg, 2008) and has recently shifted also to specifically investigate how blogging practices differ across different cultures (Russell and Echchaibi, 2009). Other studies have also investigated the practices and motivations of bloggers in specific countries from a sociological perspective through large-scale surveys (e.g. Schmidt, 2006). Blogs have also been directly employed within both K-12 and higher education, across many disciplines, as tools for reflexive learning and discussion (Burgess, 2006).

The computational turn

Over the past years, another significant approach to blog research has developed as part of what David Berry (2011) has described as the 'computational turn': the increased availability of tools for the semi-automatic capture and analysis of large corpuses of web (and other) content, and the development of research methodologies across the humanities and social sciences which exploit these new opportunities, often in interdisciplinary research teams. In blog research, the thrust of such developments is twofold: the earliest such research projects (see, for example, Adamic and Glance, 2005) focused mainly on the links found on blog sites and used them to plot the network structure which these multiple interlinkages reveal. This is done by using web crawler software – such as the freely available IssueCrawler (http://www.issuecrawler.net) – which start from a seed list of web pages provided by the researcher, and identify and follow the links present on those pages over a number of iterations to identify the wider network of sites which these seed sites link to. By analysing these linkage patterns, it is possible, for example, to identify those sites which receive the most links (and

which can therefore be understood as key providers of information or opinion), those which link the most but do not receive many links themselves (that is sites which sit on the margins, looking in), and those which both receive many incoming links *and* frequently link to others (sites which, in network analysis terms, have the greatest centrality in the network and act as its key connecting hubs). Additionally, networks may also exhibit more or less pronounced clustering patterns, where sites in specific clusters are highly interlinked with one another but not with sites in rival clusters. In their study of political blogs during the 2004 US election campaign, for example, Adamic and Glance (2005) found that bloggers on either side of US politics interlinked strongly with like-minded authors but much more rarely connected to their political foes.

Such analysis is of interest well beyond the relatively narrow field of explicitly political blogging, however: it can provide information on the structuration of the blogosphere on a much larger scale, as well as on the internal structures of its smaller subsets that are based around shared interests or identities. It is important to note in this context, however, that conventional web crawlers tend to be somewhat limited in their capabilities on several major points: first, they tend not to be able to distinguish between blogs and other types of websites, and will need to be trained to ignore links which may be commonly present in the sites analysed but are irrelevant for the study itself (for example to Google search functionality or to blog platform providers like Wordpress or Blogger). An untreated corpus of links generated by a crawler may therefore include a range of links that need to be removed manually, depending on the specific aims of the network analysis.

Second, crawlers usually also fail to distinguish between different types of links found on the same blog. A typical blog page will contain headers, footers and sidebars in addition to the blog post itself (and any comments which may have been made by readers) – however, the hyperlinks present in each of these sections fulfil vastly different discursive roles. Links in headers, footers and sidebars may mainly serve a purely navigational role, allowing readers to access different sections of the blog site, and should usually be excluded from any analysis altogether; some sidebar links (for example in blogrolls) may be relevant, but serve a very different role from links in the blog post itself: where blogroll links are affiliational (indicating the blogger's longer-term regard for or interest in another site), blog *post* links are much more directly discursive (relating immediately to the topic of the blog post itself and relevant perhaps only to that post). Indeed, some bloggers might indicate their affiliation with other blogs through the blogroll, but may only very rarely link to actual posts made by those blogs. Any analysis which treats such affiliational and discursive link types as equivalent therefore runs the risk of finding a large number of false positives: showing tight clustering between sites which are on one another's blogrolls, but hardly ever 'speak' to one another in their posts. (Finally, of course, any links provided by commenters on a blog post constitute yet another category – here, in fact, the bloggers themselves are not even the authors of these links, so that the links indicate neither a blogger's affiliation nor their discursive interest in the linked site.) More advanced crawling and capturing technology which reliably distinguishes between these different link types and dismisses those links which do not contribute to the questions at hand is required, therefore, and is being developed by a number of projects, even if it is not yet widely available.

Third, the crawling process itself also provides no opportunity for researchers to set temporal limits on the range of blog posts which are to be included in the corpus, even though this would be of significant interest in many contexts. As we have described it above, crawlers take the URL for a given web page, identify the links on that page and then repeat the process (over multiple iterations) with any of the new pages identified by those links; even if all of the seed URLs are blog posts from a specific period (say, the last week), then, if one or more of those posts link to substantially older posts, the corpus of links produced by the crawler may point to a network of posts which spreads over several months or even years. By contrast, however, researchers may well be interested to study only the interlinkages between blogs during the current week or month – for example to identify which blogs are key opinion leaders on the topics that currently excite the community, and how such opinion leadership may shift over time. Further development of research tools and methodologies will need to address such limitations and may lead to a move from crawling-based methods towards approaches which capture new blog posts from across a large collection of blogs *as they are made*, and which are thus able to capture the timestamp of those posts; this, then, enables researchers to select for analysis from a larger corpus of data only those posts which were made within a set timeframe (we describe such a system in Kirchhoff et al., 2009; and Bruns et al., 2008b).

By using tools other than (or in addition to) web crawlers, it also becomes possible to study more than simply the patterns of interlinkage between the blogs, but to examine the blog content more directly, and on a large scale. If blog posts can be captured (that is, accessed and stored in a local database for further study), this enables the use of tools which provide automatic textual analysis. Tools which enable this are usually a form of web content scraper – software that takes a list of URLs and captures the content of those web pages (usually as plain text or HTML). Here, too, it is important to ensure that the scraper distinguishes between the discursive textual content of blog posts themselves and the simply functional or phatic texts found in headers, footers and sidebars, as well as from comments made by readers – in almost all research scenarios, only the texts of the blog posts themselves will be relevant for the analysis. Further, in using scrapers, researchers must also consider the legal and ethical implications of their actions, of course (which we address in more detail below): for example, whether capturing such content is permissible under relevant 'fair use' or 'fair dealing' provisions in applicable copyright laws, and whether (even though the material captured is openly available online) posts should be de-identified or authors' identities otherwise concealed.

If acceptable approaches can be found, then the generation of a body of textual content – in addition to the information about interlinkage patterns which may be generated by scrapers or similar tools – opens further opportunities for research. Semi-automated textual analysis tools can extract ranked lists of the most frequently used keywords within a specific blog, across a group of blogs or during a specific timeframe; this provides information on bloggers' core topics (and can be used to examine whether bloggers belonging to different clusters in a link network have different topical emphases) as well as on shifts in overall interest over time (for example in response to external stimuli, such as news or current events). Textual analysis softwares such as *Leximancer* also include the functionality to assess patterns of co-occurrence between individual keywords: this enables researchers to identify clusters of key terms which are commonly used in close proximity, and thus to develop a better picture of topical preoccupations within a single blog (or a group of blogs, or during a set time period) than a mere ranking of keywords by frequency can provide (cf. Bruns et al., 2008a). It may even offer first insights into how specific themes are framed – co-occurrence of the names of specific persons or organisations with emotionally loaded terms ('clever', 'dishonest', 'sexy', 'strong', . . .) may point to how they are generally perceived by the bloggers whose posts are being studied.

Combining quantitative and qualitative approaches

Such examples also make clear that a merely computational, quantitative approach to blog research is rarely sufficient. Link network mapping and textual keyword analysis, even where they utilise highly sophisticated tools for capturing data on a large scale, only provide overall approximations of bloggers' and blog users' activities, and should never be regarded as entirely conclusive in their own right. First, while clustering tendencies in link networks and among keyword terms may appear to paint a convincing picture of affiliations and associations, it is necessary at the very least to verify through qualitative spot-checking how such close connection between nodes in the network is to be interpreted. In link networks, for example, frequent and reciprocated linking between two blogs may be the sign of close affiliation – of two bloggers in a cordial and meaningful conversation – but it could also indicate a bitter, drawn-out war of words. Similarly, the co-occurrence of a political leader's name and key terms such as 'clever' and 'smart' in the textual data could be a sign of high levels of approval – but then, such terms could also have been used in a highly ironic way and mean exactly the opposite. An accurate picture will only emerge if researchers examine at least some of the captured material *in situ* to verify what interpretation is correct.

Second, and more fundamentally, the use of automated tools at least for part of the analysis – while inherently necessary to process the potentially very large datasets which the computational approach can generate – also raises the threat that researchers may treat these tools as black-box technologies whose inner workings need not be understood as long as they produce outcomes that 'look right'. Indeed, to a significant extent the computational turn could also be described as a shift towards data visualisation – but any even casual glance at visualisation research clearly shows that there is a very wide variety of approaches to turning raw data into graphs. Far from constituting a neutral step in the analytical process, choices made during the data visualisation stage may have significant impacts on how the research outcomes are interpreted, and may well lead researchers to form conclusions about their objects of study that are not supported by a closer look at the source data themselves. When generating graphical maps of link networks or keyword co-occurrences, for example, researchers must question on what mathematical and network-theoretical basis individual nodes in the network are placed at specific distances from one another or grouped into particular clusters. This is also a call to form interdisciplinary research teams, of course, combining skills in areas such as cultural studies, communication studies, sociology and network mapping.

Finally, it is also crucial to note that the data gathered by the methodologies which we have described – however sophisticated the research tools may be – remain only approximations of actual activity by bloggers and their readers. While blog posts are clearly intended as more or less public statements of the blogger's views, we should not fall into the trap of understanding these individuals to be constituted of no more than their stated opinions: their blog content merely represents the – or, more precisely, *one* – public face of the author, who may privately or in other public contexts hold some very different opinions. Similarly, in analysing the network of links between blogs what we are actually interested in is a sense of the likely traffic of readers which may follow these links, which in turn provides us with an idea of the respective level of influence of specific bloggers and their points of view over the wider community (of writers *and* readers) populating the blogosphere. Short of gaining access to the often highly prized (and expensively priced) traffic data gathered by online market analysis companies such as Alexa or Hitwise, researchers are able to use linkage patterns as a reasonably accurate indication of likely traffic: both because higher levels of incoming links to a site from other blogs make it more likely that blog readers will find the site and, because more inlinks also increase the site's overall ranking in search engines like Google, the assumption that inlinks correlate with traffic is acceptable. Beyond this, we may further expect that the higher visibility that results from a greater number of visitors also provides sites with a better ability to influence and act as opinion leaders for their readers; this necessarily is another assumption only, but one which cannot be tested with any better accuracy unless researchers are prepared to take an excursion into the realms of cognitive science, where the question of the media's effects on audiences remains hotly contested.

Implications of the computational turn

Influenced by differing disciplinary emphases and research agendas, the emerging field of online research which bases its work on this computational augmentation (or, for some, supplantation) of more conventional social science research methodologies has been described as 'Web Science' (Hendler et al., 2008). This paradigm shift is paralleled by similar moves in the 'digital humanities', where the availability of huge, digitised datasets is transforming not only the specific methods, but is reframing the methodologies of particular sub-disciplines as a whole (Manovich, 2007; Moretti, 2005). Manovich (2005) specifies the term 'Cultural Analytics' in order to describe the ways in which computer-assisted approaches transform not only the methods, but in some ways even the object of study of humanities research. While in the present chapter we lack the space to chart in detail the range of epistemological and methodological approaches associated with the 'computational turn', researchers seeking to explore the opportunities inherent in this field would do well to understand the varying

configurations of existing discipline knowledge which may be brought to bear on their work; they need to do so with the understanding, too, that methods and methodologies as well as disciplinary framings still remain highly mobile in this new area of research activity.

What is already becoming evident, however, is that whatever the field may be called in the future, one area which needs to be addressed with some urgency is that of research ethics. The computational research tools which are applied in this area are powerful and should not be used without due consideration. Already, over the past few years we have seen major controversies over the public release of major datasets and/or the large-scale gathering of personal data – from search engine queries (van Wel and Royakker, 2004), Facebook data (Zimmer, 2010a) and Twitter updates (Zimmer, 2010b) – using computational tools similar to those we have described here for blog research.

Because of the power of these new research tools and the scale at which they can be employed, these new controversies dramatically exacerbate existing difficulties in applying standard research ethics protocols to online human research. Ethical issues arise at every stage of online research that deals with user-created content and communication. For computer-assisted approaches to blog research, they concern two main interconnected problems, each of which has implications for how we might understand various choices made in the research process to be ethical. First, are blogs 'publications' or something more akin to personal communication? Second, should individual bloggers therefore be considered to be authors or treated as research 'subjects'?

To illustrate how this dilemma plays out, computer-assisted blog research may involve gathering, aggregating and analysing the actual content of a large number (hundreds or even thousands) of blogs. Depending on the form the eventual analysis will take, a decision may need to be made about whether this content can then be quoted (perhaps to illustrate findings), and if so, whether or not the content should be attributed to its author or anonymised. In order to answer these questions, the researcher must address issues both of privacy and of authorial agency (for example, in regard to copyright) with regard to the aggregation and later public availability of the data. This is far from straightforward, however, and has proven contentious even in small-scale qualitative research projects (see an extended discussion in Bruckman, 2002). One point of view would hold that blogs are simply publications and therefore their contents can be quoted and repurposed within the limits of copyright law; indeed, such reuse of blog material may confer additional attention on the creative work of the blog's author or authors. But another point of view, one that is sensitive to the diversity in actual practices and discourses of bloggers themselves (van Dijck, 2004), might be that while some blogs, particularly those concerned with politics and journalism, are clearly 'public' in nature, others might function as personal media produced with a limited imagined audience in mind, so that further dissemination of blog content in a different context from that originally intended may infringe the privacy or agency of their authors. It is impossible to determine the answers to these questions in advance, as blogging is culturally complex and diverse, and even in the case of individual blogs the answers may change over time and as a result of other highly specific circumstances. Further, in the context of a very large-scale project relying on automated data-gathering and analysis, the standard solution to ethical dilemmas – seeking and obtaining informed consent from each research participant – is usually impractical. Because of this complexity, standard social science research protocols are rarely adequate to deal with these issues, so it is essential that aspiring blog researchers familiarise themselves thoroughly with the scholarly debates and current thinking on best practice in Internet research ethics in order to take a well-grounded position within them when mounting a case to their ethical review board. There are several authoritative online research handbooks that synthesise these unfolding debates (see, for example, Buchanan, 2004; Burnett et al., 2010). Additionally, the Association of Internet Researchers working party on research ethics provides a useful guide to reasonably current areas of consensus and ongoing deliberation among the Internet research community (Ess et al., 2002).

Another problem with the standard ethical review process as it operates in most universities is that, particularly for large-scale, exploratory projects in a field of research that is only now emerging, it is not always possible at the planning stage to anticipate and address all the ethical issues – let alone solutions to them – that will arise in the course of the project. For one thing, the object of study is itself continually in flux. Researchers employing the kinds of large-scale computer-assisted methods we have described here will not only be directly negotiating, but also helping to shape complex ethical issues with each methodological and consequent technological choice they make. Hence it is important that a reflexive and open approach that is both informed by and responsive to the debates around Internet research ethics be built into the methodology as it unfolds throughout the research process.

Questions for further investigation

1. What analytical frameworks exist for interrogating and evaluating the data which may now be gathered from blogs and other social media platforms in large volumes?
2. What differences or similarities exist between specific (topical, demographic or otherwise defined) segments within the overall blogosphere, and/or between different blogospheres as distinguished by ethnicity, language, geography or nationality?
3. What are the dynamics of blogging: what seasonal patterns does blogging activity exhibit, and how does prominence in the blogosphere wax and wane?
4. How do blogs interrelate with other mass or social media spaces: how does information travel across the wider media ecology, and how is blogging affected by developments in more recent social media platforms?
5. What are the research ethics of capturing, analysing and otherwise engaging with content which, while publicly available, might only have been intended for a small personal audience?

Suggested further reading

Baym, N. K. (2010) *Personal Connections in the Digital Age*. Cambridge: Polity. Situating social and mobile media in the wider media ecology of which they are a part, Baym demonstrates the growing importance of non-mass media forms for everyday life, relationships and communication. She shows clearly why further research in this field is necessary and important.

Rogers, R. (2009) *The End of the Virtual: Digital Methods*. Inaugural lecture, University of Amsterdam, 8 May 2009. Available at: http://www.govcom.org/publications/full_list/ oratie_Rogers_2009_preprint.pdf (accessed 15 December 2010). Rogers, the founder of Govcom.org, the independent organisation which makes available the IssueCrawler research tool, describes the computational turn in Internet research methods and outlines its implications.

Shadbolt, N. and Berners-Lee, T. (2008) 'Web science emerges', *Scientific American*, October, pp. 32–7. Co-authored by Tim Berners-Lee, the inventor of the World Wide Web, this brief article outlines the ideas behind the 'Web Science' initiative for quantitative, data-driven research into uses of the web. It also contains useful further references.

Walker Rettberg, J. (2008) *Blogging*. Cambridge: Polity. One of the first scholars to research blogs and blogging, Walker provides an in-depth introduction to the history of the form and outlines current themes, issues and research possibilities.

References

Adamic, L. and Glance, N. (2005) 'The political blogosphere and the 2004 U.S. election: divided they blog'. *Proceedings of the 3rd International Workshop on Link Discovery 2005* (online). Available at: http://www.blogpulse.com/ papers/2005/AdamicGlanceBlogWWW.pdf (accessed 19 January 2009).

Berry, D. M. (ed.) (2010) *The Computational Turn: The Digital Humanities and New Technology*. London: Palgrave Macmillan.

Bruckman, A. (2002) 'Studying the amateur artist: a perspective on disguising data collected in human subjects research on the Internet', *Ethics and Information Technology*, 4(3): 217–31.

Bruns, A. and Jacobs, J. (eds) (2006) *Uses of Blogs*. New York: Peter Lang.

Bruns, A., Wilson, J., Saunders, B., Kirchhoff, L. and Nicolai, T. (2008a) *Australia's Political Blogosphere in the Aftermath of 2007 Federal Election* (online). Paper presented at the AoIR 2008 conference, Copenhagen, 18 October 2008. Available at: http://snurb.info/files/aoir2008/Australia%27s%20 Political%20Blogosphere%20in%20the%20Aftermath%20 of%20the%202007%20Federal%20Election%20(AoIR%20 2008).pdf (accessed 7 April 2010).

Bruns, A., Wilson, J., Saunders, B., Highfield, T., Kirchhoff, L. and Nicolai, T. (2008b) *Locating the Australian Blogosphere: Towards a New Research Methodology* (online). Paper presented at the ISEA 2008 conference, Singapore, 25 July–3 August 2008. Available at: http://snurb.info/ files/Locating%20the%20Australian%20Blogosphere%20 (final%20-%20long).pdf (accessed 7 April 2010).

Buchanan, E. (ed.) (2004) *Readings in Virtual Research Ethics: Issues and Controversies*. London: Information Science Publishing.

Burgess, J. (2006) 'Blogging to learn, learning to blog', in Bruns, A. and Jacobs, J. (eds) *Uses of Blogs*. New York: Peter Lang, pp.105–14.

Burnett, R., Consalvo, M. and Ess, C. (2010) *The Handbook of Internet Studies*. London: Wiley-Blackwell.

Ess, C. and AoIR Ethics Working Group (2002) *Ethics Guide* (online). Available at: http://aoir.org/documents/ethics-guide/ (accessed 27 May 2010).

Gurak, L. J., Antonijevic, S., Johnson, L., Ratliff, C. and Reyman, J. (eds) (2004) *Into the Blogosphere: Rhetoric, Community, and Culture of Weblogs* (online). Available at: http://blog.lib. umn.edu/blogosphere/ (accessed 27 May 2010).

Hendler, J., Shadbolt, N., Hall, W., Berners-Lee, T. and Weitzner, D. (2008) 'Web Science: an interdisciplinary approach to understanding the web', *Communications of the ACM*, 51(7).

Kirchhoff, L., Nicolai, T., Bruns, A. and Highfield, T. (2009) *Monitoring the Australian Blogosphere through the 2007 Australian Federal Election* (online). Paper presented at ANZCA 2009, Brisbane, 8 July 2009. Available at: http:// snurb.info/files/talks2009/Monitoring%20the%20 Australian%20Blogosphere%20through%20the%20 2007%20Australian%20Federal%20Election.pdf (accessed 7 April 2010).

Manovich, L. (2007) *Cultural analytics* (online). Available at: http://www.manovich.net/cultural_analytics.pdf (accessed 24 April 2010).

Moretti, F. (2005) *Graphs, Maps, Trees: Abstract Models for a Literary History*. London: Verso.

Russell, A. and Echchaibi, N. (eds) (2009) *International Blogging: Identity, Politics, and Networked Publics*. New York: Peter Lang.

Schmidt, J. (2006) *Weblogs: Eine kommunikationssoziologische Studie*. Konstanz: UVK.

Van Dijck, J. (2004) 'Composing the self: of diaries and lifelogs', *Fibreculture Journal*, 3. Available at: http://www.journal.fibreculture.org/issue3/issue3_vandijck.html (accessed 16 November 2011).

van Wel, L. and Royakker, L. (2004) 'Ethical issues in web data mining', *Ethics and Information Technology*, 6: 129–40.

Walker Rettberg, J. (2008) *Blogging*. Malden, MA: Polity.

Zimmer, M. (2010a) '"But the data is already public": on the ethics of research in Facebook', *Ethics and Information Technology*, 4(3): 205–16.

Zimmer, M. (2010b) *Is it Ethical to Harvest Public Twitter Accounts Without Consent?* (online). Available at: http://michaelzimmer.org/2010/02/12/is-it-ethical-to-harvest-public-twitter-accounts-without-consent/ (accessed 16 November 2011).

Documentary methods

Gary McCulloch

Introduction

This chapter is designed to provide an introduction to documentary methods, including the use of online archival resources, in education (see also McCulloch, 2004 and 2011, for more detailed treatments of historical and documentary research). A document may be defined briefly as a record of an event or process. Such records may be produced by individuals or groups and take many different forms.

Broad distinctions may be drawn between types of documents and it is important for the researcher to observe these, although they are not always rigid typologies. One distinction that can be made, for example, is between the documents created by private individuals and family groups in their everyday lives, and the records produced by local, national and international authorities and small or large organisations (Hodder, 1998). The former class of personal or private documents might include diaries, letters, photographs, blogs, autobiographies and suicide notes (Plummer, 2001). The latter group of public and official records would include committee minutes, reports and memoranda, but also formal items such as birth, marriage and death certificates, driving licences and bank statements (Scott, 1990). Media documents, either printed like newspapers and magazines or visual such as television, operate at the interface of the private and public, and record aspects of both types of domain.

There are preliminary issues around ascertaining the authenticity of the document, that is verifying the author, place and date of its production. In some cases the document may have been forged or the authorship be in doubt. The researcher also seeks to take into account the reliability of the document, for example the credibility of the account of an event in terms of the bias of the author, the access to the event and the interpretation of the observer. The differential survival rate of documents creates a further issue of reliability, and raises questions about how representative, typical and generalisable the surviving documents may be (Scott, 1990: 7).

A distinction may also be drawn between documents that are based on written text and other forms produced through other means. Until very recently, most written documents were produced on paper or similar materials, either by hand or mechanically. The past two decades have witnessed the exponential growth of electronic documents such as electronic mail and data communicated and stored through the Internet. This constitutes a contemporary revolution in the nature of documents, albeit that electronic documents may well retain and incorporate elements of the print culture developed over the past five centuries (McCulloch, 2004: 2). Such written, printed and electronic texts might be contrasted with visual documents such as photographs, cartoons, paintings and films (Prosser, 1998; Grosvenor, 2007), although it should be noted that texts in contemporary society have become increasingly multi-semiotic in combining and juxtaposing language and visual forms (Fairclough, 1995). They also differ from oral sources such as sound recordings of speeches. One may also distinguish textual records from material artefacts like fossils, slates, desks and buildings.

A further distinction is between documents produced independently of the researcher for a range of possible purposes outside the researcher's control and those produced by researchers themselves as data for their research. Transcripts of interviews or completed questionnaires are examples of documents prepared by researchers for the purposes of their research (Silverman, 2001: 119). Electronic technology facilitates the rapid interchange of solicited documents in a wide variety of formats. Documentary methods generally make use of documents produced previously and by others, rather than in the process of the research or by the researcher.

There is also an established difference between primary documents and secondary documents, although this difference is more complex than it may at first appear. Primary documents are produced as a direct record of an event or process by a witness or subject involved in it. Secondary documents are formed through an analysis of primary documents to provide an account of the event or process in question, often in relation to others. However, many documents do not fit easily into this basic dichotomy. For example, autobiographies are primary documents by virtue of the author being a witness or participant in the relevant events, but are often produced years or even decades later and so may be affected by memory or selective recall. They might also be regarded as secondary documents to the extent that they seek to analyse the changing times through which the autobiographer has lived (for instance Hobsbawm, 2002).

Moreover, some documents are edited and collected versions of diaries, letters and autobiographies. These might be described as hybrid documents. These are more widely accessible than the original primary document but have gone through an editing process that may alter some of their characteristics, whether subtly or substantially. In producing a published work of this kind, editors may tend to emphasise particular types of material to make it more interesting or more or less flattering to the authors of the document, or else to reflect specific interests (Fothergill, 1974). In such cases, one might say that some features of the primary document have been compromised by the process of being edited and presented in this way.

Virtual documents, that is, primary documents stored electronically for access through the Internet, are available through 'the click of a mouse' (*Guardian*, 2007). These are often most valuable for researchers, although government and other organisational websites which store documents in this way may seek to cast the government or organisation in a favourable light. On the other hand such digital documents lose the immediacy of the original paper document that they represent (McCulloch, 2004: 34–42).

Personal documents

Diaries, letters and autobiographies are generally regarded as personal documents, although they can often reveal a great deal about public issues and debates. In some cases, they may provide commentary on contemporary social developments and they often record meetings or other events in which the author has been involved. Diaries are generally produced soon after the event, although this varies, and may give detailed and intimate evidence of individuals and daily life for women no less than for men (Blodgett, 1988). In many cases, as with the published diaries of the composer Benjamin Britten, they document the tensions of adolescence and early adulthood (Britten, 2009). Political diaries, such as those of the British politician Tony Benn, can be highly revealing about policy changes, as in the case of the self-styled 'Great Debate' on education in Britain in 1976 (Benn, 1990). They also reveal much, often unintentionally, about the diarists themselves (Pimlott, 2002). School log books have an official function in that they are generally required to include specific information about the pupils, teachers and management of the school, but in some cases they may reveal the everyday life and interactions of the head teacher concerned (see, for example, McCulloch, 1989: chapter 8).

Letter writing as a means of communication has generated a further type of documentary source, one that has been rivalled in recent times by devices such as the telephone and transformed through electronic media. They are interactive in character, forming explicitly part of a dialogue, and may again be both personal and formal in their style and substance (Earle, 1999; Dobson, 2009). Many letters relating to education, such as those from parents to a school or to a newspaper or to a Minister of Education, reflect the interaction between the personal or family domain and the concerns of an established institution (see, for instance, Heward, 1988). By contrast, autobiographies and memoirs are essentially introspective and provide an inside account of lives and relationships. They often give particular emphasis to the early life and schooling. For example, David Vincent's major study of working-class autobiographies in nineteenth-century England, based on 142 accounts of this kind, demonstrates the nature of their involvement in a social network of family, friends, colleagues and acquaintances (Vincent, 1981).

Fictional works might also be classed as personal documents. Although not intended to convey the literal truth about particular events, these may represent deeper realities about social experiences. In relation to education, they can provide insights into everyday life from the imagined viewpoints of pupils and teachers, notwithstanding the dramatisation and stereotyped forms that it generally depends upon for plots and characterisation. Novels and plays have been especially useful for their depiction of teachers and teaching. James Hilton's *Goodbye, Mr Chips*, for example, is a classic account of the life story of a male veteran teacher in an elite English boarding school (Hilton, 1934), while the plays of Alan Bennett such as *Forty Years On* (1969) and *The History Boys* (2004) have evoked resilient cultural images (McCulloch, 2009). Susan Ellsmore has also explored representations of the teaching profession in films, including the film of *Goodbye, Mr Chips* produced in 1939 (Ellsmore, 2005).

The public record

The printed press embodies a further important source of primary documentary evidence. This provides a day-to-day public record very soon after the event being studied (Vella, 2009: 194), albeit one that caters for particular kinds of public taste and interest and is by no means comprehensive in its coverage. Peter Cunningham has made interesting use of newspapers as a documentary source by examining the development of the image of the teacher in the British press from 1950 to 1990 (Cunningham, 1992). Cunningham's work compares newspaper coverage of teachers in 1950, 1970 and 1990, using *The Times* in its unofficial capacity as a newspaper of record as well as major mass-circulation newspapers of the political left and right. This has been taken further in other work that examines political cartoons involving teachers in the British press since the 1970s (Warburton and Saunders, 1996). Other particular features of newspapers also offer interesting and useful material for researchers, including leading articles, letters columns and advertisements.

School magazines have a limited circulation in and around their own institution but constitute a significant record on behalf of the institution itself, with detailed information on everyday life and interests as well as transmitting the received values of the school. J. A. Mangan's research on English public schools in the late nineteenth century demonstrated the role of school magazines as the official record of school life, reflecting in many cases an emphasis on games and sports as opposed to examinations (Mangan, 1986). Nevertheless, unofficial magazines may also provide important clues to debates and differences within the school (see, for example, McCulloch, 2007: chapter 6).

Over the past five hundred years, books in their modern printed format have been repositories of knowledge and scholarship, besides also being a key means of challenging established orthodoxies. Tracts and treatises are important sources of documentary evidence that often embody the principal themes of debate in politics and society, although they do not always fully convey wider attitudes in a particular context, and their representative nature and influence are often exaggerated. A specific type of book that is often useful for researchers in education is the textbook, produced for schools and other educational institutions since the 1830s when the term itself appeared (Stray, 1994: 2). They are generally used to support teachers, lecturers, pupils and students to follow a syllabus, and are significant partly for the way in which they present information but also for how they project approved values and ideologies. Stuart Foster, for example, has investigated the treatment of ethnic groups in history textbooks in the United States in terms of a struggle for American identity, arguing that such works have represented the views and interests of a white, male, Protestant middle or upper class, and have tended to support the capitalist system, traditional lifestyles and western traditions (Foster, 1999).

Published reports are a further significant source of research evidence in this area of study. Governments as well as organisations and pressure groups produce reports in order to examine particular defined problems and to propose solutions. The information that they provide is often very helpful, although it cannot be assumed that this is always accurate, and it should be checked against other sources. Policy reports are also important for revealing the kinds of assumptions that underlie policy reforms. They represent an outlook or ideology (Scott, 2000: 27) and also embody the contradictions and tensions that are inherent in state policy (Codd, 1988). Some reports are voluminous, taking up several volumes including appendices of oral and written evidence provided by witnesses, whereas in recent decades reports have tended to become shorter in length, more limited in focus and more reader-friendly in format to promote their public appeal. Again, care needs to be taken to resist assuming that such reports reflect educational practices in a straightforward manner.

The proceedings of parliamentary debates and committees provide another kind of official publication. In Britain, these are known as Hansard, after Thomas Hansard, who began publishing the debates of the House of Commons and House of Lords in 1812, and are now available online (http://www. parliament.the-stationery-office.co.uk; see also http://www.parliament.uk). In the USA, the Congressional Record provides a similar service, also available on the Internet (http://www.gpoaccess.gov/crecord/index. html). This was first published in 1873 and provides up-to-date and complete proceedings of debates in the House of Representatives and the Senate. Many datasets produced by governments, organisations and research project teams are also readily accessible, and these lend themselves to secondary analysis. Hakim has defined this in terms of the further analysis of existing datasets which develops the original interpretations and findings of the enquiry in a different way (Hakim, 1982). These include population census reports and datasets specially related to education such as that of the National Child Development Study in Britain (http://www.data-service.ac.uk).

Much research employs one or two of these kinds of document as the principal source of data, but different combinations of personal and public documents may be applied depending on the problem being studied. For example, an education policy report may be examined through the study of the report itself, of the files of the committee that produced it, and of newspapers relating to its reception after publication. The changes in the curriculum at a university might be appraised through institutional records, lecture notes and student diaries where these exist (see, for example, Slee, 1986). The different perspectives of parents, children and teachers may also be revealed through a combination of such methods, as in the case of the Simon family and their experiences with Gresham's School in the 1930s (McCulloch and Woodin, 2010). Moreover, documentary research may frequently be allied to good effect with other research methods in education (see, for example, Saran, 1985, on combining archive and interview research). Interviews with teachers about their curriculum and pedagogic practices may be compared with documentary evidence of changing policy in these areas over the past thirty years, as in the case of research by McCulloch et al. (2000).

Archival documents

As we have seen, many documentary records are available quite readily through research libraries or the Internet. In other cases, they are stored in an organised format, usually in numbered files for identification, in archives and record offices. Archives are repositories of accumulated knowledge, in many ways the institutional memory of modern societies, and these also exist in a number of forms.

National archives preserve the official records of government departments, and local record offices those of the particular location where appropriate, and in many countries around the world these are preserved carefully and methodically to store the collective memory. In some cases they date from the nineteenth century or even earlier, and they often reflect the specific national and social characteristics (Joyce, 1999). The French Archives Nationales, set up in 1790, developed with a strong focus on the centralised state (Sheppard, 1980). Much documentary evidence has been lost for a number of reasons, whether due to being discarded by the original owners, failing to survive changes of location or for lack of space or resources. Thus the researcher is left with only the documents, whether recent or from earlier periods of time, that remain to be examined today. There are many silences in the documents that do survive (Andrew, 1985: 156). The experience of working in an archive can also be a challenge. Beyond the costs and the time that may be involved in reaching an archive, it is often difficult to anticipate the amount and quality of documentary material that is available on a particular topic (Steedman, 2001: 29).

At the same time, the establishment and spread of online archives over the past ten years have transformed the nature of archival research. In many cases the archive catalogue or inventory of holdings is available in searchable form on the Internet so that the researcher is able to check in advance before travelling to the archive. Increasingly also the documents themselves may be researched digitally. For example, in Britain the results of the Census up to and including 1911 (http://www.census.pro.gov.uk) and more than 150 years of the newspaper *The Guardian* (http://www.guardian.co.uk/archive; see also *Guardian*, 2007) have been made available online. Cabinet minutes and discussions are also accessible by this means (http://www.pro.online.pro.uk). For example, Cabinet discussion of the Conservative government on education policy in the early 1970s (Cabinet file CAB.128/50/55) may be consulted in this way. However, there are some restrictions in terms of coverage and a subscription or other cost may often be applied.

Conclusion

Documents are a significant and often underused resource for research in education. An enormous range of primary documents is available for researchers to examine and evaluate. Diaries, letters, autobiographies and fictional writings offer many insights into both the personal and the public domains, while documents based on the media, books, reports and proceedings of debates and committees also provide extensive source material. Often, it is helpful to combine different kinds of documents to develop a fuller and more comprehensive account of specific themes. Archival documents can support research on many topics, and the scope for such research has been greatly enhanced by the online revolution of the early twenty-first century.

Questions for further investigation

1. Select one key individual or organisation and search for different types of primary documentary source that help to highlight their contributions to education. How would you seek to combine these sources in researching this topic?
2. How would you make use of the Internet to support an archive-based research study? Explain with detailed reference to one study of your choice.

Suggested further reading

McCulloch (2004) provides a detailed discussion of documentary research in relation to education, history and the social sciences; Scott (1990) is dated in some respects but still useful. Analysis of a wide range of primary sources in their historical context is given in Dobson and Ziemann (2009), while Steedman (2001) reflects on the experience of archival research.

References

Andrew, A. (1985) 'In pursuit of the past: some problems in the collection, analysis and use of historical documentary evidence', in Burgess, R. G. (ed.) *Strategies of Educational Research*. London: Falmer Press, pp. 153–78.

Benn, T. (1990) *Against the Tide: Diaries 1973-76*, ed. R. Winstone. London: Arrow.

Bennett, A. (1969) *Forty Years On*. London: Faber & Faber.

Bennett, A. (2004) *The History Boys*. London: Faber & Faber.

Blodgett, H. (1988) *Centuries of Female Days: Englishwomen's Private Diaries*. Brunswick, NJ: Rutgers University Press.

British Census (2011). Available at: http://www.ons.gov.uk/ons/guide-method/census/2011/index.html.

British official records (2011). Available at: http://www.nationalarchives.gov.uk/default.htm.

British Parliamentary committee proceedings, evidence and reports. Available at:
http://www.parliament.uk (accessed 17 November 2011).

British Parliamentary debates. Available at: http://www.parliament.the-stationery-office.co.uk (acessed 17 November 2011).

Britten, B. (2009) *Journeying Boy: The Diaries of the Young Benjamin Britten, 1928–1938*, ed. J. Evans. London: Faber.

Burgess, R. (ed.) (1985) *Strategies of Educational Research: Qualitative Methods*. London: Falmer.

Codd, J. (1988) 'The construction and deconstruction of educational policy documents', *Journal of Education Policy*, 3(3): 235–47.

Cunningham, P. (1992) 'Teachers' professional image and the Press, 1950–1990', *History of Education*, 21(1): 37–56.

Dobson, M. (2009) 'Letters', in Dobson, M. and Ziemann, B. (eds) *Reading Primary Sources: The Interpretation of Texts from Nineteenth and Twentieth-Century History*. Abingdon: Routledge, pp. 57–73.

Dobson, M. and Ziemann, B. (eds) (2009) *Reading Primary Sources: The Interpretation of Texts from Nineteenth- and Twentieth-Century History*. Abingdon: Routledge.

Earle, R. (ed.) (1999) *Epistolary Selves: Letters and Letter-Writers, 1600–1945*. Aldershot: Ashgate.

Ellsmore, S. (2005) *Carry On, Teachers! Representations of the Teaching Profession in Screen Culture*. Stoke-on-Trent: Trentham.

Fairclough, N. (1995) *Critical Discourse Analysis: The Critical Study of Language*. London: Longman.

Foster, S. (1999) 'The struggle for American identity: treatment of ethnic groups in United States history textbooks', *History of Education*, 28(3): 251–78.

Fothergill, R. (1974) *Private Chronicles: A Study of English Diaries*. London: Oxford University Press.

Gosden, P. (1981) 'Twentieth-century archives of education as sources for the study of education policy and administration', *Archives*, 15: 86–95.

Grosvenor, I. (2007) 'From the "eye of history" to a "second gaze": the visual archive and the marginalized in the history of education', *History of Education*, 36(4–5): 607–22.

Guardian (2007) 'The Archive', *Guardian*, 3 November.

Guardian Archive. Available at: http://www.guardian.co.uk/archive (accessed 17 November 2011).

Hakim, C. (1982) *Secondary Analysis in Social Research: A Guide to Data Sources and Methods with Examples*. London: George Allen & Unwin.

Heward, C. (1988) *Making a Man of Him: Parents and their Sons' Education at an English Public School, 1929–50*. London: Routledge.

Hilton, J. (1934) *Goodbye, Mr Chips*. London: Hodder & Stoughton.

Hobsbawm, E. (2002) *Interesting Times: A Twentieth-Century Life*. London: Allen Lane.

Hodder, I. (1998) 'The interpretation of documents and material culture', in Denzin, N. K. and Lincoln, Y. S. (eds) *Collecting and Interpreting Qualitative Materials*. London: Sage, pp. 110–29.

Joyce, P. (1999) 'The politics of the liberal archive', *History of the Human Sciences*, 12(2): 35–49.

McCulloch, G. (1986) '"Secondary education without selection"? School zoning policy in Auckland since 1945', *New Zealand Journal of Educational Studies*, 21(2): 98–112.

McCulloch, G. (1989) *The Secondary Technical School: A Usable Past?* London: Falmer.

McCulloch, G. (2004) *Documentary Research in Education, History and the Social Sciences*. London: Routledge.

McCulloch, G. (ed.) (2005) *The RoutledgeFalmer Reader in the History of Education*. London: RoutledgeFalmer.

McCulloch, G. (2007) *Cyril Norwood and the Ideal of Secondary Education*. New York: Palgrave Macmillan.

McCulloch, G. (2009) 'The moral universe of Mr Chips: veteran teachers in British literature and drama', *Teachers and Teaching*, 15(4): 409–20.

McCulloch, G. (2011) 'Historical and documentary methods', in Cohen, L., Manion, L. and Morrison, K. (eds) *Research Methods in Education* (7th edn). London: Routledge.

McCulloch, G. and Woodin, T. (2010) 'Learning and liberal education: the case of the Simon family, 1912–1939', *Oxford Review of Education*, 36(2): 187–201.

McCulloch, G., Helsby, G. and Knight, P. (2000) *The Politics* of Professionalism: Teachers and the Curriculum. London: Continuum.

Mangan, J. A. (1986) Athleticism in the Victorian and Edwardian Public School: The Emergence and Consolidation of an Educational Ideology. London: Falmer.

National Child Development Study, Britain. Available at: http://www.data-service.ac.uk.

Pimlott, B. (2002) 'Dear diary . . .', Guardian G2, 18th October, pp. 2–3.

Plummer, K. (2001) Documents of Life 2: An Invitation to a Critical Humanism. London: Sage.

Prosser, J. (ed.) (1998) Image-Based Research: A Sourcebook for Qualitative Researchers. London: Falmer.

Saran, R. (1985) 'The use of archives and interviews in research on education policy', in Burgess, R. (ed.) Strategies of Educational Research: Qualitative Methods. London: Falmer, pp. 207–41.

Scott, D. (2000) Reading Educational Research and Policy. London: RoutledgeFalmer.

Scott, J. (1990) A Matter of Record: Documentary Sources in Social Research. Cambridge: Polity Press.

Sheppard, J. (1980) 'Vive la difference?! An outsider's view of French archives', Archives, 14: 151–62.

Silverman, D. (2001) Interpreting Qualitative Data: Methods for Analysing Talk, Text and Interaction (2nd edn). London: Sage.

Slee, P. (1986) Learning and a Liberal Education: The Study of Modern History in the Universities of Oxford, Cambridge and Manchester, 1800–1914. Manchester: Manchester University Press.

Steedman, C. (2001) Dust. Manchester: Manchester University Press.

Stray, C. (1994) 'Paradigms regained: towards a historical sociology of the textbook', Journal of Curriculum Studies, 26(1): 1–29.

Travis, A. (2003) 'Online archive brings Britain's migration story to life', Guardian, 30 July, p. 7.

US Congressional Record. Available at: http://www.gpoaccess.gov/crecord/index.html.

Vella, S. (2009) 'Newspapers', in Dobson, M. and Ziemann, B. (eds) Reading Primary Sources: The Interpretation of Texts from Nineteenth- and Twentieth-Century History. Abingdon: Routledge, pp. 192–208.

Vincent, D. (1981) Bread, Knowledge and Freedom: A Study of Nineteenth-Century Working Class Autobiography. London: Methuen.

Warburton, T. and Saunders, M. (1996) 'Representing teachers' professional culture through cartoons', British Journal of Educational Studies, 44(3): 307–25.

Systematic reviews

Carole Torgerson, Jill Hall and Kate Light

Overview

Systematic reviews are rigorously designed and conducted literature reviews that aim to exhaustively search for, identify, appraise the quality of and synthesise all the high-quality research evidence in order to answer a specific research question. Systematic reviews are designed to limit all potential sources of bias in reviewing a body of literature.

Introduction

Traditional literature reviews

Literature reviews seek to consolidate existing theoretical and empirical knowledge on specific issues. 'Traditional' literature reviews, sometimes termed 'narrative' or 'expert' reviews, are generally based on expert substantive knowledge in a given area. Generally, there is little or no clear rationale for the design and methods of such reviews. Typically, an expert in a substantive topic area gathers together and interprets previous research in the field and draws conclusions about the studies selected. However, the selection of studies for inclusion is usually not explicit, and whether the included studies are a truly representative or a 'biased' sample of the existing literature is often not clear. There are a number of potential problems with traditional literature reviews, including pre-existing author bias towards a particular hypothesis, which may in turn lead to a biased review.

Systematic reviews

A systematic review has been defined as '. . . the application of strategies that limit bias in the assembly, critical appraisal and synthesis of all relevant studies on a given topic' (Chalmers et al., 2002). The philosophy underpinning systematic review design is based on the scientific principle of replication. Systematic reviews are designed to be explicit, transparent and replicable in order to overcome many of the potential problems associated with the design of traditional reviews. If a review is to be replicable it needs to be explicit about how the various studies included in the review were identified and synthesised. All assumptions and reviewer judgements are made explicit and open to scrutiny and replication. Systematic reviews also seek to search exhaustively for all the relevant studies, whether formally published or listed in the 'grey' literature, and to include the 'totality' of studies in a field. Therefore systematic review design is less likely to suffer from reviewer selection bias. In addition, the exhaustive nature of the review process offers some protection against other forms of potential bias, in particular publication bias (see below).

Systematic reviews have a long history, with some of the first being reported in astronomy more than 100 years ago (Petticrew, 2001; Chalmers et al., 2002). Glass first invented meta-analysis, a statistical method for combining similar studies, for use in the field of education/psychology in the 1970s (Glass, 1976; Glass et al., 1981), and he pioneered the use of systematic reviews and meta-analysis in the field of education. After a period in which systematic reviews and meta-analyses tended to fall out of use, in the last 20 years or so their use has increased in prominence, first in the field of healthcare research and more recently in education and the social sciences.

Focus of this chapter

Systematic review methodology can be used to inform the design of a number of types of review. Scoping reviews can map out the research in a field while tertiary reviews can locate, critically appraise and synthesise existing systematic reviews in a field. Systematic reviews vary in emphasis in terms of their design and the inclusion of studies selected for specific kinds of research questions. It should be noted that systematic reviews can answer questions of 'why?' or 'how?', where it might be appropriate to identify empirical research using qualitative designs. Much of the information on the design and methods of systematic reviews contained within this chapter can be applied to systematic reviews of this nature. However, this chapter focuses on effectiveness questions and therefore on experimental research, as those studies most likely to be included in systematic reviews address these types of questions. These designs offer the potential of a counterfactual to demonstrate what would have happened to the participants had the intervention not been introduced. Ideally the same school, class or group of individuals would be observed under one condition and then observed again under the alternative condition. However, this is generally not possible (except in the relatively unusual circumstances of a cross-over trial). Consequently it is necessary to assemble two or more groups, with one group receiving the intervention and the other receiving an alternative intervention or 'business as usual'. It is then possible to compare the groups to see if there are any differences and potentially ascribe these differences to the intervention under evaluation.

Systematic review design and methodology

The rationale for systematic reviews focuses on the key principles of objectivity and scientific rigour. Systematic review design enables potentially unmanageable amounts of literature to be managed in a scientifically credible and reliable way and it enables the consistency and generalisability of research findings to be tested and all potential sources of bias to be minimised (Mulrow, 1994; Chalmers et al., 2002).

Systematic reviews use explicit methods to locate, appraise the quality of and synthesise the results of relevant research. To minimise the risk of bias the methods are pre-defined. This is important because once studies are identified it is critical that the inclusion/exclusion criteria are not changed in order to support a hypothesis that has been developed through exposure to some of the studies identified. There is a consensus regarding the design, methodology and methods of systematic reviews, a generally accepted set of core principles, underpinned by philosophy, methodological work and expert opinion. A considerable amount of work by leading review methodologists has been undertaken in developing guidance in the design and conduct of systematic reviews. Such guidance has been codified to enable researchers to judge whether a given systematic review is likely to be of high or low quality.

Key features of systematic reviews

1. A transparent, comprehensive search strategy.
2. Clear pre-specified inclusion/exclusion criteria.
3. Explicit methods for coding, quality appraising and synthesising included studies.

Quality of systematic reviews

Systematic reviews, like any other form of research, can be of variable quality. To ensure the highest quality in design and methods in undertaking a systematic review methodologists have developed a number of guidance statements.

The Preferred Reporting Items for Systematic

Reviews and Meta-Analyses (PRISMA) Statement (Moher et al., 1999; Shea et al., 2001) (which supersedes the QUOROM Statement) is a minimum set of items for reporting systematic reviews and meta-analyses, developed through methodological work. The aim of the PRISMA Statement is to help authors improve the reporting of their systematic reviews and meta-analyses. PRISMA focuses on systematic reviews of randomised controlled trials but it can also be used as a basis for reporting systematic reviews of other types of research, particularly evaluations of interventions. PRISMA may also be useful for critical appraisal of published systematic reviews. The PRISMA Statement consists of a 27-item checklist and a four-stage flow diagram. The 27 items are included under seven subsections: title, abstract, introduction, methods, results, discussion, funding. So, for each stage of the systematic review, explicit guidance is given on how it should be reported. Authors of systematic reviews in any field, including education, are recommended to use the PRISMA checklist in the design, conduct and reporting of their reviews. The PRISMA flow diagram depicts the flow of information through the four different phases of a systematic review, including the number of records identified in the searches, the number assessed for eligibility, inclusion and exclusion, and the reasons for the exclusions.

Stages of a systematic review

A systematic review can be seen as having seven main stages which are well established in health care, education and social science research:

1. *Research question.* Development of a well focused, clear research question which can be addressed by a systematic review; establishing the review team and the parameters of the review.
2. *Protocol.* Development of a protocol or plan of the review, including an *a priori* statement of the design and methods for each stage of the review.
3. *Information retrieval and study selection.* Development of a search strategy, searching and screening to identify/select the studies included in the review.
4. *Coding.* Extraction of data from each of the included studies using a coding form developed for the review.

5. *Quality appraisal.* Assessment of risk of bias in each of the included studies using, for example, a tool developed from the CONSORT Statement (see below).
6. *Synthesis.* Results of all the included studies are combined (this may include a meta-analysis).
7. *Report writing.* The systematic review is disseminated through a report or published article.

Detailed guidance on methods for undertaking a systematic review

In the following, detailed guidance on methods for undertaking the seven stages of a systematic review have been applied to an exemplar review in the field of educational research.

Exemplar: Writing review

The title for the exemplar review is: 'A systematic review of the effectiveness of writing interventions on written composition' (hereafter 'writing review'). This is an effectiveness review which means that the primary studies included in the review would be studies using an experimental design.

1. Research question

The research question is the first stage in any systematic review. Once a question is established which is of substantive, methodological or policy importance, a rapid scope (preliminary search of the main electronic databases) can be undertaken to check whether any previous systematic reviews have already been undertaken. If no previous reviews exist or if any previous reviews are out of date, a systematic review is justified and the parameters of the review can be established. The parameters limit the scope of the review, and include such items as the language and publication dates of the studies to be included. All parameters require a justification. The research question can be framed in terms of the participants, interventions, outcomes, study designs (PICOS) categories (Moher et al., 1999 – see below).

Once it has been established that a systematic review is justified, the review team can be set up.

An important aspect of the design of a systematic review is that it should be undertaken by a team of researchers rather than by a single researcher. This is because more than one person is required to assure the conduct of the review is of the highest quality. For example, double screening and coding (data extraction) are recommended to ensure that there is minimal error or bias in the review. Both substantive and methodological experts are required to work as a team to develop the research question, develop the search strategy and interpret the findings of the review; methodological experts are required to quality assure the review and statistical experts are necessary to undertake any meta-analysis.

Summary

- The research question should be an important substantive, methodological or policy question.
- It establishes the parameters and restricts the scope of the review; it drives all the subsequent stages of the review.
- The research question can be framed in terms of the PICOS categories.

2. Protocol

The protocol or plan for the research describes the design and methods of the systematic review in advance of the identification of the studies included in the review. The design of the review will include such features as the conceptual underpinning of the review, the parameters of the review and the rationale for the research question being addressed by the studies included in the review. In addition, the protocol specifies the study characteristics, using the categories participants, interventions, outcomes, study designs (PICOS) (Moher et al., 1999) and these will be used as criteria for eligibility for inclusion in the review. The research question and objectives, the scope of the review, its parameters and strategy for information retrieval, inclusion/exclusion criteria, methods for searching, coding (data extraction) and the development of an assessment of risk of bias tool for quality appraisal of included studies are all pre-stated in the protocol.

This will reduce the possibility of reviewer selection bias and inclusion bias.

The main reason for developing a protocol in advance of undertaking the review is to limit bias potentially introduced by the reviewers. If the main research question is developed and the methods are specified in advance *before* the literature is identified, this prevents the research question being altered by the data. For example, if it is pre-specified that only randomised controlled trials (RCTs) will be included but during the search a large quasi-experimental study is found the results of which support a prior hypothesis, including this study at this stage would require a change to the methods of the review and this may introduce a potential source of bias. While the review might refer to the quasi-experiment to set the experimental studies in context, the main finding should, in this case, be based on a synthesis of the experimental studies. Reviewers may go on and develop a further review protocol that states that quasi-experiments will be included in an update of the review but they should not be included in the current review as they were not pre-specified.

Although the process of undertaking a systematic review can include an iterative process, any changes after the finalising of the protocol have to be made explicit and justified, and for this reason the protocol is generally sent for peer review and 'published' in a public place (website or online journal) to increase the rigour and transparency of the review.

The background to the review will include its rationale in the context of what is already known, previous theoretical and empirical research including previous systematic reviews, informed by a 'rapid scope' of the literature and the policy and practice context to the review. The protocol also includes the parameters of the review, the inclusion criteria (with justifications), the categories for coding and the criteria for assessing risk of bias in the included studies. The proposed nature of the synthesis is also pre-specified in the protocol. In Figure 30.1 a brief exemplar protocol for the writing review is presented.

The inclusion and exclusion criteria are developed alongside the protocol and are based on the research question and parameters of the review. The inclusion and exclusion criteria are used for checking all studies

Research question: What is the effectiveness of writing interventions on the written compositional skills of children aged 7 to 16 in mainstream school settings?

Objective: The objective of the review is to systematically search for, identify, locate and quantitatively synthesize (meta-analyse) the high-quality evidence of the effectiveness of writing interventions aimed at either improving or reducing or preventing writing difficulties of children and young people aged between 7 and 16 in mainstream school settings.

Rationale for review/background: Confidence and accuracy in written expression should be an attainable outcome for all children in mainstream education. In addition, quality of written expression is related to children's ability to access and achieve in all areas of the curriculum in both the primary and secondary phases of education. A number of interventions have been developed for those target groups which researchers have identified as underachieving at writing. Although there have been a number of systematic reviews and meta-analyses in the topic area of writing, a tertiary review identified no review that synthesised the experimental research on the effectiveness of writing interventions in all writing genres (Torgerson, 2007). There is therefore a need for such a review to be undertaken in order to inform policy and practice.

Conceptual issues: The conceptual issues include the nature of writing development in a variety of genres, theories of the development of writing abilities, writing interventions and outcomes, potential mediators and moderators, and conceptual issues regarding appropriate research designs to address an effectiveness question.

Design and method: The design of the review is a full systematic review; design and methods of the review are informed by the Campbell Collaboration policy briefs (see http://www.campbellcollaboration.org/); 'Systematic reviews: CRD's guidance for undertaking reviews in health care' (see http://www.york.ac.uk/inst/crd); the 'Cochrane Collaboration Handbook' (see http://www.cochrane-handbook.org/); the (1994) *Handbook of Research Synthesis* (eds) Cooper, H, Hedges, L. and Torgerson, C. (2003) *Systematic Reviews*. London: Continuum.

Design of studies included: Studies that can adequately address the research question (which is an effectiveness question) are high-quality evaluations of interventions to improve the quality of expression in pupils' written work using experimental designs: randomised controlled trials and quasi-experiments. This is because, in order to establish causality (i.e. to be able to state that a specific teaching practice *causes* an improvement in written outcomes) study designs which can adequately control for all other known and unknown variables that could affect outcome are required (Cook and Campbell, 1979; Shadish et al., 2002). The review will focus on research evidence from academic journals and other published research and, in order to limit the possibility of publication bias, research from the difficult-to-locate 'grey' literature:

1.   Randomised controlled trials (allocated at either the individual level or cluster level e.g. class/school/district).
2.   Quasi-experimental studies of any design (including regression discontinuity design, interrupted time series design).

Studies in which at least one of the groups received a writing intervention compared to standard practice ('business-as-usual') or an alternative writing intervention will be included. Studies in which the control group did not receive any writing instruction will be excluded. Citation searches will be conducted on any located previous systematic reviews/meta-analyses.

Figure 30.1   Exemplar protocol

Types of participants in included studies: Studies in which participants have English as a first, second or additional language will be included. Studies evaluating interventions in children or young people aged 7 to 16 years in a full-time mainstream educational setting will be included. Studies evaluating interventions in children of all learner characteristics attending mainstream schools and classes will be included.

Types of interventions (and comparisons) included: Studies evaluating any whole text writing intervention will be included, for example: provision of model writing structures; guided practice; advanced planning strategies (strategies for developing, evaluating and organising ideas); collaborative or cooperative editing and revision; self-regulated strategy development (e.g. goal setting, self-monitoring, self-regulation), strategies for editing and revision, text analysis, writing prompts, strategies for composing, editing and revising different text types, strategies for directing processes for planning and composing. Strategies for improving writing in the following genres will be included: descriptive writing, expository writing, narrative writing, poetry, drama, instructional writing, argumentation, letter writing, discursive writing and persuasive writing.

Types of outcomes included: Studies will be included if they contain at least one of the following kinds of quantified outcomes: holistic writing quality, length of composition, planning and composing times, essay elements, essay coherence, maturity of vocabulary, reader sensitivity, productivity, elements or features of writing in different genres, e.g. quality of argument, quality of persuasiveness, quality of description, quality of narrative writing, text structure.

Proposed codings for assessment of risk of bias in included studies: A modified version of the CONSORT Guidelines will be used in order to develop a tool to assess the risk of bias in the included randomised and quasi-experimental studies. This assessment of methodological quality of the included studies will include reviewer judgement of the following: method to generate allocation to groups and concealment of that allocation; evidence of sample size calculation; eligibility criteria specified; blinding of intervention provider, participants and outcome assessor; presentation of estimate of effect size and its precision; attrition; primary analysis, i.e. intention-to-treat or on-treatment analysis. A subgroup analysis of the higher quality trials will be undertaken, if appropriate.

Methods for coding (extracting data from) included studies: Data from the included studies will be extracted onto a specially designed coding form. Data to be extracted will include: country, setting, aims and objectives, research design, participants, inclusion criteria, interventions and control or comparison conditions, outcomes, results.

Synthesis: A narrative synthesis will be undertaken to combine the results of the included studies and, if appropriate a meta-analysis (statistical synthesis) will be undertaken.

Proposed quality assurance procedures: Independent double screening, data extraction, quality appraisal (assessment of risk of bias) and extraction of quantified outcomes will be undertaken. Procedures to assure the quality of each stage of the review will be set up.

References

Cook, T. D. and Campbell, D. (1979) *Quasi-Experimentation: Design and Analysis Issues for Field Settings.* Boston, MA: Houghton-Mifflin.

Shadish, W. R., Cook, T. D. and Campbell, T. D. (2002) *Experimental and Quasi-experimental Designs for Generalized Causal Inference.* Boston, MA: Houghton-Mifflin.

Torgerson, C. (2007) 'The quality of systematic reviews of effectiveness in literacy learning in English: a "tertiary" review', *Journal of Research in Reading,* 30(2).

Figure 30.1 (*cont.*) Exemplar protocol

Inclusion criteria

(1) Topic: Studies about writing in English-speaking countries (English as *first, second or additional language*).

(2) Study design: Studies with designs where there is a control or comparison group – randomised controlled trials (individual or cluster); quasi-experiments (case control studies, cohort studies, regression discontinuity studies, interrupted time series).

(3) Participants: Studies where the participants are aged between 7 and 16 years (inclusive) and in full-time mainstream education.

(4) Interventions: Studies evaluating whole-text writing interventions in the following genres: description, expository writing, narrative writing, poetry, drama, instructional writing, writing argument, letter writing, discursive writing and persuasive writing.

(5) Intervention and control or comparison treatments: Studies in which at least one of the groups received a writing intervention compared to standard practice ('business-as-usual'), or an alternative writing intervention.

(6) Outcome: Studies in which participants are measured at post-test on a writing outcome, e.g., holistic writing quality, length of composition, planning and composing times, essay elements, essay coherence, maturity of vocabulary, reader sensitivity, productivity, elements or features of writing in different genres, e.g. quality of argument, quality of persuasiveness, quality of description, quality of narrative writing, text structure.

Exclusion criteria

(1) Topic: Studies about writing English as a *foreign language*.

(2) Study design: Studies with designs where there is no control or comparison group.

(3) Participants: Studies in which the participants are below the age of 7 or above the age of 16 or in which the participants do not attend mainstream schools.

(4) Interventions: Studies which do not evaluate whole-text interventions in the stated writing genres.

(5) Intervention and control or comparison treatments: Studies in which the control group did not receive any writing instruction.

(6) Outcome: Studies in which participants are not measured at post-test on a writing outcome.

Figure 30.2 Exemplar inclusion and exclusion criteria

---

that could be potentially included in the review in order to determine eligibility for inclusion. In Figure 30.2 the inclusion and exclusion criteria for the exemplar writing review are presented. The criteria focus on the topic area, the study design, the participants, the interventions, the comparison or control conditions and the outcomes. Each inclusion criterion is mirrored by an exclusion criterion, which enables the process

of screening to be operationalised and the reasons for exclusion to be documented.

Summary

- The protocol is a plan of the review, written in advance of study identification or selection in order to limit bias.

- It contains the design and methods of the review, including the research question, search strategy, inclusion/exclusion criteria and proposed methods for synthesis.
- The protocol can be changed during the course of the review but all changes should be documented and justified.

3. Information retrieval and study selection

Information retrieval and study selection refers to the methods for searching, locating and checking the inclusion eligibility of potentially relevant studies. These methods should be rigorous to ensure that a high proportion of the eligible published and unpublished studies will be located, retrieved and included. Systematic information retrieval is critical to a systematic review as it ensures an unbiased compilation of potentially relevant research by minimising bias and maximising coverage. The main thrust of the search is likely to use the electronic sources, although other methods of retrieval can supplement the electronic searches. For the electronic searches, an exhaustive search strategy is important. High sensitivity, that is identifying as many relevant papers as possible, may result in low precision (i.e. most papers identified are not relevant to the review), so a judicious balance between the two is recommended. Ideally, an experienced information scientist should be consulted for this aspect of the review.

The strategy used to search the electronic databases is usually based on one or more of the PICOS elements used to produce the inclusion and exclusion criteria (see above). The information contained in database abstracts is limited and rarely reports all of the inclusion criteria required by the review. For this reason it is advisable to use as few PICOS elements as possible, to avoid missing relevant material. The search strategy constructed for the exemplar writing review used only two facets, intervention (writing interventions) and outcome (writing composition). Each facet should contain a variety of terms to capture that element of the review question. Terminology will differ from article to article, even when the same topic is being addressed, so it is important to use synonyms to capture as many relevant papers as possible. The use

of indexing terms can help with this, so where they are available they should be used alongside free text (or natural language) terms.

The creation of the search strategy is an iterative process and the strategy may go through a number of versions in response to feedback on the material retrieved. Ideally, the search strategy should be peer-reviewed, and it may evolve still further in the light of this process. Copies of all search strategies should be kept, along with information about which databases were searched and when the searching was undertaken. This will assist with the writing of the final report and enable critical appraisal of the search element of the review. Once the basic search strategy for the electronic databases has been finalised, the searches can be undertaken.

As mentioned above, the main thrust of identifying research studies is likely to be on the electronic searches, but these can be supplemented through hand searching of key journals. This may be of particular benefit if the area is a 'niche' subject with a few specialist journals publishing relevant material or if the subject is difficult in terms of key words that can be used to identify relevant material. Furthermore, older publications, in particular, may not specify their design particularly well, making some relevant studies difficult or impossible to locate using electronic means. Relevant studies can also be identified through citation searching and checking the bibliographies of previous systematic reviews and seminal studies. Also, reviewers may contact authors of relevant publications to ask them if they are aware of any other relevant studies, including their own, particularly unpublished studies. Nevertheless, however rigorous the method of searching, a number of potential sources of bias can be introduced through the search. These include publication bias, language bias, time lag bias and database bias, all of which have the potential to introduce a source of bias into the review.

Publication bias is the phenomenon whereby studies with 'positive' findings are more likely to be reported in the peer-reviewed literature than studies with null or negative effects. If primary research studies remain unpublished and if there is a relationship between non-publication and their outcomes this can, in turn, affect the findings of systematic reviews. In systematic reviews potential sources of publication bias are not

searching the grey literature for unpublished (but in the public domain) reports and studies not having been published (therefore not able to be included in the review). Publication bias has been described as the Achilles' heel of any literature review (Torgerson, 2006). If non-publication was a random event this would only matter in our level of uncertainty. A meta-analysis that indicates a non-statistically significant benefit of an intervention may, in fact, be recording a Type II error, i.e. concluding erroneously there is no statistically significant difference, when in fact, if all of the studies ever undertaken had been assembled, then the difference would have been statistically significant. However, this is the lesser of the two problems: the second problem of bias is more serious. Usually there is a reason why studies are not published and this often relates to the study's findings. A study that finds either no effect or a difference going in the opposite direction to that hypothesised has a lower possibility of being published. Authors of such studies may feel journals are less likely to accept such studies (a self-fulfilling prophecy) and not submit them, while

editors and reviewers may be more likely to reject them. Even when negative studies are published the process often takes longer than for positive studies. In contrast, studies that have a positive result, especially a statistically significant one, are often fast-tracked by the authors for submission and are more likely to be accepted by referees and editors than negative studies. Consequently, at any one time the published literature is more likely to be over-representative of positive results than negative findings.

The other biases that can affect systematic reviews include language bias, time lag bias and database bias. It may be the case that important papers are not published in English and are excluded from the review because of the cost of requiring necessary translations. Time lag bias is a form of publication bias described above whereby 'negative' studies take longer to publish than positive studies. Database bias may occur if the choice of databases means that a significant proportion of unpublished (or 'grey' literature) studies are excluded because they are not present in the narrow choice of databases used for the search.

Search strategy for ERIC (Dialog DataStar):

1. writing-composition.de.
2. writing-processes.de.
3. (descriptive near (write or writing or written or essay or essays or composition or paper or papers or text or texts or assignment or assignments or document or documents or prose)).ti,ab.
4. (discursiv$ near (write or writing or written or essay or essays or composition or paper or papers or text or texts or assignment or document or documents or prose)).ti,ab.
5. (written adj expression).ti,ab.
6. 1 or 2 or 3 or 4 or 5 **[brings together all the terms for writing composition]**
7. (model$ near (write or writing or written) near structure$).ti,ab.
8. collaborat$ near (edit or editing or revision$)
9. ((strategy or strategies) near (edit or editing or edits or compose or composition or revise or revision or write or written or writing)).ti,ab.
10. 7 or 8 or 9 **[brings together all the terms for writing interventions]**
11. 6 and 10 **[retrieves papers that include terms for both a writing intervention and a writing outcome]**

Key:

.de.	= restrict search to index term	**adj**	= finds terms next to each other
.ti,ab.	= restrict search to title or abstract	**near**	= finds terms within five words of each other
$	= truncate term		

Figure 30.3   Exemplar search strategy

Details about how the search strategy was developed and which databases and journals will be searched should be clearly described in order to permit scrutiny and replication. To ensure that any search is replicable the PRISMA Statement recommends that all information sources are described in detail, including the date the searches were undertaken. It also recommends that at least one full electronic search strategy is presented in the report, together with any limits in order that it could, in theory, be replicated. A simplified version of a search strategy for the exemplar writing review is reproduced in Figure 30.3. (This is for illustrative purposes only – the original contained many more search terms.)

During screening the inclusion criteria are applied to the results of the searches in a three-step process which should be pre-specified in the protocol: pre-screening (to filter out studies that are immediately and easily identified as being irrelevant to the review), first-stage screening (of titles and abstracts) and second-stage screening (of full papers). The identified articles are checked against the predetermined criteria for eligibility and relevance. This process should be undertaken rigorously and quality assured in order to minimise bias. It is recommended that two reviewers screen at each stage independently and then compare their decisions. If this is not possible due to resource constraints the database of potentially relevant studies can be screened by one reviewer, with a random sample of studies screened by a second reviewer at each stage. If this process is adopted the inter-rate reliability of the screening of the two reviewers should be checked through, for example, the calculation of a Cohen's Kappa statistic, and if agreement is low (as demonstrated by a low Cohen's Kappa statistic), then the entire dataset will need to be screened by two reviewers (independent double screening).

Summary

- The research question determines the limits of the search which should be comprehensive, explicit and replicable.
- The main focus of the search strategy is likely to be on the electronic searches, but these should be supplemented by other means, such as hand searching of key journals or citation searching.

- Studies should be screened for selection into the review using pre-specified inclusion and exclusion criteria.

4. Coding

Once the screening has been completed the included studies should be coded. Coding, or data extraction, is the process by which the included studies are described and classified. A paper-based or electronic coding instrument should list all the items for which data will be sought. This will include, as a minimum, data extraction of information about the bibliographic details of the study and its aims and objectives, and key items using the PICOS categories (see above): participants, intervention, control or comparison conditions, outcomes and study designs. It will also state the quantified outcomes which will be extracted (e.g. the means and standard deviations of all pre- and post-tests for all groups).

In addition, the items which will be used to appraise the quality of the included studies (see below) should be coded, and the quality assurance procedures for ensuring the reliability of the coding should be recorded. Ideally this should involve independent double coding, with a plan for comparing information on the coding form and procedures to follow when two reviewers disagree. The coding instrument should ideally be piloted using draft versions to extract data from a dozen or so papers to test the efficacy of the instrument with a relatively small sample of studies: it can then be amended if necessary. If possible, the coding should be undertaken 'blind' to authors of the included studies, although to do this may be costly and time-consuming.

5. Quality appraisal

In order to limit the potential for introducing bias into a systematic review because of design bias it is necessary to critically appraise the included studies in order to assess the potential for risk of bias. In the case of randomised controlled trials, which vary in quality, pooling the results of a number of RCTs with risk of bias due to methodological shortcomings in their design needs to be explored in the review. Methodological work, mainly in the field of healthcare research, has

| Study characteristics (e.g. publication year) |
| Methodological characteristics (e.g. method of assignment to condition, study design) |
| Participant characteristics (e.g. gender, SES, baseline writing) |
| Intervention characteristics and implementation fidelity |
| Control/comparison characteristics and implementation fidelity |
| Outcome measures |

Figure 30.4 Exemplar coding book

led to the development of a number of tools designed to quality appraise RCTs. The Consolidated Standards of Reporting Trials (CONSORT) Statement (Schultz et al., 2010) is not a quality assessment tool, but a minimum set of recommendations for reporting RCTs in a standardised way in order to increase transparency and to help with critical appraisal of trials. A form of the CONSORT Statement, adapted to make it relevant to educational research, can be used to develop a quality appraisal (or assessment of risk of bias) tool. The CONSORT Statement comprises a 25-item checklist and a four-stage flow diagram. The tool should focus on the most important reporting issues such as trial design and analysis, for example whether the allocation was independent and concealed, whether a sample size calculation was undertaken, whether the unit of analysis matched the unit of allocation, and whether there was high or differential attrition between the arms of the trial. The four-stage flow diagram depicts the flow of participants through the key stages of the trial: enrolment, allocation, follow-up and analysis. Quality appraisal of studies should include whether or not a CONSORT-type flow diagram was included in the report. This is important as a significant source of bias can be introduced through high attrition and the flow diagram is a visual way of presenting these data. The potential impact of the quality of the included studies should be considered in the synthesis.

Summary

- Coding involves extraction of information from the included studies to describe and classify the studies.

- The kind of data extracted will depend on the research question and the type of synthesis that will be undertaken.
- The categories for coding should be pre-specified, piloted on a sample of studies and based on the PICOS categories.
- Quality appraisal involves assessing the included studies for key sources of risk of bias and methodological rigour.
- It can be undertaken using a tool developed from the CONSORT Statement.
- Methods for quality assuring the coding and quality appraisal should be predetermined, and rigorously undertaken and reported.

6. Synthesis

The synthesis involves combining the results of the individual studies using a framework or structure. This can be done in a number of different ways. For example, a 'qualitative' or 'narrative' synthesis may be undertaken, or a quantitative or statistical 'meta-analysis' may be used to combine the results of homogeneous studies and increase the power and precision in the measurement of effect sizes.

In a 'narrative' synthesis the included studies are grouped thematically in terms of their characteristics; for example different varieties of the intervention being evaluated and different learner characteristics, and then commonalities between studies (whether of all the studies or a sub-group of them) can be described. However, systematic reviews of randomised controlled trials and quasi-experiments often, but not always, use statistical techniques (meta-analysis) to combine quantitatively the results of the eligible studies. Whether a narrative or a statistical synthesis is undertaken, the strengths and limitations of each of the included studies (based on the quality appraisal undertaken in step 5 –see above) should be taken into account in drawing conclusions based on the results of the synthesis.

Meta-analysis

Probably the most frequently used method of synthesising quantified data is meta-analysis. Simply put, a meta-analysis combines all the studies to give an overall or summary estimate of effect. Generally, meta-analyses use a process of giving greater weighting to larger studies as these are usually likely to be the most reliable studies in the review. Authors of the systematic review should consider, first, whether a meta-analysis is appropriate, given that in any systematic review the included studies may not be homogeneous in terms of participants, interventions and outcomes, etc. If a meta-analysis is deemed to be appropriate, authors should include, as a minimum, the following: a pooled effect size of all studies eligible to be included in the meta-analysis, with confidence intervals; an indication of how heterogeneity between the studies was explored; whether a fixed-effect model or a random-effects model was used for the meta-analysis; and the pre-specified sub-group and sensitivity analyses that were undertaken. An indication of whether and how the potential for publication bias has affected the results of the meta-analysis should be included, for example through the use of a 'funnel plot'. Given sufficient numbers of studies, a meta-regression analysis can be undertaken to explain some of the heterogeneity observed within the component studies. For example, in the writing review whether or not age of pupil affects outcomes or whether underlying ability interacts with the intervention could be explored through a meta-regression. Furthermore, it is possible to see if the results are affected by the underlying quality of the component studies. Do methodologically weak studies, for example, generate larger effect sizes? The advantage of a meta-regression is that it may help to explain the heterogeneity of findings. However, there does need to be caution when interpreting any findings

from a meta-regression. First, the statistical power of any meta-regression is relatively small; consequently there may be relatively important interactions that the analysis does not uncover. Second, some false positive interactions may be observed. Despite there being a statistically significant interaction with, say, gender, in truth no such relationship may exist. Therefore such findings should be used to generate hypotheses and be confirmed, ideally, in a large robustly designed RCT.

There are a number of different techniques that can be used to undertake a meta-analysis, a detailed description of which is beyond the scope of this chapter (see Chapter 46 in this book for detailed guidance on the use of meta-analytical techniques; see also Lipsey and Wilson, 2001 for a detailed text on meta-analysis).

Summary

- The synthesis involves the combining of the results of the review.
- Where possible, the nature of the synthesis should be proposed in advance.
- It can take a variety of forms, including a 'narrative' synthesis or a meta-analysis.
- The quality appraisal judgements for each included study should be taken into consideration in the synthesis.
- Meta-analyses are sometimes appropriate in systematic reviews of experimental research in order to provide a pooled effect size of a group of homogeneous studies.
- If a meta-analysis is undertaken, the possible presence of publication bias should be investigated.

7. Report writing

Like all primary research, systematic reviews should be written up and published as soon as possible after their completion. Indeed, there is, arguably, a stronger imperative for publishing reviews as swiftly as possible as they will tend to become outdated more quickly than primary research as the search strategy for the systematic review is time limited. The process of writing up the final report ought to be guided by the PRISMA Statement to ensure its results are deemed to be of high quality. The report should refer to the existing protocol and be written so that it is as accessible as possible to the widest audience, including policy-makers and practitioners.

Summary

- The design, methodology and methods of a systematic review should be written up in a report and published and disseminated widely in a timely manner, as reviews soon become outdated.
- The process of writing the report can be guided by the PRISMA Statement which will increase the rigour of its reporting.
- The report should be accessible to the widest possible audience, including policy-makers, practitioners and researchers.

Conclusion

With the explosion of research endeavour across the world it is difficult or impossible for researchers, practitioners and policy-makers to keep abreast of new research findings by reading all of the primary research. Systematic reviews enable researchers and others to access the literature in a comprehensive and unbiased manner. In this chapter the basic design and methods underpinning a systematic review have been described. Systematic reviews are an essential precursor to sophisticated synthesis methods such as meta-analysis. A meta-analysis is only as good as its component studies. Should these be from a biased sample of studies then even the most sophisticated statistical techniques cannot rescue the results. Consequently meta-analysts should pay careful attention to how the studies they are including in their statistical synthesis were identified.

In summary, systematic reviews are scientific reviews which have explicit, transparent and theoretically replicable designs and methods. The key features of their design limit any potential biases. They can increase evidence-based education by synthesising a body of literature in a topic area to address a specific research question. They can also identify 'gaps' in the literature, inform the design of a randomised controlled trial or a future research agenda. However, systematic reviews, like all forms of research, can vary in terms of their quality. Therefore any users of systematic reviews should pay critical attention to the quality of their design, conduct and reporting.

Questions for further investigation

1. Find a systematic review in your area of interest. Prepare a critique of the review in terms of transparency, explicitness and replicability. Make an assessment of the reliability of the findings of the review.
2. Write a research question for a systematic review in a topic area of interest together with a compelling rationale for its significance. Develop the following: parameters for the review; inclusion and exclusion criteria; methods for searching, screening, coding and synthesis. Note any challenges to designing this review.

Suggested further reading

Campbell Collaboration at: http://www.campbellcollaboration. org/. The Campbell Collaboration prepares, maintains and disseminates systematic reviews in education, crime and justice and social welfare.

Cochrane Collaboration at: http://www.cochrane-handbook. org/. The Cochrane Collaboration prepares, updates and promotes systematic reviews in health care. See also: Higgins, J. P. T. and Green, S. (eds) *Cochrane Handbook for Systematic Reviews of Interventions*, Version 5.0.2 (updated September 2009).

Meta-analysis in Education Research at: http://www.dur. ac.uk/education/meta-ed/. The Economic and Social Research Council (ESRC) Researcher Development Initiative (RDI): Training in Quantitative Synthesis (Meta-analysis) aims to develop understanding of the design, methodology and methods of meta-analysis.

Moher, D., Liberati, A., Tetzlaff, J., Altman, D. G., PRISMA Group (2009) 'Preferred Reporting Items for Systematic Reviews and Meta-Analyses: The PRISMA Statement', *BMJ*, 339.

References

Chalmers, I., Hedges, L. V. and Cooper, H. (2002) 'A brief history of research synthesis', *Evaluation and the Health Professions*, 25: 12–37.

Cooper, H. and Hedges, L.V. (eds) (1994) *The Handbook of Research Synthesis*. New York: Russell Sage Foundation.

Glass, G. V. (1976) 'Primary, secondary and meta-analysis', *Educational Researcher*, 5: 3–8.

Glass, G. V., McGaw, B. and Smith, M. L (1981) *Meta-analysis in Social Research*. Beverly Hills, CA: Sage.

Lipsey, M. W. and Wilson, D. B. (2001) *Practical Meta-analysis*, Applied Social Research Methods Series 49. London: Sage.

Moher, D., Cool, D. J., Eastwood, S., Olkin, I., Rennie, D., Stroup, D. F. (1999) 'Improving the quality of reports of meta-analyses of randomized controlled trials: the QUOROM Statement', *Lancet*, 354: 1896–900.

Mulrow, C. (1994) 'Rationale for systematic reviews', *BMJ*, 309: 597.

Petticrew, M. (2001) 'Systematic reviews from astronomy to zoology: myths and misconceptions', *BMJ*, 322: 98.

Schultz et al. (2010) *CONSULT Statement* (online). Available at: http://www.consort-statement.org/ (accessed 20 September 2011).

Shea, B., Dube, C. and Moher, D. (2001) 'Assessing the quality of reports of systematic reviews: the QUOROM statement compared to other tools', in Egger, M., Davey-Smith, G. and Altman, D. (eds) *Systematic Reviews in Healthcare: Meta-analysis in Context* (2nd edn). London: BMJ Publishing Group.

Torgerson, C. (2003) *Systematic Reviews*. London: Continuum.

Torgerson, C. (2006) 'Publication bias: the Achilles' heel of systematic reviews?', *British Journal of Educational Studies*, 54(1).

Torgerson, D. and Torgerson, C. (2008) *Designing Randomised Trials in Health, Education and the Social Sciences*. London: Palgrave Macmillan.

31

Questionnaires

Peter Tymms

Introduction

Questionnaires are tools for collecting information and this chapter outlines the reasons for using them, the formats that are employed, administration methods, response rates, lengths of questionnaires, scale formation and the number of items needed to create measures. Technological advances have resulted in computer delivery gradually overtaking paper-based questionnaires and statistical techniques are advancing which can inform the development of instruments and the analysis of data. Other key issues such as research design are briefly mentioned and readers are referred to other chapters.

Purposes

The reasons for using questionnaires can be divided into four and each is outlined below.

Exploratory work

When starting an investigation the researcher may be unsure about the best way to proceed. At this stage he or she would start to read the relevant literature and talk to colleagues and perhaps some individuals from the population which is the focus of the proposed

work. Then, depending on what exactly is envisaged, it might make sense to collect some questionnaire data. At this exploratory stage collecting information from a small number of people, either using paper questionnaires or by interviews, could be helpful. This would be followed up by more serious work, but in the first instance a little information might help to start to define a problem.

Describing a population

Sometimes it is important to establish a general pattern across a population. In that case one could administer a questionnaire to a representative sample of that population. If one wanted a breakdown of the UK population by ethnic origins, or a breakdown by age, then an exercise which collected data from a sample of the population is appropriate. Some studies try to collect data on the whole population – the UK Census does this every ten years and is based on a questionnaire to each household (Census, 2011). Other well-known examples of questionnaires which involve samples include polling for election purposes by various organisations such as Ipsos MORI (2010).

As an aside it is interesting to recall one of the most notorious mistakes made in sampling which resulted from an attempt to establish who was going to win the US election in 1936. The Literary Digest had correctly predicted the outcomes of the previous five elections and having polled 10 million voters confidently announced that Landon would win. In fact Roosevelt won – a sobering result for all those who would use questionnaires (Freedman et al., 2007) A correct prediction was made by George Gallup who carefully sampled 50,000 people.

Outcomes or controls in studies

Questionnaires can also be used as part of an intervention study or a quasi-experiment which need outcome measures (see my Chapter 19 on 'Interventions' in this volume) and, perhaps, control (baseline) measures. In such cases, the measures may be of a construct such as motivation or mental health or self-esteem. It is probable that the questionnaire would involve a series of items which are combined together to form a scale. Additionally some contextual information is usually collected.

At this point it is worth noting that tests can be very similar to questionnaires differing mainly in style. In a test one would generally assess somebody's knowledge or understanding whereas the word questionnaire is generally reserved for something less pressured and often more diverse. Both can generate outcome measures formed from items.

Feedback

It is common for in-service and other courses to ask attendees to complete a questionnaire. These are very often intended for formative purposes, so that better experiences may be experienced next time round, although the results can also be used summatively. The formats vary dramatically from some in which attendees are asked to rate the presenters on a scale from 1 to 5, to those that simply ask open-ended questions such as 'what was good for you?' or 'what could have been better?' Such exercises can be extended to whole conferences, where samples are sometimes asked to complete ratings on individuals or break-out sessions. In higher education courses questionnaires are often used as part of quality assurance processes. Recently the National Student Survey (2010) has assumed a position of importance among universities as they vie for position in league tables.

There is a growing literature surrounding students' ratings with questions over the reliability, validity and impact.

Formats

Questionnaires come in a bewildering array of formats, which can broadly be divided into those that are open-ended and those that are closed. In the former the person responding is simply given a prompt and asked to write what they feel is appropriate. These prompts allow the respondent free rein. The contrasting approach constrains the response to tick-boxes, rank ordering or writing one or just a few words. This approach can certainly facilitate the analysis of large amounts of data and should only really be used if the investigator has a clear idea of the kinds of responses that are likely to appear. It would be most appropriate to start with open-ended, qualitative work before one focuses on closed items in a questionnaire. Various formats are outlined below together with examples and associated advantages and disadvantages.

Open-ended questions

Such questions might look like this:

> **What did you like about the course that you just attended?**

Or it might be something which asked 'How do you feel about having attended this college?'

Short written response

Between the open-ended and closed questionnaire items comes the short response in which one is constraining the amount that somebody might write. Two examples follow.

How would you describe President Obama? Use three words.

1 _____   2 _____   3 _____

Use one sentence in the two lines below to describe how you feel about going into a pub.

_____

_____

Likert-type responses

This is a closed format which involves a question such as:

We have good science teachers at this school.

Strongly agree   Agree   Not sure   Disagree   Strongly disagree

A Likert-type question involves presenting answers on a scale where the number of possible responses can vary from three up to seven or more. As a general principle one should provide as many responses as the respondents are able to cope with and anything beyond seven would seem to be problematic. Five is commonly used, as is three. Some writers advise researchers to use an even number of possibilities in order to force a decision from the respondents. But the job of Likert-type questions is to gauge a respondent's feeling and if they sit on the fence then the researcher should know that!

When analysing the data, it is possible to assess the extent to which the various options on the Likert scale are used. There should be some variation otherwise the item is providing no information and it is expected that all possibilities will be used to some extent. Generally a well-worded question using a five-point

scale will be managed well, but younger children might have difficulty and it may also be that the use of faces, as in the example below, is better.

I like school.

A complication arises from subjects who have no opinion or simply don't know how to respond. This can be different from a neutral response such as 'not sure'. It is possible to emphasise that respondents do not have to answer all questions. But it can also be useful to add a response option which says 'No response'.

Multiple choice

Multiple choice is very similar to the Likert-type response, but there is no continuum. For example:

What is your country of birth?

England	☐
Wales	☐
Scotland	☐
Northern Ireland	☐
Republic of Ireland	☐
Elsewhere	☐

please write in the present name of the country _____.

Sometimes the multiple choices will be exclusive, as above, where it is not possible to be born in more than one country. But sometimes it is possible to pick more than one.

Rank ordering

It is fairly common to see questionnaires in which people are asked to rank order a series of factors. For example:

Please rank the following in order of importance for good classroom teaching using the numbers 1 to 7 where 1 is the most important.

	Rank
Maintaining order	
Teaching subject matter	
Motivating the students	
Getting good inspection ratings	
Getting good test marks for the pupils	
Keeping the class quiet	
Making sure there is good discussion	

As a general rule, the results from this kind of item are more difficult to analyse than from Likert-type questions or multiple-choice responses. The data do not lend themselves to the usual analyses, and it would be good to avoid this kind of question. Rank ordering can nearly always be established *post hoc* from Likert-type questions and so little is lost by their avoidance.

Semantic differentials

A really nice way to get people to respond about their feelings is to put in opposing statements or opposing words and ask to which end their views are most applicable (Osgood et al., 1957).

Example

How do you feel about ice cream?

Hate it	X Love it

The cross shows that the respondent feels more inclined towards loving rather than hating ice cream.

Your perception of work

Relaxing	X Stressful

Enjoyable X	Unpleasant

On top of things	X Overwhelmed

This approach can be quite motivating and interesting for respondents as well as easy to analyse. This can

be done in a computer or on paper. In both cases the distance of the cross from one end is the measure. The format has been used very widely in psychological research.

An interesting feature of this format is that the analyst can place a cross on the diagram to represent the average response; this has been done in the 'Your perception of work' example above for teachers of Year 2 children.

Forced choice

Q Sort, also known as Q methodology, was created by a physicist by the name of Stephenson working in the social sciences. One is given a normal distribution and a series of statements on pieces of paper which, when laid out, will just fit in under the normal distribution (Stephenson, 1952). The respondent is asked to arrange the statements in an order going from 'Statement applies extremely well' to 'Statement applies very poorly'.

Once completed, the analyst automatically has a score for each of the items derived from the position on the distribution and this is a major advantage. The process prevents an individual describing themselves or others in consistently positive terms. Because the respondent is required to put in opposing items, if one is trying to assess a trait which someone might hide this may be an approach which helps.

Wording

Anyone who has designed and used a questionnaire knows that there is considerable scope for alternative interpretations of wordings and it is therefore really important to aim to keep statements and questions brief and direct so that they are readily understood. It also means that questionnaires need to be trialled before they are used and that only a single piece of information is collected for each statement. Despite this, it is common to see questions which have two parts to them even in some that are widely used.

It is well known that people are prepared to give opinions about things about which they have no knowledge and it is important to make sure that when we ask for information the respondent is in a position to answer. If, for example, one wants to ask about attitudes towards the content of a novel it is useful to know if they have read the book. One tactic is to ask them about other books including non-existent books. One can expect a proportion to say that they have read the non-existent book as well as real books and by doing this one can get a better estimate of the numbers who have read the book which is the focus of the question.

Textbooks sometimes advise questionnaire designers to make sure that some questions are worded positively and some negatively. A reason for this is to avoid respondents falling into a 'response set' whereby they start ticking all the boxes, say, on the right-hand side of the column without thought. One has to be very careful about that advice because a negatively worded item which should result in a 'strongly disagree' response can confuse even very bright respondents, lowering the validity of the data. It is better to word questions in different ways. Rather than reversing 'I am happy' to 'I am not happy' it is worth trying 'I am sad'. In other words, try to word items in a way which does not require the respondent to double-think their answer.

Administration

Questionnaire data can be collected in four major ways which are outlined below. Each has their strengths and weaknesses outlined in the Table 31.1 which follows the descriptions. In some cases these methods can be used simultaneously or consecutively.

Paper-based

Traditionally questionnaires have been administered on paper. They can be given out by hand or sent by post. After completion the data are usually entered into a computer and then analysed. Sometimes the results are scanned in and for large-scale exercises this makes sense, but the scanning machines tend to be uncompromising and require that the marks on the papers are accurate to an exacting degree.

Computer-delivered

It is increasingly popular to send out requests to answer questionnaires by email, directing respondents to a website and there are numerous software packages designed for this purpose. Some, such as Survey Monkey (2010), have a basic free option. This approach has great appeal because one can reach large audiences very rapidly. It was used recently to survey all the Malaysian academics of a set university from the UK (Hassan et al., 2008). The major downside of the use of computer-delivered questionnaires is the extent of access to computers by the people in whom the researcher is interested.

Face-to-face

It might be that the investigator actually holds the paper-based questionnaire, perhaps on a clipboard or computer in front of him/her, and asks a respondent what their answers are.

By phone

An alternative approach is to phone people and to administer the questionnaire verbally (Frey, 1989; Sturman and Taggart, 2008). The investigator can enter the answers straight into a computer or, possibly, write them down.

Length of questionnaires

Researchers often want to find out as much as possible when collecting data and this can result in very long questionnaires. But such instruments tend to get short shrift from respondents and, even if they do opt for completion, there are other problems with long questionnaires. Respondents may lose interest in what is being asked and they may start ticking boxes without thinking or tick the same position on a page – generating a 'response set'.

The length of the questionnaire, then, is important for response rates and for validity. It is also important from an ethical point of view to avoid asking for information which the analyst is not going to use. It would be wasting people's time.

Table 31.1 Advantages and disadvantages of the various forms of administration

Administrative procedure	Advantages	Disadvantages
Paper-based	Easy to administer to small samples. Simple to run off copies. Well established. Tried and tested.	Cost of paper and data entry. Difficult to use over large distances such as overseas. Scanning can be troublesome. Papers can be lost in transit.
Computer delivered	Useable on a very wide scale. Very economic. Rapid data collection. No data entry. Branching questionnaires are possible.	A major problem is the potential bias because those who don't have computers would not be able to respond.
Face-to-face	A skilled interviewer can encourage responses. He/she can flip between open and closed questions without difficulty. Additional notes can be taken relating to information that doesn't appear in a questionnaire. People can be approached in the street, in the pub or elsewhere.	An interviewer can be off-putting. An individual asked sensitive questions may be less likely to be honest. It can be expensive.
Phone	Perhaps surprisingly phones can generate more revealing responses than face-to-face interviews. As with interviews points of interest can be followed up. Can be recorded although by law one must ask permission and a reminder beep must be put on the line. Can be automated.	Some people may not want to respond on the phone. Phone numbers may not be readily available. It can be expensive.

Response rates

Researchers need meaningful data and low response rates threaten the validity of the information which they collect. When sending out questionnaires one wants to get back a fair proportion of those that were sent out but inevitably one very rarely gets them all back. It is possible in a constrained situation such as a classroom to ensure nearly 100 per cent response rates, though some students may opt not to complete it. Often questionnaires are collected in a less controlled way: they are sent out, perhaps by post, and the researcher waits for responses. The Canadian Medical Association Journal's medical policy states that 'Except in unusual circumstances, surveys are not considered for publication in *CMAJ* if the response rate is less than 60% of eligible participants' (Houston, 1996).

But it is common in social science to see response rates lower than that and response rates as low as 20% are sometimes published.

How to increase the response rate

There have been very clear and informative studies of how to increase the rate of response, especially when it comes to postal questionnaires, and these are well summarised in an article in which meta-analyses of the various investigations have been conducted. The recommendations are (Edwards et al., 2002):

- Keep the questionnaire short or at least make it look as though it is short and easy to complete. The shorter it is, the higher the response rate. The best response rate that the author of this chapter has had to a questionnaire is to send out a post-card with a return address and stamp on it which simply asks the respondent to tick five Likert-type questions .

- Use coloured paper.
- Use a handwritten envelope.
- Include a first-class stamp for return.
- Use a named respondent. If one addresses a specific person rather than the Head of Physics at Bog Standard Comprehensive, the response rate is going to be better.
- Promise feedback.

For online questionnaires and other formats the ways to increase response rates have not been so thoroughly investigated.

Scales

As noted earlier, Likert-type responses and semantic differentials are often used to create a scale. A scale is formed to measure a construct which represents an idea that we have about a person or a place or a thing which isn't immediately apparent – a latent trait. It is not like height which can be measured directly with a ruler, rather it might be an attitude or some aspect of personality such as introversion. We try to get at it by asking a series of questions and then aggregate those questions. Traditionally the procedure has involved checking that the items hang together well, checking the validity of items, as well as checking the scale's relationship to other measures. The process is well described in Spector (1992). More recently Item Response Theory and more specifically Rasch measurement has provided a modern way to approach the issue of measuring in the social sciences (Bond and Fox, 2007). This approach can help enormously when developing measures.

How many items are needed in a scale?

How many items are needed to get a reliable measure of a construct? Before answering this question, it is important to distinguish two things: one relates to the unit of analysis and the second to the construct being measured.

The unit of analysis

Typically, questionnaires have been designed to measure individuals. But in surveys we may be more interested in the measures of groups. For example, the focus may be on pupils in a school as a whole, or the average level of the measure within the school. Interest may also focus on a sub-group within that school within a year. The distinction between measuring individuals and measuring groups might seem obscure but it really matters because if we are to measure a pupil, then one set of rules comes into operation, but if we are to measure a school, then another set of rules is needed. We might be able to measure individual pupils well but schools not so well, and the opposite may also be true. To give a couple of examples: we can measure the height of an individual accurately and quickly, but to distinguish one school from another on the basis of the pupils' heights would not be easy. On the other hand, we don't measure a pupil's background very well by knowing if they have access to free school meals, but this poor pupil measure behaves quite well at the aggregate level in helping to characterise a school.

The construct

It is really important to be clear about what the questions in a survey are designed to measure or what the construct is that the measure is trying to assess. Such careful definition will inform the measure's development and use.

Measuring pupils

If we were interested in measuring pupils then we can reasonably ask a question such as: 'How many items are needed to reliably measure pupils' emotional problems?' We can try to answer that by saying that we would be pleased if we had a valid measure with reliability of, say, 0.9. The 0.9 figure is somewhat arbitrary but would be widely accepted by psychometricians and others as an indication of a very reliable assessment of individuals.[1] Quite often well-established instruments do not have reliabilities as high as that but are regarded as being acceptable. For example, the Strengths and Difficulties Questionnaire (SDQ; Goodman, 1997) uses five items to measure emotional problems and has an internal reliability of about 0.7 with secondary school pupils. This is satisfactory albeit short of the high target of 0.9. We can estimate how many items would be needed to get a reliability of 0.9 using the Spearman-Brown formula:

$$\rho_{new} = \frac{k\rho_{old}}{1+(k-1)\rho_{old}}$$

where

- ρ_{new} is the reliability of the new measure;
- k is how many times longer the new measure is;
- ρ_{old} is the reliability of the old measure.

This indicates that the more items we have, the more reliable the measure, and if we wanted to have a measure of reliability of 0.9 for the emotional problems measure of the SDQ we would need approximately 2.9 times as many similar items (assuming the same level of inter-item correlations). That is 14 items.

Measuring schools

How many items are needed to measure a school? Now the above formula is not appropriate. Rather the reliability[2] is given by:

$$Reliability = \frac{n\sigma_u^2}{n\sigma_u^2 + \sigma_e^2}$$

where:

- n is the number of pupils in the school;
- σ_u^2 is the school level variance;
- σ_e^2 is the pupils' level variance.

In order to apply the formula Figure 31.1 can be used (Tymms, 1995). This relates the number of pupils in the school to the reliability of a school-level average for different levels of intra-school correlations.[3] The latter is a measure of how different schools are from one another. If we are looking at something like achievement on maths tests, having taken into account pupils' earlier scores, then the intra-school correlation would be between 0.09 and 0.15 for a secondary school. This is sometimes stated as 'between 9 and 15% of the variance is linked to schools'.

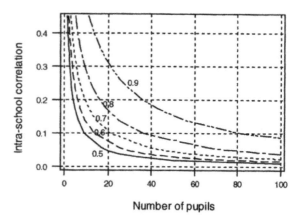

Figure 31.1   Look-up graph for indicator reliabilities

The chart tells us that if we had a measure of maths which, controlling for prior attainment, had an intra-class correlation of 0.15, then to get a reliability of 0.9 for the school measure we would need approximately 50 pupils. It also tells us that if the intra-school correlation is 0.01 then we are going to need a very large number of pupils in order to be able to assess a school very reliably. If we have 100 pupils in a school the reliability of our estimate of that school is about 0.5. It seems unlikely that we would have enough pupils in a school to get to a point where we would have a reliability of 0.9. This is because the very low intra-school correlation indicates that school averages hardly vary at all compared to the variation in pupil scores.

A complication

The school level section above has been set out without reference to the number of items that were used in the test. To some extent the number of items is not important provided an adequate set have been asked. An informal simulation was carried out and it indicated that after we have got a few items the intra-school correlation remains fairly constant. In other words, when we are measuring schools, we don't need large numbers of items, we simply need a few good ones. The key is the number of pupils.

Could we manage with one item? Here the validity

of the measure is important. A single item on a questionnaire is unlikely to capture enough of the construct that we are interested in. Ideally we would have a series of items all sampling different features of the key construct. If we are interested in emotional problems, for example, we might ask questions that relate to worries, happiness, tearfulness, nervousness, and fears. Each item is designed to sample a different aspect of the construct. By assessing a range, we get a better measure.

In conclusion, in order to measure schools reliably it is important to assess an adequate number of pupils. What that number should be depends on the extent to which schools differ on the construct in question. The construct itself should be addressed using a group of items that assess the construct as broadly as possible.

Conclusion and links to other methodology

Questionnaires are one way to collect data and other sections in this book deal with interviews (Mears, Chapter 24 in this volume), which can be linked to questionnaires. In fact questionnaires can sometimes be seen as a form of interviewing. Other data such as that from tests are dealt with elsewhere in this volume. Questionnaires are also relevant to experimental design and sampling elsewhere in this volume.

A further consideration when dealing with questionnaires is bias. This can come in two forms. One relates to the representativeness of those who return data and this is covered under the heading of sampling. The other relates to the wording. If questions are interpreted differently by different groups then there is a problem. This issue is discussed in the chapter on testing elsewhere in this volume.

Questions for further investigation

1. How can the response rates for online questionnaires be increased? There is a considerable amount of research suggesting how the response rates of paper-based questionnaires can be increased but the methods which have been investigated may not be relevant to online surveys and there may be other approaches which are relevant.

2. When are mobile phones suitable for collecting data? In formulating a response to this question consider the ways in which a research project might access the sample of subjects as well as the facilities available on modern mobile phones and the capacity of programmers to generate innovative approaches.

Notes

1. How high a reliability is acceptable depends on what it is to be used for. High-stakes decisions about individuals may need above 0.9; for everyday decisions 0.9 is probably adequate; if just for information, or indicative diagnosis, below this may be fine.
2. This is the 'shrinkage' formula from Goldstein (1987).
3. More generally called the intra-class correlation or ICC.

Suggested further reading

Bond, T. G. and Fox, C. M. (2007) *Applying the Rasch Model: Fundamental Measurement in the Human Sciences* (2nd edn). Mahwah, NJ: Lawrence Erlbaum Associates. This book is an introduction to Rasch measurement and is very relevant to researchers who wish to measure attitudes using Likert-type response formats. It also has an interesting section about converting interviews into quantitative data linked to Piaget's work.

Edwards, P., Roberts, I., Clarke, M., DiGuiseppi, C., Pratap, S., Wentz, R. and Kwan, I. (2002) 'Increasing response rates to postal questionnaires: systematic review', *British Medical Journal*, 324: 1183–211. A key paper in synthesising the research on increasing response rates to questionnaires.

Frey, J. H. (1989) *Survey Research by Telephone*. London: Sage. Telephone interviews have much to be said for them and much good advice can be found in this text.

References

Bond, T. G. and Fox, C. M. (2007) *Applying the Rasch Model: Fundamental Measurement in the Human Sciences* (2nd edn). Mahwah, N.J: Lawrence Erlbaum Associates.

Census (2011). Available at: http://www.ons.gov.uk/census/index.html (accessed 1 January 2011).

Edwards, P., Roberts, I., Clarke, M., DiGuiseppi, C., Pratap, S., Wentz, R. and Kwan, I. (2002) 'Increasing response rates to postal questionnaires: systematic review', *British Medical Journal*, 324: 1183–211.

Frey, J. H. (1989) *Survey Research by Telephone.* London: Sage.

Goldstein, H. (1987) *Multi-level Models in Educational and Social Research.* London: Griffin School Effects.

Goodman, R. (1997) 'The strengths and difficulties questionnaire: a research note', *Journal of Child Psychology and Psychiatry*, 38: 581–86.

Hassan, A., Tymms, P. and Ismail, H. (2008) 'Academic productivity as perceived by Malaysian academics', *Journal of Higher Education Policy and Management*, 30(3): 283–96.

Houston (1996) The Canadian Medical Association Journal Medical Policy. Available at: http://www.cmaj.ca/ (accessed 20 September 2011).

Ipsos MORI (2010). Available at: http://www.ipsos-mori.com/ (accessed 27 December 2010).

National Student Survey (2010). Available at: http://www.thestudentsurvey.com/ (accessed 27 December 2010).

Osgood, C. E., Suci, G. J. and Tannenbaum, P. H. (1957) *The Measurement of Meaning.* Urbana, IL: University of Illinois.

Spector, P. E. (1992) *Summated Rating Scale Construction: An Introduction.* Newbury Park, CA: Sage.

Stephenson, W. (1952) 'Some observations on Q-Technique', *Psychological Bulletin*, XLIX: 483–98

Sturman, L. and Taggart, G. (2008) 'The professional voice: comparing questionnaire and telephone methods in a national survey of teachers' perceptions', *British Educational Research Journal*, 34(1): 117–34.

Sudman, S. and Bradburn, N. M. (1982) *Asking Questions. A Practical Guide to Questionnaire Design.* San Francisco: Jossey-Bass.

Survey Monkey (2010). Available at: http://www.surveymonkey.com/ (accessed 27 December 2010).

Tymms, P. (1995) *Technical Report: Primary.* London: School Curriculum and Assessment Authority.

32

Measurement and validity

Ronald K. Hambleton

Introduction

All of the steps in the research process, from identifying a problem to investigate and writing a research purpose, through sampling, data collection and analysis, to preparing the final report, are critical, and to skip one or complete one step poorly can have a devastating impact on the overall value of that study. But some of the steps, if completed poorly, can be corrected without having to spend a lot of time or money. For example, if the statistical analyses are incomplete or carried out incorrectly, they can be fixed. If a final report is poorly written, the organisation and writing can be improved. But some steps, such as the measurement of the variables of interest in the study (e.g. reading achievement, motivation level assessment or attitudes about sport), if done poorly, are impossible to fix without collecting more data, and often this is not possible because of time, access and/or cost.

Of course to get the correct data, the variables of interest must be specified and clear. Measurement is about assigning numbers to persons or groups to represent their characteristics on these variables of interest in a research study. These variables can span the range from achievement, to aptitudes, to attitudes and personality, to psychomotor skills. These numbers often serve as the link between a researcher's purposes and the conclusions he/she wants to make.

For example, a researcher may be studying the impact of a new children's reading programme on reading comprehension. Measurements or scores provided by a reading comprehension test administered before and after the instruction provide the numbers for the researcher to analyse any gains that may have been made.

Of course not all measurements are equally useful. It is important that the measurements provided by the administration of the reading comprehension test to the participants in the study have desirable properties—there needs to be evidence that the test is in fact providing measurements that actually measure the construct of interest (that is the measurements must be valid) and can be shown to be consistent, for example be similar to scores obtained from administering the test again or administering an equivalent form of the test (that is the measurements must be reliable).

Approaches to collecting data

Once the outcome variables of a study are specified, then it is possible to consider ways in which the data of interest can be collected. Researchers have many options available to them when making measurements of human characteristics in their studies, though of course all of these options are not always feasible or reasonable for a given study. What follows are some options with very brief descriptions:

- *Norm-referenced achievement and aptitude tests.* Normally, these types of tests are commercially available and there are thousands available. A good reference for these tests would be the Buros Mental Measurement Yearbooks found in the reference section of university libraries (also, see the website: http://www.unl.edu/buros/) or the commercial publishers who all have websites that can be explored. The quality of these tests is generally high though the costs of the tests can often be substantial. The availability of score norms to aid in test score interpretation can be especially valuable.

- *Criterion-referenced achievement tests* (e.g. competency tests, basic skills tests, commercially available credentialling exams). Sometimes a researcher is interested in the level of accomplishment of participants in relation to a domain of content, for example high school mathematics, and levels might be failing, basic, proficient and advanced. Sometimes the test data come from existing files, such as might be available from an education department, or sometimes these tests need to be constructed by the researcher (e.g. Shrock and Coscarelli, 2007). These types of tests are prominent in the schools, training programmes, and credentialling agencies.

- *Classroom tests.* These tests may be constructed by teachers or by researchers and are often intended for one-time use. Rarely are the tests of the same high quality of commercial tests, but often they can be constructed to match exactly the needs of the researcher.

- *Performance tests* (e.g. writing tests, tests of psychomotor skills). These types of tests require the respondents to write something, to perform something, to construct a response to a question, etc.

- *Personality tests* (e.g. assessments of motivation, school anxiety or self-concept). These tests are typically constructed by test publishers, of high quality and with norms to aid in score interpretation.

- *Attitude scales.* So often researchers have an interest in assessing the attitudes of participants in their research, attitudes towards sports, religion, computers, etc. They can be available commercially but more often researchers construct these types of instruments themselves so that they can assess exactly the construct of interest. In a typical attitudinal survey, respondents are presented with a series of statements (e.g. 'Watching sports on television is a big waste of my time') to which they provide one of five responses, 'strongly disagree', 'disagree', 'undecided', 'agree' or 'strongly agree'.

- *Interest inventories.* These types of instruments are normally available from commercial test publishers.

- *Questionnaires* (structured as well as unstructured). Questionnaires (often called 'surveys') are among the most common ways that researchers compile data for their studies. They can be tailored exactly to the needs of the researcher. The questions themselves come in two forms: structured and unstructured. Structured questions provide both a question and set of responses from which the respondent makes a choice. Sometimes the responses are unordered such as 'What is your favourite sport?' (1) hockey, (2) soccer, (3) baseball, (4) basketball, (5) other. Other times the choices are ordered. For example, how often do you get to go to the movies? (1) never, (2) rarely, (3) sometimes, (4) frequently. Other times, a question or prompt is presented to the respondent and he/she answers in his/her own words. For example, write 500 words or so on the similarities and differences in the educational policies of the last two Presidents of the United States: George Bush and Barak Obama. Both structured and unstructured questions have their advantages and disadvantages in research studies. Often researchers will use a mix of formats to capitalise on their advantages and minimise their disadvantages (see, for example, Gay et al., 2006). What researchers seem to like most about questionnaires is the ease with which they can be constructed to meet their own research objectives. Of course, questionnaires still benefit from careful reviews and pilot-testing prior to actual use in a study.

- *Observational methods.* Researchers conducting

qualitative studies may want to collect their data through observational methods. Often this involves the development of an instrument focused on the variables of interest. For instance, a researcher may be interested in focusing on children in a classroom and their activities – listening to the teacher, talking with other children in the classroom, reading a book, looking out of the window, etc. An observation form can be constructed that identifies possible activities of children, and then observers can note the percentage of time individual children are engaged in these activities. Normally, training of observers must be done, and multiple observers are used to ensure that the observations noted by one observer are replicated by others.

• *Interviews* (structured and unstructured). Interviewing respondents is another very effective way to collect data for a research study. Questions can be structured or unstructured just as with questionnaires. This data collection method does tend to be time-consuming and often more expensive than questionnaire research.

Research methods textbooks usually have a chapter, and often more than one, on modes of data collection for research studies. Factors such as cost to purchase, required time to administer, time to development and validate, and the match between an instrument and the informational needs it addresses are the sorts of factors considered in ultimately deciding upon the mode or modes of data collection in a research study.

Scales of measurement

The measurements researchers work with (i.e. the numbers obtained from the data collection initiatives) have different properties and these need to be known or assumed prior to conducting any statistical analyses. When numbers are used to simply distinguish individuals or groups from each other, we say that the numbers are on a *nominal scale*. For example, we often code gender data by recording females as '1' and males as '2'. These numbers provide no information about order. They are simply labels we use to distinguish our research sample by gender. Because the numbers are simply labels, we

do not use them to carry out any statistical operations other than counting the number of participants in each category. Nominal numbers have value for helping to describe the research sample and in conditioning the data for some analysis (e.g. splitting a sample of data into combinations of gender and ethnicity) but there is little that can be done otherwise.

Sometimes the numbers we use inform about order (e.g. the order of finish of participants in a race or on a test). We may ask participants to rank order the preferences they have for their teachers, sports they play or subjects they have studied. Asking participants to order lists on a questionnaire is common. Measurements that inform about order are referred to as measurements on an *ordinal scale*. Again, these numbers are limited statistically but medians can be calculated, and there are statistics that can be used to obtain score variability information. One downside to measurements on an ordinal scale is that the differences between scores of 1, 2, 3, etc. cannot be assumed to be equal. Suppose the numbers represent the placing of individuals on a test. But it should not be assumed that these differences in performance are equal. It is possible, for example, that the individual who was first may have performed substantially better than the second place participant in the study, whereas the second and third best-performing participants may have been close. These numbers, 1, 2, 3, etc. communicate the ordering of performance, but they do not communicate any information about the actual performance differences.

If the numbers do communicate information about the differences, as they might on an achievement test or personality survey, we say the numbers are being reported on an *interval scale*, sometimes called an *equal-interval scale*. Now an equal interval scale for the scores on a test is probably not strictly true. For example, gaining points at the lower end of an achievement test score scale is often easy whereas gaining points at the higher end is often more difficult to obtain. But it is common to assume that equal differences along an achievement, aptitude, attitude and personality scale represent equal differences in the construct. So, on an achievement test score scale, it is common to assume that it takes the same change in achievement knowledge or skills to move from 30 to 40, 60 to 70 and 90 to 100. This surely isn't strictly true, but researchers commonly assume that it is. This assumption permits the usual array of descriptive and inferential statistics to be used on the measurements. It is common to assume that these statistical methods are robust to violations in the assumption that the measurements are being reported on an equal-interval scale. The one shortcoming with equal-interval measurements is that the zero score is arbitrary and so ratios of scores are not acceptable. It makes no sense to say that one participant has twice the attitude of another based on scores from the administration of an attitudinal survey.

Finally, if the score scale on which measurements are made does contain a well-defined zero score then, in addition to treating the data as equal interval, ratios can be carried out. This type of scale is called a *ratio scale*. Well-known examples of measurements that are reported on ratio scales include the measurement of weights, lengths and time. In these examples, a zero score is well-understood. So not only do we recognise that the numbers on these scales represent equal changes in the construct from one number to the next, we can make ratio statements too such as one participant completed the task of interest in twice the time of another participant.

All four scales of measurement are valuable in social science research because they have major implications for the handling of measurements in any statistical analyses.

Criterion-referenced vs. norm-referenced measurement

Over the years, two frameworks for interpreting measurements on equal-interval scales have emerged: criterion-referenced and norm-referenced (Shrock and Cascarelli, 2007). Norm-referenced measurements are the better known of the two and lead to a comparison of participants to a reference group of persons on the construct measured by the test of interest. For example, suppose researchers were using an intelligence test in their study. The publisher of that test has compiled 'norms' on the test which, for a fully described reference group, provide the basis for interpreting individual test scores. We might say, for example, that an individual scored about as well as a

person in the reference group at the 90th percentile. Individual scores derive meaning by comparing them to a reference group. For some tests too, there may be 'norms' for multiple reference groups. This is common with some popular aptitude and personality tests.

In contrast to norm-referenced tests, criterion-referenced tests provide a basis for interpreting individual measurements in relation to a well-defined body of content, for example the mathematics content required for high school graduation. Tests are constructed, a scoring scheme is developed and performance standards, sometimes called 'cutscores', are set on the test score scale (or perhaps on a derived scale) for distinguishing among failing, basic, proficient and advanced candidates. Individual scores are used to place those individuals into performance categories. The interpretation of the individual score is made using the performance standards which were set in relation to the body of content that the test measures.

Depending on the purpose of the research study, either or both norm-referenced and criterion-referenced measurements may be of interest. Because the purposes of these two types of measurement are very different, it should come as no surprise that the approaches to constructing and evaluating each kind of test are different (Hambleton and Zenisky, 2003).

Score reliability

Numerous books have been written about score reliability, so this section will attempt to cover only a few main points. If you wish to further your interest in this area, the best place to start would be with Thorndike and Thorndike-Christ (2010). Score reliability is about the 'consistency' of the measurements obtained from a test administration. Consistency has a meaning that shifts depending on the use of the measurements. With many achievement, aptitude and personality tests, consistency may have to do with the similarity of scores over time. With achievement tests, sometimes there is concern about the consistency of scores over parallel forms of the test. With observational data there may be concern about consistency of the measurements across observers or interviewers. In scoring performance data when judgement is involved, the concern may focus on the consistency of scores assigned to individual work across graders or raters.

There are several important points to remember about reliability. First, score reliability is measured by degree (between 0 and 1). Researchers may say that their test is reliable or not, but the reality is that it is measured from one end of a continuum (0) to the other (1). Second, a high level of score reliability is important but does not guarantee that the resulting scores have some level of validity. Score validity is a more important characteristic of scores than reliability. All the same, some level of reliability of scores is required, or score validity will be very limited. Third, reliability is really a function of the scores themselves, the kind of reliability being reported and the group to which the test was administered. For example, test-retest reliability may differ from parallel-form reliability, and the results may be different for Black, White and Hispanic students.

Why might the scores from a test be inconsistent? Sometimes the directions or the items may be ambiguous; attention, effort or health can fluctuate from one administration to the next; a restrictive time limit could cause guessing, or quitting; observers or raters may adopt different strategies for doing their work; unforeseen interruptions can occur; and so on. Researchers must strive for high consistency or reliability in the data they are using.

Researchers have access to many designs for compiling their reliability data: test-retest (often used with standardised tests), parallel-form (often used with achievement tests), inter-rater reliability (often used with observational data or when scoring performance data) and internal consistency (e.g. coefficient alpha) are used when there is only time for a single administration of a test. Often too, reliability for standardized tests can be found in technical manuals. With questionnaires, it would be rare to readminister them a second time. Sometimes they are completed anonymously and so it would be difficult to match up responses from the first and second administration. In addition, getting response rates up high is hard, and the idea of getting respondents to participate twice is difficult to imagine. Often reliability is checked by asking some similar questions in different parts of the questionnaire to check on the extent to which respondents are consistent in their answers.

Score validity

Ultimately, researchers must be concerned about the extent to which the measurements they are using are accurate representations of the constructs they want to include in their research. They can try hard to construct or select instruments for their studies, but hard work is not sufficient to defend sets of scores in a research study. Hard work and following the main steps in either selecting or constructing tests and questionnaires are important, but additional evidence for score validity is needed.

There are important features of score validity to remember. First, test score validity is judged by how useful the scores are for addressing an intended purpose or use. There may be some great tests in the field for assessing the personality of adults. But these same tests would likely be completely inappropriate for children. Test score validity is very much specific to a particular group and a particular use. As with test score reliability, test score validity is very much assessed by degree, even though it is common in practice to describe a test as 'valid' or 'invalid'. There is no critical correlation that must be obtained or particular result obtained. Test score validity is about compiling evidence and then making a professional judgement about the worth of that evidence for supporting use of the measurements to accomplish some particular goal of a study. Finally, and again just like test score reliability, there are several types of evidence that can be compiled and the evidence may not always be consistent.

Historically, there are three major categories of evidence that are recognised by researchers. *Content validity* evidence has to do with the extent of overlap between the content that a test or questionnaire measures and the domain of content that is of interest. Measure too little and the critics argue that the test does not constitute a representative sample; measure too much and the critics argue that the test measures more than was intended by the construct. Assessing content validity is a judgemental activity. With an observational instrument, questionnaire or interview, often content validity is addressed by matching up the content of the instrument to features or criteria that are deemed important to measure.

Criterion-related validity evidence concerns studying

the relationship between the scores on the test of interest and scores measuring variables that they might be expected to predict (e.g. a study about predicting college grades from a predictor test) or variables that a test might be expected to correlate with at the present time (e.g. a competitor to the test of interest or perhaps high school grades). Other names for these types of studies are convergent and divergent validity investigations.

Construct validity evidence has to do with evidence that scores from a test can be interpreted in terms of the construct the test was intended to measure, for example correlations with tests that purport to measure the same construct (here we might expect the correlations to be relatively high) or even different constructs (here, we might expect the correlations to be modest or low). Content validity evidence is always valued in construct validation investigations. In addition, evidence shows that scores from the test or questionnaire function as they might do if they were measuring the construct of interest – they should go up and/or down (over groups perhaps and over time; testable hypotheses come from the theory associated with the construct) when expected, they should correlate with tests measuring similar constructs, and they should not correlate with tests measuring unrelated constructs. There is no end to the amount of evidence that can be compiled to investigate the construct validity of scores from a test. The amount surely depends on professional judgement considering the importance of the test and the resources available to the researchers. But do too little, and the credibility of the research study is severely weakened because of questions about the validity of the measurements being used in the study.

Conclusion

So much more is known about measurement than is contained in this chapter, and many have spent their careers working only on this single topic. They are called 'measurement specialists' or 'psychometricians' and become deeply involved in instrument development, the assessment of reliability and validity of instrument scores, the uses of measurement, and the development of professional standards for developing and using tests and questionnaires. Of course they also become involved in expanding the field through developing new psychometric theories and models, e.g. generalisability theory (Brennan, 2001) and item response theory (Osterlind, 2006), and other types of research (e.g. development of new modes of instrumentation, new methods of collecting data from participants and automated scoring of participant responses) (see, for example, Brennan, 2001; Mills et al., 2002).

Questions for further investigation

1. Discuss the pros and cons of criterion-referenced and norm-referenced measurements and for which types of research they are best suited.
2. Discuss score validity and score reliability. Which do you consider more important and why?

Suggested further reading

Brennan, R. L. (2001) *Generalizability Theory*. New York: Springer. This book offers an extensive conceptual framework and a powerful set of statistical procedures for characterising and quantifying the fallibility of measurements within the social sciences.

Osterlind, S. J. (2006) *Modern Measurement: Theory, Principles, and Applications of Mental Appraisal*. Upper Saddle River, NJ: Pearson Education. This text presents a wide array of information on diverse but fundamental aspects of test theory and its application to practical problems in mental measurement for the advanced student and measurement professional.

References

Brennan, R. L. (2001) *Generalizability Theory*. New York: Springer.

Gay, L. R., Mills, G. E. and Airasian, P. (2006) *Educational Research: Competencies for Analysis and Applications* (8th edn). Upper Saddle River, NJ: Pearson Education.

Hambleton, R. K. and Zenisky, A. (2003) 'Issues and practices of performance assessment', in Reynolds, C. R. and

Kamphaus, T. W. (eds) *Handbook of Psychological and Educational Assessment of Children* (2nd edn). New York: The Guilford Press, pp. 377–404.

Mills, C. N., Potenza, M., Fremer, J. J. and Ward, W. C. (2002) *Computer-based Testing: Building The Foundation for Future Assessments*. Mahwah, NJ: Lawrence Erlbaum Associates.

Osterlind, S. J. (2006) *Modern Measurement: Theory, Principles, and Applications of Mental Appraisal*. Upper Saddle River, NJ: Pearson Education.

Shrock, S. A. and Coscarelli, W. C. (2007) *Criterion-referenced Test Development: Technical and Legal Guidelines for Corporate Training* (3rd edn). San Francisco: John Wiley & Sons.

Thorndike, R. M. and Thorndike-Christ, T. (2010) *Measurement and Evaluation in Psychology and Education* (8th edn). Boston: Pearson.

Dimension 3

Analysis methods

33

Software and qualitative data analysis

Graham R. Gibbs

Computer-Assisted Qualitative Data Analysis (CAQDAS) programs have been developed to help with the sheer amount of data to be analysed and its complexity and density. There are many different programs available but some are better than others at some kinds of analysis and for some purposes. If you are able to choose what software to use before you start analysis then it is important to know which is good at what. Download trial versions and try them out. (See the resources section at the end of the chapter.) The rest of this chapter, however, focuses on one of the most popular, NVivo, now in version 9, but much of the advice applies to any software you might use. There is a very full interactive help system with the NVivo program. There is a pdf version of all the help information which can be downloaded from the website of the publishers of NVivo, QSR. Unfortunately, at the moment this is only available for version 8. The functionality of version 9 is similar to version 8, but version 9 now uses a ribbon bar instead of the menus of version 8. References below are to pages in the 'Using the software' manual, for version 8, abbreviated to NVUS.

While there are many benefits to be gained from using CAQDAS, there are dangers too. Fielding and Lee have examined the history of the development of qualitative research and its support by computers in the light of the experience of those interviewed in their study of researchers using CAQDAS (Fielding and Lee, 1998). Among the issues they identified was a feeling of being distant from the data. Researchers using paper-based analysis felt they were closer to the words of their respondents or to their field notes than if they used computers. This is probably because many of the early programs did not make it easy to jump back to the data to examine the context of coded or retrieved text. In contrast, recent programs excel at this. A second issue, as many users and some commentators have suggested, was that much software seemed too influenced by grounded theory. This approach has become very popular among both qualitative researchers and software developers. However, as Fielding and Lee point out, as programs have become more sophisticated, they have become less connected to any one analytic approach. A related danger that some have pointed to is the over-emphasis on code and retrieve approaches. Indeed, these are core activities of CAQDAS. Some commentators have suggested that this militates against analysts who wish to use quite different techniques (such as hyperlinking) to analyse their data. But it is clear that coding is central in the kind of analysis best supported by most CAQDAS and although some software does have linking facilities, these are not as well developed as those that support coding.

To use CAQDAS or not

There are several considerations to examine when deciding whether to use software with your project. You might consider your project too small to justify its use. This does not simply mean a small number of participants. Interviews and observations can be long, complex and intensive and produce lots of data to analyse. On the other hand you may intend to use simple structured questionnaires, in which case the data may be quite easy to analyse without computer support.

Above all you need to ask if the software supports your analytic approach or does it help sufficiently to make its use worthwhile. Code and retrieve or thematic coding approaches are well served by the software.

These include grounded theory, interpretative phenomenological analysis, framework analysis, template analysis and many kinds of ethnographic approaches that tend to analyse data thematically. Less well served are more intensive and discursive approaches such as discourse analysis and narrative and conversation analysis. Some software does support the special mark-up needed by, for example, conversation analysis and even supports the process of transcription, but these approaches are not reliant on thematic coding and thus the core function of most CAQDAS is of little use.

Setting up the project in NVivo

Start the program and in the welcome screen that appears select New Project and give it a title and description (NVUS, pp. 42–4, 56–7, 63–4). Use the Browse button to save it where you want it. Then the main NVivo window opens (see Figure 33.1).

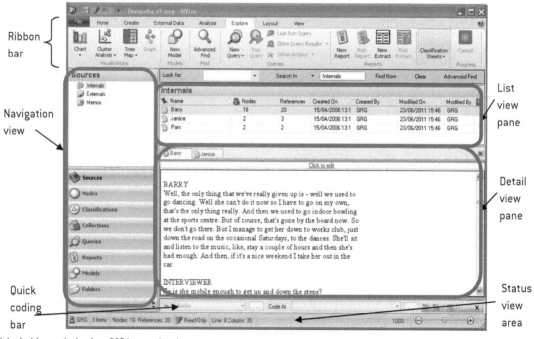

Ribbon bar

Navigation view

List view pane

Detail view pane

Quick coding bar

Status view area

Published with permission from QSR International.

Figure 33.1 The NVivo main window

The new project is just a container for your data. The next step is to introduce some data into it. These data are called sources in NVivo and include documents, video, audio and images as well as a special kind of document called memos. Most commonly the sources are text, including interviews (usually audio or video recordings), observations (including those recorded by video) and field notes. NVivo can import a variety of types of documents including plain text (.txt), rich text format (.rtf) and Word format, both old and new (.doc and .docx) (NVUS, pp. 72–3, 87–95). Once introduced, documents can be examined at any time and their contents appear as tabs in the Detail view pane (NVUS, pp. 82–5). You can also introduce sources that are video, audio or images in a digital format. Many of these will be at a much higher quality than you need in the project for display on screen. If you can, make the video files smaller by resaving as small mp4 files. For the audio use mp3 files. Images from cameras can be quite large. Again for the purposes of showing on screen these can be resaved at much lower quality and resolution jpegs. You will need to make the changes outside NVivo before you import them into the project (NVUS, pp. 73–6, 96–102).

Units of analysis

You need to decide what are the cases in your study because in NVivo cases can have attributes and can combine together several different sources (documents, video, images, etc.) This analytically separates the sources of information about the cases (e.g. the transcripts of your interviews or your video of interaction in the classroom) from the cases themselves. By the time you start using NVivo you should have a pretty good idea what these cases are. Sometimes they reflect your sampling strategy, for example you may have undertaken snowball sampling of young people who played truant when at school age, in which case people are your cases. More commonly cases reflect your research questions or your research design. For instance, you may be investigating differences in classroom innovation between different teachers and different schools. Then your cases will probably be teachers (or classes) and schools. It is usually best to set up these cases when setting up the project, although if

more appear or additional values for existing cases are discovered during the study these can be added to the project. In NVivo cases are a kind of node and they are found in the nodes list pane (NVUS, pp. 160, 162–72).

Attributes means variables, usually categorical variables, about the cases. For example, if the cases are people they might be age, gender, education or work experience of the people, or if they are places they might be population, crime rate or state, or if events they might be date, duration, size, type, etc. (NVUS, pp. 160–3). In a mixed-methods study you might well have collected some attribute data of this kind about the cases in the quantitative part of the study. In this case you can introduce this data to the NVivo project as a spreadsheet or an SPSS data file called a casebook (NVUS, pp. 165–72). Normally it is best to introduce this data before any qualitative data as it is a quick way of establishing cases. But you can also add attributes to cases after you have set up the project, either from data you have collected in the field or on the basis of analysis of your qualitative data (see Miles and Huberman, 1994: 102–9).

Security

As you build your project and develop your analysis, you will create files and structures you won't want to lose. Do regular saves of your data. By default, NVivo prompts every 15 minutes for you to save your data or produce backup files, so that if the program or the computer crashes at any time, you will not lose all your work.

Most of the data you create is very compact. Information about coding and links takes only a little space. Along with the documents you have introduced, this information is all kept together in the project file. However, you may opt to keep larger files you may have, such as video and audio files, outside the project file. You should keep backups of both the project file (for NVivo this is the .nvp file) and other large data items that you are keeping outside the NVivo project file. You don't normally change primary data such as audio and video after it has been introduced into the project so these may only need occasional backups. But the main project file will change every time you do some analysis so this needs regular backing up. The most convenient backup media are flash memory – usually in the form of memory sticks – and removable hard disks. Memory sticks will be fine if you just have documents and a few pictures, but if you have lots of video or audio files then a removable hard disk will be needed.

Also keep the data confidential. Don't allow others to see your data if you have given respondents assurances that what they have told you is confidential or will be kept anonymous. Password protect your computer and your NVivo project if you can and don't leave the program running unattended on a PC in an open office.

Coding

Coding is one of the core activities in most CAQDAS programs and NVivo is no exception. Coding means applying labels, the codes, to passages of text, sections of video or audio, or regions of images. Most commonly this is done as a way of indicating all the content that is about some theme you have identified. At its simplest, this labelling or coding process enables researchers quickly to retrieve and collect together all the text and other data that they have associated with some thematic idea so that they can be examined together and different cases can be compared.

NVivo calls codes 'nodes'. Typically when you first create nodes they can just be kept in a list. As you develop your coding ideas you can arrange the nodes into a hierarchy or tree shown in the node list view pane (NVUS, pp. 137–40). Nodes can be reordered, renamed, deleted, split and combined and nodes in a hierarchy can be reorganised by moving them from one branch of the tree to another (NVUS, pp. 145–52).

You can separate out the construction of a coding scheme (the nodes) from the act of coding the text and other sources. Thus you can create nodes in NVivo, perhaps with definitions and even attached memos, without any coding, i.e. without using them to label any sources. Such nodes, often called a priori codes, are based on your literature review, your experience in the field or your initial hunches and can be used later for coding. On the other hand, a very common approach and one often combined with a priori codes is to read the text (or view the video) directly and create new nodes and code the source content to them and/or to a priori codes as you do so (NVUS, pp. 182–92, 197–200).

Once some sources have been coded, you can inspect what you have done in a couple of ways. With

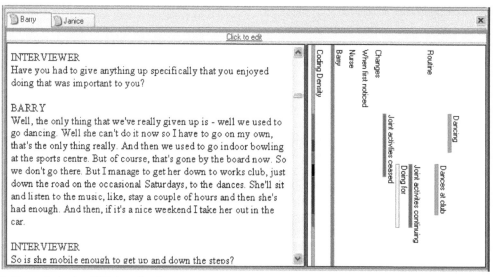

Published with permission from QSR International.

Figure 33.2   Document showing coding stripes

text that has been coded you can display coding stripes, to the right of the text, to show how the passages have been coded (NVUS, pp. 202–5) (see Figure 33.2). Alternatively you can retrieve all the sources coded at a specific node. Just double-click the node name (in the node list pane) and a new tab will open in the detail view pane showing the text and other sources that have been coded at that node (NVUS, pp. 153–8).

This code and retrieve activity is a central one in the analytic process. First, it enables you to check that the theme you have identified makes sense, is well evidenced by the sources you have coded and that the coding has been done consistently. It is thus a way of checking the quality of your analysis. Second, you can begin to look for patterns within the data sources coded to the same theme. For example, you can compare the results across different cases to see whether there are differences in what has been coded between groups of cases – perhaps all the older cases talk about this thematic issue in a different way from the younger ones. In this way you can build up a more sophisticated account of what is happening among the cases in your study.

Coding crisis

A common problem experienced by many researchers doing qualitative analysis and especially those using software to help them is to end up with too many codes and/or disorganised codes. This is not necessarily a bad thing. It may simply reflect the heterogeneity of the data you are analysing and the complexity of your analysis. However, it can be a barrier to further analytic work and especially to developing a clear understanding and explanation of your data. There are several things you can do. For example, you could print out all the codes you have (possibly with definitions and even short samples of the coded text), cut them up and then try rearranging them. Alternatively you might cut and paste such details into a spreadsheet where you can use rows for each code and columns for things like definitions and examples and for other thoughts about the code. In both cases you are looking to rearrange and sort the codes or sometimes to re-express them. You should look for patterns and categories among the codes. One reason some researchers like to move away

from the software to do this is that you are attempting to rethink the analysis you are doing and moving away from the existing project stops it interfering in the rethink. Other things that might help with this rethink are re-examining the literature for ideas or talking about your research to colleagues or your supervisor.

Some heuristics that are useful here have been suggested by supporters of grounded theory: for example, the idea of dimensions of codes (Corbin and Strauss, 2008). This is the notion that codes can be of different kinds of thing or refer to different contexts etc. of the same thing. It is quite common in the early, open stages of coding to note down all the different varieties of things without noticing that they have anything in common. Thus you might have codes for note taking, summarising, writing prompt cards, re-reading and quizzing as ways of revising for exams. In this case there can be an overall code called 'Revising' and the others can be simply ways of doing that. In NVivo this can be done easily using the hierarchical coding system (the node tree) to make 'Revising' a parent node and 'note taking', 'summarising', etc. its children nodes (NVUS, pp. 145–52).

In other cases you may find that nodes are actually about the same thing but you didn't notice you had two of them when you were coding (perhaps they relate to different cases). In this case they can simply be combined. On the other hand, when looking carefully at both the definition of a node and the text that has been coded at it you might realise that there are two (or more) distinct analytic things represented by the coded items. In this case you can split the node by creating a new one and moving some of the coded items to the new node (and removing them from the old node).

Searching

CAQDAS programs, NVivo included, support two kinds of searching, searching for text, also called lexical searching, and searching for codes. Both can be used as ways of advancing the analytic process. In NVivo they are both types of query. Lexical searching is rather like the word searching facility in a word processor, only more powerful. In NVivo you can search for a number of different terms (perhaps synonyms) at the same time, search for word roots (and find all the words with different endings) and even search for words spelt like the terms you are using (NVUS, pp. 242–50). After the search NVivo lists all the terms it has found and you can then display these finds and look at each, in turn, in its context.

Lexical searching can help the analysis in a number of ways. First, it can be used a way of getting familiar with the text (in addition to reading the text, of course). Search for terms that are connected with your theoretical hunches and then inspect the passages where the terms are found in the original documents. This might produce new ideas or candidates for new nodes. Second, such searching can be used as a way of looking for passages similar to those you have already coded. Passages already coded will contain terms, words or phrases that might occur elsewhere and indicate similar topic matter. Put these terms and others you can think of into the text search tool to find all the further occurrences. Of course, this won't guarantee that you find all relevant passages but it can complement your reading of the data. Beware, sometimes the search will find passages that contain the term but just aren't relevant. You need to read each in turn and decide about its relevance. Third, you can use this approach as a way of checking the validity of your analysis and in particular you can check for the occurrence of negative cases – that is instances that are inconsistent with your explanations. You may have missed these because you just weren't expecting them in the context they appear. But if they use the same terms as other instances then lexical searching will find them. However, beware, this approach is not infallible. Relevant passages of text might just not use the terms you are searching for and so you won't find them. In the end you still need to read the text and inspect the other sources in a comprehensive way.

Searching for coded text and attributes

It is quite common, even in published work, for researchers just to summarise the major thematic codes in the report on their study. This expresses what they have found and, naturally, tends to be quite descriptive. Sometimes that is interesting, but qualitative studies can go a lot further and offer accounts of the patterns of the occurrence of such themes and, perhaps, suggest causes for those patterns. In CAQDAS programs it is searching for coded text and searching for attributes (often combined together) that support this. In this case what is compared in the search is the actual text coded at or linked to the node or attribute. Thus, in the simplest case, if you search for one node or another, what is compared is the text coded with those nodes. The search will find all the text coded at either node, if any (including that coded at both nodes, if any).

NVivo allows two or more nodes (and sometimes attributes too) to be searched for in combination (NVUS, pp. 233–7, 250–8). Such combination is divided into two kinds, Boolean and proximity. Boolean searches combine codes using the logical terms like 'AND', 'OR' and 'NOT'. Proximity searches rely on the coded text being near, after or perhaps overlapping some other coded text. Commonly used proximity searches are 'followed by' (also referred to as 'sequence' or 'preceding') and 'near' (also referred to as 'co-occurrence') (NVUS, pp. 263–6). Boolean searches are most useful in examining hypotheses or ideas about the data and rely on consistent and accurate coding, whereas proximity searches can be used more speculatively and to explore the data, often at an early stage of coding.

For instance, in a study of teachers' career development, you might wonder if male teachers had a different view from female teachers about career development courses. Assuming you had a node for 'career development courses' with lots of coding done and an attribute for gender, then you could search for text coded at the node 'career development courses' AND in cases with the attribute female, and then repeat it for the male cases and compare the two sets of data you have retrieved.

Teamwork

Using computers to assist with analysis is particularly useful when working in teams on projects. Partly this is because teams tend to work on larger projects with more respondents and more settings so the database is simply larger. However, teams need to be properly coordinated and can undertake certain kinds of cross checking – the software can be of crucial help here.

When working in a team, it makes sense, very early on in the project to create a model template for everyone to work on. This can be done in NVivo using the Project Properties (NVUS, pp. 51–6). Here you can set up all the users who are entitled to use and work on the project. You should password protect the project and decide whether each researcher has read only access to the data or whether they can edit the data as well. Of course it makes sense to have a convention for how you name sources (documents, videos, etc.) and cases and how you organise them in the project. One person, perhaps the senior researcher (or the NVivo expert), can set up the cases and import the documents available so far, and even establish some preliminary codes in the project along with associated definitions and linked memos about them. This project can then be shared with others in the team and those who you decide may do so can add more sources, coding and cases as appropriate.

When several people are working on the analysis then consistency in approach becomes an issue. This may be down to simple things like how large are the chunks of text that get coded. You might decide that a minimum size might be a sentence, or that where possible and appropriate several sentences or even whole paragraphs or speeches should be coded. In other cases, it is possible to assess the reliability of coding by comparing one coder's work with that of another (NVUS, pp. 267–8).

Resources

The CAQDAS Networking Project provides practical support, training and information in the use of a range of software programs designed to assist qualitative data analysis and has links to all the manufacturers' websites (see caqdas.soc.surrey.ac.uk).

QSR is the publisher of NVivo and on their website you will find pdf versions of the help files. For version 8 these are 'NVivo 8 Help – Using the Software' and 'NVivo 8 Help – Working with Your Data' and can be found by searching for the titles in the Resource Articles section. These documents are not available for version

9 yet, but you will find the video tutorials for version 9 very helpful. They can be found under Tutorial: NVivo 9 (see http://www.qsrinternational.com).

Questions for further investigation

1. Can software help with your project's analysis? Which software will support what you need to do and which do you have access to?
2. How will you set up your data set in the software program you are using? What are the main groups of documents? What are the cases? What initial, a priori codes will you use?
3. How can you use the software to ensure that your analysis is of high quality and any conclusions you draw from it are justified?
4. If you are working in a team, how will you organise the analytic work? Will you share the coding and, if so, how will you compare and combine the coding you have done?

Suggested further reading

NB: All the books mentioned here cover older versions of the software. However, their advice and much of the detailed instructions will still apply to the most recent versions.

Bazeley, P. (2007) *Qualitative Data Analysis with NVivo*. London: Sage. This works through all the stages of undertaking an analysis using one program, NVivo. There are detailed instructions on how to use the software at each step of your research.

di Gregorio, S. and Davidson, J. (2008) *Qualitative Research Design for Software Users*. Maidenhead: Open University Press, McGraw-Hill. Focuses on the issues around the ways that your research design will influence and be influenced by the use of software. In particular it contains sage advice about things to consider when first setting up your data in a new computer project.

Gibbs, G. R. (2007) *Analyzing Qualitative Data*. London: Sage. This is a more general book on qualitative analysis, but the last few chapters provide step-by-step instructions on how to get started in your analysis using either NVivo, MAXQDA or Atlas.ti.

Lewins, A. and Silver, C. (2007) *Using Software in Qualitative Research: A Step-by-Step Guide*. London: Sage. Written by two experts from the CAQDAS Networking Project, this covers in detail the three most popular programs, NVivo, MAXQDA and Atlas.ti, as well some discussion of other programs. There is good advice on how to choose which program is right for your analysis and how to set up and use the programs for your project. A new edition, covering the latest versions of the software is due out soon.

References

Corbin, J. M. and Strauss, A. L. (2008) *Basics of Qualitative Research: Techniques and Procedures for Developing Grounded Theory*. Thousand Oaks, CA: Sage.

Fielding, N. G. and Lee, R. M. (1998) *Computer Analysis and Qualitative Research*. London: Sage.

Miles, M. B. and Huberman, A. M. (1994) *Qualitative Data Analysis: A Sourcebook of New Methods*. Beverly Hills, CA: Sage.

34

Statistical analysis tools

Paul Connolly

Introduction

The purpose of this chapter is to provide you with a brief overview of a number of software packages available for statistical analysis. Having been introduced to a wide range of statistical techniques in previous chapters, this chapter takes a much more practical look at how you would go about performing some of these techniques. To do this we will take some real data and explore how they can be analysed with four statistical software packages: Excel, SPSS, Stata and MLwiN. The data are taken from a cluster randomised controlled trial that sought to evaluate the effects of a pre-school programme on improving young children's socio-emotional development, respect for cultural diversity and willingness to be inclusive of others.

Given the limited space available, this chapter is not intended to provide detailed guidance on how to use each of the four packages being featured. There already exist excellent introductory and advanced texts that do this for each of these packages and some suggested reading in this regard is provided at the end of the chapter. Rather, the purpose of this chapter is just to give you an overall sense of how researchers actually handle quantitative data and how they go about running the types of statistical analyses covered in previous chapters. In organising the chapter around

an analysis of some real data, the aim is to enable some comparisons to be made between the different software packages and their respective strengths and limitations. It is assumed that you already have some familiarity with the statistical techniques that will be used here (summary statistics, independent samples t-test, linear regression, and multilevel analysis) and, if not, you are encouraged to refer back to the relevant chapters that feature these techniques before continuing with this one.

The quantitative dataset

The first thing we need to do is to input our quantitative data into a file and prepare it ready for analysis. The data we will be analysing in this chapter form just a small part of a much larger cluster randomised controlled trial. The trial itself took place over a whole academic year (October 2008 to May 2009) and involved 1,081 children aged 3–4 years attending 74 pre-school settings. The settings were initially recruited to the trial and then randomly assigned either to be trained in and then undertake the pre-school programme for the year (the intervention group) or to continue with their normal activities (the control group). The programme itself – the *Media Initiative for Children Respecting Difference Programme* – is aimed at 3–4 year olds and seeks to increase their: socio-emotional understanding, respect for cultural diversity, and willingness to be inclusive of others. For this chapter we will focus on just three outcomes relating to their socio-emotional understanding which were:

- children's ability to recognise emotions in others;
- children's ability to recognise instances of exclusion;
- children's ability to recognise how being excluded makes someone feel.

The first outcome, emotional recognition, was measured on a continuous scale with a range of 0 to 8 while the other two outcomes were simple binary measures indicating whether a child was able to demonstrate awareness of exclusion (or of how being excluded made someone feel) or not. Data were collected through interviews with each of the children individually prior to the commencement of the programme in September 2008 and then again at the end of the programme in June 2009. More details on each of these measures, together with further information on the programme and full details of the research instrument and data collection methods, are provided in the main report of this trial that is available to download online (see Connolly et al., 2010).

The data relating to these variables have been entered into a simple Excel spreadsheet as shown in Figure 34.1. This is the typical format of a quantitative dataset and one recognised and used by nearly all statistical software packages. As can be seen, the dataset comprises an array of numbers organised into rows and columns. Each row (running horizontally) represents an individual case (in this instance a child) and each column (running vertically) represents a variable. It can be seen that, barring the first row of variable names, data for the first 25 children are visible. This is just a small fraction of the dataset, however, and it is possible in Excel to use the right-hand scrollbar to move right down the dataset to view the final 1,081st child.

In relation to the columns, it can be seen that there are nine variables in total with the final six variables representing each child's pre-test and post-test scores for the three outcome variables described above

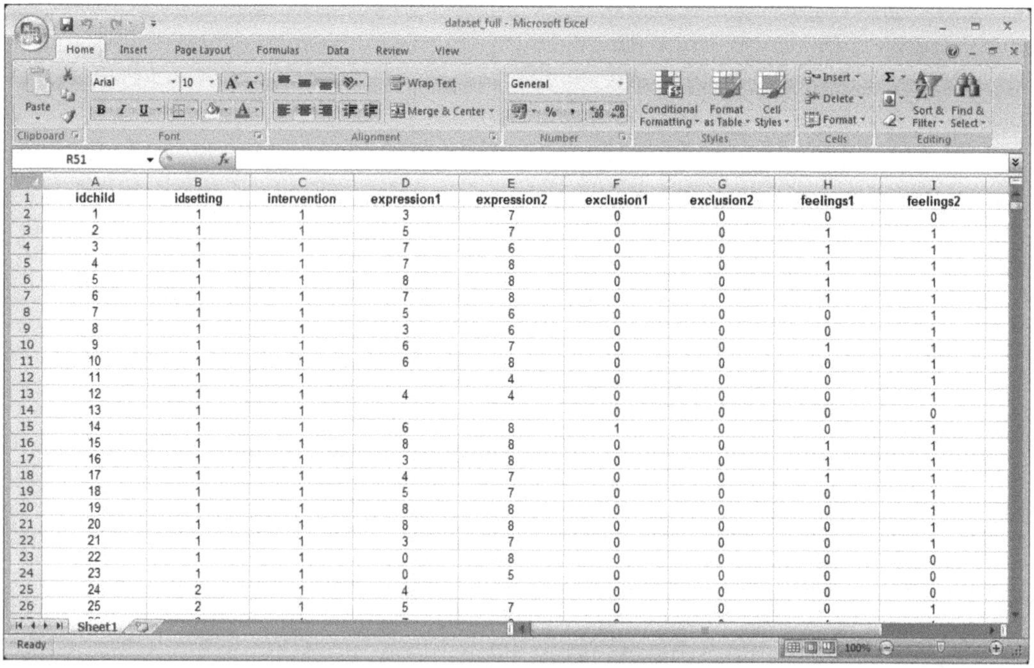

idchild	idsetting	intervention	expression1	expression2	exclusion1	exclusion2	feelings1	feelings2
1	1	1	3	7	0	0	0	0
2	1	1	5	7	0	0	1	1
3	1	1	7	6	0	0	1	1
4	1	1	7	8	0	0	1	1
5	1	1	8	8	0	0	1	1
6	1	1	7	8	0	0	1	1
7	1	1	5	6	0	0	0	1
8	1	1	3	6	0	0	0	1
9	1	1	6	7	0	0	1	1
10	1	1	6	8	0	0	0	1
11	1	1		4	0	0	0	1
12	1	1	4	4	0	0	0	1
13	1	1			0	0	0	0
14	1	1	6	8	1	0	0	1
15	1	1	8	8	0	0	1	1
16	1	1	3	8	0	0	1	1
17	1	1	4	7	0	0	1	1
18	1	1	5	7	0	0	0	1
19	1	1	8	8	0	0	0	1
20	1	1	8	8	0	0	0	1
21	1	1	3	7	0	0	0	1
22	1	1	0	8	0	0	0	0
23	1	1	0	5	0	0	0	0
24	2	1	4		0	0	0	0
25	2	1	5	7	0	0	0	1

Figure 34.1 The first 25 cases of the dataset as they appear in Excel

(indicated with the suffixes '1' and '2' respectively). If you look at the numbers in each column then you can see that they range from '0' to '8' for the two expression variables and take on the values of '0' or '1' for the exclusion and feelings variables. The first three variables in the dataset represent a child's unique identifying number, a unique identifying number for the pre-school setting they attended and a dichotomous variable coded '1' if that setting was part of the intervention group and '0' if it was part of the control group. It can also be seen that some of the individual boxes (called 'cells') are empty, indicating that some data are missing.[1]

By way of illustration let us take the first child in the dataset (with the unique identifying number '1'). It can be seen from Figure 34.1 that this child attended setting number '1' that was, in turn, part of the intervention group and that his/her emotional recognition score changed from '3' at pre-test to '7' at post-test. Interestingly, this child failed to demonstrate recognition of an instance of exclusion or of understanding how it feels to be excluded at pre-test and this did not change at post-test (with all four variables coded '0').

Statistical analysis with Excel

We have begun with Excel as this is likely to be the software package that students are most familiar with and the one they are also likely to have used the most. While you may well have used it previously as a simple spreadsheet, it is easy to overlook the fact that Excel is also capable of performing most of the common forms of statistical analysis that you are likely to wish to undertake for a simple quantitative education research project. To illustrate this, Figure 34.2 shows how Excel can be used to perform an initial analysis of the present data. Simply for the purposes of fitting all of the relevant information onto one screen, I have removed all but three of the original variables.

The first piece of analysis we can perform is to compare the two groups of children at post-test to see if their scores in relation to the first outcome variable – emotional recognition – differ. As the two groups of children have been allocated randomly then we would expect them to be broadly similar (although we should never assume this) and so a simple comparison of their post-test scores should provide the first indication of

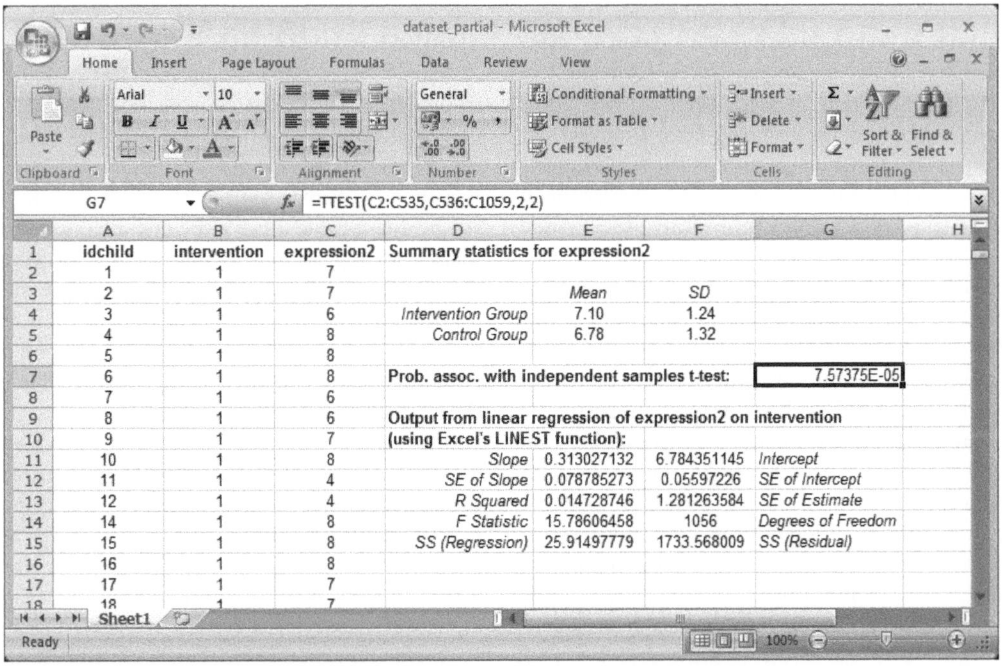

Figure 34.2   Statistical analysis in Excel

whether the programme has been more effective in improving the children's ability to recognise emotions in comparison with what pre-schools will have normally done.

To calculate the mean post-test emotional recognition score for children in the intervention group, you begin by clicking in any empty cell (I chose cell E5), and then typing in the formula '=AVERAGE(C2:C535)' before pressing the return key. This formula tells Excel to calculate the average (in this case the mean score) for all of the numbers in cells C2 through to C535 inclusive (i.e. all of those in the intervention group) and to display the resultant score in this cell. The dataset has been sorted so that all of the children in the intervention group come first, followed by all those in the control group.

In a similar vein, the mean score for those in the control group is calculated by clicking in another cell (in this case I chose E4) and typing in the formula '=AVERAGE(C36:C1059)' and pressing return.[2] The standard deviations associated with both these mean scores are also calculated in a similar way by clicking in empty cells (F5 and F4 respectively) and typing in the formulae 'STDEV(C2:C535)' and 'STDEV(C536:C1059)' respectively. It can be seen from Figure 34.2 that, in addition to entering these four formulae, I have also just added some text in the accompanying cells to label each of the scores generated. Also, and for completeness, I should say that I have also formatted these cells (by selecting the 'Format' option from the menu above the spreadsheet) so that the figures are only reported to two decimal places.

As can be seen, at first sight there does seem to be a positive effect associated with the programme, with the children in the intervention group having a mean emotional recognition score of 7.10 (sd = 1.24) compared to 6.78 (sd = 1.32) among those in the control group. Of course there is the possibility that this difference could have occurred randomly, with the original process of random allocation possibly creating two slightly different groups of children. We can assess what evidence there is for this by conducting an independent samples t-test. To do this, we simply select any empty cell (cell G7 in my case) and type in the following formula before clicking return: '=TTEST(C2:C535,C536:C1059,2,2)' It can be seen in Figure 34.2 that as cell G7 has been selected, then the reference 'G7' appears in the window immediately above the column headers and this is followed, to the right, by the formula that has been entered into that cell.

This TTEST function returns the probability associated with an independent samples t-test that compares the mean scores of the two groups of cases 'C2:C535' and 'C536:C1059' against a two-tailed test, assuming that the variances of the two groups of cases are similar (the last two digits in the formula – '2' and '2' respectively – specify these two options). The figure that is produced, 7.57375E-05, is interpreted as 7.57375×10^{-5} or 0.0000757375. As such, with $p = 0.000076$ we can conclude that the difference in mean scores between the children in the intervention and control groups is highly unlikely to have occurred by chance.

Another way of conducting the same test for statistical significance is by using linear regression. This can also be undertaken in Excel by selecting ten empty available cells (organised in five rows and two columns) and entering the following formula into the top left cell of those selected: '=LINEST(C2:C1059,B2:B1059,TRUE,TRUE)'. This formula tells Excel to regress the variable found in cells 'C2:C1059' (the response or dependent variable, 'expression2' in this case) on those found in cells 'B2:B1059' (the predictor or independent variable, 'intervention' in this case) and then to display various statistics associated with the resultant model in the ten cells selected. It can be seen from Figure 34.2 that the ten cells selected in this case were E11:F15 and the formula was therefore entered into cell E11. Unfortunately, Excel simply returns the statistics without any labels. To help interpretation I have therefore typed in labels for each of the statistics produced.

For now, we shall just concern ourselves with the estimates produced through the linear regression for the intercept and slope. These, in turn, give us the following formula for a child's predicted post-test emotional recognition score, based on whether they were a member of the control or intervention group:

$$\text{expression2} = 6.78435 + 0.31303 * \text{intervention}$$

As the variable 'intervention' was coded '0' for those in the control group, we can use this formula to predict that the mean emotional recognition score for a child in the control group at post-test will be: 6.78435 + 0.31303*(0) = 6.78435, or 6.78 if we round it up to two decimal places. Similarly, as those in the intervention group were coded '1', we can use the formula to predict their mean post-test score as: 6.78435 + 0.31303*(1) = 7.09738, or 7.10 if we again round this up to two decimal places. Not surprisingly, these two mean scores tally with those calculated earlier. It can be seen that the coefficient for 'intervention' (0.31303) therefore represents the average increase in a child's emotional recognition score for those in the intervention group compared to those in the control group. Unfortunately, Excel does not report whether this coefficient is significant as part of the output it produces for the LINEST function. However, this can be calculated using some of the other information provided and this would give us the same significance value of p = 0.000076.[3]

Whichever way we test the difference in mean emotional recognition scores between the intervention and control group, we thus arrive at the same result which is that the difference is highly statistically significant. This, then, is where we can draw our first tentative conclusion based upon the logic of randomised controlled trials. In essence we can assume that if our sample is large enough then the random allocation of the children will have produced two well-matched groups who are only likely to differ due to random variation. The significance test reported above tells us that such random variation is unlikely to be the cause of the difference in post-test scores that we have found. Thus, as the only other difference between the children is that one has participated in the Media Initiative programme for the last year while the other has not, we can therefore conclude with a degree of confidence that the higher emotional recognition scores found among those children in the intervention group must be due to the effects of the programme.

Statistical analysis with SPSS

There are, however, two limitations with the logic outlined above. The first is that the random allocation

procedure may still have created two groups that are different at pre-test and so, at the very least, simply comparing post-test scores like this may give inaccurate estimates of the size of the differences found between the groups. The second is that this particular trial was actually a *cluster* randomised trial meaning that the units of randomisation were the 74 pre-school settings rather than individual children. While this could increase the risk of producing two groups that may differ at pre-test, a more serious concern is that unless the clustered nature of the data is accounted for in the analysis then this is likely to produce findings that can be misleading (most simply, findings that may be statistically significant when they should not be).

One way to address the first issue is to control for any pre-test differences in the analysis. This can be done very simply by extending the linear regression model described above to include an additional independent variable representing the children's pre-test scores. While we can perform this analysis in Excel, we will use the opportunity to illustrate the second software package, SPSS. The main SPSS environment is shown in Figure 34.3. Ignoring the drop-down menus for the moment, it can be seen that the dataset is essentially in the same format as that for Excel. Each row represents one case and the names of the nine variables can be seen running across the top of the first nine columns. When you open SPSS for the first time, it is possible to select the option of just typing in data into the cells just as you would in Excel. However, one useful feature of SPSS is that you can import existing datasets, including those created in Excel. In addition, and in this present case, it is as easy just to select and copy all of the data in the Excel worksheet and then simply paste it into SPSS.

If you look to the bottom left of the SPSS window shown in Figure 34.3, you can see two tabs. The one currently selected is 'Data View' and this is why the data is currently being displayed in the main area of the window. However, if you selected 'Variable View' you would see a list of the variables instead. It is in Variable View where you would create or edit the names of your variables ('idchild', 'idschool' and so on) and also where you can set labels for particular values of a variable (i.e. in relation to 'exclusion1' we could label '0' as 'Did not recognize exclusion' and '1' as 'Recognized exclusion').

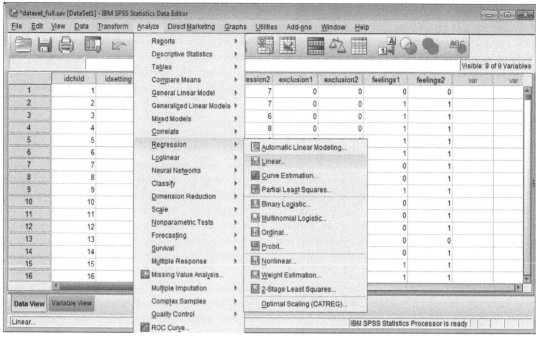

Reprint courtesy of International Business Machines Corporation, © SPSS, Inc., an IBM Company.

Figure 34.3   Undertaking linear regression in SPSS

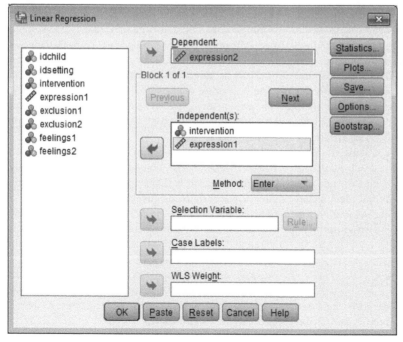

Reprint courtesy of International Business Machines Corporation, © SPSS, Inc., an IBM Company.

Figure 34.4   The Linear Regression window in SPSS

One of the benefits of SPSS over software packages like Excel is the drop-down menu system that tends to make performing statistical analysis much simpler. In relation to the present case where we wish to undertake a linear regression, it can be seen from Figure 34.3 that we just need to select 'Analyze → Regression → Linear . . .' This opens up the second window shown in Figure 34.4. As can be seen, all of the variable names are listed to the left and all we need to do is to select the relevant variables and use the arrow buttons to move them across to the windows to the right to designate them either as dependent or independent variables. For the default model and output we then just need to click the 'OK' button and the results appear in a separate SPSS Output Window that is shown in Figure 34.5.

As can be seen, SPSS presents the output from the linear regression in a very clear way. For the purposes of the present analysis, our main interest is the coefficients table and, particularly, the unstandardised coefficient for the independent variable 'intervention' (0.453) that now represents the difference in mean scores between the control and intervention groups once any variations in the children's pre-test scores ('expression1') have been controlled for. As can be seen, this difference is now greater than the raw difference between the mean post-test scores for the two groups (which was 0.313 from the earlier analysis in Excel). Moreover, we can calculate the standardised effect size for this difference of 0.453 simply by dividing it by the standard deviation of the post-test variable 'expression2' for the sample as a

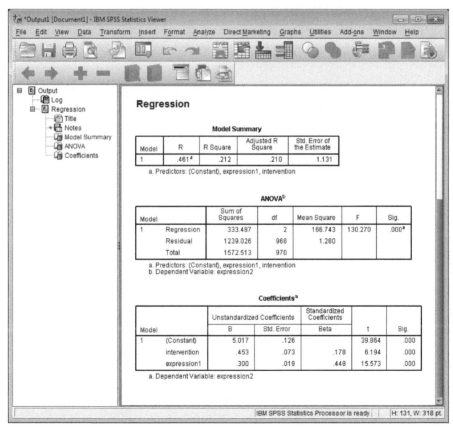

Reprint courtesy of International Business Machines Corporation, © SPSS, Inc., an IBM Company. Connolly, Statistical Analysis Tools.

Figure 34.5   SPSS output for a linear regression

whole.[4] Thus as the standard deviation for the sample as a whole is 1.290 then this gives us an estimated effect size of d = 0.453/1.290 = 0.351. Hence we can use this to conclude that participating in the Media Initiative programme is likely to lead to an increase in children's emotional recognition scores by 0.351 of a standard deviation. Interestingly, had we not controlled for differences in pre-test scores then this would have resulted in an under-estimated effect size of d = 0.313/1.290 = 0.243.

Statistical analysis in Stata

Another specialist software package for statistical analysis is Stata. The main Stata environment is shown in Figure 34.6. As can be seen, the Stata environment comprises four main windows: the Variables Window (bottom left) where all of the variables included in the dataset are listed; the Command Window (bottom right) where specific commands can be entered

directly; the main Output Window (top right) where the output generated by the commands appear; and the Command Window (top left) which keeps a running record of each command. The actual dataset can be viewed by clicking on the view dataset icon (third from the right in the row of icons immediately above the four main windows). The format of the dataset is just the same as it is in Excel and SPSS and data can either be typed directly into the separate dataset window once it is opened or copied and pasted into it. Stata also has the facility to import datasets in a variety of formats.

Just as with SPSS, Stata also has a simple to use drop-down menu system that can be used to perform statistical analyses. However, one of the strengths of Stata is its simple and intuitive command language that often makes it much quicker to run analyses by typing commands directly into the Command Window. Thus to run the simple linear regression we conducted earlier in Excel, where the variable 'expression2' was regressed on 'intervention', we simply type in the

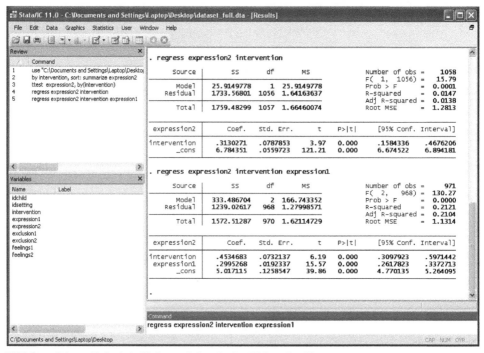

StataCorp. 2009. Stata: Release 11. Statistical Software. College Station, TX: StataCorp LP.

Figure 34.6 Linear regresson in Stata

```
. xtmixed expression2 intervention expression1, || idsetting:, mle variance

Performing EM optimization:

Performing gradient-based optimization:

Iteration 0:   log likelihood = -1486.6935
Iteration 1:   log likelihood = -1486.693
Iteration 2:   log likelihood = -1486.693

Computing standard errors:

Mixed-effects ML regression              Number of obs      =        971
Group variable: idsetting                Number of groups   =         73

                                         Obs per group: min =          1
                                                        avg =       13.3
                                                        max =         48

                                         Wald chi2(2)       =     255.21
Log likelihood = -1486.693               Prob > chi2        =     0.0000

------------------------------------------------------------------------------
 expression2 |      Coef.   Std. Err.      z    P>|z|     [95% Conf. Interval]
-------------+----------------------------------------------------------------
intervention |   .4323839   .1024158     4.22   0.000     .2316525    .6331152
 expression1 |   .3034466   .0192968    15.73   0.000     .2656255    .3412677
       _cons |    4.97564    .136818    36.37   0.000     4.707482    5.243798
------------------------------------------------------------------------------


------------------------------------------------------------------------------
  Random-effects Parameters  |   Estimate   Std. Err.     [95% Conf. Interval]
-----------------------------+------------------------------------------------
idsetting: Identity          |
                 var(_cons)  |   .0807659   .0303175      .0386997    .1685575
-----------------------------+------------------------------------------------
               var(Residual) |   1.196758   .0562816      1.09138     1.312312
------------------------------------------------------------------------------
LR test vs. linear regression: chibar2(01) =    18.88 Prob >= chibar2 = 0.0000
```

StataCorp. 2009. Stata: Release 11. Statistical Software. College Station, TX: StataCorp LP.

Figure 34.7   Output of multilevel linear regression model in Stata

command: 'regress expression2 intervention' (i.e. the command 'regress' followed by the dependent variable and then any independent variables in the model). In a similar vein, to run the extended regression model we illustrated with SPSS we simply type in 'regress expression2 intervention expression1'. As can be seen, each of these commands appears in the Output Window followed by the relevant output. For the interested reader, the output for both of these models can be compared with the same models generated in Excel and SPSS respectively. Fortunately, the results are all the same!

One of the benefits of Stata over SPSS is that it is better able to handle and run a range of multi-level models. This takes us on to the second concern raised earlier regarding the simple analysis of post-test scores undertaken in Excel: the need to address the effects of clustering. One way of doing this is to run the same extended linear regression model but as a multi-level model with children (level one) nested within pre-school settings (level two). The command for doing this in Stata and the resultant output are shown in Figure 34.7. It can be seen that the first part of the command is similar to that for a single-level linear

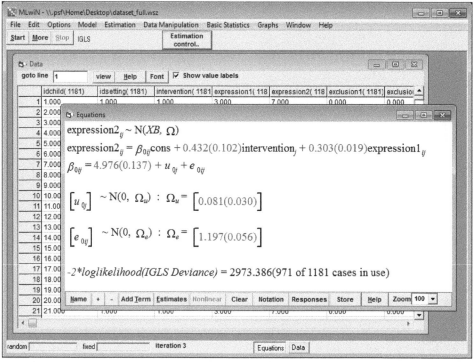

Rasbash, J., Charlton, C., Browne, W. J., Healy, M. and Cameron, B. (2005) MLwiN Version 2.02. Centre for Multilevel Modelling, University of Bristol.

Figure 34.8 Multilevel linear regression with MLwiN

regression, but just starting with the command name 'xtmixed'. What follows is the name of the level two variable ('idsetting') and then, after the final comma, any options that you wish to specify (in this case we have just asked Stata to use maximum likelihood estimation, 'mle', and to report variances and covariances for the random parts of the model). It does not take long to learn the format of commands like this. However, for those new to Stata it is always possible to run the first model using the drop-down menu and then to cut and paste the resultant commands into the Command Window and adapt them when wishing to run further models.

The model reported in Figure 34.7 now represents the appropriate way of analysing a cluster randomised controlled trial as it not only controls for any pre-test differences but also properly takes into account the clustered nature of the data. As can be seen, there is a slight change in the coefficient for 'intervention'

(changing from 0.453 to 0.432) and also, as expected, the standard error of this estimate has increased (from 0.073 for the single level model to 0.102 for this multi-level model). As it happens, given that the original difference was highly statistically significant then this increase in the standard error has had little effect on the findings. However, for effects that are smaller and/or that are only marginally statistically significant then appropriately accounting for the clustering of the data in this way can change the findings notably (see Bland, 2010).

Statistical analysis with MLwiN

Finally, it is worth briefly introducing the more specialist multi-level software package MLwiN just to illustrate another type of user interface. The main MLwiN environment is shown in Figure 34.8. As can be seen, MLwiN uses a windows-based system. In Figure 34.8 there are currently two windows open within the main MLwiN environment: the Data Window and the Equations Window. The former simply displays the dataset in exactly the same format as with the other software packages covered in this chapter. This is the window that one would open to type in data directly and/or copy and paste data. There is also a separate Names Window (similar to the Variable View feature in SPSS) which includes a list of variables in the dataset and that can be used to rename variables and assign labels to particular values within variables.

Perhaps the most notable difference between MLwiN and the other packages featured in this chapter is the Equations Window. This is, in essence, where the statistical models are generated and then estimated. When this window is first opened it simply has the following information:

$$y \sim N(XB, \Omega)$$
$$y = \beta_0 x_0$$

This is the default starting point based on an assumption that the response variable, y, is normally distributed. If the variable follows a different distribution (i.e. binomial or poisson) then you simply click anywhere on 'N(XB, Ω)' and a pop-up window appears allowing you to set a different distribution ('binomial', for example, if you wished to undertake a logistic regression). The model is then built up in a similar interactive way. Thus to set the response variable you simply click on 'y' and a pop-up window opens that allows you to select the variable you require from a list of all variables in the dataset. It also asks you to specify how many levels are in the model and which variables represent which levels (in our case there are two levels with 'idchild' representing level one and 'idsetting' representing level two). You then build up the right-hand side of the model in the same way. You can click on the 'Add Term' button at the bottom of the Equations Window to add additional new terms and then clicking on each term will open a pop-up menu to allow you to select which variable you wish to include.

As you build the model in the first instance each term will be preceded by the numbers '1.000(1.000)'

that will appear in blue. These represent the estimated coefficient and associated standard error for that term. When they are coloured blue this indicates that the model has yet to be estimated. Once the model has been built up as required the last step in the process is to run the algorithm to estimate the model parameters and this is done by clicking the 'Start' button at the top of the main MLwiN Window. Once the model has been estimated, all of the parameters turn green in colour. Figure 34.8 illustrates this by showing the estimated multi-level model that we generated earlier in Stata. You can compare the parameters estimated here with those in the same model estimated with Stata. Reassuringly once more, the figures are all the same!

Conclusion

Given the limits of space it has only been possible to provide the very briefest of overviews of software packages that can be used to undertake statistical analysis. As has been seen, at the heart of all of the packages featured here is the dataset that takes the same format each time of individual cases organised into rows and variables into columns. Once you have a dataset ready to analyse you are faced with the decision of which statistical software package to use. In this chapter we have looked at four of them – Excel, SPSS, Stata and MLwiN – and shown that each has its particular strengths and limitations. Perhaps the main strength of Excel is its wide availability and the likelihood that many people reading this book will already have it on their laptop or PC, or have something very similar (like 'Numbers' for Macs). As shown in this chapter, for simple statistical analysis it has much to commend it. However, if you are planning to undertake a fair amount of statistical analysis, and/or analysis that is more advanced, then a dedicated statistics software package with a simple graphical user interface like SPSS or Stata (or other packages such as Minitab) will be more appropriate. Given the types of analysis most students in education are likely to perform – such as standard hypothesis testing and common multivariate techniques such as multiple regression, factor analysis and cluster analysis – then there is little to distinguish between packages like these. However, it is also likely that there will be occasions when some students may need to supplement one of these generic statistics packages should they wish to undertake more specialist statistical analysis. While Stata can handle much multi-level modelling, it is arguably the case that more specialist multi-level modelling packages such as MLwiN and HLM have a greater degree of flexibility and range of options available. Moreover, some techniques such as structural equation modelling require more specialist statistics packages like Amos or Lisrel.

Perhaps the main advice is for you to 'shop around' and try out some of these packages for yourself to see what suits your own style and requirements the most. Fortunately, trial versions of most of the statistics packages available can be downloaded free of charge in order for you to try them for yourself. Prior to doing this, you should consult some of the many reference books out there that will provide you with a practical orientation to the software you are interesting in trying out, whether that be Excel (Schmuller, 2009), SPSS (Muijs, 2004; Connolly, 2007) or Stata (Acock, 2010; Kohler and Kreuter, 2009). For MLwiN there is a dedicated website (http://www.cmm.bristol.ac.uk) where a trial version of the package can be downloaded and also where the User Manual is available for free, as well as a wide range of online resources provided to guide you through your first analyses with MLwiN.

Questions for further investigation

1. Try using the statistics software packages mentioned above (Excel, SPSS, Stata, etc.). Which do you find easiest to use, and for what purposes? List the pros and cons of each package.

Notes

1. While there are various options available in relation to how best to deal with missing data like this, including in-putting values, these are beyond the scope of this present chapter. As such, and for the purposes of the analyses to follow, all missing data are simply left as they are.
2. You may have noticed that there are now just 1,058 cases whereas the original sample comprises 1,081 children. The reason for this is that I have deleted all cases where

there is a missing value for the variable 'expression2'. If you compare Figures 34.1 and 34.2, for example, you will see that child '13' has been deleted. It is not necessary to do this before using the AVERAGE function in Excel; however, it is necessary before the LINEST function can be used that will be discussed shortly.

3. In this case, the test statistic for calculating the significance of the slope term is calculated by dividing the value of the slope by its standard error, which is 0.07879 in this case as shown in Figure 34.2. The test statistic, t, is therefore $0.31303/0.07879 = 3.973$. This, in turn, can then be used to calculate the probability associated with this statistic for 1,056 degrees of freedom which is $p = 0.000076$.

4. This effect size measure is Cohen's d that represents the difference between two mean scores divided by their pooled standard deviation.

Suggested further reading

Connolly, P. (2007) *Quantitative Data Analysis in Education: A Critical Introduction Using SPSS*. London: Routledge. This text provides illustrated step-by-step guides showing how to use SPSS, with plenty of exercises to encourage the reader to practise and consolidate their new skills.

Schmuller, J. (2009) *Statistical Analysis with Excel for Dummies* (2nd edn). Hoboken, NJ: Wiley. This book makes it easy to crunch numbers and interpret statistics with Excel, information that will help readers improve their performance on the job or in the classroom.

References

Acock, A. C. (2010) *A Gentle Introduction to Stata* (3rd edn). College Station, TX: Stata Press.

Bland, J. M. (2010) 'Analysing cluster randomized controlled trials in education', *Effective Education*, 2: 165–80.

Connolly, P. (2007) *Quantitative Data Analysis in Education: A Critical Introduction Using SPSS*. London: Routledge.

Connolly, P., Miller, S. and Eakin, A. (2010) *A Cluster Randomised Trial Evaluation of the Media Initiative for Children: Respecting Difference Programme*. Belfast: Centre for Effective Education, Queen's University Belfast. Available at: http://www.qub.ac.uk/cee (accessed 19 November 2011).

Kohler, U. and Kreuter, F. (2009) *Data Analysis Using Stata* (2nd edn). College Station, TX: Stata Press.

Muijs, D. (2004) *Doing Quantitative Research in Education with SPSS*. London: Sage.

Rasbash, J., Charlton, C., Browne, W. J., Healy, M. and Cameron, B. (2005) MLwiN Version 2.02. Centre for Multilevel Modelling, University of Bristol.

Schmuller, J. (2009) *Statistical Analysis with Excel for Dummies* (2nd edn). Hoboken, NJ: Wiley.

Discourse analysis

Elaine Vaughan

Introduction

Discourse is all around us, as McCarthy et al. (2002: 55) so succinctly put it: 'Life is a constant flow of discourse – of language functioning in one of the many contexts that together make up a culture.' In an obvious, though nevertheless taken-for-granted, way, language is intrinsic to the creation and maintenance of the institutions and practices that we may wish to investigate as educational researchers; hence the importance of discourse analysis, and its critical contribution to our analytical toolkit. But discourse analysis is a teeming field, as Taylor (2001: 10) suggests that any budding researcher who has attempted a literature search on the topic will attest, made up of a variety of disciplinary fields, all of which take a specific view of what *discourse* and *discourse analysis* means. In this chapter, an overview of the provenance of what has come to be termed discourse analysis will be outlined. As it is not possible to deal with all of these in detail, a selection of fields, their theoretical backgrounds and methodological concerns will be discussed. Research methods are rarely, if ever, independent of some epistemological stance (Gee, 2005: 6), and so this direction is taken in order to illustrate how the findings a researcher might arrive at

by using a particular discourse analytic approach are inextricably linked to the theory that underlies their method.

If we start with what is meant by the term *discourse analysis*, we will find that it is defined by Stubbs (1983: 1) as referring to the study of '. . . the organisation of language above the sentence'; Brown and Yule (1983: 1) see the analysis of discourse as '. . . necessarily, the analysis of language in use', while for Fairclough (1992: 28), discourse itself is '. . . more than just language use: it is language use, whether speech or writing, seen as a type of social practice.' Schiffrin (1994: viii) provides a useful way of conceptualising what discourse analysis is about in her identification of some of the questions that discourse analysts, whatever their disciplinary origin or theoretical bent, attempt to answer: 'How do we organise language into units that are larger than the sentence? How do we use language to convey information about the world, ourselves, and our social relationships?' Jaworski and Coupland (1999: 3) state that the reason that discourse 'falls squarely within the interests not only of linguists, literary critics, critical theorists and communication scientists, but also of geographers, philosophers, political scientists, sociologists, anthropologists, social psychologists and many others' (we might add here 'and educational researchers') is because 'despite important differences of emphasis, discourse is an inescapably important concept for understanding society and human responses to it, as well as for understanding language itself.' Therefore, for linguists and those interested in how language works, and for those whose research agenda foregrounds how language is implicated in social processes, discourse analytic methods are relevant.

Approaches to discourse analysis

As previously mentioned, the ways in which discourse is conceptualised and studied have emerged from the theoretical viewpoint of many different disciplines, and though the approaches that have spread tentacle-like from these disciplines may differ, they are united in that now, on the whole, they prioritise naturally occurring language, as opposed to abstract formulations. The fact that there are such a range theoretical stances on discourse, situated in sometimes quite distinct perspectives which influence how discourse is defined, viewed and analysed, raises a very practical issue for the researcher: it can be difficult to ascertain where in the discourse analytic literature to start. As Gee (2005: 5) points out, no one approach to discourse analysis is '. . . uniquely "right." Different approaches fit different issues and questions better or worse than others. And, too, different approaches sometimes reach similar conclusions though using different tools and terminologies connected to different "micro-communities" of researchers.' There is a lot to be said, in fact, for taking an eclectic approach to discourse-based analysis (see also the suggested further readings at the end of the chapter). Eggins and Slade (1997: 24) present a useful schematic which positions their own eclectic approach to the analysis of casual conversation in relation to the theoretical origins of each discourse analytic approach they consider relevant to it, and this contributes to creating a coherent picture of discourse-focused research studies and the theoretical foundations they are built on (see also McCarthy et al. 2002: 60). Briefly then, and in very broad strokes, they describe the field of discourse analysis as being populated by work in:

- ethnomethodology (Garfinkel, 1967), a movement within the discipline of sociology, via *conversation analysis* (dealt with in more detail below);
- sociology and anthropology, via *interactional sociolinguistics* (concerned generally with how language is affected by the social context in which it takes place) and *variation theory* (which in its early stages, for example, was characterised by work which focused on the relationship between social and geographical factors and phonological patterns, e.g. Labov, 1972);
- the philosophy of language, via *Speech Act Theory* (which centres around the fact that we can 'do' things with words, like apologise, criticise or compliment) and *pragmatics* (a branch of analysis interested in the relationship between what is said and what is meant);
- linguistics, via structural-functional approaches to the analysis of language, such as the Birmingham School (see below for a more detailed view) and a research agenda which has come to be known as Critical Discourse Analysis, now quite distinct from, but originating in, critical linguistics.

For a more detailed and comprehensive overview of each of these discourse analytic areas, see Schiffrin (1994), Eggins and Slade (1997), Jaworski and Coupland (1999), Wetherell et al. (2001a, 2001b) or Schiffrin et al. (2003); for an excellent guide which situates discourse analysis for language teachers, see McCarthy (1991). The areas that will be discussed in greater detail here, along with a focus on how discourse is approached theoretically and methodologically and in terms of data collection and analysis, are Birmingham School discourse analysis and conversation analysis. This selection of approaches may seem quite random; however, one of the critical touchstones for any researcher seeking to explore discourse analysis in relation to educational research is Sinclair and Coulthard's (1975) pioneering work on discourse structures in the classroom (this approach is frequently glossed as the Birmingham School of discourse analysis, the driving force having been a group of researchers at the University of Birmingham). Conversation analysis has contributed enormously to what has been described as 'institutional talk' –

arguably, what any educational researcher will be dealing with as data may well be broadly categorised thus.

Birmingham School

In 1975, Sinclair and Coulthard published a seminal paper describing a structural approach to the description of classroom discourse (Sinclair and Coulthard, 1975). The aim of this work was to investigate the structure of verbal interaction in the classroom and, crucially, anchor it to the discipline of linguistics (Coulthard, 1985: 120). The data they analysed was from traditional teacher-fronted lessons in England, the teacher asking 'display' questions (i.e. questions to which they know the answer) and the pupils answering these questions when nominated by the teacher. Below is an extract typical of the data they analysed (Extract 1):

Extract 1

T = Teacher; P = any pupil who answers

T: Now then. I've got some things here too. Hands up. <u>What's that? What is it?</u>
P: <u>Saw.</u>
T: <u>It's a saw. Yes this is a saw</u>. What do we do with a saw?
P: Cut wood.
T: Yes, you're shouting though. <u>What do we do with a saw? Marvelette?</u>
P: <u>Cut wood.</u>
T: <u>We cut wood.</u>
(Sinclair and Coulthard, 1975: 93–4)

The boundary of the lesson is realised in 'Now then' these boundaries are categorised as *transactions*. Sinclair and Coulthard called the question-answer-feedback sequences (underlined in the extract) *exchanges*. These exchanges are made up of different *moves*, a questioning move, an answering move and a feedback move. Finally, within these moves, we can see individual actions, such as the nomination of a student to answer a question, or an instruction to the students to raise their hands, even an admonishment to the pupil who shouts his or her answer – these they classified as *acts*. The status and relationship of moves and acts in discourse is very similar to that of words and morphemes in grammar (Coulthard, 1985: 125) 'whereby words combine to make groups, groups combine to make clauses and clauses combine to make sentences' (Hoey, 1993: 115). In this respect, Sinclair and Coulthard draw heavily on the early descriptive work of Halliday (1961; the Hallidayan approach to discourse has been very influential, and is strongly connected to an approach to discourse analysis termed *Systemic-Functional Linguistics*). This is very clearly evidenced in the model they developed to describe how smaller units combine with other units of the same size to form larger units; *lesson* is at the 'top' of their rank-scale model for classroom discourse. In descending order of size, their analytical units are *transaction*, *exchange*, *move* and *act*: *acts* combine to form *moves* which in turn combine to form *exchanges*, and so on.

Sinclair and Coulthard see the exchange as the heart of classroom discourse (Hoey, 1993: 116). A three-move structure was proposed for exchanges – *Initiation*, *Response* and *Feedback* (IRF). They posited that all exchanges will feature Initiation and Response but not necessarily Feedback, later Follow-up. As Hoey observes (1993: 118), 'Feedback is uncommon in some interactive genres, while in others, like classroom discourse and quiz shows, it is virtually compulsory.' They distinguish between free and bound exchanges and teaching and boundary exchanges, which mark the boundaries of the major sections of the lesson. Stubbs (1983: 146) suggests that Sinclair and Coulthard's model is most suited to what he calls 'relatively formal situations in which a central aim is to formulate and transmit pieces of information' and so is ideal when analysing the structure of classroom discourse, doctor–patient interaction or service encounters (such as the interaction which occurs when we buy something in a shop or go to a hairdresser's, etc.). Casual conversation, however, does not necessarily lend itself to this type of analysis, given that its general aim could be said to be 'a phatic or social one rather than the transmission of information' (Clancy, 2004: 138). Stubbs (1983) and Hoey (1991 and 1993) have adapted Sinclair and Coulthard's model in order to analyse conversation in more informal settings. What they suggest is that exchange structure in everyday, naturally occurring spoken discourse is more complicated than the simple three-part exchange of Initiation – Response – Feedback. Hoey (1991: 74) states that:

> Just as most naturally occurring sentences are complex, that is, constructed out of one or more clause, so also most naturally occurring exchanges are complex – the result of combining two or more simple exchanges. The simple exchange is characterised by having a single initiation and response, while complex exchanges have one or more of each.

Hoey claims that speakers combine exchanges and in doing so make discourse more complex and flexible. The example from a study of family discourse (Clancy, 2004: 139) given in Extract 2 illustrates this complexity. In this extract, two family members, Susan and Tom, are discussing whether or not you can use a steam cleaner to clean a car.

Extract 2

S = Susan; T = Tom

T: Handy now if you had a what d'you ma call it? You know if you got a second hand car or anything like that.   Initiation

S: You're not supposed to be able to use it on a car on the outside of a car.   Response

T: I mean on the inside of it.   Feedback treated as Initiation

S: Oh yeah. It'd | it would clean the inside of a car no bother. But it's supposed to be too hot for the outside of a car.   Response

Here, *Feedback* is treated as *Initiation* and therefore the listener treats the *Feedback* as if a new exchange has been started. The discrepancy between the ad hoc nature of this tiny sliver of casual conversation and the excerpt from Sinclair and Coulthard's data is conspicuous. As Walsh (2006: 47) points out there is, furthermore, a major discrepancy between the

context of the 1960s primary school classroom and the contemporary, in Walsh's context, language classroom, which displays far more 'equity and partnership in the teaching-learning process' (2006: 47). Despite the fact that it has been shown to be perhaps too rigid for modern classroom discourse, Sinclair and Coulthard's model still has resonance for discourse analysts. Their theorising of the components of the exchange has been highly influential, and no discussion of discourse analysis, particularly as it relates to educational discourse, would be complete without it.

Conversation analysis

Conversation analysis (CA) has its theoretical roots in ethnomethodology, which itself is a hybrid research approach. The originator of the approach, sociologist Harold Garfinkel, modelled this hybrid label after existing terms in research concerned with cross-cultural analyses of 'doing' and 'knowing'. Essentially, it presupposes people have a reserve of common-sense knowledge regarding their activities and how those activities are organised within enterprises. It is this fundamental reserve which makes the knowledge orderable. Ethnomethodological research is thus concerned with revealing what it is that we know. Another suggestion within this area is that 'knowledge is neither autonomous nor decontextualised; rather, knowledge and action are deeply linked and mutually constitutive' (Schiffrin, 1994: 233). Furthermore, participants continuously engage in interpretive activity, negotiating and creating knowledge during the course of their social action; this action and interaction in turn generates the knowledge by which further activity can be created and sustained. Therefore, 'social action not only displays knowledge, it is also critical to the creation of knowledge' (Schiffrin, 1994: 233).

These precepts were then applied specifically to conversation, most significantly by Harvey Sacks, Emmanuel Schegloff and Gail Jefferson. To connect the principal ideological tenets of ethnomethodology and CA, let us assume that our knowledge manifests itself publicly in our utterances. These utterances are designed to occur in particular sequential and social contexts. Here, CA and ethnomethodology converge: conversation is how our sense of the world in general, and social order in particular, is both constructed and negotiated – we create our world with words. CA at this point diverges in its theoretical construction of underlying 'patterns' of conversation and its methods of analysis. It employs its own esoteric transcriptions, and notation of relevant features and '. . . its broader provenance extends to . . . the disposition of the body in gesture, posture, facial expression, and ongoing activities in the setting . . .' (Schegloff, 2002: 3).

Its catholic concerns mean there is much to interest the discourse analyst. Where it is most obviously at variance with other methods of discourse analysis is in the fact that it is wary of linguistic categorisation, namely in the categorisation of the linguistic function of specific items or phrases, believing categorisations may be over-generalised, indeed may not at all reflect the actual uses of the items or phrases. Conversation analysts also avoid making generalisations about what interactants (or participants) 'know', and deny that social 'identity' is necessarily a factor, insofar as 'social identity' is a problematic construct; more cautiously again, as Schegloff (1987: 219) asserts, '. . . the fact that they [social interactants] are "in fact" respectively a doctor and a patient does not make these characterisations *ipso facto* relevant.'

Heritage (1984: 241) lists three assumptions of CA:

- interaction is structurally organised;
- contributions to interaction are contextually oriented; and
- these two properties inhere in the details of interaction so that no order of detail can be dismissed a priori as disorderly, accidental or ir-relevant.

What is said not only constitutes data for analysis but also the basis of the development of hypotheses and conclusions for CA as a discipline. CA believes that interaction (conversational or otherwise) is 'structurally organised'. It articulates this *structure* through the isolation and analysis of certain features of conversation, for example, adjacency pairs. Schegloff and Sacks' (1973: 295–6) work on adjacency pairs defines them as two-part sequences, ordered as first part and second part. The presence of a first part requires the corollary presence of a second part, or one of an appropriate range of second parts. In other words, the first part of a pair *predicts* the occurrence of the second: 'Given a question, regularly enough an answer will follow' (Sacks, 1967, cited in Coulthard, 1985: 69). Adjacency pairs are integral to the turn-taking system in conversation (discussed below) and the absence of a second part is noticeable in conversation, if only for practical reasons (an unanswered question may stall the development of the conversation). Further work in analysing adjacency pairs (Pomerantz, 1984; Atkinson and Drew, 1979; Levinson, 1983) has developed the notion of preferred and dispreferred second parts. For example, an invitation first part 'prefers' an acceptance second part, as opposed to a refusal (even when this refusal is not a 'flat' refusal but tempered with an 'account' of the refusal). Hoey (1993) has also mentioned 'adjacency pairs' such as 'hi/hi' and 'how are you/fine' and defines them as 'frozen exchanges' – there is no need to actively process this type of interaction, though they are necessary procedural preambles to the development of the exchange (see section above for more on exchange structure analysis).

The most fundamental aspects of the *organisation* of conversation are, according to Schegloff (2002: 4–5):

(a) Turn-taking (the organisation of participation)

(b) Turn organisation (forming talk so that it is recognisable as a unit of participation)

(c) Action formation (forming talk so that it accomplishes one or more recognisable actions)

(d) Sequence organisation (deploying resources for making contributions cohere, for example, topically)

(e) Organisation of repair (dealing practically with problems in interaction, for example problems in hearing and/or understanding)

(f) Word/usage selection (selection, usage and understanding of words used to compose the interaction)

(g) Recipient design (all of the above as they relate to our co-participants in talk-in-interaction).

To extrapolate from these, the turn-taking system is of immediate concern to any analysis of talk in general, and of course institutional talk in particular. CA attempts to explain how participants in talk decide who talks, how the flow of conversation is maintained and how gaps and overlaps are avoided. It has posited '. . . a basic set of rules governing turn construction, providing for the allocation of a next turn to one party, and co-ordinating transfer so as to minimise gap and overlap' (Sacks et al., 1974: 12). A full discussion of these rules is not possible here. Probably the most salient aspect of the discussion of these turn-taking rules ('taking' in its literal sense) is the ability of participants to identify and seize upon 'transition-relevance places', i.e. points in the interaction where it is possible and/or appropriate to take or resume a turn so that the interaction runs smoothly.

Another of the above aspects that is particularly interesting is the idea of recipient design – the design of utterances or turns with a view to our co-participants. Tannen and Wallat for example, have studied how a paediatrician selects and switches between different linguistic registers according to whether she is addressing the mother or the child during the consultation (Tannen and Wallat, 1987, cited in Drew and Heritage, 1992: 9). In institutional talk, recipient design may not only be an asymmetrical phenomenon (where we, consciously or unconsciously, consider what the effect of our contributions on our superiors will be), but also of consideration in maintaining and enhancing our institutional and social profiles with regard to our colleagues. In terms of institutional talk, Heritage (2004: 225) suggests a number of dimensions of analysis that can reveal the 'fingerprint' (cf. Heritage and Greatbatch, 1991: 95–6) of the institutional situation under analysis. These are:

- its turn-taking system;
- the overall structure of the interaction;
- sequence organisation;
- turn design;
- lexical choice; and
- epistemological and other forms of asymmetry.

As an example of how CA-type analysis can be applied to real data, consider this extract from a staff meeting in the English language department of a public university. The meeting is drawing to a close, and the chair of the meeting is Peter, the head of department. Rita, Olivia, Harry and Julia are teachers in the department who are present at the meeting.

Extract 3

[Note: <\$O> marks the beginning of an overlapped utterance; <\\$O> marks the end of an overlapped utterance]

(1) **Peter: I'm teaching this after** I'll write that down chapter four done. Eh I think maybe should we I think we should meet maybe a little bit regularly. <\$O30> When could we meet again? <\\$O30>. **Is a weekly meeting maybe a little bit too maybe once a fortnight at least?**
(2) **Rita:** <\$O30> I think that would be a good idea <\\$O30>.
(3) **Olivia:** Yeah. Once a fortnight.
(4) **Peter:** Once a fortnight **okay**.
(5) **Harry:** Yeah we should try to start preparing for that PET exam like we need.
(6) **Julia:** We need to get all the resources.
(7) **Peter:** And resources for that as well. **Okay**.
(8) **Rita: Okay. Thank you**.
(Vaughan, 2009)

We can note a number of features of this closing phase. From the point that we pick up the interaction, there are eight turns which accomplish the closing of the meeting. Researchers have identified making arrangements as one of the sequence types regularly used to move out of closings along with back-references, topic initial elicitors (e.g. *yeah*, *okay*), in-conversation objects (e.g. minimal response tokens), solicitudes (*drive carefully*, *take care*), re-iterating the reason for a phone call and appreciations (*thank you*). At the end of the meeting, Peter (the head of department) moves to close by making an arrangement for the next meeting (*when could we meet again? Is a weekly meeting maybe a little bit too maybe once a fortnight at least?*). When two of the participants answer his question – Rita (3) and Olivia (4) – Peter summarises the response and this is bounded by *okay* suggesting a final turn. Harry, however, initiates a new topic (6) and this is supported by Julia (7); Peter moves to shut this topic down fairly decisively by summarising it and again bounding the move with *okay*. The meeting closes when Rita echoes the boundary marker and thanks Peter. The hierarchical, institutional nature of the talk is evident in the way that Peter, as head of department, takes control of the closing phase of the meeting (for more on meetings as interactional events and phases within them, see Bargiela-Chiappini and Harris, 1997). The relationship between language and power, both at the micro- and macro-level, is very much a concern of Critical Discourse Analysis (Fairclough, 1995, 2001; for an extensive overview of Critical Discourse Analysis in educational research, see Rogers et al., 2005).

Discourse analysis and teacher language: data and analysis

Turning our attention briefly to research on the topic of how teachers use language is helpful in terms of conceptualising what type of research is being done, how discourse analytic data is collected and analysed, and the ethical concerns that are implicated in accessing and using this type of data. Frequently, discourse analysis is categorised as an exclusively qualitative method; however, this is not always the case (as will be seen below). In addition, this sphere of research highlights how central understanding teacher language is in connection to how classrooms work, and how the profession considers its practices within them reflexively. Walsh (2006) in relation to English language teaching suggests that teachers' classroom language is characterised in the following ways:

- teachers control patterns of communication in the classroom;
- the classroom is dominated by question and answer routines;
- 'repair' or correction of learner errors is a prerogative of the teacher;
- teachers typically modify their speech to accommodate learners.

Walsh's own research proposes a framework (Self-Evaluation of Teacher Talk, or SETT) to aid teachers in their description of language used in this classroom context and as a conduit for understanding the complex interactional processes that occur within it (Walsh, 2006: 62–92). SETT is a very useful framework for

educators with an interest in researching teacher language in the classroom context, though most particularly so for those engaged in language teaching and learning.

More findings from the field of language teacher education (LTE) are also illuminating in terms of the professional concerns of language teachers. In the initial stages of LTE, the development of trainees' language awareness is obviously a priority. Trappes-Lomax and Ferguson (2002) highlight practical concerns in language education for trainees, such as meta-linguistic awareness, target language proficiency and pedagogical skills with regard to teaching language. While these concerns take centre stage, concepts such as language as a social institution, as verbal and reflexive practice and its position as the medium of classroom communication are considered neglected, though essential, aspects of teachers' language awareness. An example of the extent to which trainee teachers are required to be reflexive in their awareness of language and its use in the classroom is evident in Extract 4, which is taken from Farr's (2005a) analyses of trainer–trainee interaction in LTE in the Irish context (see also Farr, 2003, 2005b).

Extract 4

Tr = Trainer; Tee = Trainee

Tr: . . . now one area that I want you to try a difficult area to work on+
Tee: My voice is it? I noticed.
Tr: The sounds you know the pronunciation of the T H sounds+
Tee: Mmhm.
Tr: +ah don't don't do you ever use them correctly? You're from Cork are you?
Tee: Killarney.
Tr: Killarney.
(Farr, 2005a: 198)

The discourse of teacher training has huge potential as a route for investigation in educational research. Farr's work is focused on a specific event, feedback meetings on trainees' observed classes, an event within the initial training of teachers which is inherently face-threatening (Reppen and Vásquez, 2007:16). This is manifestly evident in the extract from Farr's data above: here the trainer is required to criticise the trainee's regional accent and contrast it with the 'correct' pronunciation she/he should be modelling for her/his students. Also in the teacher training context, Vásquez and Reppen (2007) report on collecting recordings of post-observation meetings. Both researchers were teaching on an MA in TESL (Teaching English as a Second Language) as part of which students gain practical English as a Second Language (ESL) teaching experience. The post-observation meetings conducted by them, as supervisors, were intended to engender a reflective rather than evaluative model of feedback, and so as supervisors/mentors they wished to create an open, discursive space to facilitate this (Vásquez and Reppen, 2007: 159). However, an analysis of the participation patterns in the meetings indicated that, in fact, the supervisors/mentors did more of the talking than the trainees. This empirical insight led to an actual change in practices for the supervisors/mentors involved. They increased the number of questions they asked the trainees, and thus they were able to turn the floor over to the trainees by creating more effective discursive conditions for reflection.

All discourse analysts use texts – whether spoken or written. Many of the spoken texts have been, in the past, transcriptions of interviews, for example, but also transcriptions of naturally occurring events and interactions. The act of transcribing these spoken interactions represents the final stage in data collection for analysts, the initial stages being the negotiation of access to the situation that will yield the desired spoken data and obtaining consent to record from potential participants. All academic institutions will have their own ethical guidelines and procedures, but the fundamentals of ethical access to and use of data require that participants are guaranteed anonymity – in transcribing the event participants should naturally be given pseudonyms; however, any other references within the transcript that could potentially identify the speakers should also be removed, such as institutional names, geographical references and so on. Transcription itself is, as Roberts (2010) points out, a great deal more and a great deal less than talk written down. The way in which an event is transcribed can bias how it is read and interpreted, and any transcription represents an event that has been reduced in two

ways: firstly, the recording removes it from its original context (live, online production of talk), and secondly, it is further reduced by being orthographically transcribed. In addition, transcriptions that attempt to be faithful to the original event by including pauses, hesitations, false starts, ellipses and contractions, to name but a few, run the risk of appearing 'messy' or 'incoherent'; however, as Cameron (2000: 33) points out, we frequently think transcribed talk is 'incoherent' and not communicatively efficient because the written form is our model of coherence and this is a bias we need to 'unlearn':

> Analysts of talk must work from the assumption that if communication is not breaking down in a given instance than participants must be able to make sense of it, no matter how incoherent it must seem; and if certain features recur in spoken language data, they must serve some purpose, however obscure we find it.

For example, in an investigation of the workplace meetings of English language teachers, the present author found laughter to be a frequent feature within the transcripts (Vaughan, 2007, 2008). This prompted a focus on the interactional implications of humour and laughter in the meetings in terms of when they occur and who produces them. This study, and also the studies carried out by Vásquez and Reppen, and Farr, mentioned above, share a common characteristic. They synthesise quantitative methodologies derived from the area of corpus linguistics (referred to variously as a methodology and a discipline in the literature – see Tognini-Bonelli, 2001, for a full discussion of this issue) with discourse analytic methods. As mentioned, discourse analysis has frequently been referred to as a qualitative method; however, many discourse analysts have always integrated some form of quantitative analysis to complement the qualitative insights that the data they collect yield. Corpus-based studies store the transcriptions of spoken text, or selections of written text, as text files and use specialised software such as WordSmith Tools (Scott, 2008). Previously, corpora, defined by Tognini-Bonelli (2001: 55) as 'computerised collections of authentic texts, amenable to automatic or semi-automatic processing or analysis . . . selected according to specific criteria in order to capture the regularities of a language, a language variety or sub-language', were by definition large, expensive to compile (particularly spoken components) and the preserve of researchers working at the level of word or clause. However, in recent times more researchers have been fruitfully using corpora large and small to investigate discourse-level phenomena (Ädel and Reppen, 2008). For an overview of how to build spoken and written corpora, and using corpus analysis tools to retrieve information about linguistic patterns from computerised collections of texts, see O'Keeffe and McCarthy (2010). For an overview of issues in how teachers can use corpora for their own research see Vaughan (2010).

Discourse analysis is not, therefore, a discrete research 'tool' as such, but a label that glosses a teeming and heterogeneous field of research. What the various approaches to language now have in common is a focus on naturally occurring language-in-use. The two approaches summarised here – Birmingham School discourse analysis and conversation analysis – derive from a broadly linguistic and broadly sociological theoretical basis respectively, and the approaches produce different ways of understanding how language is organised above the sentence. While discourse analysts of the Birmingham School are interested in how language is structured according to the genre in which it occurs (owing much to the Systemic Functional Linguistics that underpins it), conversation analysts have concerned themselves much more with how speakers naturally and instinctively navigate interaction, the careful observation and consideration of which reveals an order to the ostensible chaos of conversation. Both approaches are descriptive in this way. Research into the language used in educational contexts has also been exemplified, in terms of initial teacher training, the post-observational meeting, with teachers analysing their own use of language in the classroom (Walsh's SETT approach) in addition to data from outside the classroom, e.g. teacher's speech in meetings.

Language is never neutral, and as researchers using language we strive to acknowledge and mitigate our biases in analysing it – it is, however, fundamental to social life and the institutions that it permeates.

Questions for further investigation

1. In the context that you are researching, what types of talk or written text are embedded in it (e.g. policy documents, textbooks, meetings, informal situations of talk within an institution)?

2. How might you 'capture' some of this spoken or written discourse? What might a sufficient sample of it be?

3. If you are recording spoken discourse, how will you present your aims to participants in order to gain consent to record? How much input will your participants have into the research? Will they have access to the transcriptions? Will you follow up with them in terms of interviews or question-naires?

4. As you read your transcriptions/collections of written discourse, what are the first things that strike you about them? Can you identify any particular lexical items (particular words or phrases) or linguistic strategies (such as indirect-ness or questions) that appear to be frequent?

5. How will you code and investigate those items? When you do a literature search on the item/strategy, what tradition or approach to discourse analysis does research on this particular item seem to 'fit' into, if any?

Suggested further reading

Cole, K. and Zuengler, J. (eds) (2008) *The Research Process in Classroom Discourse Analysis: Current Perspectives*. London: Routledge. This edited volume is made up of multiple discourse analyses of the same classroom-derived data (a high school biology lesson). The discussions of the theory–practice nexus that are interspersed in the chapters should be of critical interest to educational researchers with a focus on discourse analytic research.

Gee, J. P. (2005) *Discourse Analysis* (2nd edn). London: Routledge. Gee distinguishes between Discourse ('big D Discourse') and discourse ('little d') in this introductory text – a useful distinction for newcomers to discourse analysis and its quite broad field of literature. Gee's work more generally will be of particular interest to educational researchers.

Wetherell, M., Taylor, S. and Yates, S. J. (eds) (2001) *Discourse as Theory and Practice*. London: Sage/Open University Press. Wetherell, M., Taylor, S. and Yates, S. J. (eds) (2001) *Discourse as Data*. London: Sage/Open University Press. These companion volumes cover a large amount of ground theoretically and methodologically on discourse analysis as an approach to social scientific research more generally. The *Discourse as Theory and Practice* volume takes the reader through the foundations of discourse analytic research and includes classic articles. The *Discourse as Data* volume focuses on analytic approaches in discourse analysis more generally, and covers fundamental issues in treating spoken or written discourse as data.

References

Ädel, A. and Reppen, R. (eds) (2008) *Corpora and Discourse: The Challenges of Different Settings*. Amsterdam: John Benjamins.

Atkinson, J. and Drew, P. (1979) *Order in Court: The Organisation of Verbal Interaction in Judicial Settings*. London: Macmillan.

Bargiela-Chiappini, F. and Harris, S. (1997) *Managing Language: The Discourse of Corporate Meetings*. Amsterdam: John Benjamins.

Brown, G. and Yule, G. (1983) *Discourse Analysis*. Cambridge: Cambridge University Press.

Cameron, D. (2000) *Working with Spoken Discourse*. London: Sage.

Clancy, B. (2004) 'The exchange system in family discourse', *Teanga*, 21: 134–50.

Coulthard, M. (1985) *An Introduction to Discourse Analysis* (2nd edn). London: Longman.

Drew, P. and Heritage, J. (1992) *Talk at Work: Interaction in Institutional Settings*. Cambridge: Cambridge University Press.

Eggins, S. and Slade, D. (1997) *Analysing Casual Conversation*. London: Continuum.

Fairclough, N. (1992) 'Introduction', in Fairclough, N. (ed.) *Critical Language Awareness*. London: Longman.

Fairclough, N. (1995) *Critical Discourse Analysis: The Critical Study of Language*. London: Longman.

Fairclough, N. (2001) 'The discourse of New Labour: critical discourse analysis', in Wetherell, M., Taylor, S. and Yates, S. J. (eds) *Discourse as Data*. London: Sage/Open University Press, pp. 228–66.

Farr, F. (2003) 'Engaged listenership in spoken academic discourse', *Journal of English for Academic Purposes*, 2(1): 67–85.

Farr, F. (2005a) 'Reflecting on reflections: the spoken word as a professional development tool in language teacher education', in Hughes, R. (ed.) *Spoken English, Applied Linguistics and TESOL: Challenges for Theory and Practice*. Hampshire: Palgrave Macmillan, pp. 182–215.

Farr, F. (2005b) 'Relational strategies in the discourse of professional performance review in an Irish academic environment: the case of language teacher education', in Schneider, K. P. and Barron, A. (eds) *Variational Pragmatics: The Case of English in Ireland*. Berlin: Mouton de Gruyter, pp. 203–34.

Garfinkel, H. (1967) *Studies in Ethnomethodology*. Englewood Cliffs, NJ: Prentice Hall.

Gee, J. P. (2005) *Discourse Analysis* (2nd edn). London: Routledge.

Halliday, M. A. K. (1961) 'Categories of the theory of grammar', *Word*, 17: 241–92.

Heritage, J. (1984) *Garfinkel and Ethnomethodology*. Cambridge: Polity.

Heritage, J. (2004) 'Conversation analysis and institutional talk: analysing data', in Silverman, D. (ed.) *Qualitative Research: Theory, Method and Practice* (2nd edn). London: Sage, pp. 222–45.

Heritage, J. and Greatbatch, D. (1991) 'On the institutional character of institutional talk: the case of news interviews', in Boden, D. and Zimmerman, D. H. (eds) *Talk and Social Structure: Studies in Ethnomethodology and Conversation Analysis*. Cambridge: Polity, pp. 93–137.

Hoey, M. (1991) 'Some properties of spoken discourses', in Bowers, R. and Brumfit, C. (eds) *Applied Linguistics and English Language Teaching*. London: Modern English Publications in association with the British Council, pp. 65–84.

Hoey, M. (1993) 'The case for the exchange complex', in Hoey, M. (ed.) *Data, Description, Discourse: Papers on the English Language in Honour of John McH Sinclair*. London: Harper-Collins, pp. 115–38.

Jaworski, A. and Coupland, N. (1999) *The Discourse Reader*. London: Routledge.

Labov, W. (1972) *Sociolinguistic Patterns*. Oxford: Blackwell.

Levinson, S. (1983) *Pragmatics*. Cambridge: Cambridge University Press.

McCarthy, M. (1991) *Discourse Analysis for Language Teachers*. Cambridge: Cambridge University Press.

McCarthy, M., Matthiessen, C. and Slade, D. (2002) 'Discourse analysis', in Schmitt, N. (ed.) *An Introduction to Applied Linguistics*. New York: Arnold, pp. 55–73.

O'Keeffe, A. and McCarthy, M. (2010) *The Routledge Handbook of Corpus Linguistics*. London: Routledge.

Pomerantz, A. (1984) 'Agreeing and disagreeing with assessments: some features of preferred/dispreferred turn shapes', in Atkinson, J. M. and Heritage, J. C. (eds) *Structures of Social Action: Studies in Conversation Analysis*. Cambridge: Cambridge University Press, pp. 57–101.

Reppen, R. and Vásquez, C. (2007) 'Using corpus linguistics to investigate the language of teacher training', in Waliński, J., Kredens, K. and Goźdź-Roszkowski, S. (eds) *Corpora and ICT in Language Studies*, PALC 2005. Frankfurt am Main: Peter Lang, pp. 13–29.

Roberts, C. (2010) *Qualitative Research Methods and Transcription: Issues in Transcribing Spoken Discourse*. Available at: http://www.kcl.ac.uk/schools/sspp/education/research/projects/dataqual.html (accessed 26 May 2010).

Rogers, R., Malancharuvil-Berkes, E., Mosley, M. Hui, D. and O'Garro Joseph, G. (2005) 'Critical Discourse Analysis in education: a review of the literature', *Review of Educational Research*, 75(3): 365–416.

Sacks, H., Schegloff, E. A. and Jefferson, G. (1974) 'A simplest systematics for the organisation of turn-taking for conversation', *Language*, 50(4): 696–735.

Schegloff, E. A. (1987) 'Between macro and micro: contexts and other connections', in Alexander, J., Giesen, B., Munch, R. and Smelser, N. (eds) *The Micro-Macro Link*. Berkeley and Los Angeles, CA: University of California Press, pp. 207–34.

Schegloff, E. A. (2002) 'Conversation analysis and applied linguistics', *Annual Review of Applied Linguistics*, 22, 3–31.

Schegloff, E. A. and Sacks, H. (1973) 'Opening up closings', *Semiotica*, 8(4): 289–327.

Schiffrin, D. (1994) *Approaches to Discourse*. Oxford: Blackwell.

Schiffrin, D., Tannen, D. and Hamilton, H. E. (eds) (2003) *The Handbook of Discourse Analysis*. Oxford: Blackwell.

Scott, M. (2008) *WordSmith Tools Version 5*. Liverpool: Lexical Analysis Software Ltd.

Sinclair, J. McH. and Coulthard, M. (1975) *Towards an Analysis of Discourse*. Oxford: Oxford University Press.

Stubbs, M. (1983) *Discourse Analysis: The Sociolinguistic Analysis of Natural Language*. Oxford: Blackwell.

Taylor, S. (2001) 'Locating and conducting discourse analytic research', in Wetherell, M., Taylor, S. and Yates, S. J. (eds) *Discourse as Data*. London: Sage/Open University Press, pp. 5–48.

Tognini-Bonelli, E. (2001) *Corpus Linguistics at Work*. Amsterdam: John Benjamins.

Trappes-Lomax, H. and Ferguson, G. (2002) *Language in Language Teacher Education*. Amsterdam: John Benjamins.

Vásquez, C. and Reppen, R. (2007) 'Transforming practice: changing patterns of interaction in post-observation meetings'. *Language Awareness*, 16,(3): 153–72.

Vaughan, E. (2007) '"I think we should just accept our horrible lowly status": analysing teacher–teacher talk in the context of community of practice', *Language Awareness*, 16(3): 173–89.

Vaughan, E. (2008) 'Got a date or something? An analysis of the role of humour and laughter in the workplace', in Ädel, A. and Reppen, R. (eds) *Corpora and Discourse: The Challenges of Different Settings*. Amsterdam: John Benjamins, pp. 95–115.

Vaughan, E. (2009) *Just Say Something and We Can All Argue Then: Community and Identity in the Workplace Talk of English Language Teachers*, PhD thesis, Limerick, Ireland: Mary Immaculate College, University of Limerick.

Vaughan, E. (2010) 'How can teachers use corpora for their own research?', in O'Keeffe, A. and McCarthy, M. (eds) *The Routledge Handbook of Corpus Linguistics*. London: Routledge, pp. 471–84.

Walsh, S. (2006) *Investigating Classroom Discourse*. London: Routledge.

Wetherell, M., Taylor, S. and Yates, S. J. (eds) (2001a) *Discourse as Theory and Practice*. London: Sage/Open University Press.

Wetherell, M., Taylor, S. and Yates, S. J. (eds) (2001b) *Discourse as Data*. London: Sage/Open University Press.

Media analysis

Michael Atkinson

Introduction

The analysis of (mass) media production, the meaning of its content and its varied effects on audiences as interpretive communities have mushroomed in popularity within the academy over the last three decades. The burgeoning interest is due, in part, to the growth and proliferation of media technology, the shrinking of cultural space between groups through ongoing globalisation processes, and the nature of everyday life within information obsessed and consumer-driven late-market capitalist societies. Quite some time ago, Stuart Hall (1980) pointed to the power of the media in constructing and disseminating social knowledge in late-modern societies, commenting on how the media deliberately assemble (or *encode*) information and then how audiences are encouraged to receive (decode) the information in a narrow range of manners. Today, the media function as more than a one-way assemblage of cultural information distribution and education portals in our societies. Sociologist Pierre Bourdieu (1993) notes that the media constitute, for all intents and purposes, an 'autonomous [popular] cultural' field, endowed with the ability to entertain, provoke, distract, produce, connect and of course educate people in unique manners.

Debates concerning the media as a primary definer or director of culture or central educator about a broad range of social issues continue. Media critics cite how theorists including Louis Althusser, Jean Baudrillard and Guy DeBord cleverly exposed the media's overarching, coercively ideological and top-down impact on public behaviours and attitudes while others call attention to theorists including Marshall McLuhan, Manuel Castells and Douglas Kellner, who respectively heralded the growth of 'new media' as a watershed moment in the extension of human agency and cultural self-determination. Some researchers view television, radio, popular music, print media, the Internet and other mass mediators of culture as sites of suffocating and hegemonic social reproduction, and yet others see the possibility for many cultures and ideological positions and possibilities to be represented, negotiated, contested and resisted in increasingly democratic (or at least more 'open' and accessible) media spaces. Cutting across differences of opinion regarding the social functions and impacts of the media are, nevertheless, a series of core questions or substantive concerns driving most research:

- What are people exposed to by the media (i.e. the *encoded* messages)?
- How do audiences actively interpret media content (i.e. how are interpretive communities constituted)?

- How are media messages actively used by people and when do they become incorporated into [popular] cultural practice?
- Are cultural differences and spaces eroding between groups as a result of the mass mediation of cultures in an increasingly global society?
- What systems of representation, ideology or discourse dominate in the media?
- How and why are people (especially youth) producing their own media, and exploring the link between new social media and human agency?

From the outset, we must be mindful that the systematic analysis of media forms, their content and impacts is not one methodology but rather a house of interrelated techniques. While researchers grant, in varying degrees and forms, baseline attention to the encoding-decoding-usage process in most active research on media, no one style of, or approach to, media analysis reigns supreme as proto-typical. There are quantitative, qualitative, historical, semiotic, structural, poststructural, feminist, critical realist, post-positivist, existential and a full range of other ways of performing media research. Whatever the orientation, those conducting media research strive to better understand how the mass circulation of images, messages, discourses and symbols through societies creates, disrupts, reflects, reproduces, distributes and aligns collective definitions of reality (or simply knowledge) for people. In this pursuit, media research ranges from very politically and ideologically passionate efforts to quasi-neutral and purely descriptive reports. Students often complain that media research is densely theoretical and conceptually labyrinth-like at times. Such is unfortunate, as much media research sheds considerable light on the real-world influence of media on human groups, cultural practices and social structures.

For the remainder of this chapter, I briefly address several of the most common methods employed in/ as media research, and address their strengths and limitations. The aim is to illustrate a cross-section of the broader panorama of media analysis methods and techniques available, and their widespread applicability to a host of substantive areas of investigation.

Conducting media analysis

Students are immediately drawn to media analysis as many of them have practised it informally for years as voracious media consumers in their own right. However, they quickly realise that the systematic analysis of the media is much more murky, complicated and conceptually taxing than lay interpretations of the relative palatability of selected popular media content. Most research projects drawing upon media analysis commence in a relatively common manner; one determines the explicit substantive focus of the project and the parameters of the case study in question (i.e. is it a project focusing on media encoding, distribution or reception?) and then chooses representative or at least conceptually appropriate units/texts to sample. The arduous methodological trench work begins when researchers are forced to address how they will analyse media data!

Among the most straightforward media analytic designs is *manifest content analysis*. Here, the goal of the research is to examine the overt or surface-level characteristics of media texts. For example, one might be interested in studying whether patriarchal ideologies still dominate in media representations of amateur or professional sport. To investigate the question further, a researcher could sample ten years of Summer and Winter Olympic Games television coverage in Britain as the case study data. Before analysing any of the television content, the researcher would have to decide what would be examined in the broadcasts, and how to 'count' the presence of patriarchy. One might suggest that the percentage of men's versus women's sports coverage, the gender of athletes interviewed or showcased in special stories, whether one gender is featured in more 'primetime' events than the other are all empirical indicators of patriarchal attitudes. These are easily recognised by a researcher, and could be tallied quite quickly across the broadcasts. At the end of the study, basic descriptive statistical and impressionistic analysis could be offered to conclude whether, on the surface, Olympic television broadcasts in Britain seemed to privilege men over women, potentially indicating the enduring face of patriarchy in the representation of Olympic sport. A number of studies have conducted such an analysis of patriarchy and sport media, and found vast discrepancies in the media coverage of men and women in organised sport (see Coakley and Pike, 2009).

Discourse analysis

Discourse analysis is a technique inspired by French structuralists including Ferdinand de Saussure, Jacques Lacan and Roland Barthes, and critical poststructuralists including Judith Butler, Julia Kritseva and Michel Foucault. Discourse analysis is not a single method, but rather a series of complementary techniques focusing on the interpretive 'reading' of a sample of media texts in order to expose the dominant *episteme* (knowledge), assumptions, ideologies or values underwriting them. Another way of describing discourse analysis is to call it the study of the 'dominant languages' or ideologies in media texts that frame how audiences are supposed to understand and use them. Hall (1980) refers to this process as the encoding of 'preferred' meanings in a text that limit alternative (or 'resistive') readings and understandings of a represented subject. For discourse analysts, the exposure of dominant discourses in texts is critically important, as those who tend to control how something is spoken about (and thus thought about and known) have immense social power to frame reality and dictate policy. Discourse analysts see mass circulated media texts as connected through and composed by socially diffuse – what Deleuze and Guattati (1987) call 'rhizomatically' creeping – systems of language encoded with dominant ideologies. Discourse analysts assert that no media text is ever 'neutral' or outside the trappings of language/ideology. Research on the medicalisation of cyberspace illustrates how governmental ideologies of self-surveillance and associated neo-liberal discourses of healthism abound online. Research has also highlighted how the Internet has become a zone for spreading dominant, conservative and self-blaming health messages, and as such how they systematically blur and eschew real material differences in people's access to quality, state-provided healthcare schemes and styles of healthy living. Giroux's (2005) work on discourses of neo-liberalism in stories about education cutbacks in the United States and Canada exposes how the slashing of public school budgets is largely framed by late-modern, supply-side economics

mantras and principles. Giroux illustrates how stories are embedded with neo-liberal understandings of the role of 'waste and fat cutting' in the school system as something positive, while obfuscating the real-world impact of the erosion of the social safety net on children's futures. To be sure, discourse analysis is the most commonly cited technique of media analysis in much of the social science and education literature today.

Narrative analysis

Narrative analysis is similar to, and yet importantly different from discourse analysis. Narrative analysis – the examination of how stories are told through the media, or a specific set of media texts – looks and feels like discourse analysis, but their respective emphases on how power is related to discourse/narrations in the media are quite different. Narrative analysis tends to focus on how and why individuals, groups, organisations or others choose specific language and symbols to represent something about themselves. Whereas the approach in discourse analysis tends to be rather top-down (that is, focusing how discourses wrapped in ideologies are spread through society by powerful or elite groups), narrative analysis tends to home in on how media may be used to create and disseminate a wide range of cultural identities, images and opportunities for social storytelling. Gillett (2003), for example, argues that the media are a critical cultural context where gay men are able to write their social selves in empowering manners, especially in the case of telling different (that is non-medically pathological) stories about life with HIV/AIDS. Gillett's (2003) examination of how men narrate gay identities through magazines and websites attests to the emancipatory potential of public storytelling as a form of claims-making and knowledge production for socially marginalised communities. Gillett (2003) calls attention to how narrative work serves as a vital technique for publicly distancing gay sexualities and identities from medicalised understandings of the 'diseased' body. As the narrations show the human, mundane, emotional and 'everyday' aspects of being HIV+, different realities about being gay in society are offered.

While the techniques of media analysis listed

above, by and large, emphasise how media produce or shape cultural meaning and social practices, *audience ethnography* strives to understand how people actively receive, decode and use media texts. An audience ethnography might be designed as a one-shot case study, or be structured as a long-term panel study of how a group interprets media over the course of time. In the typical scenario, participants in an audience ethnographic project are asked to collectively or individually watch, read or listen to select media and then respond to its content. A researcher acts as a facilitator in these scenarios, prompting questions among respondents about what the messages or symbols in the media might mean to them and how they actively decode them from a variety of cultural standpoints (i.e. age, race, sexuality, gender, class). The underpinning logic of doing audience ethnography is that by observing and questioning how people make sense of media data 'live' and *in situ*, researchers compile a more valid understanding of the process of immediate reception and the cognitive processing of media content. Wilson and Sparkes (1996), for example, illustrate how African-Canadian teenage boys fashion their own constructions of, and lived experiences with, Black masculinity to interpret mass mediations of 'Blackness' in basketball shoe advertisements. Wilson and Sparkes (1996) discuss how the boys find humour, reality and frequent inferential racism in the depictions of Black masculinity in the advertisements. They also attest to how the youth selectively take from the commercials what makes sense to them culturally, and how they negate or resist supposedly preferred images and constructions of 'Blackness' in the commercials. Through Wilson and Sparkes' audience ethnographic analysis, an understanding of people's creative capacities to make sense of media in complex and nuanced ways results, thus challenging simplistic readings and portrayals of people as merely unreflexive cultural dupes of dominant media discourses and images. Still, what is especially curious about audience ethnography is that media and visual culture methodologists have championed the approach for well over two decades, but very few actively pursue audience ethnographic methods.

Photo elicitation

Photo elicitation, like audience ethnography, is designed to stimulate conversation about how media are actively received and decoded by people. Here, a researcher will show subjects a series of pictures and ask them what they see in them, what the images mean to them or to provide an account of what is happening in the picture. Rather than ask a question, then, the researcher asks a person to respond to something visual in the hope it will stir alternative ways of thinking about the subject at hand. *Photovoice* is a similar method to photo elicitation, by which researchers encourage or ask participants in a project to take their own pictures of, video record or draw people, places, events or images which mean something to them (that is, related to a well-specified and overarching research project). For example, I have conducted research with chronically ill athletes – people living with cancer, liver disease, HIV and other conditions. At one stage of the research process I asked several participants to take one of my video cameras and film their own mini-documentaries of a week in their lives. The participants did so with much enthusiasm and produced amazing short features of their lives as wounded athletes. By having the subjects highlight what they understand to be the relevant day-to-day structures and meanings of their lives as wounded athletes, I gained a deeper understanding of how illness and sport identities must be negotiated daily (Atkinson and Young, 2008). Researchers have similarly used drawing as a technique of personal expression and knowledge production. Studies focusing on youth constructions of drugs and alcohol have involved children drawing out pictures of what comes to their mind when a word like 'drugs' is mentioned. Children might not be able to verbally articulate how they understand drugs as well as they may be able to represent it graphically through a series of mental maps. In such cases, the methodological point of photovoice or drawing is to access subjects' ways of knowing a topic.

With the rise of new online media the practice of *netnography* is gaining popularity as a technique of analysis. Netnography is literally an online ethnography of Internet sites, wherein a researcher does not simply observe the content of websites, but actively contributes to them as a registered or recognised member. Wilson and Atkinson (2005), for example, studied the online recruiting and social connecting mechanisms provided by Rave and Straightedge blogs and chat forums/rooms. In both subcultures, youth use Internet sites as a technique of performing community and fostering bonds between members across great spaces. Both of the researchers participated and chatted with members online as a means of conducting quasi-interviews, but more importantly, in gaining a first-hand understanding of how new media space is produced by groups in 'real time' as a vehicle for developing a sense of mutual identification and commitment. Bennett's (2008) book *Civic Life Online* presents a series of chapters detailing the emancipatory potential of new media forms such as personal websites, blogs, social networking sites and other forms of computer-mediated communication (CMC) for youth in particular. The separate chapters in the book attest to how the development of online space provides an opportunity for people to be their own media producers, and thus become public knowledge producers and cultural claims-makers. To date, very few inside the academy have rigorously attended to the study of how, why and when youth choose to become media encoders and how this may impact systems of ideological production and dissemination within popular culture. Ohler (2007) has extended the study of new media into the classroom. His work advocates the use of computer programs and Internet space as a means of teaching students how to create and publish avant garde digital stories. Ohler's (2007) emphasis is on the creation of dynamic texts, embedded with movies, images, digital interviews and other visual-spoken forms of knowing. Ohler (2007) further emphasises the creative and knowledge-production capabilities of new, digital stories in that they are for the producers to play around with sound, speed, camera angles and other cinematic techniques in order to create desired feels, moods or atmospheres in stories. New media analytic methods advocated by Bennett (2008) and Ohler (2007) establish exciting ways of knowing and seeing subjects of interest, and illustrate the potential for knowledge production and translation once representations of lived experience and the human condition are liberated from one-dimensional written/textual ways of knowing.

A final series of comments about the role of theory in conducting media analysis are warranted. The lion's share of media analytic research is interpretive and qualitative in orientation; that is to say, researchers are not so concerned with testing formal hypotheses derived from theory against media data in most cases. So, it is fair to suggest that media analysis is based more on the use of media research to explore, probe and extend the empirical applicability of particular concepts, axioms or ideas from extant theories. More often that not, researchers have particular penchants for proscribed theoretical ideas they regularly employ in order to make sense of emergent data. For instance, poststructural, neo-Marxist and neo-Gramscian, cultural studies, feminist, queer and postcolonial/critical race theories are used quite extensively to wade through and interpret the potential significance of media texts. The vast majority of projects are not, despite internal claims otherwise, 'grounded theoretical' examinations of media production and dissemination. Grounded theory is a very special data analytic procedure (Charmaz, 2006), and it has come to be lazily used among qualitative researchers and conflated with interpretive analysis or hermeneutics in general. When a set of theoretical decisions about how to read and report media data is sorted a priori to the data collection process, or a pre-existing theoretical schema is applied to emergent media data in a project, such is not in the spirit of grounded theoretical development.

Critiques

Media analysis receives substantial criticism from academics who consider themselves dyed-in-the-wool scientists. Due in large part to the extensive amount of reflexively interpretive analysis in most media studies projects, the overall methodology is prone to contestation from researchers searching robustly objective, reliable and generalisable data. While there are many criticisms of media analysis studies, five are especially common. *First*, quarrels about the rigours of sampling in media projects are practically inevitable. The sampling approach underpinning many media-based projects is almost always non-probability based, but researchers nevertheless tend to make grand claims about the generalisability of their data and theoretical conclusions. Further, very little theoretical or conceptual rationale is offered as to why the sample data have been collected, or why they may be representative of 'something' at all. *Second*, the question of how theory guides media research looms large. Even though many researchers purport to conduct 'grounded theory' through the data analysis process, their studies read as if the theoretical reading had been determined well in advance (see above). In this instance, one is led to question whether or not media studies are simply vehicles for reifying, rather than testing, expanding or amending, extant theories of cultures, individuals and societies.

Third, questions of the internal validity and reliability of researchers' readings of media texts, or interpretations of audience interpretations of texts, chase practically all media-based studies. If, as semioticians instruct, media texts are indeed polysemic or 'floating' and thus open to countless cultural interpretations, then how is one researcher's set of conclusions any more reality-congruent than another's? If a thousand media researchers might decode the significance of, say, media accounts of the obesity epidemic in the London broadsheets in a thousand different ways, what is the legitimate role of media analysis in the academy? What trustworthy, usable, intersubjectively agreed upon or definitive knowledge does it generate? *Fourth*, new questions of best ethical practice (especially around participant anonymity and confidentiality) surround media projects in which photographs, film, blogs, websites, and other Internet spaces are employed as data. While the use of new media and their forms of representation well and truly open up representational practice in our research efforts, the 'public' nature (and therefore 'free to use' nature) of online material – and our ability to 'invade' personal webspace for our research purposes – remain grey areas in research ethics debates. *Fifth*, even the most ardent defenders of media analysis struggle with how best to represent visual, spoken, moving, ambiguous and mass distributed media texts as academic papers. Thrift (2007) like Richardson (1999) challenges all qualitative researchers to seek new forms of moving, emotional, aesthetic and personally compelling academic writing/representation that bring audiences 'closer' to that which has been studied in the here and now of everyday life. Their criticism is based on the idea that researchers take very complex, visceral and sensual practices like media reception and usage and then transform it/represent it as a theoretically obtuse written, textual analysis. Atkinson (2010), for example, has explored the role of 'infographics' (i.e. using pictures and selected field notes as the main body of a research report) in the effort to reduce the author's own theoretical voice in the academic text.

Conclusion

In sum, media analysis continues to develop and flourish within universities, drawing more practitioners on a yearly basis across a swathe of academic departments. Advocates call attention to the insights offered by such research in societies obsessed with and saturated by the mass mediation of culture while critics continue to question the scientific legitimacy and rigour of much media-focused research.

Questions for further investigation

1. Do you think media producers actually encode and communicate preferred meaning into texts, or are audiences simply able to read media freely?

2. Select any edition of a popular magazine for teenage boys and one for teenage girls. Examine the advertisements in each of the magazines and 'read' any messages or discourses about gender in the ads. Compare and contrast between the boys' magazine ads and the girls' magazine ads.

3. If you were asked to conduct an audience ethnography of popular movies, how would you design and implement the project?

4. Select a subject of interest to you and think of how you might use either photovoice or photo elicitation to produce data for a study on the subject.

5. How do you think the rise in popularity of new media creates both challenges and possibilities for enhanced learning in the classroom?

Suggested further reading

Bennett, W. L. (2008) *Civic Life Online: Learning How Digital Media Can Engage Youth*. Cambridge, MA: MIT Press. Bennett's book provides a much-needed call for the exploration of mass media technologies and ways of knowing in the classroom. As each successive generation of students is more media savvy than previous generations, Bennett's arguments regarding the ways in which children can connect with new media in the learning process are especially relevant.

Hall, S. (1980) 'Encoding/decoding', in *Culture, Media, Language: Working Papers in Cultural Studies, 1972–79*, Centre for Contemporary Cultural Studies. London: Hutchinson, pp. 128–38. Hall's 1980 essay is a must read for students as they first encounter mass media research. Among other contributions to the field of media research, this article carefully and thoughtfully outlines the ways in which media messages are produced and received in the transmission process.

Richardson, L. (1999) 'Feathers in our CAP', *Journal of Contemporary Ethnography*, 28: 660–8. Richardson's article is a path-breaking challenge to socio-cultural researchers and their preferred systems of social representation through writing. Richardson argues for more open, creative and artistic methods of representing lived realities and cites, for example, the potential of visual/mass media modes of representation.

References

Atkinson, M. (2010) 'Fell running in post-sport territories', *Qualitative Research in Sport and Exercise*, 2:109–32.

Atkinson, M. and Young, K. (2008) *Sport, Deviance and Social Control*. Champaign, IL: Human Kinetics.

Bennett, W. L. (2008) *Civic Life Online: Learning How Digital Media Can Engage Youth*. Cambridge, MA: MIT Press.

Bourdieu, P. (1993) *The Field of Cultural Production*. New York: Columbia University Press.

Charmaz, K. (2006) *Constructing Grounded Theory: A Practical Guide Through Qualitative Analysis*. London: Sage.

Coakley, J. and Pike, L. (2009) *Sports in Society: Issues and Controversies*. London: McGraw-Hill.

Deleuze, G. and Guattari, F. (1987) *A Thousand Plateaus*. Minneapolis, MN: University of Minnesota Press.

Gillett, J. (2003) 'Media activism and Internet use by people with HIV/AIDS', *Sociology of Health and Illness*, 25: 608–24.

Giroux, H. (2005) 'The politics of public pedagogy', in Di Leo, J. (ed.) *If Classrooms Matter: Place, Pedagogy and Politics*. New York: Routledge, pp. 15–36.

Hall, S. (1980) 'Encoding/decoding', in *Culture, Media, Language: Working Papers in Cultural Studies, 1972–79*, Centre for Contemporary Cultural Studies. London: Hutchinson, pp. 128–38.

Ohler, J. (2007) *Digital Storytelling in the Classroom*. Thousand Oaks, CA: Corwin Press.

Richardson, L. (1999) 'Feathers in Our CAP', *Journal of Contemporary Ethnography*, 28: 660–8.

Thrift, N. (2007) *Non-Representational Theory: Space, Politics, Affect*. London: Routledge.

Wilson, B. and Atkinson, M. (2005) 'Rave and Straightedge, the virtual and the real: exploring on-line and off-line experiences in Canadian youth subcultures', *Youth and Society*, 36: 276–311.

Wilson, B. and Sparkes, R. (1996) 'It's gotta be the shoes: youth, race, and sneaker commercials', *Sociology of Sport Journal*, 13: 398–427.

Visual methodologies and social change

Claudia Mitchell

Introduction: visual methodologies

'Draw a scientist'. 'Take pictures of where you feel safe and not so safe'. 'Produce a video documentary on an issue "in your life"'. 'Find and work with seven or eight pictures from your family photographs that you can construct into a narrative about gender and identity'. Each of these prompts speaks to the range of tools that might be used to engage participants (learners, teachers, parents, pre-service teachers) in visual research (a drawing, simple point-and-shoot cameras, video cameras, family photographs) and suggests some of the types of emerging visual data: the drawing, the photographic images and captions produced in the photovoice project, the video texts produced in a community video project, and the newly created album or visual text produced by the participants in an album project.

In each case there is the immediate visual text (or primary text as John Fiske, 1989, terms it), the drawing, photo image, collage, photo-story, video narrative or album, which can include captions and more extensive curatorial statements or interpretive writings that reflect what the participants have to say about the visual texts. In essence, their participation does not have to be limited to 'take a picture' or 'draw

a picture', though the level of participation will rest on time, the age and ability of the participants and even their willingness to be involved, and a set of drawings or photos produced in isolation of their full participatory context (or follow-up) does not mean that they should therefore be discarded, particularly in large-scale collections (Mitchell et al., 2005a).

Each of these examples can also include what Fiske (1989) terms 'production texts' – or *how* participants engaged in the process describes the project, regardless of whether they are producing drawings, photographic images or video narratives, or 'reconstructing' a set of photographs into a new text, and indeed what they make of the texts. These production texts are often elicited during follow-up interviews. The production texts can also include secondary visual data based on the researcher taking pictures during the process and can show levels of engagement, something Pithouse and Mitchell (2007) in an article called 'Looking at looking' describe as a result of the visual representations of the engagement of children looking at their own photographs. Each of the visual practices noted above and described in more detail below brings with it, of course, its own methods, traditions and procedures. Taken as a whole these approaches all fall under the umbrella term 'visual methodologies'. Clearly, as noted above, such approaches can range from those which are relatively 'low tech' and which can be easily carried out without a lot of expensive equipment through to those which require more expensive cameras, from those that are camera-based to those that provide for a focus on things and objects (including archival photographs), from those where participants are respondents to the visual (in the case of photo elicitation) to those which fully engage participants as producers. The constant is some aspect of the visual.

Mapping the terrain of visual methodologies

There is a variety of visual methodologies, each with its own advantages, challenges and limitations. This section offers a map of the range of approaches followed by a section on interpretive possibilities and another on challenges and limitations.

Visual approaches

Drawings

The use of drawings to study emotional and cognitive development, trauma and fears, and more recently issues of identity has a rich history, and using drawings in participatory research with children and young people along with adult groups, such as beginning teachers, is a well-established 'low-tech' methodology. As a recent Population Council study points out, drawings offer children an opportunity to express themselves regardless of linguistic ability (Chong et al., 2005). They also point out that work with drawings within visual methodologies is economical as all it requires is paper and a writing instrument. Drawings have been used with pre-service teachers in South Africa to study their metaphors on teaching mathematics in the context of HIV and AIDS (Van Laren, 2007), with children and pre-service teachers to study images of teachers, and with children to study their perceptions of illness, of living on the street and of violence in refugee situations, and on the perceptions of girls and young women in Rwanda on gender violence (Mitchell and Umurungi, 2007).

Photovoice

Made popular by the award-winning documentary *Born into Brothels*, photovoice, as Caroline Wang (1999) terms the use of simple point-and-shoot cameras in community photography projects, has increasingly become a useful tool in educational research in South Africa. Building on Wang's work, which looks at women and health issues in rural China, Mary Brinton Lykes's (2001) work with women in post-conflict settings in Guatamela, Wendy Ewald's (2000) photography work with children in a variety of settings, including Nepal, the Appalachian region of the US and Soweto, and James Hubbard's (1994) work with children on reservations in the US, researchers in South Africa have worked with rural teachers and community healthcare workers to examine the challenges and solutions in looking at HIV and AIDS (Mitchell et al., 2005a; De Lange et al., 2007), with teachers exploring gender, with learners in a variety of contexts, including exploring stigma and HIV and AIDS (Moletsane, 2007), with rural learners, and with teachers addressing poverty and safe and unsafe spaces in schools (Mitchell et al., 2005b), to name only some of the school-based research using photo-voice.

Family photographs

Clearly much has been done already on family albums, particularly in the area of the visual arts and art history. These studies range from work on one's own family album(s) (Spence, 1988) to the work of Hirsch (1997) and Langford (2001), to name only a few of the scholars who examine 'other people's albums'. These various album projects have highlighted the personal aspect in looking at or working with one's own photographs, but there is also, as in the case of Langford, the idea of explicitly looking at 'other people's photo albums' through a socio-cultural lens. The issues that they have explored range from questions of cultural identity and memory, through to what Spence (1988) has described as 'reconfiguring' the family album. Research on family albums in South Africa points to the rich possibilities for this work in exploring apartheid and post-apartheid realities. Mitchell and Allnutt (2007) have applied this work on family albums to participatory work with teachers in Canada and South Africa.

Participatory video

The use of participatory video in educational research (beyond the use of videotaping classrooms and other settings or videotaping interviews) may be framed as collaborative video, participatory video, indigenous video or community video. Sarah Pink (2001) argues that video within ethnographic research can break down traditional hierarchies between visual and textual data. She maintains that these hierarchies are irrelevant to a reflexive approach to research that acknowledges the details, subjectivities and power dynamics at play in any ethnographic project. What runs across this work is the idea of participants engaged in producing their own videos across a variety of genres, ranging from video documentaries, video narratives (melodramas or other stories) or public service narratives. As with the work with photovoice, both the processes and the products lend themselves to data analysis within visual studies.

In terms of process and video-making in Southern African schools, Mitchell et al. (2007) and Moletsane et al., (2009) write about the ways in which young people might participate in this work, noting the particular relevance of this work to addressing gender violence and HIV and AIDS. Equally, though, the work with adults, teachers, parents and community healthcare workers is also critical, as can be seen in the work of Olivier et al. (2007) on poverty and Moletsane et al. (2009). Building on the work of Jay Ruby (2000) and others in relation to the idea of the ethnographic video as text, researchers have reflected on what might be described as a meta-narrative on working with community-based video through the researcher-generated production of a composite video of each project. The production of these composite videos is an interpretive part of the process (in relation to the research team). These composite videos become tools of dissemination but also serve to become new tools of enquiry when community participants view them.

Material culture

How objects, things and spaces can be used within visual research in education draws on work in socio-semiotics, art history and consumer research. Stephen Riggins' generative and groundbreaking essay on studying his parents' living room offers a systematic approach to engaging in a denotative and connotative reading of the objects and things in one physical space. This work can be applied to a variety of texts, ranging from clothing and identity, bedrooms, documents and letters, and even desks and bulletin boards as material culture. However, some of the 'photo subjects' are objects: a school bus, empty chairs and hair dryers in a beauty salon, or a shrivelled tree. Weber and Mitchell (2004), in the edited book *Not Just any Dress: Narratives of Memory, Body and Identity*, offer a series of essays on the connotative meanings of various items of clothing. The collection of dress stories – divided into 'growing up with dresses', 'dress and schooling', 'dress rituals and mothers', 'of dresses and weddings', 'dressing identity' and 'bodies, dress and mortality' – offers a reading on a wide range of issues of identity (mostly women's) across the lifespan.

Interpretive processes and visual research

There is no quick and easy way to map out the interpretive processes involved in working with visual research any more than there is a quick and easy way to map out the interpretive processes for working with any type of research data, though Jon Prosser (1998), Marcus Banks (2001), Gillian Rose (2001) and Sarah Pink (2001), among other researchers working in the area, offer useful suggestions and guidelines. Some considerations include the following:

1. At the heart of visual work is its facilitation of reflexivity in the research process. Situating oneself in the research texts is critical to engaging in the interpretive process.
2. Close reading strategies (drawn from literary studies, film studies and socio-semiotics, for example) are particularly appropriate to working with visual images. These strategies can be applied to working with a single photograph, a video documentary text or a cinematic text (Mitchell and Weber, 1999).
3. Visual images are particularly appropriate to drawing in the participants themselves as central to the interpretive process. In work with photovoice, for example, participants can be engaged in their own analytic procedures with the photos: which ones are the most compelling? How are your photos

the same or different from others in your group? What narrative do your photos evoke? Similarly with video documentaries produced as part of community video, participants can be engaged in a reflective process, which also becomes an analytic process: what did you like best about the video? What would you change if you could? Who should see this video? The interpretive process does not have to be limited to the participants and the researcher. Communities themselves may also decide what a text means.

4. The process of interpreting visual data can benefit from drawing on new technologies. Transana, for example, is a software application that is particularly appropriate to working with video data. The use of digitising and creating metadata schemes can be applied to working with photovoice data.

5. Archival photos (both public and private) bring their own materiality with them and may be read as objects or things. Where are they stored? Who looks after them? (See also Rose, 2001.)

6. Visual data (especially photos produced by participants), because it is so accessible, is often subjected to more rigorous scrutiny by ethics boards than most other data. There are many different ways of working with the visual and the choice of which type of visual approach should be guided by, among other things, the research questions, the feasibility of the study, the experience of the researcher and the acceptability to the community under study.

On the limitations and challenges in working with the visual

Lister and Wells (2001) stress the unprecedented importance of imaging and visual technologies in contemporary society and urge researchers to take account of those images in conducting their investigations. Over the last three decades, an increasing number of qualitative researchers have indeed taken up and refined visual approaches to enhance their understanding of the human condition. These uses encompass a wide range of visual forms, including films, videos, photographs, drawings, cartoons, graffiti, maps, diagrams, cyber graphics, signs and symbols.

Although many of these scholars normally work in visual sociology and anthropology, cultural studies, and film and photography, a growing body of interdisciplinary scholarship is incorporating certain image-based techniques into its research methodology. Research designs which use the visual raise many new questions and suggest new blurrings of boundaries: is it research or is it art? Is it truth? Does the camera lie? Is it just a 'quick fix' on doing research? How do you overcome the subjective stance? The emergence of visual and arts-based research as a viable approach is putting pressure on the traditional structures and expectations of the academy. Space, time and equipment requirements, for example, often make it difficult for researchers to present their work in the conventional venues and formats of research conferences.

Applying the methods: a case for photovoice – the Friday Absenteeism Project

In this project children from an informal settlement in rural South Africa became involved in a photovoice project which led to several policy changes in relation to food security and gender violence – both critically linked to HIV and AIDS (see also Mitchell et al., 2006; Mitchell et al., 2005b; Moletsane and Mitchell, 2007). A key issue in the school was the fact that many of the children in the senior primary school missed school on Fridays. This was perhaps understandable in a community where problems of poverty, unemployment and high rates of HIV infection and illness abound, and where, as the principal and staff noted, children missed school on Friday – market day – when many of them were often called on to work in the market to earn money to provide for at least the basic nutritional needs of the families over the weekend. This is an important point since although there was a school feeding-scheme from Monday to Friday, no provision existed for help with food over the weekends. The principal was concerned because the learners could not afford to miss a day a week of school, and because this behaviour also sent a message to other learners that school wasn't important. From this understanding of the issues, the principal saw the potential for the children to use photography not only to document the problems they faced, but also to identify and/or influence the development of strategies within the school and the community, as well as in the government departments responsible for their well-being. So, through a photovoice project, the children worked in small groups with disposable cameras to document their community. Once they had taken the photographs they were involved in analysing their own photos according to the problems and possible solutions affecting the community, and writing captions. Each group produced a poster where they analysed the issues.

The children's narratives in the photographs, posters and writing revealed a variety of issues. These included alcoholism among adults in the community; this is captured in a caption to a photograph: 'If we look at these people who are living in this shack, they are drinking alcohol. They are not working. The schoolchild cannot survive in this condition.' Other issues they identified included high levels of unemployment, the need for housing, the lack of clean water and sanitation, the danger to children of even coming to school because they have to cross a wide highway that has no bridge over it. Most importantly, the photographs draw attention to the effects of poverty, and they provide visual evidence of why children as young as 11 or 12 must supplement the family income. Poverty also led to some of them having to miss school to take care of younger siblings. In a caption to one of the photographs, the students note: 'This photo shows us the rate of children who are absent from schools. These children are absent because they have to look after their baby sister or brother while their parents are working.' The photographs taken in the market not only showed images of the adults who run the market trying to make a living, but also showed the children's peers at work, so, very obviously, not at school. The children also took pictures of learners from nearby schools, demonstrating that Friday absenteeism was a widespread problem in the district. One particular photograph was of a boy who was working in the market to raise money for a school trip to Durban, which he could not otherwise afford: 'He absented himself from school because they had a trip to Durban. He decided to look for a part-time job because he

needs the money. He has no parents.' The photographs and captions also reflected upon the conditions of the school itself. For example, one of the girls who was working in the market spoke about issues of safety and security in her classroom. Her teacher, she indicated, had been making sexual advances towards her. Being away from school on Fridays was an escape from this unwanted attention. The rich insider data produced by the children in the photovoice project had major implications for policy development at the school and community level. For example, from the data, the principal instituted disciplinary action against the teacher who allegedly was sexually harassing a female learner. He also raised the issue of absenteeism with other principals in the district, and planned for a community-based stakeholders' forum where the children were to present their posters. From this work he was able to approach donors and corporate funders with the children's images and captions and attract financial support for a feeding scheme for the weekends as well as during the week.

Conclusion

The overview of visual methodologies has focused largely on the use of such methods in the service of social change and where the visual can serve as a mode of enquiry as well as a mode of dissemination. Many would also argue that much of the work, whether it is with drawings or cameras, also has the potential to serve as transformative for the participants who are, in a sense, the principal actors in the process. More than anything, the use of the visual also means that participants can be engaged in the process of interpretation: 'this is why I took the photograph'. For researchers seeking approaches that have the potential to bring about change in the process of doing, visual methodologies are ideal.

Questions for further investigation

1. Do we as researchers conduct ourselves differently when the participants of our studies are 'right there', particularly in relation to the photos or videos they have produced?

2. How can visual interventions be used to educate community groups and point to ways to empower and reform institutional practices?

3. What ethical issues come to the fore in these action-oriented studies? How do we work with such concepts as 'confidentiality' and 'anonymity' within visual work?

Suggested further reading

De Lange, N., Mitchell, C. and Stuart, J. (eds) (2007) *Putting People in the Picture: Visual Methodologies for Social Change.* Amsterdam: Sense. This collection, while focused primarily on South Africa, offers an overview of many different methodologies and critical issues, using case studies. It has a strong education focus.

Ewald, W. (2000) *Secret Games: Collaborative Works with Children, 1969–99.* Berlin and New York: Scalo. For anyone working with children as photographers, this book is key. We get to appreciate the photographers as artists and not just as social documentarians.

Prosser, J. (ed.) (1998) *Image-Based Research: A Sourcebook for Qualitative Research.* London: Falmer Press. Jon Prosser was one of the first to publish in the area of visual research and education. This book, while having been around for a while, nonetheless offers a very comprehensive overview of work in the area of visual and educational research.

Knowles, G. and Cole, A. (eds) (2007) *Handbook of the Arts in Qualitative Research: Perspectives, Methodologies, Examples and Issues.* London: Sage. This is one of the most comprehensive books on arts-based methodologies, including many visual approaches.

Rose, G. (2001) *Visual Methodologies.* London: Sage. The book has a strong theory base. For anyone who is interested in applying discourse anlaysis to working with visual images, this book is key.

Sontag, S. (1977) *On Photography.* New York: Doubleday. Sontag's work is a classic in doing visual studies. The book provides an excellent theoretical base for any visual work.

Wang, C. (1999) 'Photovoice: a participatory action research strategy applied to women's health', *Journal of Women's Health,* 8(2): 85–192. Caroline Wang coined the term 'photovoice' and as such her work is basic in the whole area of photography and photo elictation.

References

Banks, M. (2001) *Visual Methods in Social Research.* London: Sage.

Chong, E., Hallman, K. and Brady, M. (2005) *Generating the Evidence Base for HIV/AIDS Policies and Programs.* New York: Population Council.

De Lange, N., Mitchell, C. and Stuart, J. (eds) (2007) *Putting People in the Picture: Visual Methodologies for Social Change.* Amsterdam: Sense.

De Lange, N., Mitchell, C., Moletsane, R., Stuart, J. and Buthelezi, T. (2006) 'Seeing through the body: educators' representations of HIV and AIDS', *Journal of Education,* 38: 45–66.

Emmison, M. and Smith, P. (2000) *Researching the Visual: Images, Objects, Contexts and Interactions in Social and Cultural Inquiry.* London: Sage.

Ewald, W. (2000) *Secret Games: Collaborative Works with Children, 1969–99.* Berlin and New York: Scalo.

Fiske, J. (1989) *Understanding Popular Culture.* Boston: Unwin.

Hirsch, M. (1997) *Family Frames: Photography, Narrative and Postmemory.* Cambridge, MA: Harvard University Press.

Hubbard, J. (1994) *Shooting Back from the Reservation.* New York: New Press.

Knowles, G. and Cole, A. (eds) (2007) *Handbook of the Arts in Qualitative Research: Perspectives, Methodologies, Examples and Issues.* London: Sage.

Langford, M. (2001) *Suspended Conversations: The Afterlife of Memory in Photographic Albums.* Montreal: McGill-Queen's Press.

Lister, M. and Wells, L. (2001) 'Seeing beyond belief: cultural studies as an approach to analysing the visual', in van Leeuwen, T. and Jewitt, C. (eds) *Handbook of Visual Analysis.* London: Sage, pp. 61–91.

Lykes, M. B. (2001) 'Creative arts and photography in participatory action research in Guatemala', in Reason, P. and Bradbury, H. (eds) *Handbook of Action Research: Participative Inquiry and Practice.* Thousand Oaks, CA: Sage, pp. 363–71.

Mitchell, C. and Allnutt, S. (2007) 'Working with photographs as objects and things: social documentary as a new materialism', in Knowles, G. and Cole, A. (eds) *Handbook of the Arts in Qualitative Research: Perspectives, Methodologies, Examples and Issues.* London: Sage, pp. 251–63.

Mitchell, C. and Umurungi, J. P. (2007) 'What happens to girls who are raped in Rwanda', *Children First*, pp. 13–18.

Mitchell, C., Moletsane, R. and Stuart, J. (2006) 'Why we don't go to school on Fridays: youth participation and HIV and AIDS', *McGill Journal of Education*, 41(3): 267–82.

Mitchell, C., Walsh, S. and Weber, S. (2007) 'Behind the lens: reflexivity and video documentary', in Knowles, G. and Cole, A. (eds) *The Art of Visual Inquiry*. Halifax: Backalong Press, pp. 281–94.

Mitchell, C., Weber, S. and Pithouse, K. (2009) 'Facing the public: using photography for self-study and social action', in Tidwell, D., Heston, M. and Fitzgerald, L. (eds) *Research Methods for the Self-Study of Practice*. New York: Springer, pp. 119–34.

Mitchell, C., De Lange, N., Moletsane, R., Stuart, J. and Buthelezi, T. (2005a) 'The face of HIV and AIDS in rural South Africa: a case for photo-voice', *Qualitative Research in Psychology*, 3(2): 257–70.

Mitchell, C., De Lange, N., Moletsane, R., Stuart, J. and Buthelezi, T. (2005b) 'Taking pictures/taking action! Using photo-voice techniques with children', *ChildrenFIRST*, 9(60): 27–31.

Moletsane, R. and Mitchell, C. (2007) 'On working with a single photograph', in De Lange, N., Mitchell, C. and Stuart, J. (eds) *Putting People in the Picture: Visual Methodologies for Social Change*. Amsterdam: Sense, pp. 131–40.

Moletsane, R., De Lange, N., Mitchell, C., Stuart, J., Buthelezi, T. and Taylor, M. (2007) 'Photo-voice as a tool for analysis and activism in response to HIV and AIDS stigmatization in a rural KwaZulu-Natal school', *Journal of Child and Adolescent Mental Health*, 19(1): 19–28.

Moletsane, R., Mitchell, C., De Lange, N., Stuart, J., Buthelezi, T. and Taylor, M. (2009) 'What can a woman do with a camera? Turning the female gaze on poverty and HIV/AIDS in rural South Africa', *International Journal of Qualitative Studies in Education*, 22(3): 315–31.

Pink, S. (2001) *Doing Visual Ethnography*. London: Sage.

Pithouse, K. and Mitchell, C. (2007) 'Looking into change: studying participant engagement in photovoice projects', in De Lange, N., Mitchell, C. and Stuart, J. (eds) *Putting People in the Picture: Visual Methodologies for Social Change*. Amsterdam: Sense, pp.141–51.

Prosser, J. (ed.) (1998) *Image-Based Research: A Sourcebook for Qualitative Research*. London: Falmer Press.

Rose, G. (2001) *Visual Methodologies*. London: Sage.

Ruby, J. (2000) *Picturing Culture: Explorations of Film and Anthropology*. Chicago: University of Chicago Press.

Schratz, M. and Walker, R. (1995) *Research as Social Change: New Opportunities for Qualitative Research*. London: Routledge.

Sontag, S. (1977) *On Photography*. New York: Doubleday.

Spence, J. (1988) *Putting Myself in the Picture: A Political, Personal and Photographic Autobiography*. Seattle: Real Comet Press.

Van Laren, L. (2007) 'Using metaphors for integrating HIV and AIDS education in mathematics curriculum in pre-service teacher education: an exploratory classroom study', *International Journal of Inclusive Education*, 11(4): 461–79.

Wang, C. (1999) 'Photovoice: a participatory action research strategy applied to women's health', *Journal of Women's Health*, 8(2): 85–192.

Wang, C. C. and Redwood-Jones, Y. A. (2001) 'Photovoice ethics: perspectives from Flint photovoice', *Health Education and Behaviour*, 28(5): 560–72.

Weber, S. and Mitchell, C. (eds) (2004) *Not Just Any Dress: Narratives of Memory, Body and Identity*. New York: Peter Lang.

Grounded theory

Michael Waring

Introduction

Grounded theory continues to be an extremely influential and highly regarded method of social analysis, and a popular methodology predominantly but not exclusively used as part of qualitative enquiry in educational research (Douglas, 2003; Thomas and James, 2006). However, there remains a degree of confusion and uncertainty about the interpretation and implementation of grounded theory (Babchuk, 2009; Buckley and Waring, 2009). This chapter will explore issues associated with the evolving (re)interpretation of grounded theory which is currently taking place. It will identify the philosophical location of the grounded theory researcher, the (mis) use of terminology in defining grounded theory, and the identification of essential elements that make up a grounded theory methodology. In addition, it will provide a pragmatic overview of the 'grounded theory process of analysis' using a model which is particularly helpful to the novice grounded theory researcher, offer advice on writing a grounded theory and supply an outline of key criticisms of grounded theory.

(Re)interpretations of grounded theory

Almost every chapter or article on grounded theory starts with a historical overview of its development. This may be repetitive, but it is important for at least two reasons. Firstly, it acknowledges the context and how the development of the seminal text on grounded theory: *The Discovery of Grounded Theory: An Approach to Qualitative Research* (Glaser and Strauss, 1967) was presented at the time to articulate a credible alternative to the considerable dominance of positivistic paradigms and their associated assumptions of the time. Glaser and Strauss attempted to articulate a merger of different epistemologies involving their pragmatist (Strauss) and positivistic (Glaser) backgrounds via a set of systematic procedures to generate theory from empirical data, and in so doing enhance the status of interpretive research (e.g. Thomas and James, 2006). They did not, however, articulate their ontological or epistemological assumptions at that time.

Secondly, it highlights the inherent ethos of grounded theory to be flexible, creative and evolutionary in its approach. As Morse (2009) notes the demands of a particular context, researcher, participants and research focus will require certain adaptations in the use of grounded theory. Therefore any (re)articulation of grounded theory should not be seen as a negative thing, but as a positive and constructive dimension of its development. Also any researcher employing grounded theory has to be informed of and able to locate themselves and their research within the contested and complicated landscape of grounded theory methodology and methods (Morse et al., 2009).

Grounded theory should therefore not only be seen as a methodology to study process but also as a methodology *in* process (Charmaz, 2009). Bryant and Charmaz (2007: 11) reinforce the challenge facing the researcher considering the use of grounded theory when they note that, 'anyone who is contemplating the grounded theory method (GTM) landscape must grasp the inherent complexity of what might be termed the 'family of methods claiming the GTM mantle'. So grounded theory is in transition, with many researchers developing their interpretations of grounded theory as part of an ongoing shift and articulation about the assumptions and methods that underpin it. Babchuk (2009) also refers to grounded theory as a 'family of methods' as he succinctly and effectively identifies the historical progression and evolution of grounded theory. Morse (2009: 17) also offers a very helpful illustration of the 'genealogy' of grounded theory which sets out major milestones. In it she clearly and succinctly identifies how in the form of subsequent publications from *The Discovery of Grounded Theory*, Glaser and Strauss and other authors (many of whom were students of Glaser and Strauss) have (re)interpreted grounded theory to reveal a landscape of 'different' grounded theories: Straussian (Strauss, 1987; Strauss and Corbin, 1990, 1997, 1998; Corbin and Strauss, 2008); Glasarian (also referred to as 'classic' GT by its advocates) (Glaser, 1978, 1992, 2004, 2005, 2008); constructivist (Bryant and Charmaz, 2007; Charmaz, 2009); situational analysis (Clarke, 2007).

Locating yourself as a grounded theorist

As we know, a rudimentary prerequisite for any researcher is a depth of understanding of the con-figuration of the methodology and associated methods they adopt. Therefore, in order to achieve this, a researcher must be able to articulate their ontological and epistemological positions as these will inform their methodological preferences.

If one looks at the language in *The Discovery of Grounded Theory*, Glaser and Strauss, (even though they did not articulate it at the time), the ontological assumptions being made are realist in nature, that is they assume that there is a single objective reality that exists independently of individuals' perceptions of it.

The epistemological assumptions are positivistic in nature. That is the investigator and the investigated are considered to be independent entities and enquiry takes place as if in a one-way mirror. Strauss and Corbin on the other hand would say that they are firmly located within an interpretive epistemology because they acknowledge and include the perspectives and voices of the individuals that they study. However, it has also been pointed out by Annells (1997) and Charmaz (2000) that the language which is used by these authors, such as 'recognising bias', is very much realist in nature. So, Strauss and Corbin (e.g. 1998) (and other Straussian grounded theorists) have adopted the somewhat contradictory epistemology known as post-positivism. That is, they make interpretive assumptions in that not all aspects of the social world can be measured, as well as contradicting this by attempting to maintain an approach which is objective and free from bias. That is, where the data are real and represent objective facts and the researcher is an impartial observer who maintains a distance from those being researched and their realities (the data is uncovered and a theory developed from them) (Charmaz, 2006; Hildenbrand, 2007). Glaser (1992) is a realist and positivist. Other grounded theorists such as Charmaz and Bryant propose constructivist grounded theory, an interpretation of grounded theory that offers a moderate constructivist ontology and interpretivist epistemology. This means that both data and analyses are seen as social constructions reflecting their process of production, and each analysis is specific to the time, space, culture and situation.

What is grounded theory?

As the originators of grounded theory, Glaser and Strauss (1967) distinguished their methodology from that of others by highlighting the evolutionary nature of the research process through the identification of a set of 'interpreted' procedural steps, rather than the verification of a preconceived theory. One does not begin with preconceived ideas or extant theory and then force them on data for the purpose of verifying them or rearranging them into a corrected grounded theory (Glaser, 1992: 15). Their claim is that data shapes the research process and its product in an innovative way. This allows data that is grounded to be identified, discarded, clarified and elaborated upon (relative to that situation) through simultaneous data collection and analysis. As a result, it differs from those theoretical frameworks which are developed deductively, evolved prior to or in isolation from engagement in the field. From the accumulation of data the researcher develops or 'discovers' the grounded theory (Martin and Turner, 1986: 143). One starts with an area of investigation and begins to evolve an appropriate theory from the relevant data specific to the situation under investigation. Thus a grounded theory is

> . . . discovered, developed, and provisionally verified through systematic data collection and analysis of data pertaining to that phenomenon. Therefore, data collection, analysis, and theory stand in reciprocal relationship with each other. One does not begin with a theory, and then prove it. Rather one begins with an area of study and what is relevant to that area is allowed to emerge. (Strauss and Corbin, 1990: 23)

Remember, the data is collected in the same ways, using the same techniques as with other research methodologies. Data may be qualitative or quantitative or combinations of both types.

Grounded theory is often said to be rooted in a symbolic interactionist perspective (Clarke and Friese, 2007; Parker and Myrick, 2011). This is a contentious issue and many would disagree with it (Bryant and Charmaz, 2007; Glaser, 2005). However, grounded theory and symbolic interactionism are very similarly positioned and highly compatible in many respects. They both signify the importance of asking what is happening and why it is happening, assume the capacity of an agent to act in a world and be producers as well as products of social systems, the exploration of process, the building of theory from empirical observations and the development of conditional theories that address specific realities (Bryant and Charmaz, 2007: 21).

Grounded theory has been described as a method comprising a systematic, inductive and comparative approach for conducting enquiry for the purpose of constructing theory (Bryant and Charmaz,

2007; Charmaz and Henwood, 2007). Glaser and Strauss (1967: vii) note that a central feature of this analytic approach is a 'general method of [constant] comparative analysis'. It has also been described as a simultaneous set of assumptions about the production of knowledge and a set of guidelines for empirical research work (Tesch, 1990: 58), a general methodology for developing theory that is grounded in data systematically gathered and analysed (Glaser, 1992; Strauss and Corbin 1994), and a set of relationships among data and categories that proposes a plausible and reasonable explanation of the phenomenon under study (Moghaddam, 2006). Grounded theory is said to be a general methodology for developing theory that is grounded in data systematically gathered and analysed. The theory that evolves during actual research, does so through continuous interplay between analysis and data collection (Strauss and Corbin, 1998).

The use of the terms method and methodology have often been used interchangeably and inappropriately so in the literature on grounded theory. In the scheme of things the ontological assumptions (the nature of the social world) informs the epistemological assumptions (how knowledge of the social world is possible), which in turn informs the methodology (which procedures and logic to follow), which informs the methods (the specific techniques used to collect data). There is clearly confusion as to whether grounded theory is a methodology or a set of methods. The short answer is that it is a methodology. However, Weed (2009) develops this further noting that a better term for what is an integrated research strategy that assumes the principles of grounded theory have been followed from the start would be a 'total methodology' that provides a set of principles for the entire research process and not, as he puts it, 'a pick and mix' box.

Having acknowledged the differences between some of the various interpretations of grounded theory, there are also similarities between them: an iterative process (concurrent data generation or collection and analysis); theoretical sampling; theoretical sensitivity; coding and categorisation of data, writing memos and concepts; constant comparative analysis using inductive and deductive logic (abduction); theoretical saturation; fit, work, relevance and modifiability; substantive theory (Birks and Mills, 2011; Bryant and Charmaz, 2007; Weed, 2009). These can be considered to be the essential elements which together are considered conditions for grounded theory research and are core parts of grounded theory methodology. Therefore, when reading or constructing a grounded theory, you should use them to critique the 'grounded theory'.

The helix model: a framework for enquiry

The novelty of grounded theory exists not in the mode of the investigation associated with it but, as Turner (1983) points out, in the manner in which the information is collected and analysed. This theme has been developed further by Martin and Turner (1986) when they use, quite appropriately, the phrase 'grounded theory *craft*'. The framework of data collection and analysis you are about to be presented with is systematic; however, within it there is flexibility which increases proportionally to the researcher's understanding of and familiarity with the methodology, methods and the research setting.

The helix model (see Figure 38.1) draws heavily on the work of Strauss and Corbin (1990) to illustrate the systematic and flexible nature of grounded theory analysis. There can and should be movement backwards and forwards within the helix to suit the research situation and expertise of the researcher. The adoption of a spiral emphasises the notion of continually revisiting aspects of the theory, while maintaining progression towards a substantive theory. However, as has been pointed out, theory is a process, an 'ever developing entity, not a perfected product' (Glaser and Strauss, 1967).

Theoretical sensitivity

The term 'theoretical sensitivity' is one which is closely associated with grounded theory (e.g. Glaser, 1978; Glaser and Strauss, 1967; Strauss, 1987). Everyone not only brings to (due to the accumulation of their past experiences and attitudes) but generates within each research context (as a result of an increased awareness of relevant aspects) theoretical sensitivity. This is something that cannot and should not be ignored.

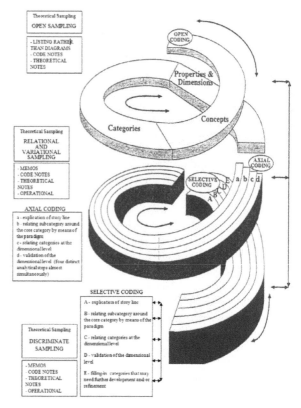

Source: Waring (1995).

Figure 38.1   The helix model

Theoretical sensitivity is defined as 'sensitive thinking about data in theoretical terms' (Strauss, 1987) or 'the personal quality of the researcher' (Strauss and Corbin, 1990). Due to the accumulation of past experiences people bring theoretical sensitivity to each context, which can increase with their exposure to the research setting. Interpersonal interaction is an essential feature of these experiences, therefore the researcher must not only observe the behaviour of their subjects, but reflect critically on themselves. This necessitates awareness of one's own preconceptions, which Hutchinson (1988) refers to as 'bracketing'. It would be unrealistic to expect these preconceptions, regardless of how careful the researcher was, to be completely abandoned when entering a research project.

The heart of the matter – coding

If we assume that the experiences which construct each person's reality have patterns, grounded theory makes sense of them. Data analysis is the process of bringing order, structure and meaning to the mass of collected data (Marshall and Rossman, 1989: 112). You should consider carefully the data that you will gather. The nature of the data can be qualitative or quantitative and extremely varied, in terms of the means – for example, from interviews, images from video, stills, hand drawings, policy documents, observations, field notes, academic literature, informal discussions, etc. However, regardless of how it is gathered, the data needs to be fit for purpose. That means the data that is gathered should allow for the researcher to capture relevant, substantial and rich data which involves varied contexts and the detailed views and actions of the participants so as to allow the researcher to fully engage in the process of analysis. The analysis portion of grounded theory is referred to as 'coding'. The focus of analysis is *not* merely on the collecting or ordering of '. . . a mass of data, but on *organising many ideas*, which have emerged from analysis of data' (Strauss, 1978: 23). This represents the complex operation by which data are broken down, conceptualised and put back together in new ways (Strauss and Corbin, 1990: 57). This is developed by Charmaz (1983: 112) when she comments on the way in which codes provide the pivotal link between the data collection and its conceptual rendering. Thus coding becomes the fundamental means of developing the analysis.

Open coding

Once the researcher has collected their initial set of data, they embark on open coding which is the initial coding that takes place in the research project. During this process Strauss suggests that 'the point is not so much in the document as in the relationship between it, the inquiring mind and the training of the researcher who vigorously and imaginatively engages in the open coding' (Strauss, 1987). The data that has already been gathered is then broken down, examined, compared, conceptualised and categorised. Glaser (1978) classifies open coding under the heading substantive coding, describing the process as 'running the data open'. He defines this as coding the data in every way possible in order to work towards the generation of an emerging set of categories and their properties. Breaking down the data in order to conceptualise it refers to the process of taking an observation, a sentence or a paragraph and giving each of the individual events, ideas and incidents that exist in it a name that represents that phenomenon. Every incident is compared and contrasted with others as the conceptualising process develops. This allows the researcher to take similar phenomena and give them the same conceptual names. When 'labelling the phenomena' in this way, the researcher must endeavour to conceptualise the data (Strauss and Corbin, 1990). This is more than using the remnants of sentences that are being analysed, it requires conceptualisation. Strauss and Corbin (1990) refer to this grouping of concepts around particular phenomena as 'categorising'. The degree of abstraction associated with the concepts is less than with the categories in which they are grouped.

Having begun to identify concepts and then create categories in this open coding portion of the helix model, the next section of it deals with the properties and dimensions of the categories. Relationships between categories need to be discovered so that the researcher can move towards a single category. The basis on which this is done is the systematic development of their properties and dimensions. The process of open coding stimulates the discovery not only of categories but also of their properties and dimensions. General properties pertain to a category regardless of the situation in which the category is found (Strauss and Corbin, 1990: 70). Each of these general properties exists along a continuum (a dimensional continua). Having identified the dimensional continua many specific instances identified within a general property can exist at different points along it. This gives rise to the notion of a 'dimensional profile'. As Strauss and Corbin (1990: 70) point out: several of these profiles can be grouped to give you a *pattern*. The dimensional profile represents the specific properties of a phenomenon under a given set of conditions. Open coding is conducted alongside open sampling.

Open Sampling

Open sampling is part of the notion of theoretical sampling, that is sampling on the basis of concepts that have proven theoretical relevance to the evolving theory. Proven theoretical relevance indicates that concepts are deemed to be significant because they are repeatedly present or notably absent when comparing incident after incident, and are of sufficient importance to be given the status of categories (Strauss and Corbin, 1990: 176). Open sampling maintains a high degree of flexibility while attempting to uncover as many potentially relevant categories (and their related properties and dimensions) as possible. The researcher must remain open to all possibilities at this stage because all the sources (places, people, circumstances) which yield the necessary evidence for concepts will not be fully appreciated.

Memos and diagrams (the product of analysis) in open coding

The written forms of abstract thinking about data are known as memos. There can be virtually no limit to the kind of memos written in open coding. They can be as uncertain as the researcher likes, i.e. the noting of first impressions and any other thoughts they have had. These should not be considered as 'the' answer, for if they were, there would be no need to do the research in the first place. Three 'types' of memo can be defined: *code notes* – memos containing the actual products of the three types of coding, such as conceptual labels, paradigm features and indications of process; *theoretical notes* – theoretically sensitising and summarising memos that contain the products of inductive or deductive thinking about relevant categories, their properties, dimensions, relationships, variations, processes and conditional matrix; *operational notes* – memos containing directions to the researcher (or research team) regarding sampling, questions, possible comparisons, leads to follow up on, and so forth (Strauss and Corbin, 1990: 197). All of these can appear within the same memo; however, such a situation would diminish the potential value of each of them, because of the ambiguity it would create.

Diagrams are the visual representation of relationships between concepts. Two kinds of diagrams are employed in open coding: *logic diagrams* and *integrative diagrams*. These visually identify relationships between categories and the analytical thinking with conceptual linkages respectively. A list of the categories, their properties and dimensions is drawn to create the foundation for the logic diagrams that will be developed in axial coding.

Theoretical notes extend code notes. Even though they are provisional and in need of verification, these notes can increase the theoretical sensitivity of the researcher. They do this by making them ask more questions about the categories (their properties and dimensions) generated in the interview and/or observational data. Literary sources such as articles can be used to achieve the same results. Importantly, from theoretical notes the researcher can manoeuvre and direct further sampling. For example, having pursued certain questions in one interview the researcher can identify that which appears to be relevant to their work and worth further investigation. Operational notes direct questions and avenues of enquiry in future interviews, representing the point where theoretical notes lead to sampling notes. The process of open coding and sampling could be perpetuated indefinitely; however, once the categories and sub-categories have been sufficiently reinforced by subsequent data the researcher will move into the axial coding phase.

Axial coding

The helix model illustrates the four distinct analytical phases of axial coding that are conducted almost simultaneously: (a) using the paradigm model relating sub-categories to categories; (b) verification of hypotheses against actual data; (c) continued search for the properties of categories and sub-categories and dimensional locations of data; (d) the beginning of the exploration of variation in phenomena. The procedures of axial coding enable the data to be 'put back together' in new ways after open coding and consist of four distinct analytical stages applied almost simultaneously. Once again this is conducted at the same time as sampling procedures (relational and variational sampling) and the development of memos and diagrams.

The paradigm model

The paradigm model (Strauss and Corbin, 1990) enables systematic thinking about the data, which generates more complex relationships between the sub-categories and categories. The model involves the following: the identification of the causal conditions associated with the occurrence or development of a phenomenon; the specification of a category for the phenomenon; the specific set of properties that pertain to a phenomenon; the structural conditions bearing on action/interactional strategies that pertain to the phenomenon; action/interactional strategies devised to manage/respond to a phenomenon under certain circumstances; and the consequences of action and interaction. By asking questions and making comparisons (i.e. those basic analytic procedures mentioned in open coding) links between categories and their development take place. Within axial coding this process becomes much more complicated because there are four quite separate analytical steps conducted almost simultaneously. The whole process of relating sub-categories to categories in axial coding is one which requires complex inductive and deductive thinking, facilitated by asking questions and making comparisons.

Relational and variational sampling

Relational and variational sampling is the theoretical sampling that takes place during the second phase of the helix model. Relational and variational sampling maximises differences at the dimensional level. The researcher has a choice of two approaches to achieve this aim as they sample on the basis of theoretically relevant concepts. Firstly, because of the limitations of time, access and availability, a highly systematic approach can be employed. This would involve a predetermined list of situations/people/documents to be visited. Secondly, the opposite situation may arise, where no such preconceived restrictions exist. This allows for a deliberate selection from a variety of sites, documents and/or people which are believed to be the most appropriate as the research continues.

Memos and diagrams in axial coding

The verification of relationships between a category and its sub-categories promoted in axial coding is mirrored in the kind of memos used. They identify all the attempts made to associate each different aspect to the paradigm model. The sophistication of the code notes and theoretical notes increases as the theoretical sensitivity of the researcher develops. The subsequent directness and ability to focus on the most relevant context, people and places highlights this. Operational notes develop in much the same manner, suggesting particular categories to focus upon when conducting further sampling, or to investigate those hypotheses generated and in need of verification in future interviews. As with the memos, the diagrams used in axial coding start by being simplistic in nature, i.e. in the form of a table of rows and columns of certain aspects, but they become much more complex over time.

Selective coding

In the helix model selective coding follows axial coding, but they only really differ in terms of their more abstract level of analysis; axial coding is the foundation on which selective coding takes place. Selective coding involves the selection of a core category and systematically relating it to other categories. Figure 38.1 illustrates how this involves the simultaneous use of five stages, together with discriminative sampling and associated memos and diagrams.

Integrating categories

Strauss and Corbin (1990) suggest that there are systematic guidelines that can be used to achieve what is a difficult and complex part of the research; that is 'the final leap between creating a list of concepts and producing a theory.' The steps suggested (which occur at the same time, with movement back and forth between them) are:

1. Explication of a story line. Write thoughts down on paper; use an existing category or create a new category which is abstract enough to consume

all that which has been described in the story (this category is the core category that is the central phenomenon around which all the other categories are integrated (Strauss and Corbin, 1990: 116). Once the properties of the core category are identified, the next step is to relate the other categories to it, thereby making them *subsidiary categories.*

2. Relating the subsidiary categories around the core category by means of the paradigm. The existing categories are matched to relevant portion(s) of the paradigm, i.e. either to conditions, context, strategies or consequences. This may appear straightforward; however, those conditions which influence the action/interactional strategies ('intervening conditions') make it complicated.

3. Relating categories at the dimensional level. During selective coding, the categories that were integrated in axial coding by identifying the matrix of conceptual relationships existing between them are refined further through the juxtapositioning between asking questions, generating hypotheses and making comparisons as a result of the inductive and deductive thinking going on. This refinement is necessary to enable the theory to cover what will occur in given instances within the research setting. Strauss and Corbin (1990: 131) emphasise that it is very important to identify these patterns and to group the data accordingly, because this is what gives the theory its specificity.

4. Validating the relationships against the data. The grounding of the theory is completed once it is validated against the data. This is achieved by drawing or writing memos which represent the theory, then writing statements about the relationships between categories in a variety of contexts which are validated against the data.

5. Filling in categories that may need further development and/or refinement. This is necessary in order to achieve *conceptual density* in the theory and to promote *conceptual specificity.*

The sampling that occurs in selective coding is known as discriminative sampling and it is used for verificational purposes. In discriminative sampling, a researcher chooses the sites, persons, and documents that will maximise opportunities for verifying the story line, the relationships between categories and for filling in poorly developed categories (Strauss and Corbin, 1990: 187). Something may be discovered which does not fit the story line and those relationships that have frequently been found. If this situation occurs those factors leading to the occurrence of such an instance must be uncovered to determine whether or not it is due to incorrect thinking or an instance of a variation. Categories are considered theoretically saturated and so make the theory conceptually adequate when: there is no more new or relevant data emerging regarding a category; each category has been linked with the paradigm model and each of its elements are catered for, including the variation and process; relationships between categories are well established and validated. Sampling continues until the researcher can theoretically saturate each category.

Memos at this stage of the analysis are complex, illustrating the depth of thought that mirrors the evolving theory. Code notes in the context of selective coding relate mainly to the filling-in role, i.e. filling in those categories which are not sufficiently saturated. Theoretical notes on the other hand are much more extensive during this period of the analysis. 'It is in the form of theoretical memos that we write the first descriptive rendition of what the research is all about' (Strauss and Corbin, 1990). These memos enable the researcher to identify the core category and its host of sub-categories, as well as elaborate these relationships as hypotheses. The operational notes during this phase are very much more succinct. The exploration phase is now over, and it is a matter of validating and refining the theory.

Diagrams also reflect complexity at this stage. The transference of this complexity from writing to an accurate, but concise, graphic format (a diagram) is difficult. However, the process of doing this aids the classification of many of the relationships between the core category and other categories. Hence, this diagram will not only clarify the theory to other people, but act as a guide to enable the researcher to keep the nature of the relationships clear when writing the theory. General reading of the memos leads to the writing of a descriptive story which is translated into an analytical one using the categories.

Writing a grounded theory

Writing a grounded theory 'right' is, on the face of it, even more complicated than writing up the more usual types of qualitative research (Strauss and Corbin, 1990: 233). Writing in grounded theory is a continual process throughout the analysis, i.e. coding, memos, field notes. However, there comes a point when analytical writings need to be translated into a written form that can be digested and understood by its designated audience. Charmaz (1990) develops this further when she comments '. . . writing and rewriting actually become crucial phases of the analytic process.' Therefore, analysis never really stops and it would be wrong to suggest that it did when one comes to write the final document.

Numerous questions arise during the writing up phase such as: 'What is to be communicated?', 'What order should it take?' and 'Who is to be its audience?' Strauss and Corbin (1990) suggest four things which writing a grounded theory text requires: (1) a clear analytic story; (2) writing on a conceptual level, with description kept secondary; (3) the clear specification of relationships among categories, with levels of conceptualisation also kept clear; (4) the specification of variations and their relevant conditions, consequences and so forth, including the broader ones. May (1986: 150) proposes the following structure for writing up a grounded theory study: (1) clear statement of the major research question and key terms defined; (2) literature review section (presents the pertinent literature in the area); (3) methodology section (the process of grounded theory); (4) findings section (includes the presentation of the theoretical scheme). There is not usually a separate 'discussion section' as there is with most hypothetico-deductive studies because in the course of presenting the theoretical scheme, findings are usually presented in sufficient detail.

The audience to which the theory is being presented is also very important, because it will help to determine its format. For example, when writing a 'thesis', something of a standardised format is usually expected, i.e. introduction, review of literature, methodology, analysis, discussion, conclusion/implications. This would make the third of the procedures suggested by Strauss and Corbin (1990) (clear specification of relationships among categories, with levels of conceptualisation also kept clear) much more difficult when writing up a grounded theory investigation. The language employed in the theory will be loaded with certain meanings and interpretations. It is, therefore, the unenviable task of the grounded theory writer to not only accommodate the contextual meaning in the form of terms (categories/concepts) for the researched audience, but to do so in a way that others outside of the context can appreciate their meanings, interpreting them in the way they were intended. There is a very delicately drawn line between 'coining a term and inventing jargon' (May, 1986).

Criticisms of grounded theory

Many criticisms of grounded theory turn on misunderstandings or misuse of the methodology. The major problems with the grounded theory method lie in the limited explication of its epistemological assumptions and in minimising its relation to extant sociological theory (Bryant and Charmaz, 2007; Charmaz, 1990).

Charmaz (1990) has emphasised that a number of criticisms of grounded theory stem from an incomplete understanding of the logic and strategies of the methodology. For example, most authors discussing grounded theory have drawn attention to the *tabula rasa* (blank slate) view of enquiry which grounded theory espouses (e.g. Bulmer, 1979; Charmaz, 1990; Hammersley, 1992). Glaser and Strauss (1967: 33) advocated that the researcher goes into the research setting 'without any preconceived theory, that dictates prior to the research 'relevancies' in concepts and hypotheses'. Grounded theory is not pure induction, but a matter of 'maintaining the balance between the two logics (*inductive and deductive*)' (Glaser, 1978: 90), even though it is inductive as a theory emerges after the data collection has started. However, deductive work guides theoretical sampling. Sparkes (1987: 138) notes that inductive theory formation is open to criticism centring on the notion of 'underdetermination' and that no process is ever completely reliant upon either induction or deduction.

Grounded theory's apparent affinity with positivism, or viewing it as a form of 'inductivist positivism' (Stanley and Wise, 1983: 152), creates problems for theorists (see Roman and Apple, 1990;

Henwood and Pidgeon, 1993; Woods, 1992). Glaser and Strauss (1967: 3) acknowledge in a footnote the use of existing knowledge, as long as it is well grounded. However, Charmaz (1990: 1163) emphasises a delay and not the complete removal of the literature review from the whole process.

Sanger (1994: 179) notes, 'their [Strauss and Corbin's] view conflates creativity with "theoretical sensitivity"'. Strauss and Corbin (1990) facilitate creativity within a systematic analysis by suggesting that the manipulation of categorised data is a creative enterprise. This creativity involves an open-minded, generative approach, which not only entertains alternative notions, but is able to cope with them in its framework relative to the perspective of the researcher and their interpretive skills. Catering for this creativity is a compromise not only for Strauss and Corbin (1990), but for any researcher between a systematic structure and freedom. To systematise this creativity, however, runs the risk of the criticism that one might as well adopt a computer program that categorises key words and phrases.

Another criticism levelled at grounded theory is the lack of rigour associated with it (e.g. Hammersley, 1989). There is no rigid divorce between discovery and verification. Yes, Glaser and Strauss (1967) do contrast the discovery and verification approaches, but this was to emphasise the desire and need to develop new avenues of theoretical development. Grounded theory specifically, and qualitative research generally, do not employ the hypothetico-deductive verification model. It emphasises inductive, open-ended, intuitive approaches to data gathering. Grounded theory does provide a rigorous method; however, it must be assessed from the internal logic of its own method (Charmaz, 1983) and not by criteria found in and appropriate to other methods.

Conclusion

The (re)interpretation and evolution of grounded theory methodology is a positive and constructive dimension of its development. However, any researcher employing grounded theory has to fully understand and articulate their ontological, epistemological and methodological location within that changing landscape. Writing a grounded theory is challenging and complicated in that it is part of a continual process throughout the analysis and actually forms part of that analysis. The form of the final report or dissertation will be determined very much by the particular audience and the substantive theory. It therefore does not usually adhere to the standard modes of presentation. Those criticisms of grounded theory methodology mainly stem from a lack articulation or thought about the assumptions which underpin the methodology. The misinterpretations which form many of the criticisms are being eroded by the (re)interpretation and greater clarification of grounded theory methodology by researchers.

Questions for further investigation

1. Why have you selected/considered grounded theory methodology? What is it about the methodology that is attractive to you in terms of addressing the particular area of research, as well as yourself as a researcher?

2. What are the ontological and epistemological differences between the main (re)interpretations of grounded theory (constructivist, Glasarian, Straussian)? Where would you locate yourself and why?

3. What is theoretical sensitivity and how will your ontological and epistemological assumptions influence your interpretation of it?

4. Relative to an area of investigation of your choice, consider how and what different kinds of data you would need to gather to ensure that it was relevant, had depth and provided a detailed viewpoint of the participants.

Suggested further reading

Birks, M. and Mills, J. (2011) *Grounded Theory: A Practical Guide*. London: Sage. A good starting point for researchers unfamiliar with grounded theory. This text offers an accessible, logical and succinct practical guide addressing those questions and aspects of grounded theory a researcher familiarising themselves with it would ask.

Bryant, A. and Charmaz, K. (eds) (2007) *The Sage Handbook of Grounded Theory*. London: Sage. An excellent text which draws together chapters from leading researchers and practitioners in grounded theory, providing a comprehensive overview of the major perspectives on grounded theory from across the world.

Morse, J. M., Stern, P. N., Corbin, J., Bowers, B., Charmaz, K. and Clarke, A. E. (2009) *Developing Grounded Theory: The Second Generation*. New York: Left Coast Press. This text is a result of a meeting of the 'second generation' of grounded theory methodologists (many students of Glaser and Strauss) in 2007. It is very helpful in that it shares those experiences, thoughts and insights of key protagonists involved in the evolution of grounded theory.

Strauss, A. and Corbin, J. (1990) *Basics of Qualitative Research: Procedures and Techniques* Thousand Oaks, CA: Sage. Strauss, A. and Corbin, J. (1998) *Basics of Qualitative Research: Techniques and procedures for developing Grounded Theory* (2nd edn). Thousand Oaks, CA: Sage. Corbin, J. and Strauss, A. (2008) *Basics of Qualitative Research: Procedures and Techniques* (3rd edn). Thousand Oaks, CA: Sage. These three texts illustrate the progression of an interpretation of grounded theory which has strongly influenced the organisation and formulation of the helix model presented here to illustrate grounded theory analysis and substantive theory generation.

References

Annells, M. (1997) 'Grounded theory methods, part 1: within the five moments of qualitative research', *Nursing Inquiry*, 4(2) 120–9.

Babchuk, W. A. (2009) *Grounded Theory for Practice-Based Application: Closing the Embarrassing Gap Between Theory and Empirical Research*. Paper presented at the Midwest Research-to-Practice Conference in Adult, Continuing, Community and Extension Education, Northeastern Illinois University, Chicago, 21–23 October.

Birks, M. and Mills, J. (2011) *Grounded Theory: A Practical Guide*. London: Sage.

Bryant, A. and Charmaz, K. (eds) (2007) *The Sage Handbook of Grounded Theory*. London: Sage.

Buckley, C. and Waring, M. (2009) 'The evolving nature of grounded theory: experiential reflections on the potential of the method for analysing children's attitudes towards physical activity', *International Journal of Social Research Methodology*, 12(4): 317–34.

Bulmer, M. (1979) 'Concepts in the analysis of qualitative data', *Sociological Review*, 27: 651–77.

Charmaz, K. (1983) 'The grounded theory method: an explication and interpretation', in Emerson, R. M. (ed.) *Contemporary Field Research: A Collection of Readings*. Boston: Little Brown.

Charmaz, K. (1990) '"Discovering" chronic illness: using grounded theory', *Social Science and Medicine*, 30(11): 1161–72.

Charmaz, K. (2000) 'Grounded Theory: objectivist and constructivist methods', in Denzin, N. K. and Lincoln, Y. S. (eds) *Handbook of Qualitative Research* (2nd edn). London: Sage.

Charmaz, K. (2006) *Constructing Grounded Theory: A Practical Guide Through Qualitative Analysis*. Thousand Oaks, CA: Sage.

Charmaz, K. (2009) 'Shifting grounds: constructivist grounded theory methods', in Morse, J. M. et al. (eds) *Developing Grounded Theory: The Second Generation*. New York: Left Coast Press, pp. 127–54.

Charmaz, K. and Henwood, K. (2007) 'Grounded theory in psychology', in Willing, C. and Stainton-Rogers, W. (eds) *Handbook of Qualitative Research in Psychology*. London: Sage.

Clarke, A. (2007) 'Grounded theory: critiques, debates and situational analysis', in Outhwaite, W. and Turner, S. P. (eds) *Handbook of Social Science Methodology*. Thousand Oaks, CA: Sage, pp. 423–42.

Clarke, A. and Friese, C. (2007) 'Grounded theorizing using grounded theory', in Bryant, A. and Charmaz, K. (eds) (2007) *The Sage Handbook of Grounded Theory*. London: Sage, pp. 363–97.

Corbin, J. and Strauss, A. (2008) *Basics of Qualitative Research: Techniques and Procedures For Developing Grounded Theory* (3rd edn). Thousand Oaks, CA: Sage.

Douglas, D. (2003) 'Reflections on research supervision: a grounded theory case of reflective practice', *Research in Post-Compulsory Education*, 8(2) 213–29.

Glaser, B. G. (1978) *Theoretical Sensitivity: Advances in the Methodology of Grounded Theory*. Mill Valley, CA: Sociology Press.

Glaser, B. G. (1992) *Basics of Grounded Theory Analysis*. Mill Valley, CA: Sociology Press.

Glaser, B. G. (2004) 'Remodelling grounded theory', *Forum: Qualitative Sozialforschung/Orum: Qualitiative Social Research*, 3(3).

Glaser, B. G. (2005) *The Grounded Theory Perspective III: Theoretical Coding*. Mill Valley, CA: Sociology Press.

Glaser, B. G. (2008) *Doing Quantitative Grounded Theory*. Mill Valley, CA: Sociology Press.

Glaser, B. G. and Strauss, A. L. (1967) *The Discovery of Grounded Theory: An Approach to Qualitative Research*. New York: Aldine.

Hammersley, M. (1989) *The Dilemma of Qualitative Method: Herbert Blumer and the Chicago Tradition*. London: Routledge.

Hammersley, M. (1992) *What's Wrong With Ethnography?* London: Routledge.

Henwood, K. L. and Pidgeon, N. F. (1993) 'Qualitative research and psychological theorizing', in Hammersley, M. (eds) *Social Research: Philosophy, Politics and Practice*. London: Sage, pp. 14–32.

Hildenbrand, B. (2007) 'Mediating structure and interaction in grounded theory', in Bryant, A. and Charmaz, K. (eds) *The Sage Handbook of Grounded Theory*. London: Sage, pp. 539–64.

Hutchinson, S. A. (1988) 'Education and grounded theory', in Sherman, R. R. and Webb, R. B. (eds) *Qualitative Research in Education: Focus and Methods*. London: Falmer Press.

Marshall, C. and Rossman, G. B. (1989) *Designing Qualitative Research*. Newbury Park, CA: Sage.

Martin, P. Y. and Turner, B. A. (1986) 'Grounded theory and organisational research', *Journal of Applied Behavioural Science*, 22(2): 141–57.

May, K. A. (1986) 'Writing and evaluating the grounded theory research report', in Chentiz, C. W. and Swanson, J. M. (eds) *From Practice to Grounded Theory: Qualitative Research in Nursing*. Menlo Park, CA: Addison-Wesley, pp. 146–54.

Mogghadam, A. (2006) 'Coding issues in grounded theory', *Issues in Educational Research*, 16(1): 52.

Morse, J. M. (2009) 'Tussles, tensions and resolutions', in Morse, J. M., Stern, P. N., Corbin, J., Bowers, B., Charmaz, K. and Clarke, A. E. *Developing Grounded Theory: The Second Generation*. New York: Left Coast Press, pp. 13–19.

Morse, J. M., Stern, P. N., Corbin, J., Bowers, B., Charmaz, K. and Clarke, A. E. (2009) *Developing Grounded Theory: The Second Generation*. New York: Left Coast Press.

Parker, B. and Myrick, F. (2011) 'The grounded theory method: deconstruction and reconstruction in a human patient simulation context', *International Journal of Qualitative Methods*, 10(1): 73–85.

Roman, L. G. and Apple, M. W. (1990) 'Is naturalism a move away from positivism? Materialist and feminist approaches to subjectivity in ethnographic research', in Eisner, E. W. and Peshkin, A. (eds) *Qualitative Inquiry in Education: The Continuing Debate*. New York: Teachers College Press, pp. 38–73.

Sanger, J. (1994) 'Seven types of creativity: looking for insights in data analysis', *British Educational Research Journal*, 20(2): 175–85.

Sparkes, A. C. (1987) *The Genesis of An Innovation: A Case of Emergent Concerns and Micropolitical Solutions*. PhD thesis, Loughborough University.

Stanley, L. and Wise, S. (1983) *Breaking Out: Feminist Consciousness and Feminist Research*. London: Routledge & Kegan Paul.

Strauss, A. L. (1987) *Qualitative Analysis for Social Scientists*. New York: Cambridge University Press.

Strauss, A. and Corbin, J. (1990) *Basics of Qualitative Research: Procedures and Techniques*. Thousand Oaks, CA: Sage.

Strauss, A. and Corbin, J. (1994). 'Grounded theory methodology', in Denzin, N. K. and Lincoln, Y. S. (eds), *Handbook of Qualitative Research*. Thousand Oaks, CA: Sage, pp. 273–85.

Strauss, A. and Corbin, J. (eds) (1997) *Grounded Theory in Practice*. Thousand Oaks, CA: Sage.

Strauss, A. and Corbin, J. (1998) *Basics of Qualitative Research: Techniques and Procedures for Developing Grounded Theory* (2nd edn). Thousand Oaks, CA: Sage.

Tesch, R. (1990) *Qualitative Research: Analysis Types and Software Tools*. London. Falmer Press.

Thomas, G. and James, D. (2006) 'Reinventing grounded theory: Some questions about theory, ground and discovery', *British Educational Research Journal*, 32(6): 767–95.

Turner, B. A. (1983) 'The use of grounded theory for the qualitative analysis of organisational behaviour', *Journal of Management Studies*, 20(3): 333–48.

Waring, M. (1995) 'Gatekeeping Processes: Grounded Theory, Young People and Physical Activity'. Unpublished PhD thesis, Loughborough University.

Weed, M. (2009) 'Research quality considerations for grounded theory research in sport and exercise psychology', *Psychology of Sport and Exercise*, 10: 509–10.

Woods, P. (1992) 'Symbolic interactionism: theory and method', in LeCompte, M. D., Millroy, W. L. and Preissle, J. (eds) *The Handbook of Qualitative Research in Education*. San Diego, CA: Academic Press, pp. 337–404.

Ethnography as epistemology

Judith L. Green, Audra Skukauskaite and W. Douglas Baker

Introduction to educational ethnography

What makes a study ethnographic? How do researchers engage in ethnographic inquiry? In this chapter, we provide an introduction to ethnography as epistemology, that is, as a way of knowing (Agar, 2006b) or, as Anderson-Levitt (2006) argues, as a philosophy of research, not a method. Ethnography is a recursive, iterative and abductive reasoning process (logic), a logic-in-use (Kaplan, 1964/1998), not a predefined set of steps or fieldwork methods. Although specific theories or disciplinary perspectives guiding a particular study differ across traditions, ethnographers share *a common goal*: to learn from the people (the insiders) *what counts as cultural knowledge* (insider meanings). This goal guides ethnographers, whether they are constructing a study of a society, family, social group, classroom or social process (e.g. literacy, science or learning), or tracing an individual (Mitchell, 1984). To identify cultural knowledge that members need to know, understand, predict and produce (Heath, 1982), the ethnographer engages in a range of decisions, including:

- selecting phenomena to study ethnographically;
- constructing an orienting framework to guide participant observation processes;
- selecting methods and resources (e.g. interview-

ing, writing field notes, video/audio recording, collecting artefacts, documents and/or photographs);
- identifying angles of recording (e.g. teacher's, student(s)', a particular group's or individual's);
- examining how factors outside of observed spaces impact what is happening;
- archiving records (present and historical);
- identifying rich points as anchors for analysis;
- constructing data sets from archive for analysis (i.e. producing data);
- constructing grounded accounts to develop explanations of observed events and/or phenomena;
- making transparent the logic-in-use in published accounts.

The particular ways that ethnographers engage in each process depend on theoretical and disciplinary perspectives guiding their logic-in-use.

On ethnography as a logic-in-use

In arguing that ethnography is not a method but a logic-in-use, we draw on Agar's (2006) conceptualisation of ethnography as a non-linear system, guided by an iterative, recursive and abductive logic. Ethnographers construct systems to learn what members of particular groups need to know, understand, produce and predict as they participate in events of everyday life within a group. Thus ethnographers strive to identify patterned ways of perceiving, believing, acting and evaluating what members of social groups develop within and across the events of everyday life (Anderson-Levitt, 2006; Atkinson et al., 2007; Heath and Street, 2008; Walford, 2008). From this perspective, cultural knowledge is socially constructed in and through languacultures of particular social groups (Agar, 1994, 2006a). As Agar (1994) argues, *language* is imbued with culture and *culture* is constructed through language-in-use; the two are interdependent and cannot be separated.

In education, ethnographers enter a classroom, school, family group or community setting to identify insider knowledge by asking questions such as:

- What is happening here?
- What is being accomplished, by and with whom, how, in what ways, when and where, under what conditions, for what purposes, drawing on what historical or current knowledge and resources (e.g. artefacts, meanings, tools), with what outcomes or consequences for individuals and the group?
- To what do individual members of sustaining groups have access, orient and hold each other accountable?
- What makes someone an insider or outsider of particular groups (e.g. class, group within a class, peer group or social network)?
- What counts as disciplinary knowledge (i.e. mathematics, science, social science or art) in this particular group or classroom?
- What roles and relationships, norms and expectations, and rights and obligations are constructed by and afforded members?
- How does previously constructed cultural knowledge support or constrain participation in, or create frame clashes with, local knowledge being constructed in a particular event (or social group)?
- How do decisions beyond the group support and/or constrain ways of knowing, being and doing afforded members?

Questions such as these have been used to guide ethnographic research *in* education as well as ethnography *of* education in other disciplines (e.g. anthropology, sociology, applied linguistics and technology-based disciplines) (Green and Bloome, 1997; Heath and Street, 2008; Warschauer, 2004). Walford (2008) argues that by asking such questions the 'ethnographer tries to make sense of what people are doing . . . and hopes gradually to come to an understanding of "the way we do things around here" (Deal, 1985)' (Walford, 2008: 7). These questions acknowledge the dynamic processes involved in constructing *common knowledge* (Edwards and Mercer, 1987) within social groups, and how, through a process of acculturation, knowledge in classrooms and other social spaces is constructed against a tapestry of cultural knowledge developed previously by members in other social contexts (e.g. other classrooms, families, peer or community groups) both in and out of schools (Lima, 1995).

By exploring common cultural knowledge through a non-linear, abductive, iterative and recursive logic-in-use, ethnographers develop grounded explanations for patterns of practice, or roles and relationships, and other social phenomena. To construct such explanations, ethnographers make principled decisions about records to collect and pathways to follow in order to explore the roots or routes associated with a particular meaning, event or cultural process/practice. Ethnographers also make decisions about ways of archiving, analysing and reporting accounts of phenomena studied.

Central to the ethnographic logic-in-use are moments where ethnographers are confronted with a surprise or something that does not go as expected. Such moments of frame clash become *rich points* as the ethnographer strives to shift his/her point of view (POV1) to that of the insiders' (POV2) in order to resolve the clash in expectations, frames of reference or understandings of what is happening. At such moments, Agar (1994) argues, cultural expectations, meanings and practices are made visible to ethnographers (as well as members). Rich points, therefore, provide anchors for tracing roots and routes of developing cultural knowledge to build warranted accounts of phenomena from an insider point of view.

Exemplars of educational issues, topics and directions

To make visible a range of topics, issues and directions that have been studied ethnographically in education, we present a sketch map of programs of research across national contexts:

- cross-national comparative studies of education and policy–practice relationships (Alexander, 2001; Anderson-Levitt, 2002; Castanheira, 2004; Kalman and Street, 2010; Rockwell, 2002; Street, 2005; Tobin et al., 2009);
- community-based studies of cultural processes and practices (Brayboy and Deyhle, 2000; Delamont, 2002; Heath, 1983; Philips, 1983; Spindler and Hammond, 2006);
- impact of changing policies on opportunities for learning and teaching (Carspecken and Walford, 2001; Levinson et al., 2002; McNeil and Coppola, 2006; Smith et al., 1987; Stevick and Levinson, 2007; Troman et al., 2006);
- linguistic and cultural differences between home and school (Cazden et al., 1972; Gonzalez et al., 2005; Vine, 2003);
- literacy and discourse practices in homes, schools and communities (Barton and Tusting, 2005; Bloome et al., 2005; Jennings et al., 2010; Martin-Jones et al., 2008; Orellana, 1996);
- peer culture and social development in school and community contexts (Corsaro, 2003);
- learning and teaching relationships as social constructions in classrooms and other educational settings (Edwards and Mercer, 1987; Green and Wallat, 1981; Jeffrey and Woods, 2003; Mehan, 1979; Rex, 2006; Santa Barbara Classroom Discourse Group, 1992a, 1992b);
- disciplinary knowledge in science (Brown et al., 2005; Freitas and Castanheira, 2007; Lemke, 1990), mathematics (Street et al., 2005), medicine (Atkinson, 1995) and literacy (Bloome et al., 2005; Cochran-Smith, 1984), among other subject matter, as social constructions in educational contexts;
- ways that access to technology in schools is shaped by policy decisions and instructional processes inside and outside of classrooms (Kitson et al., 2007; Warschauer, 2004).

These studies demonstrate the breadth of *ethnographic research in education* and the range of questions of global,

Table 39.1 Principle one: ethnography as a non-linear system

Principle of operation	Conceptual issues	Actions implicated
Abductive logic guides identification of pieces of cultural knowledge which are made visible when the ethnographer identifies a frame clash which cannot be understood without further exploration.	To construct an explanation of cultural processes, practices, meanings and knowledge previously unknown, the ethnographer uses abductive logic, and recursive and iterative processes.	Using abductive logic involves: • examining differences in expectations and understandings (points of view) between the ethnographer (outsider) and member(s) of the group being studied (insiders); • following historical and future pathways (roots and routes) to uncover insider (emic) knowledge through iterative actions and recursive logic; • constructing grounded connections among cultural processes, practices and local knowledge among members to develop explanations of what was previously unknown to the ethnographer.

national and local concern arising in the complex social, cultural, linguistic, economic and political contexts in which education is conducted.

Principles of operation guiding the actions of the ethnographer

In this section, we describe the principles of operation (Heath, 1982) guiding the decisions ethnographers make in constructing their logic-in-use. To make visible how the proposed principles of operation guide decisions and actions in the field and during analysis, we present an *if . . . then . . .* logic that links the principles of operation to conceptual issues and then to actions implicated by the principle. This approach to linking principles and actions can be stated as follows: *if* x is a principle, *then* y are particular kinds of decisions ethnographers make in planning, undertaking, analysing and constructing warranted accounts using ethnographic records. As part of this process, we refer to a range of tools and methods ethnographers draw on to record everyday life within a group, and to gather insider information about meanings of the processes and practices, norms and expectations, and roles and relationships constructed, and used by, members of social groups.

Principle of operation one: ethnography as a non-linear system

The first principle of operation is framed by Agar's (2006b) conceptualisation of ethnography as a non-linear system guided by abductive, recursive and iterative logic-in-use (see Table 39.1).

Implicated in this principle is the time needed in the field for a particular ethnographic study. Given the ethnographic goal of following full cycles of activity to explore cultural knowledge, ethnographers have engaged in principled studies with different time scales. Some have undertaken longitudinal studies of one to ten years (e.g. Anderson-Levitt, 2002; Green and Heras, 2011; Heath, 1983; Smith et al., 1987); others have used an ethnographic logic-in-use to examine smaller segments of life (Mitchell, 1984); still others have elected to trace individual actors across particular social spaces as they learn how to engage in particular

activities (e.g. juggling: Heath and Street, 2008; being a principal: Wolcott, 2003). Additionally, some have examined artefacts/records (video or written) of life in social groups collected by others (Castanheira et al., 2001; Skukauskaite and Green, 2004). From this perspective, what makes a study ethnographic is not the length of time involved but the logic-in-use guiding the researcher's decisions, actions and work across all phases of the study.

Principle of operation two: leaving aside ethnocentrism

Principles two to four were proposed by Heath (1982) in her seminal article 'Ethnography: Defining the Essentials'. Principle two captures a stance that ethnographers take to *bracket* their own points of view, expectations or interpretations in order to identify insider knowledge.

As indicated in Table 39.2, the principle of leaving ethnocentrism aside is a goal that leads to a range of actions designed to support ethnographers in uncovering and identifying insider knowledge as proposed by members and made visible in the chains of actions and discourse among members. This principle is designed to remind ethnographers that setting aside their own expectations is critical so that they can explore insider points of view.

Principle of operation three: identifying boundaries of what is happening

One challenge facing ethnographers is the identification of event boundaries. This process involves identifying how members signal what they are doing together and when they are changing their collective activity. Furthermore, by examining the discourse of a developing event, ethnographers are able to identify references to previous events, meanings previously constructed or actions previously taken related (i.e. intertextually tied) to the developing event. Through this process of examining how and what members propose, recognise, acknowledge, interactionally accomplish and mark as socially significant, ethnographers examine multiple levels of timescale and knowledge made visible in a particular social event (Bloome and Egan-Robertson, 1993).

Table 39.2   Principle two: leaving ethnocentrism aside

Principle of operation	Conceptual issues	Actions implicated
Fieldworkers (and analysts) should attempt to uphold the ideal of leaving aside ethnocentrism and maintaining open acceptance of the behaviours (actions) of all members of the group being studied (Heath, 1982: 35).	To suspend belief, ethnographers strive to use emic, or insider language and references, whenever possible by: • identifying insider names (folk terms) for particular activities or phenomena (e.g. 'the Island History Project', 'continuous lines', 'first year students'); • locating verbs (and their objects) to identify past/present/future actions and connected activities (e.g. 'take out your learning logs', 'we'll plan a fashion show', 'when we do public critique'); • tracing chains of interactional exchanges (not individual behaviours) to explore what counts as local knowledge.	Bracketing one's expectations about what is happening involves examining what members: • propose, orient to, acknowledge and recognise as socially (academically, institutionally or personally) significant within and across times and events; • jointly (discursively) construct and name as actions and events; • construct as norms and expectations, roles and relationships, and rights and obligations; • draw on past events in a developing event; • make visible to the ethnographer (or other members) in points of emic-etic (insider–outsider) tensions.

Challenges facing ethnographers in identifying the boundaries of events, and making them transparent, are presented in Table 39.3.

As indicated in Table 39.3, central to the chain of reasoning associated with identifying and establishing boundaries is a conceptual argument that events are constructed by members in and through discourse and actions among participants, and that an event may involve multiple levels of timescale and activity. This conceptualisation of events as dynamic and

Table 39.3   Identifying boundaries of events

Principle of operation	Conceptual issues	Actions implicated
When participation in, or adequate description of, the full round of activities of the group is not possible, fieldworkers should make principled decisions to learn (from participants) and to describe as completely as possible what is happening in selected activities, settings, or groups of participants (Heath, 1982: 35).	To make transparent the logic-in-use constructed in deciding boundaries of events, ethnographers make principled decisions about: • what and whom to observe, examine closely or trace across times and events; • how boundaries of the *field* for a particular observation are being proposed, recognised and acknowledged; • how members of a developing event signal to each other (contextualise) what is said or done.	Constructing records for analysis depends on: • how fieldnotes are written; • what is recorded on video/audio, from whose perspective, focusing on what objects, actors or activity; • what artefacts, documents or photographs are collected; • how event maps of activity are constructed to locate actors in time(s) and space(s); • what kinds of interviews are conducted of whom, under what conditions and for what purposes; • how records from the field are archived to permit search and retrieval of interconnected texts, contexts and events.

developing, as potentially existing across time(s) or as interconnected texts or processes, means that ethnographers, as part of *fieldwork*, need to make transparent the boundaries of particular events (i.e. units of analysis). Thus, to trace cycles of events and to identify levels of analytic scale necessary to understand the knowledge members are drawing on to participate in a developing event requires that ethnographers remain in the field for extended periods of time (Smith, 1978).

Principle of operation four: building connections

The fourth principle, *building connections*, captures the ethnographic goal of making connections between one *bit of* life and others in order to construct, through a process of contrastive relevance (Hymes, 1982), warranted claims about what counts as cultural knowledge and to develop grounded explanations of social phenomena. Ethnographers (or analysts using an ethnographic logic-in-use), whether participating in the field or reconstructing a data set from archived

records, select rich points around which the data set for a particular analysis will be constructed or additional records collected. This final principle, like the previous ones, involves an iterative, recursive, abductive logic to construct explanations of previously unknown knowledge of cultural activity and meanings that insiders know, understand, predict and produce to participate in everyday events. Table 39.4 describes the principle and the implicated logic and actions.

As indicated in Table 39.4, the development of an archiving system that supports ethnographers in searching and retrieving bounded events or bits of social life observed in time and space is a critical dimension of ethnographic work. This archive is important given that, while connections may be traced in the field, the analysis most often occurs after ethnographers leave the field or between planned fieldwork sessions. The final principle of operation, therefore, lays a foundation for a key aspect of the ethnographers' task: connecting different cultural activities, actions and meanings through a process of contrastive analysis in order to construct conceptually framed explanations or accounts of the cultural phenomena under study.

Table 39.4 Principle of operation four: building connections

Principle of operation	Conceptual issues	Actions implicated
Data obtained from study of pieces of the culture should be related to existing knowledge about other components of the whole of the culture or similar pieces studied in other cultures (Heath, 1982: 35).	Ethnographers construct evidence of connections among events to develop grounded claims and explanations of cultural phenomena and local knowledge. Ethnographers create an archiving system that permits search and retrieval of relevant records by including: • cross-reference of records by date and place of collection; • event maps and transcripts of events, activity and actors; • citations to particular bodies of literature informing the work.	To analyse particular bits of cultural knowledge, discourse or social life, ethnographers engage in contrastive analysis that includes tracing developing cultural knowledge, processes or practices across time(s), actors, and events. Each analysis in an ongoing ethnographic study involves making visible relationships among: • questions brought to and identified *in situ* • types and amount of data collected; • analysis processes/approaches used for each question and data analysed; • literature guiding each dimension of ethnographic work.

Table 39.5   Interconnected analyses of student performance

Frame clash/rich points identified year two: 1999–2000	Guiding research questions generated for each analysis	Data retrieved and/or generated from archived records
Analysis 1 Kristen, a fourth-year student, told the ethnographer that if he wanted to understand what was important to know, then he needed to look at public critique (Baker, 2001).	What were the roots of public critique? What were the connections between public critique and earlier cycles of activity? What knowledge was necessary to participate in public critique from an emic perspective?	Transcription of public critique. Provide demographic information that includes percentage of new students each year entering class and teacher's history with programme. Construct event maps at different levels of timescale: <ul><li>identify critique cycles for two years of observation;</li><li>construct detailed event maps of each day;</li><li>identify cycles of critique leading to public critique.</li></ul>
Analysis 2 Kristen's performance differs from students with 1, 2, 3 years in programme, which surprised the ethnographer (Baker and Green, 2007).	How did students with differing years in the programme present their public critique? How, and in what ways, was performance across students similar or different? What contributed to the difference between the teacher's and ethnographer's interpretation of Kristen's performance?	Transcript constructed for each student's performance and for question-and-answer segment following performance. Analysis of transcript of teacher's responses to students. Contrastive analysis of public critique performances and teacher feedback for four students with different amounts of time in programme. Interview with teacher to discuss differences in interpretation of Kristen's (a fourth-year student) performance in contrast to other students with less time in the programme.
Analysis 3 The teacher responds differently to the performance of two first-year students, suggesting need to identify possible factors contributing to differences identified (Baker et al., 2008).	How did differences in the teacher's response to two first-year students create a frame clash for the ethnographers? How did the performance of the two first-year students differ, when compared to the rubric for presentation? How was time of entry socially and academically significant for student performance?	Transcript constructed for each student's performance and for question-and-answer segment following performance. Differences in teacher role in providing feedback to students. Student performance compared to rubric elements given to students to guide presentations. Contrastive analysis of teacher feedback and rubrics for two first-year students. Backward mapping to identify points of entry and cycles of critique experienced (or not).

A telling case of a logic-in-use:

Connecting three analyses of student performance

In this section, we draw on a two-year ethnographic study in an inter-generational, advanced placement studio art class to demonstrate how the principles of operation provide a basis for examining *what counts as studio art to members of the class*. We draw on three ethnographic analyses to demonstrate why multiple levels of analytic scale were needed to explore what contributed to observed differences in student performance in one key event, public critique.

By exploring relationships between and among analyses for three interconnected studies, we make visible the logic-in-use of each analysis. Together the analyses presented constitute a telling case (Mitchell, 1984) about how individual–collective relationships are critical to identify factors that support or constrain student learning across times and events. This telling case also makes visible how contrastive analysis was central to constructing an explanation of what contributed to the observed differences in performance. Table 39.5 provides a description of the rich point (a frame clash) identified for each study, the questions asked and the specific archived resources selected for the contrastive analysis of student performance.

As indicated in Table 39.5, in the first study comments by Kristen, a fourth-year student, led to the identification of public critique as an anchor for over-time analysis of connections shaping performance of public critique.

Figure 39.1 graphically presents interconnected chains of cycles of activity, folk terms and insider language associated with each cycle. It also provides a detailed description of the initiating events on the first day of school as well as different points of entry of two first-year students. This figure was used for all three analyses presented, each focusing on a different root or route to public critique.

Analysis 1: Locating intertextually tied events leading to public critique

As indicated in Figure 39.1, backward mapping from public critique to the first day of school made visible how on the first day, through letters, the Disney video and the introduction of necessary work and materials, the teacher initiated and foreshadowed an intertextual web of processes and practices culminating with public critique. As indicated in the demographic information, across the four years of the programme, there was a growing number of new students entering the programme, creating a continually changing inter-generational community. Analysis of these data indicated that each year the class consisted of overlapping groups of students with 1–4 years of experience with the programme. Given the differences in time in the programme, students with 2–4 years were able to revisit key cycles and expand their knowledge, contributing, as the teacher argued, to differences in performances. Figure 39.1 represents the bounded events identified in Analysis 1, and provides a basis for answering the question about the roots of public critique and the inter-connections between bounded events. Therefore this analysis identified the interconnected cycles of activity on which students drew in performing public critique.

Analysis 2: From frame clash to rich point

Analysis of student performance observed during public critique in Analysis 1 led to identifying a frame clash and creating a rich point for Analysis 2, which focused on differences in teacher (insider) and ethnographer (outsider) interpretations of Kristen's performance. In analysing the similarities and differences in student performance, the ethnographer was confronted with a surprise: Kristen's performance did not meet his expectations and differed from the performance of students with 1–3 years of experience in the programme. Kristen did not provide details of each action she took but rather presented a more synthesised description of her process (Table 39.5). This contrast in performance led the ethnographer to interview the teacher, who characterised Kristen's performance as 'light years ahead' of the others and characterised Kristen as speaking *as an artist*, not talking *about* doing the steps or practices of art (Baker and Green, 2007). Analysis 2 therefore raised questions about limits to certainty of observed actions for the ethnographer with two years in the class, in contrast to the teacher and students with longer

LIFE HISTORY OF CLASS: TIMELINE OF INTERGENERATIONAL STUDIO ART CLASS [1997–2000]

Teacher – 29 years of teaching	1996–1997 [5% of students enter]	1997–1998 [12% of students enter]	1998–1999 [35% of students enter]	1999–2000 [53% of students enter]

ENTERING THE FIELD: TIMELINE OF THE ETHNOGRAPHY 1998–2000

Academic Year One [1998–1999]									Academic Year Two [1999–2000]									
Sept	Oct	Nov	Dec	Jan	Feb	Mar	Apr	May	Jun	SEP	OCT	NOV	Dec	Jan	Feb	Mar	Apr	May	Jun

Clock time	**Running record of events [bold] and phases of activity**
	T preparing
9:09–9:18	
9:18–9:22	**Students arriving; T greeting students at door** T talking about class preparation T instructing students to pick up two index cards and select a workbench
9:22–9:30	**T taking roll and initiating 'Index card activity'** Students writing two questions T giving students envelopes Students returning index cards
9:30–9:44	**T welcoming, presenting agenda and introducing self and programme** *T presenting overview day and programme Introducing Disney video Explaining links with video
6 min.	**Teacher plays Disney Video of teacher receiving award**
9:44–9:55	**T reading and commenting on excerpts from letters of past students** T reading letters from four past students T explaining connections
9:55–10:00	**T introducing work of class** Letter of intent Handout; quoting Z. Hurston 'Student agendas'
10:00–10:09	**T presenting four needs for class** T introducing sketchbooks Notebooks: connection to AP and areas of concentration Folders: value of handouts Fee: cost of materials
10:09–10:15	**T discussing 'highlights' of upcoming year** Mini-chalk festival Superintendent's visit Presentations from students who attended art summer school

Note (for 9:30–9:44): *T initiates cycles of friendly sharing: 'to-morrow I'll have a short activity that's kind of a creative activity' [occurs on 9/3]

Cycles of critique

Framing class 9/2: James enters	Friendly sharing 9/10, 9/13	Gentle critique	Maya enters 10/11	Deep critique 11/16–19 Maya & James present

Figure 39.1 Intertextual cycles of activity of public critique

histories. This analysis also raised questions about the need for triangulation across actors and sources of data, in addition to tracing actors' actions and intertextual ties across times and events in order to bracket ethnocentric interpretations.

Analysis 3: Consequences of differing entry points

Analysis 3 explored differences in the performance of two first-year students, Maya and James, differences that were not easily explained by analysis of the observed performances. In-time analysis of the developing event of public critique showed that not only was there a pattern of difference in their presentations but also a difference in the patterns of interaction of the teacher with each of these students. That is, the teacher played the questioner role almost exclusively for Maya, while students initiated questions and comments to James, with two exceptions.

The differences in both the students' performances and the teacher responses created a rich point for tracing how student points of entry contributed to the differences in observed performances. Analysis of entry points showed that James entered on the first day of class, while Maya entered one month later. The impact of the missed knowledge was identified through a contrastive analysis of the rubric given to students the day before the deep critiques began. Analysis of what each student included in their public performance showed that James included concepts introduced in all cycles of activity pre-dating public critique, including cycles presented on the first day of class. Analysis of Maya's performance showed a series of omitted elements suggested in the rubric. The missing information in Maya's presentation was traced to cycles of activity introduced during the month of school prior to her entry. Additionally, although the language and processes were present in the talk and actions of other students, the fact that she did not include them in her presentations suggested that, for Maya, they were unmarked, and were not viewed as socially or academically relevant or significant to public critique. The late entry point therefore created *missed opportunities* for Maya to learn particular aspects of studio art presented in the first two cycles of activity (Figure 39.1). This analysis demonstrated

the importance of contrastively examining both the performance differences among students and tracing the history of particular students in order to construct grounded explanations of what accounted for the observed differences.

Together the three studies provide a telling case of the need for multiple levels of analytic scale, for contrastive analyses and for tracing histories of observed phenomena and actors in order to identify relationships among time, actions, entry, access and performance. The intertextual ties among the three studies demonstrate the generative nature of ethnographic research as well as the non-linear, abductive, iterative, recursive logic guiding an ethnographic logic-in-use, including:

- how each analysis required particular types of records and data collection;
- how different records analysed represented particular levels of analytic scale;
- how each analysis generated questions for further analysis and the construction of a new data set from archived records;
- how different levels of timescale provided a grounded basis for constructing warranted claims about factors contributing to observed differences in student performance.

Through this telling case, we also demonstrated how graphic representations provide analytic texts to explore rich points and their pathways, both within a particular analysis and across a series of inter-connected analyses. The multiple levels of analyses constituting this telling case make *transparent* the recursive and iterative logic-of-inquiry necessary to develop evidence of factors leading to observed differences in student performance.

Conclusion

In this chapter, we introduced readers to ways of thinking as ethnographers and to principles of operation guiding the logic-in-use that ethnographers bring to and construct during ethnographic research. Through recommended readings we invite readers to explore these issues further. These readings provide insights into the ways that ethnographic research has been conceptualised, conducted and reported across national borders and disciplines.

Questions for further investigation

1. What do you think are the best ways to generate research-specific questions in an ethnographic study?
2. In an exploratory data study, debate the pros and cons of structured and unstructured data collection.
3. What are the benefits and limitations of archival data collection?

Suggested further reading

Atkinson, P. (1990) *The Ethnographic Imagination: Textual Constructions of Reality*. London: Routledge. Atkinson argues that all texts are rhetorical representations, shaped by authors' disciplinary backgrounds, research purposes and implicit or explicit sociological theories. Citing classic and contemporary ethnographies, Atkinson demonstrates how ethnographic texts persuade readers and create particular views of reality.

Bloome, D., Carter, S. P., Christian, B. M., Otto, S. and Shuart-Faris, N. (2005) *Discourse Analysis and the Study of Classroom Language and Literacy Events: A Microethnographic Perspective*. Mahwah, NJ: Lawrence Erlbaum. The volume presents theoretically grounded analyses of classroom literacy events. By drawing on socio-cultural, socio-linguistic and discourse theories, the authors demonstrate how microethnographic research reveals the complexity of life and learning in linguistically diverse classrooms.

Emerson, R. M., Fretz, R. I. and Shaw, L. L. (1995) *Writing Ethnographic Fieldnotes*. Chicago: University of Chicago Press. This book encompasses theoretical, practical, methodological and representational issues of conducting ethnographic observation, constructing and analysing ethnographic field notes and writing ethnographic reports.

Heath, S. B. and Street, B. V. (2008) *On Ethnography: Approaches to Language and Literacy Research*. New York: Teachers College Press. Drawing on their own and a novice

ethnographer's fieldwork, the authors provide theoretically grounded practical suggestions for developing and sustaining a constant comparative perspective in ethnographic work that examines co-occuring patterns of individual and community knowledge.

Walford, G. (ed.) (2008) *How to Do Educational Ethnography*. London: Tufnell. This edited volume presents central processes in doing educational ethnography, including site selection, ethics, observing, interviewing, video-enabled research, the role of theory in ethnographic research, the characterisation of social settings and a critical examination of representation in ethnography.

References

Agar, M. (1994) *Language Shock: Understanding the Culture of Conversation*. New York: Quill.

Agar, M. (1996) *The Professional Stranger: An Informal Introduction to Ethnography* (2nd edn). San Diego, CA: Academic.

Agar, M. (2006a) 'Culture: can you take it anywhere?', *International Journal of Qualitative Methods*, 5(2): 1–12.

Agar, M. (2006b) 'An ethnography by any other name . . .', *Forum Qualitative Sozialforschung/Forum: Qualitative Social Research*, 7: 4.

Alexander, R. (2001) *Culture and Pedagogy: International Comparisons in Primary Education*. Malden, MA: Blackwell.

Anderson-Levitt, K. (2002) *Teaching Cultures: Knowledge for Teaching First Grade in France and The United States*. Cresskill, NJ: Hampton.

Anderson-Levitt, K. (2006) 'Ethnography', in Green, J. L., Camilli, G. and Elmore, P. B. (eds) *Handbook of Complementary Methods in Education Research*. Mahwah, NJ: Lawrence Erlbaum, pp.279–96.

Atkinson, P. (1995) *Medical Talk and Medical Work*. London: Sage.

Atkinson, P., Coffey, A., Delamont, S., Lofland, J. and Lofland, L. (eds) (2007) *Handbook of Ethnography*. London: Sage.

Baker, W .D. (2001) 'Artists in the Making'. Unpublished dissertation.

Baker, W. D. and Green, J. L. (2007) 'Limits to certainty in interpreting video data: interactional ethnography and disciplinary knowledge', *Pedagogies*, 2(3): 191–204.

Baker, W. D., Green, J. L. and Skukauskaite, A. (2008) 'Video-enabled ethnographic research: A microethnographic perspective', in Walford, G. (ed.) *How to Do Educational Ethnography*. London: Tufnell, pp.77–114.

Barton, D. and Tusting, K. (eds) (2005) *Beyond Communities of Practice: Language, Power and Social Context*. New York: Cambridge University Press.

Bloome, D. and Egan-Robertson, A. (1993) 'The social construction of intertextuality in classroom reading and writing lessons', *Reading Research Quarterly*, 28(4): 305–33.

Bloome, D., Carter, S. P., Christian, B. M., Otto, S. and Shuart-Faris, N. (2005) *Discourse Analysis and the Study of Classroom Language and Literacy Events: A Microethnographic Perspective*. Mahwah, NJ: Lawrence Erlbaum.

Brayboy, B. M. and Deyhle, D. (2000) 'Insider-outsider: researchers in American Indian communities', *Theory into Practice*, 39(3): 163–9.

Brown, B. A., Reveles, J. M. and Kelly, G. J. (2005) 'Scientific literacy and discursive identity: a theoretical framework for understanding science learning', *Science Education*, 89(5): 779–802.

Carspecken, P. F. and Walford, G. (eds) (2001) *Critical Ethnography and Education* (Vol. V). Greenwich, CT: JAI.

Castanheira, M. L. (2004) *Aprendizagem contextualizada: Discurso e inclusão na sala de aula*. Belo Horizonte, Brazil: Ceale; Autêntica.

Castanheira, M. L., Crawford, T., Dixon, C. N. and Green, J. L. (2001) 'Interactional ethnography: an approach to studying the social construction of literate practices', *Linguistics and Education*, 11(4): 353–400.

Cazden, C., John, V. and Hymes, D. (eds) (1972) *Functions of Language in the Classroom*. New York: Teachers College Press.

Cochran-Smith, M. (1984) *The Making of a Reader*. Norwood, NJ: Ablex.

Corsaro, W. (2003) *We're Friends, Right? Inside Kids' Culture*. Alex, AL: Joseph Henry.

Delamont, S. (2002) *Fieldwork in Educational Settings: Methods, Pitfalls And Perspectives* (2nd edn). London: Routledge.

Edwards, D. and Mercer, N. (1987) *Common Knowledge: The Development of Understanding in the Classroom*. New York: Falmer.

Freitas, C. A. and Castanheira, M. L. (2007) 'Talked images: examining the contextualised nature of image use', *Pedagogies*, 2(3): 151–64.

Gonzalez, N., Moll, L. C. and Amanti, C. (eds) (2005) *Funds of Knowledge: Theorizing Practices in Households, Communities, and Classrooms*. Mahwah, NJ: Lawrence Erlbaum.

Green, J. L., & Bloome, D. (1997) 'Ethnography and ethnographers of and in education: a situated perspective', in Flood, J., Heath, S. B. and Lapp, D. (eds) *Handbook of Research on Teaching Literacy Through the Communicative and Visual Arts*. New York: Macmillan, pp. 181–202.

Green, J. L. and Heras, A. I. (2011) 'Identities in shifting educational policy contexts: the consequences of moving from two languages, one community to English only', in Lopez Bonilla, G. and Englander, K. (eds) *Discourses and Identities in Contexts of Educational Change*. New York: Peter Lang.

Green, J. L. and Wallat, C. (eds) (1981) *Ethnography and Language in Educational Settings* (Vol. V). Norwood, NJ: Ablex.

Heath, S. B. (1982) 'Ethnography in education: defining the essentials', in Gilmore, P. and Glatthorn, A. A. (eds) *Children In and Out of School: Ethnography and Education*. Washington, DC: Center for Applied Linguistics, pp. 33–55.

Heath, S.B. (1983) *Ways with words: Language, life, and work in communities and classrooms*. Cambridge: Cambridge University Press.

Heath, S. B. and Street, B. V. (2008) *On Ethnography: Approaches to Language and Literacy Research*. New York: Teachers College Press.

Heras, A. I. (1993) 'The construction of understanding in a sixth grade bilingual classroom', *Linguistics and Education*, 5(3 & 4): 275–99.

Hymes, D. (1982) 'What is ethnography?', in Gilmore, P. and Glatthorn, A. A. (eds) *Children In and Out of Schools*. Washington, DC: Center for Applied Linguistics.

Jeffrey, B. and Woods, P. (2003) *The Creative School*. London: Falmer.

Jennings, L. B., Jewett, P. C., Laman, T. T., Souto-Manning, M. and Wilson, J. L. (eds) (2010) *Sites of Possibility: Critical Dialogue Across Educational Settings*. Creskill, NJ: Hampton.

Kalman, J. and Street, B. V. (eds) (2010) *Lectura, escritura y matemáticas como prácticas sociales: Diálogos con América Látina*. Pátzcuaro, Mexico: CREFAL.

Kantor, R. and Fernie, D. (eds). (2003) *Early Childhood Classroom Processes*. Cresskill, NJ: Hampton.

Kaplan, A. (1964) *The Conduct of Inquiry*. San Francisco: Chandler.

Kitson, L., Fletcher, M. and Kearney, J. (2007) 'Continuity and change in literacy practices: a move towards multiliteracies', *Journal of Classroom Interaction*, 41/42 (2/1): 29.

Lemke, J. L. (1990) *Talking Science: Language, Learning, and Values*. Norwood, NJ: Ablex.

Levinson, B. A. U., Cade, S. L., Padawer, A. and Elvir, A. P. (eds) (2002) *Ethnography and Education Policy Across the Americas*. Westport, CT: Praeger.

Lima, E. S. (1995) 'Culture revisited: Vygotsky's ideas in Brazil', *Anthropology and Education Quarterly*, 26(4): 443–57.

McNeil, L. M. and Coppola, E. M. (2006) 'Official and unofficial stories: getting at the impact of policy on educational practice', in Green, J. L., Camilli, G. and Elmore, P. B. (eds) *Handbook of Complementary Methods in Education Research*. Mahwah, NJ: Lawrence Erlbaum/AERA, pp. 681–700.

Martin-Jones, M., De Mejia, A. M. and Hornberger, N. H. (eds) (2008) *Encyclopedia of Language and Education: Discourse and Education* (Vol. III) (2nd edn). Birmingham: Springer.

Mehan, H. (1979) *Learning Lessons*. Cambridge, MA: Harvard University Press.

Mitchell, C. J. (1984) 'Typicality and the case study', in Ellen, P. F. (ed.) *Ethnographic Research: A Guide to General Conduct*. New York: Academic, pp. 238–41.

Orellana, M. F. (1996) 'Negotiating power through language in classroom meetings', *Linguistics and Education*, 8: 335–65.

Philips, S. (1983) *The Invisible Culture: Communication in Classroom and Community on the Warm Springs Reservation*. New York: Longman.

Rex, L. A. (ed.) (2006) *Discourse of Opportunity: How Talk in Learning Situations Creates and Constrains – Interactional Ethnographic Studies in Teaching and Learning*. Creskill, NJ: Hampton.

Rockwell, E. (2002) 'Learning for life or learning from books: reading practices in Mexican rural schools (1900 to 1935)', *Pedagogica Historica: International Journal of the History of Education*, 38(1): 113–35.

Santa Barbara Classroom Discourse Group (1992a) 'Constructing literacy in classrooms: literate action as social accomplishment', in Marshall, H. (ed.) *Redefining Student Learning: Roots of Educational Change*. Norwood, NJ: Ablex, pp. 119–50.

Santa Barbara Classroom Discourse Group (1992b) 'Do you see what we see? The referential and intertextual nature of classroom life', *Journal of Classroom Interaction*, 27(2): 29–36.

Skukauskaite, A. and Green, J. L. (2004) 'A conversation with Bakhtin: on inquiry and dialogic thinking', *Journal of Russian and East European Psychology*, 42(6): 59–75.

Smith, L. M. (1978) 'An evolving logic of participant observation, educational ethnography, and other case studies', *Review of Research in Education*, 6: 316–77.

Smith, L. M., Prunty, J. J., Dwyer, D. C. and Kleine, P. (1987) *The Fate of an Innovative School: The History and Present Status of the Kensington School*. London: Falmer.

Spindler, G. and Hammond, L. (eds) (2006) *Innovations in Educational Ethnography: Theory, Methods and Results*. Mahwah, NJ: Lawrence Erlbaum.

Stevick, E. D. and Levinson, B. A. U. (eds) (2007) *Reimagining Civic Education: How Diverse Societies Form Democratic Citizens*. Lanham, MD: Rowman & Littlefield.

Street, B. V. (ed.) (2005) *Literacies Across Educational Contexts: Mediating, Learning and Teaching*. Philadelphia: Caslow.

Street, B. V., Baker, D. and Tomlin, A. (2005) *Navigating Numeracies: Home/School Numeracy Practices*. Netherlands: Springer.

Tobin, J., Hsueh, Y. and Karasawa, M. (2009) *Preschool in Three Cultures Revisited: China, Japan and the United States*. Chicago: University of Chicago Press.

Troman, G., Jeffrey, B. and Beach, D. (eds) (2006) *Researching Education Policy: Ethnographic Experiences*. London: Tufnell.

Vine, E. (2003) '"My partner": a five-year-old Samoan boy learns how to articulate in class through interactions with his English-speaking peers', *Linguistics and Education*, 14(1): 99–121.

Walford, G. (ed.) (2008) *How to Do Educational Ethnography*. London: Tufnell.

Warschauer, M. (2004) *Technology and Social Inclusion: Rethinking the Digital Divide*. Boston: MIT.

Wolcott, H. F. (2003) *The Man in the Principal's Office: An Ethnography* (updated edn). Walnut Creek, CA: Altamira.

Biographical research methods

Michael Tedder

Introduction

The intrinsic subjectivity of biography means that researchers who consider using biographical methods as part of an enquiry in education are quickly immersed in some fundamental issues: they have to consider what tests for 'truth' may be possible given the nature of the data they are collecting; they need to think whether it is possible to be 'objective' or whether the process of undertaking their enquiry is inevitably 'subjective'. Biographical research inhabits an interdisciplinary academic field, drawing theoretical framings from a range of academic disciplines and sub-disciplines. Researchers can draw on sociological and anthropological traditions or they can draw on the possibilities opened by psychological and psycho-analytical theories. There is related work in oral history, in literature and cultural studies that needs to be recognised. This context means that there are many practical and theoretical issues to be resolved when biographical methods are planned.

The distinctive feature of biographical research is that it enquires into the way that people make sense of their lives through the collection, analysis and representation of data about individual experiences of life. Such research can be regarded as a kind of ethnography if we take that as signifying that the main concern is with *meaning*, that the enquiry is interested in the ways that people describe and understand themselves and their actions and their interactions with others. It is not necessarily the factual accuracy of descriptions and explanations that interests biographical researchers but rather the expressions of understanding that research participants make and the forms that such expressions take. The research challenge is to decide how to use such data in suitably systematic and rigorous ways.

The most common data collection method is the personal interview, an invitation to someone to tell stories about their life, and a biographical interview might be a singular event or part of a series in a longitudinal study. Other documentary sources might also be used, such as personal diaries, letters and autobiographies or, in this digital age, blogs and tweets. Collecting data from focus group interviews and observation may also have a role to play. In his introduction to the field, Norman Denzin (1989) outlines a comprehensive listing of artefacts, methods and key concepts in the traditions of collecting and representing biographical data; included in his list are biography and autobiography, life story and life history, narrative as well as oral history and personal history, case history and case study. Each of these means something subtly different – and would signify different approaches to different researchers – but all are outcomes of biographical research.

The appeal of biographical research

Historians of social science research comment on the ebb and flow of biographical methods. In the early twentieth century, a study of Polish migrants by Thomas and Znaniecka and of a juvenile delinquent called Stanley by Clifford R. Shaw are often quoted as milestones in the development of the Chicago School of sociology. The writings of George Herbert Mead are cited for the importance they place on understanding individuals through their participation in social acts. There was a reaction against forms of research that focused on the individual and the personal in the latter half of the twentieth century but biographical methods have undergone a resurgence in recent decades to the extent that some writers (such as Chamberlayne et al., 2000) have observed a 'biographical turn' in the social sciences.

The 'biographical turn' can be understood in several ways. Some commentators characterise interest in the personal as a feature of the individualisation and commodification of modern life. The preoccupation of popular media with celebrity and the public appetite for disclosure of emotion and interpersonal conflict might be regarded as facets of these trends. Social networking through the Internet has opened new avenues for personal disclosure. The growing popularity throughout the UK of oral history projects and tracing family genealogies suggests that there is greater valuing of individual stories within British culture. That popularity is evident also in the US in the operation of an organisation like StoryCorps that is dedicated to recording discussions between two people who are relations or friends in order to articulate the diverse community voices that can be heard in modern America. Participants each receive a CD copy of their discussion while a second copy is archived in the Library of Congress and more than 50,000 such recordings have been made.

For social scientists, biographical methods offer a means of exploring questions about identity and sense of self in a fragmented, rapidly changing world. Giddens (1991) famously wrote of the 'reflexive project of the self' that he sees as characterising individuals and their moulding of lifestyles in late-modern society. Bauman (2004) has written extensively of the 'liquid' qualities of late modernity and offers a critical perspective on the personalisation of modern society. Biographical research offers empirical means for enquiry into such issues; it offers an approach to understanding how people come to terms with uncertainties about identity and change in contemporary society. It generates data about how far people have or think they have influence and control over the kinds of change they experience.

This brings us to an important proposition that interests many biographical researchers: that the narration of a life story not only enables people to articulate their identity but also offers the possibility of learning from their life and the potential to effect change as a consequence. Among the leading contributors to the field is Peter Alheit whose work explores the relationship of biography to learning in the workplace and across the life-course (see Alheit, 1994, 2005; Alheit and Dausien, 2002). Pierre Dominicé (2000) has worked particularly with teachers in Switzerland in the development of 'educational biographies' and he also argues that the practice of telling stories about life and experience enables adult learners to effect change. Biographical research and the notion that developing life stories has agentic possibilities has great appeal to adult education researchers committed to ideals of emancipatory and transformative education.

For Chamberlayne et al. (2000), the concern of social scientists to link micro and macro levels of socio-political analysis explains the recent burgeoning of interest in biographical research methods. It is part of a long-established concern of sociologists, evident in writers like C. Wright Mills who is often quoted for emphasising the interconnection of private and public domains:

> . . . many personal troubles cannot be solved merely as troubles but must be understood in terms of public issues – and in terms of the problems of history making. Know that the human meaning of public issues must be revealed by relating them to personal troubles and to the problems of individual life. (Wright Mills, 1970: 248)

Another reason that biographical research appeals to researchers is that it appears easy. What could be more straightforward in carrying out a research project than asking people to tell you stories about themselves? However, as Harry Wolcott wryly observes:

Qualitative approaches beckon because they appear easy or natural. And were it not for the complexity of conceptualising qualitative studies, conducting the research, analysing it, and writing it up, perhaps they would be. (Wolcott, 1990: 11)

It may seem 'easy and natural' to collect biographical data but no one who engages seriously in such research should underestimate the challenge of collecting data in a sensitive and ethical manner, of managing and archiving quantities of recordings and transcriptions, of discerning analytical sense in disparate data sources, or of interpreting and writing with meaning and rigour for different audiences.

Conducting biographical research

In collecting data for an oral history or a life story, interviewing is the central – though not the only – method of collecting data and an interviewer needs to be familiar with the strengths, possibilities and limitations of interviewing. Introductory literature on research methods tends to suggest that conducting an interview is essentially a technical procedure: interviewing is portrayed as managing a kind of oral questionnaire for which the requisite skills are structuring questions and developing codes. However, experience of interviewing usually develops an awareness of the complexity of such meetings. Ellis and Berger (2002) said of interviews that:

The interviewing process becomes less a conduit of information from informant to researchers that represent how things are, and more a sea swell of meaning making in which researchers connect their own experiences to those of others. (Ellis and Berger, 2002: 853)

The meaning and significance of what is said at a particular time and place between different individuals reaches far beyond the moment. Firstly, what the researcher brings to the encounter is as significant to the interview as what the participant says. In addition, there is great diversity in what interviewees bring: responses to questions about past, current or anticipated experiences may be tentative or speculative,

particularly if the interview offers an unprecedented opportunity to discover and construct coherence within a life story. Alternatively, an interviewee may have stories that have been reviewed and rehearsed, introspectively or with others, and the stories may have achieved a degree of coherence through reflection and repetition. Whether a narrative is newly minted or recycled, the teller engages in processes of selection and interpretation structured by the norms and values of the culture of which he or she is part.

Some scholars use different terms to distinguish different stages of biographical research. Denzin (1989) makes a distinction between an 'oral history', which he said can be obtained through conversations and interviews, and 'life history' or 'personal history' that builds on such conversations and interviews to construct a written account of a person's life. A similar distinction is made between 'life story' and 'life history' by Goodson and Sikes (2001). They propose that a 'life story' might be conceived as a simple narrative, a personal reconstruction of what an individual considers significant about his or her life. A 'life history', however, moves through stages of interpretation: it may be co-constructed by the researcher and project participant, with the researcher using a range of data sources. The outcome is a narrative that becomes contextualised and theorised and in the process becomes a history rather than a story.

Biographical research projects are often interested in the way that human experience is temporally situated, that our experiences happen in time (Biesta et al., 2010). People are invited to talk about how they see their lives progressing and changing. We tend to assume that everyone shares interior thought processes through which each person makes sense or constructs meaning from 'real-life' experiences. Listening to the interweaving of stories about the past, the present and the future offers a means of unravelling how change is perceived and understood. Some biographical research has focused on the nature of memory and the manner in which individuals telling their stories adapt them over time to accommodate changing social and cultural conditions. While some might see the unreliability of individual memory as a problem, a factor of unreliability in the research, others would argue that biographical research gives us a vital tool to explore the meaning and significance of such change.

There are always important ethical issues to be considered in biographical research. Clearly, the researcher needs to observe the relevant codes of the organisation undertaking the research. However, while a code provides rules to follow, the real challenge is to have the sensitivity and skill to ensure such guidance becomes operational.

Analysing and writing up biographical research

Part of the researcher's task in the analysis of biographical data is to render as clearly as possible what participants have said in the stories collected. However, it is clear that there are processes of selection and decisions about meaning at every stage. Life stories cannot be treated as an objective account of the facts of a life; rather, they are 'lives interpreted and made textual' and represent 'a partial, selective commentary on lived experience' (Goodson and Sikes, 2001). It is standard practice to transcribe interviews and the transcriber also undertakes analysis as decisions that affect possible meaning are made about matters such as what level of detail to include, what to do about non-grammatical structures, whether to indicate pauses and non-verbal signifiers.

Once there is an artefact – whether a transcribed text, or audio or video recording – it is possible to undertake coding, to identify what the researcher finds are significant themes and patterns within the data. Some choose to delay coding on the grounds that they want to avoid reorganising and probably distorting the participant's voice. For such reasons, many are attracted to grounded theory (Glaser and Strauss, 1967; Strauss and Corbin, 1998) for the notion that analysis and interpretation can evolve naturally from the data of a research project, that the data should 'speak for itself'. Grounded theory offers an approach in which substantive theory is constructed from immersion in the data: by repeated listening to audio tapes, viewing of videos and reading of transcripts, themes and patterns will emerge as potential categories for organising the data. Additional appropriate cases may be sought to 'saturate' the categories. It becomes possible to use set processes, such as the 'constant comparative method', for more general analysis and computer programs are available that have been specifically designed to facilitate such analysis.

While some researchers claim they use adapted versions of 'grounded theory', others claim it is impossible for a researcher not to have a framework of pre-formed ideas, values and beliefs that will influence what she or he thinks is significant in the data and therefore what categories emerge.

Important questions are raised by Marxist, feminist and postmodern researchers about the power relationship between researcher and researched in deciding what is significant for inclusion in a research narrative. Marxists tend to question how far research participants can articulate the social divisions of which they are part. For feminists, it has been crucial to give prominence to women's stories about such matters as domestic life, about maternity or about female labour that have been excluded from most accounts of social history. Postmodern critics draw attention to the way practices of storytelling are deeply embedded within our culture and referential to particular cultural narratives. Researchers from critical perspectives tend to argue for social justice, for hearing the voice of 'the other', of people on the margins of society, of giving proper attention to the excluded and unheard. They argue also the importance of researchers being aware of their role in what becomes articulated, that they are part of the social matrix that permits some forms of expression and not others. Some biographical researchers have adopted the term 'Auto/biography' (with forward slash) to convey the idea that the researcher is aware of the reflective and self-reflexive nature of their role.

Exemplary studies

An evaluation of sure start

Linden West and colleagues have used biographical methods to research the experiences of adults in higher education, the lives of GPs working in inner-city communities and, more recently, the perceptions of families and professional workers of a Sure Start project based in a community in Kent (West and Carlson, 2006, 2007). Their approach to interviewing and analysis of data is framed by their awareness of the psychoanalytical potential of biographical interviews.

Sure Start was a UK government initiative to engage with parents who are defined as 'hard to reach' and are deemed to need particular support if they are to ensure their children's well-being and transcend 'cycles of dependence'. The overall aim of the programme, as summarised in national statements, was to 'achieve better outcomes for children, parents and communities'. West and his colleagues asked some basic questions about the initiative as experienced by the people affected, whether it was intrusive or empowering, whether it offered new resources and hope or whether, in effect, it was a form of social control.

In four years of fieldwork, the research team conducted over 100 interviews with parents (several with both partners and children present) and 54 with Sure Start staff. They interviewed over half of the parents and staff more than once, and ten up to five times and more. They used a variety of methods in the evaluation: focus groups and participant observation as well as auto/biographical interviews. The study had a three-part focus. First, they wanted to illuminate the meaning and significance of Sure Start in the lives of a sample of local families. Participants were asked what they thought of its purpose and to what extent they felt supported and empowered by it. The researchers wanted to find out how perceptions changed over time in the light of specific interventions and relationships with professionals. Second, they wanted to document the life history of Sure Start through the eyes of the professionals directly responsible for providing services. Third, they sought to chronicle the community's involvement in the development of the project, including its governance, through a period when funding bodies changed.

The final report uses metaphors of space to discuss outcomes, including 'sustaining space' to describe how Sure Start provided a lifeline to parents, especially those struggling with mental health problems or domestic violence; 'transitional space' to describe circumstances in which children and adults learned to think and feel about themselves in new ways; and 'transactional space' to describe how family learning projects like Sure Start may enable parents to learn how to act as citizens.

Sure Start has been criticised for inefficiency and ineffectiveness. National evaluations of the programme found it not to be cost-effective and failing to engage the 'hard to reach'. According to some criteria, the programme appeared to have minimal impact and parents living in Sure Start communities sometimes felt worse about where they live. West and Carlson were able to question the methodology of national evaluations and to exemplify a different approach by which biographical methods illuminate changes in the quality of what was done rather than relying on the counting of outcomes.

Learning in the life-course

The project 'Learning Lives: Learning, Identity and Agency' was a longitudinal study of adult learning biographies conducted between 2004 and 2008 by a team of researchers from four UK universities (Biesta et al., 2011). A total of 528 interviews were carried out with 117 people, 59 male and 58 female, aged between 25 and 84. Some participants were interviewed as many as nine times. The official aim of the project was to deepen understanding of the complexities of learning in the life-course and to investigate what learning 'means' and 'does' in the lives of adults. This was particularly relevant at a time when 'lifelong learning' had become part of the rhetoric of government policy and education management.

The interviews used a combination of life-history and life-course approaches. The first interview with each participant focused on the life story ('Tell me about your life . . .') while subsequent interviews increasingly focused on ongoing events in the life-course of interviewees. Sometimes the events were structured transitions within life and sometimes they were changes of a more incidental and possibly critical nature, such as redeployment or illness. Such events offer opportunities for learning, both formal and informal, and longitudinal interviews monitored the stories that people told about such opportunities.

One of the central themes explored in the project concerned the nature of narrative and its significance for learning (Goodson et al., 2010). Unsurprisingly, the researchers found that some people are more adept at telling stories about their lives than others but this suggested that the potential for learning from narrative also varies. They propose that a life story can be conceived as a 'site for learning' within which learning can take place both during the creation of a story (i.e. within the *narration* of a life story) and in the telling and retelling of such stories with others (i.e. in having a *narrative* to tell). Two analytical tools were developed by the researchers, one for the analysis of the *narrative quality* of narration and narrative and the other for the analysis of the *efficacy* of narrative and narration. Within the latter a distinction was made between the *learning potential* and the *action potential* of narrative and narration (Tedder and Biesta, 2009). The writers suggest that narration is not only about the construction of a particular version of one's life, it is at the same time a construction of a particular version of the self.

Goodson et al. (2010) state that the 'Learning Lives' project found only a small number of participants actually identified their storying as a learning process, although the stories they told contained abundant evidence of learning and of the impact of this learning on people's lives. It was also evident that having a narrative in the form of sophisticated, well-developed stories was no guarantee of effective learning: some people were found to be 'caught' in their stories, unable to use them to generate new perspectives and insights, and there was thus little 'action potential' from such storying. Equally, not providing a narration or narrative did not prevent people from being able to learn or from being effective and influential members of their community.

Conclusion

Biographical research can produce vivid research data in the form of stories that are engaging and that resonate strongly with contemporary social and cultural mores. For social science and education researchers, such stories can provide insights into individual experiences of change, whether the change is personal, psychological and educational, or social, political and cultural. No other form of research focuses so explicitly on the relationship between the personal and the social, on exploring the way that social 'context' permeates the way people construct meaning from their individual experience and the way

that social norms find expression through individual sense-making and action-taking.

Biographical research tends to be theoretically eclectic, drawing from multidisciplinary sources, overlapping with psychology and psychotherapy, history, literature and cultural studies. The inherent appeal of narrative and the eclectic theoretical framing can give to biographical research qualities of narrative richness and depth of insight that help persuade a reader of the authenticity and credibility of its depiction of the complexities of the 'real world'. Biographical research challenges epistemological reductionism and superficiality.

The very appeal of narrative, however, makes biographical research susceptible to over-reliance on description and vulnerable to being dismissed as merely anecdotal. For some academics and for many policymakers a biographical approach scarcely registers as legitimate research. At a time when much research effort is directed towards securing straightforward solutions to difficult problems, research that actively seeks to portray complexity may hold little appeal to some research funders. A researcher in education using biographical methods needs to be prepared to argue for the legitimacy of individual stories and for the significance in research narratives of the personal domain.

There is a well-established tradition of biographical research among teachers and educational professionals and much interesting work has been undertaken with other professional groups, particularly in northern Europe (see West et al., 2007). There has been much less research among the wider population that addresses questions of learning and education. Existing research shows how narrative learning can contribute to certain forms of learning and suggests that life-storying is a genre that can be practised. However, we know little about how far story-telling has importance for different forms of learning or for the learning of people in different cultures and social groups. We have yet to address what the implications might be for the organisation of the curriculum and for formal education. The task of undertaking biographical research that is carefully analysed and critically theorised in order to address educational questions has scarcely begun.

Questions for further investigation

1. What are the strengths and limitations of interviewing for the life story of someone who is different from you in terms of (a) age; (b) gender; (c) ethnicity; (d) social group?
2. How would you address the ethical issues of interviewing someone in terms of (a) ensuring the confidentiality of their part in data collection; (b) respecting their rights in data analysis and interpretation?
3. How far would you say your life is influenced by social forces? How far do you have influence over such forces and how might biographical research help with the recognition of such processes?
4. What educational issues or research questions can be usefully addressed through collecting biographical interviews and constructing life histories?

Suggested further reading

Chamberlayne, P., Bornat, J. and Wengraf, T. (eds) (2000) *The Turn to Biographical Methods in Social Science*. London: Routledge.

Goodson, I. and Sikes, P. (2001) *Life History Research in Educational Settings*. Buckingham: Open University Press.

Goodson, I., Beista, G. J. J., Tedder, M. and Adair, N. (2010) *Narrative Learning*. London/New York: Routledge.

Harrison, B. (ed.) (2009) *Life Story Research*, Sage Benchmarks in Social Research Methods series, 4 vols. London: Sage.

Merrill, B. and West, L. (2009) *Using Biographical Methods in Social Research*. London: Sage.

Roberts, B. (2002) *Biographical Research*. Buckingham: Open University Press.

West, L. and Carlson, A. (2007) *Claiming Space: An In-depth Auto/biographical Study of Sure Start Millmead 2001–2006*. Canterbury: Canterbury Christ Church University.

References

Alheit, P. (1994) *Taking the Knocks. Youth Unemployment and Biography – A Qualitative Analysis*. London: Cassell.

Alheit, P. (2005) 'Challenges of the postmodern "learning society", a critical approach', in Bron, A., Kurantowicz, E., Olesen, H. S. and West, L. (eds) *'Old' and 'New' Worlds of Adult Learning*. Wroclaw: Dolnoslaskiej Szkoly Wyzszej Edukacji.

Alheit, P. and Dausien, B. (2002) 'The "double face" of lifelong learning: two analytical perspectives on a "silent revolution"', *Studies in the Education of Adults*, 34(1): 1–20.

Bauman, Z. (2004) *Identity*. Cambridge: Polity Press.

Biesta, G. J. J., Field, J. and Tedder, M. (2010) 'A time for learning: representations of time and the temporal dimensions of learning through the lifecourse', *Zeitschrift für Pädagogik*, 56(3): 317–27.

Biesta, G. J. J., Field, J., Hodkinson, P., Macleod, F. and Goodson, I. F. (2011) *Improving Learning Through the Life Course. Learning Lives*. London: Routledge.

Chamberlayne, P., Bornat, J. and Wengraf, T. (eds) (2000) *The Turn to Biographical Methods in Social Science*. London: Routledge.

Denzin, N. (1989) *Interpretive Biography*. London: Sage.

Dominicé, P. (2000) *Learning from Our Lives*. San Francisco: Jossey-Bass.

Ellis, C. and Berger, L. (2002) 'Their Story/My Story/Our Story', in Gubrium, F. G. and Holstein, J. A. (eds) *Handbook of Interview Research*. San Francisco: Sage.

Giddens, A. (1991) *Modernity and Self-Identity*. Oxford: Blackwell.

Glaser, B. and Strauss, A. (1967) *The Discovery of Grounded Theory*. London: Weidenfield & Nicholson.

Goodson, I. and Sikes, P. (2001) *Life History Research in Educational Settings*. Buckingham: Open University Press.

Goodson, I., Beista, G. J. J., Tedder, M. and Adair, N. (2010) *Narrative Learning*. London/New York: Routledge.

Merrill, B. and West, L. (2009) *Using Biographical Methods in Social Research*. London: Sage.

Strauss, A. L. and Corbin, J. (1998) 'Grounded theory methodology: an overview', in Denzin, N. K. and Lincoln, Y. S. (eds) *Strategies of Qualitative Inquiry*. Thousand Oaks, CA: Sage.

Tedder, M. and Biesta, G. (2009) 'Biography, transition and learning in the lifecourse: the role of narrative', in Field, J., Gallacher, J. and Ingram, R. (eds) *Researching Transitions in Lifelong Learning*. London: Routledge.

West, L. and Carlson, A. (2006) 'Claiming and sustaining space? Sure Start and the auto/biographical imagination', *Auto/Biography*, 14: 359–80.

West, L. and Carlson, A. (2007) *Claiming Space: An In-depth Auto/biographical Study of Sure Start Millmead 2001–2006*. Canterbury: Canterbury Christ Church University.

West, L., Alheit, P., Andersen, A. S. and Merrill, B. (eds) (2007) *Using Biographical and Life History Approaches in the Study of Adult and Lifelong Learning: European Perspectives.* Frankfurt am Main: Peter Lang.

Wolcott, H. F. (1990) *Writing up Qualitative Research.* San Francisco: Sage.

Wright Mills, C. (1970) *The Sociological Imagination.* Harmondsworth: Penguin.

Statistical hypothesis tests

Michael Borenstein

Introduction

Statistical analysis in educational research is usually conducted within either of two frameworks. One is significance testing, where the researcher poses a null hypothesis and then attempts to reject that hypothesis. The other is effect-size estimation, where the researcher reports the magnitude of the treatment effect and its confidence interval. My first goal in this chapter is to introduce the two frameworks. My second goal is to explain why researchers in the field of education (as well as many other fields) should focus primarily on effect size estimation rather than tests of significance.

Motivational example

Suppose that students enrolled in a SAT preparatory course currently use one curriculum and we anticipate that a modified curriculum will yield higher test scores. We draw a sample of students, assign the students randomly to either of the two curricula, and then compare the SAT scores for the two groups at the conclusion of the course. There are one hundred students in each group, the standard deviation within groups is known to be 100, and the mean SAT scores for the two groups are 420 vs 400, for a difference of 20 points.

As always, our goal is to make inferences from this sample to the larger population from which the sample was drawn. To distinguish between the sample and the population I will follow the convention of using Greek letters for population parameters and Roman letters for the sample statistics. The mean difference in the population is denoted Δ (delta), while the mean difference in the sample is denoted D.

Significance tests

One approach to the analysis is the significance testing framework (formally, the null hypothesis significance test, or NHST). Under this paradigm we pose the null hypothesis that the effect size (here the mean difference in SAT scores for the two curricula) is zero, and then attempt to disprove this hypothesis.

The fact that the mean difference in the sample (D) is not zero does not, in itself, tell us that the mean difference in the population (Δ) is not zero. This is because even if Δ is zero, in any given sample D will be lower or higher than zero due to random sampling error. Rather, to establish that Δ is not zero, we need to assess D in relation to its sampling error.

Concretely, if we were to draw an infinite number of samples from a population where Δ is zero, we can anticipate how the sample Ds would be distributed, and identify the range within which (for example) 95% of all Ds would fall, and define this as the 'acceptable' range. If D in our study falls inside this range we will conclude that there is no reason to reject the null (the result is not statistically significant). If D in our study falls outside of this range, there are two possible reasons. Either the null hypothesis is true and our study is among the 5% that happen to fall at the extreme, or the null hypothesis is false – one curriculum really does yield a higher mean score than the other, and this is the reason that our study yielded a mean difference so far from zero. We reject the first option in favour of the second (the result is statistically significant).

To implement this strategy we need to identify the *acceptable* range, and we do so using:

$$\Delta \pm SE_D \times Z_{1-\alpha}$$

The first element in this formula, Δ, is the mean difference under the null hypothesis (that is, zero). The sample Ds will be distributed about this value.

The second element, SE_D, is the standard error of D, and reflects the width of the distribution of D. The standard error, SE_D, is defined as:

$$SE_D = SD_W \sqrt{\frac{1}{n_T} + \frac{1}{n_C}}$$

where SD_W is the standard deviation of scores within groups, while n_T and n_C are the sample size within each group. If the standard deviation of scores within each group is relatively small, and/or the sample size within each group is relatively high, then the estimate of the group means (and of D) will tend to be relatively precise, leading to a smaller SE_D and relatively narrow width for the acceptable range.

The third element in the formula is $Z_{1-\alpha}$, where Z is the standard normal deviate corresponding to $1-\alpha$ (one minus alpha) and α is the criterion for significance. If we set α at 0.05, then the acceptable range includes ($1-\alpha$, or) 95% of the distribution of Ds, and the corresponding Z-value is 1.96. If we set α closer to zero (for example 0.01 rather than 0.05) the Z-value increases (for $\alpha = 0.01$, $Z = 2.58$), the acceptable range gets wider and we require a higher (absolute) value of D to reject the null hypothesis.

In the SAT example:

$$SE_D = 100\sqrt{\frac{1}{100} + \frac{1}{100}} = 14.14$$

If we set α at 0.05, then $Z_{1-\alpha}$ is 1.96, and the limits for the acceptable range are

$$\text{Lower} = 0.00 - 1.96 \times 14.14 = -27.72$$

and

$$\text{Upper} = 0.00 - 1.96 \times 14.14 = +27.72$$

In words, if the null hypothesis is true ($\Delta = 0$) and we were to perform an infinite number of studies, in 95% of those studies D would fall in the range of -27.72 to $+27.72$. In our example D is 20 points, and so we do not reject the null hypothesis – we conclude that Δ might (or might not) be zero. If D had been a difference of 30 points, then we would have rejected the null hypothesis – we would have concluded that Δ is probably not zero.

The NHST framework is sometimes presented using a 2×2 format (Table 41.1). The row labelled $\Delta = 0$ addresses the case where the null hypothesis is true. We hope that when Δ is zero, D will fall within the acceptable range (Cell B) and yield a non-significant result. However, we recognise that it may fall outside that range, leading to us to reject the null hypothesis (Cell A), which is called a Type I error. If the null hypothesis is true and α is set at 0.05, then 5% of studies will result in a Type I error. If the null hypothesis is false, then the Type I error rate is zero by definition.

The row labelled $\alpha \neq 0$ addresses the case where the null hypothesis is false. We hope that when Δ is not zero, D will fall outside the acceptable range (Cell C) and yield a significant result. However, we recognise that it may fall inside that range (Cell D). In this case we do not reject the null, and this is called a Type II error. The proportion of studies that will yield a significant result (and fall into Cell C rather than Cell D) is the power of the test, while 1-power, the type II error rate, is called β (beta).

Power depends on the true mean difference (the larger the value of Δ, the larger the expected value of

Table 41.1 Table of possible outcomes under NHST

	Result	
	Significant	**Not significant**
$\Delta = 0$	(A) Type I error	(B) Correct
$\Delta \neq 0$	(C) Correct	(D) Type II error

D and the greater the likelihood that it will fall outside the acceptable range), on the sample size (the larger the sample size, the narrower the acceptable region and the more likely that D will fall outside its bounds) and the value of α (when α is set at 0.05 rather than 0.01, the narrower the acceptable region and the more likely that D will fall outside its bounds). If a study has a power of 90% to reject the null then 90% of studies will yield effects outside the acceptable range and result in a correct conclusion, while 10% will yield effects within the acceptable range and result in a type II error.

I have presented the logic of the significance test by showing how we define an acceptable range based on SE_D and Z, and then see where D falls relative to this range. This approach lends itself to a clear explication of the significance test framework. In practice, one would typically reverse the process, computing a test statistic Z based on D and SE_D and then comparing this with the Z distribution. The two approaches are mathematically identical to each other.

To apply the traditional approach, we compute the test statistic Z, defined as:

$$Z = \frac{D}{SE_D}$$

where D and SE_D have the same definitions as before. If the test statistic Z is greater than the Z-value corresponding to $1-\alpha$ (or equivalently, if the p-value corresponding to Z is less than α) the result is statistically significant.

In the SAT example,

$$Z = \frac{20}{14.14} = 1.41$$

The test statistic Z is 1.41, which does not meet the threshold of $Z = 1.96$ (equivalently, the corresponding p-value is 0.157, which is greater than 0.05) and therefore the result is not statistically significant.

In sum, under the NHST framework we focus on the question of whether or not the difference in means is precisely zero. A non-significant result leads us to conclude that the true difference may be zero. A significant result leads us to conclude that the true difference is probably not zero.

NHST: the wrong framework for educational research

I have dedicated this much space to NHST because it is ubiquitous in social science research and is therefore important to understand. However, NHST is a very poor framework for the vast majority of analyses in this field, for the following reason. The null hypothesis significance test addresses a question that we typically don't care about and neglects the question that we do care about.

The *only* question addressed by NHST is the question of whether or not the effect size is *precisely* zero. For some studies, this is indeed the question of interest. For example, if the null hypothesis is that people who purport to have paranormal abilities will have the same accuracy in reading minds as 'normal' people, or that people treated with homeopathic medicine will have the same outcomes as people treated with placebo, then the question of interest *really is* whether or not the effect is precisely zero. In these cases NHST *is* the appropriate framework.

However, in the vast majority of social science research, the researcher has little (if any) interest in whether or not the effect size is precisely zero. Rather, the goal of the research is to estimate the actual size of the effect, since this is the issue that tells us whether or not the intervention's impact is of substantive importance. In the SAT study, for example, the p-value can only tell us that the impact of the intervention is (probably) not zero. Simply knowing that the effect is not zero does not tell us whether or not we should go to the expense of implementing the new curriculum. Rather, we want to know if the new curriculum increases the mean SAT score by zero points, 20 points, 50 points or 80 points. This is the issue addressed by effect size estimation.

Effect size estimation

An effect size is a value that reflects the magnitude of the relationship between two variables. It captures the substantive finding that the research is intended to address, and it does so using a metric that is meaningful and intuitive. In the SAT example we can use D, the difference in means, as the effect size. Other common effect sizes include the standardised difference in means, the risk difference and the correlation coefficient.

Recall that under the NHST framework we built a distribution of Ds (the *acceptable region*) around the null hypothesis – thus focusing on a specific effect size (zero) that is usually of little interest. By contrast, under the framework of effect size estimation we build a distribution of Ds (a confidence interval) around the observed effect size – thus focusing on the actual effect, which is what we care about. The lower and upper limits for the interval (D_{LL} and D_{UL}) are given by:

$$D_{LL} = D - SE_D \times Z_{CI\,Level}$$

$$D_{UL} = D + SE_D \times Z_{CI\,Level}$$

where SE_D is the same as before and $Z_{CI\,Level}$ is the Z value corresponding to the confidence level (for example, 1.96 for the 95% confidence interval).

In the SAT example, where D is 20 points and SE_D is 14.14, the 95% confidence interval is given by:

$$D_{LL} = 20 - 14.14 \times 1.96 = -7.72$$

$$D_{UL} = 20 + 14.14 \times 1.96 = 47.72$$

This means that the true effect probably falls in the range of −7.72 (in favour of the old curriculum) to 47.72 (in favour of the new curriculum). Formally, it means that in 95% of all possible studies, the confidence interval computed in this way will include the true effect, Δ.

These two approaches, NHST on the one hand, and effect-size estimation on the other, are in many ways the same. In one case we focus on the null, identify a range of likely D values under the null and then ask whether or not the observed D falls inside that range. In the other we focus on D, and identify a range of likely Δ values given D.

Importantly, since SE_D is identical in the two approaches, the 95% distribution about the null will include D if and only if the 95% distribution about D includes the null. Put another way, the p-value will be less than 0.05 if and only if the 95% confidence interval for D does not include zero. As such, the two approaches are completely congruent with each other mathematically, and the difference between them is one of form rather than substance (see Figure 41.1).

Nevertheless, this difference in form – whether to focus on the viability of the null hypothesis or to focus on the estimate of the effect size – turns out to be critically important for two reasons.

Effect size estimation addresses the question of interest

First, effect size estimation addresses the question that we intend to address ('What is the magnitude of the effect?'), while the NHST does not. The only information provided by the NHST (that we can or cannot rule out an effect size of precisely zero) is of little practical use.

Consider the four SAT studies in Figure 41.2, and assume that a 25-point difference in means would have practical importance. Using the effect size framework, two studies (A and D) show that the intervention may (or may not) be useful while two (B and C) show clearly that it is not useful. This speaks to the question of interest.

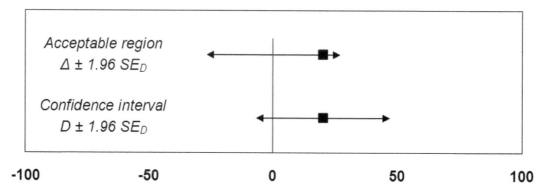

Figure 41.1 NHST (acceptable region) versus effect size estimation (conference interval)

By contrast, under the NHST framework two studies (A and B) allow us to reject the null hypothesis while two (C and D) do not. As such, we are grouping studies A and B together despite the fact that the substantive implications of the two are very different (one tells us that the effect size is trivial while the other tells us that it could be as large as 94 points). Similarly, we are grouping studies C and D despite the fact that the substantive implications of the two are very different (again, one tells us that the effect is trivial and the other tells us that it could be as large as 74 points).

NHST lends itself to mistakes of interpretation

The second reason that the difference in format (effect size estimation rather than NHST) is important is because the NHST lends itself to mistakes of interpretation and these mistakes are common.

The NHST, when interpreted properly (that we can or cannot rule out a zero effect), often tells us nothing of practical importance. Since this would imply that the study provides nothing of real value, researchers often assume that the results *must be* telling us something about the magnitude of the effect and press the results

Mean difference (D) and 95% confidence interval

	D	N*	p-value	95% CI
A	50	40	0.025	6 to 94
B	10	1000	0.025	1 to 19
C	6	1000	0.180	−3 to 15
D	30	40	0.180	−14 to 74

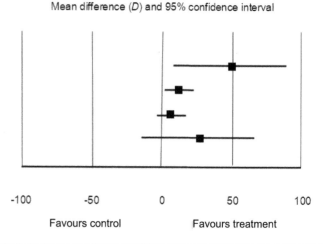

Figure 41.2 Four fictional studies to assess the impact of curricula on SAT scores

into service as an indicator of effect size. If the effect is (or is not) *statistically* significant, this information is interpreted as meaning that the effect is (or is not) of *substantive* significance. Similarly, the *p*-value is often pressed into service as an index of effect size, with a *p*-value of 0.05 taken to reflect a moderate effect, 0.01 a strong effect and 0.001 a very strong effect.

However, these interpretations are not justified. The *p*-value depends on both the size of the effect and the size of the sample. This is appropriate (indeed necessary) when the *p*-value is used in the context of NHST, since it is the combination of these factors that tells us that the null hypothesis is (or is not) probably false. By contrast, the fact that the *p*-value depends on both the size of the effect and the size of the sample makes it a poor choice as an index of effect size since it makes it difficult for us to distinguish between the two factors. While a p-value of 0.02 *could* reflect a large effect size, it could also reflect a small (or even trivial) effect size in a large study.

Again, consider the four studies in Figure 41.2. Suppose you were told that a study yielded a *p*-value of 0.02. Many people would envision the results as looking like Study A, where the difference in means is substantial. But the results might also look like Study B, where the difference in means is trivial. Similarly, suppose you were told that a study yielded a *p*-value of 0.18. Many people would envision the results as looking like Study C, where the treatment effect is shown to be small. But the results might also look like Study D, where the observed effect is substantial, and the true effect could be as high as 74 points.

By contrast, when we use the effect size approach, we report the effect size and its precision (or confidence interval) as two distinct values, and thus avoid these mistakes of interpretation. In A and D the effect is large whereas in B and C the effect is small. In B and C the effect size is known precisely, whereas in A and D it is not known precisely.

In context

Readers who have been trained to work exclusively within the NHST framework may find the previous sections surprising. In fact, though, these ideas have been expressed many times by scores of researchers over a period of decades. At the end of this chapter I have listed a few of the papers and books that deal with this subject.

Why does it work at all?

Given that NHST focuses on a question with little (if any) relevance to practical issues in education and that the *p*-values reported by studies are often misinterpreted, one might wonder how educational research has managed to make any progress at all over the past decades.

David Rindskopf (1970) argues that when the system works, it works because of a set of happy coincidences. Recall that the power of a study depends on the sample size, on alpha and on the true effect size. In educational research, many studies tend to have varied sample sizes and α is usually set at 0.05. Once these two factors are set, power tends to be poor (say, 20%) when the true effect is small, somewhat better (50%) when the true effect is moderate and better (80%) when the true effect is large. As such, the system will tend to weed out the less effective interventions while identifying those with real potential.

When this set of coincidences allows NHST to work *at all*, it does work very well. If an intervention is moderately effective, so that power is around 50%, then half the studies will yield a significant result while half will not. The correct interpretation, of course, is that some studies allow us to reject the null while others do not (presumably because of low power). In practice, researchers often see the results as 'conflicting', with some studies rejecting the null and others (making the mistakes outlined above) suggesting that the null is true. Even when the results are interpreted properly, focusing on the *p*-value rather than the size of the effect is a poor practice. Decisions about the utility of an intervention should be based on the magnitude of the effect size, not on evidence that the effect is (or is not) zero.

Effect sizes and research synthesis

While there has been only modest progress over the past few decades in moving from NHST to effect-size estimation, there is reason to expect that this trend will accelerate. Over the past two decades researchers have embraced the importance of research synthesis (or systematic reviews) which serve as the basis for evidence-based practice. The goal of research synthesis is to study the pattern of effects – if the treatment effect is consistent across studies, then we can report that the effect is robust across the kinds of studies included in the analysis. If the treatment effect varies, then we can report that the effect varies, and possibly identify factors associated with this variation. In order to perform a research synthesis of this kind we need to start with the effect size for each study, and so the importance of presenting this information is becoming more widely recognised (see, for example, Schmidt, 1996; Harlow et al., 1997).

Statistical notes

In this chapter I focused on the effect size D, which is a raw difference in means. There are many other effect sizes (see Chapter 45 by Rob Coe in this volume; Borenstein, 2009a; Borenstein et al., 2011) but the issues raised in this chapter apply to those as well.

My goal in this chapter has been to introduce NHST and effect size estimation, and to show why the latter is a better match for most social science research. To keep the focus on these goals I used an example (the SAT study) where the effect size is the raw mean difference, D. The formula for the standard error of D does not depend on D (only on the standard deviation and the sample size) and therefore the standard error is identical for NHST (where Δ is zero) and for effect size estimation (where D is the observed effect). By contrast, for many effect sizes (including the standardised mean difference and effect sizes for binary data) the standard error does depend on the effect size (though the impact is usually small). Therefore it is possible to have the case where the 95% confidence interval includes zero while the p-value is less than 0.05. For this reason, if one needs to report a p-value, then the p-value should be based on NHST formulas. This is a technical statistical matter and does not detract from the basic theme of this chapter.

I also made the assumption that the standard deviation of SAT scores within-groups is known (rather than estimated from the sample), which allowed me to use the Z-distribution rather than the t-distribution for computing the acceptable range and the confidence interval. Typically, we do need to estimate the standard deviation from the sample and therefore use the t-distribution for both.

Conclusion

The question addressed by NHST – '*Is the effect size precisely zero?*' – is of little relevance to most education research. When interpreted properly, NHST tells nothing about the substantive import of an intervention or relationship. When interpreted improperly (as is often the case) NHST can lead to incorrect conclusions. In particular, because the p-value reported for the significance test combines information about the effect size with information about the sample size, people often equate a significant p-value with a large effect size and a non-significant p-value with a small effect size, when these conclusions may not be justified.

By contrast, when we report an effect size with its confidence interval we focus on the question of interest – '*What is the magnitude of the effect?*' Additionally, we report a confidence interval that speaks to the precision of the estimate. Because the effect size and the precision are reported as distinct values, the mistakes of interpretation that are common for NHST are less likely for effect size estimation.

NHST and effect size estimation are congruent with each other. The key difference is not in the mathematics, but rather in the focus of the report. However, this change in focus, because it directs attention to the relevant question and helps avoid mistakes of interpretation, is critically important.

Questions for further investigation

1. What are the fundamental differences between a statistical significance and a practical significance?
2. See the suggested readings below. View the papers by Jacob Cohen and discuss the effects of the misapplication of p-values.

Suggested further reading

Two of my favourite readings on NHST are papers written by my mentor, Jacob Cohen, entitled 'The Earth Is Round (p < .05)' (1990) and 'Things I have learned (so far)' (1994). Jack shows how p-values have been misapplied over a period of decades and how this has served to undermine science and confuse generations of researchers.

The next two readings are collections of essays on the use (and misuse) of significance tests. *The Significance Test Controversy – A Reader* (Morrison and Henkel, 1970) is a collection of early essays that expand on the issues raised in this chapter and also provide some historical context. *What If There Were No Significance Tests?* (Harlow et al., 1997) is a similar collection of essays published 30 years later.

The final two readings are books on research synthesis and meta-analysis. In this chapter I've discussed why we need to report an effect size for each study. These books show how we can use that effect size, in concert with effect sizes from other studies, to get a more appropriate picture of an intervention's effect. The books are *The Handbook of Research Synthesis* (2nd edn) (Cooper et al., 2009) and *Introduction to Meta-analysis* (Borenstein et al., 2009).

References

Borenstein, M. (1994) 'The case for confidence intervals in controlled clinical trials', *Controlled Clinical Trials*, 15: 411–28.

Borenstein, M. (2009) 'Effect sizes for continuous data', in Cooper, H., Hedges, L. V. and Valentine, J. C. (eds) *The Handbook of Research Synthesis and Meta-Analysis* (2nd edn). New York: Russell Sage Foundation, pp. 221–35.

Borenstein, M., Hedges, L. V., Higgins, J. and Rothstein, H. R. (2009) *Introduction to Meta-analysis*. Chichester: Wiley.

Borenstein, M., Hedges, L. V., Higgins, J. and Rothstein, H. R. (2011) *Computing Effect Sizes for Meta-analysis*. Chichester: Wiley.

Cohen, J. (1990) 'Things I have learned (so far)', *American Psychologist*, 45: 1304–12.

Cohen, J. (1994) 'The earth is round (p < .05)', *American Psychologist*, 49: 997–1003.

Cooper, H. M., Hedges, L. V. and Valentine, J. C. (2009) *The Handbook of Research Synthesis and Meta-Analysis* (2nd edn). New York: Russell Sage Foundation.

Harlow, L. L., Mulaik, S. A. and Steiger, J. H. (1997) *What If There Were No Significance Tests?* Mahwah, NJ: Lawrence Erlbaum Associates.

Morrison, D. E. and Henkel, R. (eds) (1970) *The Significance Test Controversy – A Reader*. Chicago: Aldine.

Rindskopf, D. (1970) 'Testing "small": not null hypotheses: classical and Bayesian approaches', in Morrison, D. E. and Henkel, R. (eds) *The Significance Test Controversy – A Reader*. Chicago: Aldine.

Schmidt, F. L. (1996) 'Statistical significance testing and cumulative knowledge in psychology: implications for training of researchers', *Psychological methods*, 1: 115–29.

Analysis of variance (ANOVA)

H. J. Keselman and Lisa Lix

Introduction

Assessing whether treatment groups are equivalent on some measure of central tendency is a common problem for researchers in many fields. The classical method for examining this question has been the analysis of variance (ANOVA) F-test.

Consider a study in which a randomised trial is undertaken to compare a control group, an intervention group receiving a standard treatment and an intervention group receiving a new treatment on a single continuous outcome measure such as health status. How can we determine whether there is a statistically significant difference in the mean outcome score among the three groups? The conventional method of analysis for these data is ANOVA. ANOVA encompasses a broad collection of statistical procedures used to partition variation in a dataset into components due to one or more categorical explanatory variables (i.e. factors). The topics covered in this chapter are: (1) a description of the applications of ANOVA in research; (2) considerations in applying ANOVA to a dataset; (3) the basic computations that underlie ANOVA along with ancillary procedures; and (4) criteria to assess the reporting of ANOVA results in the education literature.

Applications of ANOVA

Data arising from many different types of studies can be analysed using ANOVA, including the following:

* *One-way independent groups design*, in which three or more groups of study participants are to be compared on a single outcome measure (or dependent variable). This is the simplest type of design in which ANOVA is applied.
* *Factorial independent groups design*, in which two or more factors (or independent variables) are crossed so that each combination of categories, or cell of the design, comprises an independent group of study participants. Interaction and main effects will usually be tested in factorial designs. A statistically significant two-way interaction implies that the effect of one factor is not constant at each level of a second factor.
* *One-sample repeated measures design*, in which a single group of study participants is observed on two or more measurement occasions. The measurements for each participant are typically correlated.
* *Mixed design*, which contains both independent groups and repeated measures factors. Within-subjects interaction and main effects as well as the between-subjects main effect may be tested in a

mixed design. A significant within-subjects two-way interaction effect implies that the repeated measures effect is not constant across groups of study participants.

Considerations in applying ANOVA

The assumptions that underlie validity of inference for the ANOVA F-test in independent groups designs are:

- The outcome variable follows a normal distribution in each population from which the data are sampled.
- Variances are equal (i.e. homogeneous) across the populations.
- The observations which comprise each sample are independent.

In one-sample repeated measures and mixed designs, measurements obtained from the same study participant are usually correlated, but it is assumed that measurements from different study participants are independent. In these designs it is also assumed that the data follow a multivariate normal distribution and conform to the assumption of multisample sphericity. Multivariate normality is satisfied when the marginal distribution for each measurement occasion is normal and the joint distributions of the measurement occasions are normal. For multisample sphericity to be satisfied, pairs of repeated measurements are assumed to exhibit a common variance. Furthermore, this variance is assumed to be constant across independent groups of study participants.

How it works/the basics

Variability in the outcome variable scores is used to determine whether there is an effect due to one or more independent variables (e.g. Method of Instruction: Method 1, Method 2, Method 3) and/or the combined effects of multiple independent variables (i.e. Method of Instruction *and* Hours Studied per Week: less than or equal to 10, greater than 10). In other words, the null hypothesis of equality of the population means (e.g. $H_0 : \mu_1 = \mu_2 = \ldots = \mu_A$) is tested by examining variation in the data.

We begin by focusing on the one-way independent groups design that contains a single independent variable denoted by A with A groups or levels. The ANOVA F-test compares a variance (i.e. MS_{BG}) whose magnitude is due to the (systematic) treatment effect (*when it exists*) as well as uncontrolled non-systematic effects (i.e. error) to a variance (MS_{WG}) whose size is only a function of non-systematic effects (i.e. error). The former, between groups variance, is calculated from the variability that exists between the means of the treatment groups, while the latter, within groups variance, is calculated from the variability that exists among the scores within each of the groups. These variances, in the ANOVA context, are denoted as mean squares (MS) because the sums of the squared deviation scores are divided by the degrees of freedom (df; i.e. MS=SS/df). The between groups MS, whose magnitude is a function of treatment variance and error variance, equals SS_{BG}/df_{BG}, while the within groups MS, whose magnitude is only due to error variance, equals SS_{WG}/df_{WG}. In the population, treatment variance and error variance are denoted as σ_A^2, and σ_e^2 respectively. The df for MS_{BG} is equal to the number of levels of variable A minus one. The df for MS_{WG} equals the total number of observations in the study, N, minus the number of levels of the independent variable. The statistic to test the null hypothesis of mean equality is the ratio of MS_{BG} to MS_{WG}. This ratio will be approximately equal to one when there are no effects due to the independent variable, because each MS will be estimating error variance. This ratio will be greater than one when a treatment effect exists, that is when the null hypothesis is false.

How does one answer the following question: Is the value of the F-test greater than one merely by chance (for example, because of sampling variation) or because a treatment effect really exists in the population? One answers this question by calculating the probability of observing the test statistic by chance assuming the null hypothesis of no treatment effect is true. If this probability is less than the criterion of significance, denoted by the Greek letter alpha (α), then one concludes there is sufficient evidence of a treatment effect and the null hypothesis is rejected in favour of the alternative hypothesis (H_A) that not all population means are equivalent. Typically, α is set equal to 0.05.

Having laid out the mechanics of an ANOVA F-test, the results of the analysis are typically reported in a tabular format that includes information about the sources of variation in the data and their associated df, MS and the F-test value (see Table 42.1). For completeness, we have included the population variances that contribute to each MS so that readers can see how the rule for forming the test statistic applies to our exemplar designs; the column containing this information is denoted E(MS). The expectation operator (i.e. E) indicates what we 'expect' the value of the MS to be in the long run.

Now consider the factorial independent groups design containing independent variables, A (e.g. method of instruction) and B (e.g. hours studied per week). Prior to the time of the well-known statistician Ronald Fisher, experimenters would manipulate only one variable at a time. Fisher proved that two or more variables could be examined simultaneously, without the effects of one variable confounding the other. Furthermore, in addition to examining the effect of each variable (i.e. each *main effect*) on the variability in the dependent scores, Fisher noted that researchers could also determine whether the variables interact to produce a unique effect on the scores above and beyond what one would predict from knowing the main effects.

To illustrate, consider the schematic in Figure 42.1. To test whether there is an effect due to variable A, the marginal means for this variable are used to compute the ANOVA F-test. (*Note*: Sample means

are depicted with a caret ($\wedge$) over the population mean (μ).) Likewise, to test whether there is a B main effect, the marginal means for this variable are used to compute the ANOVA F-test. To test if there is an A×B interaction, the cell means are used to compute the ANOVA F-test; this is done by examining whether the simple effects (differences between the means of one variable at a fixed level of the other variable, e.g. the differences between the A means at a fixed level of, say, B_1 – in other words comparing $\hat{\mu}_{11}$ and $\hat{\mu}_{21}$) of one variable are constant across the levels of the other variable. The three null hypotheses tested in a two-way independent groups factorial design are: (a) $H_A : \mu_{1.} = \mu_{2.} \ldots = \mu_{A.}$, (b) $H_B : \mu_{.1} = \mu_{.2} = \ldots = \mu_{.B}$, and (c) $H_{AB} : \mu_{jk} - \mu_{j.} - \mu_{.k} + \mu_{jk}$, (for all j and k) where $j = 1, \ldots, A$ and $k = 1, \ldots, B$. A dot notation replacing a subscript indicates that that variable has been summed over; thus $\mu_{1.}$ is the A_1 population marginal mean. The null hypothesis for the interaction effect is not intuitively obvious but, needless to say, it tests, as we have stated previously, whether the simple effects of one variable are constant across the levels of the other variable. Also note from the ANOVA summary table (Table 42.2) that the df and F-tests are formed in the manner previously described for the one-way independent groups design. That is, the main effect df are the number of treatment levels minus one, i.e. (A−1) and (B−1). The interaction df is equal to the product of the df for the effects that comprise the interaction, i.e. (A−1)(B−1). The df for the denominator MS (no longer called the within groups ms but now the within *cells* MS) for the F-tests are arrived at in a manner that is consistent with what we stated for the one-way independent groups design, i.e. N−AB, that is the df

Table 42.1 ANOVA summary table for a one-way independent groups design containing Factor A

Source of variation	Sums of squares (SS)	df	Mean square (MS)	E(MS)	F-test
Between groups	SS_{BG}	A−1	SS_{BG}/df_{BG}	$\sigma_e^2 + \sigma_A^2$	MS_{BG}/MS_{WG}
Within groups	SS_{WG}	N−A	SS_{WG}/df_{WG}	σ_e^2	

Note: It is assumed that Factor A is a fixed-effect variable, meaning levels of the variable have not been sampled from a larger pool of levels, and consequently all levels of interest are contained in the study.

df = degrees of freedom. N = total sample size. In the df column, A = number of levels of Factor A.

		Variable B		Marginal A means
	Variable values	B_1	B_2	
Variable A	A_1	$\hat{\mu}_{11}$	$\hat{\mu}_{12}$	$\hat{\mu}_{1.}$
	A_2	$\hat{\mu}_{21}$	$\hat{\mu}_{22}$	$\hat{\mu}_{2.}$
Marginal B means		$\hat{\mu}_{.1}$	$\hat{\mu}_{.2}$	

Note: Dot notation is used to indicate that the variable that the dot replaced has been summed over, e.g. a dot in the first subscript indicates that A has been summed over to get the B marginal value.

Figure 42.1   Schematic of cell and marginal means for a factorial independent groups design with independent variables A and B

are the total number of observations (N) minus the total number of treatment combination cells (AB).

This approach to assessing effects generalises to higher-order factorial ANOVA designs. For a three-way independent groups design containing independent variables A, B, and C, there are three two-way interaction effects: A×B, A×C and B×C, and one three-way interaction effect: A×B×C.

ANOVA summary tables for a two-way independent groups factorial design, a one-way repeated measures design and a mixed design containing one between-subjects variable and one repeated measures variable are presented in Tables 42.2 to 42.4, respectively.

For mixed designs (i.e. Table 42.4), all other things constant, within-subjects effects are typically easier to detect than between-subjects effects because differences between individuals do not contribute to a repeated measures error term. Both the B main effect and the A×B interaction effect are within-subjects effects and are easier to detect than if both A and B were between-subjects variables (see Maxwell and Delaney, 2004). For this design two different MSs are used as denominator values to calculate the F-tests because the mixed design is a combination of a one-way independent groups design [MS_A and ($MS_{S/A} = MS_{WG}$)] and a one-way repeated measures

Table 42.2   ANOVA summary table for a factorial independent groups design containing Factors A and B

Source of variation	Sums of squares (SS)	df	Mean square (MS)	E(MS)	F-test
A	SS_A	$A-1$	SS_A/df_A	$\sigma_e^2 + \sigma_A^2$	MS_A/MS_{WG}
B	SS_B	$B-1$	SS_B/df_B	$\sigma_e^2 + \sigma_B^2$	MS_B/MS_{WG}
A×B	SS_{AB}	$(A-1)(B-1)$	SS_{AB}/df_{AB}	$\sigma_e^2 + \sigma_{A\times B}^2$	MS_{AB}/MS_{WG}
Within groups	SS_{WG}	$N-AB$	SS_{WG}/df_{WG}	σ_e^2	

Note: See Table 42.1 note. In the df column, A = number of levels of Factor A, B = number of levels of Factor B.

Table 42.3 ANOVA summary table for a one-sample repeated measures design containing the within-subjects Factor A

Source of variation	Sums of squares (SS)	df	Mean square (MS)	E(MS)	F-test
A	SS_A	$A-1$	SS_A/df_A	$\sigma_e^2 + \sigma_A^2 + \sigma_{A\times S}^2$	$MS_A/MS_{A\times S}$
S	SS_S	$N-1$	SS_S/df_S	$\sigma_e^2 + \sigma_S^2$	*
A×S	$SS_{A\times S}$	$(A-1)(N-1)$	$SS_{A\times S}/df_{A\times S}$	$\sigma_e^2 + \sigma_{A\times S}^2$	

Note: There is no proper test for the Subject (S) effect. However, we expect study participants to differ from one another – one reason why a simple repeated measures design was likely selected by the experimenter. Thus researchers would not typically be interested in testing this effect. The Subjects factor is a random-effects variable since study participants are sampled from a larger pool of participants. See Table 42.1 note.

design (MS_A and $MS_{A\times S}$). Accordingly, the between-subjects effect (A) has a between-subjects error term ($MS_{S/A}$) and the within-subjects effects (B and A×B) have a within-subjects error term ($MS_{B\times S/A}$). The df for $MS_{B\times S/A}$ is the product of the df for the effects that comprise the interaction, namely $(B-1)$ and $(N-A)$.

As we indicated previously, ANOVA F-tests require that certain characteristics (e.g. normality, homogeneity of variances, etc.) prevail in the population in order to obtain valid results. Prior to adopting the ANOVA F-test, the researcher should carefully evaluate whether the study data satisfy these

Table 42.4 ANOVA summary table for a two-way mixed design containing between-subjects (A) and within-subjects (B) factors

Source of variation	Sums of squares (SS)	df	Mean square (MS)	E(MS)	F-test
Between subjects					
A	SS_A	$A-1$	SS_A/df_A	$\sigma_e^2 + \sigma_A^2$	$MS_A/MS_{S/A}$
S/A	$SS_{S/A}$	$N-A$	$SS_{S/A}/df_{S/A}$	σ_e^2	
Within subjects					
B	SS_B	$B-1$	SS_B/df_B	$\sigma_e^2 + \sigma_{B\times S/A}^2 + \sigma_A^2$	$MS_B/MS_{B\times S/A}$
A×B	SS_{AB}	$(A-1)(B-1)$	SS_{AB}/df_{AB}	$\sigma_e^2 + \sigma_{B\times S/A}^2 + \sigma_{A\times B}^2$	$MS_{AB}/MS_{B\times S/A}$
B×S/A	$SS_{B\times S/A}$	$(N-A)(B-1)$	$SS_{B\times S/A}/df_{B\times S/A}$	$\sigma_e^2 + \sigma_{B\times S/A}^2$	

Note: S/A is read as S 'within' A, meaning subjects are nested within groups, and this value is equivalent to MS_{WG}. See the notes from Table 42.1 and 42.3.

assumptions. For example, within the context of a one-way independent groups design, the normality and homogeneity of variance assumptions should be examined. A prevalently used statistical package for obtaining numerical results is PASW (formerly known as SPSS). This package provides tests of normality (Komolgorov-Smirnov and Shapiro-Wilk) through its Descriptive Statistics/Explore program and a test for variance homogeneity (i.e. Levin) is obtained from its programs which compute ANOVAs (Compare Means/Oneway or General Linear Model/Univariate programs) (see Norusis, 2008). Similar diagnostic procedures are available in other software packages. Descriptive tools such as box plots, normal probability plots and histograms can also provide valuable insights into the characteristics of the study data.

Ancillary procedures

Effect size (ES) and proportion of variance accounted for statistics

Researchers are encouraged to supplement tests of significance with statistics that quantify the magnitude of effect associated with an independent variable. According to *The Publication Manual of the American Psychological Association* (2001) 'it is almost always necessary to include some index of ES or strength of relationship in your Results section.' (APA, 2001: 25). The practice of reporting ESs has also received support from the APA Task Force on Statistical Inference (Wilkinson and the Task Force on Statistical Inference, 1999).

Cohen (1965) defined one well-known test statistic that quantifies mean differences (e.g. $\bar{A}_1-\bar{A}_2$ – a difference between the A_1 and A_2 marginal means) in standard deviation units (typically called Cohen's *d*). If the measurement scale is meaningful (i.e. not arbitrary), the mean difference need not be standardised. Other ES measures include omega squared (ω^2) and eta squared (η^2), which quantify the proportion of variation explained by an independent variable (see Howell, 2008: 402–6).

ES measures are important to report alongside tests of statistical significance. The latter are sensitive to sample size. Even a small treatment effect may be statistically significant if the sample size is sufficiently large. Thus we want to know that the effect is not only statistically significant, but that the magnitude of the effect is noteworthy. Guidelines are given by numerous authors for interpreting the magnitude of treatment effects (i.e. small, medium, large ESs) for social science data (Howell, 2008).

Confidence intervals (CIs)

The American Psychological Association's Task Force (Wilkinson and the Task Force on Statistical Inference, 1999) also recommends that tests of significance be supplemented with CIs for various statistics. For example, a 95% CI may be estimated for the difference statistic $\bar{A}_1-\bar{A}_2$. A CI establishes an upper and lower limit for the population value of interest, such as the mean difference (e.g. $\mu_1-\mu_2$). CIs assume a common form: the statistic (e.g. $\bar{A}_1-\bar{A}_2$), plus and minus a critical value from the appropriate sampling distribution of the statistic, times the standard error. (Standard deviations of statistics are referred to as standard errors.) For example, assume one wants to set an interval around $\bar{A}_1-\bar{A}_2$. The 95% CI would be:

$$(\bar{A}_1 - \bar{A}_2) \pm \sqrt{F_{\acute{a};1,N-A}} \sqrt{MS_{WG} \sum (c_j^2 / n_j)}$$

Because $(\bar{A}_1-\bar{A}_2)$ is a contrast (i.e. comparison) among means having one numerator df, where the c_js and n_js are the contrast coefficients (+1 and −1) and group sizes, respectively, the standard error of the contrast equals $\sqrt{MS_{WG} \sum (c_j^2 / n_j)}$ (see Maxwell and Delaney, 2004: 170).

Power to detect treatment effects

The power of a statistical test is the probability of detecting the effect of an independent variable(s) when it is present in the population. In other words, statistical power is the probability of rejecting the null hypothesis of no treatment effects in favour of a true alternative hypothesis that states that there are treatment effects. When designing their experiments, researchers should determine the conditions of the experiment so that if there is an effect due to their independent variable(s) it/they would be detected. That is, why put time and effort into designing and running an experiment if you do not have a high chance of detecting a true population effect? In particular, after diligently making sure that extraneous variables are controlled through appropriate experimental design procedures, so that variability in the dependent scores can only be due to the independent variable(s), researchers must decide on their criterion of significance (i.e. α) and how many subjects they need in order to detect the effect some percentage of the time when it exists. Because it is customary to set the criterion of falsely rejecting the null hypothesis at 0.05, and because researchers typically believe that the probability (Pr) of falsely rejecting the null hypothesis (a type I error = α) is a mistake that is four times as serious as falsely accepting the null hypothesis when an alternative hypothesis is indeed true (i.e. a type II error = β), the power $1-\Pr(\beta)$ that researchers typically strive to achieve is 0.80 (or greater). Researchers can postulate the magnitude of the effect that they believe exists (from prior research or a pilot study) with effect size/proportion of variance accounted for statistics (e.g. d, ω^2 or η^2), and then refer the value to an appropriate table or graph to determine how many subjects are required to detect the effect with the specified probability (Howell, 2008: 545; Maxwell and Delaney, 2004: Table A.11). Software programs that calculate power for popular statistical tests, including ANOVA F-tests, are readily available. For example, GPOWER can be freely obtained from http://www.psycho.uni-duesseldorf.de/aap/projects/gpower/.

Robust analogues to ANOVA F-tests

Many studies have demonstrated that the F-test and associated procedures (i.e. ES statistics, contrasts on means, CIs) are not robust to assumption violations, meaning that they are sensitive to changes in those factors that are extraneous to the hypothesis of interest. The F-test may become seriously biased when assumptions are not satisfied, resulting in spurious decisions about the hypothesis under consideration (see Erceg-Hurn et al., 2011; Keselman et al., 2008a, 2008b; Wilcox, 2003).

The assumptions which underlie the ANOVA F-test are unlikely to be satisfied in many studies. Outliers or extreme observations are often a significant concern because they can result in a substantial loss of power to detect a treatment effect. For example, in studies about reaction times, a few very large or small values may be observed. Furthermore, study participants who are exposed to a particular treatment or intervention may exhibit greater (or lesser) variability on the outcome measure than study participants who are not exposed to it. Heterogeneity of variance can have serious consequences for control of the type I error rate.

Researchers who rely on the ANOVA F-test (and ancillary procedures) to test hypotheses about equality of means may therefore unwittingly fill the literature with non-replicable results or at other times may fail to detect effects when they are present. In this era of evidence-informed decision-making, it is crucial that the statistical procedures applied to a set of data produce valid results.

Applied researchers often regard non-parametric procedures based on rank scores, such as the Kruskal-Wallis test or Friedman's test, as appealing alternatives to the ANOVA F-test when the assumption of normality is suspect. However, non-parametric procedures test hypotheses about equality of distributions rather than equality of means. They are therefore sensitive to variance heterogeneity, because distributions with unequal variances will necessarily result in rejection of the null hypothesis. Rank-transform test procedures are also appealing because they can be implemented using existing statistical software. A rank-transform ANOVA F-test is obtained by converting the original scores to ranks prior to applying the conventional ANOVA F-test to the data. One limitation of rank-transform procedures is that they cannot be applied to tests of interaction effects in factorial designs. The ranks are not a linear function of the original observations, therefore ranking the data may introduce additional effects into the statistical model. Furthermore, ranking may alter the pattern of the correlations among the measurement occasions in repeated measurement designs. Rank-transform tests, while insensitive to departures from normality, must therefore be used with caution.

Transformations of the data, to stabilise the variance or reduce the influence of extreme observations on estimation and inference, are another popular choice. Common transformations include logarithmic, square root and reciprocal transformations. The primary difficulty with applying a transformation to one's data is that it may be difficult to interpret the null hypothesis when the data are no longer in the original scale of measurement.

When variance equality cannot be assumed, robust parametric procedures such as the Welch test for the one-way independent groups design are recommended as alternatives to the ANOVA F-test. Welch's test does not pool the group variances in the computation of the test statistic error term, and modifies the degrees of freedom using a function based on the sample sizes and the variances. However, Welch's test assumes that the data satisfy the assumption of normality. If normality is not tenable, then a modification of the Welch test should be considered. One alternative involves substituting robust measures of location and scale for the usual mean and variance in the computation of the test statistic. Robust measures are less affected by the presence of outlying scores or skewed distributions than traditional measures of location and scale. There are a number of robust estimators that have been proposed in the literature; among these, the trimmed mean has received substantial attention because of its good theoretical properties, ease of computation and ease of interpretation. The trimmed mean is obtained by removing (i.e. censoring) the most extreme scores in the distribution, which have the tendency to 'shift' the mean in their direction. Current recommendations are to remove between 10 and 20% of the observations in *each* tail of the distribution. A consistent robust estimator of variability for the trimmed mean is the Winsorised variance, which is computed by replacing the most extreme scores in the distribution with the next most extreme observations. While robust estimators are insensitive to departures from a normal distribution, they test a different null hypothesis than traditional estimators. *The null hypothesis is about equality of trimmed population means.* Many researchers subscribe to the position that inferences pertaining to robust parameters (i.e. population trimmed means) are more valid than inferences pertaining to the usual least squares parameters (the μs) when they are dealing with populations that are non-normal in form (e.g. Huber, 1981; Wilcox, 2004). Thus one is testing a hypothesis that focuses on the majority (i.e. central part) of the population rather than the entire population.

Finally, computationally intensive methods, such as the bootstrap, have also been used to develop alternatives to the ANOVA F-test (and ancillary procedures). Under a bootstrap methodology, the usual ANOVA F-test is computed on the original observations, but statistical significance is assessed using the empirical distribution of the test statistic rather than the theoretical sampling distribution (i.e. F distribution) of the statistic. The empirical distribution is obtained by generating a large number (e.g. 1,000) bootstrap datasets; each dataset is a random sample (sampling with replacement) from the original observations. The F-test is computed for each bootstrap dataset. The resulting bootstrapped test statistics are ranked in ascending order; the critical value for assessing statistical significance corresponds to a pre-selected percentile of the empirical distribution, such as the 95th percentile. Research has shown that bootstrap test procedures have good properties in the presence of assumption violations. For example, the bootstrapped ANOVA F-test for repeated measures designs will effectively control the rate of type I errors to α, the nominal level of significance, under departures from both normality and sphericity.

Assessing ANOVA results reported in empirical research

For decision-makers to have confidence in ANOVA results reported in the empirical literature, it is important that the choice of test procedures is justified and the analytic strategy is accurately and completely described. The reader should be provided with a clear understanding of the characteristics of the data under investigation. This can be accomplished by reporting exploratory descriptive analysis results, including standard deviations (or variances), sample sizes, skewness (a measure of symmetry of the distribution) and kurtosis (a measure of peakedness of the distribution), and normal probability plots. As a general rule of thumb, skewness and kurtosis measures should be within the range from +1 to −1 in order to assume that the data follow a normal distribution. The normal probability plot is a graphic technique in which the observations are plotted against a theoretical normal distribution; if all of the points fall on an approximate diagonal line, then normality is likely to be a tenable assumption.

While, preliminary tests of variance equality, such as Levene's test, or tests of sphericity, such as Mauchly's test, are available in statistical software packages, their use is not always recommended. Many tests about variances are sensitive to departures from a normal distribution, and those that are insensitive to non-normality may lack statistical power to detect departures from the null hypothesis of equal variances which can result in erroneous decisions about the choice of follow-up tests.

For factorial designs, unless there is theoretical evidence that clearly supports the testing of main effects only, the analysis should begin with tests of interactions among the study factors. Graphic presentations of the cell means may be useful to characterise the nature of the interaction for readers.

Tests of main and interaction effects should be completely described. This includes reporting the value of the test statistic, degrees of freedom and p-value or critical value for each effect that is tested.

A statistically significant ANOVA F-test is routinely followed by multiple comparisons to identify the localised source of an effect. The choice of a multiple comparison test statistic and procedure for controlling the familywise error rate, the probability of making at least one type I error for the entire set of comparisons, should be explicitly identified in the reporting of results. A simple Bonferroni approach may suffice, in which each of p comparisons is tested at the α/p level of significance. However, this multiple comparison procedure is less powerful than stepwise Bonferroni procedures, such as Hochberg's (1988) procedure.

Conclusion

The ANOVA F-test (and its ancillary procedures) is one of the most popular test procedures for analysing behavioural and social science data because it can be used in a wide variety of research applications. Researchers may be reluctant to bypass the conventional ANOVA F-test in favour of an alternative approach. This reluctance may stem, in part, from the belief that the F-test is robust to departures from derivational assumptions (see, for example, Aron et al., 2009). While the type I error rate, the probability of erroneously rejecting a true null hypothesis, *may* be relatively insensitive to the presence of non-normal distributions, power rates can be substantially affected. This is a critical issue, particularly for small-sample designs which are common in behavioural and social science research. Departures from variance homogeneity and multi-sample sphericity can result in seriously biased tests of between-subjects and within-subjects effects, respectively. Statistical procedures that are robust to assumption violations have been developed for both simple and complex factorial designs and are now routinely available in many statistical software packages (Erceg-Hurn et al., 2011; Keselman et al., 2008a, 2008b; Wilcox, 2004).

In conclusion, we wish to note that the ANOVA layout, effect size measures, confidence intervals and statistical power analyses which were the focus of this chapter provide the basic schemata for a variety of analyses, whether one adopts the classical ANOVA F-test or one of its robust counterparts. As we stated previously, there are different perspectives as to whether the ANOVA F-test and its ancillary procedures are robust to derivational assumptions. Applied researchers must be able to make an appropriate justification for the choice of testing procedures based on a careful examination of the study data. We recommend that researchers consider adopting *both* classical and robust procedures. When the results of the two approaches agree, researchers can be more confident in their conclusions.

Questions for further investigation

1. Discuss the different types of testing procedures detailed in this article. List the pros and cons of the robust and classical procedures. When would one be prevalent over the other and what are the benefits of using both techniques in data analysis?

Suggested further reading

There is a wealth of reading available if you are interested in furthering your studies in this area. Please see the papers and texts referenced below, as well as Chapter 45 by Robert Coe, Effect Size, in this volume, which will prove a sound starting point.

References

American Psychological Association (APA) (2001) *Publication Manual of the American Psychological Association* (5th edn). Washington, DC: American Psychological Association.

Aron, A., Aron, E. N. and Coups, E. J. (2009) *Statistics for Psychology* (5th edn). Upper Saddle River, NJ: Pearson.

Conover, W. J. and Iman, R. L. (1981) 'Rank transformation as a bridge between parametric and nonparametric statistics', *American Statistician*, 35: 124–9.

Erceg-Hurn, D. M., Wilcox, R. R. and Keselman, H. J. (2011 forthcoming) 'Robust statistical estimation', in Little, T. (ed.) *The Oxford Handbook of Quantitative Methods.* New York: Oxford University Press.

Hill, M. A. and Dixon, W. J. (1982) 'Robustness in real life: a study of clinical laboratory data', *Biometrics*, 38: 377–96.

Hochberg, Y. (1988) 'A sharper Bonferroni procedure for multiple tests of significance', *Biometrika*, 75: 800–2.

Howell, D. C. (2008) *Fundamental Statistics for the Behavioral Sciences* (6th edn). San Francisco: Thomson Wadsworth.

Huber, P. J. (1981) *Robust Statistics*. New York: Wiley.

Keselman, H. J. (2005) 'Multivariate normality tests', in Everitt, B. S. and Howell, D. C. (eds). *Encyclopedia of Statistics in Behavioural Science* (Vol. 3). London: Wiley, pp. 1373–79.

Keselman, J. C., Lix, L. M. and Keselman, H. J. (1996) 'The analysis of repeated measurements: a quantitative research synthesis', *British Journal of Mathematical and Statistical Psychology*, 49: 275–98.

Keselman, H. J., Wilcox, R. R. and Lix, L. M. (2003) 'A generally robust approach to hypothesis testing in independent and correlated groups designs', *Psychophysiology*, 40: 586–96.

Keselman, H. J., Algina, J., Lix, L. M., Wilcox, R. R. and Deering, K. (2008a) 'A generally robust approach for testing hypotheses and setting confidence intervals for effect sizes', *Psychological Methods*, 13: 110–29.

Keselman, H. J., Algina, J., Lix, L. M., Wilcox, R. R. and Deering, K. (2008b) 'Supplemental material'. A SAS program to implement a general approximate degrees of freedom solution for inference and estimation. Available at: http://dx.doi.org/10.1037/1082-989X.13.2.110.supp (accessed 21 November 2011).

Lix, L. M. and Keselman, H. J. (1998) 'To trim or not to trim: tests of mean equality under heteroscedasticity and non-normality', *Educational and Psychological Measurement*, 58: 409–29.

Lix, L. M., Keselman, J. C. and Keselman, H. J. (1996) 'Consequences of assumption violations revisited: a quantitative review of alternatives to the one-way analysis of variance *F* test', *Review of Educational Research*, 66: 579–619.

Maxwell, S. E. and Delaney, H. D. (2004) *Designing Experiments and Analyzing Data* (2nd edn). Mahwah, NJ: Lawrence Erlbaum.

Norusis, M. J. (2008) *SPSS statistics 17.0: Guide to Data Analysis*. Upper Saddle River, NJ: Prentice Hall.

Scariano, S. M. and Davenport, J. M. (1987) 'The effects of violations of independence assumptions in the one-way ANOVA', *American Statistician*, 41: 123–9.

Toothaker, L. E. (1991) *Multiple Comparisons for Researchers*. Newbury Park, CA: Sage.

Wasserman, S. and Bockenholt, U. (1989) 'Bootstrapping: applications to psychophysiology', *Psychophysiology*, 26: 208–21.

Wilcox, R. R. (1995) 'ANOVA: a paradigm for low power and misleading measures of effect size?', *Review of Educational Research*, 65: 51–77.

Wilcox, R. R. (2003) *Applying Contemporary Statistical Techniques*. New York: Academic Press.

Wilcox, R. R. and Keselman, H. J. (2003) 'Modern robust data analysis methods: measures of central tendency', *Psychological Methods*, 8: 254–74.

Wilkinson, L. and the Task Force on Statistical Inference (1999) 'Statistical methods in psychology journals', *American Psychologist*, 54: 594–604.

Zimmerman, D. W. (2004) 'A note on preliminary tests of equality of variances', *British Journal of Mathematical and Statistical Psychology*, 57: 173–81.

43

Multiple linear regression

Stephen Gorard

Introduction

This chapter provides a brief and basic introduction to regression techniques and to the use of several variables in one consolidated analysis, focusing here on multiple linear regression. There are, of course, many other kinds of regression and even more ways of conducting multiple variable analysis, and some of these are referenced later in the chapter. However, most of the advice given in this chapter, about interpretation and judgement for example, would apply equally to all of these other techniques of analysis as well. For the benefit of some readers the chapter starts with a reprise of the ideas of correlation and two-variable regression. The next section describes a basic multiple linear regression, and ensuing sections look at the interpretation of results and some of the potential dangers of being misled.

Correlation and simple regression

There is a correlation between people's height and their foot length. In general, taller people tend to have bigger feet (and vice versa). This correlation is not perfect, and some tall people have quite dainty feet, for example. But imagine you were told that three people have heights of 2m, 1.7m and 1.2m, and

that the same three people have foot lengths of 0.2m, 0.25m and 0.3m. You are asked to guess which foot size matches which height. In the absence of any other evidence you would be wise to place the smallest foot size with the shortest person and so on. Imagine that this is correct, and that a fourth person has a foot size of 0.3m. You are asked to estimate how tall they would be. In the absence of any other evidence, you would be wise to imagine them as near the height of 2m. This, in essence, is a simple regression. You use an existing correlation between two measures to estimate an unknown value of one measure from a known value of the other measure for the same case or individual.

Several things should be clear from this example. First, regression is rather easy and intuitive in nature. Second, it can easily yield an incorrect answer. How likely it is that the fourth person is near 2m in height depends upon the representativeness of the first three cases, the accuracy of all of the measurements involved, the variability of all measures involved and the strength of the correlation. Third, regression is not a definitive test of anything, and it does not prove anything. It is only of use for estimating, or best guess in the absence of any other evidence. Fourth, it is impossible to demonstrate causes using regression alone. An individual's height does not cause their foot size or vice versa. However elaborate a regression model is, it is merely an expression of association between the two variables. We may imagine in some regression models that the link is a causal one, but the indications of this causality come from our knowledge of the real world outside the regression model, not from the model itself. For example, imagine that a pupil's repeated absence from school is correlated with their examination performance. This might be a negative correlation, meaning that the two measures are related inversely, so that an individual with higher recorded absence from school would tend to attain fewer GCSE passes (the GCSE is a standard national examination in each curriculum subject for 16 year olds in England). We might imagine that absence from school therefore impairs examination performance. But that explanation must be based on our wider knowledge of the mechanisms involved, not on the regression pattern alone. Otherwise, it could be that failure at school leads to school avoidance, or the two measures could be mutually reinforcing, or there might be any number of other things affecting both measures (poverty, illness and so on).

The most commonly used technique for correlation/regression is based on the Pearson's R correlation coefficient. An R score of 1 means perfect correlation or even identity, an R of −1 means perfect inverse, and an R of 0 means no correlation at all between the two variables. Usually you will uncover R values between these extremes. For example, using data from an imaginary 400 pupils, the correlation between the precise age of a pupil in months and their examination score (measured as number of GCSEs passed, as above) might appear as Table 43.1 (using SPSS). The correlation between the two measures is 0.643, meaning that any relationship is positive (a higher age is linked to better GCSE scores). It also means that any relationship is imperfect. If we square the R value of 0.643 we get an R^2 value of just over 0.4. This 'effect size' tells us that around 40 per cent of the variation in the two measures is common to both, and that around 60 per cent is independent. Even if higher age were assumed to *cause* better performance, the R^2 tells us that there are other factors involved as well, including errors in measurement and recording (Gorard, 2010a).

Table 43.1 also reports 'Sig.' or significance; it marks significant values with ** and includes an explanatory footnote that this means significant at the 0.01 level. SPSS generates these items automatically, and there

Table 43.1   Correlation between age in months and number of GCSEs passed

		Age	GCSEs
Age	Pearson Correlation	1	.643(**)
	Sig. (2-tailed)		.000
	N	400	400
GCSEs	Pearson Correlation	.643(**)	1
	Sig. (2-tailed)	.000	
	N	400	400

**Correlation is significant at the 0.01 level (2-tailed).

is no way of switching them off at present, so you must just ignore them when they are not relevant. They are only relevant when the measures are very accurate, come from a sample drawn randomly with full response from a known population, and you want to estimate the likelihood that *if* there is no sizeable correlation in the population you would obtain an R value at least as large as the one in the table. Why anyone should want to know the latter is inconceivable and I have never encountered such a situation – my advice is that you should usually ignore these items to focus on judgement based on the values of N and R and the accuracy and distribution of your two measures. The key point is that you must not mistake the Sig. as being any indication of the importance of your results (Gorard, 2010b). It also means that you do not need to repeat a table like this in any report. The R (0.643) and N (400) figures will suffice.

The calculation of R is based on two key assumptions. The two sets of values used for the correlation/regression must be real measures, in the way that height or number of days missing from school are real numbers, and that the ethnic origin of an individual or their shoe size are not. And the two sets of values must cross plot to form an approximate straight line. Figure 43.1 shows a cross plot of our imaginary data on pupil age and GCSE passes. Although there is variation in the number of passes for each age value, and a cluster of pupils

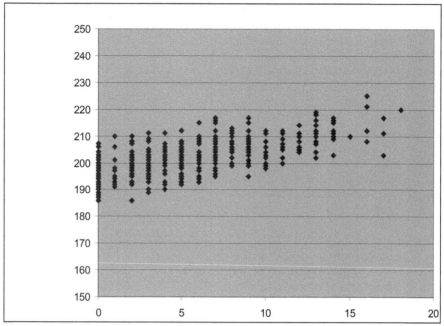

N = 400

Source: hypothetical data.

Figure 43.1 Cross plot of pupil age in months (y axis) and number of GCSE passes (x axis)

with zero passes, the graph shows a small near linear positive relationship between age and GCSE passes (as we would expect from the correlation coefficient of 0.643). Note that a very low or zero value of R does not mean that the two measures are not related, merely that they are not obviously linearly related. In situations where the two measures form a curve when cross plotted it is sometimes possible to transform the variables (e.g. by conversion to logarithms) to make a better line of fit, although this can introduce further problems (Harwell and Gatti, 2001). In addition, there are correlation and regression techniques available for use with categorical variables (Siegel, 1956).

There is a line of best fit that is usually seen as the line on a graph like Figure 43.1 that minimises the mean deviation of all points from the line. Once this line has been calculated as part of the regression analysis, it is possible to use it to read off the values of one variable (such as height, the dependent variable in our example) from the values of the other (such as foot length, the independent variable). The words dependent and independent are traditional, but do not be confused into thinking that they mean one measure is caused by the other or that the other measure could not equally well be the dependent one. The key output from SPSS when conducting a simple bivariate linear regression, using the same data as Table 43.1 but shorn of items relating to significance and standard errors, could appear like Table 43.2. The dependent (predicted) variable is the number of GCSE passes per individual, and the independent (predictor) variable is the number of half days absent from school. In this example the model R value is 0.643, also shown as beta in Table 43.2.

The R value, identical to that in Table 43.1, is an estimate of how closely correlated the two measures are. What is new in this regression analysis is the B column. This gives a theoretical coefficient (or multiplier) for the pupil age to yield the best estimate of the number of GCSE passes for all cases. The constant yields the intercept on the graph (see below). So our

Table 43.2   Regression analysis, predicting GCSE passes from school absence

Model		B	Beta
1	Constant	-78.185	
	Age	.414	.643

Dependent variable: GCSEs.

best estimate for any pupil, ignoring measurement and other errors that we cannot estimate, is:

Number of GCSE passes = −78.185 + (0.414 * Age)

Using this equation we can estimate the number of GCSE passes for individuals whose results we do not know but whose ages we do know. Someone who is 189 months old would be predicted to achieve −78.185 + (0.414 * 189) GCSE passes. This is very near zero, as we would expect from Figure 43.1, since the imagined line of best fit crosses the y axis (a value of zero GCSE passes) at around 189. On the other hand, someone aged 210 months would be predicted to gain around 9 GCSE passes, since −78.185 + (0.414 * 210) is near 9. Again this makes sense looking at the data in Figure 43.1. However, age is not the only thing related to examination outcomes. Even if it is a contributory factor, there may be many other measures which could help to make our estimate even more accurate. This leads us to consider multiple linear regression.

Multiple regression

Going back to the very first illustration, imagine you were told that four people have heights of 2 m, 2 m, 1.7 m and 1.2 m, and that the same four people have foot lengths of 0.2 m, 0.25 m, 0.27 m and 0.3 m. You are asked to guess which foot length matches which height. Here you have two individuals with the same height who must have different foot lengths. How do you decide which matches which? What you really need is more information. Knowing the individual's sex, ethnicity or age may help here. Factoring a third, fourth or fifth variable into your calculation at the same time as the original two measures is what

multiple regression does. Using the same approach as simple regression, the model could calculate the best single predictor, and then keep adding the next best predictor to the model to make the estimates more accurate, until either we run out of possible predictors or the model cannot improve (its R^2) any further with the available predictors.

For example, we might improve our estimate of GCSE passes by adding more independent variables to our main predictor of pupil age in months. Perhaps, as suggested earlier, a pupil's pattern of absences from school makes a difference to their GCSE attainment. A practical problem is that this new variable might be correlated with pupil age as well as with GCSE passes. We cannot therefore simply total the correlations of each independent variable with the GCSE passes. For example, if pupil absence is negatively correlated with their GCSE passes, we cannot simply add this to the correlation for pupil age. If age and absences have some correlation between themselves, then using both together means we end up using their common variance twice. The real multiple correlation between age and absence on the one hand and GCSE passes on the other is likely to be less than the sum of the two correlations. This is one key reason for using multiple linear regression, since it takes into account the correlations between multiple independent variables when combining them to predict/explain the variance in the dependent variable. In fact the number of days absent from school correlates with GCSE passes at R of −0.455, and it correlates with pupil age at R of −0.321. So, multiple regression is clearly indicated if we wish to use both predictors at once.

Multiple regression is done in the same way as simple regression (using SPSS) but with more than one independent variable. The output, continuing the GCSE passes example, could look like Tables 43.3 and 43.4 (as above, shorn of items relating to standard errors and significance). Table 43.3 shows the value of R (0.712), which means the same as it does in simple regression, except that it now expresses the multiple correlation between GCSE passes on the one hand, and all independent variables in combination on the other. Note that adding the second predictor variable leads to a better model (R), 0.712 rather than 0.643, with more accurate estimates of the dependent variable, but does

Table 43.3 Summary model for multiple regression analysis

Model	R	R square
1	.712	.506

Predictors: (Constant), Absences, Age.

Table 43.4 Coefficients for multiple regression analysis

Value	B	Beta
Constant	-66.845	
Age	.364	.566
Absences	-.244	-.315

Dependent variable: GCSEs.

not increase R by as much as its simple correlation with the dependent variable.

Table 43.4 is like Table 43.2, but here shows the coefficients (or multipliers) for more than one predictor variable. Given the values in Table 43.4, you can therefore calculate (or use the computer to calculate) expected GCSE passes for any pupil, as long as you know their precise age and number of absences from school. And you can do so more accurately than you could using either age or absences alone.

The multiple regression equation would be of the form:

$$\text{GCSE passes} = -66.845 + (0.364 * \text{Age}) - (0.244 * \text{Absences})$$

If more explanatory variables are available you can simply add them to this analysis. Each will yield a further row in Table 43.4 and a B coefficient that can be added to the equation and used to help predict the dependent value for any case. Each explanatory variable added should substantially increase the R value in Table 43.3. If it does not, then that variable is not really 'explanatory' (but see below for discussion about the order of entering variables into your model).

Basic assumptions

The underlying assumptions for an analysis are the things that the analytical software needs to be true in order for the calculated result to be correct. Most basic assumptions for multiple linear regression are the same as for correlation and simple regression (Maxwell, 1977; Achen, 1982).

- All variables used should be real numbers.
- All variables are measured as far as possible without error.

- There is an approximate linear relationship between the dependent variable and the independent variables (both individually and grouped).

To these is added one more basic one.

- No independent variable is a perfect linear combination of another (not perfect 'multicollinearity').

If the basic assumptions are not true, or at least nearly so, then the regression results can be very misleading. Regression does not work well with categorical independent variables having more than two values (Hagenaars, 1990), but if a variable (such as sex) has only two possible values it can be treated as an equal interval variable (since there is only one interval). Further, even variables with more than two categories can be used by converting them to a series of dummy variables. A social class scale with three categories, for example, could be treated as two dummy variables. The first dummy is a yes/no variable representing being in the 'Professional' class or not, and the second dummy represents being in the 'Intermediate' class or not. 'Working' class is therefore defined as being not Professional and not Intermediate class. Some writers have argued that this treatment is a distortion and not really appropriate, especially now that newer methods have been developed specifically to deal with categorical variables (such as logistic regression). Since it is assumed in regression that the variables are normally distributed (Lee et al., 1989), and dummy variables cannot have such a distribution then simply converting a categorical variable into a set of dummies is not the solution. These dummy variables add to the measurement error (Blalock, 1964). For more on this, and other potential flaws in regression analysis such as omitted variable bias, heteroskedasticity and multicollinearity, see Maddala (1992).

The full set of assumptions underlying regression techniques is large and therefore can be rather off-putting. But unless the standard error or significance is an issue for you most of these further assumptions are less important, or indeed completely irrelevant like the first one below.

- The measurements are from a random sample (or at least a probability-based one).
- There are no extreme outliers.
- The dependent variable is approximately normally distributed (or at least the next assumption is true).
- The residuals for the dependent variable (the differences between calculated and observed scores) are approximately normally distributed.
- The variance of each variable is consistent across the range of values for all other variables (or at least the next assumption is true).
- The residuals for the dependent variable at each value of the independent variables have equal and constant variance.
- The residuals are not correlated with the independent variables.
- The residuals for the dependent variable at each value of the independent variables have a mean of zero (or they are approximately linearly related to the dependent variable).
- For any two cases the correlation between the residuals should be zero (each case is independent of the others).

However, these assumptions are the subject of some dispute, both over what the assumptions really are and the implications for running an analysis that does not meet them (Menard, 1995; Miles and Shevlin, 2001; de Vaus, 2002). In any real research project involving multiple regression, at least some of the assumptions are likely to be violated (Berry and Feldman, 1985). This, in itself, may not be fatal to the validity of the work, and even where the regression is flawed it is sometimes only the intercept (or constant) that is affected while the derived coefficients may still be used with care. On the other hand, some commentators insist that regression analysis only makes sense when the variables are precisely measured, otherwise the

coefficient values will be misleading. As with almost any technique, the best defence against any such problems is a large high-quality sample and using only the best measurements possible. In general, if any assumptions are not true for any analysis, the impact is to reduce the apparent size of any relationship uncovered. Therefore, and in general, if you obtain a powerful result it is still relatively safe to proceed to investigate it.

Cautions and interpretations

Multiple regression is powerful, easy to use and reasonably tolerant in its assumptions (or relatively unaffected by violation of them). Nevertheless, it is still often used poorly, with incorrect conclusions drawn from weak findings. This section raises some cautions for the interpretation of regression data. Three of these have been outlined before. A zero or weak correlation coefficient does not mean that there is no interrelationship between the variables involved. It might just mean that the interrelationship is more complex than a simple linear correlation. Also, regression does not test anything. It merely models a relationship that we prescribe as analysts. The fact that there is such a model is therefore weak evidence in itself. It is certainly not evidence of a specific, or indeed any, causal relationship between the variables involved. For any study, the regression model explaining the greatest variance in the dependent variable (e.g. exam score) will use all available independent variables. This is the model you get if you simply enter all of the variables at once. However, it is possible to create simpler models containing fewer variables but still explaining a large proportion of the variance. These models are easier to use and understand, and so more practical. In several forms of multivariate analysis, the order in which independent variables are entered into the explanatory model can also make a very substantial difference to the results obtained. It is always worth changing the order of entry of your variables to see how robust the findings are.

Another problem is that because regression models are fitted to the data after collection, it is possible to use the natural but often meaningless variation in the independent variables to match individual scores in the purportedly dependent variables. The ensuing model is completely irrelevant but can have a very high R-value (and of course misleading probabilities). For example, a dataset with as many independent variables as cases will *always* yield an R of 1, even if the scores are randomly generated (Gorard, 2006a). This is why reputable texts emphasise that the number of cases in any study must outnumber the number of variables by an order of magnitude. If we vary the analysis to use 'backward' elimination of any redundant variables, it is possible to reduce the number of independent variables in the model without substantially reducing the R-square value. In other words, we can still create a perfect prediction/explanation for the dependent variable, but this time using fewer variables than cases. If we are happy to allow the R-squared value to dip below 1.0 then the number of variables needed to predict the values of the dependent variable can be reduced dramatically. It is easily possible, in this way, to produce a model with an R-value of 0.6 or higher using only 10 or fewer variables for 100 cases, even where all of the values are nonsensical random numbers. This R-value is higher than many of those that are published in journals and that have been allowed to affect policy or practice. Many of these remaining variables will be labelled 'significant' by the software. And the ratio of cases to variables is 10:1, which can be considered reasonably healthy.

This is part of the reason for being very cautious about small values of R^2. Unfortunately, there is no standard scale of substantive importance for effect sizes like R^2 (Gorard, 2006b), and things like significance tests are no use here even if the data meet the requirements, such as being based on a good random sample (Gorard, 2010b). That is why the judgement to publish a regression model needs to be justified in terms of N, R^2, the quality of the measures, the theoretical explanation, its practical importance or the steps taken to test the association more rigorously via a randomised controlled trial or similar.

Conclusion

I have used simple linear regression in this explanation for clarity and familiarity, but the danger of spurious findings is a general one and cannot be overcome by using alternative forms of regression. Similar arguments apply to logistic regression or to multilevel modelling. In fact, more complex methods can make the situation worse, because they make it harder to establish how many cases (sampling units) there are. Complex statistical methods cannot be used *post hoc* to overcome design problems or deficiencies in datasets. It is worth stating this precisely because of the 'capture' of funders by those pushing for more complex methods of probability-based traditional analysis, whereas of course 'in general, the best designs require the *simplest* statistics' (Wright, 2003: 130). A good defence is, as always, to increase the number of cases and minimise the number of variables. Another defence is to look at the same variables in another way, using a complementary method. This is one of the strengths of mixed methods work, wherein a tentative, theoretical or statistical result can be tested by a field trial and/or in-depth observation, for example.

Multiple regression is an easy to use and powerful method for summarising patterns in large datasets. It is also a fascinating entry into the world of modelling and complex multivariate analysis. I recommend it as a useful tool to help you think about your data and form judgements about what the data might mean (Gorard, 2001). However, despite talk of predictions, regression has rarely if ever been used to predict real-life events such as stock market crashes, eclipses or even a thunderstorm (Brighton, 2000). This limited practical success in isolation is to be expected if you understand what regression is and is not. Imagine it like drawing a graph. The graph does not really tell you anything new, and it is not a test of anything. But it can help you think about the meaning of your results. Regression can do the same with more variables than a graph usually can, and it can encourage you to consider interactions between variables. No more, no less. It is more likely to be the start of your investigation trying to explain the pattern uncovered than an end in itself.

Questions for further investigation

1. Find a dataset in your own area of interest that contains a large number of cases and at least three real-number variables. Select three such variables, and draw a cross-plot graph of each pair. Note any

near linear patterns. Run a correlation analysis for each pair. Run a regression analysis with one variable as the imagined dependent variable and one as the predictor. Note the relationship to correlation. Now run a regression with two predictors. Note the differences to bivariate regression results.

2. Find an article in your area of interest that uses regression. Prepare a critique, noting how well and fully the paper presents the methods, whether the paper includes undigested computer output or whether the tables are made easy to read, whether the paper uses significance incorrectly (with population data or a convenience sample) and whether the paper uses causal words like 'influence' or 'impact' without justification.

Suggested further reading

Gorard, S. (2006) *Using Everyday Numbers Effectively in Research*. London: Continuum. This book illustrates how numbers can be used routinely and successfully for research purposes – without your ever having to consider confidence intervals, probability densities, Gaussian distributions or indeed any of those complicated and generally useless things that appear in treatises on statistics. This no-nonsense guide should prove essential reading for all educational and social science researchers.

Hancock, G. and Mueller, R. (2010) *The Reviewer's Guide to Quantitative Methods in the Social Sciences*. London: Routledge. Designed for evaluators of research manuscripts and proposals in the social and behavioural sciences, and beyond. Covering virtually all of the popular classic and emerging quantitative techniques, thus helping reviewers to evaluate a manuscript's methodological approach and its data analysis.

References

Achen, C. (1982) *Interpreting and Using Regression*. London: Sage.

Berry, W. and Feldman, S. (1985) *Multiple Regression in Practice*. London: Sage.

Blalock, H. (1964) *Causal Inferences in Nonexperimental Research*. Chapel Hill, NC: University of North Carolina Press.

Brighton, M. (2000) 'Making our measurements count', *Evaluation and Research in Education*, 14(3 & 4): 124–35.

de Vaus, D. (2002) *Analyzing Social Science Data: 50 Key Problems in Data Analysis*. London: Sage.

Gorard, S. (2001) *Quantitative Methods in Educational Research: The Role of Numbers Made Easy*. London: Continuum.

Gorard, S. (2006a) *Using Everyday Numbers Effectively in Research: Not a Book About Statistics*. London: Continuum.

Gorard, S. (2006b) 'Towards a judgement-based statistical analysis', *British Journal of Sociology of Education*, 27(1): 67–80.

Gorard, S. (2010a) 'Measuring is more than assigning numbers', in Walford, G., Tucker, E. and Viswanathan, M. (eds) *Sage Handbook of Measurement*. Los Angeles: Sage, pp.389–408.

Gorard, S. (2010b) 'All evidence is equal: the flaw in statistical reasoning', *Oxford Review of Education*, 36(1): 63–77.

Hagenaars, J. (1990) *Categorical Longitudinal Data: Log-linear, Panel, Trend and Cohort Analysis*. London: Sage.

Harwell, M. and Gatti, G. (2001) *Review of Educational Research*, 71(1): 105–31.

Lee, E., Forthofer R. and Lorimor, R. (1989) *Analyzing Complex Survey Data*. London: Sage.

Maddala, G. (1992) *Introduction to Econometrics*. New York: Macmillan.

Maxwell, A. (1977) *Multivariate Analysis in Behavioural Research*. New York: Chapman & Hall.

Menard, S. (1995) *Applied Logistic Regression Analysis*. London: Sage.

Miles, J. and Shevlin, M. (2001) *Applying Regression and Correlation*. London: Sage.

Siegel, S. (1956) *Nonparametric Statistics*. Tokyo: McGraw-Hill.

Wright, D. (2003) 'Making friends with your data: improving how statistics are conducted and reported', *British Journal of Educational Psychology*, 73: 123–36.

Multilevel analysis

Michael Seltzer and Jordan Rickles

Introduction

The data that we encounter in educational research often have what is termed a multilevel, nested or hierarchical structure. One source of multilevel data structures is the kinds of sampling and data collection designs employed in educational surveys such as High School and Beyond (HSB) and the Early Childhood Longitudinal Study (ECLS) (e.g. cluster sampling designs). For example, in their study of the effects of teachers' literacy instructional practices on kindergarten students' language and literacy skills, Xue and Meisels (2004) conducted analyses using a sample from ECLS consisting of over 13,000 kindergarten students nested within 2,690 classrooms which in turn were nested in 788 schools.

A multilevel structure can also arise from an experimental or quasi-experimental research design that involves, for example, assigning intact classrooms or schools to treatment and comparison conditions and assessing student-level outcomes. For example, to study the effectiveness of Comer's School Development Program (CSDP), Cook et al. (1999) randomly assigned 23 middle schools to treatment (CSDP) and control conditions. The sample for this study comprised of approximately 12,000 students and 2,000 staff members nested within these 23 schools.

Similarly, many studies in education – surveys as well as experimental studies – entail collecting measures of key constructs at multiple points in time for each student in a sample (e.g. measures of student achievement in reading or mathematics across a series of grades). This gives rise to a multilevel structure in which longitudinal data are nested within each student.

In many studies in which students are nested within a sample of different groups (e.g. classes or schools), we often find that there are appreciable differences across groups in students' prior educational experiences and background characteristics, in contextual factors such as normative climate, and in the quality of the curricula and instructional practices that students in these different groups encounter. Such factors give rise to a certain degree of similarity among the outcome scores for the students nested within a given group, i.e. student outcome scores are dependent to some extent on group membership. This is referred to by statisticians as intra-class correlation. When we ignore such dependencies in our analyses – that is, when we use standard regression methods to analyse the student-level data in a sample and ignore the fact that students are nested within different groups – we run the risk of obtaining standard errors for estimates of key parameters (e.g. programme effects) that are too small. That is, we underestimate the statistical uncertainty. This, in turn, can give rise to spuriously significant results.

A second problem that arises when we ignore the nested structure of our data – one that we emphasise in this chapter – is connected with Cronbach's (1976: 1) concern that the analyses we conduct in educational research might often conceal more than they reveal. For example, minority gaps in achievement, and gender gaps in mathematics and science achievement are important educational policy issues in the US. Often overall estimates of minority or gender gaps based on large-scale survey data sets receive appreciable attention. However, such single-number summaries conceal the fact that differences in achievement between minority and non-minority students, for example, may vary extensively across schools; in some schools the difference may be substantial, but in others there may be no gap at all. Approaching such policy issues from a multilevel perspective encourages us to attend to differences in the magnitude of minority gaps across schools, and to try to identify those school policies and practices that are systematically related to differences in the magnitude of minority gaps (e.g. Lee and Bryk, 1989). Along these lines, interest might also centre on the relationship between student socio-economic status (SES) and achievement, and why differences in SES might be associated with large differences in achievement between students in some schools, but negligible differences in achievement in others.

Thus multilevel modelling enables us to study differences across groups in how equitably outcomes of interest are distributed with respect to various demographic characteristics. In the following section, in an extended example of the logic and application of multilevel modelling, we show how such models enable us to investigate the extent to which the effects of programmes vary across sites, and identify key factors that might underlie such variability. We then briefly discuss several other types of applications, including a school effects application from work by Lee and Bryk (1989) and Raudenbush and Bryk (1986) that investigated whether 12th grade mathematics achievement is higher in Catholic high schools than in public high schools, and whether differences in student SES are less consequential with regard to student achievement in Catholic versus public high schools. At the end of the chapter, questions to follow up this introduction to multilevel

modelling are asked and a variety of further reading sources are provided.

Before turning to our extended example, we wish to point out that multilevel models are also often referred to as hierarchical models and mixed models. The term mixed models helps convey the idea that multilevel models combine key elements of standard regression models (i.e. fixed effects regression models) with key elements of ANOVA models with random effects (see Raudenbush, 1993).

Two key papers that help lay the conceptual groundwork and initial analysis strategies for multilevel modelling are papers by Cronbach (1976) and Burstein (1980). Also, see Raudenbush and Bryk (2002: chapter 1) for a discussion of important technical work connected with the development and implementation of more comprehensive multilevel modelling frameworks.

In the example that follows we employ a software program developed by Raudenbush et al. (2004) called HLM. A list of several other available programs is provided later in the chapter.

An illustration of multilevel modelling via analyses of the data from a multi-site evaluation of the Transition Mathematics curriculum

In this example, we focus on a subset of the data from an evaluation of an innovative pre-algebra curriculum called Transition Mathematics (TM). Specifically we present a series of analyses using a sample of 19 carefully matched pairs of classrooms located in various school districts throughout the United States.[1] (Note that in this section we use the terms sites and matched pairs of classes interchangeably.) Within each pair, one class was taught by a teacher who implemented TM and the other was taught by a teacher who used the pre-algebra curriculum already in place at that site. In the case of ten pairs, the decision as to which teacher would use TM with his or her class was based on random assignment; various logistical factors precluded random assignment in the case of nine pairs. One question we will explore later is whether the effects of TM in sites in which assignment was random are similar to the effects in sites where random assignment was not feasible.

We begin by focusing on the following question: On a 19-item post-test assessing student readiness for geometry, what is the expected difference in outcomes when students work with TM materials versus when they work with more traditional materials?

We first conduct an analysis that ignores the nested structure of the data. Specifically, to compare the mean geometry readiness scores for the 273 students in the sample who worked with TM materials and the 276 students who did not, we fit the following simple regression model to the sample of 549 student-level observations:

$$Y_i = \beta_0 + \beta_1 X_i + r_i \quad r_i \sim N(0, \sigma^2) \qquad (44.1)$$

where Y_i is the geometry readiness score for student i; X_i is a treatment indicator variable that takes on a value of 1 if student i is a TM student or a value of 0 if student i is a comparison group student; β_0 is the intercept parameter in the model, representing the expected geometry score when students work with traditional materials, i.e. when $X_i = 0$. β_1 is the parameter of primary interest and captures the expected difference in geometry readiness scores when students work with TM materials ($X_i = 1$) vs. using more traditional materials. Note that the r_i are residuals assumed independent and normally distributed with mean 0 and variance σ^2, where σ^2 represents the amount of variance in student outcome scores that remains after taking into account TM/comparison group membership. When we fit this model to the data, the resulting estimate of β_1 and its standard error are: $\beta_1 = 1.39$ and SE = 0.36 ($t = 1.39 / 0.36 = 3.56$, $df = 547$, $p < 0.001$). Note that these results are identical to what we would obtain conducting a standard two-group comparison of the mean geometry readiness score for the 273 students who worked with TM materials ($\bar{Y}_{TM} = 10.1$) and the mean geometry readiness score for the 276 students who worked with more traditional materials ($\bar{Y}_c = 8.7$).

In the above analysis, it is assumed that the outcome scores for students in the sample, after taking into account whether students worked with TM or more conventional curricular materials, are independent. But since the 549 students in our sample are nested in

different pairs, we might very well suspect that how well TM or comparison group students perform on the post-test may depend on pair or site membership. Thus we now fit the above regression model in equation 44.1 to each site's data to obtain an estimate of the TM effect for each site and its SE. These results appear in Table 44.1. As can be seen, the site TM effect estimates vary substantially, ranging from a negative value of −2.21 points for site 10 to a positive value of 4.56 points for site 19. (Note that the negative estimate for site 10 indicates that the TM students in that site scored approximately 2.21 points lower on the geometry readiness post-test.)

The TM effect estimate for a given site ($\hat{\beta}_{1j}$) provides us with an estimate of the true TM effect for that site. The standard error for ($\hat{\beta}_{1j}$) conveys how precise the estimate is, i.e. how much the estimate might differ from the true effect for that site.

Importantly, the standard error provides the basis for forming a confidence interval that gives us a sense of how big or little a site's true TM effect might be. For example, if we take the TM effect estimate for site 8 (4.25 points), and add and subtract 2 standard errors (i.e. 2×0.85), this yields an approximate 95% interval with lower and upper boundaries of 2.58 points and 5.92 points, respectively. On the basis of this confidence interval, the idea that the true TM effect for site 8 equals 0, for example, is highly doubtful. As can be seen in Figure 44.1, all six sites with TM effect estimates greater than 2 points have intervals that lie above a value of 0, and the intervals for two of those sites lie completely above a value of 1.39 (i.e. the estimate of the overall effect of TM obtained in the traditional analysis). For the other sites in the sample, the 95% intervals include a value of 0, and the intervals for two of those sites lie completely below a value of 1.39. (See Denson and Seltzer, 2011: 221, for a discussion of these concepts in the context of meta-analysis.)

Thus the above results indicate that there is likely substantial variability in the true effects of TM across sites. Given, for example, that teachers may vary substantially in their patterns of implementation, and that the quality of students' prior educational experiences might differ appreciably across sites, the results that we see in Table 44.1 and Figure 44.1 are in some respects not very surprising.

Table 44.1   Site-by-site analysis: OLS estimates of means and TM effects

Site (j)[a]	Size (n_j)	Site mean $(\hat{\beta}_{0j})$	SE $(\hat{\beta}_{0j})$	TM effect $(\hat{\beta}_{1j})$	SE $(\hat{\beta}_{1j})$	95% CI $(\hat{\beta}_{1j})$	Implementation of reading (0 = low, 1 = high)
1	31	13.52	0.48	−0.23	0.96	(−2.10, 1.65)	0
2	27	6.59	0.46	2.12*	0.93	(0.31, 3.93)	1
3	34	5.15	0.38	0.33	0.77	(−1.18, 1.84)	0
4	44	7.86	0.49	−0.24	0.99	(−2.18, 1.70)	0
5	17	8.47	0.61	0.29	1.22	(−2.09, 2.67)	0
6	35	11.54	0.57	1.50	1.15	(−0.76, 3.76)	1
7	37	13.97	0.39	1.27	0.79	(−0.27, 2.81)	1
8	42	6.98	0.43	4.25*	0.85	(2.58, 5.92)	1
9	17	8.71	0.73	4.06*	1.54	(1.05, 7.07)	1
10	28	6.68	0.56	−2.21	1.13	(−4.43, 0.01)	0
11	31	14.42	0.50	1.20	1.00	(−0.75, 3.15)	1
12	31	10.87	0.76	1.15	1.52	(−1.83, 4.12)	0
13	25	10.12	0.58	4.20*	1.29	(1.66, 6.73)	1
14	23	10.83	0.71	1.11	1.43	(−1.70, 3.92)	0
15	33	11.45	0.64	−1.61	1.28	(−4.12, 0.90)	0
16	33	8.70	0.56	1.90	1.13	(−0.31, 4.11)	0
17	27	6.81	0.56	0.93	1.14	(−1.30, 3.15)	1
18	17	5.29	0.53	2.69*	1.08	(0.57, 4.80)	0
19	17	7.12	0.82	4.56*	1.72	(1.18, 7.94)	1

a. The subscript j is used to reference each of the sites in the sample.

* Denotes a TM effect estimate that is more than twice its standard error.

Adapted from Seltzer (1994)

But note that the single-number summary based on the traditional analysis concealed this heterogeneity. On the basis of that analysis, decision-makers might mistakenly conclude that the effects of TM are uniform across sites. Furthermore, the results from such an analysis do not encourage us to ask whether, and if so why, TM may be more successful in some sites than others.

We now show how multilevel models enable us to represent the location (nesting) of students in different sites, and investigate the variability in programme effects across sites. We begin by specifying a within-site (level-1) model. The regression model that we fitted to each site's data in the previous analysis provides the basis of our level-1 model. In addition to a subscript (i) that indexes students, we also need to include a subscript (j) denoting the site membership of students. Thus:

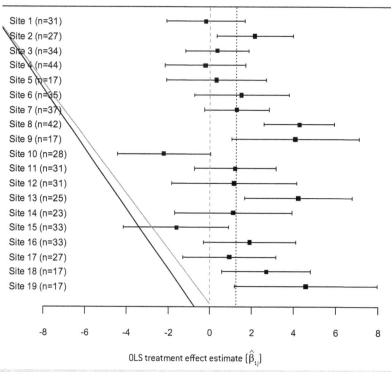

Figure 44.1 OLS estimate and 95% confidence interval for the TM treatment effect in each site (the vertical dark dashed line marks the treatment effect grand mean (1.39))

$$Y_{ij} = \beta_{0j} + \beta_{1j}(X_{ij} - \bar{X}_{.j}) + r_{ij} \quad r_{ij} \sim N(0, \sigma^2) \quad (44.2)$$

where Y_{ij} is the geometry readiness score for student i in site j; since there are 19 sites in our sample, our subscript or index for sites takes on values from 1 to 19 ($j = 1, \ldots, 19$) and X_{ij} is a treatment indicator that takes on a value of 1 if student i in site j is a TM student (0 otherwise). β_{1j}, which is the parameter of primary interest in the level-1 model, represents the true TM effect for site j. Note that the predictor X_{ij} is centred around its site mean ($\bar{X}_{.j}$). This type of centring, which is termed group-mean centring, is widely used in HLM analyses. As Raudenbush and Bryk (2002) note, group-mean centring of predictors at level-1 gives the intercept term β_{0j} a useful interpretation, i.e. β_{0j} represents the mean outcome score for site j. While β_{1j} is of primary interest in our application, as will be seen later, in some applications group mean outcome scores as well as slopes are of substantive interest. Finally, in

the above model σ^2 represents within-site variance of geometry readiness score.

If we fit the above model to each site's data using a standard regression program, we obtain the OLS estimates of the site TM effects shown in Table 44.1 and, furthermore, the resulting OLS estimate of β_{0j} for a given site will simply be equal to the mean geometry readiness outcome score for the sample of students in that site.

As discussed above, each site's TM effect estimate contains a certain degree of error (see Table 44.1). A key question is: To what extent is the variation in TM effect estimates across sites due to such error, and how much is connected with differences in the true effects of TM across sites? Raudenbush and Bryk term the latter type of variability parameter variance (e.g. heterogeneity in the true effects of TM). How might we obtain an estimate of the amount of parameter variance in TM effects?

A key feature of multilevel models is that they enable us to represent the fact that level-1 parameters (e.g. site TM effects (β_{1j}) and site means (β_{0j})) may vary across groups (e.g. sites). In particular, level-1 parameters are treated as outcomes in a between-group (level-2) model. We first specify a between-site model in which level-1 parameters (e.g. site TM effects) are viewed as varying around a corresponding grand mean (e.g. a mean TM effect):

$$\beta_{0j} = \gamma_{00} + u_{0j} \qquad u_{0j} \sim N(0, \tau_{00}) \qquad (44.3)$$

$$\beta_{1j} = \gamma_{10} + u_{1j} \qquad u_{1j} \sim N(0, \tau_{11}) \qquad (44.4)$$

In Equation 44.4, for example, γ_{10} represents an overall, average TM effect, and u_{1j} is a level-2 residual that captures the deviation of the true TM effect for site j from the average TM effect; the level-2 residuals allow for the possibility that the true TM effect for some sites may lie close to the average effect, but may be substantially larger or smaller than the average effect in the case of other sites. The variance term in this equation (τ_{11}) represents the amount of heterogeneity in the true effects of TM across sites. As noted above, the variability in TM effect estimates that we see across sites in Table 44.1 is attributable in part to estimation error (error variance) connected with each of the estimates and to differences in the true effects of TM termed parameter variance. τ_{11} represents the latter source. Similarly, γ_{00} in equation 44.3 is the grand mean for geometry readiness scores, u_{0j} is a residual term representing the deviation of the true mean outcome score for a given site (β_{0j}) from the grand mean, and τ_{00} represents the amount of variance connected with underlying differences in mean outcome scores across sites, i.e. it is the parameter variance in site mean outcome scores.

The above level-1 and level-2 models comprise the first multilevel model that we will fit to the data; we term this Model A. In the parlance of multilevel

Table 44.2   Multilevel Model A for the TM evaluation data

Fixed effects	Estimate	SE	t-ratio	Approx. df	p-value
Grand mean (γ_{00})	9.22	0.66	13.97	18	0.000
Overall TM effect (γ_{10})	1.34	0.43	3.14	18	0.006

Variance components	Estimate	df	Chi-square	p-value	
Between-site:					
Site mean geometry readiness (τ_{00})	7.94	18	494.8	0.000	
Site TM effects (τ_{11})	2.12	18	47.5	0.000	
Within-site:					
Residual variance (σ^2)	9.09				

modelling, γ_{00} and γ_{10} are referred to as fixed effects, u_{0j} and u_{1j} are termed random effects, and σ^2, τ_{00} and τ_{11} are termed variance components. The key level-2 parameters in our model are γ_{10} (i.e. the average TM effect) and τ_{11} (i.e. the parameter variance in site TM effects).

In Table 44.2 we see that the resulting estimate of γ_{10} is 1.34 points (SE = 0.43; $t = 3.14$, approx. $df = 18$, p. = 0.006). To help grasp how this average effect was computed, note that the HLM program essentially used the TM effect estimates for the 19 sites shown in Table 44.1 to compute a weighted average, where those sites whose TM effects were estimated with more precision received more weight.[2]

While this estimate of the average TM effect is similar to the one obtained in the analysis in which we ignored the nested structure of the data, note that the standard error of HLM's estimate is approximately

Table 44.3 Multilevel Model B for the TM evaluation data

Fixed effects	Estimate	SE	t-ratio	Approx. df	p-value
Model for site mean readiness:					
Grand mean (γ_{00})	9.21	0.29	31.90	17	.000
Between-site pre-test/post-test slope (γ_{01})	0.60	0.07	8.99	17	.000
Model for site TM effects:					
Expected TM effect at low impl. sites (γ_{10})	0.23	0.46	0.50	17	0.620
Expected increase in effect of TM at high impl. sites (γ_{11})	2.29	0.65	3.52	17	0.003

Variance components	Estimate	df	Chi-square	p-value	
Between-site:					
Site mean geometry readiness (τ_{00})	1.24	17	81.83	.000	
Site TM effects (τ_{11})	0.87	17	28.13	.000	
Within-site:					
Residual variance (σ^2)	9.10				

20% larger. To help understand this difference, we first turn to HLM's estimate of the heterogeneity in site TM effects, i.e. $\hat{\tau}_{11} = 2.12$. A chi-square test of the hypothesis that τ_{11} is equal to 0 (i.e. the hypothesis of no variability in the true effects of TM across sites) yields a p-value less than 0.001, which points to strong evidence against this hypothesis.

Since it is easier to interpret standard deviations rather than variances, we take the square root of our estimate of τ_{11} (2.12), which yields a value of 1.46. This standard deviation, combined with our estimate of the average TM effect, provides a 'best guess' regarding the distribution of site TM effects. For example, based on our results, a site whose true TM effect is 2 standard deviations above the average would be equal to $1.34 + (2 \times 1.46) = 4.26$ points; similarly a site whose true effect is 2 standard deviations below the average effect would be equal to $1.34 - (2 \times 1.46) = -1.58$ points. This suggests that a substantial amount of the variability that we see in the TM effect estimates in Table 44.1 is connected with parameter variance, i.e. heterogeneity in the true effects of TM across sites.

In contrast to the analysis that ignores the nesting of individuals in different sites, the standard error for the average TM effect based on the above HLM analysis reflects the fact that how well TM students fare relative to comparison group students depends substantially on site membership. Specifically, HLM's estimate of τ_{11} is a key component of the standard error. Furthermore, when this component is large, the magnitude of the standard error – the precision with which we are able to estimate the average effect – depends not only on how many students there are in our sample but, crucially, on how many sites there are in our sample as well. In this connection, the *df* for hypothesis tests regarding γ_{10} is equal to the number of sites minus 1, i.e. 18.

The results based on Model A, along with the exploratory analyses that we conducted, point to substantial variability in the effectiveness of TM across sites. This variability encourages us to ask: Why might TM be appreciably more effective at some sites than others? What factor(s) might be critical with respect to the success of the programme? We now show how such questions can be addressed by adding predictors to the level-2 (between-site) model.

The reading material contained in the TM text is viewed as a key component of TM by its programme developers. We now model differences in the effects of TM as a function of a measure of implementation that takes on a value of 1 if the TM teacher at a site indicated that she discussed the reading in the text on a daily basis ($IMPLRDG_j = 1$, i.e. high implementation), and a value of 0 if the reading was discussed frequently but was not part of the daily routine ($IMPLRDG_j = 0$, i.e. low implementation).

As can be seen in Table 44.3, TM effect estimates tend to be higher in those sites in which the reading in the text is discussed on a daily basis. This pattern is also evident in the plot of TM effect estimates versus level of implementation in Figure 44.2. We now investigate more formally whether increases in level of implementation are systematically related to increases in the effectiveness of TM by including $IMPLRDG_j$ as a predictor in the level-2 equation for site TM effects (β_{1j}):

$$\beta_{0j} = \gamma_{00} + \gamma_{01} \overline{PRE}_j + u_{0j} \qquad u_{0j} \sim N(0, \tau_{00}) \tag{44.5}$$

$$\beta_{1j} = \gamma_{10} + \gamma_{11} \overline{IMPLRDG}_j + u_{1j} \qquad u_{1j} \sim N(0, \tau_{11}) \tag{44.6}$$

Based on the 0/1 coding scheme for $IMPLRDG_j$, γ_{10} is the expected effect of TM at low implementation sites and γ_{11} is the expected increment in the effect of TM at high implementation sites. Similar to a regression model, u_{1j} is a residual capturing the deviation of the site TM effect for site j from an expected value based on $IMPLRDG_j$. Thus τ_{11} now represents the remaining parameter variance in site TM effects after taking into account $IMPLRDG_j$.

While the level-2 equation for site TM effects is of primary interest in this analysis, there are many applications, as will be seen in the rest of this chapter, where interest might centre on mean outcome scores (β_{0j}) and modelling them as a function of various group characteristics. To help illustrate such possibilities, we model β_{0j} as a function of site mean pre-test scores on a 40-item general mathematics test ($\overline{PRE}_j$). Thus, as in a regression analysis, the coefficient γ_{01} captures the expected change in site-mean readiness scores when site pre-test means increase 1 unit, and τ_{00} now represents the parameter variance in site mean

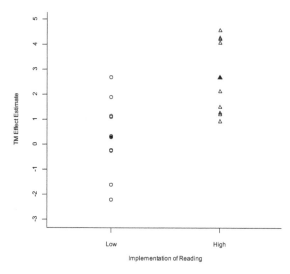

Adapted from Seltzer and Rose (2006).

Figure 44.2   Site TM effect estimates by level of implementation of reading

Circles and triangles are used to represent low- and high-implementation sites, respectively. The mean of the TM effect estimates for the ten low-implementing sites is represented by a dark circle, and the mean of the TM effect estimates for the nine high-implementing sites is represented by a dark triangle

readiness scores that remains after taking into account site mean pre-test scores.[3]

We term the multilevel model defined by equation 44.2 (level-1) and equations 44.5 and 44.6 (level-2) Model B. In Table 44.3, we see that the estimate of the expected effect of TM in low implementation sites (γ_{10}) is extremely small (i.e. 0.23 points; SE = 0.46), and is clearly not statistically significant; this suggests that given a low level of implementation, TM and more traditional curricula may, on average, be equally effective. In contrast, the estimate for the expected increase in TM given a high level of implementation (γ_{11}) is 2.29 points (SE = 0.65). Thus while the results based on Model A point to an overall average effect of 1.34 points, the results based on Model B point to an expected effect that is negligible when implementation

is low, and an effect of approximately two and a half points given a high level of implementation (i.e. 0.23 + 2.29 = 2.52 points).

We also see that the inclusion of $IMPLRDG_j$ in the model results in a substantial reduction of parameter variance in site TM effects, i.e. while the estimate of τ_{11} based on Model A is 2.12, the estimate based on Model B is 0.87, which represents a reduction of nearly 60%.

From a substantive standpoint, the amount of parameter variance in site TM effects that remains is appreciable. Some of the remaining variance may be due to unique site characteristics or events (e.g. perhaps the principals at one or two sites were extremely supportive of the TM programme). However, some may be due to factors that are systematically related to differences in the effect of TM. Thus, akin to multiple regression analyses, we can specify multiple predictors in level-2 models. This is especially important. For example, if we are concerned that a particular factor may be confounding the relationship between a key level-2 predictor (e.g. $IMPLRDG_j$) and the magnitude of within-group relationships of interest (e.g. site TM effects), we can attempt to control for that factor by including it as a predictor in the model. Thus, for example, as noted earlier, the assignment of teachers to TM comparison conditions was random in some sites but not in others. In an analysis controlling for type of assignment, Seltzer (2004) found that the results concerning the relationship between implementation of reading and the magnitude of site TM effects remained virtually unchanged.

Note that we can also specify multiple predictors in level-1 models. For example, as in an analysis of covariance (ANCOVA), we could expand the level-1 model specified in equation 44.2 to include student scores on a pre-test as a covariate; thus β_{1j} would represent the TM effect for site j holding constant student pre-test scores.

Additional applications and examples

School effects research

The kinds of two-level multilevel models that we employed in the analyses of the TM data can be directly used in various school effects research applications. In particular, we can employ these models in investigating the extent to which minority gaps, gender gaps and/or SES-achievement slopes vary across schools, and in attempting to identify those school policies and practices that underlie this variability. Thus, for example, in an analysis based on a sample from the HSB study consisting of over 7,000 students nested within 90 public and 70 Catholic high schools, Raudenbush and Bryk (1986, 2002) specified a level-1 (within-school) model in which student 12th grade mathematics achievement scores were modelled as a function of student SES:

$$Y_{ij} = \beta_{0j} + \beta_{1j}(SES_{ij} - \overline{SES}_{.j}) + r_{ij} \qquad r_{ij} \sim N(0, \sigma^2)$$
$$\text{(44.7)}$$

where Y_{ij} and SES_{ij} represent, respectively, the 12th grade mathematics achievement score and SES value for student i in school j. This model is formally identical to the level-1 (within-site) model employed in the multilevel analyses of the TM data. In equation 44.7, β_{1j} is the SES-achievement slope for school j capturing the expected increase in student achievement when SES increases 1 unit and, by virtue of centring SES around its group mean, β_{0j} is the school mean achievement score for school j. Note that a relatively flat SES-achievement slope for a given school would suggest that differences in SES are fairly inconsequential with respect to student achievement. To investigate whether school mean achievement tends to be higher and SES-achievement slopes flatter in Catholic schools, Raudenbush and Bryk posed level-2 (between-school) equations in which school mean achievement (β_{0j}) and SES-achievement slopes (β_{1j}) were modelled as a function of sector (i.e. $SECTOR_j$, where $SECTOR_j = 1$ if school j was a Catholic school and 0 otherwise). Since Catholic schools tend to serve students with higher SES values, Raudenbush and Bryk controlled for differences among schools in their mean SES values $(\overline{SES}_{.j})$ by also including $(\overline{SES}_{.j})$ as a predictor in each level-2 equation. The results based on their analysis pointed to higher school mean achievement in Catholic schools as well as a more equitable distribution of achievement within Catholic schools (i.e. flatter slopes). Note that such models can be expanded by including additional predictors in the within-school and between-school models (see, for example, Lee and Bryk, 1989).

Standard errors for estimates of fixed effects

As noted earlier, when we ignore the fact that students are nested within different groups, we run the risk of obtaining standard errors for estimates of fixed effects (e.g. sector effects) that are too small. This is especially so when interest centres on drawing inferences concerning the coefficients for predictors in level-2 equations for group-mean outcome scores (β_{0j}) (e.g. the fixed effect relating differences in sector to differences in school-mean achievement). For an example, see Seltzer's (2004) analyses of the data from a study of reform-minded mathematics instruction.

Longitudinal analysis

The kinds of multilevel models discussed above can also be used in studies of change. Consider, for example, one of the cohorts in the LSAY sample that Seltzer et al. (2003) focused on in their analyses of patterns of student change in mathematics achievement across grades 7 through 10. In this cohort, mathematics achievement scores collected in grades 7–10 are nested within each student. In a level-1 (within-student) model, we can model each student's time series as a function of grade, capturing, for example, a rate of change for each student (i.e. a slope relating mathematics achievement to grade). In a level-2 (between-student) model, we can model differences among students in their rates of change as a function of differences in their home environments and educational experiences. See Singer and Willett (2003) for an accessible treatment of the use of multilevel models in investigating patterns of change.

Three-level models

Multilevel models can be expanded to accommodate three or more levels of nesting. For example, in the case of the NELS sample where we have time-series data nested within students who, in turn, are nested in different high schools, we can pose three-level models consisting of a level-1 (within-person) model, which enables us to estimate a rate of change for each student, a level-2 (within-school) model that captures variability in student growth rates within schools, and a level-3 (between-school) model that enables us to investigate factors associated with differences across schools in their mean rates of change.

Note also that various commonly employed experimental designs in studies of instruction yield data that necessitate the use of three-level models. Consider, for example, a study in which schools are randomly assigned to an innovative or traditional first-grade reading programme, yielding a three-level data structure, i.e. students nested within different first-grade classrooms which, in turn, are nested within schools that have been assigned to treatment or comparison conditions (see Spybrook et al., 2009; Nye et al., 2004).

Conclusion

Multilevel modelling encourages us to attend to differences in relationships of interest across groups, and open up possibilities for investigating why programs of interest are more successful in some sites than others, and why student achievement is more equitably distributed with respect to SES and other student background characteristics than others. Multilevel modelling also provides us with more appropriate standard errors for estimates of varions between group effects of interest.

Questions for further investigation

1. Think about an issue or set of questions in education that you are interested in studying. How might what you have learned about multilevel modelling help to broaden the questions you wish to investigate and design a study to investigate these questions?
2. How might you proceed in analysing the data from your study?

Notes

1. Note that this is the same data set used in Seltzer (1994, 2004), but for the analyses in this chapter we have omitted an outlying site.

2. Note that the weights used in estimating fixed effects are based on HLM's estimates of the variance components in the model; for details, see Raudenbush and Bryk (2002: chapter 3).
3. As in the case of level-1 equations, we can choose various centrings for predictors in the level-2 equations. Though not shown in Equation 6, we centered $\overline{PRE}_j$ around the grand mean pretest score $(\overline{PRE})$. By virtue of this centring, γ_{00} retains its meaning as the grand mean for geometry readiness scores. See Raudenbush and Bryk (2002) for further details regarding centring level-2 predictors.

Support for Jordon Rickles' work on this chapter was provided through an Institute of Education Sciences training grant fellowship.

Suggested further reading

Raudenbush and Bryk (2002) provide a detailed, comprehensive discussion of the logic of multilevel modelling and present an array of applications. In addition they provide coverage of various advanced topics including multilevel modelling for categorical (e.g. binary) outcomes, and estimation theory for multilevel models. Snijders and Bosker (1999) also provide a comprehensive and accessible treatment of multilevel models that covers a range of applications. For a very clear book-length introduction to multilevel modelling see Kreft and DeLeeuw (1998).

In addition to the HLM program, there are many other available programs for multilevel analysis, including MLwiN developed by Goldstein and his associates, SuperMix developed by Hedeker and Gibbons, SAS Proc Mixed, the *xtmixed* module in STATA, the *mixed* procedure in SPSS and the *lme4* package in R developed by Bates and Maechler.

There are several websites that provide very useful, freely available materials and on-line courses on multilevel modelling and the use of various software packages in estimating multilevel models:

Academic Technology Services at UCLA: http://www.ats.ucla.edu/stat/seminars/
Stat/Math Center at Indiana University: http://www.indiana.edu/~statmath/stat/all/hlm/
Center for Multilevel Modelling: http://www.cmm.bristol.ac.uk/

References

Burstein, L. (1980) 'The analysis of multi-level data in education research and evaluation', *Review of Research in Education*, 8: 158–233.

Cook, T., Habib, F., Phillips, M., Settersten, R., Shagle, S. and Degirmencioglu, S. (1999) 'Comer's school development program in Prince George's County, Maryland: a theory-based evaluation', *American Educational Research Journal*, 36: 543–97.

Cronbach, L., Deken, J. and Webb, N. (1976) *Research on Classrooms and Schools: Formulations of Questions, Design, and Analysis* (Occasional Paper). Stanford, CA: Stanford Evaluation Consortium.

Denson, N. and Seltzer, M. (2011) Meta-analysis in higher education: An illustrative example using hierarchical linear modeling. *Research in Higher Education*, 52: 215–44.

Kreft, I. and DeLeeuw, J. (1998) *Introducing Multilevel Modeling*. Thousand Oaks, CA: Sage

Lee, V. and Bryk, A. (1989) 'A multilevel model of the social distribution of educational achievement', *Sociology of Education*, 62: 172–92.

Nye, B., Konstantopoulos, S. and Hedges, L. (2004) 'How large are teacher effects?', *Educational Evaluation and Policy Analysis*, 26: 237–57.

Raudenbush, S. (1993) 'Hierarchical linear models and experimental design', in Edwards, L. (ed.) *Applied Analysis of Variance in Behavioral Science*. New York: Marcel Dekker, pp. 459–96.

Raudenbush, S. and Bryk, A. (1986) 'A hierarchical model for studying school effects', *Sociology of Education*, 59: 1–17.

Raudenbush, S. and Bryk, A. (2002) *Hierarchical Linear Models: Applications and Data Analysis Methods*. Thousand Oaks, CA: Sage.

Raudenbush, S., Bryk, A., Cheong, Y. and Congdon, R. (2004) *HLM 6: Hierarchical Linear and Nonlinear Modeling*. Lincolnwood, IL: Scientific Software International.

Seltzer, M. (1994) 'Studying variation in program success: a multilevel modeling approach', *Evaluation Review*, 18: 342–61.

Seltzer, M. (2004) 'The use of hierarchical models in analyzing data from experiments and quasi-experiments conducted in field settings', in Kaplan, D. (ed.) *The Handbook of Quantitative Methods for the Social Sciences*. Thousand Oaks, CA: Sage, pp. 259–80.

Seltzer, M. and Rose, M. (2006) 'Constructing analyses: developing thoughtfulness in working with quantitative methods', in Conrad, C. and Serlin, R. (eds) *Handbook for Research in Education: Engaging Ideas and Enriching Inquiry*. Thousand Oaks, CA: Sage, pp. 477–92.

Seltzer, M., Choi, K. and Thum, Y. M. (2003) 'Examining relationships between where students start and how rapidly they progress: using new developments in growth modeling to gain insight into the distribution of achievement within schools', *Educational Evaluation and Policy Analysis*, 25: 263–86.

Singer, J. and Willett, J. (2003) *Applied longitudinal analysis: modeling change and event occurrence*. New York: Oxford University Press.

Snijders, T. and Bosker, R. (1999) *Multilevel Analysis: An Introduction to Basic and Advanced Multilevel Modeling*. Thousand Oaks, CA: Sage.

Spybrook, J., Raudenbush, S., Congdon, R. and Martinez, A. (2009) *Optimal Design for Longitudinal and Multilevel Research: Documentation for the 'Optimal Design' Software*. New York: William T. Grant Foundation.

Xue, Y. and Meisels, S. (2004) 'Early literacy instruction and learning in kindergarten: evidence from the Early Childhood Longitudinal Study – kindergarten class of 1998–1999', *American Educational Research Journal*, 41: 191–229.

45

Effect size

Robert J. Coe

Introduction

'Effect size' is simply a way of quantifying the size of the difference between two groups. It is easy to calculate, readily understood and can be applied to any measured outcome in education or social science. It is particularly valuable for quantifying the effectiveness of a particular intervention relative to some comparison. It allows us to move beyond the simplistic, 'Does it work or not?' to the far more sophisticated, 'How well does it work in a range of contexts?' Moreover, by placing the emphasis on the most important aspect of an intervention – the size of the effect – rather than its statistical significance (which conflates effect size and sample size), it promotes a more scientific approach to the accumulation of knowledge. For these reasons, effect size is an important tool in reporting and interpreting effectiveness.

The routine use of effect sizes, however, has generally been limited to meta-analysis – for combining and comparing estimates from different studies – and is all too rare in original reports of educational research (Keselman et al., 1998). This is despite the fact that measures of effect size have been available for at least 70 years (Huberty, 2002) and the American Psychological Association has been officially encouraging authors to report effect sizes since 1994 – but with limited success (Wilkinson et al., 1999). Discussion of the use

and calculation of effect sizes is absent from many statistics textbooks (other than those devoted to meta-analysis) while calculations are not featured in many statistics computer packages and are seldom taught in standard research methods courses. For these reasons, even the researcher who wants to use and interpret effect size and is not afraid to confront the orthodoxy of conventional practice may find that it is quite hard to know exactly how to do so.

This chapter is written for non-statisticians and is intended to be introductory, although it does assume familiarity with the statistical ideas of the mean and standard deviation. It describes what effect size is, what it means and how it can be used and outlines some potential problems associated with using it.

Why do we need 'effect size'?

Perhaps the most obvious motivation for the use of effect size is that it allows meaning to be given to a difference recorded by an unfamiliar instrument and reported on an unknown scale. By using the familiar concept of the standard deviation, it allows the difference to be calibrated in terms of the amount of variation within the overall population.

To illustrate this, consider a hypothetical experiment to evaluate a new reading scheme. Children in

Table 45.1   Reading comprehension and effect

Outcome measure	Treatment group			Control group			Significance
	Mean	n	SD	Mean	n	SD	
Overall reading score	26.9	104	6.9	24.8	105	7.6	p < 0.05
Reading comprehension sub-score	7.5	105	3.1	5.6	105	3.5	p < 0.01
Reading comprehension sub-score (school 1)	8.1	59	3.2	5.6	59	3.0	p < 0.01
Reading comprehension sub-score (school 2)	6.7	46	3.6	5.6	46	3.5	ns

each school were randomly allocated to use the new scheme (treatment) or continue with the old (control). The main outcome was an overall measure of reading, which included a reading comprehension subtest. The researchers also wanted to know whether the effects varied in different schools. Results are shown in Table 45.1.

On both the overall score and the comprehension subtest the difference between the means for the two groups is about 2 points, but these points are hard to interpret. If we use the standard deviation as a reference, we see that the former is about 0.3 of a standard deviation, the latter about 0.6 – the effect is around twice as big on the comprehension subtest when calibrated against the spread of scores on each test.

A second reason for using effect size is that it emphases amounts, not just statistical significance. It is often more useful to know how big a difference is between two groups rather than just whether it is beyond what might reasonably occur by chance. An example can be seen in Figure 45.1, which shows the effect sizes for the comparisons in Table 45.1, together with their confidence intervals (see below for explanation of confidence intervals).

It is immediately clear that the effect on comprehension is bigger than on overall reading, though their confidence intervals do overlap. It is also clear that the overall effect on reading was about the same as the effect on reading comprehension in school 2 (both around 0.3). The traditional interpretation of these comparisons might be that the former showed an effect (p < 0.05) while the latter did not (see the significance column in Table 45.1). In fact, the effect

was about the same in both cases – only the smaller sample size in the latter case increased the margin of error to the point where the range of plausible values for the effect includes zero.

Further reasons for using effect sizes include that they draw attention to statistical power (Cohen, 1969), that they may reduce the risk of pure sampling variation being misinterpreted as a real difference, that they may help to reduce the under-reporting of 'non-significant' results (Rosenthal, 1979; Ioannidis, 2005) and that they allow ready accumulation of knowledge from multiple studies using meta-analysis (see Chapter 46 on meta-analysis' by Hedges, in this volume). Effect sizes are also generally required for a power calculation, i.e. to estimate the sample size required to have a reasonable probability of finding an effect that is both practically important and statistically significant.

How is it calculated?

The most common measure of effect size is the *standardised mean difference* between the two groups, in other words the difference between the means for each group, divided by the standard deviation. Algebraically:

$$d = \frac{m_1 - m_2}{s}$$

The *standard deviation* is a measure of the spread of a set of values. In the context of an experiment in which the effect size is the difference between treated and control groups it might be thought that the control group would provide the best estimate of standard

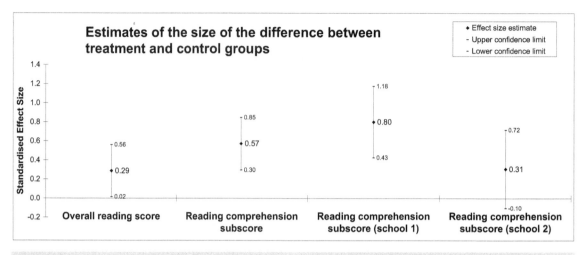

Figure 45.1 Effect sizes for the comparisons of Table 45.1

deviation, since it consists of a representative sample of the population who have not been affected by the experimental intervention. This is the approach used by Glass et al. (1981), sometimes referred to as *Glass' Δ (delta)*.

However, unless the control group is very large, the estimate of the 'true' population standard deviation derived from only the control group is likely to be appreciably less accurate than an estimate derived from both the control and experimental groups. Moreover, in studies where there is not a true 'control' group (for example when two different treatments are compared) then it may be an arbitrary decision which group's standard deviation to use and it may make an appreciable difference to the estimate of effect size.

For these reasons, it is often better to use a 'pooled' estimate of standard deviation. The pooled estimate is essentially an average of the standard deviations of the experimental and control groups. If the two groups are not the same size this average is weighted to reflect the imbalance. If more than two groups are compared, there is a further choice about which ones to use in the pooled estimate. Slight differences in this choice and in the choice of weightings give rise to *Cohen's d* (Cohen, 1969) or *Hedges' g* (Hedges and Olkin, 1985), though different sources differ in the precise definitions of each. The latter is given by taking:

$$s = \sqrt{\frac{(n_1 - 1)s_1^2 + (n_2 - 1)s_2^2}{(n_1 - 1) + (n_2 - 1)}}$$

Note that a pooled standard deviation is not the same as the standard deviation of all the values in both groups 'pooled' together. If, for example, each group had a low standard deviation but the two means were substantially different, the true pooled estimate would be much lower than the value obtained by pooling all the values together and calculating the standard deviation. The implications of choices about which standard deviation to use are discussed by Olejnik and Algina (2000).

The use of a pooled estimate of standard deviation depends on the assumption that the two calculated standard deviations are estimates of *the same* population value. In other words, that the experimental and control group standard deviations differ only as a result of sampling variation. Where this assumption cannot be made (either because there is some reason to believe that the two standard deviations are likely to be systematically different or if the actual measured values are very different), then a pooled estimate should not be used.

How can effect sizes be interpreted?

One feature of an effect size is that it can be directly converted into statements about the overlap between the two samples in terms of a comparison of percentiles.

An effect size is exactly equivalent to a 'Z-score' of a standard normal distribution. For example, an effect size of 0.8 means that the score of the average person in the experimental group is 0.8 standard deviations above the average person in the control group, and hence exceeds the scores of 79% of the control group.

Figure 45.2 illustrates how effect sizes correspond to percentiles of a normal distribution and the equivalent change in rank order for a group of 25. For example, for an effect size of 0.6, the value of 73% indicates that the average person in the experimental group would score higher than 73% of a control group that was initially equivalent. If the group consisted of 25 people, this is the same as saying that the average person (i.e. ranked 13th in the group) would now be on a par with the person ranked 7th in the control group. It should be noted that these values depend on the assumption of a normal distribution. The interpretation of effect sizes in terms of percentiles is very sensitive to violations of this assumption (see below).

Another way to interpret effect sizes is to compare them to the effect sizes of differences that are familiar. For example, Cohen (1969: 23) describes an effect size of 0.2 as 'small' and gives to illustrate it the example that the difference between the heights of 15-year-old and 16-year-old girls in the US corresponds to an effect of this size. An effect size of 0.5 is described as 'medium' and is 'large enough to be visible to the naked eye'. A 0.5 effect size corresponds to the difference between the heights of 14-year-old and 18-year-old girls. Cohen describes an effect size of 0.8 as 'grossly perceptible and therefore large' and equates it to the difference between the heights of 13-year-old and 18-year-old girls. As a further example he states that the difference in IQ between holders of the PhD degree and 'typical college freshmen' is comparable to an effect size of 0.8.

Cohen does acknowledge the danger of using terms like 'small', 'medium' and 'large' out of context. Glass et al. (1981: 104) are particularly critical of this approach, arguing that the effectiveness of a particular intervention can only be interpreted in relation to other interventions that seek to produce the same effect. They also point out that the practical importance of an effect depends entirely on its relative costs and benefits. In education, if it could be shown

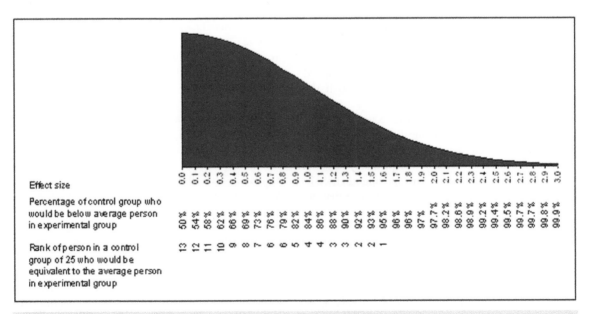

Figure 45.2   How effect sizes correspond to percentiles of a normal distribution

Table 45.1 Examples of average effect sizes for different interventions on learning

Intervention	Effect size	Comments
Ability grouping: dividing teaching groups by ability or attainment	0.09	Extensive evidence shows small or even negative effects on learning and other outcomes, but cost is low
Learning styles: matching teaching approaches to individual learning style	0.14	Good evidence shows small effects which may be due to the range of approaches rather than the matching per se, but cost is low
Reducing class size: from 30 to 15	0.21	Good evidence shows modest effects, but cost is extremely high
Assessment for learning: using formative assessment and feedback to inform teaching and learning	0.32	Limited evidence shows moderate impact for moderate cost
ICT: using technology (e.g. computers) in teaching	0.37	Extensive evidence of moderate overall effects, but wide diversity of interventions and effects are present here. Overall, moderate impact for high cost
One-to-one tutoring: one teacher giving remedial support to one pupil	0.41	Good evidence shows moderate impact for very high cost
Peer tutoring: learners teach each other	0.55	Extensive evidence shows high impact for low cost
Meta-cognitive strategies: teaching learners to think explicitly about learning	0.66	Extensive evidence shows high impact for low cost

Adapted from Higgins et al. (2011)

that making a small and inexpensive change would raise academic achievement by an effect size of even as little as 0.1, then this could be a very significant improvement, particularly if the improvement applied uniformly to all students, and even more so if the effect were cumulative over time.

Glass et al. (1981: 102) give the example that an effect size of 1 corresponds to the difference of about a year of schooling on the performance in achievement tests of pupils in elementary (i.e. primary) schools. However, an analysis of a standard spelling test used in Britain (Vincent and Crumpler, 1997) suggests that the increase in spelling age from 11 to 12 corresponds to an effect size of about 0.3, but seems to vary according to the particular test used.

In England, the distribution of GCSE grades in compulsory subjects (i.e. Maths and English) have standard deviations of between 1.5 and 1.8 grades, so an improvement of one GCSE grade represents an effect size of 0.5–0.7. In the context of secondary schools

therefore introducing a change in practice whose effect size was known to be 0.6 would result in an improvement of about a GCSE grade for each pupil in each subject. For a school in which 50% of pupils were previously gaining five or more A*–C grades, this percentage (other things being equal and assuming that the effect applied equally across the whole curriculum) would rise to 73%.[1] Even Cohen's 'small' effect of 0.2 would produce an increase from 50% to 58% – a difference that most schools would probably categorise as quite substantial. Olejnik and Algina (2000) give a similar example based on the Iowa Test of Basic Skills.

Finally, the interpretation of effect sizes can be greatly helped by a few examples from existing research. Table 45.2 lists a selection of these, adapted from Higgins et al. (2011). The examples cited are given for illustration of the use of effect size measures; they are not intended to be the definitive judgement on the relative efficacy of different interventions. In interpreting them, therefore, one should bear in mind that most of the meta-analyses from which they are derived can be (and often have been) criticised for a variety of weaknesses, that the range of circumstances in which the effects have been found may be limited and that the effect size quoted is an average which is often based on quite widely differing values.

It seems to be a feature of educational interventions that very few of them have effects that would be described in Cohen's classification as anything other than 'small'. This appears particularly so for effects on student achievement. No doubt this is partly a result of the wide variation found in the population as a whole, against which the measure of effect size is calculated. One might also speculate that achievement is harder to influence than other outcomes, perhaps because most schools are already using optimal strategies, or because different strategies are likely to be effective in different situations – a complexity that is not well captured by a single average effect size.

What is the margin for error in estimating effect sizes?

Clearly, if an effect size is calculated from a very large sample it is likely to be more accurate than one calculated from a small sample. This 'margin for error' can be quantified using the idea of a 'confidence interval', which provides the same information as is usually contained in a significance test: using a '95% confidence interval' is equivalent to taking a '5% significance level'. To calculate a 95% confidence interval, you assume that the value you have (e.g. the effect size estimate of 0.8) is the 'true' value, but calculate the amount of variation in this estimate you would get if you repeatedly took new samples of the same size (i.e. different samples of 38 children). For every 100 of these hypothetical new samples, by definition, 95 would give estimates of the effect size within the '95% confidence interval'. If this confidence interval includes zero, then that is the same as saying that the result is not statistically significant. If, on the other hand, zero is outside the range, then it is 'statistically significant at the 5% level'. Using a confidence interval is a better way of conveying this information since it keeps the emphasis on the effect size – which is the important information – rather

than the p-value. It is important to remember that this statistical confidence interval captures the variation in the effect size estimate that would arise purely as a result of re-sampling, assuming that every other aspect of the study were unchanged (and this limitation applies to the traditional significance test as well). A sensible estimate of the amount of variation in the effect that should be expected if we were to implement or replicate the intervention would therefore probably be quite a bit larger, given inevitable variations in context, population, implementation, etc.

Technically, estimating confidence intervals for effect sizes requires the use of a non-central t-distribution which is quite complex to calculate. Fortunately, however, a simple formula given by Hedges and Olkin (1985: 86) provides an excellent approximation to the standard error of the effect size, d:

$$S_d \cong \sqrt{\frac{n_1 + n_2}{n_1 n_2} + \frac{d^2}{2(n_1 + n_2)}}$$

Hence a 95% confidence interval for d would be from

$$d - 1.96\, S_d \quad \text{to} \quad d + 1.96\, S_d$$

Figure 45.3 shows the size of the margin of error with different sample sizes. For example, with two groups of 50 each (total 100) the margin of error is 0.4. Hence an effect size estimate of, say, 0.5 would have a 95% CI from 0.1 (i.e. $0.5 - 0.4$) to 0.9 ($0.5 + 0.4$).

What other factors can influence effect size?

Although effect size is a simple and readily interpreted measure of difference, it can also be sensitive to a number of spurious influences, so some care needs to be taken in its use. Some of these issues are briefly outlined here.

Restricted range

If the samples being compared have too narrow a range of values, the estimate of the standard deviation will be too low. The standardised mean difference, calculated by dividing by this standard deviation, will

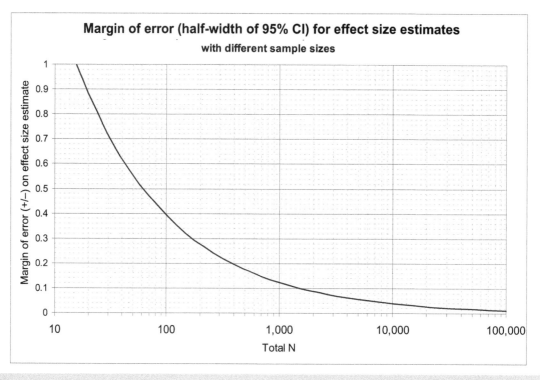

Figure 45.3 Approximate half-width of 95% confidence intervals with sample size, assuming equal numbers in each group, for small effect sizes (<1)

therefore be inflated. For example, in considering the effect of an intervention with university students, or with pupils with reading difficulties, one must remember that these are restricted populations: an effect size calculated from an intervention using these 'restricted range' groups will be larger than would be seen for the same intervention with a fully representative sample.

Ideally, in calculating effect size one should use the standard deviation of the full population in order to make comparisons fair. However, there will be many cases in which unrestricted values are not available, either in practice or in principle. In reporting the effect size, one should draw attention to this fact; if the amount of restriction can be quantified it may be possible to make allowance for it. Any comparison with effect sizes calculated from a full-range population must be made with great caution, if at all. One particular case where this issue arises is when a regression or ANCOVA model has been used to estimate effects after adjusting for covariates. Here the

standard deviation to use in calculating an effect size should normally be from the unadjusted outcome, not the residuals.

Non-normal distributions

The interpretations of effect-sizes given in Table 45.1 depend on the assumption that both control and experimental groups have a 'normal' or Gaussian distribution – the familiar 'bell-shaped' curve. Needless to say, if this assumption is not true then the interpretation may be altered, and in particular it may be difficult to make a fair comparison between an effect size based on normal distributions and one based on non-normal distributions.

Measurement reliability

A third factor that can spuriously affect an effect size is the reliability of the measurement on which it is based. According to classical measurement theory, any measure of a particular outcome may be considered to consist of the 'true' underlying value together with a component of 'error'. The problem is that the amount of variation in measured scores for a particular sample (i.e. its standard deviation) will depend on both the variation in underlying scores and the amount of error in their measurement. With an unreliable measure, the standard deviation is inflated, thereby reducing the effect size.

In interpreting an effect size, it is therefore important to know the reliability of the measurement from which it was calculated. This is one reason why the reliability of any outcome measure used should be reported. It is theoretically possible to make a correction for unreliability (sometimes called 'attenuation'), which gives an estimate of what the effect size would have been had the reliability of the test been perfect. However, in practice the effect of this is rather alarming, since the worse the test was, the more you increase the estimate of the effect size. Moreover, estimates of reliability are dependent on the particular population in which the test was used, and are themselves anyway subject to sampling error. For further discussion of the impact of reliability on effect sizes, see Baugh (2002).

Are there alternative measures of effect size?

A number of statistics are sometimes proposed as alternative measures of effect size, other than the 'standardised mean difference'. Some of these will be considered here.

Perhaps the most widely used is the proportion of variance accounted for: R^2. If the correlation between two variables is 'r', the square of this value (usually denoted with a capital letter: R^2) represents the proportion of the variance in each that is 'accounted for' by the other. In other words, this is the proportion by which the variance of the outcome measure is reduced when it is replaced by the variance of the residuals from a regression equation. This idea can be extended to multiple regression (where it represents the proportion of the variance accounted for by all the

independent variables together) or ANOVA (e.g. 'eta-squared', η^2).

A simple formula (for example, see Cohen, 1969) can be used to convert between d and R^2. Because R^2 has this ready convertibility, it (or alternative measures of variance accounted for) is sometimes advocated as a universal measure of effect size (e.g. Thompson, 1999). One disadvantage of such an approach is that effect size measures based on variance accounted for suffer from a number of technical limitations, such as sensitivity to violation of assumptions (heterogeneity of variance, balanced designs) and their standard errors can be large (Olejnik and Algina, 2000). They are also generally more statistically complex and hence perhaps less easily understood. Further, they are non-directional; two studies with precisely opposite results would report exactly the same variance accounted for. There is also scope for confusion in the use of the word 'effect' to describe a relationship that is essentially correlational.

It has been shown that the interpretation of the 'standardised mean difference' measure of effect size is very sensitive to violations of the assumption of normality. For this reason, a number of more robust and non-parametric alternatives have been suggested. An example of a simple, non-parametric effect size statistic, based on dominance, is given by Cliff (1993). In recent years, interest in and advocacy for the use of robust statistics has grown (Wilcox, 1998). These allow many of the advantages of using classical parametric statistics to be maintained while reducing their sensitivity to common violations of their assumptions. Algina et al. (2005) describe a robust equivalent to Cohen's d, which uses trimmed means with a Winsorised standard deviation, rescaled to make it comparable with the more familiar Cohen's d and confidence intervals estimated by bootstrapping.

Conclusion

There are also effect size measures for multivariate outcomes. A detailed explanation can be found in Olejnik and Algina (2000). A method for calculating effect sizes within multilevel models has been proposed by Tymms et al. (1997). Good summaries of many of the different kinds of effect size measures that can be used and the relationships among them can be found in Snyder and Lawson (1993), Rosenthal (1994) and Kirk (1996).

Finally, a common effect size measure widely used in medicine is the 'odds ratio'. This is appropriate where an outcome is dichotomous: success or failure, a patient survives or does not. Explanations of the odds ratio can be found in a number of medical statistics texts, including Altman (1991), and in Fleiss (1994).

Questions for further investigation

1. Why are unstandardised measures (regression coefficients or mean differences) preferred to standardised ones (*r* or *d*) with meaningful units of measurement?
2. Discuss your understanding of odds ratios before and after reviewing Altman (1991) and Fleiss (1994).

Note

1. This calculation is derived from a probit transformation (Glass et al., 1981: 136), based on the assumption of an underlying normally distributed variable measuring academic attainment, some threshold of which is equivalent to a student achieving 5+ A*–Cs. If $\Phi(z)$ is the standard normal cumulative distribution function, p_1 is the proportion achieving a given threshold and p_2 the proportion to be expected after a change with effect size, d, then:

$$p_2 = \Phi\{\Phi^{-1}(p_1) + d\}$$

Suggested further reading

There is an abundance of additional reading on the areas suggested in this chapter. Please see the papers and texts referenced below, as well as Chapter 42, by Keselman and Lix on ANOVA, this volume.

References

Algina, J., Keselman, H. J. and Penfield, R. D. (2005) 'An alternative to Cohen's standardized mean difference effect size: a robust parameter and confidence interval in the two independent group case', *Psychological Methods*, 10(3): 317–28.

Altman, D. G. (1991) *Practical Statistics for Medical Research.* London: Chapman & Hall.

Baugh, F. (2002) 'Correcting effect sizes for score reliability: a reminder that measurement and substantive issues are linked inextricably', *Educational and Psychological Measurement*, 62(2): 254–63.

Carpenter, J. and Bithell, J. (2000) 'Bootstrap confidence intervals: when, which, what? A practical guide for medical statisticians', *Statistics in Medicine*, 19: 1141–64.

Cliff, N. (1993) 'Dominance statistics – ordinal analyses to answer ordinal questions', *Psychological Bulletin*, 114(3): 494–509.

Cohen, J. (1969) *Statistical Power Analysis for the Behavioral Sciences.* New York: Academic Press.

Cumming, G. and Finch, S. (2001) 'A primer on the understanding, use, and calculation of confidence intervals that are based on central and noncentral distributions', *Educational and Psychological Measurement*, 61: 532–74.

Fleiss, J. L. (1994) 'Measures of effect size for categorical data', in Cooper, H. and Hedges, L. V. (eds) *The Handbook of Research Synthesis.* New York: Russell Sage Foundation.

Glass, G. V., McGaw, B. and Smith, M. L. (1981) *Meta-Analysis in Social Research.* London: Sage.

Grissom, R. J. (1994) 'Probability of the superior outcome of one treatment over another', *Journal of Applied Psychology*, 79(2): 314–16.

Grissom, R. J. and Kim, J. J. (2001) 'Review of assumptions and problems in the appropriate conceptualization of effect size', *Psychological Methods*, 6: 135–46.

Grissom, R. J. and Kim, J. J. (2005) *Effect Sizes for Research: A Broad Practical Approach.* Mahwah, NJ: Erlbaum.

Hedges, L. V. and Olkin, I. (1985) *Statistical Methods for Meta-Analysis.* New York: Academic Press.

Higgins, S., Kokotsaki, D. and Coe, R. (2011) *Toolkit for strategies to improve learning. Summary for schools spending the pupil premium.* May 2011. London: Sutton Trust.

Huberty, C. J. (2002) 'A history of effect size indices', *Educational and Psychological Measurement*, 62(2): 227–40.

Ioannidis, J. P. A. (2005) 'Why most published research findings are false'. *PLoS Med*, 2: 8. Available at: http://www.plosmedicine.org/article/info:doi/10.1371/journal.pmed.0020124 (accessed 21 September 2011).

Keselman, H. J., Huberty, C. J., Lix, L. M., Olejnik, S. et al. (1998) 'Statistical practices of educational researchers: an analysis of their ANOVA, MANOVA, and ANCOVA analyses', *Review of Educational Research*, 68(3): 350–86.

Kirk, R. E. (1996) 'Practical significance: a concept whose time has come', *Educational and Psychological Measurement*, 56(5): 746–59.

Kulik, J. A. and Kulik, C. C. (1982) 'Educational outcomes of tutoring: a meta-analysis of findings,' *American Educational Research Journal*, 19: 237–48.

Olejnik, S. and Algina, J. (2000) 'Measures of effect size for comparative studies: applications, interpretations and limitations', *Contemporary Educational Psychology*, 25: 241–86.

Rosenthal, R. (1979) 'The file drawer problem and tolerance for null results', *Psychological Bulletin*, 86(3): 638–41.

Rosenthal, R. (1994) 'Parametric measures of effect size', in Cooper, H. and Hedges, L. V. (eds) *The Handbook of Research Synthesis*. New York: Russell Sage Foundation.

Smith, M. L. and Glass, G. V. (1980) 'Meta-analysis of research on class size and its relationship to attitudes and instruction', *American Educational Research Journal*, 17: 419–33.

Snyder, P. and Lawson, S. (1993) 'Evaluating results using corrected and uncorrected effect size estimates', *Journal of Experimental Education*, 61(4): 334–49.

Thompson, B. (1999) Common Methodology Mistakes in Educational Research, Revisited, Along with a Primer on Both Effect Sizes and the Bootstrap. Invited address presented at the annual meeting of the American Educational Research Association, Montreal.

Tymms, P., Merrell, C. and Henderson, B. (1997) 'The first year as school: a quantitative investigation of the attainment and progress of pupils', *Educational Research and Evaluation*, 3(2): 101–18.

Vincent, D. and Crumpler, M. (1997) *British Spelling Test Series Manual 3X/Y*. Windsor: NFER-Nelson.

Wilcox, R. R. (1998) 'How many discoveries have been lost by ignoring modern statistical methods?', *American Psychologist*, 53(3): 300–14.

Wilkinson, L. and Task Force on Statistical Inference, APA Board of Scientific Affairs (1999) 'Statistical methods in psychology journals: guidelines and explanations', *American Psychologist*, 54(8): 594–604.

Meta-analysis

Larry V. Hedges

Introduction

Independent replication of results has long been considered a central feature of scientific enquiry. A body of replicated results presents the question of how best to interpret those results. Standard statistical methods focus on the results of single studies in isolation. For example, standard statistical methods might be suitable for testing hypotheses about the existence of treatment effects in each study but do not provide methods for dealing with multiple studies. To deal with statistical evidence from several independent studies, special statistical methods are needed. Meta-analysis is the use of statistical methods to combine the results of a set of research studies that examine the same question. Meta-analysis is often used for carrying out the synthesis of results in systematic reviews and the term has sometimes been used to encompass the entire process of carrying out a research review using statistical methods. However, we use the term meta-analysis to refer only to the statistical aspects of systematic reviews: combining evidence across independent studies using statistical methods.

The term meta-analysis was suggested by Glass (1976) to describe the process of combining the results of statistical analyses in different studies for the purpose of drawing general conclusions. Although the term meta-analysis dates from 1976, the process

of using statistical methods for combining evidence across studies has a much longer history. Early examples of published work meta-analysis (described not as meta-analysis but as combining information across studies) include Pearson (1904) in medicine, Tippett (1931) and Fisher (1932) in statistics, Birge (1932) in physics and Cochran (1937) in agriculture.

Why is meta-analysis necessary?

Statistical significance tests are often used to help interpret the results of individual research studies. It therefore seems quite intuitive to use the outcomes of significance tests in each study to assess results across studies. Consider a series of studies all of which evaluate the effect of the same treatment via a hypothesis test. Intuitively, if a large proportion of studies obtain statistically significant results, then this should be evidence that there is a (non-zero) effect in these studies. Conversely, if few studies find significant results, then the combined evidence for a non-zero effect would seem to be weak. In spite of the intuitive appeal of this logic, it has very undesirable properties as a method of drawing inferences about treatment effects from a collection of studies. Not only does this strategy have exceptionally low sensitivity (low power in the statistical sense), its sensitivity can actually decline as the amount of evidence (the number of studies) increases (Hedges and Olkin, 1980).

Similarly, it seems intuitively sensible to say that if both study A and study B find statistically significant effects of a treatment, then study B has replicated the finding of study A. Similarly, it seems intuitive to say that if study A finds a statistically significant effect of a treatment and study B does not, then study B has failed to replicate. This intuition is also faulty. Significance tests compare an observed effect with a null (typically zero) effect. However, it is easy to find examples where two studies both have significant treatment effects (meaning that they are both reliably different from zero) but these two effects are themselves significantly different (meaning that they are reliably different from each other). Moreover, the fact that one effect is statistically significant (reliably different from zero) and the other is not does *not* imply that they are significantly different from each other.

More fundamentally, the use of statistical significance to represent the outcomes of studies is problematic in this context because statistical significance values (*p*-values) confound information about two aspects of a study: features of the design (principally the sample size) and a feature of the outcome that is independent of the design (the effect size). Highly statistically significant results can occur because the sample size is large (even if the effect size is small) or because the effect size is large (even if the sample size is small). Meta-analysis attempts to combine the information about study outcomes that is independent of the particular design used (and in particular is independent of sample sizes) by explicitly focusing on effect size.

Effect sizes

In order to use statistical methods to combine the results of studies, it is essential that the results of each study be described by a numerical index and that these indexes have the same meaning across studies. In education and the social sciences, these numerical indexes of study outcomes are called effect sizes. Simple effect sizes include the correlation coefficient and the difference between treatment and control group means divided by the standard deviation

(often called the standardised mean difference or the *d*-index). Effect sizes are discussed more extensively in Chapter 45 on effect size by Robert Coe in this volume.

An important distinction is the difference between the observed effect size (the sample effect size) and the underlying parameter that it estimates. For example, consider a study that estimates the correlation between two variables (such as socio-economic status and achievement). Such a study, with a particular sample of individuals would compute a value of the correlation. If that study were replicated with a different sample of individuals (sampled from the same population as the first sample), it is unlikely that the value of the correlation computed in the replication would be the same as with the original sample. In fact, if we replicated the study a very large number of times (each time using a different sample from the same population), we would get a range of values of the correlation. This range of values is what statisticians call the sampling distribution of the estimate. The average of all these correlation values is what we call the effect size parameter, and any one of the correlations computed from a particular sample is an effect size estimate. The standard deviation of the collection of estimates is called the standard error of the estimate and is used to quantify the variation of the observed effect sizes from sample to sample. (Another way to define the effect size parameter is as the correlation that would be obtained from an indefinitely large sample.)

One way of thinking about the distinction between the effect size estimate and the effect size parameter is that the difference between the effect size estimate and the corresponding parameter is an estimation error. Thus if d is the effect size estimate, δ is the effect size parameter, and ε is the estimation error, then $\varepsilon = d - \delta$ or $d = \delta + \varepsilon$. In this framework, the standard error of the estimate describes the variation in the estimation errors.

Typically, we will have only one effect size estimate from a study but the thought experiment above is meant to clarify the distinction between the effect size parameter and the observed effect size and to define the standard error. It may not be obvious therefore how one might obtain the standard error of an effect size estimate. As it turns out, statisticians have been able to deduce formulae for these standard errors (or more typically the variance which is the square of the standard error) in terms of sample sizes and effect sizes. For example, the variance of the correlation is $(1 - r^2)^2/(n - 1)$, where n is the sample size and the variance of the standardised mean difference is $2(1 + d^2/8)/n$, where n is the sample size in each group. For a more extensive discussion of computing effect sizes and their variances see Borenstein et al. (2009).

We emphasise the difference between an effect size estimate and the corresponding effect size parameter by using Roman letters for the effect size estimates and the corresponding Greek letters for the effect size parameter (r and ρ or d and δ).

In meta-analysis, the results of each study are summarised by its effect size. The data provided by each study is then an effect size estimate and its standard error.

Procedures in meta-analysis

The typical meta-analysis starts by assembling the effect size estimates from each study and their standard errors (or the square of the standard error, also known as the variance of the effect size). Sometimes additional information about each study is collected in the form of study characteristics that are potential moderators of the effect size.

The first analytic step in many meta-analyses is to examine the effect sizes descriptively. Effect size estimates will typically differ somewhat across studies. Because most meta-analyses involve collections of studies with (somewhat to profoundly) different sample sizes, and because standard errors depend on the sample size, the standard errors of the effect sizes will also typically differ. One way to characterise the range in which the effect size parameter for a study is likely to lie is by computing a (95%) confidence interval for the effect size parameter based on the estimate and its standard error. If d is the effect size estimate, v is its variance so that $S = \sqrt{v}$ is its standard error, then the 95% confidence interval for the effect size parameter δ is

$$d - 2S \leq \delta \leq d + 2S$$

Often the effect sizes and their confidence intervals are displayed together in a graphic called a forest plot.

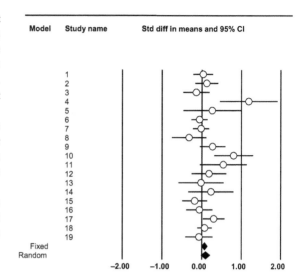

Figure 46.1   Forest plot of teacher expectancy data

Because the confidence intervals reflect a range of uncertainty of the estimates, the forest plot permits the analyst to see how similar the effect size estimates are and to see the range of uncertainty of each estimate. Figure 46.1 is an example of a forest plot.

Combining effect size estimates across studies

Effect size estimates are usually combined across studies by taking an average. However, the estimates from different studies have quite different uncertainties (that is, have different standard errors) which is indicated by confidence intervals having different widths on the forest plot. Therefore in combining (averaging) estimates across studies, it makes sense to give more weight to the effect size estimates that have less uncertainty (smaller standard errors). The weights that produce the most precise weighted estimate are inversely proportional to the variance (the square of the standard error) of the effect size estimates. This is why meta-analyses use inverse variance weights to compute a weighted average of the effect size estimates.

The weighted average estimate of k effect size

estimates $d_1, ..., d_k$ that have variances $v_1, ..., v_k$ is given by:

$$d. = \frac{\sum_{i=1}^{k} w_i d_i}{\sum_{i=1}^{k} w_i}$$

and the variance of this weighted average is:

$$v. = \frac{1}{\sum_{i=1}^{k} w_i}$$

where the weights are given by $w_i = 1/v_i$ and the standard error is $S. = \sqrt{v.}$. The standard error $S.$ can be used to construct a confidence interval for $d.$ or to test hypotheses about the average effect size parameter (e.g. that the average effect size is zero). The 95% confidence interval for the average effect size is:

$$d. - 2\,S. \leq \delta \leq d. + 2S.$$

Assessing heterogeneity

A logical question that arises in carrying out meta-analyses is whether the effect sizes are consistent across studies (this corresponds to the question, for example, of whether the treatment effect sizes are consistent across studies). However, even if the effect size parameters in every study were identical, the observed effect size estimates would be expected to differ due to estimation error. Therefore it is not always obvious whether a set of effect size estimates indicates that the underlying effect size parameters are likely to be different or if the values of the effect size estimates are likely to have occurred because of estimation errors.

One approach to this problem is to use a statistical test of heterogeneity of effect sizes (see Hedges and Olkin, 1985). This test computes a statistic that is a weighted sum of squared deviations from the weighted mean effect size:

$$Q = \sum_{i=1}^{k} (d_i - d.)^2$$

When the effect size *parameters* are identical across studies, the Q-statistic has a chi-square distribution with $(k - 1)$ degrees of freedom, which is used to get critical values to determine when an obtained value of Q is large enough to indicate heterogeneity at a particular significance level.

The statistical test based on the Q-statistic can give an indication that the effect size parameters are not identical, but it does not describe *how different* the effect size parameters might be across studies. To describe the amount of heterogeneity in effect size parameters in meta-analysis, one can estimate the actual variation of the underlying effect size parameters, often called the between-studies (effect size) variance component and symbolised by τ^2. One use for the variance component (or rather its square root τ) is to characterise the plausible range in which the effect size parameters might lie. Approximately 95% of the effect size parameters might be expected to lie in the range from $d. - 2\tau$ to $d. + 2\tau$ (note the use of τ not τ^2).

Quantifying the variation of the effect size parameters via τ^2 leaves open the question of how much of the variation in the observed effect size estimates is real variation (variation in effect size parameters) and how much is due to estimation error. One way to quantify the proportion of real variation is the index I^2, which is an estimate of τ^2 divided by the total variation of the effect size estimates. It can be computed very simply as:

$$I^2 = \frac{Q - (k-1)}{Q}$$

Fixed versus random effects

Practitioners of meta-analysis sometimes take different perspectives on whether the heterogeneity of effect size parameters should be counted as random variation in meta-analysis. One perspective is that heterogeneity is due to real differences between studies that are consequences of study design, even if we do not understand exactly what they were. A different perspective is that if we do not understand the sources of these differences, it is safer to treat them as if they were random disturbances. The first perspective (between-study differences are systematic) implies that any heterogeneity of effect size parameters is not a random phenomenon and therefore does not add statistical uncertainty to the analysis. This is sometimes called the *fixed effects* analysis strategy and was described above.

The second perspective (between-study differences need to be treated as unsystematic) implies that heterogeneity of effect sizes is a random phenomenon that must add to the statistical uncertainty of the analysis. This is called the *random effects* analysis. The random effects analysis is analogous to the fixed effects analysis in every way except the weights used. In the random effects analysis, the variance of the effect size estimate is defined as $v_i + \tau^2$ (as opposed to just v_i in the fixed effects analysis). Therefore the weights used in the random effects analysis are $w_i = 1/(v_i + \tau^2)$ (as opposed to just $w_i = 1/v_i$ in the fixed effects analysis). The process of computing the weighted mean, its standard error, confidence intervals for the mean and tests for the mean effect size is exactly the same as in the fixed effects analysis.

The fixed and random effects analyses yield identical results if $\tau^2 = 0$, because then the weights are identical in the two analyses. If $\tau^2 > 0$, then the random effects weights are each larger and tend to be more equal than the fixed effects weights. More equal weights often lead to slightly different weighted means in the random effects analysis than in the fixed effects analysis, but they may be either smaller or larger. The generally larger weights imply that the variance of the weighted average (and its square root, the standard error) will be larger in the random effects analysis than in the fixed effects analysis. This reflects the fact that there is an additional source of uncertainty for each estimate in the random effects analysis (quantified by τ^2) and therefore the uncertainty of the weighted mean is larger.

While researchers who use meta-analysis disagree about whether random effects analyses are preferable, there is general agreement that meta-analyses are more interpretable when there is less unexplained heterogeneity. Many specialists in meta-analysis recommend generally using random effects analyses because they are generally more conservative. For a broad discussion see Hedges and Vevea (1998).

Analysis of variance and regression analyses in meta-analysis

One approach to dealing with heterogeneity of effect sizes in meta-analysis is to use statistical models to explain this variation as attributable to differences in study characteristics such as type of sample, intensity or duration of the treatment, characteristics of the measurement of the outcome or features of the study design. While standard analysis of variance and multiple regression analyses are not directly applicable in meta-analysis, generalisations of these methods are available that are designed for meta-analysis (see, for example, Cooper et al., 2009). These methods make it possible to determine whether variables describing studies are related to effect size and to estimate the remaining level of heterogeneity after the effects of study-level variables have been accounted for.

Both fixed effects and random effects analogues to analysis of variance and regression analysis are available and differ in whether or not they treat the heterogeneity in effect sizes as a random phenomenon that contributes uncertainty to the analysis. If the remaining level of heterogeneity is large, then many researchers would argue for the use of random effects analyses which are more conservative.

Publication bias

A challenge to the interpretation of published scientific findings is that they may not be representative of the studies actually conducted. This challenge obviously applies to summaries of such findings, including meta-analyses. For example, if studies with positive findings are more likely to be published and therefore available for inclusion in meta-analyses, the findings of individual published studies and any summaries of them will tend to be positively biased. Often publication bias is tied to statistical significance testing: studies that do not obtain statistically significant results are less likely to be published (or even submitted for publication). Unfortunately there is evidence of such bias in many areas of scientific work, including education and the social sciences (see Rothstein et al., 2005). However, while it is difficult to understand whether publication bias may be operating when interpreting a single study, there are methods for detecting and even adjusting for the effects of publication bias in meta-analysis.

One of the most useful tools for detecting publication bias is the funnel plot. A funnel plot is a plot of each study's effect size versus its standard error (or its sample size). If there is no publication bias, the plot should look like a funnel, because the studies whose effect sizes have larger standard errors should exhibit more variation and those effects have smaller standard errors. If there is publication bias in which statistically insignificant effects are less likely to be observed, effect sizes with large standard errors and small effect sizes (which will tend to be statistically insignificant) will be less likely to be observed. Thus part of the funnel plot will be missing (the part of the upper corner nearest to the vertical line representing zero effect size). Consequently this plot can be used for a visual indicator of possible publication bias. There are also statistical tests for publication bias based on funnel plots (e.g. Begg, 1994).

A great deal of work has been devoted to adjustment for the effects of publication bias in meta-analysis. The simplest of such methods is called the trim and fill procedure (Duval, 2005). The idea of trim and fill is to use the funnel plot to estimate the number of effect sizes that are missing due to publication bias, then fill them in (impute the missing values) using values on the opposite side of the funnel plot (and presumably not subject to publication selection). There are also more sophisticated methods involving estimation based on non-parametric selection models which are more persuasive but also more complex (see, for example, Hedges and Vevea, 2005).

Example

Raudenbush (1984) reported a meta-analysis of 19 experimental studies of teacher expectancy effects on pupil IQ. Using the fixed effects analysis of these standardised mean difference effect sizes, the weighted mean was $d. = 0.06$, with a standard error of $S = 0.036$, which corresponded to a confidence interval for the mean effect size of -0.01 to 0.13. This analysis would suggest that the average effect size was not significantly different from zero. The random effects analysis yielded a similar conclusion with a weighted mean effect size of 0.11 with a standard error of 0.079, and a 95% confidence interval for the weighted mean effect size of -0.04 to 0.27. The standard error was more than twice as large in the random effects analysis because there was considerable heterogeneity in the results. The Q-statistic was $Q = 35.83$, which was large enough to indicate heterogeneity at the 0.001 level of statistical significance. The value of the variance component was $\tau^2 = 0.082$, so that the standard deviation of the distribution of effect size parameters across studies was $\tau = 0.286$. The value of I^2 was $I^2 = 49.8\%$, meaning that about half the total variation of the observed effect sizes was due to variation in the effect size parameters across studies.

Conclusion

Raudenbush showed that a crucial variable in explaining the variation in effect sizes across studies was the amount of prior contact that the teachers had had with the students before the expectancy effect was experimentally induced. Producing an effect on students required that teachers believed the information the experimenters gave them to try to change their expectations about the students. Consequently, teachers who had had enough experience with students to form expectations before the experimenters tried to change them were not influenced by what the experimenters told them. For students of these teachers, there were essentially no effects. For students of teachers who had been with their class for a week or less, analysis of variance methods showed that there was a substantial and consistent positive effect size. In this analysis there was essentially no heterogeneity of effects once the amount of prior teacher contact with their class was taken into account.

Questions for further investigation

1. Discuss your understanding of the usefulness of meta-analysis in statistical testing and analysis. Has it improved in light of the information in this chapter and elsewhere in this volume?

2. Discuss the benefits of employing meta-analysis to a study over a traditional literature review.

Suggested further reading

Borenstein, M., Hedges, L. V., Higgins, J. P. T. and Rothstein, H. (2009) *Introduction to Meta-analysis*. London: Wiley. This book provides a clear and thorough introduction to meta-analysis, the process of synthesising data from a series of separate studies.

Cooper, H. (1989) *Integrating Research*. Thousand Oaks, CA: Sage. An invaluable tool for learning the techniques of researching, reviewing and analysing research literature. Applying basic tenets of sound data gathering to a comprehensive synthesis of past research on a topic, from conceptualisation of the research problem to the concise summary of the research review.

Lipsey, M. and Wilson, D. (2001) *Practical Meta-analysis*. Thousand Oaks, CA: Sage. By integrating and translating the current methodological and statistical work into a practical guide, the authors provide readers with a state-of-the-art introduction to the various approaches to doing meta-analysis.

Rothstein, H., Sutton, A. and Borenstein, M. (eds) (2005) *Publication Bias in Meta-analysis*. New York: John Wiley. Adopts an inter-disciplinary approach and makes an excellent reference volume for any researchers and graduate students who conduct systematic reviews or meta-analyses.

References

Begg, C. B. (1994) 'Publication bias', in Cooper, H. and Hedges, L. V. (eds) *The Handbook of Research Synthesis*. New York: Russell Sage Foundation, pp. 399–410.

Birge, R. T. (1932) 'The calculation of errors by the method of least squares', *Physical Review*, 40: 207–27.

Borenstein, M., Hedges, L. V., Higgins, J. P. T. and Rothstein, H. (2009) *Introduction to Meta-Analysis*. London: Wiley.

Cochran, W.G. (1937) 'Problems arising in the analysis of a series of similar experiments', *Journal of the Royal Statistical Society* (*Suppl.*), 4: 102–18.

Cooper, H., Hedges, L. V. and Valentine, J. (2009) *The Handbook of Research Synthesis and Meta-analysis* (2nd edn). New York: Russell Sage Foundation.

Duval, S. (2005) 'The trim and fill method', in Rothstein, H., Sutton, A. and Borenstein, M. (eds) *Publication Bias in Meta-analysis*. New York: John Wiley, pp. 127–44.

Fisher, R. A. (1932) *Statistical Methods for Research Workers* (4th edn). London: Oliver & Boyd.

Glass, G. V. (1976) 'Primary, secondary, and meta-analysis of research', *Educational Researcher*, 5: 3–8.

Hedges, L. V. and Olkin, I. (1980) 'Vote counting methods in research synthesis', *Psychological Bulletin*, 88: 359–69.

Hedges, L. V. and Olkin, I. (1985) *Statistical Methods for Meta-analysis*. New York: Academic Press.

Hedges, L. V. and Vevea, J. L. (1998) 'Fixed and random effects models in meta analysis', *Psychological Methods*, 3: 486–504.

Hedges, L. V. and Vevea, J. L. (2005) 'Selection model approaches to publication bias', in Rothstein, H., Sutton, A. and Borenstein, M. (eds) *Publication Bias in Meta-analysis*. New York: John Wiley, pp. 145–74.

Pearson, K. (1904) 'Report on certain enteric fever inoculations', *British Medical Journal*, 2: 1243–6.

Raudenbush, S. W. (1984) 'Magnitude of teacher expectancy effects on pupil IQ as a function of the credibility of expectancy induction: a synthesis of findings from 18 studies', *Journal of Educational Psychology*, 76: 85–97.

Rothstein, H., Sutton, A. and Borenstein, M. (eds) (2005) *Publication Bias in Meta-analysis*. New York: John Wiley.

Tippett, L. H. C. (1931) *The Method of Statistics*. London: Williams & Norgate.

Software for meta-analysis

Comprehensive Meta-Analysis (CMA), developed by Borenstein, Hedges, Higgins and Rothstein – see: http://www.Meta-Analysis.com

Metawin Version 2.0, developed by Rosenberg, Adams and Gurevitch – see: http://www.metawinsoft.com

RevMan, developed by the the Cochrane Collaboration – see http://www.cc-ims.net/RevMan

Index

Note: the letter 'f' after a page number refers to a figure; the letter 't' refers to a table.